STREETWISE
SPANISH
DICTIONARY/THESAURUS

STREETWISE
SPANISH
DICTIONARY/THESAURUS

The User-Friendly Guide to Spanish Slang and Idioms

Mary McVey Gill
Brenda Wegmann

McGraw-Hill

Chicago New York San Francisco Lisbon London Madrid Mexico City
Milan New Delhi San Juan Seoul Singapore Sydney Toronto

Library of Congress Cataloging-in-Publication Data

Gill, Mary McVey.
    Streetwise Spanish dictionary/thesaurus / Mary McVey Gill and Brenda Wegmann;
with illustrations by Norma Vidal.
       p.   cm.
    Includes index.
    ISBN 0-8442-2551-7
    1. Spanish language—Slang—Glossaries, vocabularies, etc.   2. Spanish
language—Idioms—Glossaries, vocabularies, etc.   3. Spanish
language—Dictionaries—English.   I. Wegmann, Brenda, 1941–   II. Title.

PC4971.G55   2000
463'.21—dc21
                  00-63699

McGraw-Hill

A Division of The **McGraw·Hill** Companies

1 2 3 4 5 6 7 8 9 0 LBM/LBM 0 9 8 7 6 5 4 3 2 1

ISBN 0-8442-2551-7

Other titles in the **Streetwise** series:
Streetwise Spanish, Mary McVey Gill and Brenda Wegmann
Streetwise Spanish audio package, Mary McVey Gill and Brenda Wegmann
Streetwise French, Isabelle Rodrigues and Ted Neather
Streetwise French Dictionary/Thesaurus, Ian Pickup and Rod Hares
Streetwise German, Paul G. Graves

This book was set in Minion and Myriad by Village Typographers, Inc.
Printed and bound by Lake Book Manufacturing.

Cover design by Nick Panos
Cover photograph by Farrell Grehan/FPG International LLC
All illustrations are by Norma Vidal, with the following exceptions: pages 172, 201, and
210, cartoons by Oscar Sierra Quintero ("Oki").

McGraw-Hill books are available at special quantity discounts to use as premiums and
sales promotions, or for use in corporate training programs. For more information, please
write to the Director of Special Sales, Professional Publishing, McGraw-Hill, Two Penn
Plaza, New York, NY 10121-2298. Or contact your local bookstore.

This book is printed on acid-free paper.

Contents

Contents

Preface

Have you ever wanted to thank a friend in Spanish for a fantastic evening, say that the food was "super," the music was "awesome," or that you had a "cool" time? Have you ever searched for words in Spanish to mean "a drag," "loser," "on cloud nine," or "the cream of the crop"? Or do you want to be able to understand Spanish speakers when they use this kind of informal language? If so, *Streetwise Spanish Dictionary/Thesaurus* is for you!

The Spanish language is one of the world's richest when it comes to lively, humorous, and inventive expressions for everyday use. *Streetwise Spanish Dictionary/Thesaurus* includes roughly 5,500 such words and expressions, primarily slang, along with idiomatic expressions that are used colloquially. It is not just a dictionary of slang and idiomatic Spanish terms. It was designed also as a thesaurus to help readers increase their active colloquial vocabulary and understand regional variations in the many different areas in which the language is spoken. Specific country references are included for each entry. The entries listed are in use today on TV and radio programs, in movies, in daily conversation, and in informal writing, such as in magazine articles or on the Internet.

Organization

Thesaurus

The main body of the book is the Thesaurus, which is organized into 156 general categories or themes (for example, happiness, selfishness, time, work), arranged alphabetically. The categories, all in noun form, typically are divided into subcategories. Each expression includes a literal translation when helpful or possible (placed in parentheses), the actual English definition, and the countries or regions in which the expression is used. Examples and their accompanying English translations are given as needed. While no attempt has been made to sanitize the language by eliminating off-color expressions, words considered vulgar are marked with the word "vulgar" in parentheses.

A typical entry is shown on the following page.

creerse la última Coca-Cola en el de- ← word/expression
sierto (to think one is the last Coca- ← literal translation
Cola in the desert) to think one is hot ← actual translation
stuff, God's gift ◄ Mex, ES, Nic, Pan, DR, PR, ← countries/regions used
Col ►

Carmen se ve muy bonita, ¿no? Su vestido ← example
es de París. —¡Pero es tan engreída! Se
cree la última Coca-Cola en el desierto.
Carmen looks very pretty, doesn't she? Her ← example translation
dress is from Paris. —But she's so stuck-up!
She thinks she's God's gift.

Definite articles indicate gender of nouns. Feminine forms of nouns are given in parentheses:

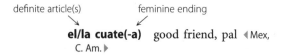

definite article(s)   feminine ending

el/la cuate(-a) good friend, pal ◄ Mex,
C. Am. ►

The feminine ending is typically added after dropping **-o** or **-e**; for example, the feminine form of **el cuate** is **la cuata**. If no feminine ending is given, the noun is invariable (the same in the feminine as in the masculine): **el/la hincha** (fan, sports enthusiast). When an expression requires a specific verb form in the second person ("you" in English), the **tú** form is normally used rather than **usted**, as slang is primarily informal. Notes referring to register (level of formality) or to specific country variations are given in parentheses.

Spanish-English Dictionary/Index

This alphabetical listing of all the Spanish words and expressions included as entries provides abbreviated English translations. Page numbers refer the reader to full entries within the Thesaurus.

English Topic Index

The English Topic Index can be used to find specific kinds of expressions. Most categories are divided into subcategories, and these are listed here. For instance, the reader looking for slang words for cars will be referred to the travel and transportation category. Likewise, the reader trying to find out how to say "fed up" or "wimp" or "chutzpah" will be referred to the appropriate category.

Say It with Slang!

These short articles highlight specific linguistic or cultural features, such as "Latin hospitality," "Using last names for subtle criticism," or "Rhyme time." They provide glimpses into how the language is used in various regions of the Spanish-speaking world—for instance, how names of vegetables or names of amphibians are used in different ways in different places. They point out humorous use of the language and provide insights into how slang language is invented—such as by shortening words or reversing their syllables.

Test Your Slang Power!

Each of these short self-tests focuses on a group of related categories, such as "Feelings and emotions," "The working world," or "Celebrations, parties, and having fun." Answers and a rating scale are provided. Readers can use these self-tests to work on their active colloquial vocabulary.

Native Readers

Native readers from many different Spanish-speaking countries helped to create the final manuscript. Each word or expression is accompanied by a list of abbreviations representing the countries and regions in which the word or expression is used. However, because slang by its very nature is continually spreading and disappearing and since we were not able to have readers from every Latin American country read the entire manuscript, there may be cases where a word is currently used in a certain country but not listed as such. We are deeply indebted to our Hispanic friends for all their help and advice.

Country/regional abbreviations

Arg	Argentina	Mex	Mexico
Bol	Bolivia	Nic	Nicaragua
C. Am.	Central America	Pan	Panama
Ch	Chile	Para	Paraguay
Col	Colombia	PR	Puerto Rico
CR	Costa Rica	S. Cone	Southern Cone (Argentina,
DR	Dominican Republic		Chile, Paraguay, Uruguay)
Ec	Ecuador	S. Am.	South America
ES	El Salvador	Sp	Spain
G	Guatemala	U	Uruguay
Hond	Honduras	Ven	Venezuela
L. Am.	Latin America		

(The following are not abbreviated: chicano, Caribbean, Cuba, Florida, and Peru.)

The regional markers for any specific entry are listed roughly from north to south, with Spain following the Southern Cone countries.

Grammar abbreviations

adj.	adjective	n.	noun	inf.	infinitive

Streetwise Spanish: Speak and Understand Everyday Spanish

This dictionary/thesaurus accompanies the original *Streetwise Spanish* book, which consists of fifteen chapters, each focusing on a language function (such as greetings, expressing sympathy, expressing anger, and so forth) and on a specific country or region. Each chapter includes conversations illustrating key vocabulary, cultural and linguistic notes, vocabulary exercises, and occasional jokes or anecdotes. Interspersed among the chapters are short essays on vocabulary and culture, plus review sections with exercises. The book is also available with an accompanying recording that includes the conversations performed by native speakers from each of the countries represented, oral exercises not found in the book, and explanations of the various accents and dialects.

Acknowledgments

We would like to thank Christopher Brown, our editor at McGraw-Hill, for his constant support, good cheer, advice, and editorial insight from the inception of the project through its completion. Without him, this book would not have been possible. Thanks also to illustrator Norma Vidal for her wonderful "translation" of word to art. We would like to thank our project editor, Heidi Bresnahan, for so competently carrying the book to completion, and the copyeditor, Lisa Dillman, for her careful reading of the manuscript. We also extend our deep appreciation to the following native readers who read the material and gave us many comments and suggestions:

Adriana de Álvarez, Anna Colom, Sofía Domínguez de Málvarez, Dolores Fernández, Pilar Hernández, Llanca Letelier, Yolanda Magaña, Fernando Moscoso, Anna Elisa Ordóñez, Armando Sánchez Lona, Elka Scheker, and María Teresa Varese.

The following people deserve a special thank-you for contributing many colorful expressions from their native countries and answering our endless questions about usage and meaning:

María Elena Alvarado, Raimundo Arredondo, Ingrid de la Barra, Cristina Cantú, Miriam Castillo, Lucy Flores, Nidia González Araya, Sylvia Henríquez Rivas, Wilma Hernández, Iván H. Jiménez Williams, Alejandra Kerr, Naldo Lombardi, Alex Machado, Delia Magaña, Lucrecia Mendoza, Gilda Mesa de Yi, Feruz Mouselli, Manuel Palos, Ofelia Romero, Beatriz Rosales de Kelly, Luciana Sacchi, Susana Singer, Humberto Somarriba, Januaria de Somarriba, Cristina Stricker de Márquez, Agustín and María Dolores Vela-López, Edgar Villanueva, and Cecilia Walter.

Thesaurus

absurdity

See also "unusualness."

como a un santo cristo un par de pistolas (like a couple of pistols for a statue of Christ) phrase indicating that something is not appropriate with respect to something else ◄ Sp ►

parecer un arroz con bicicleta (to be like rice with a bicycle) to seem absurd ◄ Florida, Col ►

pegar una cosa como guitarra en un entierro (to stick like a guitar at a funeral) to be out of time or place ◄ Sp ►

ser como chancho en misa (to be like a pig in mass) to be out of place ◄ Ec, Ch ►
Ese tipo vino a la fiesta y parecía más perdido que chancho en misa. That guy came to the party and stuck out like a sore thumb.

tirado(-a) de las mechas (pulled by the locks of one's hair) absurd, crazy ◄ Ch ►
Esas ideas me parecen muy tiradas de las mechas. Those ideas really seem out in left field to me.

activity

See also "busyness."

apiolarse to be a go-getter, be clever and try hard to get something ◄ Mex, Arg ►
Esos comerciantes se están apiolando. Those businesspeople are really wheeling and dealing.

comosellamear, chunchear (to what's-its-name) to do something undefined ◄ Nic ►

En la cancha se ven los gallos. (It's in the ring that we see the roosters.) Actions speak louder than words. ◄ Ch ►

enrollarse con (to get rolled up with) to get mixed up or involved with ◄ ES, DR, Sp ►

estar en tránsito (to be in transit) to be under way (said of a project) ◄ Mex, Col, Ch ►

meter la mano hasta el codo en algo (to put one's hand up to the elbow in something) to do something with great dedication; to take something selfishly ◄ most of L. Am., Sp ►

no estar quieto(-a) ni a la de tres (to not be still even for that of three) to not be quiet for even one minute ◄ Sp ►

quedarse a medio camino (to end up in mid road) to not finish ◄ Mex, DR, PR, Ch, Sp ►

torear (to fight a bull; to provoke) to manage, manipulate people or a situation ◄ Mex, DR, Col, Ch, Sp ►

Zapatero a tus zapatos. (Shoemaker to your shoes.) Mind your own business. Let's stick to what we know best. ◄ L. Am., Sp ►

getting going or getting active

apuntarse to join in, do something with others ◄ most of L. Am., Sp ►
¿Van al concierto de Gloria Estefan? Me apunto. Are you going to the Gloria Estefan concert? Count me in.

enchufarse (to plug into) to join in (conversation, etc.) ◄ S. Cone ►

enchufarse

menearse to get moving, get a move on ◄ L. Am., Sp ►
Menéate, que no quiero llegar tarde. Get a move on because I don't want to be late.

meterle mano (to put in hand) to take, undertake ◄ Mex, G, Cuba, DR, PR, Col ►
Señores, vamos a meterle mano al proyecto, que hay que entregarlo mañana. Gentlemen, let's get going on the project since we have to hand it in tomorrow.

mojarse el culo en algo (to wet one's ass in something) to get involved in something (vulgar) ◄ Sp ►
No se puede pescar sin mojarse el culo. (You can't fish without getting your ass wet.) You don't achieve anything without getting involved. (saying in ES)

mover el esqueleto (to move one's skeleton) to get going, get a move on ◄ Mex, U, Ch, Sp ►
¡Muevan el esqueleto! Es hora de irnos. Get a move on! (Get your buns in gear!) It's time to go.

ponerse en algo (to put oneself in something) to get with it ◄ DR, Col ►
Ponte en algo. Get with it.

admiration

See also "attractiveness," "good," "good character."

¡Cámara!, ¡Camaronchas! Wow! (seeing a beautiful woman, etc.) ◄ Mex ►

chochear to dote on (e.g., a grandparent to grandchildren) ◄ Col, S. Cone ►

chocho(-a) doting, proud (like a grandparent), gaga; senile ◄ Mex, Col, CR, DR, PR, S. Cone ►
Está chocho con su nieta. He's gaga over his granddaughter.

mirarse en alguien como en un espejo (to see oneself in another as in a mirror) to have great love for someone and be pleased with their actions or good qualities (Sp); to look like someone (Mex) ◄ Mex, Sp ►
Me miro en ella como en un espejo. I love her like my own daughter.

ser la luz de los (sus) ojos to be the light of one's life (eyes) ◄ Mex, ES, S. Cone ►
El hijo de Eduardo es la luz de sus ojos. Eduardo's son is the light of his life.

ser la niña de los (sus) ojos to be the apple (pupil) of one's eyes ◄ Mex, ES, DR, Sp ►

ser santo de su devoción (to be the saint of one's devotion) to be someone looked up to, an idol ◄ ES, Nic, S. Cone, Sp ►

affection

See also "friendship," "romance."

hugging and kissing

apretar to hug, kiss ◄ Mex, CR, Col, U, Arg ►

besar con la lengua (to kiss with the tongue) to French-kiss; also, **beso de lengua**, a French kiss ◄ L. Am., Sp ►

besos y abrazos (kisses and hugs) hugs and kisses (common ending for a letter to a friend) ◄ L. Am., Sp ►

los besotes (big sloppy kisses) smooches ◄ Mex, C. Am. ►

besuquearse to smooch ◄ C. Am., DR, PR, S. Cone, Sp ►

el besuqueo necking, smooching, repeated kissing ◄ L. Am., Sp ►
Estoy harta de tanto besuqueo de mi madre. I'm sick of so much smooching from my mother.

chapar to make out, hug and kiss with boyfriend or girlfriend ◄ Bol, Arg ►

darse el lote (also, **el filete**, less commonly) (to give each other the lot) to hug and kiss ◄ Sp ►

fajar (to girdle, wrap) to make out ◄ Mex ►

Fajé con mi novio. I made out with my steady boyfriend.

grajearse to make out ◄ PR ►

¡Qué chisme tengo! ¡Anoche vi a Julio grajeándose con Anita en el carro! What a bit of gossip I have! Last night I saw Julio making out with Anita in his car!

el jamón (ham) French kiss ◄ Ven ►

pastelear (to cake) to hug and kiss (boyfriend and girlfriend), to pet ◄ Mex ►

el pico (beak) kiss ◄ Col ►

romancear to get romantic ◄ ES, Nic, Pan ►

Fueron a romancear a un sitio solitario. They went off by themselves to get romantic.

rumbiarse to French-kiss ◄ Col ►

pampering

el/la alcahuete(-a) (procurer, pimp) person who spoils or pampers someone, gives in to their wishes or goes along with them; also, teacher's pet in Col ◄ Mex, G, ES, DR, PR, Col, Ec, Ch ►

alcahuetear (to procure, pimp) to give in or go along (with something) ◄ Mex, ES, DR, Col, Ch ►

No le alcahueteas eso. Ese niño es un malcriado porque sus padres le alcahuetean todo. Don't go along with him and give him that. That boy is a spoiled brat because his parents give in to him on everything.

llevar en palmas (palmitas) (to carry with palm leaves) to please, pamper ◄ Sp ►

el regalón, la regalona (big gift-getter) pet, favorite, pampered one ◄ Ch ►

regalonear (to big gift) to spoil, pamper ◄ Ch ►

terms of endearment

chato(-a) (pug-nosed) affectionate nickname ◄ most of L. Am., Sp ►

corazón (heart) darling ◄ L. Am., Sp ►

dulzura (sweetness) sweetie, honey ◄ L. Am., Sp ►

flaco(-a) (skinny) affectionate nickname ◄ L. Am., Sp ►

gordito(-a) (chubby) honey, dear ◄ L. Am., Sp ►

gordo(-a) (fat) fat plum; darling ◄ L. Am., Sp ►

luz de mi vida light of my life, dear ◄ L. Am., Sp ►

m'ijo, m'ija (short for **mi hijo, mi hija**) my son, my daughter; used to show affection even to people who are not related ◄ L. Am., Sp ►

Gracias, m'ijo. Thank you, dear.

mamacita (little mama) term of address derived from **mamá**, used with affection to a girl or woman; also, sometimes used as a come-on by a man to a good-looking woman ◄ L. Am. ►

mami, mamita term of affection for girl or woman, even a young girl ◄ Mex, G, CR, Cuba, DR, PR, Col, S. Cone ►

Mamita, tú te ves bien buena. Pretty mama, you're looking really good.

mi alma (my soul) darling, dear ◄ L. Am. ►

mi amor my love ◄ L. Am., Sp ►

mi amorciano (my Martian love, used instead of **mi amorcito**, sounds like **amor** and **marciano**, Martian) my darling, my love (used mostly by women) ◄ Mex, Col ►

mi amorcito (little love) sweetheart ◄ L. Am., Sp ►

mi amorciano

mi bomboncito (my little piece of candy) darling love ◀ U ▶

mi cielo (my heaven) sweetheart, darling ◀ L. Am., Sp ▶

mi pichón (my pigeon; Mex: **pichoncito**) my turtledove, love ◀ parts of L. Am. ▶

mi rey (reina) (my king [queen]) my dear, sweetheart ◀ L. Am., Sp ▶

mi tesoro (my treasure) my dear ◀ L. Am., Sp ▶

mi vida (my life) sweetheart, darling ◀ L. Am., Sp ▶

muñeco(-a) (doll) term of affection ◀ Mex, G, Cuba, Col ▶

negro(-a) (black one) term of affection like sweetheart, used for people of any skin color ◀ L. Am., Sp ▶

papacito term of affection for a man ◀ Mex, G, ES, DR, PR ▶
Ese papacito me trae loca. That sweetie is driving me crazy.

papazote big daddy ◀ Mex, G, DR, PR, Col ▶

papi (dad) term of affection used by women to men ◀ Mex, G, ES, Pan, Cuba, DR, PR ▶
Ay, papi, te amo mucho. Oh, big daddy, I love you so much.

papucho daddy-o, big daddy (for boyfriends, not dads) ◀ Mex, ES, CR, Col ▶

affirmation: yes

ajá uh-huh ◀ L. Am., Sp ▶

cilindro, cirilo, ciro, sirope used instead of **sí** ◀ Cuba ▶

cinta used instead of **sí** ◀ Peru ▶

ey yeah ◀ most of L. Am. ▶

sifón, cintas variants of **sí**, yes ◀ Mex, Col ▶

simón used instead of **sí** ◀ most of L. Am. ▶

sincho of course ◀ chicano, Mex, Col ▶
¿Vas al cine con nosotros? —¡Sincho! You going to the movies with us? —Natch!

sirol, simonetes used instead of **sí** ◀ chicano, Col ▶

age

See also "youth."

la cabeza de cebolla (onion head) someone with gray hair ◀ Mex, ES ▶
Soy cabeza de cebolla pero con tallo verde. I'm a gray-headed senior (onion head) but with the fire of youth (a green stem).

carroza (carriage) old, mature; describing someone middle-aged who tries to be young ◀ Mex, Sp ▶

el cascarón, la cascarona (thick rind or bark) old man, old woman ◀ Mex, PR ▶

chochear to be a bit senile, forgetful because of age ◀ Mex, S. Cone, Sp ▶
El abuelo ya chochea y dice algunas tonterías. Grandpa is already getting forgetful and saying some foolish things.

chocho(-a) old, senile, gaga ◀ Mex, Nic, CR, DR, PR, Col ▶
Ya está chochita. She's gotten a bit gaga.

cincuentón, cincuentona fiftyish (the -ón is an augmentative, emphasizing age) ◀ L. Am., Sp ▶

El que va pa' viejo va pa' pendejo. (Whoever is getting old, is getting to be a fool.) Old age brings woe. (ES: also, **Más viejo, más pendejo.**) ◀ Mex, ES, Nic, Ven ▶

entradito(-a) en años (a little bit entered into years) getting up there (euphemism) ◀ most of L. Am., Sp ▶

estar hecho(-a) un cascajo (to be made a piece of junk) to be decrepit ◀ PR, Sp ▶

estar para sopitas y buen vino (to be for light soup and good wine) to be old, on his (her) last legs ◀ Sp ▶

cincuentona

los rucos old folks, fogies ◀ Mex, ES, Col ▶

tener abriles (to have Aprils) to have a certain age ◀ L. Am., Sp ▶
Tiene unos cuarenta abriles. He's (She's) around forty years old.
Tiene sus abriles, pero es bonita. She has a few years on her, but she's pretty.

traqueteado(-a) (clattered) old, used or worn out (CR: tired or badly made) ◀ Mex, ES, S. Cone ▶
Ese carro está traqueteado. That car is worn out (ready for the junk yard).

vejestorio(-a) geezer, fogy ◀ ES, Nic, DR, S. Cone, Sp ▶

el vejete old man ◀ L. Am. ▶

vetusto(-a) (bat) old and worn out, old goat (a bit old-fashioned) ◀ Sp ▶

Ya le han caído cincuenta castañas (tacos). (Fifty chestnuts [bad words] have fallen on him or her.) He or she is fifty. ◀ Sp ▶

más viejo(-a) que el pargo de la meseta older than the snapper on the mesa ◀ PR ▶

más viejo(-a) que el pinol (older than pinol, toasted corn drink) as old as the hills ◀ Nic ▶

más viejo(-a) que Matusalén older than Methuselah ◀ L. Am., Sp ▶
Me siento más viejo que Matusalén. I feel older than Methuselah.

la momia (mummy) geezer, old fogy ◀ Mex, Col ▶

la momiza geriatric set, fogies; opposite of **la chaviza**, young people ◀ Mex ▶

el pellejo (skin) old geezer ◀ Mex ▶

ponerse carcamán (to become an old tub) to be getting old-looking and shriveled up, to be on one's last legs (DR: **carcamal**) ◀ Arg ▶

la reliquia (relic) geezer, old person ◀ Mex, ES, Col, S. Cone ▶

rondar los cincuenta (cuarenta, etc.) (to round the fifty, forty, etc.) to be pushing fifty (forty, etc.) years old ◀ ES, S. Cone, Sp ▶

el ruco, rucailo geezer, old guy (CR: **roco** or **rocolo**) ◀ Mex, G, ES, Nic ▶

agreement

agreeing, going along

bailar al son que le tocan (to dance to the sound that is played) to go along with others, do whatever is appropriate ◀ L. Am., Sp ▶
Esteban siempre baila al son que le tocan. Esteban always goes along with the others.

cuadrar con alguien to agree, make a deal, square things (also, in Cuba; **cuadrar la caja con**, to make peace with) ◀ Mex, Cuba, Col ▶
Cuadramos con el jefe para salir temprano hoy. We squared things with the boss to leave early today.

decir amén a todo (to say amen to everything) to always agree, be a yes man (Ch: more common, **llevar el amén**) ◀ ES, DR, S. Cone, Sp ▶
Ella nunca busca problemas; a todo dice amén. She never looks for problems; she always goes along with things.

seguirle a alguien la corriente (to fol-low someone's current) to follow some-one and agree with him or her, go along (sometimes just to humor someone) ◀ Mex, ES, Nic, DR, S. Cone, Sp ▶

making up

arreglar el pastel (to fix the cake) to patch things up ◀ S. Cone ▶

hacer las paces (to make peace) to bury the hatchet ◀ L. Am., Sp ▶

ponerse en buena (to put oneself in good) to make up, reconcile ◀ DR, Ch ▶

Tengamos la fiesta en paz. (Let's have the party in peace.) Don't cause trou-ble. (ES: **Llevemos la fiesta en paz.**) ◀ ES, DR, Sp ▶

terms of agreement

¡Allí está el detalle! (There's the de-tail!) That's the point! (a saying popu-larized by the actor Cantinflas) ◀ Mex, DR, S. Cone ▶

¡Ándale! (¡Ándate!) Right! That's it! ◀ chicano, Mex, Col ▶

Clarisa se llamaba... (la que me lavó el pañuelo). (Clarisa was the name . . . [of the one who washed my handker-chief].) You are right! Correct! (pun on **claro** meaning clearly) ◀ Nic, Ch ▶

Conforme. (Agreed.) OK. ◀ Ch ▶
¿Nos vamos ahora? —Conforme. Shall we go now? —OK.

¡De bola! (Of the ball!) Absolutely! Agreed! ◀ Ven ▶

Igual Pascual. (Equal Pascual.) Me too. The same. ◀ Ch ▶

Iguanas ranas. (Iguanas frogs; **iguanas** sounds like **igual**) Me too. The same. ◀ Mex, Col ▶

¡Juega! (Play!) Done deal! Agreed! ◀ Mex, ES, Col ▶

No tiene(s) que jurarlo. (You don't have to swear it.) said when something is agreed, obvious ◀ Mex, Col ▶

Okei. OK. (from the English expres-sion) ◀ L. Am. ▶

Oquey, maguey. (All right, maguey cactus.) Okey-dokey. ◀ Mex, Col ▶

¡Papas! (Potatoes!) Great! You're on! Agreed! ◀ Mex, ES, Col ▶

Sale y vale. (It goes/turns out and it's worth it.) It's a deal. (Mex, ES: sometimes shortened to **Sale**) ◀ Mex, C. Am., Col ▶
¿Cinco mil pesos? Okei, sale y vale. Five thousand pesos? —OK, it's a deal.

Sobres. Right. ◀ Mex, ES ▶

Trato hecho. (Agreement made.) It's a deal. ◀ L. Am., Sp ▶

Vale. (It is worth something.) All right. OK. ◀ Col, Sp ▶

¡Vaya! Good, great, agreed, under-stood. ◀ Mex, G, DR, Col ▶

Váyalo. (Go it.) All right. Agreed. ◀ Ven ▶

Ya. (Already, now.) OK. ◀ Ch ▶

Ya lo creo. (I already believe it.) I should say so. ◀ L. Am., Sp ▶
Nunca fui a una cantina. —¡Ya lo creo! I never went to a bar. —I believe it!

Ya se ve. (It's already seen.) expression of agreement, I see. ◀ L. Am., Sp ▶

Ya vas, Barrabás. All right. Agreed. (ES: usually ironic, meaning There you go again! Same old story!) ◀ Mex, Col ▶

anger

See also "annoyance," "criticism," "hostility," "insults."

el berro anger, bad temper ◀ Cuba ▶

la chicha anger ◀ CR, Col ▶

el coraje (courage) anger ◀ parts of L. Am., Sp ▶
Me da coraje que me engañen. It makes me mad when I get taken advantage of.

dejar como Dios pintó al perico (to leave [someone] the way God painted the parakeet, i.e., green) to make (someone) mad ◀ Nic ▶

la descarga (discharge, unloading) scolding ◀ Cuba, PR, Col ▶

Say it with slang!

Reptiles, upright and lowdown

Snakes make plenty of appearances in Spanish slang and not always in a negative way. To talk about the times long past, Nicaraguans sometimes say: **cuando las culebras andaban a pie** (when snakes used to walk upright). To describe someone trying to do the impossible, a Mexican may say: **Está buscando chichis a las culebras** (He/She is looking for breasts on snakes). The winding and unwinding movement of serpents suggests something that goes on and on in a repetitive way, which must be why the soap operas so popular in many places are called **culebrones** (literally, big snakes) or **teleculebras** (tele-snakes). In Chile a person who talks on and on without letting anyone else get a word in edgewise is described as **una persona que suelta la culebra** (someone who lets loose the snake). Of course, ever since the Garden of Eden, reptiles have had a pretty bad reputation. Just as in English we speak about a lowdown creep as a "snake in the grass," in Spanish a nasty person is **una víbora**, and a place where many such people hang out can be called **un nido de víboras** (a nest of vipers).

descargar (to discharge, unload) to let loose with emotion, positive or negative, let it all out (Mex: usually negative emotion, like **desahogarse**) ◀ Mex, Cuba, PR, Col ▶
Llegó furiosa y descargó todo en su esposo. (Mex) She was furious when she arrived and took it all out on her husband.

tenerle una bronca a alguien to be upset with someone ◀ U, Arg ▶

angry

bravo(-a) angry ◀ L. Am., Sp ▶
Se puso bravo cuando le acusaron de ese robo. He got mad when they accused him of that robbery.
¿Por qué andas tan brava? Why are you so upset?

cabreado(-a) angry; also, horny ◀ Mex, CR, Col, Sp ▶
Está muy cabreado por la putada que le hiciste. (Sp) He's very angry because of the dirty trick you played on him.

choreado(-a) angry, mad ◀ CR, Ch ▶

de rompe y rasga (of break and tear) determined and angry ◀ CR, Sp ▶

emperrado(-a) (made into a dog) wildly mad, angry (like a dog) ◀ ES, Nic ▶

encabronado(-a) angry ◀ Mex, C. Am., PR, many S. Am. countries ▶

enchilado(-a) (sick from hot chilies) angry (CR: curious or with interest piqued) ◀ Mex, G, Nic ▶
Rosa no permitió que José la besara y él se quedó enchilado. Rosa didn't allow José to kiss her and he got all hot under the collar.
Pepe está enchilado porque no puede averiguar cómo el mago hace sus trucos. (CR) Pepe is angry because he can't figure out how the magician does his tricks.

encohetado(-a) angry, furious ◀ CR, ES ▶

encojonado(-a) angry, furious (vulgar, from **cojones**) ◀ DR, PR ▶
Mejor volvemos otro día. Parece que su papá esta encojonadísimo porque Luis llegó tarde ayer. We'd better come back another day. It seems his dad is really pissed off because Luis was late yesterday.

estar ardido(-a) (mordido[-a]) (to be burned [bitten]) to be angry ◀Mex, G, CR▶

estar cabreado(-a) como una mona (to be angry as a monkey) to be very angry ◀Sp▶

estar como agua para chocolate (to be like water for chocolate) to be at the boiling point because of either anger or passion ◀Mex, CR▶
Cuando Miguel llegó a la casa, su esposa estaba como agua para chocolate. When Miguel got home, his wife was ready to explode.

estar como energúmeno (to be like one possessed) to be hysterical ◀Mex, ES, Ch▶

estar como un león (de bravo) (to be like a lion) to be very angry ◀Mex, G▶

estar jetón, jetona (to be big mouth) to be angry (CR: **ser jetón, jetonear,** to be a liar) ◀Mex, G, ES▶
Está jetón porque no puede salir. He's angry because he can't go out.

estar que ladra (to be barking) to be angry ◀Mex, Sp▶
Ni le hables a Norma porque está que ladra. Don't even talk to Norma because she's ready to bite your head off.

fúrico(-a) furious ◀Mex▶

llevarse (a alguien) el demonio (to be taken by the devil or demon) to be angry or very irritated ◀Mex, Sp▶

llevarse (a alguien) el diablo (to be taken by the devil) to be angry or very irritated (Mex: also, **llevarse la trompada, la tostada, la trampa**) ◀Mex, S. Cone▶
El jefe estaba que se lo llevaba el diablo cuando vio que no terminé el trabajo. The boss was as angry as heck when he saw that I hadn't finished my work.
Anda que se lo lleva la tostada desde que perdió el trabajo. She acts like she's mad as can be since she lost her job.

tener una cara de teléfono ocupado (to have a face like a busy telephone) to be angry, annoyed ◀PR▶

trompudo(-a) (with a big snout) loud-mouthed or bigmouthed; someone sounding off threats ◀Mex, C. Am., Col▶
Cada vez que lo veo, está trompudo. Every time I see him, he's yelling and screaming.

expressions of anger

¡A la verga! (to the male organ) interjection of anger or surprise (critical and negative, to react to something you don't like [vulgar]) ◀ES, Nic, Ven▶
¡Vete a la verga! Go piss off!
Ya me voy a la verga. Now I'm gonna go to the devil.

¡Caracoles! (snails) Darn it! euphemism for **¡Carajo!** ◀Mex, DR, Col, U, Arg, Sp▶

¡Carajo! (male organ) common expression of anger (vulgar) ◀L. Am., Sp▶

¡Cojones! (testicles) Damn! common expletive (vulgar) ◀Cuba, Sp▶

¡Coña! (female organ) expletive (vulgar) ◀Sp▶
Vaya coña tener que ir al cine con Jaime. Damn my luck to have to go to the movies with Jaime.

¡Coño! (female organ) interjection of anger, surprise, pain (vulgar, especially in L. Am.) ◀Mex, Caribbean, Col, Sp▶
¡Coño! ¡Qué suerte has tenido! ¡Qué guapa que estás! Damn! What luck you've had! How gorgeous you look!

¡Diablo! (Devil!) expression of surprise (Mex: more common, **¡Diablos!**) ◀Mex, DR, PR, Col▶

¡Dianche!, ¡Diantre! (Devil!) Holy smoke!, used instead of **¡Diablo!, ¡Demonio!** to express surprise, dismay (DR: **diache;** Mex: **diantres**) ◀Col, PR, Mex, DR▶
¡Diantre! (¡Diache!, ¡Diablo!) ¡Tú no sabes de lo que te pierdes! (DR) Holy smoke! You just don't know what you're missing!
¡Diantres! (Mex) Dang!

¡Esto es el colmo! (This is the limit, culmination!) This is the last straw! ◀L. Am., Sp▶

¡Hostia puta! (Host whore! religious reference) Goddamn it! (vulgar) ◀Sp▶
¡Hostia puta, me han robado la cartera! Goddamn it! They stole my wallet!

¡La chucha! (female organ) Crap! (very common, vulgar) ◀Ch▶

¡Maldito(-a) sea! (May it be cursed!) Damn it! exclamation of anger ◀Mex, G, DR, PR, Col, Sp▶

¡Me cago en Dios! (I shit on God!) strong expletive implying sacrilege (vulgar) ◀Sp▶

¡Me cago en la puta (diez, leche)! (I shit on the whore [ten, milk]!) expression of anger (vulgar) ◀Sp▶

narices (noses) dickens, often a euphemism for **cojones** ◀Sp▶
¿Qué narices ha pasado? What the dickens happened?

¡Ostras! (Oysters!) euphemism for **¡Hostias!,** Darn! ◀Sp▶

¡Puta! (Whore!) Damn! (vulgar) ◀L. Am., Sp▶

¡Puta la huevada (güea)! (Whore the bunch of testicles!) Goddamn it to hell! (vulgar but common, like Mexican **hijo de la gran chingada**) ◀Ch▶

¡Puta madre! (Mother whore!) expression of surprise or anger (vulgar) ◀Mex, C. Am., S. Cone▶

¡Qué gran cagada! (What a pile of shit!) What a piece of shit! What a dirty trick! (usually refers to a lie or betrayal, although in Sp it's often used to imply a big mistake) ◀ES, S. Cone, Sp▶
La gran cagada de mi vida fue casarme con Luis. (Sp) The big screwup of my life was marrying Luis.

¡Qué huevada (güea)! (What a bunch of testicles!) Oh, shit! (vulgar) ◀Ch▶

¿Qué huevonada (verga) es ésta? (What screwup [thing, male organ] is this?) What the hell is happening? What's going on? ◀Ven▶

¿Qué vaina (mierda) es ésta? (What screwup [thing, shit] is this?) What the hell is happening? What's going on? ◀ES, Ven▶

fuming

echar chispas (to throw off sparks) to show signs of anger or bad temper, to fume ◀Mex, ES, DR, Ch, Sp▶
Siempre echo chispas por la mañana. I'm always grouchy in the morning.
Esa mujer anda echando chispas de enojada. That woman walks around fuming with rage.

echar fuego por los ojos (to be fiery-eyed) to show fury or anger ◀Mex, Sp▶

echar humo (to throw off steam or smoke) to be furious ◀Mex, ES, DR, Sp▶
No me hables, que vengo echando humo. Tuve un problema con la profesora de español. Don't talk to me because I'm hopping mad. I had a problem with the Spanish professor.

echar lumbre (to throw fire) to show signs of anger or bad temper ◀Mex, ES, Sp▶
Anda tan enojada que hasta echa lumbre por los ojos. She is so angry that she's giving everyone dirty looks.

echar rayos (to throw off lightning rays) to show great anger (Mex: **rayos y centellas,** lightning rays and sparks) ◀Mex, ES, Sp▶

subírsele a alguien el humo a las narices (a la cabeza) (to have smoke rising up to one's nostrils [to one's head]) to be very annoyed, steamed (CR: **a la cabeza** instead of **a las narices;** Ch: **írsele el humo a la cabeza**) ◀CR, Sp▶
A Sergio se le subió el humo a las narices cuando supo que su hija le había mentido. Sergio got all steamed up when he found out his daughter had lied.

hothead

acalorado(-a) (heated up) someone who gets upset easily, excitable, a hothead, temperamental ◀U, Arg, Sp▶

el calentón, la calentona (big hot one) person who gets angry easily, hothead; also, sexy ◀Arg▶
Es un calentón. He's a hothead.

el/la chinchudo(-a) (big ugly bedbug) person who gets angry easily, hothead, person with a short fuse ◀U, Arg▶
Juan es muy chinchudo. Juan is very hot-headed.

enojón, enojona hostile, easily angered ◀L. Am., Sp▶

fosforito (little match) quick-tempered, hotheaded (also, in PR, witty) ◀PR, Ven, U, Arg▶
¡Cuidado con Iván! Es muy fosforito. Watch it with Iván! He has a short fuse.

fosforito
(See page 11.)

losing it

agarrarse una chinche (to grab one-self a bedbug) to get very angry, blow a gasket ◄ U, Arg ►
María se quedó plantada y se agarró una chinche. María got stood up and she blew a gasket.

arrecharse (to get horns like an ani-mal) to get very angry, to lose it ◄ Nic, Ven, Ec ►
Cuando esa chica me insultó, me arreché. When that babe insulted me, I lost it.
Hombre, ¡no te arreches! No es para tanto. Man, don't hit the roof! It's no big deal.

cabrear(se) (to act like a goat) to make angry (become angry) (vulgar) ◄ CR, Ec, Arg, Ch, Sp ►
Ese chico se cabrea por nada. That guy loses it over nothing.
No me cabrées. Don't get my goat.

chorearse to lose patience, get angry (a bit vulgar) ◄ Ch ►

darle una arrechera (to give a horni-ness, heat) to upset, make angry or hot under the collar (vulgar) ◄ Ven ►
Vi que me habían robado la bicicleta, ¡y me dio una arrechera! I saw that my bike was stolen, and I went ballistic!

encabronar(se) to make (someone) angry, furious (wild, like a goat), to be-come furious ◄ Mex, C. Am., PR, many S. Am. countries ►
¡Ya me encabronaste! Now you got my goat!
El jefe se va a encabronar si el reportaje no está listo a las cuatro. The boss is going to fly off the handle if the report isn't ready by four o'clock.

encachimbarse to get enraged ◄ ES, Nic ►

enchicharse (also, **enchichado[-a]**) to get mad ◄ Mex, Col, U ►
Me tuvieron allí esperando hasta que me enchiché. They had me waiting there until I lost it.
La mamá de Juliana sigue enchichada por lo que le rompimos el vidrio. Juliana's mom is still hot under the collar because of our breaking her windowpane.

encojonarse to get angry, furious (vul-gar, from **cojones**) ◄ DR, PR ►

enfogonarse to get angry ◄ Mex, PR, Col ►
No tienes que enfogonarte conmigo; yo estaba gufeando. You don't have to lose your cool with me; I was just fooling around.

engorilarse (to become like a gorilla) to get mad suddenly, snap, go ballistic over a situation ◄ Ven ►

engranar to react angrily to a provoca-tion ◄ Arg ►

entromparse to get angry ◄ Mex, ES, Col, Ec ►
Los dos ex-novios se entromparon en-frente de ella. The two ex-fiancés tore into each other in front of her.

explotarse to explode, blow up (with anger) ◄ G, Cuba, Col ►

írsele la olla (to have the pot fly off or go off on one) to lose it, fly off the han-dle ◄ Sp ►
Se le va la olla de vez en cuando, pero no es mal tío. He flies off the handle every once in a while, but he's not a bad guy.

jalarse los pelos (to pull one's hair out) to be furious (S. Cone, Sp: more com-mon, **tirarse de los pelos**) ◄ Mex, ES, Sp ►
Estoy que me jalo los pelos de coraje. (Mex) I'm so angry that I'm tearing out my hair.

perder los estribos (to lose the stir-rups) to lose patience, lose your cool ◄ L. Am., Sp ►

Si no dejas de molestar, voy a perder los estribos. If you don't stop bugging me, I'm going to lose my cool.

picarse (to become piqued) to get angry, be annoyed ◀ PR, Col, Ch, Sp ▶
No te piques, que no es para tanto. Don't get steamed up because it's not a big deal.

ponerse como una fiera (to become like a wild animal) to get very angry ◀ ES, Ch, Sp ▶

retorcer el hígado (to have one's liver twist) to get angry (CR: **tener un ataque de hígado**) ◀ Mex ▶
Se me retorció el hígado de coraje cuando lo vi. I had an attack of anger when I saw him.

sofocarse (to get suffocated) to get upset, worked up ◀ Mex, ES, DR, Col, S. Cone, Sp ▶
No te sofoques. Don't hit the ceiling.

subírsele el apellido (to raise the last name) to get angry ◀ CR, Col ▶
A Víctor se le sube el apellido a menudo. Víctor often blows his top.

subírsele la mostaza (to have the mustard rise up) to get angry ◀ Peru, Sp ▶
Perdona que se me subiera la mostaza ayer. Excuse me for blowing my top yesterday.

sulfurarse to get steamed up (sulfured) ◀ L. Am., Sp ▶

tantrums, fits, outbursts

el ataque de caspa (dandruff attack) fit, tantrum ◀ S. Cone ▶
Tuvo un ataque de caspa porque nos faltaba un documento. He (She) had a fit because we were missing a document.

el cabreo monumental huge outburst of anger ◀ Sp ▶
Cogió un cabreo monumental cuando se canceló el concierto. He (She) threw a major tantrum when the concert was canceled.

darse (agarrarse) una rabieta to have a fit, tantrum ◀ L. Am., Sp ▶
Le dio una rabieta porque no había chocolate en casa. He (She) threw a fit because there wasn't any chocolate in the house.

formar un berrinche to have a fit, tantrum ◀ PR, Col, Sp ▶

El niño de la vecina forma un berrinche cada vez que ella se va al trabajo. The neighbor's little boy has a tantrum every time she goes to work.
Siempre igual con tus berrinches. Always the same with your tantrums.

hacer un berrinche to have a tantrum ◀ Mex, DR, Col, Sp ▶
Marta hizo un berrinche enorme cuando le dijeron que se fuera. Marta threw an enormous tantrum when they told her to leave.

hacer un coraje to pick a fight; to get very angry ◀ Mex, G ▶

la pataleta (kicking fit) fit, tantrum (DR, Col: also, **patalear**) ◀ L. Am., Sp ▶
El niño hizo una pataleta. The boy had a tantrum.

el patatús tantrum, (fainting) fit ◀ Mex, ES, CR, DR, PR, Col, Ch ▶

patear la perra (to kick the female dog) to do something as an outlet for repressed anger, blow off some steam ◀ Ch ▶

la venada fit ◀ Sp ▶
A Hugo le dio una venada y rompió su examen. Hugo threw a fit and ripped up his exam.

---

annoyance

See also "anger," "criticism," "hostility," "insults."

amoscado(-a) irritated (as if by flies, moscas) ◀ PR ▶

encimoso(-a) insistent person who keeps coming back for something ◀ Mex, ES ▶

la fregadera the act of continuously asking for something (slightly vulgar) ◀ chicano, Mex, G, CR, ES ▶
Sigues con la misma fregadera. You keep on with your same old nagging.

¡Huy! Ouch! (expression of pain) ◀ L. Am., Sp ▶

amoscado
(See page 13.)

No juegues. Don't play around.
◀ Caribbean ▶

picado(-a) (piqued, stung) annoyed, resentful ◀ Mex, G, CR, Col, Ven, Bol, Ch, Sp ▶
El perro no te obedece y ya estás picado. (CR) The dog won't obey you and now you're annoyed.

¿Qué bicho te ha picado? (What insect has bitten you?) What's bothering you? ◀ Mex, G, DR, S. Cone, Sp ▶

sacar a alguien de sus casillas (de quicio) (to take someone out of their pigeon holes [out of joint]) to change someone's way of doing things or drive them crazy, rattle their cage ◀ L. Am., Sp ▶
Mi primo me sacó de mis casillas con sus preguntas. My cousin drove me nuts with his questions.

¿Tengo monos en la cara? (Do I have monkeys on my face?) Why are you staring at me? ◀ Mex, Ch, Sp ▶

annoying

el/la alborotado(-a) (made upset) troublemaker, someone who upsets others ◀ Mex, ES, DR, Arg ▶

chavón, chavona annoying, irritating ◀ PR ▶

chayote (vegetable with prickly skin) bothersome ◀ Mex, PR ▶

el chicle (chewing gum) person who sticks like glue, annoying person ◀ Mex, G, Cuba, DR, PR ▶
Vámonos de aquí que ya llegó Tomás. —Ay, ¡ese chicle! Si nos ve, no se nos despega. Let's get out of here because Tomás has already arrived. —Oh, that pest! If he sees us, he'll stick to us like glue.

chingón, chingona annoying or bothersome ◀ chicano, Mex, C. Am. ▶

el/la muy condenado(-a) (the very condemned) that darn guy (girl, man, woman, etc.) ◀ Florida, Mex, G, CR, DR, Col, U, Ch ▶
La muy condenada ganó un viaje a Hawai como premio. That darn chick won a trip to Hawaii as a prize.

el pelma (pelmazo) (mass of undigested food) idiot, boring person ◀ Sp ▶
No seas pelmazo/pelma. Don't be a pain (bore).

fregón, fregona (scrubber) annoying ◀ Mex, G, Col ▶

el/la hincha (hinchapelotas) (inflator [of balls]) irritating person, pest (vulgar) ◀ Arg ▶
No invites a Mario; es un hincha (hinchapelotas). Don't invite Mario; he's a pain in the ass.

la jodedera impertinence, annoyance (vulgar) ◀ ES, CR, PR, Col ▶
Esta nueva regla es una jodedera. This new rule is a damn nuisance.

jodón, jodona bothersome, annoying (vulgar) ◀ Mex, G, DR, Col ▶
La cosa está muy jodona últimamente; han habido varios atracos en la ciudad. The situation is damn annoying lately; there've been several muggings in the city.

la ladilla (leech) pain in the neck, insistent person ◀ Mex, G, Cuba, DR, PR, Col, Ven, Peru ▶
¡Qué ladilla! What a pain in the neck!

la lapa (barnacle) person who is hard to shake off, pest ◀ Mex, DR, PR, Col, Ch, Sp ▶
¡Qué lapa! What a pest!

latoso(-a) boring, bothersome, a pain ◀ Mex, ES, DR, Col, Ec, Ch ▶
Esa muchacha es bien latosa. That girl is a big pain.

mamón, mamona (sucker, like a suckling baby) tiresome, annoying, or ridiculous ◄ chicano, Mex, Col, Peru, ES ►

molón, molona bothersome, annoying ◄ Mex ►

pegajoso(-a) (sticky) always at your side, saying silly things or overly attentive; also, something that sticks in your mind ◄ Mex, Col, Ch ►
un chico pegajoso, una canción pegajosa a pesky kid, a catchy song

pega-pega used like **pegajoso** ◄ ES, Col ►
No seas tan pega-pega. Don't be such a pest.

ser la última gota (to be the last drop) to be the last straw ◄ Sp ►

ser pesado(-a) (to be weighty) to be a pain, a drag, boring, or unpleasant ◄ L. Am., Sp ►

ser un(a) fregado(-a) (to be a scrubber) to be an annoying, demanding, or bossy person ◄ Mex, Nic, CR, Peru, Ch ►

ser una lata (to be a tin can) to be a pain, drag, bore, annoyance (G, ES, Sp; also, **pura lata**) ◄ Florida, Mex, G, ES, DR, Col, Ch, Sp ►
Ese chico es pura lata. That boy is a real pain.
Levantarse todos los días para ir a trabajar es una lata. Getting up every day to go to work is a drag.

don't bug me

No chaves. Don't bother me. ◄ PR, Col ►
No chaves. ¡Déjame en paz! Don't bug me. Leave me in peace!

No fuñas. Don't be a pain. ◄ DR, Col ►
Muchacho, ¡no fuñas! ¡Déjame tranquila! Man, don't be a pain! Leave me alone!

No mames. (Don't suckle.) That's enough. Don't be so tiresome. Don't talk nonsense. (used like **No seas cansón.**) ◄ Mex, ES, Col ►

No mameyes en tiempos de melones. (Don't "mamey fruits" in times of melons.) euphemism for ¡No mames! That's enough. Don't go on and on. ◄ Mex ►

No me busques. (Don't look for me.) Don't get on my bad side. Don't go

there. (also, **No le busques.**) ◄ Mex, DR, PR, Col, U ►
Ando cabreadísima, así que no me busques, ¡que me encuentras! (DR) I'm really furious, so don't get on my bad side because you won't like it! (literally, because you'll find it!)
No le busques. (Mex) Don't go there with him (her). (Don't mention that subject that he's [she's] sensitive about.)

No me cargues. (Don't load me up.) Don't bother (bug) me. ◄ U, Arg ►

No me jodas. (Don't screw me.) Don't bother me. ◄ most of L. Am. ►

expressions of annoyance

¡Caramba! Jeez! Darn it! (euphemism for ¡Carajo!, vulgar) ◄ L. Am., Sp ►

¡Caray! (euphemism for ¡Carajo!) Jeez! Darn it! ◄ Mex, Cuba, DR, PR, Col, Sp ►

¡Chin! ¡Chihuahua! ¡Chispas! euphemisms for **chinga'o**, screwed ◄ Mex ►

¡Chis! exclamation of annoyance, disgust ◄ Mex, G, ES ►
¡Chis! No jodas. Jeez! Don't bug me.

el coñazo (blow, from **coño**, vulgar) drag, something bothersome or bad; also, hard time (vulgar) ◄ Sp ►
¡Qué coñazo! No recibí las entradas a tiempo. What a bitch of a problem! I didn't get the tickets on time.

Esto es la hostia. (This is the Host.) This is the damn limit. This is too much. (vulgar) ◄ Sp ►

Hasta aquí llegó mi (el) amor. (My love lasted this far, up to here.) This was the last straw. ◄ Florida, Mex, G, DR, Col, U, Arg ►

¡Hostia(s)! (Host[s]!) a strong expletive implying religious sacrilege (vulgar) ◄ Sp ►

¡Joer! from **joder**; interjection used in Spain, something like Damn! ◄ Sp ►

¡Miércoles! (Wednesday!) Heck! euphemism for ¡Mierda! ◄ L. Am., Sp ►

¡Mierda! Shit! (vulgar) ◄ L. Am., Sp ►

¡Porras! exclamation of disgust or anger ◄ Sp ►

¡Pucha! ¡La pucha! (softened form of ¡La puta!, the whore) equivalent to Darn it! ◀ L. Am. ▶

¡Puñeta! (masturbation) Damn! (slightly vulgar, although less so in CR) ◀ CR, PR ▶

¡Puñeta! No traje mi cartera. Damn! I didn't bring my wallet.

puñeta(s) (masturbation) devil, dickens (vulgar) (note: in Sp, **coño** is more common but also more vulgar) ◀ PR, Sp ▶

¿Dónde puñetas estabas? Where the devil were you?

¡Qué barbaridad! (What barbarity!) Good grief! ◀ L. Am., Sp ▶

¡Qué bárbaro! (How barbarous!) Good grief! ◀ L. Am., Sp ▶

¡Qué cruz! What a drag (cross)! ◀ Mex, DR, PR, Col, U, Sp ▶

¡Qué cruz tener un marido borracho! What a drag to have a drunk for a husband!

Qué fregado(-a) eres. How shameless (fresh, annoying) you are. ◀ G, Col, Ch ▶

¡Qué jodienda! What a nuisance/pain! (vulgar, from **joder**) ◀ Cuba, DR, PR, Col, Ven, Para, U, Sp ▶

¡Qué joroba! What a pain! How annoying (person)! ◀ Mex, DR, PR, Col, U ▶

¡Qué joroba tener que trabajar los fines de semana! What a pain to have to work on weekends!

¡Qué vaina! (What a husk, sheath!) expression of surprise, unpleasantness, anger, annoyance, disagreement ◀ G, Nic, CR, DR, Col, Ven ▶

¡Rayos! (Lightning rays!) Good grief!, Blast! (a bit old-fashioned, used to express surprise or a problem) ◀ L. Am., Sp ▶

¿Qué rayos pasa? What the dickens (lightning rays) is happening?

¡Uff! Oh dear! Oops! ◀ Mex, Col ▶

¡Válgame Dios! Good grief! ◀ L. Am., Sp ▶

fed up

estar harto(-a) to be fed up ◀ L. Am., Sp ▶

estar hasta arriba to be fed up (up to here) ◀ Col, Sp ▶

estar hasta el copete

estar hasta las cejas (to be up to the eyebrows) to be up to here, fed up; to have had it ◀ Sp ▶

estar hasta el cogote to be fed up (to the crest, top of the head) ◀ Mex, ES, PR, Ch, Sp ▶

estar hasta los cojones to be fed up (to the testicles, vulgar) ◀ Mex, Sp ▶

estar hasta el (mismísimo) coño to be fed up (to the female organ, vulgar) ◀ Sp ▶

estar hasta el copete to be fed up (to the forelock, top of the hair) ◀ Mex, G, Nic, CR, Peru, Para ▶

estar hasta la coronilla to be fed up (to the top of the head, crown) ◀ L. Am., Sp ▶

¡Ya me tiene cansada hasta la coronilla! Now it's (you've, he's, she's) got me totally fed up, up to the eyebrows!

estar hasta el gollete to be fed up (to the gullet) ◀ Sp ▶

estar hasta el gorro to be fed up (to the cap) ◀ Mex, ES, Sp ▶

Estoy hasta el gorro con tus quejas. I'm sick and tired of your complaints.

estar hasta los huevos (to be up to the eggs [testicles]) to be fed up (vulgar) ◀ Sp ▶

estar hasta la madre (to be up to the mother) to be up to here, fed up; to have had it ◀ Mex, C. Am. ▶

estar hasta el moño to be fed up (to the bun, roll of hair tied up in back) ◀ Sp ▶

estar hasta las narices to be fed up (to the nose) ◀ Mex, Sp ▶

estar hasta el tope to be fed up (to the top) ◀ Mex, ES, DR, U ▶

estar hasta los topes to be fed up (to the top) ◀ CR, Col, Sp ▶

estar hinchado(-a) (con) (to be swollen up [with]) to be fed up (with something) ◀ Ec, Ch ▶

estar negro(-a) (to be black) to be fed up, sick of something ◀ Sp ▶
Estoy negra con toda esa publicidad que me echan en el buzón. I've had it with all that advertising they stick in my mailbox.

no poder más to not be able to take any more, be fed up ◀ L. Am., Sp ▶
Esta situación es insoportable. No puedo más. This situation is unbearable. I can't take it any longer.

tener las bolas llenas (to have your balls full) to be fed up (vulgar) ◀ U, Arg ▶
Naldo tiene las bolas llenas con ese contador. Naldo is royally pissed off at that accountant.

getting upset

agitarse to get agitated, upset, worked up ◀ Mex, G, ES, DR, Col ▶
No te agites. Don't get upset.

andar mosca (to go fly) to be upset ◀ PR, Sp ▶
Andaba un poco mosca. He (She) was a little bit upset.

estar que cortar las huinchas (to be ready to cut the starting wires [on a race course]) to be in desperate straits, ready to lose control ◀ Ch ▶
Estoy que corto las huinchas. (Está que corta las huinchas.) I'm at my wits' end. (He's at his wits' end.)

hacerse mala sangre (to make bad blood for oneself) to get upset, ticked off, rattled ◀ L. Am., Sp ▶
No te hagas mala sangre. No es tan tremendo. Don't get ticked off. It's not so awful.

picarle a alguien una mosca (to have a fly biting or stinging someone) to be bothered, to have something be the matter ◀ L. Am., Sp ▶

¿Qué mosca te está picando? What's bugging you?
¿Qué mosca te ha (habrá) picado? What could have been the matter?

picarse (to get the itch) to get mad, upset ◀ Ch ▶

subirse por las paredes to be crawling up the walls (with annoyance) ◀ U, Sp ▶

tener hormigas en el culo (to have ants in your ass) to be impatient, have ants in your pants (vulgar) ◀ U, Arg ▶

giving someone a hard time

bajar un número (to lower a number) to give someone bad news or ask for something difficult to give ◀ Cuba ▶

buscarle las pulgas a alguien (to look for someone's fleas) to provoke or irritate someone ◀ Mex, Cuba, Sp ▶

dar carrete a alguien (to give someone a reel, coil) to put someone off, make them wait or keep them dangling ◀ Sp ▶

dar lata (to give tin can) to give someone a hard time; to annoy; to bore by talking a lot (Sp: **dar la lata**) ◀ L. Am., Sp ▶

dar picones (to give scratches) to provoke, antagonize, rile up, excite (ES: also, **dar chile**) ◀ Mex, ES ▶
En la fiesta mi ex-novia me daba picones. At the party my ex-girlfriend was bugging (provoking) me.

escorchar to bother, annoy, bug ◀ Arg ▶

hacer cototo (to give a bump on the head) to give (someone) a hard time ◀ Bol ▶
¡No me hagas cototo, contándome todos tus problemas! Don't give me a hard time, telling me all your problems!

hacer la puñeta a alguien to bother, beg (vulgar) ◀ Sp ▶

hacerla de tos (de pedo) a alguien to give someone problems (Mex only: **de pedo**, vulgar) ◀ Mex, ES ▶
Me la hizo de tos (de pedo). He (She) caused me a lot of trouble.

hinchar las pelotas

hacerle la vida un yogurt a alguien to make someone's life bitter (a yogurt) ◀ Cuba ▶

hinchar las pelotas (to inflate the balls) to bother, bug, pester (Arg, Ch: also used without **pelotas**; Sp: always used with either **pelotas** or **huevos** [vulgar]) ◀ Arg, Ch, Sp ▶
¡**No me hinches (las pelotas) tanto!** Don't give me such a damn hard time!

hostigar to annoy, badger, bug ◀ most of L. Am., Sp ▶
¿**Por qué hostigan tanto?** Why are they badgering us so much?
Que hostigas. How you bug a person.

joder (to screw or bother) to bother, harm, beg (vulgar; Sp: also **joder la marrana**) ◀ L. Am., Sp ▶

jorobar euphemism for **joder**, to bother (to screw) ◀ Mex, G, CR, Cuba, DR, PR ▶
Esta muela me está jorobando mucho. This molar is giving me a darn hard time.

mosquear (to be like a fly) to bother, pester ◀ Ch, Sp ▶
Me mosquea que aún no me haya llamado. It bothers me that he (she) still hasn't called me.
No me mosquées. Don't pester me.

no dejar a alguien sentar el pie en el suelo to not let someone rest (put his or her foot on the floor) ◀ Sp ▶

no dejar (ni) a sol ni a sombra a alguien (to not leave someone in the sun or the shade) to hound, pursue someone at all hours and in all places ◀ L. Am., Sp ▶

picar a alguien to upset (bite, sting) someone ◀ Mex, G, DR, PR, Peru, Sp ▶
¿**Qué le picó a ese muchacho?** What's got into that boy?
¿**Qué te pica?** What's bugging you?

pisarle los callos a alguien (to step on someone's callouses) to bother someone without rhyme or reason, be all over someone ◀ Peru, Ch ▶

poner a alguien a cien (to put someone to the hundred) to excite or exasperate someone ◀ Sp ▶

putear to bother, annoy, harass (Sp: usually used for actions rather than words [vulgar]; L. Am.: usually verbal. See "insults.") ◀ Sp ▶
Ese chico siempre me está puteando en la escuela. That boy is always giving me a hell of a time at school.
La profesora me puteó al suspenderme el examen. Ahora tengo que repetir el curso entero. The teacher screwed me by flunking me on the exam. Now I have to repeat the whole course.
¡**No me putées más y dime lo que quieres!** Stop messing with me so damn much and tell me what you want!

puyar to bother, pressure ◀ CR, ES, Nic, Col ▶
Sólo andas puyando. You're only being a nuisance.

rebotar (to repel) to annoy, upset ◀ Mex, Sp ▶
Lo que me rebotó es que escogieran a ese inepto y no a ti. What really upset me was that they chose that dolt and not you.

romperle los huevos a alguien (to break someone's eggs) to bug, pester, get someone very upset (vulgar) ◀ U, Arg ▶
Por favor, no me rompas los huevos. Please stop giving me such a damn hard time.

sacar de onda to knock out of kilter, throw off ◀ L. Am. ▶

Lo siento. Es que me sacaste de onda. I'm sorry. It's just that you knocked me for a loop.

sacar la piedra (to take away the stone) to bother, try someone's patience ◀ Ven ▶

tener (traer) a alguien frito(-a) (to have [bring] someone fried) to tire someone out, bothering them ◀ Mex, DR, Sp ▶
Daniela me tiene frita con su conducta. Daniela has got me at my wits' end with her behavior.

tenérsela pelada (to have it peeled) to tire someone out repeating or insisting on something ◀ Cuba ▶
Me la tienes pela'a con el asunto de tu trabajo. You're driving me nuts with that stuff about your work.

tocar los cojones (huevos) a alguien (to touch someone's testicles) to bother someone continually (vulgar) ◀ Sp ▶

torear (to fight bulls) to provoke, upset ◀ CR, ES, Col, Ch ▶

traer de culo a alguien (to bring someone by the ass) to upset someone (vulgar) ◀ Sp ▶

arrival: showing up

asomarse to show up ◀ L. Am. ▶

caer (to fall) to visit ◀ Mex, ES, Col, S. Cone ▶
Más tarde te caigo. Later I'll drop in on you.
Le cayeron sus amigos cuando no tenía nada preparado. His friends popped in on him when he had nothing prepared.

caerse por acá (ahí) to drop in here (there) ◀ L. Am. ▶

dejarse caer (to let oneself fall) to drop by ◀ Bol, Ch, Sp ▶
Si voy a Barcelona, me dejaré caer por tu casa. If I go to Barcelona, I'll drop by your house.

descolgarse (to unhang oneself) to appear suddenly ◀ Mex, ES ▶
Estaba lavando los platos cuando mi prima se descolgó. I was washing the dishes when my cousin popped in.

Say it with slang!

Word shortening

Some words are often shortened in everyday Spanish conversation.

—Mira en el *refri, porfa,* a ver qué hay…. ¿Prendo la *tele*?
—Si quieres. Tengo que ir a la *uni* a las dos a trabajar en la *compu.*

Do you understand the shortened expressions? Here's an English translation just to make sure:

"Look in the *fridge* (**refrigerador**), *please* (**por favor**), to see what's there. . . . Shall I turn on the TV (**televisión**)?"
"If you like. I have to go to the *university* (**universidad**) at two and work on the *computer* (**computadora**)."

Other common short forms are **chasgracias, chogusto, cole, depre,** and **profe.** Can you guess what they mean? (Answers are on page 264.)

estar al caer (to be to fall) to be about to arrive ◀ Sp ▶
Mi cumpleaños está al caer. My birthday is just around the corner.

sin paracaídas (without a parachute) without prior notice, casually ◀ Col ▶

attention

attracting attention to oneself

See also "unusualness."

brillar por su ausencia to be conspicuous (shine) by its absence ◀ L. Am., Sp ▶

cantar como una almeja (to sing like a clam) to call attention to oneself and look ridiculous ◀ Sp ▶
Cantaba como una almeja con ese vestido estrafalario. She stood out like a sore thumb with that outlandish dress.

dar el cante (to give flamenco singing) to call attention to oneself and look ridiculous ◀ Sp ▶
Carlos iba dando el cante con ese sombrero de color rojo. Carlos was calling attention to himself and looked ridiculous with that red hat.

dar la nota (to give the note) to stand out in a bad way ◀ Bol, U, Arg, Sp ▶
Le gusta llamar la atención y siempre da la nota. He (She) likes to attract attention and always stands out like a sore thumb.

dar la nota alta (to give the high note) to stand out in a bad way ◀ DR, Ch ▶

ser florero (to be a flower vase) to be the center of attention ◀ Ch ▶

attracting someone's attention

See also "greetings."

¡Amigo! (Friend!) used to get a stranger's attention ◀ Mex, G, ES, DR ▶

¡Éjele! used like **¡Oye!**, Listen! Hey! ◀ Mex, PR, Col ▶

¡Epa! Hey! ◀ Caribbean ▶

¡Jefe! (Boss!) Mac! Buddy! (to a stranger) ◀ Cuba, DR, Col ▶

¡Joven! (Young person!) used to get the attention of a waiter, gas station attendant, security guard, etc., in some areas, even when the man being called is not young (Sp: a bit old-fashioned) ◀ Mex, Col, Sp ▶

mami, mamita term used to get a woman's attention ◀ L. Am. ▶

¡Oiga! (**usted** command form of **oír**; Listen!) Excuse me, may I speak with you? (used to get attention of passerby, waiter, etc.) ◀ L. Am., Sp ▶

¡Suave! used to get someone to stop or wait ◀ CR, Col ▶

marked, singled out

encarnado(-a) singled out, being watched (negative connotation) ◀ Cuba ▶
El jefe me tiene encarnado. The boss has singled me out.

fichado(-a) someone known by all; someone being watched carefully ◀ Mex, G, CR, DR, PR, Col, S. Cone ▶
Me lo traiga bien fichadito. No quiero que salga. Don't let him out of your sight. (Keep him under careful watch.) I don't want him to go out.

paying attention

aguaitar, estar al aguaite to be on one's toes, watching out for something ◀ Pan, Ec, Peru, Ch ▶

andar con ojo (to go with eye) to be always cautious and suspicious ◀ Sp ▶

chequear, chequar to check (from English) (Mex: **chequar**) ◀ Mex, C. Am., DR, PR, Ven, Ch, Sp ▶
¿A qué hora sale el autobús? —No sé, vamos a chequear. (ES) What time does the bus leave? —I don't know. Let's check.
Mi esposo me trae bien chequadita ahora que tengo mi celular. (Mex) My husband keeps tabs on me now that I have my cell phone.

dar bola a alguien (to give someone the ball) to pay attention to someone (CR, Arg: also, **dar pelota**) ◀ S. Cone ▶
Traté de explicar la situación, pero no me dieron bola. I tried to explain the situation, but they didn't give me the time of day.

darle boleto (to give the ticket to someone) to pay attention to someone ◀ Ch ▶
El candidato hablaba sin que nadie le diera boleto. The candidate went on speaking without anyone paying the slightest attention to him.

echar el ojo to eye, have one's eye on ◀ L. Am., Sp ▶
Mi tía le echó el ojo a unos pantalones y no paró hasta comprarlos. My aunt spied some slacks and didn't stop until she'd bought them.
Ya le echaste el ojo a ese muchacho, ¿no? You've already got your eye on that guy, right?

echar un lukin (to throw a looking) to have a look ◀ Ch ▶

echar un taco de ojo (to throw a taco of the eye) to look at but not obtain (e.g., to window-shop or referring to a good-looking person of the opposite sex) ◀ Mex ▶
Vamos a entrar en esta tienda de ropa, ¿no? No tengo dinero, pero quiero echar un taco de ojo. Let's go into this clothing store, OK? I don't have any money, but I'd like to browse around (do some window-shopping).

empilado(-a) dedicated to, enamored of ◀ ES ▶
Está bien empilada en el deporte. She's really crazy about sports.
Está muy empilado con esa mujer. He's totally nuts about that woman.

enchufarse (to plug in) to pay attention (also, less commonly, to have sex, as in **Me enchufé a esa chica.**) ◀ Mex, U ▶
Enchúfate. Voy a explicarte el asunto. Listen up. I'm going to explain the issue to you.

estar al cateo de la laucha (to be watching for the female louse) to be on the lookout, alert ◀ Ch ▶

estar al loro (to be at the parrot) to pay attention, be attentive ◀ Sp ▶

empilado

estar con cien (diez) ojos (to be with one hundred [ten] eyes) to be warned, alert, suspicious ◀ Sp ▶
En este barrio hay que estar con cien ojos para que no te roben. In this neighborhood you have to be on the lookout so you don't get robbed.

estar con ojo (to be with eye) to be warned, suspicious ◀ Mex, Sp ▶

estar o ponerse mosca (to be or become fly, an insect with large eyes) to be suspicious and alert to avoid something ◀ Mex, Ven, Peru, Sp ▶
Ponte mosca. ¿Ves el dire allí? Hay que estar mosca. Get with the program! Do you see the director there? You have to be alert.

estar ojo al charqui (to be eye on the beef jerky) to take special care with something ◀ Ch ▶

Fíjese (usted). Fíjate (tú). Just imagine. ◀ L. Am., Sp ▶

funar to see ◀ Peru ▶

ir de miranda to guard, watch over ◀ Sp ▶

írsele a alguien los ojos por algo o alguien (to have one's eyes go after something or someone) to desire or want something ◀ Mex, DR, Sp ▶
Cuando la vi, se me iban los ojos. From the moment I saw her, I only had eyes for her.

levantar la antena (to raise the antenna) to pay attention ◀ Mex, Col ▶

llevarle el apunte (llevar de apunte) (to keep track of the score) to pay attention to someone or something ◀ S. Cone ▶
El jefe grita mucho en esta oficina pero no le lleves el apunte. The boss shouts a lot in this office, but don't pay him any mind.

lukear, luquear (from the English "look") to look ◀ Ec, Peru, Ch ▶
¡Nos luqueamos! We'll be seeing each other! See you!

lukiar (from the English "look") to look ◀ PR ▶

meter cabeza (to put head) to pay attention (CR, Col: to persist in getting something) ◀ Mex, CR, PR, Col ▶

pajarear to observe, look at (from **pájaro**, bird); also, used to mean one is paying attention to something other than what is at hand, being distracted by something ◀ Mex, ES, Nic, Col, Ch ▶
Estás pajareando. Hazme caso. You're getting distracted. Pay attention to me.

parar bolas (to stop balls) to pay attention ◀ Nic, Ven, Ec, U ▶

parar oreja (parar las orejas, parar la oreja) to prick up one's ears, listen carefully ◀ L. Am., Sp ▶
No soy conejo pero las paro. (Ch) I'm not a rabbit, but I'm all ears.

poner la antena (to put up one's antenna) to listen (U, Arg: **parar la antena**) ◀ Mex, Sp ▶

ponerse águila (to put oneself eagle) to be on the lookout, keep one's eyes peeled ◀ Mex, G, ES ▶
Ponte águila; viene el maestro. Keep your eyes peeled; the teacher is coming.

ponerse buzo (to become a diver) to be alert (often to avoid something); to be suspicious ◀ Mex, G, ES ▶
¡Ponte buzo! Aquí tratan de venderte cualquier cosa. Be on the alert! Here they try to sell you any old thing.

ponerse para (alguien, algo) (to put oneself toward [someone, something]) to show a lot of interest in (a girl, getting something), concentrate on ◀ Cuba ▶
Ponte para Teresa; es muy simpática. Pay attention to Teresa; she's very nice.
¿Por qué no estás estudiando? Ponte para las cosas. Why aren't you studying? Get down to business.

ponerse trucha (to make oneself trout) to be aware, alert ◀ Mex, ES ▶
¡Ponte trucha! Sharpen up! (Pay attention!)

Se te están cayendo las pestañas. (Your eyelashes are falling off.) said when someone is observing something with interest ◀ Col ▶
Julián, ¡para de mirar el examen de tu compañero! Se te están cayendo las pestañas. Julián, stop looking at your classmate's exam! Your eyes are going to pop out.

wach(e)ar to watch, look (from English) ◀ chicano, ES ▶
¡Wacha eso! Look at that!

attractiveness

See also "admiration," "romance."

enganchar (to hook) to attract (someone) from the start ◀ Ch ▶

lucir (to shine) to suit, wear, or fit well ◀ CR, ES, Nic, DR, PR, Col, Sp ▶
A Rosa le lucen pantalones rojos y un collar grueso. Anda luciendo zapatos nuevos (un buen vestido). Red pants and a heavy necklace look good on Rosa. She's wearing new shoes (a good dress).

miel sobre hojuelas (honey on pastries) expression meaning that one thing goes very well with another, adding to its attractiveness ◀ Mex, DR, Sp ▶

pega-pega attractive, like **pegajoso** ◀ ES, Col ▶
Éste es bien pega-pega para las muchachas. That guy is really attractive to women.

el pegue appeal (sometimes sex appeal) ◀ Mex, ES, Col ▶
Ese chico tiene pegue. That guy has sex appeal.
Esa música tiene pegue. That music is catchy.

Se me caen las medias (los calzones). (My stockings [pants] are falling down.) I'm excited by that good-looking guy. ◀ parts of L. Am. ▶
Es tan guapo que se me caen las medias cuando lo miro. He's so handsome that my heart beats faster when I look at him.

tener gancho (to have hook) to fascinate, seduce, captivate ◀ Ch, Sp ▶

tirar (or salirle) la baba (por litros) (to throw out saliva [by the liter]) to have one's tongue hanging out (e.g., when a man has seen a beautiful woman) ◀ Mex, Col ▶
Se te salió la baba cuando viste a Cindy Crawford. Your tongue was hanging out when you saw Cindy Crawford.

good-looking, cute, pretty

el bonitillo handsome boy; man who thinks he's good-looking ◀ Mex, G, PR ▶

la buenona good-looking woman (Ch: hot, good for taking to bed [vulgar]) ◀ Mex, G, Hond, Pan, Cuba, Col, Para, Ch, Sp ▶

chulo(-a) cute, good ◀ Florida, Mex, G, DR, PR, Sp ▶
Me encanta el vestido de Sandra. ¡Está superchulo! I adore Sandra's dress. It's super cute!

el churro (fritter) attractive male ◀ Peru, S. Cone ▶
Juan es un churro bárbaro. Juan is a major stud.

estar como nunca (to be like never) to look better than ever ◀ L. Am., Sp ▶
Estás como nunca, Marisol. You look better than ever, Marisol.

estar como una reina (to be like a queen) to look beautiful ◀ L. Am., Sp ▶
Está (usted) como una reina. You look like a queen.

estar de bandera (to be with flag) to be attractive ◀ Sp ▶

estar hecho(-a) un figurín (to be made a figurine) to have a nice figure, look good physically ◀ DR, U, Arg, Sp ▶

estar muy potable (to be very drinkable) to look good physically ◀ Mex, S. Cone, Sp ▶

estar para comérselo (to be as if to eat) to be very attractive ◀ Florida, Mex, ES, Cuba, DR, U, Arg, Sp ▶
Adria está para comérselo. Adria is cute as a button.

el forro (lining) good-looking person, male or female ◀ Mex ▶

el galanazo good-looking guy, used instead of **galán** ◀ Mex ▶
¿Quién es ese galanazo? Who is that good-looking dude?

la guaguita little baby; babe (attractive female) (vulgar) ◀ Ch ▶

el mango, manguito ([little] mango) a good-looking person ◀ most of L. Am. ▶
Está hecho(-a) un mango. He's (She's) looking really good.

mono(-a) (monkey) cute ◀ L. Am., Sp ▶

la muñeca (doll) pretty girl ◀ Mex, Col, Para, U, Arg ▶

el muñeco (doll) good-looking man ◀ Mex, G ▶

el papisongo, papichulín, papisón, papisuqui, papito, papazote handsome guy ◀ DR, PR, Col ▶
Carlos Vives es un papazote. Está pa'comérselo. Carlos Vives is one handsome guy. He's gorgeous.

paquete (paqueta) (package) elegant, nicely turned out (people or things) ◀ U, Arg ▶
Esa mujer es repaqueta. That woman is super chic.

ser un paquete (to be a package) to be very attractive, chic ◀ Col ▶

ser una monada (to be a monkey face) to be cute, pretty, sweet (often used by women to describe children) ◀ Mex, S. Cone ▶

el tipazo handsome guy ◀ Mex, ES, DR, Col ▶
Jaime es un tipazo muy bueno. Jaime is a super gorgeous guy.

hot, sexy

el bizcocho (biscuit) sexy, hot, good-looking person, usually woman (also, **bizcochito**) ◀ Mex, PR, Col ▶
¡Qué bizcocho! What a babe!

la buenota (adj. or n.) stacked (woman), woman with a good figure ◀ chicano, Mex, ES, Pan, Ec, Para ▶
Esa chava está buenota. That chick is stacked.

la candela (candle) fiery woman ◀ Cuba, DR, PR ▶

el castigador (punisher) lady-killer, stud, guy who thinks women are attracted to him ◀ chicano, Mex, DR, PR, Col ▶

la castigadora (punisher) woman with an attractive body ◀ DR, PR, Col ▶
Esa mujer es una castigadora. That woman is hot.

la colita (little tail) well-formed woman (vulgar) ◀ Mex ▶

el cuero attractive man or woman ◀ Mex ▶

estar de muerte (to be of death) to be very attractive (a woman) ◀ Nic, Sp ▶

estar bomba (to be bomb) to be very attractive (a woman) (U, Arg: **ser una bomba**) ◀ DR, Sp ▶

la mamasota good-looking woman (sometimes used as a term to get a woman's attention; also, a bit vulgar) ◀ Mex, G, ES, DR, PR, Col ▶
Estás bien buena, mamasota. You're a good-looking woman, mama.

el mamito handsome or elegant young fellow; also, mommy's boy ◀ PR ▶

el mamo handsome guy, guy with a lot of women ◀ PR ▶
Ricky Martin es un mamo. Ricky Martin is a ladies' man.

el minón (big mine, like a gold mine, etc.) gorgeous babe ◀ Arg ▶
Esa morocha es espectacular, ¡un verdadero minón! That brunette is spectacular, a real sexpot!

la mujer fatal femme fatale ◀ U, Sp ▶

la pechocha (big-breasted) well-endowed woman, with a large bust ◀ Mex, ES, Col ▶

la pechugona (from **pechuga**, the breast of a fowl) big-breasted (woman) ◀ Mex, DR, Col, Ch, Sp ▶

la recalentona (very reheated) hot, sexy (woman) (**re-** used to emphasize) ◀ U, Arg ▶

la reconcheta (re- used to emphasize) hot, sexy (woman) ◀ Arg ▶

la zorra (female fox) foxy lady, party girl; also, vagina (vulgar) ◀ Ch ▶

piropos (street compliments)

Castígame. (Punish me.) said when an attractive member of the opposite sex goes by ◀ Mex, DR, PR, Col ▶

el contrapiropo amusing comment or comeback to a street compliment (**piropo**) ◀ L. Am., Sp ▶

¡Mijito(-a) rico(-a)! (My tasty little child!) Hey, babe! (vulgar) ◀ Ch ▶

¡Qué abusadora! (How abusive!) street compliment, meaning that the girl is pretty ◀ DR ▶

¡Qué bombón y yo con diabetes! (What a bonbon and me with diabetes!) street compliment ◀ L. Am., Sp ▶

Qué curvas y yo sin freno. (What curves and me without brakes.) street compliment ◀ L. Am., Sp ▶

¡Qué gallo! (What a rooster!) What a (good-looking) guy! ◀ Mex, Col ▶

¡Qué gambas! (from Italian) What (gorgeous) legs! ◀ U, Arg ▶

¿Qué habré hecho yo para merecer tal preciosura? What could I have done to deserve such beauty (such preciousness)? ◀ L. Am., Sp ▶

¡Qué piernón! (What big leg or legginess!) What shapely legs! ◀ Mex, Col ▶

authority

aflojar las riendas to loosen the reins, loosen up ◀ Mex, DR, Sp ▶

faltar el respeto a... (to lack respect) used for a child who talks back or doesn't mind ◀ L. Am., Sp ▶
No me faltes el respeto, niña. Don't disrespect me, girl.

mandón, mandona describing someone who likes to give orders, bossy ◀ L. Am., Sp ▶
Mi hermana es muy mandona. My sister is real bossy.

el mili short for **servicio militar** ◀Sp▶

el milico soldier (pejorative) ◀Ec, S. Cone▶

los verdes (the green ones) soldiers ◀U, Arg▶

bosses and big shots

el canchanchán, la canchanchana person with power in the community ◀Mex, DR▶

el mero jodón big boss (no feminine form is normally used) ◀chicano, Mex▶

los amos del cotarro (the masters of the **cotarro**, the bank of a ravine or a shelter for vagrants) the people in charge, the ones with the power ◀Sp▶
Como son los dueños del negocio, son los amos del cotarro. Since they are the owners of the business, they rule.

los jefazos, las jefazas big shots, bosses ◀Mex, Col, Sp▶

el mero mero (la mera mera); el mero mero petatero boss; main or most important one; main seller of **petates**, or mats ◀chicano, Mex, G, ES▶
Aquí soy yo el mero mero (petatero). Here I'm the top dog.

el palo grueso (thick stick) big cheese ◀Ch▶

el pez gordo (fat fish) big shot, big cheese, honcho ◀L. Am., Sp▶
Ese señor es un pez gordo en el gobierno. That gentleman is a big shot in the government.

el toqui (from Mapuche) leader of the pack, head honcho ◀Ch▶

control and power

See also "courage: brave, gutsy, ballsy."

amarrarse los pantalones (to tie up or tighten one's pants) to make one's authority felt ◀CR, ES, Ch▶
Tienes que amarrarte bien los pantalones con esa mujer. You really have to put your foot down with that woman.

cortar el queque (to cut the cake) to take control, cut to the chase ◀Ch▶

el pez gordo

dirigir el cotarro (to direct the **cotarro**, a bank of a ravine or a shelter for vagrants) to be in charge ◀Sp▶

estar subido(-a) en la poltrona to be in charge, give orders ◀Sp▶

jefear to boss around ◀CR, ES, DR▶

llevar bien puestos los pantalones (to wear the pants well placed) to impose one's authority, especially in a home setting ◀Mex, ES, DR, PR, Sp▶

llevar la batuta (to carry the baton) to be in charge, lead; be the main person (ES: bring home the bacon or wear the pants) ◀Mex, G, Cuba, ES, DR, Ch, Sp▶
En esa familia, Alfonso lleva la batuta. In that family, Alfonso is in charge.

llevar la voz cantante (to carry the melody) to be in charge in a meeting, business, etc.; to call the shots ◀L. Am., Sp▶

ponerse los pantalones (to put on one's pants) to take charge of a situation ◀DR, PR, S. Cone▶

tener banca to have influence, power, worth ◀U, Arg, Sp▶

tener en el bolsillo a alguien to have someone in one's pocket, be able to count on that person ◀Mex, ES, DR, PR, U, Arg, Sp▶
Juan tiene a la novia en el bolsillo. Juan has his girlfriend at his beck and call.
A ésos los tengo en el bolsillo; seguro que votan por mí en las elecciones. I've got those guys under my thumb; they'll vote for me for sure in the election.

tener la sartén por el mango (to have the frying pan by the handle) to be in charge of a situation, have the upper hand ◄ L. Am., Sp ►

tirar (de) la cuerda a alguien (to pull someone by the cord) to pull someone back, control ◄ Mex, Sp ►

police

See also "crime and punishment."

los hacheros police ◄ Cuba ►

los pacos police ◄ Ven, Ec, Bol, Ch ►

la pasma police ◄ Sp ►

los perros (dogs) police ◄ chicano, Mex, ES, PR, Col ►

los polis policemen, coppers ◄ Sp ►

la tira police (from **tirana**) ◄ Mex, G ►

los tombos police ◄ CR, Col, Ven, Ec, Peru ►

bad

See also "bad character."

bendito(-a) (blessed) sometimes used ironically for the opposite ◄ L. Am. ►
¡Ese bendito coche! That damn (blessed) car!

el bodrio stupid, boring thing or person ◄ S. Cone, Sp ►
Esta película es un bodrio. This film is a bore.
Ese señor es aburridísimo, un bodrio. That gentleman is totally boring, a drag.

chungo(-a) bad, inappropriate, deteriorated ◄ Mex, Sp ►
Tengo un trabajo muy chungo. I have a crummy job.
Estos zapatos están un poco chungos. These shoes are a little down at the heel.

como un (el) culo (like an [the] ass) ugly, unpleasant (vulgar) ◄ Cuba, Col, S. Cone ►
Ese tipo me cae como un culo. I think that guy is an ass.
Esa falda le queda como un culo. That skirt looks like hell on her.

El diablo anda suelto. The devil is loose. Evil is afoot. ◄ Mex ►

Está que arde. (It's burning.) It's at fever pitch and getting worse and worse. ◄ L. Am., Sp ►

estar hecho(-a) un asco (to be made into something disgusting) to look dirty, decrepit ◄ ES, S. Cone, Sp ►

estar hecho(-a) unos zorros (to be made foxes) to be in bad shape or badly dressed ◄ Sp ►
Llegó de la fiesta hecha unos zorros. She returned from the party in bad shape.

la mala junta (bad joining) bad influence ◄ Ch ►

el menudo número (diminutive number, or show) something not very nice or well done, fine state of affairs, pretty picture (ironic) ◄ Sp ►

mucho ruido y pocas nueces (a lot of noise and few nuts) said when something yields very little despite appearances or expectations ◄ Mex, Ch, Sp ►

muy especial (very special) expression sometimes used ironically to mean difficult ◄ L. Am., Sp ►

no oler bien una cosa, oler mal (to not smell good, to smell bad) to seem suspicious ◄ Mex, Ch, Sp ►
Esto me huele mal. This seems fishy to me.

saber a cuerno quemado (to taste like burned horn) to make a bad impression or give a bad feeling (news, a reproach, etc.) ◄ Sp ►
Me sabe a cuerno quemado que no nos vinieron a ver. It leaves a bad taste in my mouth that they didn't come to see us.

sacar punta a una cosa (to sharpen something, make pointed) to attribute malice or something bad to something wrongly, twist (e.g., a comment); to use it for a purpose that wasn't intended ◄ DR, PR, Sp ►

el tarambana undisciplined (person, kid) ◄ Cuba, Ch, Sp ►
Su hermano no había cambiado; seguía siendo el mismo tarambana. His (her)

brother hadn't changed a bit; he was still the same brat.

tener mala sombra (to have bad shade) to be unpleasant, a bad influence; to be unlucky ◀ ES, Sp ▶
Tiene mala sombra que vayan a construir allí. I have a bad feeling about them starting to build there.

awful, the pits

de los cojones (of the testicles) awful, damn (vulgar) ◀ Mex, Sp ▶
el tío de los cojones, la musiquita de los cojones a god-awful guy, some god-awful music

de madre indicating negative characteristics, used for things or people; difficult, bad, ugly, etc. ◀ Cuba ▶

de mierda (of shit) crappy, shitty (vulgar) ◀ ES, Nic, PR, Ch ▶
¿Cómo se puede mantener con esa pensión de mierda? How can you get along with that crappy pension?
¡Pueblo de mierda! A one-horse town!

de mil (todos los) diablos (of a thousand [all the] devils) very bad, a heck of a + noun (used to exaggerate something bad or uncomfortable) ◀ Mex, ES, Sp ▶
Ese niño se porta de lo peor. Tiene una conducta de los mil diablos. That boy acts out in the worst way. His behavior is the pits.

de perros (of dogs) very disagreeable, a bitch of a + noun ◀ Mex, ES, Sp ▶
¡Qué tiempo de perros! What crummy weather!
un humor de perros a bitch of a mood

del mero (of the mere) bad, awful ◀ PR ▶

Está cabrón. It's unbearable. (vulgar) ◀ most of L. Am. ▶
No se puede contigo. Está cabrón. You're impossible. (Nothing can be done with you.) It's a bitch of a situation.

Está el asunto feo. (It's an ugly business.) It's awful. ◀ L. Am., Sp ▶

Está por el suelo. (It's down on the floor.) It's in the pits, in a bad way. ◀ L. Am. ▶
La situación económica está por el suelo. The economic situation is at rock bottom.

fatal (fatal) awful, the pits, not well done or said ◀ Mex, G, DR, PR, Col, Sp ▶
Esa película fue fatal. That movie was the bottom of the barrel.

fu bad, bad news, yucky ◀ Cuba, Ven ▶

furris bad, horrible (Nic: **furri**) ◀ Mex, CR, Ven ▶
Su acción fue muy furris. What he did was really dumb (awful).

maldito(-a) damn(ed) ◀ L. Am., Sp ▶

maluca (malena) (from **mal**) kind of nasty, lame ◀ Ch ▶

matado(-a) (killed) awful; bad; graceless; boring ◀ Florida, CR, Cuba, DR, PR, Col ▶
Esa profesora está matada. That teacher is lousy.
Es un lugar matado. (CR) It's a crummy place.

perro(-a) (dog) rotten, mean, a bitch, a bitch of a + noun, exaggerated, tremendous, difficult ◀ Mex, G, Cuba, Col ▶
Este trabajo está perro. This job is a bitch.
una noticia perra (Col) a lousy piece of news
¡Qué perra vida! What a dog's life!

pinche blasted, damn ◀ Mex ▶
ese pinche viejo; la pinche máquina, that damn old goat; the blasted machine

puñetero(-a) lousy, terrible (vulgar) ◀ PR ▶
Hace un calor puñetero. It's damn hot.

puto(-a) (pimp or whore) blasted, damn (vulgar) ◀ L. Am., Sp ▶
Esta puta máquina no funciona. This damn machine doesn't work.
No me hizo ni puto caso. He didn't pay a damn bit of attention to me.
¿Dónde está un puto taxi? Where's a blasted taxi?

raspado(-a) de la olla (scraped from the pot) dregs, bottom of the barrel ◀ Ch ▶

ser pura mierda (ser una mierda) (to be pure shit [to be shitty]) to be very bad, worthless (vulgar) ◀ Mex, ES, DR, PR, Ch, Sp ▶
Ese tipo es pura mierda. No ayuda a nadie. That guy is a real shithead. He doesn't help anyone.

ser un petardo (to be a detonator, fire-cracker) to be bad quality, boring, or ugly ◀Sp▶
Esa película (chica) es un petardo. That movie (babe) is a dud.

bad habits

las andadas (walkings, tracks) old habits, tricks ◀L. Am., Sp▶
Alfonso volvió a sus andadas. Alfonso went back to his old tricks.

Gallina que come huevo, ni que le quemen el pico. (A hen that eats eggs, not even if its beak is burned . . . [will it stop].) Someone who once participates in some forbidden pleasure won't stop doing it even upon receiving harsh punishments. ◀ES, Nic▶

la maña (skill) bad habit ◀Mex, C. Am., DR, U, Ch▶
Marilú tiene la maña de chuparse el dedo. Marilú has the bad habit of sucking her thumb.

bad mood

See also "anger," "annoyance."

andar de maleta (to walk with a suitcase) to be in a bad mood ◀Ch▶

estar de mal humor to be in a bad mood ◀L. Am., Sp▶

estar de mal talante to be in a bad mood ◀U, Arg, Sp▶

estar de mala leche to be in a bad mood (milk) ◀Mex, Sp▶

estar de mala uva to be in a bad mood (grape) ◀Sp▶

estar de malas pulgas (to be of bad fleas) to be in a bad mood; also, **andar de** or **tener** ◀ES, CR, Col, Ch, Sp▶
Hoy está de malas pulgas. Today he (she) is in a really lousy mood.

estar como todos los diablos to be beside oneself (like all the devils), in a very bad mood ◀Mex, G, CR▶

estar que me (lo, la, etc.) lleva el diablo to be beside oneself (ready for the devil to take), in a very bad mood (CR: **que me llevan los diablos**) ◀Mex, G, CR, ES, DR▶

andar de maleta

Y anda que se la lleva el diablo. And she is ready to bite your head off.
Estoy que me lleva el diablo. I'm in a very crummy mood.

jurar en arameo (to swear in Aramaic, the language of Christ) to swear because one is in a bad mood ◀Sp▶
Cuando no me dieron el trabajo, empecé a jurar en arameo. When they didn't give me the job, I started using language that would make a sailor blush.

no estar para bromas to not be in a joking mood ◀L. Am., Sp▶

tener cara de mala leche (to have the face of bad milk) to look like one is in a bad mood ◀Sp▶
Ese señor tiene cara de muy mala leche, ¿no crees? That man looks like he's ready to bite your head off, don't you think?

tener la leche cortada (to have the milk soured) to be in a bad mood ◀Cuba▶

corny

cebollero(-a) (onion seller) schmaltzy (e.g., story or movie), overly sentimental ◀Ch▶

cursi corny, too sentimental, often referring to someone who uses overly sweet or sentimental language ◀L. Am., Sp▶

Ay, mi pichoncito dorado. —No seas cursi. Oh, my darling little turtledove. —Don't be corny.

ser un guiso (to be a stew) to be corny ◄ Col ►

old-fashioned

aguacatero(-a) old-fashioned ◄ Col ►

cafre old-fashioned, outdated, bad ◄ PR ►
¡Qué vestido más cafre tiene esa señora! ¿De dónde lo habrá sacado? What an out-of-it dress that lady has on! Where on earth did she get it?

chapado(-a) a la antigua old-fashioned ◄ L. Am., Sp ►
Es un hombre chapado a la antigua. He's an old-fashioned kind of guy.

charro(-a) relating to cowboys or country people; old-fashioned, out of it, ridiculous (Col except Medellín, where it means great, good) ◄ Mex, PR, Col ►

chimbo(-a) stupid and out of style, lame ◄ Ven, Ec ►
Esa película sí fue chimba. That movie sure was lame.

fuera de onda out of it, totally unhip, old-fashioned ◄ Mex, ES, DR, Col, Sp ►

pasadón, pasadona (way in the past) out of date, old-fashioned ◄ Mex ►
ideas pasadonas antiquated ideas

ser una rémora to be a reactionary, an obstacle to progress or advancement ◄ Peru ►

ser un atraso a la cultura (to be a setback for the culture) to be old-fashioned, out of date ◄ Col ►
¡Qué atraso a la cultura! Wow, back to the Stone Age!

tacky, low-class, poor quality

See also "uselessness: not good for anything."

balurdo(-a) weird, in poor taste, far-out, tacky (Nic, Ec: **balurde**) ◄ Ven ►

basto(-a) raunchy, tacky, vulgar ◄ Sp ►
ser más basto que matar un cerdo a besos to be tackier than a seascape painted on velvet (killing a pig with kisses)

berreta cheap, low quality; used to describe things or people ◄ Arg ►
No compres esa bolsa, que es muy berreta. Don't buy that purse because it looks very cheap.
Ese señor es muy berreta. That guy is very lowbrow.

burdo(-a) (coarse) in poor taste ◄ Mex, CR, Col ►

la caca de la vaca (cow dung) something of poor quality or someone not trustworthy (vulgar) ◄ Sp ►

el cache person or thing that is pretentious and in bad taste (something chintzy, nouveau riche) ◄ Arg ►
La casa de mi prima me pareció un cache. My cousin's house struck me as very tacky.
Ese muchacho me pareció un cache. That boy seemed like a lowlife to me.

cachudo(-a) (big horn of an animal) in poor taste ◄ U ►

charcha (fat around the waist) lame, worthless ◄ Ch ►

charralero(-a) common, of little value ◄ CR, ES ►
Es bien charralero, muy simple. It's really chintzy looking, very ordinary.

cutre poor, of low quality ◄ Sp ►
Es un bar muy cutre. It's a bar for down and outers.

de mala muerte (of bad death) of little worth, poor quality ◄ L. Am., Sp ►
No quiero ir a ese bar de mala muerte. I don't want to go to that crummy bar.

de pacotilla of bad quality or little importance ◄ DR, PR, S. Cone, Sp ►
Es un cantante de pacotilla. He (She) is a run-of-the-mill singer.

gacho(-a) bad, unpleasant, of low quality or little worth (CR: boring) ◄ Mex, G, ES ►
Su novio es bien gacho. No sé porque ella sigue con él. Her boyfriend is really a lowlife. I don't know why she keeps going out with him.

la leperada low-class action or obscene expression ◄ Mex, C. Am. ►

macarra vulgar, in bad taste ◄ Sp ►
una camisa macarra, un pantalón macarra a cheap-looking shirt, a chintzy-looking pair of pants

penca lame, boring; low quality ◄ Ch ►

picante (spicy) tacky, low-class, in bad taste (Peru: also, ill-mannered person) ◄ Mex, DR, Peru, Ch ►
un chiste picante a joke in poor taste

ser trililís to be of bad quality, junky ◄ PR ►
No, no es de oro. Es un reloj trililís que compré en Miami. No, it's not real gold. It's a junky watch I bought in Miami.

bad character

See also "bad," "drunkenness," "gossip," "pride," "pushiness," "selfishness," "uselessness."

el/la chanta someone who has very shallow values ◄ Bol ►

el/la comemierda (eat shit) proud or stupid person, snob; fake (vulgar) ◄ Mex, G, ES, Nic, Cuba, DR, PR, Col ►
No soporto al primo de Lucy. Es tremendo comemierda; se cree mejor que todo el mundo. I can't stand Lucy's cousin. He's a total jerk; he thinks he's better than everyone else.

conchudo(-a) (hard-shelled) person without shame, thick-skinned and insensitive; con man ◄ Mex, C. Am., Ven, Col, Ec, Bol ►

criado(-a) a puro machete (raised by pure machete) badly raised or brought up ◄ Mex, ES ►
Qué mal educado ese chavo. Parece que fue criado a puro machete. How rude that kid is. It looks like he was brought up in a barn.

el/la desubicado(-a) (disoriented) difficult (person), pain in the neck ◄ S. Cone ►

encholarse to become wild, a gang member for instance (usually said of youth) (note: in CR, to be wrong, **equivocarse**) ◄ ES ►
Arturo se encholó. Marta anda de chola. Arturo has fallen into bad ways. Marta is slipping off the straight and narrow.

greñudo(-a) longhaired, sloppy ◄ Mex, ES, DR, Col ►

el hojaldra (puff pastry) asshole (vulgar) ◄ Mex ►

el ojete (eyelet, hole) asshole (vulgar) ◄ Mex ►

picado(-a) de la araña (bitten by the spider) fickle and flirtatious ◄ Ch ►

el picaflor (hummingbird) fickle and flirtatious person ◄ Ch, DR ►

ser de la piel del diablo (to be of the devil's skin) to be very mischievous, a little dickens ◄ most of L. Am., Sp ►

víbora (viper) bad, insidious ◄ Cuba, Col ►

bad guys

el/la canalla (from canine, dog) person who is abject, vile, a creep (a bit old-fashioned in Sp) ◄ L. Am., Sp ►

el/la descarado(-a) scoundrel, nasty ◄ L. Am., Sp ►
¡Qué descarado! What a creep! (What a nasty person!)

el girador (rotator; also, person who writes a bad check) operator, guy involved in bad things ◄ Mex ►

el/la macarra troublemaker, person with bad manners and/or violent tendencies ◄ Sp ►

los patos malos (bad ducks) bad guys ◄ Ch ►

la rata (rat) scoundrel ◄ Col, Ven ►

el ratón (rat) scoundrel ◄ PR, Ven ►

ser el mismísimo demonio to be the devil himself, very perverse or cunning ◄ Mex, DR, PR, U, Arg, Sp ►

ser puro Satanás to be Satan himself ◄ ES ►
Mi suegro es puro Satanás. My father-in-law is the devil incarnate.

ser un mal bicho (to be a bad animal) to have bad character (people) ◄ Sp ►

Say it with slang!

Rhyme time

Rappers and poets aren't the only ones who like to speak in rhymes. Everyday Spanish is filled with rhyming similar to the English expression "See you later, alligator!" In fact, a loose equivalent of this could be the Venezuelan phrase **¡Chao, pesca'o!** (Bye, fish! The words rhyme because the "d" in **pescado** can be aspirated in Venezuela and many other parts of the Caribbean.)

Rhymes are used for many purposes. In Spain, for disbelief they might say: **Si no lo veo, ¡no lo creo!** (If I don't see it, I don't believe it!) or to describe something of poor quality: **caca de la vaca** (cow poop). In Nicaragua, people call someone's attention with **¡Epa, Chepa!** (Hey, there!) and tell people to mind their own business by asking: **¿Quién te mete, Juan Bonete?** (Who brings you into this, buddy?). In Mexico and Central America they might express agreement by saying: **¡Okei, maguey!** (All right, cactus!) or **¡Sale y vale!** (It's a done deal!). Or they might ask: **¿Qué te pasa, calabaza?** (What's up with you, pumpkin?), to which the traditional response is **Nada, nada, limonada.** Some rhymes are used in many places, like the observation **Cada oveja con su pareja** (Everyone with a partner or Like goes with like) or the warning **Te conozco, mosco** (I know you, fly; I know what you're up to).

ser un malaje   to have bad character ◀ Sp ▶

tener mala leche   to have bad intentions (vulgar) ◀ S. Cone, Sp ▶

bitches

la cabrona   bitch ◀ Mex, C. Am., Cuba, PR, Bol, Ch, Sp ▶

la maraca   whore; bitch, demanding, unpleasant woman (synonym: **maricona**) ◀ Ch ▶

la perra   (female dog) bitchy woman ◀ chicano, G, Col, Sp ▶

la puta   (prostitute) bitch ◀ L. Am., Sp ▶

la zorra   (female fox) bitch, nasty woman ◀ Sp ▶
Es una zorra; se quedó con mi dinero y se largó. She's a real bitch; she took my money and ran.

disagreeable, unpleasant

ácido(-a)   (acidic) disagreeable (person), sourpuss ◀ G, PR, Col, Sp ▶
¡Qué ácida eres! What a sourpuss you are!

bofe   unsociable, unlikeable, unpleasant ◀ Cuba, Col ▶

el/la cara de limón   (lemon face) unpleasant or annoyed appearance ◀ Mex, ES ▶

el/la cara de perro   (dog face) hostile appearance ◀ Mex, PR, Sp ▶

geniudo(-a)   bad tempered ◀ Mex, Col ▶

más pesado(-a) que cargar un elefante   (heavier than carrying an elephant) unpleasant (person) ◀ Mex, PR ▶

no ser perita en dulce   (to not be a pear in sugar) to be difficult, disagreeable ◀ Mex, ES ▶

31

¡Qué rompe grupo! (What a group breaker!) said of someone who is not sociable ◄ PR, Col ▶

sangrón, sangrona bad tempered, unpleasant, annoying (CR: usually someone who humiliates or mistreats people smaller or weaker) ◄ Mex, G, ES, CR, Cuba, Col ▶

tener buen lejos (to have a good far away) to be good only from a distance (ironic way of saying someone is not too much fun to have around) ◄ Ch ▶

tener mala leche (to have bad milk) to be bad tempered, disagreeable ◄ Mex, ES, Sp ▶

tener mala sangre (to have bad blood) to be bad tempered, disagreeable ◄ Mex, ES ▶

tener mala uva (to have bad grape) to have a gruff or severe demeanor ◄ chicano, Sp ▶
Tiene muy mala uva (leche) y se enoja por cualquier cosa. He's (She's) a real grouch and gets upset over any little thing.

fussy, uptight

balurde picky, fussy, uptight (to describe a person, the opposite of **llevadera**, meaning easygoing); dull (to describe a thing) ◄ Nic ▶
La película no fue interesante; fue balurde. The movie wasn't interesting; it was dull.

cartucho(-a) prudish, very prim about sexual behavior ◄ Ch ▶

chiveado(-a) inhibited, timid, overly proper person ◄ Mex, ES ▶
Ramona está chiveada porque le chiflaron. Ramona is embarrassed because they whistled at her.

mírame y no me toques (look at me and don't touch me) describing a very fussy person or things that break easily (Nic: **veme y no me toques**) ◄ Mex, ES, DR, PR, Ch, Sp ▶

no aguantar pulgas to not tolerate problems (fleas) ◄ Mex, Sp ▶

el/la pichiruche unimportant person who fusses about small details, lower civil servant ◄ Nic, Peru, Ch ▶

puntudo(-a) (pointed) overly sensitive, finicky ◄ Ch ▶

ser de pocas pulgas (to be of few fleas) to be fussy, delicate ◄ Mex, ES, CR, Col, U, Arg ▶
Tiene una cara de pocas pulgas. Es de pocas pulgas. He (She) looks uptight. He (She) is a fussbudget.

ser un(a) fruncido(-a) (to be a wrinkled-up person) to be very fussy, uptight, and persnickety; to be a tightass ◄ S. Cone ▶

irresponsible

el/la cantamañanas person who doesn't have much responsibility or who is unreliable, a dreamer who doesn't get things done ◄ Sp ▶

faltón, faltona irresponsible, describing someone who doesn't do what he (she) is supposed to do ◄ most of L. Am., Sp ▶

el tiro al aire (shot in the air) unreliable or unpredictable person, loose cannon; slacker type who doesn't commit ◄ S. Cone ▶

jerk, loser, worthless

el bacán (controller of a woman who earns money for him, from Lunfardo) shallow glamour boy, jerk (implies someone with money also) ◄ S. Cone ▶
El bacán de su marido tiene su casa a todo lujo. That jerk of a husband of hers has a very fancy house.
Mirá que hombre tan bacán, tiene un Mercedes Benz último modelo. Look at that shallow glamour boy; he has the newest model Mercedes Benz.

cabrón, cabrona (big goat) poor jerk, unbearable (person), SOB; as adj., damn, a bitch of a + noun; also, used with affection among males to friends jokingly; feminine form, bitch (vulgar) ◄ Mex, C. Am., Cuba, PR, Col, Bol, Ch, Sp ▶
¡Qué gusto de encontrarte aquí, cabrón! What a pleasure to find you here, you SOB!
¡Qué enfermedad más cabrona! What a bitch of an illness!

La cabrona máquina no funciona. The crappy machine doesn't work.

el cero a la izquierda (zero to the left) worthless, no good ◀ L. Am., Sp ▶

¡Qué mujeriego! Ese chico es un cero a la izquierda. What a playboy! That guy is a total loser.

el chimbarón jerk, pest ◀ Nic ▶

el/la culero(-a) lazy, uncooperative person, person who takes no initiative (vulgar, referring to **culo**; can also mean pedofile or homosexual, but not usually; commonly used in masculine) ◀ chicano, Mex, C. Am. ▶

Esos culeros no hicieron nada para ayudarnos. Those assholes did nothing to help us.

el/la gandalla loser, good-for-nothing ◀ Mex, ES ▶

el/la garra, garrapata (tick, the insect) loser, unappealing or ugly person ◀ Mex, Col ▶

los jijos de la guayaba (euphemism for **hijos de la chingada**; **guayaba** is guava) poor suckers ◀ Mex, ES ▶

los jijos de sayula (euphemism for **hijos de la chingada**) poor suckers ◀ Mex ▶

mal nacido(-a) (badly born, meaning bastard) jerk, SOB (vulgar) ◀ L. Am., Sp ▶

el/la mequetrefe just anyone, mediocre person, pretentious person who won't amount to much ◀ Mex, G, ES, Nic, DR, PR, S. Cone, Sp ▶

¿Qué quiere ese mequetrefe? What does that loser want?

naco(-a) (from **totonaco**, an Indian tribe, formerly with a racist meaning) jerk, uneducated or rude person (of any social class) ◀ Mex ▶

¿Quién es ese naco allí? Who is that boor over there?

No va pa'l baile. (He/She is not going to the dance.) He (She) is a loser, not wanted. ◀ Ven ▶

pelado(-a) (peeled, bald) shameless, rude ◀ Mex ▶

chiste pelado; ser un pelado, rude joke; to be a rude person

el/la pelagatos (cat skinner) jerk ◀ ES, PR, Ch ▶

No voy a permitir que cualquier pelagatos se case con mi hija. I'm not going to let any good-for-nothing jerk marry my daughter.

el pinche buey jerk, loser ◀ Mex, Col ▶

ser un hígado (to be a liver) to be a pain, jerk ◀ Mex ▶

phony

el diablo vendiendo cruces (the devil selling crosses) hypocrite ◀ L. Am. ▶

fantasma, fantasmón (fantasmona) (ghost) hypocritical, artificial ◀ Sp ▶

hueco(-a) (hollow, empty) phony, superficial ◀ Ch ▶

plástico(-a) (plastic) hypocritical, artificial, or superficial; sometimes used as **hijo de papi** ◀ G, DR, PR, Col, Ch ▶

Raquel es una plástica. Lo único que le interesa es la ropa, los carros y el dinero. Raquel is very shallow. The only things that interest her are clothing, cars, and money.

Es una persona plástica. She's an airhead.

piggish

el/la cerdo(-a) (pig) person who is dirty or who has bad intentions ◀ Sp ▶

Es un cerdo; se lava una vez al mes. He's a pig; he washes up once a month (whether he needs it or not).

Es un cerdo; se fue sin pagar. He's a swine; he left without paying.

el diablo vendiendo cruces

el/la guarro(-a) (pig, swine) dirty, person of loose morals ◀ Sp ▶

el marrano pig (dirty or fat); undesirable person ◀ Mex, G, Col, Sp ▶

rude, boorish, low-class

analfabestia (used instead of **analfabeta**, illiterate; **bestia** means beast) lowlife, ignorant and proud of it ◀ Mex, Col ▶

cafre rude, lacking in respect ◀ G, Sp ▶

el gorila gorilla, barbaric person, very big person ◀ Mex, G ▶

grasa (grease) low-class, common, rude ◀ U, Arg ▶
No sé como puedes andar con ese tipo tan grasa. I don't know how you can go out with such a boorish creep.

groncho(-a) low-class, common, rude ◀ Arg ▶
No salgas con él, es muy groncho. Don't go out with him. He's really crude.

guarango(-a) rude person with bad manners, boor ◀ U, Arg ▶

lépero(-a) low-class, rude ◀ Mex, C. Am. ▶

majadero(-a) ill-mannered (person) ◀ Mex, Cuba ▶
Con lo que dijiste, eres un majadero. Judging from what you just said, you're a rude boor.
El niño no había comido y se puso majadero. The child hadn't eaten and got very fussy.

el patán lowlife ◀ Mex, Nic, U, Arg ▶

ser bestia (to be a beast, animal) to be rude, a boor, someone with bad manners ◀ L. Am. ▶
No seas bestia. Don't be crude.

ser un barbaján to be coarse, rude, a dope (masculine only) ◀ Mex ▶

ser una corriente to be coarse, rude, a dope (for women) ◀ Mex ▶

torreja (variant of **torrija**, French toast) low-class ◀ Ch ▶

tráfalo(-a) low-class, like a bum ◀ PR ▶

stubborn, pigheaded

cabeza de chancho (pig head) pigheaded, stubborn ◀ Ch ▶

cabezón, cabezona (bighead) hardheaded, stubborn ◀ Florida, Mex, G, DR, PR, Col, S. Cone, Sp ▶

cabezota (bigheaded) stubborn, bullheaded ◀ Sp ▶

boasts

See also "pride."

apantallar to toot one's own horn, brag about oneself ◀ Mex, ES, DR, Col ▶

cacarear (to cackle like a hen) to boast loudly ◀ Arg ▶
Es tan orgulloso. Le encanta cacarear. He's so proud. He loves to toot his own horn.

cacarear y no poner huevo (to cackle and not lay an egg) to promise something and not fulfill it ◀ Mex, ES, Sp ▶
Ese diputado cacarea y no pone huevos. That politician talks a good game but doesn't deliver.

la cajetilla low-class braggart ◀ Arg ▶

cantar victoria (to sing victory) to brag about or rejoice in a triumph ◀ L. Am., Sp ▶
No cantemos victoria todavía. Let's not bring out the champagne yet.

Deja de decir fanfarrias (fanfarronadas). Stop bragging (saying boastful things). ◀ Mex ▶

echarse flores (to throw flowers at oneself) to brag, praise oneself ◀ L. Am., Sp ▶

echón, echona pretentious, boastful, superior acting ◀ PR ▶

postalita (little postcard) boastful ◀ Cuba ▶

tirarse el pegote (to throw oneself the add-on or crude addition) to brag or boast ◀ Sp ▶

tirarse el rollo (to throw the roll) to lie, brag ◀ Sp ▶
Mirella se tiró el rollo de que sabía cantar muy bien, y tiene una voz espantosa.

Mirella was slinging the bull about how well she can sing, and she has a horrendous voice.

showing off

balconearse (to balcony oneself) to strut one's stuff (generally used to refer to women) ◀ Mex ▶
Esa chica se puso una minifalda porque le gusta balconearse. That chick put on a miniskirt because she loves to strut her stuff.

comer delante de los pobres (to eat in front of the poor) to show off in front of less fortunate people ◀ Ch ▶

darse un quemón (to burn oneself) to show off something one has, such as a new boyfriend (girlfriend) ◀ ES ▶

pintar monos (to paint monkeys) to show off, call attention to oneself ◀ Ch ▶

body

See also "physical characteristics," "sex."

la bomba (pump) heart ◀ Cuba ▶
esos cinco (those five) the hand ◀ Sp ▶
jugar a los bomberos (jugar agua) (to play firemen [to play water]) to bathe ◀ Cuba, Col ▶
la pelada haircut ◀ CR, ES, DR ▶
el petardo (detonator, firecracker) fart ◀ G, Cuba, PR ▶
el reloj (clock) heart ◀ Cuba ▶
tirarse/echarse un caldo (to make a broth) to fart ◀ Cuba, Col ▶

above the neck

las antenas (antennas) ears ◀ CR, ES ▶
la buena portada honra la casa (the good portal honors the house) expression used to mean that large mouths are OK, generally used by those with large mouths ◀ Sp ▶

el buzón (mailbox) mouth ◀ Mex, Cuba ▶
el careto (white-faced mask) face that suggests fatigue or worry ◀ Sp ▶
la chaveta head ◀ Mex, ES, DR, PR ▶
Se me fue la chaveta. I lost my head.
la chirimoya (type of fruit) head ◀ Mex, CR, ES ▶
el coco (coconut) head (Ch: also, testicle) ◀ Mex, G, ES, Cuba, DR, PR, Col, Arg, Ch, Sp ▶
la corneta (horn, bugle) nose ◀ Cuba ▶
las cortinas (curtains) eyelids ◀ Cuba ▶
el foco (farol) (lightbulb [lamp]) eye ◀ G, Cuba ▶
la jeta face ◀ Mex, ES, Cuba, Col, Sp ▶ mouth ◀ G, CR, U, Arg ▶
la maceta head ◀ Mex, G, Nic ▶
el moropo head (from an African language) ◀ Cuba ▶
el pico (beak) mouth ◀ L. Am., Sp ▶
la sin hueso (the boneless one) tongue ◀ U, Ch, Sp ▶
el tacho, techo (vat or bowl, roof) hair ◀ Cuba ▶
el tarro head (CR: face) ◀ Sp ▶
la torta (cake) face, fat face (round) (vulgar) ◀ G, ES ▶
la trompa (trunk of an elephant) mouth (often in reference to an angry person) ◀ Mex, CR, Nic, Col ▶

bathroom talk

cambiar el agua a los peces (to change the fishes' water) euphemism for to urinate (CR: **cambiar el agua al pájaro**; U, Arg: **cambiar el agua a las aceitunas**; Ven, Sp: **cambiar el agua al canario**) ◀ Cuba, DR, PR, Col, U, Arg ▶
Un momento. Tengo que cambiar el agua a los peces. Wait a minute. I have to make a pit stop (go to the bathroom).

echar la corta (la grande) (to throw the short [the big]) to take a leak (a dump) ◀ Ch ▶

echar una meadita (to throw a little pissing) to take a leak (vulgar) ◀ L. Am., Sp ▶

el excusado (the excused place) bathroom (euphemism) ◄ Mex, Ch ►

hacer sus necesidades (una necesidad) (to do one's necessities [a necessity]) to go to the bathroom ◄ C. Am., DR ►

mear(se) to urinate ◄ L. Am., Sp ►

el mojón turd ◄ PR, Ven, Ec, Ch ►

la plasta (paste, soft mass) piece of excrement ◄ G, Ch ►

el privado the john, head, bathroom ◄ Mex, Col ►

los servicios públicos public washrooms ◄ L. Am., Sp ►

el trono, trono de los césares (throne, throne of the Caesars) toilet seat ◄ Mex, Col ►

visitar al señor Roca (to visit Mr. Rock) to go to the rest room ◄ Sp ►

el water (from water closet, pronounced with English /w/ sound) toilet, toilet bowl ◄ Ec, Ch ►

Ya me gana. (It's gaining on me.) said when one has to urinate ◄ Mex ►

below the belt

la almohada (pillow) behind, rear end ◄ Cuba ►

barrigón, barrigona potbellied; **barrigona**, pregnant ◄ L. Am., Sp ►

caerse en/lastimarse el amor propio (to fall on or hurt one's self-esteem) euphemism for to fall on or hurt one's rear end or backside ◄ Ch ►

la canilla (long bone of leg or arm) leg, skinny leg ◄ G, Nic, CR, Cuba, DR, Col, Ch ► Ella anda en minifaldas exhibiendo las canillas como si tuviera piernas. She goes around in miniskirts showing off those toothpicks as if she had legs.

la cueva (cave) anus, ass (vulgar) ◄ Ch ►

el culo ass (vulgar) ◄ L. Am., Sp ►

la guata paunch, beer belly, potbelly ◄ Peru, Bol, Ch ►

las piernas de canario (canary legs) skinny legs ◄ Col ►

el pó fanny (child's bottom, polite) ◄ Ch ►

el pompis rear end, derriere (Mex: **pompas**) ◄ Mex, Col, Ec, Ven, Sp ►

el poto base, bottom, rear end (for things or people) ◄ Ch ► **el poto de la copa,** the bottom of the wine glass **el poto de la lámpara,** the base of the lamp

el raja (split) ass (vulgar) ◄ Ch, PR ►

el siete (seven) rear end, used jokingly (ES: **ocho**) ◄ CR, ES ► **Juanito está enseñando el ocho.** (ES) Juanito is dropping a moon (has his rear end showing).

el tambembe rear end, backside ◄ Ch ►

la timba big stomach, belly (ES: also, **timbón** and **timbudo**, having a large stomach) ◄ CR, ES, Nic ► **Ese cipote tiene tamaño timba.** That kid has a big belly.

el trasero rear end ◄ L. Am., Sp ►

el traste rear end, backside ◄ Ch ►

tripón, tripona potbellied, heavy ◄ L. Am., Sp ►

bod

el cuero (hide, leather) bod (vulgar) ◄ Ch ► **Esa actriz tiene buen cuero.** That actress has a great bod.

el lomo (back of an animal) bod, body ◄ Arg, Ch ►

el pellejo (hide) body, bod ◄ Ch ►

breasts

los chicharrones female breasts ◄ Mex ►

los chiches (from Náhuatl for "to suckle") breasts ◄ G, ES ►

los chichis (from Náhuatl for "to suckle") breasts ◄ Mex, Col ►

las hermanitas Bustos (the little Bustos sisters) big boobs ◄ Ch ►

los limones (lemons) woman's breasts ◄ Cuba, Col ►

los melones (melons) woman's breasts ◄ Cuba, Col, Sp ►

Say it with slang!

Obscenity is a relative concept!

Just as "beauty is in the eye of the beholder," obscenity can be in the ear of the listener. In the Spanish-speaking world, whether a word is innocuous or obscene depends on what country the speaker is from. One of the most common verbs in Spain, the verb **coger**, which for Spaniards simply means "to take," is the equivalent of the F-word in most parts of Latin America. Another common verb, **chingar**, which in Spain or Argentina simply means "to tear" or "to break down," is the equivalent of the F-word in Mexico, but stronger. The common dessert made from sweetened milk and called **cajeta** in Mexico means something totally different in Argentina, where it refers to that particular part of a woman not spoken of in polite company. In Cuba the fruit **papaya** has the same meaning, and for that reason Cubans usually call the fruit by the euphemism **fruta bomba** (pumped-up fruit). **¡Vivan las diferencias!**

¡Qué melones tiene esa mujer! What a pair of knockers that woman has!

la pechuga almendrada (chicken breast almondine) appetizing bust ◀ Mex, Col ▶

las tetas tits (vulgar) ◀ L. Am., Sp ▶
Andaba en la playa con las tetas al aire. She was walking down the beach with her tits in the air.

tetona, tetuda big-breasted woman (vulgar) ◀ DR, PR, S. Cone, Sp ▶

feet

las lanchas (boats) big feet ◀ G ▶

las patas (paws) feet ◀ L. Am., Sp ▶

las patriarcas (patriarchs) feet ◀ CR, ES ▶

las patrullas (patrols) feet (girl chasers) ◀ Mex ▶

los pinceles (paintbrushes) feet (they paint you out of the room) ◀ Mex ▶

las planchas (boards) big feet ◀ U ▶

female conditions

dar a luz (to give to light) to give birth ◀ L. Am., Sp ▶
Mi esposa dio a luz hoy a las tres de la mañana. My wife gave birth today at three in the morning.

en estado (in a state [of maternity]) pregnant ◀ most of L. Am., Sp ▶

estar con Andrés to have one's menstrual period (vulgar) ◀ Ch ▶

estar con la ruler to have one's menstrual period (vulgar) ◀ Ch ▶

estar en varas dulces (to be in sweet rods, pun with **en-varas** sounding like **em-baraz**) to be pregnant ◀ Mex ▶

Le prendió la vacuna. (The vaccination "took.") She got pregnant. ◀ Mex, U, Arg ▶

vivir como escopeta de hacienda (to live like an old farm rifle) to be always pregnant (like an old farm rifle, always loaded and left in the corner) ◀ Nic ▶

boredom

el ahuevazón boredom ◀CR, ES▶

amuermar to bore, put to sleep ◀Sp▶
Ese tipo amuerma a cualquiera. That guy puts anyone to sleep.

a bore

aguacatón, aguacatona (big avocado) bore, party pooper ◀PR▶
Ven a la fiesta; no seas aguacatón. Come to the party; don't be a wet blanket.

aguado(-a) (watery, watered-down) simple, with no charm ◀Mex, G, Nic, CR, DR, Col, Para▶

el aguafiestas (party water, maybe implying someone who pours water over something to ruin it) party pooper; feminine form: **el/una aguafiestas** ◀L. Am., Sp▶
Como no quería ser aguafiestas, fui con ellos. Since I didn't want to be a party pooper, I went with them.

el bostezo (yawn) bore ◀CR, DR▶
Esta fiesta (clase) es un bostezo. This party (class) is a big yawn (bore).

cipeado(-a) dull ◀Nic▶

fome (styrofoam) dull, boring, lame ◀Ch▶

latero(-a) (tin canner, from **lata**, tin can) boring person or thing ◀Ch▶

muerto(-a) (dead) empty, boring ◀Mex, G, Ch▶
Este club está muerto. Vámonos. This club is dead. Let's go.

la paliza (beating) boring time (**dar la paliza**, to bore to death); boring person ◀Sp▶
María siempre nos da la paliza hablando de sus viajes. María always bores us to death talking about her trips.
Ese tío es un paliza; no lo aguanto. That guy is a bore; I can't stand him.

el pavo (turkey) boring or socially inept person ◀Ch▶

el plomazo (hit with lead) lead balloon, a drag (dull, boring thing or person) ◀DR, U, Arg▶

Qué cable. (What a cable.) How boring. ◀DR▶

Qué foco. Qué mamera. How boring. ◀Col▶
¡Qué foco farmacología hoy! Ese man habla y habla y habla y no dice nada. How dull pharmacology class was today! That man talks and talks and talks and doesn't say anything.

ser capaz de dormir a un muerto (to be capable of putting a dead person to sleep) to be very boring (people) ◀Mex, Sp▶
Ese profesor es capaz de dormir a un muerto. That prof is so dull he could put the dead to sleep.

ser un clavo (to be a nail) to be bad, boring ◀Cuba, DR▶
¡Qué clavo de película! ¡Devuélvanme el dinero! What a dud of a movie! Give me my money back!

ser como el pan sin sal (to be like bread without salt) to be bland, unattractive ◀ES▶

ser una haba sin sal (to be a bean without salt) to be a boring person ◀PR▶

ser una lata (to be a tin can) to be a pain, drag, bore, annoyance (also, **pura lata** in G, ES, Sp) ◀L. Am., Sp▶

el pavo

Ese chico es pura lata. That guy is a total drag.

Levantarse todos los días para ir a trabajar es una lata. Getting up every morning to go to work is a pain.

ser un muermo to be a drag, a snooze ◀ Sp ▶

Ese programa es un muermo. That program is a snooze.

ser un palo (to be a stick) to be boring, a drag (people or things) ◀ DR, PR, Sp ▶
Para mi es un palo tener que ir al servicio militar. For me it's a drag to have to go do military service.

ser una papa sin sal (to be a potato without salt) to be bland, unattractive ◀ G ▶

ser pesado(-a) (to be weighty) to be a pain, a drag, boring or unpleasant ◀ L. Am., Sp ▶

ser un pestiño (to be a fritter) to be a bore ◀ Sp ▶
La película era un pestiño. The movie was a bore.

ser un plomo (to be lead) to be boring ◀ DR, PR, S. Cone, Sp ▶
Ese profesor es un plomo; siempre habla de lo mismo. That professor is a dud; he always talks about the same thing.

bored

aburrirse como una ostra (to be bored as an oyster) to be or get very bored ◀ Mex, DR, Ven, Peru, Arg, Ch, Sp ▶

comerse un cable (to eat a cable) to be bored, with nothing to do, stood up ◀ DR ▶
¿Qué hiciste en Semana Santa? —Comerme un cable, ni siquiera pude ir a la playa. What did you do during Easter (Holy Week) vacation? —Twiddled my thumbs. I couldn't even go to the beach.

darse una clavada (to get hit by a nail) to have a bad or boring (crummy) time ◀ Arg ▶
Fui a una fiesta aburridísima; me di una clavada tremenda. I went to a tremendously dull party; I was bored out of my mind.

estar parquiado(-a) (parqueado) (to be parked) to be bored stiff ◀ Ch ▶

busyness

See also "activity."

andar como bola sin manija to be going around in circles, any which way (like a ball without a string) ◀ Para, Arg, U ▶
Mañana salgo para España, así que hoy ando como bola sin manija. Tomorrow I leave for Spain, so today I'm going around in circles.

bailar en la cuerda floja (to dance on the tightrope) to try to do many things at once or try to please more than one person; to be in a difficult situation ◀ L. Am., Sp ▶

el corre-corre (run-run) rat race, mess ◀ Mex, DR, PR ▶
No me gusta el corre-corre de la ciudad. I don't like the rat race of the city.
Cuando llegó la policía se armó un corre-corre en la discoteca. When the police arrived, there was a big hullabaloo in the disco.

embollado(-a) with a lot (too much) to do ◀ Col ▶
Mañana voy de viaje y tengo que terminar este proyecto; estoy embollado. Tomorrow I'm going away on a trip and I have to finish this project; I'm at the end of my tether.

estar metido(-a) hasta los codos en algo to be up to one's elbows in something ◀ Mex ▶
Estoy metida hasta los codos en este proyecto. I've got my hands full with this project.

no tener tiempo ni para rascarse (to not have time even to scratch oneself) to be very busy ◀ Mex, ES, DR, U, Sp ▶

traer a alguien de acá para allá (aquí para allí) (to bring someone from here to there) to keep someone busy, moving constantly, or confused or upset (ES: **allá para acá**) ◀ Mex, DR, PR, U, Arg, Sp ▶
Mi niño de un año me trae de acá para allá. My one-year-old son keeps me on the run.

Test your slang power!

Celebrations, parties, and having fun

«Lo pasamos bomba, ¿no?»

Relevant categories: dance, food and drink, fun, laughter, party

How much Spanish "slanguage" do you know related to this topic? Test yourself by completing the exercises. Answers and rating scale are on page 263. (If you don't do very well, read through the categories listed above and try again. The items in each exercise occur in the same order as the categories.)

A. Something's missing. *Select the appropriate word to complete the sentence.*

1. In Mexico, Ecuador, and Colombia, a lot of people like to dance to lively music. **En México, Ecuador y Colombia, a mucha gente le gusta bailar música (campanita / rayada / sacudida)** _____.

2. That gentleman wanted to dance with Rosa and he said to her, "Let's shake a leg!" **Ese caballero quería bailar con Rosa y le dijo, «Vamos a menear el (cuerpo / esqueleto / pie)** _____.»

3. Two draft beers, please. **Dos cervezas de (barril / burbuja / espuma)** _____**, por favor.**

4. It's time for the toasts. Bottoms up! **Es el momento de los brindis. ¡Fondo (abajo / blanco / cantante)** _____**!**

5. Your friend eats a lot. He's a bottomless pit. **Tu amigo come mucho. Tiene (buen diente / gran gusto / lengua larga)** _____.

6. In Mexico they serve delicious appetizers with the drinks. **En México sirven una (abreviada / botana / tentadora)** _____ **deliciosa con las bebidas.**

7. Hi, pals! How's the action? **¡Qui úbo, compadres! ¿Cómo está la (escena / movida / zumbida)** _____?

8. Our relatives had a great time. They enjoyed themselves to the max! **Nuestros parientes echaron mucho relajo. ¡Se divirtieron a sus (anchas / topes / reservas)** _____!

9. During the whole movie, I was dying with laughter. **Durante toda la película, estaba (cortada / encendida / muerta)** _____ **de risa.**

10. We had a bang-up time at the shindig last night. **Lo pasamos de peluche en la (pachanga / presurosa / puntilla)** _____ **anoche.**

B. Pick a letter! *Choose the letter of the word or phrase that best completes each sentence. Write it in the blank.*

11. _____ In Mexico, to ask someone to dance, you could say **Vamos a sacarnos**
    a. **la oxidación.**
    b. **la polilla.**
    c. **las ruedas.**
    d. **las telarañas.**

12. _____ **Un boquisabroso** (or **una boquisabrosa**) is
    a. someone who loves to eat.
    b. a picky eater.
    c. someone who talks too much.
    d. a good conversationalist.

13. _____ The last piece of food on the plate, the one that no one dares to take, is called in Spain and the Dominican Republic
    a. **la sobrasaliente.**
    b. **la de la vergüenza.**
    c. **lo dejado por la suegra.**
    d. **el resto de los restos.**

14. _____ **«Yo soy como Juan Orozco. Cuando como no conozco.»** This saying means:
    a. I never talk with my mouth full.
    b. I don't know proper table manners.
    c. I don't know whether I'm hungry or not.
    d. During a meal I pay attention to eating and nothing else.

15. _____ In many places people tell you not to eat **porquerías** (literally, things fit for pigs), but in Mexico and Colombia they call junk food
    a. **alimento basura.**
    b. **alimento cemento.**
    c. **comida chatarra.**
    d. **comida negada.**

16. _____ In Mexico, Colombia, and the Dominican Republic, a midmorning snack is called
    a. **un abrelosojos.**
    b. **una comeycanta.**
    c. **una rompemañana.**
    d. **un tentempié.**

17. _____ In Spain an area where there are lots of bars and clubs is referred to as
    a. **el camino de estrellas.**
    b. **el paseo de las girafas.**
    c. **la senda de elefantes.**
    d. **la vía láctea.**

18. _____ Clowning around or silly actions are called
    a. **bronquitas.**
    b. **camarones.**
    c. **payasadas.**
    d. **rasguños.**

19. _____ Getting a long weekend in Mexico, the Dominican Republic, and Spain by taking off the day before or after a holiday is called
    a. **abrir grieta.**
    b. **crear extensión.**
    c. **formar brazo.**
    d. **hacer puente.**

20. _____ In Spain and Latin America it is customary to have a send-off party for the bride-to-be before her wedding; this is called
    a. **la despedida de soltera.**
    b. **la jarana de la novia.**
    c. **el saludazo.**
    d. **el último brincón.**

certainty

See also "truth."

a ciencia cierta (for certain knowledge) for sure ◀ L. Am., Sp ▶
No hay duda. Lo sabemos a ciencia cierta. No doubt about it. We know it for sure.

como dos y dos son cuatro (like two and two are four) as sure as shootin', as we're standing here ◀ L. Am., Sp ▶

de plano (flatly) for sure ◀ Mex, ES, Nic ▶
De plano que sí. De plano que voy. Absolutely yes. I'm going for sure.

en redondo (in round) clearly, categorically ◀ Mex, Sp ▶

mero(-a) (mere) exact, this or that very (one) ◀ Mex, G ▶
ése mero, that exact one
en el mero momento, at the very moment
en la mera esquina, right at the corner

Son habas contadas. (They're counted beans.) They're a sure thing. They're scarce and with a fixed number. ◀ Sp ▶

change

cambiar de canal (to change the channel) to change pace or activity ◀ Mex, ES, DR, Col ▶

cambiar de casaca to leave a group, political party, etc., and go to a different one, be a turncoat (Sp and Ch: also, **cambiar de camisa, cambiar de chaqueta**) ◀ parts of L. Am., Sp ▶

el chaqueteo (jacket movements) manipulations in politics ◀ Bol, Ch ▶

dar vuelta a la página (to turn the page) to put some unpleasant experience from the past behind you and go forward, turn over a new leaf (Sp: also,

pasar o girar página) ◀ CR, ES, S. Cone, Sp ▶
Es mejor olvidarse de ese asunto y pasar (dar vuelta a la) página. It's better to forget that affair and let bygones be bygones (put the whole thing behind us).

dar la vuelta a la tortilla (to turn over the omelette) to turn the tables ◀ Ch, Sp ▶
Rosario ha dado la vuelta a la tortilla y ahora es ella que manda en esa casa. Rosario has turned the tables and now she's the one who gives the orders in that house.

darse vuelta la chaqueta (to turn the jacket inside out) to be wishy-washy, change with the tide ◀ Ch ▶

no ser ni la sombra de lo que era (to not be even the shadow of what one was) to be a shadow of one's former self ◀ L. Am., Sp ▶

sentar cabeza (to seat head) to settle down ◀ most of L. Am., Sp ▶
Por fin mi hijo se casó y sentó cabeza. Finally my son got married and settled down.

tutifruti describing someone who changes often ◀ Col ▶

changing the subject

A otra cosa, mariposa. (To another thing, butterfly.) That's that, forget it. On to a new topic. ◀ Mex, DR, Sp ▶

cambiar el cassette (to change the cassette) to change the subject ◀ U, Ch ▶

Pasemos a otro patín. (Let's go to another skate.) Let's change the subject. ◀ Mex, G, Ec ▶

Sanseacabó. (Saint it's over.) That's that; phrase used to end a discussion ◀ Mex, G, ES, DR, PR, S. Cone, Sp ▶
Esto no tiene sentido. ¡Sanseacabó! This doesn't make any sense. That's enough talk about it!

Santas pascuas. (Holy Easter or Passover) phrase to end a discussion or said when one is forced to resign oneself to something ◀ Mex, Ch, Sp ▶
Tú te quedas con la casa y yo con el Mercedes, y santas pascuas. You get the house and I get the Mercedes, and that's that.
No podemos hacer el viaje y santas pascuas. We can't go on the trip and there's an end of it.

y en paz (and in peace) that's that; phrase said to end a matter ◀ Mex, ES, Sp ▶

Yo recojo mis cosas y tú las tuyas, ¡y en paz! I'll take my things and you take yours, and that's that!

---

competence

See also "intelligence," "unusualness."

arreglárselas (to arrange them) to manage, be competent, able to do something (often something tricky) ◀ ES, DR, S. Cone, Sp ▶

Me las arreglé para convencerla. I managed to convince her.

Se las arregló para conquistarlo. She managed to win him over.

defenderse (to defend oneself) to manage, get along ◀ L. Am., Sp ▶

No te preocupes… me voy defendiendo. Don't worry . . . I'm managing.

No hablo bien el japonés, pero me defiendo. I don't speak Japanese very well, but I get along.

duro(-a) (hard, difficult) intelligent, very good at something ◀ Col, PR ▶

jugar bien sus cartas to play one's cards well, do something with astuteness ◀ Mex, DR, S. Cone, Sp ▶

llevarse todo por delante (to carry away everything in front of you) to win at everything, to take on all comers, be all things to all people ◀ S. Cone, Sp ▶

no ser cojo(-a) ni manco(-a) (to be neither lame nor one-handed) to be competent and experienced ◀ Mex, DR, PR, Ch, Sp ▶

Mamá, no puedo hacer esta tarea. —¿Y por qué, si no eres ni cojo ni manco? Mom, I can't do this chore. —And why not, if you aren't deaf or dumb?

pintarse solo(-a) para una cosa (to paint oneself alone for something) to be very apt or skillful at something ◀ Mex, U, Arg, Sp ▶

Mi hija se pinta sola en la cocina. For my daughter, cooking is right up her alley.

Mi esposo se pinta solo tocando el piano. My husband is outstanding at playing piano.

ser cachimbón, cachimbona to be good at everything, competent ◀ Mex, G, ES ▶

Ese chico es bien cachimbón para trabajar. That guy is super at working.

ser un(a) chingón (chingona) to be good at something ◀ chicano, Mex, C. Am. ▶

Juan es un chingón para la música. Juan is the best at music.

Ella es una chingona para las matemáticas. She's a whiz in mathematics.

ser un(a) duro(-a) (to be hard) to be the best, someone really good at something ◀ Col ▶

Ana es una dura en vólibol. Ana is a top player in volleyball.

ser un(a) fregón (fregona) to be good at something ◀ Mex ▶

ser Mandraque el Mago (to be Mandrake the Magician) to be a wonder worker ◀ Ch ▶

ser un manitas to be good at doing things, handy ◀ Sp ▶

ser muy cabrón (cabrona) para algo to be very good at something (vulgar) ◀ chicano, Mex, G, Col ▶

ser el putas (to be the whores) to be really good at something (vulgar) ◀ Col ▶

Eduardo es el putas del tenis en este club. Eduardo is the tennis ace at the club.

ser recábula to be convincing, a good manipulator (used for men or women) ◀ Mex ▶

tener bien puestas las pilas, estar con las pilas puestas (to have one's batteries well placed) to have one's act together, be on the ball ◀ DR, Ven, U, Ch ▶

Ese chico es muy listo; tiene las pilas bien puestas. That guy is very clever; he's really got his act together.

tener buena mano para (to have a good hand for) to have the skill for something, have the knack, the right touch ◀ DR, PR, S. Cone, Sp ▶

Ana tiene buena mano para las plantas. Ana has a green thumb.

tener colmillo (to have eyetooth) to be astute in business ◀ Mex, CR ▶

tener madera (to have wood) to have strength, aptitude, have what it takes (to do something) ◀ Mex, Col, Ven, Ch, Sp ▶
Tienes madera de músico. You have a talent for music.

tener mano (to have hand) to be competent ◀ DR, PR, Sp ▶
Elena tiene mano para la pintura. Elena has a knack for painting.

tener tablas (to have boards) to have a lot of experience at doing something; to lose one's timidity in public or to get oneself out of a jam ◀ Arg, Sp ▶
Ese conferenciante tiene muchas tablas. That speaker has what it takes.
Tienen unas tablas increíbles. They have incredible poise.

doing something outstanding

botarse to outdo oneself (dressing well, doing things well, looking good); to have something special (Mex) (CR, Col: to treat someone, invite and pay) ◀ DR, PR ▶
Bótate. You look great.
¡Qué fiestón! Esta vez se botaron los Martínez. (DR) What a super party! This time the Martínezes have outdone themselves.
Qué cuero de novia se bota Miguel. (Mex) What a gorgeous bride Miguel has.

echarse ese trompo a la uña (to put that top, the spinning toy, on one's fingernail) to perform an amazing feat ◀ Mex, ES ▶

lucirse (to shine) to stand out, do something unusual ◀ Mex ▶
Te luciste. You were outstanding.
Se lució con la comida. He (She) did a fabulous job with the dinner.

matar dos pájaros de un tiro (to kill two birds with one stone) to achieve two goals at once ◀ L. Am., Sp ▶

volarse la barda (to blow up the fence) to do something very impressive, usually good ◀ Mex ▶

Te volaste la barda con este plano (examen). You kicked over the traces with this chart (test).

complaints and crybabies

a grito pelado (to the peeled shout) yelling loudly ◀ most of L. Am., Sp ▶

chillar to squeal (inform on); to complain, cry, whine ◀ chicano, Mex, G, Col ▶

chillón, chillona crybaby, complainer (Sp: person who yells a lot) ◀ chicano, Mex, G, ES, Col, Sp ▶
¡Tan grandote y tan chillón! Such a big kid and such a crybaby (whiner)!

¡Hasta ahí podríamos llegar! (Even that far we could go!) phrase of indignation facing a possible abuse ◀ Mex, Sp ▶

llorón, llorona crybaby, whiner ◀ L. Am., Sp ▶

pegar el grito (to stick the shout) to protest, cry out ◀ CR, ES, DR, Col, U ▶

poner el grito en el cielo (to put the cry to the heavens) to complain or cry out loudly ◀ L. Am., Sp ▶

completeness

a tope totally, with all one's energy, fast ◀ Mex, Sp ▶
Aproveche a tope este sitio en la Red. Take advantage of this Web site to the max.

con pelos y señales (with hairs and gestures) in great detail ◀ L. Am., Sp ▶
Lo explicó con pelos y señales. He (She) explained it in great detail.

de remate (terminally) hopelessly, completely ◀ L. Am., Sp ▶
Es un loco de remate. He (She) is a total nut.

hasta más no poder full-fledged; all possible ◀ L. Am., Sp ▶
Es un naco hasta más no poder. (Mex) He's a complete jerk.

hasta el tope (to the top) entirely, completely, as far as it can go ◀ Mex, ES, Sp ▶

hasta los tuétanos down to the marrow (Ch: **hasta las masas**) ◀ L. Am., Sp ▶

Hay de todo como en botica. (There's everything like in a pharmacy.) It takes all kinds. There's something here for everyone. ◀ Mex, DR ▶

puritito(-a) pure, sheer ◀ Mex, G, ES ▶
Era puritita mentira. It was an absolute lie.

tal por cual (such for which) out-and-out, dyed-in-the-wool ◀ L. Am. ▶

todititito(-a) everything (variant of **todo**) ◀ Mex, ES, Nic ▶
Ya se nos arruinó todititito. The whole shooting match was wrecked for us.
Se me arruinó todititita la comida. Every last bit of my dinner was ruined.

everyone

cada hijo de vecino (any neighbor's son) any person ◀ Mex, Sp ▶

el que más y el que menos (he who most and he who least) everyone ◀ Ch, Sp ▶

hasta las piedras (even the stones) all, without exception ◀ Sp ▶

todo quisque everyone ◀ Sp ▶

from top to bottom

de cabo a rabo from top to bottom, from beginning to end, completely ◀ Mex, S. Cone, Sp ▶
Leyó el libro de cabo a rabo. He (She) read the book from beginning to end.

de (los) pies a (la) cabeza (from [the] feet to [the] head) from head to toe, entirely ◀ L. Am., Sp ▶

de pe a pa entirely; from beginning to end ◀ Mex, ES, DR, S. Cone, Sp ▶

de rabo a cabo from top to bottom, from beginning to end, completely ◀ DR, PR ▶
Se lo sabe todo, de rabo a cabo. He (She) knows everything about it, from top to bottom.

confusion

See also "mess, fuss, disorder."

confused

azurumbado(-a) confused (ES, Nic: **zurumbo[-a]**) ◀ Nic, CR, Col ▶
Bien zurumba quedé de oírlo hablar. (ES) I wound up totally muddled after hearing him speak.

como gallina en corral ajeno (like a hen in someone else's or a different pen) in a poorly adjusted way, like a fish out of water ◀ Col, Peru, Ch ▶

como gallo en patio ajeno (like a rooster in someone else's or a different patio) totally lost, like a fish out of water ◀ CR, ES, Pan, Nic ▶

hacerse bolas (to get balled up) to get confused; to complicate one's life ◀ Mex, C. Am. ▶
No te hagas bolas. Don't complicate your life.
Aquí siempre me hago bolas con el lenguaje. I always get balled up with the language here.

hacerse camote (to make sweet potato) to get confused ◀ Mex ▶
Se hizo camote en el examen y lo reprobaron. He got completely mixed up in the exam and they flunked him.

hacerse un ocho (to make oneself into an eight) to complicate one's life, get balled up ◀ DR, PR, Col ▶
Porfa, ayúdame, que yo siempre me hago un ocho con esta computadora. Pretty please, help me because I always get balled up with this computer.

hacerse un taco (to make oneself a plug) to get confused or balled up in difficulties ◄ Sp ►

norteado(-a) (northed) disoriented, confused ◄ Mex, ES ►
Ando norteada. I'm going around totally disoriented.

parecer un pato mareado (to seem like a dizzy duck) to seem confused or dim-witted ◄ Sp ►

pegado(-a) a la pared (glued or stuck to the wall) confused, not able to react ◄ DR ►

perder el norte (to lose the north) to be disoriented in what one says or does ◄ Sp ►

quedarse patidifuso(-a) (y perplejo[-a]) to be (end up) confused (and perplexed) ◄ DR, Col, Ch, Sp ►

tener un cacao mental (to have a mental cacao tree or bean) to have a confusion of ideas ◄ Sp ►

tener una empanada mental (to have a mental **empanada**, a pastry filled with meat and/or other things) to not have clear ideas or thinking ◄ Sp ►

tener mambo en la cabeza (to have mambo in the head) to be confused, disoriented ◄ Arg ►

tupirse (to get stopped up, blocked or dense) to get spaced out, confused ◄ Ch ►

volverse un etcétera (to become an etcetera) to be confused ◄ DR ►
Miss Panamá era muy bonita, pero cuando le hicieron la pregunta se volvió un etcétera y perdió muchos puntos. Miss Panama was very pretty, but she seemed completely out to lunch when they asked her a question, and she lost a lot of points.

volverse un ocho (to become an eight) to be confused ◄ PR, Col ►

confusing someone

alburear to talk with double meaning, confuse in a teasing way ◄ Mex, ES, CR ►

dar curva to evade, throw (give) someone a curve; not know ◄ Mex, Cuba ►

entuturutar to confuse, brainwash (Nic, CR: **entotorotar**) ◄ ES ►
No dejes que Felipe te entuturute. Don't let Felipe get you all mixed up.
La novia de Esteban lo tiene bien entuturutado. Ya no quiere salir con nosotros. Esteban's girlfriend has him truly brainwashed. Now he doesn't want to go out with us.

envolvente (wrapping) person who confuses others in a tricky way ◄ Mex, Cuba, Col ►

envolver en razones (to wrap in reasons) to confuse (someone) ◄ Mex, ES, Sp ►
No trates de envolverme en razones, que yo sé lo que pasó. Don't try to feed me a load of bull because I know what happened.
Trató de envolverme en razones con sus mentiras. He tried to mess up my mind with his lies.

volver a alguien tarumba (turumba) to confuse, bewilder (Ch: also, **hacerle turumba**) ◄ Ch, Sp ►

out of it

See also "lack of knowledge: in the dark, unaware."

estar colgado(-a) (to be hanging, suspended) to live without a notion of reality ◄ Ch, Sp ►

estar despistado(-a) to be lost, off the track, clueless, forgetful ◄ L. Am., Sp ►
Estoy totalmente despistada; no sé nada del asunto. I'm completely clueless; I don't know anything about the matter.

estar en otra (to be on another, with the idea of **onda** or **dimensión** understood) to feel spaced out, detached ◄ Mex, S. Cone ►

estar más despistado(-a) que un pulpo en un garaje (to be more lost than an octopus in a garage) to be lost, off the track ◄ Sp ►

flotar (to float) to not be with it or in the world, not find out about things ◄ Sp ►

fuera de base (de órbita) (off base [out of orbit]) out of it ◄ Mex, Nic, Col ►

marcando ocupado (dialing the busy signal—and just not connecting) out of it, not understanding anything ◀Ch▶
Ese chico no sabe nada. Está marcando ocupado. That guy doesn't know anything. He's temporarily disconnected (out of it).

No está en na'a (nada). He or she is out of it (not in anything). ◀most of L. Am.▶

tener la cabeza a las tres o a las once (to have one's head at three or at eleven) to be an absentminded person, a little bit out of it (from a play on words with three referring to the three-letter word **i-d-a** [gone] and eleven to the eleven-letter word **t-r-a-s-t-o-r-n-a-d-a** [disturbed, upset]) ◀Peru▶

el/la volador(a) (flyer, swinger) someone who is disorganized and forgetful, scatterbrained person, used like **despistado** ◀U, Arg▶

conversation

See also "gossip," "information."

a flor de labio (at the flower of the lip) on the tip of one's tongue ◀L. Am., Sp▶

algodón (cotton, sounds like **algo**) vague evasive answers (to indiscreet questions) ◀Mex▶
¿Qué tienes en la mano? —Algodón. What do you have in your hands? —None of your business.

barajar (to shuffle) to explain ◀Mex, G, ES, Hond, DR, PR, Col▶
No entiendo, barájeme eso. I don't understand. Lay it out for me.
Barajéamela más despacio. Run that by me a bit slower.

el caliche street slang (n.); of the street (adj., also, **calichera**) ◀Mex, ES▶
Es habla caliche. It's street slang.

destripar a alguien el cuento (to remove the stuffing or guts of the story

from someone) to steal someone's thunder (telling a story he or she began) ◀Sp▶

devolver la pelota a alguien (to return the ball to someone) to counter someone with their own arguments or reasoning ◀Mex, DR, Sp▶
Marta es un genio; cuando discute no hay quien le devuelva la pelota. Marta's a genius; when she's in a discussion, no one gets the best of her.

dos palabras (two words) short conversation ◀Mex, ES, S. Cone▶
¿Puedo hablarte? Sólo van a ser dos palabras. Can I speak to you? It's only going to take a second.

echar un fonazo to make a telephone call ◀Mex▶

echar vaina (to throw husk, sheath) to talk about nothing; to tease (somewhat vulgar but very common) ◀DR, Ven▶

enchufarse (to plug in) to join (a conversation) ◀S. Cone▶

el golpe de teléfono (hit with the telephone) phone call ◀U, Arg▶

hablar entre dientes (to talk between the teeth) to mumble, murmur, grumble ◀L. Am., Sp▶
Hablaba entre dientes y no lo entendí. He was mumbling and I didn't understand him.

muñeco viejo (old doll) old hat (something already commented on) ◀DR, Col▶

parla conversation, way of speaking ◀Mex, CR▶

parlar (from Italian and French) to talk ◀Mex, ES, Col▶

perder el hilo to lose the thread (e.g., of a conversation) ◀L. Am., Sp▶

romper el hielo to break the ice ◀L. Am., Sp▶

la sobremesa after-dinner conversation at the table ◀L. Am., Sp▶

subido(-a) de tono (heightened in tone, with a louder tone) strong language, implying vulgar expressions ◀ES, DR, Peru, Bol, Ch, Sp▶

el tiquismo Costa Rican word or expression ◀CR, ES▶

beating around the bush

andar por las ramas   to beat around the bush ◀ L. Am., Sp ▶

andarse por rodeos   to talk around the point (Mex, DR, U, Arg: **andarse con rodeos**) ◀ Ch, Sp ▶

emborrachar la perdiz   (to make the partridge drunk) to beat around the bush ◀ Ch ▶

irse por las ramas   (to go around the branches) to beat around the bush ◀ Mex, S. Cone, Sp ▶

hablar hasta por los codos

big talkers, talking at length

contar batallitas   (to recount small battles) to tell stories of one's life ◀ Sp ▶

la cotorra   (parrot) chatterbox, someone who talks a lot ◀ L. Am., Sp ▶

cotorrear   to jabber away ◀ Mex, G, DR, PR, Col, U, Arg, Sp ▶

habla que te habla   (talk that he or she talks to you) talking or nattering on, blah, blah ◀ DR, PR, Ch ▶

hablar como un papagayo (un perico)   to talk like a parrot, talk a lot (Sp: **papagayo** only) ◀ DR, PR, Sp ▶

hablar hasta por los codos   (to talk even through one's elbows) to talk a blue streak, talk someone's ear off ◀ L. Am., Sp ▶
La vecina vino a contarnos todo lo que pasó. Hablaba hasta por los codos. The neighbor lady came to tell us what happened. She talked a blue streak.

lanzar un rollo   (to throw a roll) to start a long story ◀ Mex, ES, Col ▶

No me cuentes tu vida.   Don't tell me your life story. ◀ Mex, Sp ▶

la parrafada   (paragraph) long, uninterrupted conversation ◀ Sp ▶

que si patatín que si patatán   and so on and so on; blah, blah, blah; excuses for someone who doesn't want to talk directly about something ◀ Mex, DR, PR, Sp ▶
Ramón me estuvo contando de su viaje a Chile, que visitó Santiago, que si patatín que si patatán, pero no me dijo nada del accidente. Ramón was telling me about his trip to Chile, that he went to Santiago, that blah, blah, blah, and so on and so forth, but he didn't tell me anything about the accident.

que si pito que si flauta   (that if fife then flute) yada, yada, yada; one thing and then another ◀ PR ▶

el rollo   (roll) long story or tale; bull; problem, complicated situation; also, way of being ◀ Mex, C. Am., Col, Ven, Ch, Sp ▶
Vaya rollo que tiene. Oh, my, what a story he (she) has.
Esa película es un rollo. That movie is a bore.
No me va el rollo de tus amigos (no me gustan). (Sp) I don't care for your friends.
Déjate de tanto rollo. Stop giving me such a crock.
Ese chico está metido en un rollo muy raro. That guy is mixed up in some strange monkey business.
Yo no abro la puerta a nadie porque los vendedores a domicilio tienen un rollo increíble. I don't open the door to anybody because door-to-door salesmen have such incredible spiels.

ser un pico   (to be a beak) to be a good talker ◀ Sp ▶

soltar la culebra   (to let the snake go) to talk on and on like a winding snake (or a windbag) ◀ Ch ▶
Mi tío siempre suelta la culebra. My uncle always drones on and on.

soltar el rollo (to let loose the roll) to talk at length, let out a long tale or tell all that one knows (Arg: **largar el rollo**) ◀ Mex, C. Am., Col, S. Cone, Sp ▶
Suelta el rollo, Ana. ¿Qué pasó? Tell all, Ana. What happened?

la tarabilla nonstop talker ◀ Mex, ES, Nic ▶

tener mucho rollo (to have a lot of roll) to talk a lot without saying much ◀ Mex, Sp ▶
Esa persona tiene mucho rollo; habla mucho pero no dice nada interesante. That person is a real windbag; he talks a lot but doesn't say anything interesting.

tener un pico de oro (to have a golden beak) to be a good talker, gifted speaker ◀ most of L. Am., Sp ▶

el tilín tilín (tinkle of a bell) noise, talk ◀ Col ▶
Jimena siempre promete que nos va a invitar a la casa a rumbiar. Pero eso sí: mucho tilín tilín y nada de paletas. Jimena always promises that she's going to invite us to her house to have a good time. But, what happens is a lot of yak and no action (literally, no popsicles).

volar lengua (to fly tongue) to talk, converse (CR: also, **volar lata** or **pico**; Col: **volar el pico**) ◀ CR, ES ▶

conversation gambits

See also "change: changing the subject."

a todo esto by the way, used like **a propósito**; meanwhile ◀ Mex, ES, CR, Pan, Peru, Bol, S. Cone ▶
A todo esto, ya son las cinco. By the way, it's already five o'clock.
A todo esto, los vecinos hablaban mucho de ella. In the meantime, the neighbors were talking a lot about her.

Chogusto. (short for **Mucho gusto.** Glad to meet you.) ◀ parts of L. Am. ▶

de por sí used like **de todas formas**, anyhow ◀ Mex, ES, CR, Col, Peru, Bol, U, Arg ▶
¿Dónde estabas? De por sí te estaba esperando hace días. Where were you? Anyhow, I've been waiting for you for days.
No es muy inteligente ese chico; de por sí que no lo quiero para una tesis. That fellow isn't very bright; at any rate I don't want him for a thesis.

de tocho morocho at any rate (used instead of **de todos modos**) ◀ Mex, ES ▶

encimita (a little on top) and in addition, besides all that (used as transition in conversation) ◀ ES, Nic ▶

O somos o no somos. (We are or we aren't.) phrase used to mean that because we are who we are we can or should act in a certain way or do a certain thing (e.g., get in the door at a fancy place), usually used jokingly (also: **¿Somos o no somos?** Are you with me or not? Are we on or not?) ◀ Mex, ES, Ec, S. Cone, Sp ▶

po' short for **pues**, added at end of phrases ◀ Ch ▶
Sí, po'. Right you are.
Ya po'. All right already.

¿Qué crees? (What do you think?) Guess what. ◀ L. Am., Sp ▶

¡Sopla! You don't say! ◀ Sp ▶

getting to the point

ir al chile (to go to the **chile**, slang for male organ) to get to the point ◀ Mex, ES ▶

ir al grano (to go to the grain) to get to the point ◀ L. Am., Sp ▶

ir al rollo (to go to the roll) to get to the point, the issue ◀ Mex, ES ▶
Vamos al rollo. Let's get down to brass tacks.

hinting

cahuinear (from an Indian language) to hint, insinuate, make an innuendo ◀ Ch ▶

la indirecta muy directa a very explicit hint meant not to be missed ◀ Mex, Cuba, DR ▶

tirar un palo (to throw a stick) to give a hint ◀ Ch ▶

jokes

el chiste colorado (rojo) (red joke) off-color joke (more common in Mex, ES, Ch than **chiste verde**) ◀ L. Am., Sp ▶

Say it with slang!

Family matters in Mexico

The words "child," "mother," and "father" have lots of slang power in Mexico. **¡Híjole!** (Child to you!) is one of the most common expressions for surprise or amazement, roughly equivalent to "Good heavens!" The word **madre** (mother) has multiple meanings, all of them strong and some contradictory. **Me vale (importa) madre** means "I don't give a damn" (literally, "That means mother to me"). (This attitude has a word of its own: **el valemadrismo**.) Someone who is totally shameless **no tiene madre** (has no mother), but the same phrase can also mean that he or she is extraordinarily good at something; for example, **¡Ese tenista no tiene madre!** (That tennis player is the best!) A very bad cold is **un catarro a toda madre** (a cold at full mother), but a wonderful party could be **una fiesta a toda madre**. A horrible mess is **un desmadre** (an unmothering), and the worst possible insult involves a gesture (usually the tightening and raising of one fist) that means **¡Tu madre!**, implying that the insultee's mother is or soon will be dishonored. The word **padre** (father), however, when used to describe things, generally means "super" or "marvelous," as in **¡Tu nuevo carro está muy padre!** (Your new car is marvelous!) More common would be to say that it is **padrísimo** (the fatherest), which naturally means "the very best"!

---

el chiste pelado (peeled joke) off-color joke ◀ Mex ▶

el chiste verde (green joke) off-color joke ◀ L. Am., Sp ▶
Viene tía Paulina a cenar. No estés contando chistes verdes, ¿oyes? Aunt Paulina is coming to dinner. Don't go telling off-color jokes, do you hear?

el pujo (attempt) bad joke, groaner ◀ Cuba, Col ▶

swear words

deslenguado(-a) (untongued) using strong language ◀ Mex, Ch, Sp ▶

el garabato (scribbling, graffiti) swear word, bad word ◀ Ch ▶

la grosería (gross thing, expression, etc.) vulgar or obscene word, swear word ◀ L. Am., Sp ▶

Le dijo una grosería y ella se enfadó mucho. He (She) said something obscene to her and she got really mad.

hablar como un carretero to swear like a trooper (trucker) ◀ Sp ▶

la lisura (smoothness; sincerity) obscene word, swear word ◀ Peru ▶

malhablado(-a) crude in speaking habits, using bad language ◀ L. Am., Sp ▶

la palabrota swear word, vulgar word ◀ L. Am., Sp ▶

el taco bad word, swear word ◀ Sp ▶
No me gustan los tacos. Esa película tiene muchos tacos. I don't like bad words. That picture is loaded with swear words.

el trompabulario condescending term for bad language, sounds like **trompa**, meaning mouth or angry, and **vocabulario** ◀ Mex, Col ▶

courage

accepting a challenge

aventarse to take risks ◀Mex, ES, Nic, DR, Peru▶

hacer de tripas corazón (to make heart of one's guts) to force oneself to overcome fear and adversity, pluck up courage ◀L. Am., Sp▶
A pesar del problema que tenía, hice de tripas corazón y fui a la reunión. In spite of the problem I had, I pulled myself together and went to the meeting.

ir (nadar) contra la corriente to go against the current ◀L. Am., Sp▶

recoger el guante (to pick up the glove) to accept or rise to a challenge ◀Mex, Peru, S. Cone, Sp▶

tirarse el lance (to throw oneself the spear) to try something without being sure of succeeding, take a stab or chance at ◀S. Cone▶
Me voy a tirar el lance al declararle mi amor (pedirle un aumento). I'm going to take a shot in the dark and confess my love for him (her) (ask him [her] for a raise).

brave, gutsy, ballsy

See also "authority: control and power."

aventado(-a) (thrown out) thrown into a course of action, risking oneself; (n.) risk taker ◀Mex, G, ES, Nic, Col, Peru▶
Es un aventado; no tiene miedo de nada. He's a daredevil. He's not afraid of anything.

choro(-a) brave, daring, admirable ◀Bol, Ch▶

cojonudo(-a) brave (vulgar, from **cojones**, testicles) ◀Mex, Cuba, Col, Sp▶
Eres una tía cojonuda. You're a ballsy chick.

empingado(-a) brave; with high values (vulgar) ◀Cuba▶

el gallo (rooster) brave man (ES, Sp: brave or angry) ◀Mex, G, ES, Nic, CR, Sp▶

Se puso como un gallo cuando le dijeron que bajara el volumen de su aparato de música. (Sp) He became a bulldog when they told him to turn down the volume on his boom box.

guapo(-a) (attractive, gorgeous) brave ◀Mex, Cuba, DR, PR, S. Cone▶

metelón, metelona fearless ◀Col▶

pencón(-a) (with a big male organ) dynamic, determined, full of chutzpah, hustler in a good sense (slightly vulgar) ◀ES, Nic▶

tener agallas (to have galls) to have guts, nerve ◀L. Am., Sp▶
Ese tipo tiene muchas agallas. That guy has a lot of nerve.
No tuvo agallas para hacerlo. He didn't have the guts to do it.

tener bien puestos los calzones (to have one's underwear well placed) to be worthy, have character or valor (Ch: **pantalones**, not **calzones**) ◀Mex, C. Am., Ch▶

tener bolas (to have balls) to be brave (vulgar) ◀U, Arg▶

tener las bolas bien puestas (to have one's balls well placed) to be brave, have guts (vulgar) ◀S. Cone▶

el gallo

tener los cojones bien puestos (to have one's testicles well placed) to be bold, brave (vulgar) ◀DR, Sp▶

tener huevos (to have eggs, testicles) to be bold, brave ◀Mex, ES, DR, PR, U, Arg, Sp▶

tener los huevos bien puestos (to have one's eggs, meaning testicles, well placed) to be bold, brave (vulgar) ◀Mex, ES, U, Arg, Sp▶
Nuestra secretaria tenía las bolas bien puestas cuando presentó su queja contra el jefe. Our secretary had the balls to bring a complaint against the boss.

tener los huevos cuadrados (to have square eggs, meaning testicles) to be very bold (vulgar) ◀DR▶

tener más cojones que nadie (to have more testicles than anyone) to be very brave (vulgar) ◀Sp▶

tener narices (to have noses, euphemism for **cojones**) to be brave ◀Sp▶

tener patas (to have paws) to be brash or bold ◀Ch▶

tener pelotas (to have balls) to be brave, bold (vulgar) ◀U, Arg, Sp▶

craziness

parecer chiva loca (to seem like a crazy goat) to be running around like crazy ◀Mex▶
Niña, siéntate. Pareces chiva loca. Sit down, girl. You're running around like a chicken with its head cut off.

soñar con pájaros preñados (to dream of pregnant birds) to be crazy, thinking of the impossible ◀parts of L. Am.▶
Si crees que te voy a comprar ese carro, estás soñando con pájaros preñados. If you think I'm going to buy you that car, you're dreaming.

el vato (bato) loco crazy dude ◀chicano, northern Mex▶

crazy

alocado(-a) (turned crazy) crazy for action, unpredictable ◀L. Am., Sp▶

arrebatado(-a) (carried away) crazy ◀G, Cuba, DR, PR▶

arremata'o(-a) crazy (probably from **loco de remate**) ◀ES, DR, PR▶

arrevesado(-a) crazy ◀CR, ES, DR▶

atravesado(-a) (crossed) crazy ◀Mex, Nic, CR, Col▶

boleado(-a) (balled up) half crazy, flaky ◀Arg▶

chiflado(-a) crazy; foolish; like mad ◀L. Am., Sp▶
Después de la pelea, mi hermano salió chiflado. After the fight, my brother took off like a house on fire.
Estás chiflado. You're soft in the head.

cruzarse los cables (to have one's cables crossed) to be crazy ◀L. Am., Sp▶
¿Cómo que vas a comprar otra computadora? ¿Se te cruzaron los cables? What's this about you buying another computer? Have you lost your marbles?

enfermo(-a) del mate (del chape) (sick from mate tea [from a kind of mollusk]) loose cannon, nut case ◀S. Cone▶

Ese bicho, lo que está es frito (tosta'o). (That bug, what he is, is fried [toasted].) That guy's a nut. ◀Ven▶

estar chiflado(-a) del coco to be crazy in the head (coconut) ◀Florida, Mex, G, Col, Sp▶
Estás chiflado(-a) del coco. You're touched in the bean.

estar lucas, lurias used instead of **lunático(-a)**, crazy ◀Mex▶
Está bien lucas ese hombre. That guy is really loony.

estar mal de la azotea (to be bad in the roof) to be crazy ◀DR, S. Cone, Sp▶

estar mal de la cholla (to be bad in the head) to be crazy ◀Mex, ES, PR, Sp▶

estar pirado(-a) to be crazy ◀Sp▶

fallarle la azotea (to have one's roof failing) to have bats in the belfry, be crazy ◀ Mex, DR, PR, S. Cone ▶
Le falla la azotea. His (Her) upstairs isn't fully furnished. (He's [She's] got bats in the belfry.)

faltarle a alguien un tornillo to have a screw loose (missing) ◀ L. Am., Sp ▶

faltarle cinco para el peso (to be missing five cents for the peso) to not be playing with a full deck (Ch: **faltarle una chaucha** [old-fashioned penny coin] **pa'l peso**) ◀ ES ▶
Te falta cinco para el peso. You're not playing with a full deck.

más loco(-a) que una cabra crazier than a she-goat ◀ Mex, CR, S. Cone, Sp ▶

sobado(-a) (massaged) touched in the head ◀ ES ▶

temático(-a) (thematical) obsessive, monomaniacal, crazy ◀ ES, Nic, Peru, Bol ▶
No se puede hablar con ese hombre; es bien temático. You can't talk with that man; he keeps obsessing about the same thing.

tener flojos los tornillos to have a screw (screws) loose ◀ Mex, ES, Sp ▶

tocado(-a) de la cabeza touched in the head, a bit crazy (Mex: also, just **tocado**) ◀ Mex, G, Col, U, Arg, Sp ▶

zafado(-a) crazy ◀ chicano, Mex, C. Am., Col, Ch ▶
Creo que esa cantante está bien zafada. I think that singer is off the wall.

going crazy

botar la canica (la bola) (to throw the marble [ball]) to go crazy ◀ Mex ▶
Se botó la canica y empezó a cantar en el entierro. He (She) went loopy and began to sing at the funeral.
A mi perro se le botó la canica de estar tan viejo. My dog lost his marbles from being so old.

caérsele un tornillo (to have a screw fall out) to have a screw loose ◀ Mex, CR, ES, Col, Sp ▶
Se te cayó un tornillo. You have a screw loose.

fundírsele a alguien los fusibles (to have one's fuses melt) to become crazy ◀ Mex, ES, DR, PR, Sp ▶

Se me fundieron los fusibles. No sé en qué pensaba. I got temporarily disconnected. I don't know what I was thinking.

patinarle a alguien el coco (to have one's head [coconut] skate) to be crazy, having a slipped gear mentally ◀ Mex, ES, CR, DR, Ch ▶
A Rafael le patina el coco. Rafael is driving with one headlight (has slipped a gear mentally).

patinarle a alguien el embrague (to have one's clutch [of the car] skate) to be crazy, have a slipped gear mentally ◀ Ch, Sp ▶

perder la chaveta (to lose one's head) to go crazy, be off one's rocker ◀ Mex, DR, ES, Sp ▶
¿Qué le pasa a Tito? ¿Perdió la chaveta? Lo vi salir de la casa con un vestido rosado. What happened to Tito? Is he off his rocker? I saw him leave the house in a pink dress.

rayarse to go crazy ◀ Ec, Peru, S. Cone ▶

crime and punishment

See also "authority: police."

armado(-a) hasta los dientes armed to the teeth ◀ L. Am., Sp ▶

el azote del barrio (whip of the neighborhood) person who commits crimes and repeatedly makes trouble, scourge of the neighborhood ◀ Mex, Ven ▶

chueco(-a) crooked (also, traitor in Mex, Ch) ◀ Mex, ES, DR, Col, Ch ▶
Juegan chueco. They play crooked.

el coyote (coyote) someone who takes people across the U.S. border; also, an intermediary to get things (sometimes illegally or below cost); in Nic, can be a money changer (for U.S. dollars) ◀ Mex, C. Am. ▶
El coyote que la traía la abandonó. La dejó tirada. The coyote who brought her abandoned her. He left her by the wayside.

Le pagaron a un coyote para que les consiguiera los documentos. They paid an intermediary to get the documents for them.

enhierrado(-a) (ironed-in, iron-carrier) armed, carrying a gun ◄ Ven ►

las esposas (wives) handcuffs ◄ L. Am., Sp ►

meter un paquete (to put in a package) to fine ◄ Sp ►
Le metieron un paquete de 10.000 pesetas por no llevar el casco de la moto. He (She) was fined 10,000 pesetas for not wearing a motorcycle helmet.

la movida unlawful business ◄ Mex, G, ES, Ch ►

el sistema jodicial (screwed-up system, corruption of **judicial**; **jodicial** is from **joder**, to screw up) police and legal system ◄ Mex, Col ►

catching someone

calzar a alguien (to put shoes on someone) to catch, bust, or arrest someone ◄ Ch ►

con las manos en la masa (with one's hands in the dough) caught in the act ◄ L. Am., Sp ►

encanar (to bar in) to arrest, put behind bars ◄ Arg, Ch ►

pillar (to plunder) to catch, get ◄ Mex, Col, Ch, Sp ►
Lo pillaron con las manos en la masa. They caught him red-handed.
En el super pillaron a un ratero. They caught a shoplifter in the supermarket.

in jail

estar a la sombra (to be in the shade) to be in jail ◄ Mex, G, Cuba, S. Cone, Sp ►

estar de vacaciones en el bote (to be on vacation in the jar) to be in jail ◄ Mex, Cuba ►

estar en el bote to be in jail (in the jar, container) ◄ Mex, C. Am., Cuba ►

estar en la cana (to be in a small space) to be in prison ◄ Cuba, Ec, Peru, Arg, Ch ►

estar en chirona to be in jail ◄ Mex, most of C. Am., Peru, Sp ►

estar en la jaula (to be in the cage) to be in prison ◄ chicano, Mex, Cuba, DR, Col ►

estar en el latón (to be in the brass) to be in prison ◄ Cuba ►

estar en el tambo to be in jail ◄ Mex, ES ►

guardar to keep in jail, **guardado(-a)** ◄ Mex, Cuba, DR, Col ►

irse precioso (to go precious, humorous play on **irse preso**, meaning to go as a prisoner) to go to the clink (jail) ◄ Ch ►

killing

borrar (to erase) to kill, wipe out ◄ chicano, Mex ►

dar pasaporte a alguien (to give someone passport) to kill ◄ Mex, ES, Sp ►

echarse a alguien (to throw oneself to someone) to kill ◄ Mex, G, Cuba ►

linchar to kill, lynch; in Mex, Ch, and CR, also to punish, in a threat ◄ Mex, ES, G, Cuba, DR, PR, Col, Ch, Sp ►
Expresó sus ideas y lo lincharon. (Ch) He expressed his ideas and they lynched him (verbally).

tumbar (to fell, knock down) to kill; to convince or persuade; to deceive ◄ Mex, Cuba, Col ►

estar a la sombra

robbing or mugging

afanar (from Lunfardo, to take advantage of someone) to steal, rob or mug, without violence ◀ Cuba, Peru, U, Arg, Sp ▶

ahueviar to steal ◀ ES ▶
Ya te ahueviaron la bicicleta. They already snatched your bicycle.

bolsear (to purse) to steal, pick pockets ◀ Mex, C. Am. ▶

cargar to steal ◀ CR, Col ▶

dar el golpe (to give the hit) to make a hit, steal or rob ◀ Mex, ES, Sp ▶

dar un palo (to give a stick) to strike; to make a hit, steal something ◀ Cuba, DR ▶

dejar a alguien en cueros (to leave someone naked) to rob everything ◀ Mex ▶
Me han dejado en cueros. They took me to the cleaners.

dejar a alguien sin camisa/quitarle hasta la camisa (to leave someone without a shirt/to take even someone's shirt) to ruin someone ◀ Mex, Sp ▶

levantar (to pick up) to rob, steal ◀ G, Cuba, PR, Col, Ec ▶

mafiar to steal ◀ Cuba, DR ▶
¿De dónde sacaste esas cervezas? —Se las mafié a Roberto, que compró una caja. Where'd you get those beers? —I "borrowed" them from Roberto when he bought a case.

mangar (to "sleeve") to steal ◀ Cuba, PR, Sp ▶

pinchar (to pinch) to get, take ◀ Col ▶
Me pincharon la cartera. They pinched my wallet.

quedar limpio(-a) (to be left clean) to be cleaned out, without money ◀ Mex, DR, Sp ▶
Después del robo, me quedé limpio. No sé qué hacer. After the robbery, I was cleaned out. I don't know what to do.

el/la ratero(-a) thief ◀ Mex, ES, Col, S. Cone ▶

tifitear, tifitifi (from English) to thieve ◀ Cuba, Col ▶

tumbado(-a) (lying down, knocked over) victim of a robbery ◀ PR, Col, Ven ▶

tumbar (to fell, knock down) to mug, rob ◀ PR, Col ▶
Yo no encuentro mi cartera desde ayer. Creo que me la tumbaron en la guagua. (PR) I can't find my wallet since yesterday. I think someone picked my pocket on the bus.

volar (to fly) to rob, to be robbed ◀ Mex, Col ▶
Mi bolsa voló. (Col) Me volaron la bolsa. (Mex) My purse was lifted. (They snatched my purse.)

criticism

See also "anger," "annoyance," "hostility," "insults."

Así me (te, nos) luce el pelo. (That way my [your, our] hair looks good.) used to tell that one is wasting time or not taking advantage of an opportunity ◀ Sp ▶

dar una cantaleta to give a sermon, repeat something ad nauseam ◀ Mex, C. Am., DR, Peru, Col ▶

mandarse un discurso to deliver a sermon (lecture) ◀ L. Am. ▶

chewing out, ripping apart

achurar (to eviscerate a cow) to speak badly of someone, rip someone apart ◀ U, Arg ▶
Pepito, pórtate bien porque si no, tu mamá te va a achurar. Pepe, behave yourself because if you don't, your mom is going to rip into you.

cagar (to defecate) to insult, ream out, rip apart (vulgar) ◀ Mex, Col ▶

cagar a pedos (to shit with farts) to scold and insult someone in a loud, nasty way (vulgar) ◀ U, Arg ▶
Me olvidé de pagar una cuenta y mi hermana me cagó a pedos. I forgot to pay a bill and my sister gave me a hell of a chewing out.

dar una achurada   (to eviscerate) to give (someone) a scolding or dirty deal ◀ Arg ▶
A Juan le dieron una achurada tremenda en la oficina. They gave Juan a heck of a dirty deal at the office.

darle dos hostias a alguien   (to give someone two Hosts [vulgar]) to give someone a scolding or a piece of one's mind, chew someone out ◀ Sp ▶

echar una bronca   to bawl out, reprimand ◀ parts of L. Am., Sp ▶
Me echaron una bronca espantosa por llegar tarde a casa. They gave me a terrible bawling out for getting home late.
Vaya bronca le echó a Bárbara su padre por perder las llaves. My goodness, how Barbara's father ripped her to shreds for losing the keys.

hartar   to criticize ◀ CR, ES ▶
Lo único que haces es hartarte a la gente. You spend all your time tearing down other people.

lanzar unas líneas gruesas   (to throw some thick lines) to deliver an ultimatum, say a mouthful ◀ Mex ▶

llamar a alguien a capítulo   (to call someone to chapter) to call someone on the carpet, ask someone for an accounting and reprimand him or her ◀ DR, PR ▶

poner a alguien como lazo de cochino/percha de perico   (to make someone like a pig's rope/parakeet's perch) to ream out, rip apart with insults ◀ Mex ▶

poner a alguien (quedar) como palo de gallinero   (to make someone [end up] like a perch in a chicken coop, i.e., covered with droppings) to ream out, rip apart with insults ◀ Mex, U, Ch ▶
El candidato habló tan mal en el debate que quedó como palo de gallinero. The candidate spoke so poorly in the debate that the public tore him apart.

poner a alguien como un trapo (viejo)   (to make someone like a rag [like an old rag]) to bawl someone out with offensive and angry words (U, Arg: **dejar** instead of **poner**) ◀ Mex, PR, U, Arg, Sp ▶

poner a alguien de vuelta y media   (to put someone to a turn and a half) to treat someone badly, heap insults on him or her ◀ DR, Ch, Sp ▶

poner a caldo   (to put to broth, perhaps implying someone is being scalded) to criticize, say bad things about ◀ Sp ▶

poner verde   (to make green) to heap insults or censure (on someone) ◀ Mex, Sp ▶

rajar   (to split) to speak badly of, talk about behind (someone's) back ◀ Col, Peru, Bol, U, Arg ▶

resondrar a alguien   to scold or yell at someone ◀ Peru ▶

retar (a un niño, a un subordinado)   (to challenge [a child, subordinate]) to scold ◀ S. Cone ▶

sacarle el cuero a alguien   (to take the leather out of someone) to rip someone to shreds with gossip, bad comments (DR: **sacarle las tiras del cuero**) ◀ S. Cone ▶

sacarle la piel a tiras   (to take off the skin in strips) to speak badly (of someone) ◀ PR, Sp ▶

serrucharle el piso a alguien   (to saw off the floor under someone) to undermine someone, often by saying bad things about him or her to others behind his or her back (DR: **serruchar el palo**) ◀ Hond, Nic, CR, Col, Ec, Peru, S. Cone ▶
Mireya me serruchó el piso con mi jefe cuando fui de vacaciones. Mireya cooked my goose with the boss by telling him lies when I went on vacation.

tijerear a alguien   (to cut someone with scissors) to criticize, cut down with words ◀ Mex, ES ▶

tirar arroz   (to throw rice) to criticize ◀ Peru ▶
No me gusta tirar arroz a nadie, pero ese hombre se cree mucho. I don't like to put anybody down, but that man has an inflated opinion of himself.

tirar piedras   (to throw stones) to criticize, make disparaging comments (Mex: more common, **echar pedradas**) ◀ Mex, CR, Col ▶

tronar   (to thunder, blast) to reprimand ◀ Cuba ▶

put-downs

Arrieros somos que en el camino andamos. (We are muleteers and we go down the roads.) Someday we'll meet and we'll be in the same situation. (reply after someone has criticized another, putting them in their place) ◀ Mex, ES, Ch ▶

Bájale de crema a tus tacos. (Lower or decrease the cream in your tacos.) Get off it. ◀ Mex, Col ▶

Bájale de huevos a tu licuado. (Lower or decrease the eggs in your blended drink.) Get off it. ◀ Mex, ES, Col ▶

Bájale. (Lower it.) Don't exaggerate. Come off it. ◀ Mex, ES, Col ▶

bajarle a alguien los humos (to lower someone's airs) to put someone in their place ◀ Mex, DR, PR, S. Cone, Sp ▶
La señora le bajó los humos al funcionario mal educado. The lady took that rude bureaucrat down a peg or two.

bajarle el copete (to take down his or her crest or hairpiece) to take him or her off a high horse, take down a peg ◀ S. Cone ▶

bajarle el moño (to take down his or her hair bun or twist) to take him or her off his high horse, take down a peg ◀ Ch ▶

¡Botones para los preguntones! Buttons for those who ask too many questions! (often used with children) ◀ ES ▶

¿Cuándo hemos comido en el mismo plato? (When have we eaten from the same plate?) Since when are we bosom buddies? ◀ Mex, G, ES ▶

¿Cuándo hemos gastado el dinero juntos? (When have we spent money together?) Since when are we bosom buddies? ◀ ES ▶

dar un cortón a alguien to cut someone down to size in a sharp reply (Sp: **dar un corte**) ◀ Mex ▶
La rubia me dio un cortón anoche en la fiesta. The blond cut me down to size last night at the party.

El burro delante, para que no se espante. (The burro first, so he isn't frightened, doesn't get startled.) said to someone who goes first or names himself or herself first; often just: **El burro delante.** Age before beauty. ◀ Mex, ES, DR, Arg, Ch, Sp ▶

El maestro Ciruela, que no sabe leer y pone escuela. (Master Ciruela, who can't read and has a school.) said to censure someone who is talking about something he or she doesn't know much about ◀ L. Am., Sp ▶

¡Escoba! (Broom!) Same to you, buddy! ◀ Ch ▶

hacer entrar al aro a alguien (to make someone enter into the hoop) to put someone in his or her place ◀ Mex, U, Arg ▶

¿Ladrónde compraste eso? (used instead of ¿Dónde compraste eso?, **ladrón** meaning thief) implies suspicions about the origin of something, often used in jest ◀ Mex, DR, Col ▶

¡Mira quién habla! Look who's talking! ◀ L. Am., Sp ▶

Ni el sol te va a dar. (Not even the sun will give it to you.) Don't get big ideas. (similar to **No te hagas ilusiones.**) ◀ Cuba ▶

¡Nones para los preguntones! Nothing for those who ask too many questions! ◀ Mex ▶

pedazo de... (piece of . . .) used to intensify an insult ◀ Mex, Peru, S. Cone, Sp ▶
Dile a ese pedazo de imbécil (tonto) que deje de molestar. Tell that moron to stop bothering us.

poner a alguien en su sitio (lugar) to put someone in his or her place ◀ L. Am., Sp ▶

poner a raya (to put a stripe, line) to put in his or her place, draw the line when someone is trying to take advantage ◀ Mex, Ch, Sp ▶
Me presionaba mucho, pero por fin lo puse a raya. He (She) was pressuring me a lot, but I finally drew the line.

Pon los pies sobre la tierra. (Put your feet on the ground.) said to someone who is too proud or too idealistic ◀ Mex, ES, DR, S. Cone, Sp ▶

la quemada (burn) put-down, disparaging remark ◀ chicano, Mex ▶

Say it with slang!

Shellfish: attention-seeking clams and bored oysters

Shellfish appear in English slang when we call a small person a "shrimp" or say that a cheerful person is "as happy as a clam." In Spanish, clams are seen in a different light. **Cantar como almeja** (to sing like a clam) means to call attention to oneself and look ridiculous, or, to put it into English slang, to stick out like a sore thumb. Far from being seen as happy, oysters are used as examples of boredom: **Me aburrí como una ostra** (I was bored as an oyster).

Toni se dio una buena quemada al escribir esa carta llena de errores y mandarla al jefe. Toni got her comeuppance in spades when she wrote that letter full of errors and sent it to the boss.
¿Te dijo eso? ¡Qué quemada! He (She) said that to you? What a put-down!

¿Quién te mete, Juan Bonete? (Who brings you into this, Juan Bonete?) This isn't your affair. None of your business! ◀ Mex, Nic ▶

quitar hierro (to take away iron) to take away the importance of something that one thinks was exaggerated ◀ Sp ▶

Recógete. Keep in your place. Behave yourself. ◀ Mex, PR, Col ▶

¡Tomá tu muñeca, muchacha ñoñeca! (Take your doll, silly girl!) Have it your way (but I think it's a mistake)! ◀ Nic ▶

Toma tu tomate. (Take your tomato.) Take what's coming to you. Take what you deserve. What goes around comes around. ◀ Ven ▶

Ubícate. (Find yourself.) Straighten up. Behave yourself. ◀ Mex, DR, Col, S. Cone ▶
Ésta es una reunión muy importante para mí, así que ubícate y no te pongas a hablar de política. This is a very important meeting for me, so behave yourself and don't start talking about politics.

¡Újule! expression indicating a put-down, often followed by a disparaging remark ◀ Mex, ES ▶

¡Újule! Qué bárbaro lo que me dijo. Yikes! What a nasty thing he (she) said to me.
Un poco de respeto. (A little respect.) polite way of criticizing someone ◀ L. Am., Sp ▶

dance

See also "fun," "party."

el chanclazo (blow or hit with a **chancleta**, sandal) dance ◀ chicano ▶

la música sacudida (shaken music) lively music ◀ Mex, Col, Ec ▶

patón, patona (big foot, from **pata**, usually the foot of an animal or piece of furniture) person who can't dance ◀ Cuba, Col ▶

el pulir-hebilla (buckle polishing) close dancing with rhythmic movements (cheek to cheek) (PR: **brillar-hebilla**) ◀ Ven ▶

shaking a leg

chanclear to dance ◀ chicano ▶

echar un pie (to throw a foot) to dance, shake a leg (old expression) ◀ Cuba, DR, PR ▶

menear el bote   (to rock or move the boat) to dance ◄ most of L. Am. ►

menear el esqueleto   (to shake the skeleton) to dance ◄ L. Am., Sp ►
¿Vamos a menear el esqueleto, Silvia? Are we going to shake a leg, Silvia?

mover el esqueleto   (to move one's skeleton) to dance ◄ L. Am., Sp ►

sacarse la polilla   (to get the moths off) to dance ◄ Mex ►
¿Te gusta esta música? Vamos a sacarnos la polilla, ¿no? Do you like this music? Let's cut a rug, OK?

sacudirse   (to shake oneself) to dance ◄ Col ►

death

sacar con los pies adelante a alguien (to take someone out feet first) to take someone to be buried (Sp: **sacar con los pies por delante**) ◄ Mex, DR, PR, Sp ►

el supermuertario   cemetery (sounds like a supermarket of dead people) ◄ Mex ►

el tiro de gracia   (gunshot of pity) fatal blow, coup de grace ◄ L. Am., Sp ►

kicking the bucket

cerrar el paraguas   (to close the umbrella) to die ◄ CR ►

colgar, colgar el sable   (to hang up one's saber) to die ◄ Cuba ►

colgar los guantes   (to hang up the gloves) to die (Sp: to retire) ◄ ES, Nic, Sp ►

colgar los tenis   (to hang up one's tennis shoes) to die ◄ Mex, C. Am., DR, Peru ►
El perrito de Caty colgó los tenis. Caty's little dog gave up the ghost.

dar la patada a la lata   (to kick the can) to die ◄ Cuba ►

dejar el pellejo   (to leave one's hide or skin) to die ◄ Mex, Sp ►

espantar la mula   (to scare off the mule) to die; to go away, leave ◄ Mex, Cuba, CR, DR, PR ►

estirar la pata   (to stretch out one's foot) to kick the bucket, die (also, Nic: take a walk) ◄ L. Am., Sp ►

irse para el (al) otro barrio (mundo) (to go to the other neighborhood [world]) to pass away ◄ L. Am., Sp ►

liar los bártulos   (to bundle up the household goods) to die ◄ Sp ►

liar el petate   (to roll up the **petate**, sleeping mat, but now in Spain referring to a green bag used for military service) to die ◄ Sp ►

morir con las botas puestas   (to die with one's boots on) to keep on working up to the end of one's life ◄ Mex, Nic, U, Arg, Sp ►

morir vestido(-a)   (to die dressed) to die violently ◄ Mex, Sp ►

no hacer el cuento   (to not make an account) to die ◄ Cuba, Sp ►

palmarse   to die (Sp: **palmarla**) ◄ ES, CR ►
Ya se palmó. (CR) He (She) kicked the bucket.
La palmó a los setenta años. (Sp) He (She) packed it all in at seventy years old.

pasar a mejor vida   (to go to a better life) to die ◄ L. Am., Sp ►

patalear   to die; to end ◄ CR, ES ►
La función pataleó. The performance petered out.

morir con las botas puestas

near death

a las puertas de la muerte at death's door ◀ Mex, DR, Ch, Sp ▶

cargar la lápida (to carry the tombstone) to be in danger of or singled out for death ◀ Col ▶

con un pie en el hoyo (with one foot in the hole) near death ◀ Mex, DR, PR, Sp ▶
Pobrecito don Danilo anda con un pie en el hoyo. —Bueno pero ya tiene noventa y siete años. Poor old Don Danilo has one foot in the grave. —Well, right, but he's ninety-seven years old.

con un pie en el otro mundo with one foot in the other world, near death ◀ Sp ▶

estar con un (el) pie en el estribo (to have one [the] foot in the stirrup) to be ready to die ◀ Mex, ES, S. Cone, Sp ▶

estar en las últimas (to be on the last) to be on one's last legs ◀ L. Am., Sp ▶
Doña Jacinta tiene noventa años y está en las últimas. Doña Jacinta is ninety years old and on her last legs.

hacer las cuentas (to make one's accounts) to prepare to die ◀ ES, Col ▶

the dead

criar margaritas to push up (grow) daisies, that is, to be dead ◀ Mex, Sp ▶

frito(-a) (fried) dead ◀ PR, Col, U, Arg, Sp ▶
Se cayó de la ventana y se quedó frito en el suelo. (Sp) He (She) fell out the window and wound up dead as a doornail on the ground.

Se lo llevó Pateta. (The devil took him [Pateta meaning devil].) He (She) went to the devil; said with reference to someone nasty who died. The villain got his or her just reward. ◀ Peru ▶

los tiesos (stiffs) the dead ◀ Mex, Col, Ec ▶

los tranquilos (quiet ones) the dead ◀ Col, Ec ▶

the grim reaper

la calaca death ◀ Mex, ES ▶
la calva (the bald one) death ◀ G, ES, Cuba, Col ▶

la pelona (the bald one) death ◀ Mex, C. Am. ▶

deception

See also "flattery," "persuasion."

armarla (to arm it) to cheat; to upset ◀ Mex, Sp ▶
Me la armó. He (She) pulled one over on me.

arrancarse con los tarros (to get away with the jars) to falsely take the credit ◀ Ch ▶

botarse to reveal oneself ◀ DR, Col ▶

la cascarita (little rind; bark) little trick ◀ Col ▶
Fue un examen lleno de cascaritas. It was a really tricky exam.

guillarse to cover something up, have a secret or secret relationship ◀ DR ▶
Aunque ellos se guillan, todo el mundo sabe que son novios. Although they cover it up, everyone knows that they are in a steady relationship.

llorar lágrimas de cocodrilo to cry crocodile tears (feign sadness) ◀ L. Am., Sp ▶

pintarlo (de) color de rosa (to paint it pink) to make it sound and look great, gild the lily ◀ Mex, DR, ES, PR, Col, U, Ch, Sp ▶
Todo lo pinta color de rosa; nunca habla de los problemas que tienen. He (She) really gilds the lily about how everything is going and never talks about the problems they have.

pintárselo bonito to gild the lily, present a pretty picture ◀ Mex, ES, DR, PR, Col ▶

venderle a alguien to sell someone out ◀ Mex, Cuba, Col ▶

vendido(-a) sellout, person who sells out ◀ chicano, Mex, G, DR, Col, Ch ▶
Lo acusaron de ser un vendido cuando su equipo perdió el partido. They accused him of being a sellout when his team lost the game.

con artists, swindlers, and liars

el/la afanador(a) person involved in illegal business, shady deals ◀ U, Arg ▶

el arbolito (little tree) participant (player) in illegal shady deals (person who buys and sells currency) ◀ Arg ▶
No te metas con ese hombre. Es un arbolito. Don't have anything to do with that man. He's a shady money dealer.

el chimbero fraud, someone who doesn't give back money ◀ Col ▶

el/la cobero(-a) (person from the sultan's tent) liar, scam artist, con man ◀ Ven ▶

el culebrero (snake charmer, from **culebra**) charlatan ◀ Mex, Col ▶

el/la embustero(-a) fraud, cheat, liar ◀ L. Am., Sp ▶
Tú eres un embustero; eso no pasó así. You're a big liar. That's not how that happened at all.

el/la engrupidor(a) (grouper) person who deceives you with wit or charm, smooth talker, con man ◀ S. Cone ▶

el guayabero fraud, liar ◀ Col, U ▶

el/la majadero(-a) fraud, liar ◀ Sp ▶
Manolo me vendió un coche que dijo que era casi nuevo y era mentira. Es un majadero. Manolo sold me a car he said was practically new and it was a lie. He's a fraud.

el/la mojonero(-a) (turd dealer, **mojón**, meaning turd) liar, deceitful person (vulgar) ◀ Ven ▶

el/la pajero(-a) (ES, CR, Col: also, **pajoso[-a]**) liar or someone who talks a lot with no point ◀ Mex, C. Am., Col, Sp ▶

el/la paquetero(-a) fraud; liar ◀ Cuba, PR, Col ▶

el/la timador(a) rip-off artist, con man ◀ Mex, Ch ▶

el/la tracalero(-a) swindler, cheat ◀ Mex ▶
¿Tan barato compraste el estéreo? Eres un tracalero. You bought that stereo as cheap as that? You're a con artist.

el/la tramposo(-a) (tricky) dirty player, cheater ◀ L. Am., Sp ▶

el/la transista con man, con woman ◀ Mex, Col ▶

el/la versero(-a) liar, big talker ◀ Arg ▶

viene como el tiburón (he/she comes like the shark) here comes the opportunist, fraud ◀ Col ▶

fake, false

chafo(-a) fake, ersatz ◀ Arg ▶

chimbo(-a) false ◀ Col ▶

chiveado(-a) false, fake ◀ Col ▶
un tag chiveado, a phony tag

falseta false ◀ Ec ▶

trucho(-a) (trout) fake, phony ◀ U, Arg ▶
Esta maleta no es de cuero, es trucha. This suitcase isn't real leather. It's fake.

lies and scams

la casaca (coat) false arguments, baloney ◀ G, ES ▶
No me des casaca. Don't give me that baloney.
No le creas, que es casaca. Don't believe him (her). It's a crock.

el chanchullo (piggish) rip-off; faked or rigged deal, rigged elections, or jacked-up prices ◀ Mex, CR, DR, PR, Peru, Bol, Ch ▶
Está investigando un gran chanchullo de dinero. He (She) is investigating a big money scam.

la coba (sultan's tent, from Morocco) lie, con, scam ◀ Ven, Ec ▶

el cuento chino (Chinese story) big lie, fishy story ◀ Mex, Nic, U, Arg, Sp ▶

la guayaba (guava) lie ◀ most of L. Am. (not S. Cone) ▶
No voy a tragarme esa guayaba. I'm not going to swallow that nonsense.

la macana (weapon used by the Indians, and also possibly from Sr. Macana, a famous Argentine liar) whopper, big lie ◀ Mex, Bol, Arg, Ch ▶

el marullo rip-off, setup, as an inflated price, rigged election or game ◀ Ch ▶

la paja (straw) lie, nonsense ◀ Mex, C. Am., Col ▶
No me des paja. Don't give me that baloney (straw).

el paquete (package) lie, fraud (Cuba: said also of a bad literary work or movie) ◀ Cuba, Col ▶

¡Puro cuento! (Pure story!) What a whopper! What a fib! ◀ Mex, ES, Col, U ▶

el rollo macabeo (patatero) (Maccabean [potato-seller's] roll) a lie, deception ◀ Sp ▶

la transa ruse, trick, con ◀ Mex, ES, Col ▶

la vacilada deceit, con, trick ◀ Mex, Col, Sp ▶

playing dumb, acting sweet

estar hecho(-a) un almíbar (to be made a syrup) to act very friendly and affable ◀ Sp ▶
Mi esposo está hecho un almíbar porque llegó tarde anoche. My husband has become all sweetness and light because he got home late last night.

guillado(-a) not understanding or ignorant (of something) or not wanting to tell it ◀ Cuba, DR ▶
No te hagas el guillado; sabes bien que te dije que hoy te toca trabajar en la casa. Don't play innocent; you know very well I told you you have to work at home today.

hacerse el chivo loco (to make oneself the crazy kid goat) to play the part of someone who didn't hear or see anything ◀ Mex, DR ▶

hacerse el desentendido(-a) (to make oneself the nonunderstanding one) to pretend not to notice ◀ L. Am., Sp ▶

hacerse el loco (tonto) (la loca [tonta]) (to make oneself the crazy one) to pretend not to notice (Ch: also, **hacerse el leso**) ◀ L. Am., Sp ▶
No te hagas la loca; sabes bien que Ernesto es mi novio. Don't play dumb; you know very well that Ernesto is my boyfriend.

hacerse rosca (to make oneself a doughnut) to act sweet ◀ Mex ▶

la mosquita (mosca) muerta (dead fly) person who appears to be dim or dull but who doesn't miss the chance to take advantage of someone, hypocrite (Sp: **mosquita** only) ◀ L. Am., Sp ▶

navegar con bandera de inocente (tonto) (to sail with the flag of an innocent [a fool]) to pretend to be innocent or foolish but have a motive for it ◀ Mex ▶
Navegaban con bandera de inocentes esos diablos. Those devils were pretending to be so innocent.

no darse por enterado(-a) (entendido[-a]) (to not show yourself as understanding something) to pretend that you don't understand, play dumb ◀ DR, PR, S. Cone, Sp ▶

tener cara de «yo no fui» (to have the face of "it wasn't me") humble or innocent-looking face, contrary to truth ◀ Mex, ES, CR ▶
Ésa es una hipócrita. Tiene cara de «yo no fui». That woman is a hypocrite. She has the look of "It wasn't me."
¡Qué sorpresa me dio Joaquín! Es un pícaro y con esa carita de «yo no fui». What a surprise Joaquín gave me! He's a rascal and with that expression on his face of "Who me?"

ripping off, swindling, lying

atracar (to hold up, waylay) to overcharge, take advantage of someone money-wise ◀ Mex, CR, DR ▶

bailar a alguien (to dance someone) to deceive someone ◀ Mex, G, ES ▶
Me bailaron con este producto porque era de otra marca. They ripped me off with this product because it was a different brand.

bajar la caña (to lower the reed, cane) to charge an excessive price, rip (someone) off ◀ U, Arg ▶

caribear (to caribbean) to take advantage of someone, con, scam ◀ Ven ▶

chulearle el dinero a alguien to rip someone's money off ◀ CR ▶

clavar (to nail) to swindle ◀ Mex, G, CR, Cuba, DR, S. Cone, Sp ▶
A esos turistas los clavaron con una estatua taína; ¡creen que es una pieza original! They conned those tourists with a Taino statue; they think it's an original work of art!

cobar (to act like someone from the sultan's tent) to lie; to cheat, con ◄ Ven ► **No me cobes, pana.** Don't jive me, pal.

cotorrear to jive, feed a line ◄ chicano, Mex, Col ►

currar a alguien to con or cheat someone out of their money ◄ Arg ►

dar atole con el dedo a alguien (to give someone atole [a cornmeal drink] with the finger) to deceive someone, pull the wool over his or her eyes (CR: dar atolillo) ◄ Mex, CR ►

dar una clavada (to give a nailing) to charge more than what is proper or right, rip off ◄ DR, Arg, Sp ► **En ese restaurante me dieron una clavada.** That restaurant was a real rip-off for me.

dar (pasar) gato por liebre (to give cat for rabbit) to deceive someone, giving them something inferior ◄ L. Am., Sp ► **La cámara que compré el lunes ya se estropeó; creo que me dieron gato por liebre.** The camera I bought Monday is already broken; I think I got a pig in a poke.

dormir a alguien (to put someone to sleep) to deceive someone ◄ Mex, G, Cuba, DR ►

engrupir (to group up) to fool or trick with wit or charm, to con ◄ S. Cone ►

faltar a la palabra to not keep one's word ◄ L. Am., Sp ►

fantasmear to promise something but not keep the promise ◄ DR ►

gorrear to cheat, deceive (note: elsewhere, generally means to mooch) ◄ CR, Ch ►

jugar con dos barajas (to play with two decks) to act with duplicity ◄ most of L. Am., Sp ►

jugar mente (to play mind) to deceive ◄ Cuba, Col ► **Me jugaron mente; dijeron que me iban a cobrar 500 pesos pero me cobraron 700.** They pulled one over on me; they said they were going to charge me 500 pesos and they charged me 700.

llevar a alguien al huerto (to take someone to the garden) to deceive someone making them think they are favored when they are not, to convince someone to have sex (Mex: also, **llevar al baile**) ◄ Mex, Sp ► **El vendedor cree que me va a llevar al huerto.** (Sp) The salesman thinks he's going to lead me down the garden path.

mangar to deceive ◄ Cuba, PR ►

meter la mula (to put in the mule) to betray, deceive, do a bad turn ◄ S. Cone ► **Ten cuidado que en ese negocio no te vayan a meter la mula.** Be careful in that shop that they don't pull the wool over your eyes.

meter una chiva (to put in a female goat) to make up a fib ◄ Ch ►

muletear (to move the bullfighter's cape in preparation for a kill) to deceive or fool, pull the wool over someone's eyes ◄ Mex, Col ►

paquetear to deceive ◄ CR, Col ►

transar to swindle, cheat ◄ Mex, ES ► **Este televisor no sirve. Me transaron.** This television set is no good. They conned me.

tirarse el pegote (to throw oneself the add-on or crude addition) to lie or deceive ◄ Sp ►

vacunar (to vaccinate) to deceive or cheat ◄ S. Cone ► **Ese grupiento me vacunó, vendiéndome un radio que no funciona.** That rip-off artist conned me by selling me a radio that doesn't work.

venir con cuentos (to come with stories) to tell tales ◄ Mex, G, ES, DR, PR, S. Cone, Sp ► **No me vengas con cuentos.** Don't come to me with your tall tales.

verle la cara a alguien (to see someone's face) to deceive or take advantage of (implying **verle la cara de tonto**) ◄ Mex, ES, Nic, S. Cone ► **Ese hombre me vio la cara cuando me vendió un carro tan malo.** That man saw me coming and played me for a fool when he sold me such a bad car.

two-faced

comer a dos carrillos (to eat with two cheeks) to serve two masters, work for two (often opposing) people or ideas ◄ U, Sp ►

de dos caras   two-faced ◄ Mex, ES, U, Arg, Sp ►
Javier parece honesto pero tiene dos caras y podría robarle hasta a su madre. Javier seems honest but he's two-faced and would even be capable of robbing his own mother.

ser como las hojas del yagrumo   to be two-faced, like the leaf of a trumpet-wood tree ◄ PR, Ven ►

under the table, on the sly

por debajo del agua   (underwater) under the table ◄ Mex ►
Por debajo del agua di el dinero al policía. I gave the money to the police under the table (on the QT).

por debajo de cuerda (bajo cuerda) (under cord) under the table, through hidden means, on the sly (Arg: **bajo la cuerda**; Ch, U: **bajo cuerda** only) ◄ Mex, S. Cone, Sp ►
No tiene visa; está trabajando bajo cuerda. (Ch) He (She) doesn't have a visa; he (she) is working on the sly.

por debajo de la mesa   (under the table) in a corrupt way ◄ most of L. Am. ►
Todo lo hacen por debajo de la mesa. They do everything under the table.

el/la jala-bola   (ball-puller) person who can't make up his or her mind, wishy-washy ◄ Ven ►

no cerrar la puerta   (to not close the door) to not cut down on choices or options, not burn one's bridges ◄ Ch ►

No hay vuelta de hoja.   (There's no turning of the page.) There's no turning back. There's no doubt about it. ◄ Mex, ES, Nic, U, Arg, Sp ►
Así se va a hacer y no hay vuelta de hoja. That's the way it'll be done and there's no backing out of it (second guessing).
Ya no hablemos: no hay vuelta de hoja. Let's not talk anymore about it; there's no turning back.

pupuluco(-a)   indecisive, wishy-washy ◄ Nic ►

quedar   (to remain) to leave it, agree, decide ◄ L. Am. ►
Así quedamos. (Mex, ES) So that's the way we'll leave it.
Quedamos en eso. (Ch) Then it's agreed upon.
¿En qué quedamos? ¿Nos vemos a las siete o a las ocho? So, what did we decide? We're getting together at seven or at eight?

quemar las naves   to burn one's bridges (ships) ◄ L. Am., Sp ►

decisions

See also "difficulty," "problems."

estar (poner) en tres y dos   (to be [put] in three and two) to be (put) in a decisive moment, on the spot (from baseball, three balls and two strikes) ◄ Cuba ►
Su novia lo puso en tres y dos. Le dijo que o busca un trabajo o lo deja. His girlfriend gave him an ultimatum. She told him that either he looks for a job or she'll leave him.

estar entre dos aguas   (to be between two waters) to be undecided ◄ most of L. Am., Sp ►

defeat

See also "weakness."

aplancha'o(-a)   defeated, broken in spirit ◄ Col ►

giving up or giving in

aflojar   (to loosen up) to give up (on), back down, give in ◄ Mex, ES, CR, Col, S. Cone, Sp ►
No aflojes, dale duro. Don't cave in, hang tough.

apearse del burro   (to get off the burro) to back down ◄ Sp ►

Say it with slang!

Four ways of looking at an elbow

What does an elbow mean to you? In Spanish slang, it takes on different meanings. In Mexico and parts of Central America and the Caribbean, a man who is **muy codo** (very elbow) is stingy and doesn't like to part with his money. (In an extreme case he can be called **codísimo**, the "elbow-est.") In Spain **hacer codos** (to make elbows) means to study (as we bend our elbows and rest our heads on our hands to read). In many places, **empinar el codo** (to raise one's elbow) means to do some serious drinking. Throughout the Spanish-speaking world, there are references to the person **que habla hasta por los codos**, literally, the one who talks through his or her elbows. That means a person who is going on and on or, to put it in plain English, one who talks a blue streak.

bajar el moño (to lower the bun or twist in one's hair) to give in, concede ◀ Ch ▶

bajar las orejas (to lower the ears) to give in during a dispute or response ◀ Sp ▶

bajarse del burro (to get off the donkey) to back down ◀ Mex, ES ▶

colgar la toalla to throw in (hang up) the towel ◀ Mex, U, Arg ▶
Si no gano en ésta, cuelgo la toalla. If I don't win this one, I'll throw in the towel.

darse to give up (meaning **darse por vencido**) ◀ Mex ▶
No me hagas más cosquillas. Me doy. Don't tickle me anymore. I give in.

pedir cacao (to ask for cacao) to ask for pardon, give up in a fight ◀ ES, Nic, DR ▶
No le pidas cacao. Don't say "uncle" to him (her). (Don't give up the fight.)

recoger velas (to pick up sails) to give up (an idea or course of action) ◀ DR ▶

tirar la esponja (to throw the sponge) to throw in the towel ◀ S. Cone ▶

tirar la toalla to throw in the towel, give up (Sp: also, **arrojar la toalla**) ◀ L. Am., Sp ▶

Voy a tener que tirar la toalla. Me doy por vencido. I'm going to throw in the towel. I give up.

departure

See also "good-byes."

abrir una raya (to open a stripe) to leave abruptly ◀ Cuba ▶

abrirse to leave, go off ◀ CR, S. Cone, Sp ▶

alzar vuelo (to take flight) to leave, take off ◀ Mex, ES, DR, PR ▶

aplicar (la) retirada (to apply [the] retreat) to scram, leave ◀ U, Arg ▶

arrollar los petates (to roll up the sleeping mats) to leave, move ◀ CR ▶

borrarse, borrarse del mapa (to wipe oneself off the map) to get out of a situation, leave or disappear from it quickly, take off ◀ Mex, ES, S. Cone, Sp ▶
¡Bórrense! Viene la policía. Scram! The police are coming.

Se borraron olímpicamente. They took off in grand style.

Fuimos a un parque con unos amigos, pero al llegar allí, ellos se borraron del mapa. We went to a park with some friends, but just as we got there, they disappeared.

chillar goma(s), chillarla (to burn rubber) to take off quickly ◄ Mex, PR ►
Antonio salió furioso, chillando gomas. Antonio left hopping mad, in a big rush.

darse el piro to escape, go off (like pirotécnica, fireworks) ◄ Sp ►

despintarse (to unpaint oneself) to go away ◄ Mex, PR ►
Despíntate. Clear out of here.

echarse un pollo (to throw a chicken at oneself) to scram, split ◄ Ch ►
¡Adiós! Son las once y tenemos que echarnos un pollo. Good-bye! It's eleven o'clock and we have to make like the wind and blow.

esfumarse to disappear into thin air ◄ L. Am., Sp ►
¿Dónde está tu hermanito? —No sé. Se ha esfumado. Where is your little brother? —I don't know. He's disappeared into thin air.

espantar la mula (to scare off the mule) to leave, go away ◄ Mex, CR, Cuba, DR, PR ►

evaporarse (to evaporate) to disappear from the face of the earth ◄ Mex, Ch, Sp ►
¡Este fin de semana me evaporo! This weekend I'm disappearing from the face of the earth!

hacerse humo (to become steam or smoke) to disappear ◄ L. Am., Sp ►
Los ladrones se hicieron humo. The thieves took off in a puff of smoke.
Hazte humo. ¿No sabes que ya caíste mal? Get the heck out of here. Don't you know you blew it (made a bad impression)?

ir en pira to leave, go away ◄ Cuba ►

irse con viento fresco (to go with fresh wind) to slip away easily, quickly ◄ Pan, Ch ►

largar to send to the devil, blow off ◄ U, Arg ►
Me parece que voy a largar a esta mina. I'm thinking I'm going to send this dame to the devil.

largarse to go away, move off ◄ most of L. Am., Sp ►

¡Lárgate, niño! ¿No ves que doña Carmen está muy cansada? Scram, kid! Don't you see that Doña Carmen is very tired?

liar los bártulos (to bundle up the household goods) to move ◄ Sp ►

liar el petate (to roll up the **petate**, sleeping mat or green bag used for military service) to change residence ◄ Sp ►

no vérsele a alguien el pelo to not see hide nor hair of someone ◄ Mex, Sp ►

perder de vista (to lose from view) to escape from or stop seeing someone or something ◄ ES, Sp ►
Tengo ganas de perder de vista esta escuela. ¡Estoy harto! I feel like I don't ever want to see this school again. I'm fed up!

picarla to go away ◄ CR, ES, Col ►

pintar su calaverita (to paint one's little skull) to disappear ◄ Mex ►

pintarse (to paint yourself out) to go away, leave ◄ Mex, ES ►
Se pintó de colores. (Mex) He (She) got out of there like a house afire.

pirar to disappear (probably from **pira**, funeral pyre) ◄ Mex ►

pirarse to leave, go away, beat it ◄ Cuba, Arg, Sp ►

pitar (to whistle) to go, go away or run away ◄ Cuba, Col ►

poner pies en polvorosa (to put one's feet in the dustiness) to run away ◄ Mex, Peru, U, Sp ►

quemar el tenis (to burn the tennis shoe) to leave quickly ◄ Cuba ►
Tienes que quemar el tenis para llegar a la hora. You'll have to hotfoot it to get there on time.

recoger los bates (to pick up the bats) to leave from some place ◄ DR ►
Ya es tarde. Vamos a recoger los bates. It's already late. Let's pack it in.

recoger velas (to pick up sails) to leave from some place ◄ DR ►
Esta fiesta se acabó. Vamos a recoger velas. The party's over. Let's pack it in.

salir como un bólido (to take off like a fireball) to leave or take off quickly ◄ Mex, G, CR, Cuba, DR, Col, U, Ch, Sp ►

salir como un cohete to take off like a rocket ◀ Mex, ES, DR, U, Arg, Sp ▶

salir como tío Coyote (to go away like Uncle Coyote) to make a fast getaway ◀ Nic ▶

salir pitando (to leave honking the horn or blowing a whistle) to take off quickly; also, to show anger or vehemence in a conversation ◀ Mex, Sp ▶

ser el as de la baraja (to be the ace of the deck) to make oneself scarce ◀ most of L. Am. ▶
Felipe se ha desaparecido. Es el as de la baraja. Felipe has disappeared. He's made himself scarce.

tomar el portante (to take the big door) to disappear fast, get the heck out ◀ Peru, Sp ▶

tomar las de Villadiego (to take those of Villadiego) to take to one's heels, beat it ◀ Nic, Ch, Sp ▶
Cuando Carlos vio que la relación iba en serio, tomó las de Villadiego y ya no lo vimos más. When Carlos saw that the relationship was getting serious, he flew the coop and we didn't see him anymore.

tomarse el quirse to leave, get a move on ◀ U ▶
Tengo que tomarme el quirse. I have to get a move on.

tragárselo a alguien la tierra (to be swallowed by the earth) to disappear from places one usually frequents ◀ Mex, DR, PR, S. Cone, Sp ▶
Nunca vemos a Juan; se lo tragó la tierra. We never see Juan; it's like the earth swallowed him.

tragárselo a alguien la tierra

expressions about leaving

Pies, ¿para qué os quiero? (Feet, why do I love you?) said when one is about to flee from danger (Mex, S. Cone: **Patitas, ¿pa' qué te [las] quiero?**) ◀ Mex, S. Cone, Sp ▶
Empezó el incendio y Juan salió ¿patitas pa' qué te quiero? The fire started and Juan got the heck out of there.

Pisémonos. (Let's step on ourselves.) Let's go. ◀ Col, Ec ▶

difficulty

See also "mess, fuss, disorder," "problems."

buscar una aguja en un pajar to look for a needle in a haystack ◀ L. Am., Sp ▶

Del dicho al hecho hay mucho trecho. (From what is said to what is done there is a big gap.) Easier said than done. ◀ L. Am., Sp ▶

estar peludo(-a) (to be hairy) to be difficult or complicated ◀ ES, Ven ▶
¿Qué tal el trabajo? —Estuvo bien peludo pero lo terminé. How was the work? —It was pretty hairy, but I finished it.

estar la vida muy achuchá (achuchada) to be very difficult, expensive (used mainly in the south of Sp) ◀ Sp ▶

no es soplar y hacer botellas (it's not blowing and making bottles) it's not that easy ◀ ES, Hond, Nic, Cuba, Col, Ven, Ec, U, Arg, Sp ▶

no ser cáscara (cascarón) de coco (to not be coconut shell) to not be so easy ◀ DR, PR ▶
Me retiré de la clase de estadísticas porque ese profesor no es cáscara de coco y no tengo mucho tiempo para estudiar. I dropped the statistics course because that professor is no pushover and I don't have much time to study.

parir chayotes (to give birth to chayotes, a vegetable with prickly skin) to do something very difficult ◀ Mex ▶

el parto de los montes (birth of the mountains) something very difficult ◀ Pan, Ch ▶

poner el cascabel al gato to bell the cat (do something difficult or dangerous) ◀ L. Am., Sp ▶

ser carajo(-a) (to be male organ) to be difficult (vulgar) ◀ Mex ▶
Es muy carajo que nuestro equipo llegue al campeonato. It's not too damn likely that our team'll make it to the championship.

ser un coco to be difficult (a coconut) ◀ Mex, Col ▶

ser mortal (to be mortal, deadly) to be difficult ◀ Mex, DR, Col, U, Arg ▶
Este crucigrama es mortal. Sólo he completado dos palabras. This crossword puzzle is deadly. I've only finished two words.

sus más y sus menos difficulties or complications that a matter gives ◀ Mex, Sp ▶

tener crudo algo (to have something raw) to have something be difficult to do or get ◀ Sp ▶

disagreement

See also "criticism," "hostility," "insults," "mess, fuss, disorder," "problems."

armarla (to arm it) to upset, raise a fuss ◀ Mex, Sp ▶
Me la armó. He (She) upset me.

No se puede contigo. Things are impossible with you. ◀ L. Am., Sp ▶

repelón, repelona describing someone who refuses to do things, is always negative ◀ Mex ▶

respondón, respondona uppity, describing someone who talks back unjustifiably when reprimanded ◀ Mex, Sp ▶

subir el diapasón to raise one's voice ◀ parts of L. Am., Sp ▶

tira y afloja (pull and give slack) back and forth negotiations between two people or groups having trouble arriving at a solution ◀ Mex, Peru, S. Cone, Sp ▶

defying, resisting, opposing

dar bateo (to give batting) to oppose, fight against an injustice; to present a problem ◀ Cuba ▶

estar de cuerno uno con otro (to be at horn with another) to be opposed or fighting with someone ◀ Sp ▶

estar de punta uno con otro (to be at point with another) to be at odds or on bad terms with someone ◀ Mex, U, Ch ▶

llevar la contraria (contra) (to take the contrary) to contradict, oppose (Ec: **ser un contreras**) ◀ L. Am., Sp ▶

plantar cara a alguien (to plant one's face at someone) to oppose, defy, resist someone ◀ DR, PR, Sp ▶

ponerse al tiro (to put oneself to the shot) to face the music (duel), prepare for a fight or struggle ◀ Mex, ES, Col ▶
Se puso al tiro para pasar el examen. He had to face the music and study to pass the exam.

¡Que si quieres arroz, Catalina! (So you want rice, Catalina!) sarcastic remark said when someone hasn't gotten something expected (for example, a promise has been broken) ◀ Sp ▶
¿La has llamado muchas veces por teléfono y no te ha devuelto las llamadas? ¡Que si quieres arroz, Catalina! You've phoned her many times and she hasn't returned your calls? Tough luck, but life isn't a bed of roses! (You don't always get what you want!)

ser punto y aparte (to be point and apart) to be against (something) ◀ Mex ▶
Con el problema de la droga, yo soy punto y aparte. Regarding the problem of drugs, I'm dead set against them.

fighting

andar a palos to be at blows, always fighting ◀ Mex, Sp ▶

armar o tener una bronca to have a fight, dispute ◀ L. Am., Sp ▶
Tuvieron tal bronca que las voces se oían desde la calle. They had such a big argument that their voices were heard out in the street.
Armaron una bronca tan fuerte que los vecinos llamaron a la policía. (Sp) They raised such a big fuss that the neighbors called the police.

bronquear to fight, fuss, argue ◀ Mex, Col ▶
No me gusta bronquear. I don't like to argue.

bronquearse to get angry or upset, argue, fight ◀ Mex, Arg ▶
Si me trata mal, me voy a bronquear con él. If he treats me badly, I'm going to get upset with him.

ir pa'la brea (to go to the tarpaulin) to go have a fight ◀ Col ▶

irse a la piña (to go to the pineapple) to fight (also, **dar piñazos**) ◀ DR ▶
Mario y Jorge se fueron a la piña. Mario and Jorge went to the mat (had a fight).

rifarse to fight ◀ Mex, G, ES, DR ▶
Alberto se rifa con cualquiera. Alberto will pick a fight with anybody.

tener una pelotera to have a fight, blowup, brawl ◀ S. Cone, Sp ▶
pelotera de borrachos, drunken brawl

fights, disputes, arguments

el bochinche dispute among several people, usually noisy; fuss (ES: **buchinche**) ◀ G, ES, Nic, Pan, DR, PR, Col, Ven, S. Cone ▶
Se armó un bochinche en la calle anoche. There was a noisy argument in the street last night.
No me gusta contarle nada a Luisa. ¡Siempre forma un bochinche! I don't like to tell Luisa anything. She always makes such a fuss!

la culebra (snake) misunderstanding, tense disagreement ◀ Ven ▶

el dame que te doy (give me that I give you) big fight, knock-down-drag-out ◀ ES, Pan ▶

la mocha fight ◀ Ch ▶

el rapa-polvos argument, problem ◀ DR, Sp ▶
Teresa pelea por todo últimamente. Ayer me dio un rapa-polvos porque olvidé sacar la basura. Teresa fights about anything lately. Yesterday she gave me a going over because I forgot to take the garbage out.
No quiero rapa-polvos (broncas). I don't want any arguments.

la refriega (rescrubbing) fight, blowup ◀ Sp ▶

troublemaker

bochinchero(-a) argumentative; troublemaker (Ven: also, party animal; Pan: **bochinchoso,** gossiping troublemaker) ◀ ES, Nic, DR, PR, Ven, Bol, Ch ▶

el/la broncudo(-a) someone who gets in fights ◀ Mex, ES ▶
Ese señor es un broncudo. That man is a troublemaker.

el/la bronquinoso(-a) someone who gets in fights ◀ Col ▶

el buscón, la buscona (searcher) someone who is looking for a fight ◀ Mex, DR, PR, Col, Sp ▶

el camorrero troublemaker, instigator of conflicts ◀ S. Cone ▶

el/la guaposo(-a) someone looking for a fight ◀ Cuba ▶
Roberto es un guaposo; siempre busca pleitos. Roberto is a troublemaker; he's always spoiling for a fight.

el maletero (suitcaser) dirty fighter, troublemaker who doesn't play fair ◀ Ch ▶

disbelief

See also "deception."

dejarse de cuentos (to leave off with the stories) to stop telling stories, get to the point ◀ L. Am., Sp ▶

Déjate de cuentos. That's enough of your tall tales.

fresco(-a) (fresh) cynical ◀ Mex, G, Ch ▶

porfia'o(-a) not believing, obstinate ◀ PR, Ch ▶

tomar algo con un grano de sal to take something with a grain of salt ◀ Mex, CR, DR, PR, Ch, Sp ▶
Todo lo que dice Tomás hay que tomarlo con un grano de sal porque es un chismoso. Everything that Tomás says has to be taken with a grain of salt because he's such a gossip.

expressions of disbelief

Canta, pajarito. (Sing, little bird.) No matter what you say I don't believe you; I hear you but I'm not listening. ◀ Bol, Ch ▶

Claro, y los chanchos vuelan. Right, and that's likely (pigs fly). (sarcastic) ◀ parts of L. Am. ▶

¿Cómo cree(s)? How can you think that? (disclaimer after a compliment) ◀ L. Am., Sp ▶

¿Cómo que...? What do you mean . . . ? ◀ parts of L. Am., Sp ▶
¿Cómo que perdiste el dinero? What do you mean you lost the money?

¡No habla(s) en serio! You're not serious (talking seriously)! ◀ L. Am., Sp ▶

No voy a tragar carros y carretas. I'm not swallowing that nonsense (cars and carts). ◀ Mex, Sp ▶

No voy a tragarme esa guayaba. I'm not going to swallow that nonsense (guava). ◀ L. Am. (except S. Cone) ▶

¡Pura chepa! (Pure hump!) Nonsense! ◀ Col ▶

¡Pura leche! (Pure milk!) Nonsense! ◀ Mex, Col ▶

¡Pura paja! (Pure straw!) Nonsense! ◀ Mex, C. Am., Col, Ec ▶

¡Puras vainas! (Pure husks!) Nonsense! ◀ CR, parts of S. Am. ▶

¡Qué cuento! (What a story!) expression of opposition ◀ CR, Col ▶

No puedo ir. —¡Qué cuento! Vamos. I can't go. —Yeah, right! Let's get going.

¡Qué invente! Baloney! ◀ ES, Ven ▶

¡Qué ocurrencia! (What an occurrence! What a thing to occur to you!) The very idea! (sometimes used to react to a compliment in a modest way) ◀ L. Am., Sp ▶

¡Qué tontería(s)! What nonsense! ◀ L. Am., Sp ▶

¡Qué va! Oh, come on! ◀ parts of L. Am., Sp ▶

¡Quién lo diría! (Who would say it!) Oh, come on! ◀ Mex, DR, S. Cone, Sp ▶

Vaya a contárselo a su tía (abuela). (Go tell it to your aunt [grandmother].) Oh, come on! (Ch: also, **el cuento del tío**, tall tale) ◀ Mex, S. Cone, Sp ▶

Vaya a decírselo a su abuela. (Go tell it to your grandmother.) Oh, come on! ◀ Mex, ES, U, Arg ▶

Ya está bien de cuentos. Enough stories. ◀ most of L. Am., Sp ▶

dissimilarity

confundir la gimnasia con la magnesia (to confuse gymnastics with magnesia) to confuse two very different things ◀ Mex, Sp ▶

hijos de muchas madres (sons of many mothers) describing the diversity of a group or community ◀ Sp ▶

ir (muy) lejos, estar (muy) lejos to be (very) far from what is said or done ◀ Mex, DR, S. Cone, Sp ▶
Lo que dijo va muy lejos de la verdad. What he (she) said leaves a lot to be desired (is very far from the truth).

mezclar la velocidad con el tocino (to mix speed with bacon) to mix things that are very different ◀ Sp ▶
¡Vaya! Estás mezclando la velocidad con el tocino. Aw, come on! You're mixing apples with oranges.

parecerse una cosa a otra como un huevo a una castaña (to be as similar as an egg to a chestnut) to be very different ◀ Sp ▶

another kettle of fish

Ése es otro rollo. (That's another roll.) That's another kettle of fish. ◀ Mex ▶

Eso es harina de otro costal. (That's flour from a different sack.) That's a horse of a different color, another kettle of fish. ◀ L. Am., Sp ▶

Otra cosa es con guitarra. (It's something else with a guitar.) That's a different thing, another kettle of fish. (Ch: also, it's easy to talk but harder to do something.) ◀ S. Cone ▶

Otra cosa, mariposa. (Another thing, butterfly.) Not the same thing. ◀ Mex, ES, DR, Col, Sp ▶

ser capítulo aparte (to be a separate chapter) to be another kettle of fish, different topic ◀ Mex, DR, S. Cone, Sp ▶

ser otra canción (otro cantar) (to be another song) to be another kettle of fish ◀ L. Am., Sp ▶
Ésa es otra canción. That's another kettle of fish.

Una cosa es con guitarra y otra con violín. (It's one thing with a guitar and another with a violin.) That's a different story, another kettle of fish. ◀ DR ▶

---

distance

---

close by

a pocos pasos (at a few steps) close by; without much effort ◀ Mex, S. Cone, Sp ▶

acasito used instead of **acá**, meaning here ◀ Mex, Peru, Bol ▶

ahí nomasito (over there no farther) very near ◀ ES, Nic, Peru, Bol ▶
Ponlo ahí nomasito. Put it right over there.

far away

donde Cristo perdió el gorro (where Christ lost his cap) far away ◀ Sp ▶

donde el diablo dio los tres gritos (where the devil gave the three shouts) far away ◀ Cuba, DR ▶

donde el diablo dio las tres voces (where the devil gave the three words) at the end of nowhere, far away ◀ Sp ▶

donde el diablo perdió el poncho (where the devil lost his poncho) in a far or out-of-the-way place ◀ S. Cone, Sp ▶

donde el diablo perdió el poncho y la diabla la chancleta (where the devil lost his poncho and the female devil lost her sandal) in a far or out-of-the-way place, in some godforsaken spot ◀ Ch ▶

en las chimbambas far away, on the outskirts (Cuba: **quimbambas**) ◀ DR, PR, Sp ▶

en el culo del mundo (in the world's ass) far away, in a godforsaken spot (vulgar) ◀ Nic, PR, Ven, U, Arg, Sp ▶

en el fundillo del diablo (on the buttocks of the devil) in a faraway and dreadful place, in a godforsaken spot ◀ ES, Nic ▶

en la quinta puñeta far away (vulgar) ◀ PR, Sp ▶
Acho, 'mano, y ¿dónde es que tú vives, en la quinta puñeta? Man alive, bro', where is it you live, in goddamn Timbuktu?

en el quinto coño (carajo) (in the fifth female [male] organ) far away (vulgar) ◀ DR, PR, Sp ▶

en (hasta) el quinto infierno (in [as far as] the fifth hell) far away ◀ Mex, ES, DR, PR, U, Arg ▶
Mi amiga se mudó y no la puedo ir a ver porque ahora vive en el quinto infierno. My friend moved and I can't go see her because she lives way out in the boonies.
¡Diache! Ese bar queda en el quinto infierno. ¡Llevamos dos horas buscándolo! (DR) My gosh! That bar must be at the ends of the earth. We've been looking for it for two hours!

irse a la chingada (to go to the chingada, violated woman) to go far away (vulgar) ◀ Mex, C. Am. ▶

p'allacito, de la mierda p'allacito (on over yonder, from shit on over yonder) in a faraway place, in some godforsaken place (vulgar) ◀ Nic ▶

el quinto pino (the fifth pine) far away ◀ PR, Sp ▶
Tuve que ir al quinto pino para comprar esa lavadora. I had to go to the ends of the earth to buy that washing machine.

doubt, uncertainty

See also "luck."

no saber a qué carta quedarse (to not know what card to keep) to be in doubt ◀ Sp ▶

expressions about the future

a la buena de Dios (at the good [will] of God) at random, without a plan, without preparation ◀ ES, Nic, CR, DR, S. Cone, Sp ▶
Coge el abrigo. No salgas a la calle a la buena de Dios. (Sp) Grab your coat. Don't go out on the street in such a haphazard way.
Ésos son pobres; viven a la buena de Dios (sin planes ni dinero). Those folks are really poor; they live from one day to the next (without plans or money).
Voy a viajar a Chile a la buena de Dios. I'm going to Chile by the seat of my pants.

¡Dios guarde! ¡Dios libre! God forbid! (Sp: **Dios nos guarde** or **nos libre**; PR and DR: **Dios nos libre** only) ◀ Mex, CR, ES, DR, PR, Col ▶

por si las moscas (because if the flies) just in case ◀ most of L. Am., Sp ▶

Cerramos la puerta con llave por si las moscas. Let's lock the door just to be on the safe side.

Primero Dios. (First God.) God willing. (often used when an action is proposed or some statement of optimism is made) ◀ Mex, C. Am. ▶

pueque (reduced form of **puede ser que**) maybe ◀ Mex ▶

¿Quién quita que...? (Who takes away that . . . ?) expression used to indicate the probability or chance of something happening ◀ Mex, C. Am., ES, DR, Col, Ven, Peru ▶
¿Quién quita que mañana llegue de sorpresa? Who can say that tomorrow he (she) won't show up by surprise?
Quien quita que venga mi prima. You never can tell when my cousin might show up.

Si Dios quiere. (If God wants.) God willing. (often used when an action is proposed or some statement of optimism is made) ◀ L. Am., Sp ▶
Vamos a comprar una casa más grande, si Dios quiere. We're going to buy a bigger house, if all goes well (if God wills it).

tocar madera to touch (knock on) wood (used as in English, so that something that was said shouldn't happen) ◀ L. Am., Sp ▶

Who knows?

A saber. (To be known.) Who knows? ◀ parts of L. Am., Sp ▶

Chepa la bola. Who knows? ◀ Mex ▶

Sabe Dios. God knows. ◀ most of L. Am., Sp ▶
¿Cuándo van a mandar el cheque? —Sabe Dios. When are they going to send the check? —God knows.

Sepa Chepa. (Chepa probably knows.) Who knows? ◀ chicano, Nic ▶

Sepa Judás. (Perhaps Judas knows.) Who knows? ◀ ES, Nic, CR ▶
¿Quién estuvo aquí? —Sepa Judás. Who was there? —That's anybody's guess. (Who knows?)

Sepa Moya. (Perhaps Moya knows.) Who knows? ◀ Ch ▶

Vaya uno a saber. (Go to know.) Who knows? ◀ L. Am., Sp ▶
Vaya uno a saber lo que hacen ustedes. Heaven only knows what you guys are up to.

Vaya usted (Vete) a saber. (Go to know.) Who knows? ◀ Peru, Bol, Sp ▶

dress

a pata pelada (with a peeled paw) barefoot ◀ Ch ▶

estar de coña to fit well (vulgar) ◀ Sp ▶
Este vestido te está de coña. This dress looks damn good on you.

el pitusa bluejeans ◀ Cuba ▶

quedar pintado(-a) (to remain painted) to fit very well ◀ Mex, Cuba, DR, Col, S. Cone, Sp ▶
¡Este vestido te queda que ni pintado! This dress fits you like a glove!

la ropa de semanear (de dominguear) clothes for weekdays (Sundays) ◀ CR, ES ▶

fachoso

Si se quema la casa, no pierde nada. If the house burns down, he or she won't lose anything (referring to someone who is overdressed, wearing lots of jewelry, etc.). ◀ PR ▶

socado(-a) tight (clothing) ◀ CR, ES, DR ▶

tener la farmacia abierta (y el doctor dormido) (to have the pharmacy open [and the doctor asleep]) to have an open fly in one's pants ◀ ES, Sp ▶
La farmacia está abierta y el doctor dormido. The barn door is open. (Your fly is unzipped.)

los trapos (rags) clothing ◀ L. Am., Sp ▶
Se gasta un dineral en trapos. You can spend a fortune on your duds.
Me compré algunos trapos. I bought some rags (clothes).

vestido(-a) y calzado(-a) dressed and shod, having satisfied the main things necessary for interaction with others ◀ L. Am., Sp ▶

badly dressed

andar con las hilachas colgando (to go with threads hanging) to be dressed in rags ◀ S. Cone ▶

chanclear to wear low-heeled shoes and dress badly ◀ Mex ▶

Era más grande (pequeño) el difunto. (The dead person was bigger [smaller].) said to someone when they are wearing a large (small) article of clothing ◀ Mex, ES, DR, S. Cone, Sp ▶

estar hecho(-a) unos zorros (to be made foxes) to be in bad shape or badly dressed ◀ Sp ▶
Llegó de la fiesta hecha unos zorros. She came back from the party in bad shape.

la facha ridiculous dress, outfit ◀ Mex, G, DR, PR, Col, S. Cone, Sp ▶
Con esa facha no puedes entrar en la discoteca. You can't go to the disco in that getup.
Cámbiate esa facha si quieres ir al cine conmigo. Change that ridiculous outfit if you want to go to the movies with me.

fachoso(-a) badly dressed; affected, trying to appear elegant ◀ Mex ▶

zarrapastroso

lobo(-a) (wolf) describing someone who doesn't dress well ◀ Col ▶
Ese tipo sí es mucho lobo. That guy is a really poor dresser.
Mira como está vestida Marta. Falda anaranjada, zapatos verdes y saco amarillo. ¡Mucha loba! Look how Marta is dressed. Orange skirt, green shoes, and a yellow jacket. What poor taste!

el pachuco someone who dresses in a bizarre way, not acceptable to the majority (also, in CR: slang, street talk) ◀ Mex, G, CR, Col ▶

ser un guiso (to be a stew) to be badly dressed ◀ Col ▶
Ese tipo es un guiso: ¡chaqueta de cuero, pelo engominado, botas tejanas! That guy is too much: leather jacket, slicked-down hair, Texas-style cowboy boots!

zarrapastroso(-a) (from **zarrapastra,** meaning both mud and claw, implying dirty and torn) badly dressed, dirty, having a bad appearance or looking like a slob (Mex, G: also, **salapastroso, chaparrastroso;** S. Cone: also, **zaparrastroso**) ◀ Mex, DR, PR, Col, S. Cone, Sp ▶
¿Y cómo se atreve a ir a una quinceañera así de zarrapastroso? And how dare he go to a sweet-fifteen coming-out party in a sloppy getup like that?

well dressed

a todo trapo (at full rag) with style or class ◀ S. Cone ▶

catrín elegant ◀ Mex, C. Am. ▶
¡Qué catrín va! Hoy sí va a conseguir buena morra (muchacha). (ES) How well turned-out he looks! Today he'll hook up with a gorgeous babe for sure.

de pipa y guante (with pipe and glove) all dressed up ◀ chicano, Mex ▶

empilcharse (to put on pieces of clothing) to fix oneself up to go out to a party, primp (from **pilcha,** piece of clothing) ◀ U, Arg ▶

fifí overly concerned with dressing in style (Ch: homosexual) ◀ Mex, U, Sp ▶

el paltón, la paltona (big avocado) well-dressed person ◀ Ch ▶

paquete(-a) elegant ◀ U, Arg ▶

tirar pinta (to throw spot) to dress to impress ◀ Ch ▶

drugs

el caballo (horse) heroin (also, **la farlopa, el jaco**) ◀ Sp ▶
A ese tío le gusta meterse caballo. That guy likes to take heroin.

el chocolate (chocolate) hashish ◀ Sp ▶

el chute shot (injection) of heroin or other drugs ◀ Sp ▶
Necesitaba tres chutes al día de heroína. He (She) needed three hits a day of heroin.

estar con el mono (to be with the monkey) to be in a state of abstinence from drugs ◀ Sp ▶

la pichicata illegal drug ◀ S. Cone ▶

el polvo blanco (polvo de ángel) (white powder [angel dust]) cocaine ◀ Sp ▶

el toque (touch) hit of cocaine ◀ Ch ▶

addicts

el/la chavo(-a) de onda gruesa (kid of thick sound wave) drug addict ◄ Mex ►

el drogo short for **drogadicto**, drug addict ◄ parts of L. Am. ►

el/la drogota drug addict ◄ Sp ►

el/la falopero(-a) someone who takes drugs ◄ U, Arg ►
Ese futbolista es falopero. That soccer player is a druggie.

dealers

el conecte dealer ◄ Mex ►

el doc (short for **doctor**) drug dealer (Ec: also, **el docto**) ◄ G, Ec ►

el/la narco short for **narcotraficante** ◄ L. Am., Sp ►

marijuana

el canuto marijuana cigarette ◄ Mex, Sp ►

de la verde (of the green) marijuana ◄ Mex, Col ►

la diosa verde (green goddess) marijuana ◄ Col, Ec ►

engrifarse to smoke marijuana (CR: **grifarse**) ◄ Mex ►

la fumadita (little smoke) drag on a joint of marijuana ◄ Mex ►

la grifa marijuana ◄ chicano, Mex, CR, Ec ►

la hierba (grass) marijuana ◄ Mex, G, Cuba, DR, Sp ►

la machachaca marijuana (also, **la raca, el churro**) ◄ Mex ►

el monte (brush) marijuana ◄ G, CR, ES ►

la mota marijuana ◄ chicano, Mex, G, PR ►

motearse to use marijuana ◄ Mex, PR ►

pegarse unos cuantos pititos (to stick to oneself a few little whistles) to have a few joints (of marijuana) ◄ Col, Ec ►

el pitillo marijuana cigarette ◄ Mex, G, Col ►

el pito (whistle, fife) joint (marijuana) ◄ Mex, G, Nic, Cuba, Ch ►

el porro marijuana joint ◄ U, Arg, Sp ►

el toque (touch) hit (marijuana) (also, **el toquesín**) (Mex: also, **el guato, la goma**) ◄ chicano, Mex, G, ES, Col ►

stoned

agarrar el avión (to grab the plane) to go on a (drug) trip ◄ Mex, ES ►

fuera de base (de órbita) (off base [out of orbit]) in a state of hallucination ◄ Mex, Col ►

grifo(-a) stoned on marijuana ◄ Mex, CR, Ec ►

pasado(-a) (passed) stoned, high on drugs ◄ Mex, Col ►

tener una nota (to have a note) to be high on drugs ◄ DR, PR ►
Tiene una nota que ni la toca Beethoven. He's higher than a kite with rockets attached.

tronado(-a) (blasted) stoned ◄ Mex ►

volado(-a) (blown up high or flown away) stoned, high; spaced out ◄ Ch ►

drunkenness

See also "food and drink."

ahogarse el ratón (to drown the mouse) to take a drink during a hangover or on the day after a big drinking bout ◄ Ven ►

el bazuquero (bazooka shooter) drunkard ◄ Nic ►

beber como una esponja to drink like a sponge ◄ U, Sp ►

el/la briago(-a) drunkard ◄ Mex, C. Am. ►

el colocón drunkenness ◄ Sp ►

dormir la juma to sleep it (the drunkenness) off ◄ ES, CR, Pan, Ven ►

dormir la mona (to sleep the monkey) to sleep it off ◄ Mex, G, Cuba, Col, S. Cone, Sp ►
Vete a dormir la mona, que estás muy borracho. Go sleep it off; you are really drunk.
Vaya mona que cogió anoche. (Sp) Boy, he (she) really tied one on last night.

Say it with slang!

Courtesy and comebacks

Spaniards and Latin Americans have the reputation of being very courteous. In the past, traditional phrases embodied a delicate politeness that is less common today but still present in some places. For example, in the old days if you were to compliment someone on having a beautiful object, he or she would offer it to you, although it was generally understood that you would refuse to accept it with a ritual compliment:

—¡Qué lindo reloj tiene usted!
—Es para usted.
—No, gracias. No podría mejorar de dueño.
"What a lovely watch you have!"
"It's for you."
"No, thank you. It couldn't have a better owner."

Even today, at parties or buffet suppers, Hispanic people who have to turn their backs on someone generally ask pardon for this. In Uruguay, a complimentary response is sometimes given (especially by a woman):

—Perdone la espalda.
—Los angelitos no tienen espalda.
"Excuse my back."
"Angels don't have backs."

However, because many Uruguayans have an ironic sense of humor as well as of courtesy, another person will sometimes chime in with a mild put-down:

—¡Ni las zanahorias!
"And neither do carrots [which can also mean 'simpletons' in Uruguay]."

---

hacer un cuatro (to make a four) to do the test for drunkenness, standing on one leg with arms spread out and bending the other leg at the knee in the form of a number 4 (Mex: also, **poner un cuatro**) ◄ Mex, ES, DR, Ch ►

la jaladera drunkenness ◄ Cuba ►

la juma drunkenness ◄ CR, ES, Nic, Pan, Ven, Ec ►

la nota drunkenness ◄ Cuba, PR ►

el pe'o (from **pedo**, fart) drunkenness (vulgar) ◄ Cuba, Col, Sp ►
Llegó con un pe'o tremendo. Tiene un pe'o. He (She) arrived drunk as a skunk. He (She) is smashed.

la rasca drunkenness ◄ CR, Col, Ven ►

drunk

andar bien burro (to go very donkey) to be very drunk, smashed ◄ Mex ►

andar cacheteando la banqueta (to go along with one's cheek on the sidewalk) to be drunk ◀ Mex ▶

andar con el gorila (to walk with the gorilla) to be very drunk ◀ Ch ▶

andar haciendo eses (to go around making "s"s) to be drunk ◀ Mex, S. Cone, Sp ▶

el/la curda drunk (from Lunfardo), invariable in Cuba and Arg but **curdo** is used in Ven for masculine form; drunkenness ◀ Cuba, Ven, U, Arg ▶
Siempre está curda. (Cuba) He's (She's) always bombed (drunk).
Es un(a) curda. (Arg) He (She) is a drunk.

embebido(-a) como una esponja (imbibed like a sponge) very drunk, drunk as a skunk ◀ Col ▶

en zumba habitually drunk ◀ CR, ES ▶
Éste sólo en zumba anda. This guy is a real drunk.

estar ahogado(-a) (to be drowned) to be drunk (also, **ahogado[-a] hasta el gorro**) ◀ Mex, ES, Col ▶

estar bolo(-a) to be drunk ◀ C. Am. ▶
¿Estás bolo o qué? Are you bombed, or what?

estar como una cuba (to be like a cask) to be drunk ◀ U, Arg, Sp ▶

estar curado(-a), curado(-a) como huasca (tagua) (to be cured as a whip [coot]) to be dead drunk, drunk as a skunk ◀ Ch ▶

estar geto(-a) to be drunk ◀ Col ▶

estar hasta atrás (to be behind) to be smashed, very drunk ◀ Mex, ES, Col ▶
Si se toman toda la botella, se van a poner hasta atrás. If you guys drink the whole bottle, you're going to get smashed.

estar hasta el cepillo (to be up to the brush) to be smashed, very drunk ◀ Mex ▶

estar hasta el copete (to be up to the forelock, top of hair) to be very drunk ◀ Mex, ES, Col, Sp ▶

estar hasta las chanclas (to be up to the sandals) to be smashed, very drunk ◀ Mex, ES ▶

estar hasta las manitas (to be up to the little hands) to be very drunk ◀ Mex, CR ▶

estar hecho(-a) una equis (to be made an "X") to be drunk ◀ DR ▶
Acabo de ver al tío de Ana hecho una equis en el bar de la esquina. I just saw Ana's uncle four sheets to the wind at the corner bar.

estar jalado(-a) (to be pulled) to be drunk ◀ Nic, Cuba, Col ▶

estar mamado(-a) (to be breast-fed) to be drunk ◀ U, Arg ▶

estar pedo(-a) (to be fart) to be drunk (vulgar) (U, Arg: also, **estar en pedo**; Sp: **llevar un pedo**) ◀ Mex, C. Am., U, Arg, Sp ▶
Es una vieja muy peda. (Mex) She's a lush.
Está pedo. He's drunk.

estar pica'o(-a) to be drunk ◀ PR ▶
No, gracias, no quiero más ron. Estoy medio pica'o. No, thanks, I don't want any more rum. I'm half-blasted.

estar piripi to be drunk ◀ Sp ▶

estar rascado(-a) (to be scraped) to be drunk ◀ Nic, CR, Col, Ven ▶

estar tomado(-a) to be drunk ◀ L. Am. ▶

estar trompa (also, **trompeta, tururú**) (to be trunk of an elephant) to be drunk ◀ Sp ▶

tener la mona (to have the monkey) to be drunk ◀ Ch ▶

tener la nota (to have the note) to be drunk ◀ Cuba ▶

getting drunk

ajumarse to get drunk (ES, CR: **jumarse**) ◀ Cuba, DR, PR ▶
A mi tío Felipe siempre le da con ajumarse en las fiestas de Año Nuevo. My Uncle Felipe always goes and gets blasted at New Year's Eve parties.

coger una trompa (to grab an elephant's trunk) to tie one on, get blasted, go on a bender ◀ Sp ▶

colocarse (con) (to place oneself) to get high, drunk ◀ Mex, Sp ▶
Me coloqué con dos cervezas. (Sp) I got high on two beers.
Me coloqué dos cervezas. (Mex) I drank two beers and got high.

echarse una mona encima (andar con la mona) (to throw a monkey on one-self [walk with the monkey]) to get drunk ◀ Cuba, Arg, Ch ▶

entromparse to get drunk ◀ Sp ▶
Fue a una fiesta y se entrompó. He (She) went to a party and got bombed.

jalarse (to pull oneself) to get drunk ◀ Cuba ▶

picarse (to become piqued) to get drunk ◀ Mex, G, Nic, PR ▶
Toma sólo una cerveza; no te piques con más. (Mex) Drink just one beer; don't go getting blasted by drinking more.

ponerse (estar) en curda, tener una curda to be (get) drunk ◀ U, Arg ▶

rascarse (to scratch oneself) to get drunk ◀ CR, Col, Ven ▶

high (on drugs or alcohol)

acelerado(-a) (sped up) high on alcohol or drugs ◀ Mex, G, PR, Col, Sp ▶
Ese loco parece acelerado. That dude seems stoned.

arrebatado(-a) (carried away) high on drugs or alcohol ◀ G, Cuba, DR, PR ▶
Esos tipos de la esquina siempre andan arrebata'os. ¡Qué fuerte! Those guys from the corner are always high on something. What a way to act!

colgado(-a) (hung, suspended) high on alcohol or drugs ◀ Sp ▶
Cuando está colgado, no hay quien lo aguante. When he's wasted, nobody can stand him.

completo(-a) (complete) high ◀ Mex, Ec ▶

cruzado(-a) (crossed) high (on drugs or alcohol) ◀ Mex ▶

elevado(-a) high (on drugs or alcohol) (Col: also, daydreaming) ◀ Mex, G, Col ▶

en nota high, inebriated ◀ Mex, Cuba, DR, PR ▶

en pleno vuelo (in full flight) high ◀ Mex, Col, Ec ▶

ennota'o(-a) high on drugs or alcohol ◀ PR ▶

tocado(-a) (touched) elegant; bad smelling; high (vulgar) ◀ Cuba ▶

traer una nota (to bring a note) to be high on drugs or alcohol ◀ DR, PR ▶

hung over

la cruda (rawness) hangover ◀ Mex, C. Am. ▶
El tequila me provoca una cruda espantosa. Tequila gives me a terrible hangover.

estar crudo(-a) (to be raw) to be hung over ◀ Mex, C. Am. ▶

estar de goma (to be made of gum, rubber) to be hung over ◀ C. Am. ▶
Tengo dolor de cabeza. Será que estoy de goma. I have a headache. It could be that I'm hung over.

estar enguayabado(-a) to be hung over ◀ Col ▶

estar enratonado(-a) (to be moused-in, with the mouse eating inside one's head) to be hung over ◀ Ven ▶

parecer araña fumigada (to seem like a fumigated spider) to be suffering from the effects of too much partying or drinking ◀ Mex, ES ▶

la resaca (undertow) hangover ◀ Peru, S. Cone, Sp ▶

tener chuchaqui to be hung over ◀ Ec ▶

tener guayabo (to have a guava tree) to be hung over ◀ Col ▶

tener resaca (to have undertow) to be hung over ◀ Peru, S. Cone, Sp ▶

ease

la cancha (court, field for sports) experience; **tener cancha**, to be on one's home court ◀ CR, Col, Peru, S. Cone ▶
Juan tiene cancha. Juan is on his home court (feels at ease in the present circumstances).

de perilla (of little pear) easy ◀DR, Ch▶

estar chupado(-a) (to be sucked) to be easy ◀Sp▶

estar tirado(-a) (to be pulled) to be easy ◀Sp▶

facilingo very easy ◀parts of L. Am.▶

liso y llano (smooth and flat, as a road) without difficulty ◀Sp▶

Qué lindo que canta Polo cuando está bolo. (How beautifully Polo sings when he is drunk.) Everything sounds simple when you're high and feeling good. ◀Nic▶

Se hace a ciegas. (It's done blindly.) You can do it with your eyes closed. ◀Sp▶

Se hace con la gorra. (It's done with the hat.) It's easy. ◀Sp▶

ser coser y cantar (to be sew and sing) to be child's play, a cinch ◀Sp▶

ser un guiso (to be a stew) to be easy ◀PR▶
El examen final fue un guiso. Todo el mundo sacó A. The exam was a snap. Everybody got an A.

ser un jamón (to be a ham) to be easy ◀Cuba, CR▶
Ir a San José a pie es un jamón. Going to San José on foot is a piece of cake.

ser un mamey (to be a mamey, a fruit) to be easy ◀PR, Col▶

ser un queque (to be a cake) to be easy, a piece of cake ◀CR▶

ser pan comido (to be eaten bread) to be very easy, a piece of cake (said of things) ◀Mex, DR, PR, S. Cone, Sp▶
¿Que tú no sabes usar el E-mail? ¡Eso es pan comido! So, you don't know how to use E-mail? That's easy as pie!

ser una papa (to be a potato) to be easy, a piece of cake ◀U, Ch▶
Es una papa. It's a piece of cake.

ser una papa suave (una papita) (to be a soft potato [a little potato]) to be easy ◀DR▶
El examen de español fue una papita. No había ni que estudiar. The Spanish test was as easy as pie. You didn't even have to study.

education

See also "failure," "intelligence."

aprender en cabeza ajena (to learn in another's head) to learn from someone else's experience ◀DR, U, Sp▶
Nadie aprende en cabeza ajena. (DR) Nobody learns from the experience of others.

la botella (bottle) what is memorized (as for an exam, in the short term; also, **botellar**) ◀DR, PR▶
Mario es inteligentísimo, se sabe todas las fórmulas químicas. —¡Bah! Eso es una botella; mañana se le olvida. Mario is very intelligent. He knows all the chemical formulas. —Bah! That's just crammed-in stuff; tomorrow he'll forget it.

clavar un examen to do well on (nail) an exam ◀PR▶

el/la dire short for **director** or **directora**, director or principal ◀Mex, Cuba, Sp▶
¿Cómo se llama el dire? What's the name of the principal?

estar cruda (to be raw) to take an exam without studying; to not get it ◀PR▶

estar fuera de liga (to be out of the league) to get excellent grades, be outstanding ◀Cuba▶

el insti short for **instituto**, high school ◀Sp▶

limero(-a) hard, strict ◀PR▶
Ese maestro es muy limero. Me regañó porque llegué dos minutos tarde. That teacher is really strict. He bawled me out because I arrived two minutes late.

mamar una cosa con la leche (en la leche) (to suckle something along with mother's milk) to learn something at a very young age ◀L. Am., Sp▶

las mate short for **matemáticas**, math ◀most of L. Am., Sp▶

el/la profe short for **profesor** or **profesora**, prof ◀L. Am., Sp▶

Riendo se va aprendiendo. (By laughing a person goes along learning.) Humor helps learning. ◀ Arg, Ch ▶

ser un hueso (to be a bone) to be very demanding (especially used for teachers or professors) ◀ Sp ▶
El profesor Martínez es un hueso. Professor Martínez is a tough nut.

la u short for **universidad** (Ch: U of Chile only) ◀ G, ES, Pan, Col ▶
Voy a la u. ¿Me quieres acompañar? I'm going to the university. Want to come with me?

la uni short for **universidad** ◀ Mex, DR, Sp ▶

cheating

el acordeón (accordion) crib sheet (because it's folded) ◀ Mex, G, Cuba, U ▶

el chivo (kid goat) crib sheet ◀ Cuba, DR ▶
A José lo encontraron con un chivo en el examen. José was caught with a cheat sheet in the exam.

el ventaneo (window opening) cheating on an exam by looking at another's paper ◀ Mex ▶

cutting class, playing hooky

capar clase (to neuter class) to cut class ◀ Col ▶
Voy a capar clase hoy; ese profesor es fatal. I'm going to cut class today; that professor is deadly.

capear clases (to make passes with a cape, as in a bullfight) to cut class ◀ Ch ▶

cortar to cut (class) ◀ Mex, PR ▶

echarse el día (to throw the day to oneself) to cut class for the day ◀ Cuba ▶

echarse la pera (to throw the pear) to play hooky ◀ Ec ▶

hacer campana (to make bell) to cut class ◀ Sp ▶

hacer la chancha (cimarra) (to do the pig) to play hooky, cut class ◀ Ch ▶

hacerse la pelada (to become the bald one) to play hooky ◀ U ▶

irse de pinta (to go away like spot) to play hooky ◀ Mex ▶
Me fui de pinta el lunes. I played hooky on Monday.

irse de venado (to go away like a deer) to play hooky ◀ Mex ▶

studying hard, cramming

clavarse (to be nailed) to study hard ◀ Mex, Col ▶
Me clavé para el examen de física. I buckled down to study for the physics exam.

darse un quemón (to burn oneself) to study hard ◀ Mex ▶

embotellarse (to bottle) to memorize, cram ◀ DR, PR, Col ▶
Tengo que embotellarme todas las fórmulas para el examen de química. I have to cram all those formulas into my brain for the chemistry exam.

empollar to memorize ◀ Sp ▶

estofarse (to stew oneself) to study hard, cram ◀ PR ▶

hacer codos (to make elbows) to study ◀ Sp ▶

hincar los codos (to dig in one's elbows) to study hard ◀ Mex, Sp ▶
Tengo que hincar los codos si quiero pasar el examen. I have to really dig in if I want to pass the exam.

mechar(se) (to stuff [oneself], dress a piece of meat) to study very hard ◀ Cuba ▶
Tengo que ir a mechar para el examen. I have to go cram for the exam.
Méchate, o si no vas a ponchar otra vez. Get down to business; if not, you'll flunk again.

meterle caña (to put cane) to study hard, put out some effort ◀ Mex ▶
Si quieres aprobar el examen de biología, hay que meterle caña. If you want to pass the biology exam, you have to put your nose to the grindstone.

quemarse las pestañas (cejas) (to burn one's eyelashes [eyebrows]) to study hard, burn the midnight oil, cram ◀ L. Am., Sp ▶

romperse los codos (to break one's elbows) to study diligently ◀Sp▶

tragar (to swallow) to study ◀CR, Col, U▶

types of students

el comelibros (book eater) bookworm (U, Arg: **tragalibros**) ◀most of L. Am., Sp▶

el cuadernícolas very serious student who studies a lot; from **cuaderno**, notebook ◀most of L. Am.▶

el empollón, la empollona grind, student who studies a lot (G: also, someone who works all the time) ◀G, Sp▶

el/la enchufado(-a) (plugged in) teacher's pet ◀Sp▶
Es un enchufado; hizo peor el examen pero le puso mejor nota que a mí. He's a teacher's pet; he did worse on the exam but got a better grade than I did.

estofa'o(-a), estofón (estofona) (stewed) very studious ◀PR▶

el hueso (bone) intelligent student ◀Cuba, Col▶
Pablo es un hueso; no saca menos de nueve. Pablo is a brain; he never gets less than an A (a nine in the Cuban grading system).

la polilla de biblioteca (library moth) bookworm ◀most of L. Am., Sp▶

el/la mateo(-a) bookworm ◀Ch▶

mechado(-a) (stuffed or dressed, like meat) studious ◀Cuba▶

piloso(-a) someone who studies a lot and does well in school ◀Col▶

el ratón de biblioteca (library rat) bookworm ◀L. Am., Sp▶

ponerse como un tomate

el tragón (big swallow) serious student ◀CR, Col▶

el/la turista (vacacionista) (tourist [vacationist]) someone who rarely goes to class ◀Mex, Cuba, Col▶

embarrassment

achatado(-a) (pug-nosed, with nose cut off) humbled or put down by some embarrassment ◀Arg▶
Con mi comentario, lo dejé achatado. With my comment, I took the wind out of his sails.

la aguacatona (big avocado) shy woman without much spirit ◀PR▶

ponerse como un tomate (to become like a tomato) to blush, turn red ◀Mex, DR, PR, S. Cone, Sp▶
Cuando Graciela tuvo que hablar delante de tantas personas, se puso como un tomate. When Graciela had to talk in front of so many people, she turned as red as a beet.

ponerse la cara como un chile (to have the face like a chili pepper) to turn red, blush ◀CR, Col▶

¡Qué oso! (What a bear!) How embarrassing! ◀Mex, Col▶
¡Qué oso! Empezaba a presentarle a mi profesor de inglés y no pude acordarme de su nombre. How embarrassing! I began to introduce her to my English professor and I couldn't remember her name.

la raya (lightning) embarrassment ◀Ven▶

embarrassed

achumicarse to become shy or chicken out ◀Nic▶
Mario no fue a la fiesta porque se achumicó. Mario didn't go to the party because he felt too shy.

achuncharse to become shy, embarrassed, timid ◀Ch▶
Traté de decírselo, pero me achunché. I tried to say it to them, but I got embarrassed.

chivearse

chivearse   to act ashamed or inhibited, timid ◀ Mex, ES ▶

con el rabo entre las piernas   (with one's tail between one's legs) in a humiliated, embarrassed manner ◀ DR, PR, S. Cone, Sp ▶

cortarse, sentirse cortado(-a)   (to cut oneself off, to feel cut off) to be shy, embarrassed ◀ S. Cone, Sp ▶
No te cortes y pide lo que quieras. Don't be timid, and ask for what you want.
Me corté (Me quedé cortada) cuando me hizo esa pregunta tan personal. I felt embarrassed when he (she) asked me that very personal question.
Me siento muy cortada cuando Juan está delante. I feel shy when Juan is around.

cubrirse de mierda   (to cover oneself with shit) to dishonor oneself (vulgar) ◀ Mex, Sp ▶

dar corte   (to give cut) to be embarrassed or ashamed ◀ DR, PR, Sp ▶
Me da corte hablar en público. I find it embarrassing to speak in public.

estar achunchado(-a)   to be embarrassed, shy, timid ◀ Ch ▶
En la escuela mi hija está muy achunchada. At school my daughter is very timid.

hacer el oso   (to do the bear) to embarrass oneself ◀ Mex, Col ▶
Hice el oso de mi vida. Lo confundí con su hermano. I just did the most embarrassing thing in my life. I confused him with his brother.

hacer un pancho   to do something embarrassing in front of others ◀ Mex ▶

pasar plancha   (to pass the iron) to suffer an awkward moment ◀ Ch ▶

ser plato de segunda mesa   (to be a plate of a second table) to be or feel put off or not treated with consideration (Mex: used mainly for women who are with married men) ◀ Mex, ES, DR, PR, Sp ▶
Yo no soy plato de segunda mesa. I am not a second-class citizen. (I don't play second fiddle to anyone.)

tener pena   (to have sorrow) to be shy, embarrassed ◀ most of L. Am. (not S. Cone) ▶
No tengas pena, hijo. Don't be shy, son.

tragarle la tierra a alguien   (to have the earth swallow one) used to express embarrassment, a wish to disappear from view ◀ L. Am., Sp ▶
¡Trágame tierra! Aquí viene Eduardo, y yo con esta ropa tan fea. I wish the earth would swallow me! Here comes Eduardo, and I'm wearing these ugly clothes.

el trajín   butt of a joke or of mockery ◀ Mex, Cuba ▶

teasing, embarrassing someone

See also "criticism," "harm, hurt."

balconear a alguien   (to balcony someone) to embarrass someone in front of others or put someone on the spot by asking an indiscreet question or getting the person to do something compromising ◀ Mex, ES ▶
La reportera balconeó al señor delante de sus colegas. The reporter embarrassed the gentleman in front of his colleagues.

cachondearse (de alguien)   to make fun of or tease (someone) ◀ Sp ▶
Te estás cachondeando de mí, ¿verdad? You're making fun of me, right?

cargar (to load) to tease, make fun of ◀ U, Arg ▶
¡**Me estás cargando!** You must be kidding!

chotear (to make fun of) to make someone look ridiculous (like **vacilar** in Mex), make fun of ◀ Mex, CR, Cuba ▶
Felipe me choteó. Felipe made me look like a fool.

chulear to make fun of ◀ Sp ▶

dársela a alguien con queso (to give it to someone with cheese) to deceive, make fun of ◀ Sp ▶

mamar gallo (to nurse rooster) to tease ◀ Col, Ven ▶

poner (estar) en la picota (to put [be] in the stocks or pillory) to call attention to someone's faults or problems and embarrass him or her; to be embarrassed and become the center of attention in this way ◀ Peru, U ▶

tomar el pelo a alguien to pull someone's leg (hair), tease ◀ L. Am., Sp ▶
El alumno le tomaba el pelo a la maestra. The student was pulling the teacher's leg.

vacilar to tease, trick, con, make a fool of ◀ Mex, ES, Col, Sp ▶

encouragement

dar alas (to give wings) to stimulate, inspire ◀ Mex, DR, S. Cone, Sp ▶
No le sigas dando alas a Marcelo. Don't keep leading Marcelo on.

dar marcha to give energy (march) ◀ Sp ▶
Esa música (persona) me da mucha marcha. That music (person) gives me a real lift. **Vaya marcha tienes hoy.** Wow, the energy you have today.

estar querido (to be wanted) phrase indicating that there is no problem, something will be resolved ◀ Cuba, Col ▶
No te preocupes. Eso está querido ya. Don't worry about it. That's a done deal.

levantar (el) vuelo to take flight; to raise spirits or imagination ◀ Mex, ES, S. Cone, Sp ▶

meter fuego (to put in fire) to activate or animate an enterprise, fire up ◀ Mex, Sp ▶

expressions of encouragement

Adelante con la cruz. (Forward with the cross.) Hang in there. Let's not give up. Expresses resolve to proceed in spite of difficulties ◀ most of L. Am., Sp ▶

Al agua, patos. (To the water, ducks.) Let's go to it. (S. Cone: **pato**, not **patos**.) ◀ Mex, ES, DR, S. Cone, Sp ▶
No perdamos más tiempo. ¡Al agua, patos! Let's not lose any more time. (Time's a-wastin'!) Take the plunge!

¡Así se hace! Way to go! That's the way to do it! ◀ L. Am., Sp ▶

¡Aupa! Go! (at a sports event) ◀ Sp ▶

Córrele. Go for it. (transformation of **ándale**) ◀ Mex, ES, Col ▶

¡Échale ganas! Give it all you've got! (for instance, at a sports event) ◀ Mex, ES ▶

¡Échale lo que hay que echarle! Give it all you've got! (for instance, at a sports event) ◀ Sp ▶

La otra patita. (The next step, in a plan, journey, etc.; from the **cueca**, the national dance.) Let's move on now. ◀ Ch ▶

¡Llégale! Go for it! ◀ Mex, ES, Col ▶

No te azotes, que hay chayotes. (Don't flog yourself; there are **chayotes**, a kind of squash.) Buck up! It's not that bad. ◀ Mex, Col ▶

No te rochées (e.g., con los padres). Don't let things (e.g., your parents) get you down. ◀ PR ▶
Nena, toma las cosas con calma. No te rocheés. Sweetie, take things more calmly. Don't let them get you down.

Órale. used to animate someone to do something or in accepting an invitation; all right; that's it; OK (used originally in Mex but young people now use it in C. Am. and Col; Mex: also, can be used to express surprise) ◀ Mex, G, ES, Col ▶

Say it with slang!

The importance of being cucumber (and other veggies)

How strange the movie "Gone with the Wind" would sound if Rhett Butler were to say to Scarlett O'Hara, "Frankly, my dear, I don't give a cucumber!" Yet a common way of saying, "I don't give a damn" in Spanish is **Me importa un pepino** (It matters a cucumber to me). There are other ways of saying this too (see the category "indifference").

A vegetable can also be a way of describing someone, as when a gray-haired man or woman in Mexico or El Salvador is called **una cabeza de cebolla** (an onion head). Personality traits are sometimes represented through vegetables; in Puerto Rico, **una haba sin sal** (a bean without salt) is a boring person, and **un aguacatón** or **una aguacatona** (a big avocado) is a party pooper. In a conversation in Mexico, if you want to get right to the point, you say: **¡Vamos al chile!** (Let's get to the chili pepper!). To tell someone you got confused, you say: **Me hice camote** (I became sweet potato). However, if you want to get rid of someone fast, tell him or her: **¡Vete a freír espárragos!** (Get lost! Literally, Go fry asparagus!)

So, what is the reasoning behind these phrases? Nobody really knows, but it's probably similar to what prompts us in English to talk about a "string bean" or a "couch potato."

Órale, vamos al cine. All right, then, let's go to the movies.
Órale, ¡qué coche tan lujoso te compraste! My, my! What a luxury car you bought yourself!
Sigue con la cruz a cuestas. (Continue up the hill with the cross.) Keep going in spite of problems. ◀ ES ▶

enthusiasm

afanado(-a) zealously, with enthusiasm ◀ Mex, G, ES, DR ▶

agarrar viento en la camiseta (to grab wind in the T-shirt) to get carried away ◀ U, Arg ▶

con la camiseta puesta (with the T-shirt on) describing a real fan, enthusiast ◀ S. Cone ▶

dar(se) manija (to give [oneself] a crank, pull with a string) to inspire enthusiasm (get enthusiastic about) ◀ U, Arg ▶
¡No te des manija! Don't get carried away!
No le des más manija a ese muchacho, que se va a terminar enamorando de ti. Don't go getting that boy all worked up. He's going to wind up falling in love with you.
La manija que le dio el presidente a su discurso fue exagerada. The enthusiasm that the president put into his speech was exaggerated.

emocionado(-a) excited ◀ L. Am., Sp ▶

enfiebrado(-a) (fevered) passionately enthusiastic; also, **enfiebrarse** ◀ CR, DR, Col ▶

fiebre (fever) enthusiastic, fanatical ◀ CR, Col ▶
Pedro es muy fiebre para el fútbol. Pedro is a fanatic about soccer.

el/la hincha (sports) fan ◀ S. Am., Sp ▶

picado(-a) (piqued, stung) enthusiastic or curious ◀ Mex, parts of C. Am. ▶
Estaba tan bueno el partido que todos estábamos picados viéndolo. (Mex) The game was so good that we all got carried away watching it.
Estaba picado de la curiosidad. (Mex) His curiosity was aroused.

picarse (to become piqued) to get caught up with; be interested, enthusiastic, or curious ◀ Mex ▶
Nos picamos con tu plática tan interesante. We got caught up with your talk because it was so interesting.
Estaba tan rica la sopa que nos picamos comiendo más y más. The soup was so tasty that we got carried away and ate more and more of it.

---

error

See also "failure."

abatato(-a) (sweet potatoed up) person who doesn't think before acting and makes mistakes, goofball, silly fool ◀ Para, U, Arg ▶

desubicado(-a) (disoriented) mistaken, wrong, all wet ◀ S. Cone ▶

no haber roto un plato (to not have broken a plate) to have the appearance of someone who's never made a mistake ◀ Mex, Sp ▶
Nunca ha roto un plato. He (She) is one of those perfect people who look like they've never made a mistake.

no salirle a alguien la(s) cuenta(s) (to not have the accounts come out for someone) to not turn out right for someone, said of a miscalculation that led to damages ◀ Mex, Sp ▶
No me salen las cuentas. Things are not working for me (not coming out right).

blowing it

abatatarse (to get sweet potatoed) to get upset, get flustered and make mistakes; from **batata**, sweet potato ◀ Para, U, Arg ▶

caerse (to fall down) to make a mistake ◀ Bol, Ch ▶

cagarla (to defecate on it) to make a mistake, blow it (vulgar) (sometimes used without **la**) ◀ L. Am., Sp ▶
La cagué invitándolo a la fiesta porque estuvo tan pesado como siempre. I screwed up by inviting him to the party because he was just as much of a jerk as always.

cometer una burrada (to commit a drove of donkeys) to make a gaff, mistake ◀ chicano, Mex, G, DR, Col, S. Cone, Sp ▶

dejar la escoba (to leave the broom) to screw (mess) something up ◀ Ch ▶

embarrarla (to muddy it) to goof up, make a mistake ◀ ES, Nic, Col, Peru, S. Cone ▶

escacharse to fail because of a wrong move or saying something wrong ◀ Cuba ▶

írsele a alguien la lengua to have a slip of the tongue, speak without thinking ◀ Mex, ES, U, Arg, Sp ▶
Se me fue la lengua y les conté que tú salías con Carmen. I made a little slip of the tongue and told them that you were going out with Carmen.

mear fuera del tiesto (to urinate outside the pot) to make a mistake (U, Arg: **tarro** instead of **tiesto**) (vulgar) ◀ Sp ▶

meter el cazo (to put in one's dipper) to be wrong ◀ Sp ▶

meter la pata (to put one's foot in) to put one's foot in one's mouth, make a mistake ◀ L. Am., Sp ▶

no dar una (to not give one) to goof up constantly (DR, PR: **no pegar una**) ◀Mex, U, Sp▶
No da una en matemáticas. He (She) can't get anything right in mathematics.
No doy una. I can't do anything right.

poner un huevo (to lay an egg) to make a mistake ◀DR▶
Puse un huevo cuando le pregunté a Adelia sobre su edad. I laid an egg (stuck my foot in my mouth) when I asked Adelia how old she was.

pringarla (to soak it in grease; to stab it) to make a mistake, blow it (like **cagarla**) (vulgar) ◀Sp▶
La pringó cuando se casó con ese idiota. She really goofed when she married that idiot.

regarla (to spread it) to make a big mistake, do or say something that causes a problem, blow it (original meaning was vulgar—**la** refers to **mierda**—but is now a very common expression) ◀Mex, ES, Nic, Col▶
Todos la regamos de vez en cuando. Everybody goofs up once in a while.

expressions about mistakes

Echando a perder, se aprende. (By ruining things, you learn.) People learn by trial and error. ◀DR, Ch▶

Ésa se te zafó. (That one got away from you.) You blew it. ◀Mex▶

¡Incúbalo! (Incubate it!) What a blunder! ◀DR▶

no ser el primero (to not be the first) phrase used to excuse an action because there are other examples ◀Mex, ES, DR, PR, S. Cone▶
No soy el primero ni el último. I'm not the first nor the last (to make this mistake).

No van por ahí los tiros. (The shots aren't going that way.) You're off the track, cold. ◀DR, Ch, Sp▶

Te pasaste. (You passed yourself.) You did something wrong, goofed. (Ch: also, you did something well) ◀Mex, G, DR, PR, Col, S. Cone, Sp▶

mistakes, gaffes

la barrabasada scandalous mistake (Ch: mischief, naughtiness) ◀Mex, DR, Col, Arg, Ch, Sp▶

el error garrafal huge mistake ◀Nic, DR, PR, S. Cone, Sp▶
Cometí un error garrafal en el examen. I goofed up big-time on the test.

la metida (metedura) de pata gaffe, mistake. (DR, Sp: **metida** only) ◀Mex, G, DR, S. Cone, Sp▶

el pelón (baldy) mistake, goof up, snafu ◀Ven▶

evasion, avoidance

el/la agachado(-a) (crouched down) person good at avoiding (weaseling out of) things ◀Arg▶
Esa mina es una agachada; es muy viva para zafarse de las situaciones. That dame is a conniver; she's very clever at weaseling out of situations.

dar (un) esquinazo (to hit someone with a corner) to avoid someone, go out of one's way so as not to encounter him or her ◀Arg, Sp▶
Mi amigo me dio un esquinazo. My friend went out of his way to avoid me.
Vi a ese profesor tan pesado en la calle, pero le di esquinazo. I saw that jerk of a professor walking down the street, but I gave him the cold shoulder.

mirar (ver) los toros desde la barrera (to look at [see] the bulls from behind the barrier) to participate in or witness something but avoid exposing oneself to danger ◀most of L. Am., Sp▶
Durante la Segunda Guerra Mundial, estuvimos viendo los toros desde la barrera. During the Second World War, we stayed out of harm's way (remained on the sidelines).

salirse por la tangente (to go off on a tangent) to sidestep or avoid ◄ Mex, S. Cone, Sp ►

backing out

tirar para colina (la cola) (to throw toward the hill [the tail]) to back out of some plan or commitment at the last minute ◄ Ch ►

zafarse (de) to excuse oneself, avoid or get out of; get rid of ◄ L. Am. ►
Záfate de Fernando, que no te conviene ese tipo. Stay clear of Fernando. It's not good for you to get mixed up with him.
¡Zafo! (Mex) I'm out (I won't do it)!

passing the buck

escurrir el bulto (to drain the shape or package) to avoid work or responsibility, pass the buck ◄ Ch, Sp ►
Siempre escurre el bulto cuando hay que pagar. He (She) always worms out of it when it's time to pay.

pasar to pass (on something), decline ◄ Mex, S. Cone ►
¿Te casarías con mi hermana? —No, yo paso. Would you marry my sister? —No, I pass.

pasar la bola to pass the buck (ball) in conversation ◄ Mex, Cuba, U, Arg ►

pasarse con ficha (to pass with a domino piece) to pass as in a dominoes game, avoid a response (intentionally or not) ◄ Cuba, DR, PR ►

exhaustion

aguado(-a) (watery, watered-down) tired or weak ◄ Mex, G, ES, CR, DR, Col, Para ►
agüitado(-a) down, tired, low ◄ Mex, C. Am. ►
agüitarse to be down, tired, low ◄ Mex, C. Am. ►

No te agüites, 'mana. Vamos a conseguir el dinero. Don't get down, dear. We'll get the money.

darse unas palizas (to beat oneself up with sticks) to get all worn out and sore (e.g., from walking) ◄ U, Sp ►
Se da unas palizas de caminar (trabajar). He (She) gets totally beat from walking (working).

dejar de cama (to leave in bed) to wear (someone) out physically or mentally ◄ U, Arg ►

dolerle hasta los huesos to ache all over with tiredness ◄ L. Am., Sp ►
He trabajado mucho y ahora me duelen hasta los huesos. I've worked a lot and now I'm worn to the bone (dog tired).

hacerse añicos (to break into pieces) to be exhausted physically or mentally ◄ Mex, ES, U, Arg, Sp ►

hacerse pedazos (to break into pieces) to be exhausted physically or mentally ◄ Mex, ES, U, Arg, Sp ►

matado(-a) (killed) exhausting (U, Arg: **matador[-a]**) ◄ Mex, G ►
Es un trabajo matado. It's an exhausting job.

no poder alguien con sus huesos (to not be able with one's bones) to be very tired ◄ Mex, U, Sp ►
Después de tanto trabajar, no podía ni con mis huesos. After working so much, I was bone weary.

quedar de cama (to be left in bed) to get worn out (physically, emotionally) ◄ U, Arg ►

quemarse to burn out physically ◄ G ►
El corredor se quemó antes de llegar a la meta. The runner burned out before reaching the finish line.

worn out

amolado(-a) (ground, sharpened) worn to a frazzle, ruined, exhausted ◄ Mex, C. Am. ►
Te dejaron bien amolado(-a). They left you totally worn out.

fundido(-a) (melted) exhausted (Ch: spoiled, as a child) ◄ G, Col, U, Arg ►

hecho(-a) atol (made into atol, a corn-based drink) worn out ◄ ES ►

hecho(-a) (una) mierda (made into shit) worn down, exhausted (vulgar) ◀ Mex, DR, PR, U, Arg, Sp ▶
Estoy rendido, hecho mierda. I'm wiped out, tired as hell.

hecho(-a) pedazos, añicos (in pieces) exhausted ◀ Mex, ES, U, Arg, Sp ▶

hecho(-a) pinole (made into **pinole,** an aromatic powder that used to be used in making chocolate) ground down, exhausted ◀ Mex ▶
La carrera me dejó hecho pinole. The race left me dog tired.

hecho(-a) polvo (made into dust) exhausted ◀ Mex, Cuba, DR, Sp ▶
¡Tanto trabajo! Estoy hecha polvo. So much work! I'm beat.

hecho(-a) un puré (made into a purée) exhausted, worn down (Mex: **hecho puré**) ◀ Mex, Sp ▶
El día que chocamos el coche quedó hecho puré. The day we crashed the car, he (she) was worn to a frazzle.

molido(-a) (ground down) exhausted ◀ Mex, ES, PR, Ch, Sp ▶

quemado(-a) exhausted (Sp: also, burned out) ◀ Mex, G, CR, DR, Col, Sp ▶

rendido(-a) (rendered) exhausted ◀ L. Am., Sp ▶
Trabajé siete días seguidos y estoy rendido. I worked seven days straight and I'm wiped out.

reventado(-a) (burst, blown apart) exhausted, wiped out ◀ Mex, Cuba, PR, Col, S. Cone, Sp ▶

tener un careto (to have a white-faced mask) to look really bad because of worry or lack of sleep ◀ Sp ▶

failure

See also "error."

la calabaza (pumpkin) failing grade ◀ Sp ▶

Saqué dos calabazas: en matemáticas y literatura. I got two rotten grades: in math and literature.

clavado(-a) (nailed) failing (in school); involved (in something) ◀ PR ▶

colgado(-a) (hung, suspended) failed (on an exam) ◀ PR ▶

ir abajo (to go down) to lose a position, be demoted ◀ G, Cuba, Col ▶

ir al garete to fail ◀ Sp ▶
La relación fue al garete después de tres años. The relationship failed after three years.

ir de culo (to go ass) to be wrong; to fail (vulgar) ◀ Sp ▶

irse al cuerno (to go to the horn) to come to nothing ◀ Mex, Sp ▶

llevarse el diablo (to be taken by the devil) to fail ◀ Mex, DR ▶

llevarse el demonio (to be taken by the demon) to fail ◀ Mex, Sp ▶
Si no trabajamos en serio, a este negocio se lo va a llevar el demonio. If we don't work seriously, this business is going to go to hell.

failing, flunking, washing out

batear (to hit) to fail ◀ ES ▶
Me batearon en el examen. They flunked me on the exam.

bochar to flunk (exams) ◀ U, Arg ▶

caerse con todo el equipo (to fall with the whole team or equipment) to fail totally ◀ Mex, Sp ▶

catear (to search) to fail ◀ Sp ▶
Me catearon. I failed.

clavarse (to be nailed) to fail (as on an exam), to get involved in a bad situation or problem ◀ Mex, PR ▶
Juan se clavó. Juan got nailed.

colgar (to hang, suspend) to flunk an exam ◀ Cuba ▶
¿Qué tal el examen? —Colgué. How'd the exam go? —I got nailed.

colgarse (to hang, be suspended) to fail (exam) ◀ PR ▶
Me colgué en ese examen. Cuando leí la primera pregunta me quedé en blanco. I flubbed that test. When I read the first question, my mind went blank.

echarse (to throw oneself) to fail ◀ Col ▶

Me eché el examen de historia. ¡Qué lata! I messed up on the history exam. What a drag!

echarse a alguien (to throw oneself) to fail someone (e.g., on their exams) ◀ Mex, Cuba ▶

irse al (para el) carajo (to go to the carajo, male organ) to lose something, have a bad ending, go to hell in a handbasket (vulgar) ◀ Mex, ES, DR, PR, U, Sp ▶

El negocio se fue al carajo. The business went to hell.

jalar (to pull) to fail (on an exam) ◀ Peru ▶

Yo te hubiera jalado, más bien. I would have failed you, instead.

no vender una escoba (to not sell a broom) to fail, not accomplish what was intended ◀ Sp ▶

planchar (to iron) to fail (e.g., an exam) ◀ G, U ▶

ponchar to fail (an exam) (Mex and C. Am.: also, to puncture, as a tire) ◀ Mex, G, Cuba, DR ▶

El maestro me ponchó en el examen con un 4 de calificación. (DR) The teacher failed me on the test with a D grade (4 in the usual Hispanic system).

Ponché el examen. I failed the exam.

Me poncharon en biología. (Mex) They flunked me in biology.

quemarse (to burn up) to fail or flunk (a course in school) ◀ DR ▶

rajar (to split) to fail (as on an exam) ◀ Mex, DR, Col, Ch ▶

Me rajaron en química. They failed me in chemistry.

raspar (to search) to fail ◀ Ven ▶

Me rasparon. I failed.

sonar (como tarro) (to ring [like a tin can]) to try and fail at something, fall (flat) on your face ◀ Ch ▶

suspender (to suspend) to flunk ◀ Mex, ES, Col, Arg, Sp ▶

La maestra me suspendió. The teacher flunked me.

Tres alumnos suspendieron el examen. Three students failed the exam.

tirarse (to throw oneself) to fail ◀ Col ▶

Me tiré. I failed.

tronar (to thunder) to fail (e.g., an exam, a project, in love) ◀ Mex, C. Am. ▶

Me tronaron. They washed me out.

tronar como (un) ejote (to snap like a peapod) to end badly, fail ◀ Mex ▶

Tronó como (un) ejote en el trabajo. He (She) messed up big-time at work.

Tronó con su novia como (un) ejote. He was a washout with his girlfriend.

volar (to blow up, to make fly) to flunk, fail ◀ Mex ▶

Me volaron en historia. They flunked me in history.

Volé el examen. I flunked the exam.

has-been, loser, chump

el/la aplastado(-a) (squashed, flattened person) someone who can't defend himself or herself, poor chump ◀ ES, Nic ▶

dejado(-a) (left behind) unworthy or irresponsible ◀ G, ES, Nic, Ch ▶

el/la quedado(-a) (one who's been left behind) loser, fool ◀ CR, DR, Col, Ven ▶

el/la quemado(-a) (burned-out person) has-been, someone who's lost his or her abilities ◀ Ven ▶

raspa cum laude describing a big failure ◀ PR, Col ▶

Miguelito se graduó raspa cum laude. De chepa pasó los exámenes finales. Miguelito graduated with the loser's degree. By sheer luck he passed his final exams.

fame

el pul fame (from English "pull") ◀ CR, DR ▶

Ese señor tiene mucho pul. That gentleman is really famous.

tener buena (mala) prensa to have good (bad) press or reputation ◀ most of L. Am., Sp ▶

vocea'o(-a) much voiced or commented on ◀ Col ▶

bad rep

mala ficha bad reputation ◀ ES, CR, Col ▶
Oscar tiene mala ficha. Oscar has a bad reputation.

mala nota (bad note) unpleasant thing or person, bad news, bad reputation ◀ most of L. Am. ▶
Esa escuela es (de) muy mala nota. That school has a bad rep.

rayado(-a) (striped) with a shady past (bad reputation) ◀ Ven ▶

fear

See also "weakness."

achantar to frighten ◀ Nic, Sp ▶
A mí tus chantajes no me achantan. Your blackmail threats don't scare me.
Esto a mi no me achanta. This doesn't frighten me one bit.

Deja el friqueo. Stop being freaky or afraid, stop freaking out. ◀ DR, PR, Col ▶
Deja el friqueo, que nadie nos vio con los cigarrillos. Stop freaking out. Nobody saw us with the cigarettes.

no mojarse (to not get oneself wet) to not take any risk ◀ Sp ▶
Juan no se moja para nada. Juan never goes out on a limb for anything.

No te amilanes. Don't be afraid, back down. ◀ G, S. Cone, Sp ▶

poner a alguien los pelos de punta to make someone's hair stand on end, give him or her the creeps (from fear) (Sp: also, **parar los pelos de punta**) ◀ L. Am., Sp ▶
Me contó lo que le había pasado y se me pusieron los pelos de punta. He told me what had happened to him and my hair stood on end.

Se me salió un zapato. (A shoe fell off me.) said by someone who has been frightened or has had a shock ◀ Col ▶

backing down, chickening out

achicarse (to get small) to get scared and back down, chicken out ◀ S. Cone, Sp ▶
Te voy a proponer un asunto pero sospecho que te vas a achicar. I'm going to make you a proposition but I suspect that you will chicken out.
Por favor, señora, ¡no se me achique! (Arg) Please, lady, don't cop out on me!
No te achiques por esa gente y plántales cara. (Sp) Don't back down because of those people and just face up to them.

apendejarse to back down, lose one's nerve ◀ Mex, Cuba, PR, DR, Col ▶

no tener huevos (to not have eggs, testicles) to be a coward (vulgar) ◀ Mex, DR, Sp ▶
¿A qué no tienes huevos de ir a un cementerio de noche? So, want to bet you don't have the balls to go to the cemetery at night?

rajarse (to split) to back down, chicken out, give up, take back one's words ◀ Mex, ES, Cuba, DR, Col, Peru, Sp ▶
Dijiste que vendrías al cine; no te rajes ahora. You said you'd come to the movies, so don't back out now.
Mauricio quería hacer bonjee en Costa Rica pero al final se rajó. Mauricio wanted to go bungee jumping in Costa Rica but he chickened out at the last minute.
Ay Jalisco, ¡no te rajes! Oh, Jalisco, don't let me down!

subírsele a alguien los huevos (to have one's eggs, or testicles, rise) to lose one's courage (vulgar) ◀ Mex ▶
Cuando me di cuenta de que había un ladrón en la casa, se me subieron los huevos hasta la garganta. When I realized there was a robber in the house, I got a hell of a scare.

tener los cojones por corbata (to have one's testicles as a tie) to be fearful, timid (vulgar); also, **tenerlos por corbata** ◀ Sp ▶

tener los huevos de corbata (to have one's testicles as a tie) to be fearful, timid (vulgar); also, **tenerlos por corbata** ◀ ES, Sp ▶
Cuando fui con Ricardo a la capital, manejó tan rápido que yo tenía los huevos de corbata. When I went with Ricardo to the capital, he drove so fast that it scared the hell out of me.

frightened, scared

caerse muerto(-a) de miedo (susto) (to fall dead of fear) to be very afraid (Arg, Sp: more common, **darse un susto de muerto**) ◀ Mex, ES, DR, U, Sp ▶

dar diente con diente (to have teeth hitting each other) to be very cold or to be afraid, when teeth chatter ◀ L. Am., Sp ▶

darse un cagazo (to take a big shit) to have a terrible fright (vulgar) ◀ U, Arg ▶

darse un chucho to get scared or frightened ◀ Arg, Para, U ▶
¡Pobre Pedro! Lo atacó el perro y se dio un chucho espantoso. Poor Pedro! The dog attacked him and he got a terrible scare.

escamado(-a) (scaled, like a fish) frightened, nervous, wary ◀ Mex, PR, Col ▶

escamarse (to become scaled, like a fish) to be frightened ◀ Mex, PR, Col ▶

estar achuchado(-a) to be scared stiff ◀ U, Para, Arg ▶

estar acojonado(-a) to be afraid (vulgar) ◀ PR, Sp ▶

estar cagado(-a) (to be pooped) to be scared stiff, scared shitless (U, Arg: also, **cagado[-a] hasta los pelos**) (vulgar) ◀ S. Cone, Sp ▶

hacerse un ovillo (una pelota) (to make oneself a little egg [a ball]) to shrink with fear, pain, etc.; to get confused or balled up ◀ Sp ▶

no atreverse a decir «esta boca es mía» (to not dare to say "this mouth is mine") to not dare open one's mouth ◀ L. Am., Sp ▶
Cuando vino la policía, no me atreví a decir «esta boca es mía». When the police came, I didn't dare open my mouth.

quedarse chiquito(-a) (to be left small) to be afraid ◀ CR, Col ▶

sudar frío (to sweat cold) to break out in a cold sweat, to be fearful ◀ CR, DR, Col, U, Arg ▶

tener un jabón (to have a soap) to be afraid ◀ U, Arg ▶
Tenía un jabón tremendo cuando aterrizó el avión. I was all shaken up when the airplane landed.

wimp, chicken, scaredy-cat

asustón, asustona easily frightened, scaredy-cat ◀ chicano, Mex ▶
Claudia tiene miedo de todo. ¡Qué asustona! Claudia is afraid of everything. What a scaredy-cat!

el cagón, la cagona (big shitter) scaredy-cat, chicken (Sp: also, **cagado[-a]**) (vulgar) ◀ U, Arg, Sp ▶

fruncir (to pucker) to be a coward, wimp ◀ Mex, Col ▶
¡No te frunzas! Don't be a wimp!

el gallina (hen) coward ◀ Mex, G, Nic, Cuba, DR, PR, Col, Sp ▶

el manitas (little hands) coward, sissy, wimp ◀ CR, Col ▶

el/la penco(-a) coward ◀ Cuba, Col ▶

rajado(-a) (split) describing someone who has chickened out, given up, taken back his or her words ◀ Mex, Cuba, DR, Col, ES, Sp ▶

el rajón, la rajona chicken, someone who backs down or doesn't do something promised, wimp ◀ Mex, ES, Nic, Cuba, DR, Col, Sp ▶

ser un acojonado to be a coward, timid ◀ Sp ▶
Felipe es un acojonado. Me dijo que iba a hablar con el jefe, pero no lo hizo. Felipe doesn't have any balls. He told me he was going to speak with the boss, but he didn't do it.

ser corto(-a) de genio (to be short on brilliance) to be timid, lacking in bravery ◀ Peru ▶

Test your slang power!

Feelings and emotions

Relevant categories: anger, embarrassment, enthusiasm, fear, happiness, sadness, worry

How much Spanish "slanguage" do you know related to this topic? Test yourself by completing the exercises. Answers and rating scale are on page 263. (If you don't do very well, read through the categories listed above and try again. The items in each exercise occur in the same order as the categories.)

A. Something's missing. *Select the appropriate word to complete the sentence.*

1. She's at the boiling point (about to explode). **Está como agua para (avellanas / chocolate / verdura)** _____.

2. Eduardo didn't get the check, and he's hopping mad. **A Eduardo no le llegó el cheque y está que (entona / ladra / rompe)** _____.

3. Her older sisters are always kidding her. **Sus hermanas mayores siempre la están (conciliando / modulando / vacilando)** _____.

4. We are just teasing you. **Te estamos tomando el (pie / brazo / pelo)** _____, **nada más.**

5. My aunt and uncle are very excited about their new house. **Mis tíos están muy (emocionados / excitados / enterados)** _____ **con su nueva casa.**

6. The kid got scared out of her wits. **A la niña se le pusieron los pelos de (arriba / punta / rizado)** _____.

7. He feels completely contented here. **Aquí está como pez en el (agua / cielo / plato)** _____.

8. What a bummer! (All is lost.) **¡El gozo en un (chozo / pozo / trozo)** _____!

9. My teacher makes a big deal out of every little thing. **Mi profe se ahoga en un (cubo / lago / vaso)** _____ **de agua.**

10. I'm on pins and needles, waiting for the results of the test. **Estoy en (ascuas / clavos / espinas)** _____, **esperando los resultados del examen.**

B. Pick a letter! *Choose the letter of the word or phrase that completes each sentence. Write it in the blank.*

11. ____ **Ayer vi a mi novia con otro tipo y perdí los estribos.**
    Yesterday I saw my girlfriend with another guy and
    a. I lost interest in her.
    b. I lost my cool.
    c. I got depressed.
    d. I felt relieved.

12. ____ **Mi marido hizo un berrinche anoche cuando llegué a la casa.**
    My husband _____ last night when I got home.
    a. had a surprise for me
    b. jumped for joy
    c. gave me the silent treatment
    d. threw a fit

13. ____ **Qué oso.** How
    a. cool.
    b. depressing.
    c. frightening.
    d. embarrassing.

14. ____ **Llegamos temprano pero ya había muchos hinchas allí.**
    We got there early but there were already a lot of _____ there.
    a. sports fans
    b. hustlers
    c. eager customers
    d. politicians

15. ____ **No me atrevía a decir «esta boca es mía».**
   a. I just couldn't stop talking.
   b. I was in seventh heaven.
   c. I didn't dare open my mouth.
   d. I was fainting with hunger.

16. ____ **Desde que asumió el control del comité, el jefe está como niño con zapatos nuevos.** Since he assumed control of the committee, the boss seems
   a. very happy.
   b. very sad.
   c. confused.
   d. uncomfortable.

17. ____ **Beatriz fue al funeral vestida de amarillo, pero yo comprendí que la procesión iba por dentro.** Beatriz went to the funeral dressed in yellow, but I understood that
   a. she wasn't really sad.
   b. she was sad but wasn't showing it.
   c. she was making a show of her sadness.
   d. she was secretly relieved.

18. ____ **Mi madrina siempre toma las cosas a la tremenda.** My godmother always
   a. looks at things through rose-colored glasses.
   b. takes everything with a grain of salt.
   c. gets all worked up about things.
   d. tries to remain detached.

19. ____ **Mi jefe siempre le busca tres pies al gato.** My boss always
   a. looks for cats.
   b. acts like a nitpicker.
   c. seeks praise.
   d. works too hard.

20. ____ **Mi hermana siempre le ve pelos a la sopa.** My sister always
   a. refuses to eat soup.
   b. finds something wrong.
   c. obsesses about food.
   d. gets nervous about cleanliness.

flattery

See also "deception," "persuasion."

arrimarse al sol que más calienta (to put oneself by the sun that heats the most) to serve and flatter the most powerful ◀ Mex, Sp ▶

hacer la pata (to do the paw) to brownnose ◀ Ch ▶

ir donde calienta el sol (to go where the sun heats up) to go with the winner, change sides for benefit (pejorative) ◀ U, Ch ▶

lamber ojo (to lick eye) to lick someone's boots, kiss up to ◀ PR, Col ▶

lamer/lamber el culo (trasero) a alguien to kiss (lick) someone's ass (vulgar) (Sp: more common, **lamer**) ◀ Mex, ES, S. Cone, Sp ▶
Sigue ahí, lamiéndole el culo a la profesora. He's (She's) still there, brownnosing the teacher (kissing the teacher's ass).

kiss-up, suck-up

barbero(-a) sucking up ◀ Mex ▶
Pasé el examen de química por estar barbero con la maestra. I passed the chemistry exam by sucking up to the teacher.

el/la chupamedia(s) (stocking sucker) kiss ass, person who does anything to please people in authority, brownnoser (also, **chupar media**) ◀ Bol, Peru, S. Cone ▶
Agustín le chupa las medias al director. Agustín really kisses ass with the director.

la guata de callo (guata de foca) (belly with calluses [belly of a seal]) brownnose, sycophant, person so servile that he grovels on the ground (like a seal) or gets calluses on his stomach ◀ Ch ▶

el/la jala-bola (ball-puller) brownnoser ◀ Ven ▶

el lambeojo, lameojo bootlicker, kiss-up ◀ PR, Col ▶

el chupamedias

el lambiscón, la lambiscona flatterer, suck-up (Arg: **la lambiscona** only) ◀ Mex, G, ES, Arg ▶

food and drink

See also "drunkenness."

a la suerte de la olla (to the luck of the pot) potluck ◀ Ch ▶
Te invitamos a comer a la suerte de la olla. We invite you over to eat potluck.

asustado(-a) (frightened) half-cooked or -baked ◀ Mex, Col ▶

el/la boquisabroso(-a) person who loves food ◀ Mex, Col ▶
Yo soy un boquisabroso. Me encanta probar comidas exóticas. I'm a gourmand. I love trying exotic foods.

la de la vergüenza (the one of shame) the last portion of food on a plate that no one dares to take ◀ DR, Sp ▶

la dolorosa (the painful one) the check, bill ◀ Sp ▶

estar en blanco (to be blank) to have not eaten (Mex: also, to have not slept) ◀ Mex, G, Cuba ▶

Say it with slang!

What a mess! What an unmothering!

Frustration is a universal experience. You enter a room expecting to find it orderly and instead you find everything is out of place; or you plan a logical agenda for a meeting and it spins out of control, so you scream, "What a mess!" What do people in other cultures scream? Well, in the Spanish-speaking world, there are many variations. Here are six of them:

1. (Mexico) **¡Qué desmadre!** (What an unmothering!)
2. (Spain) **¡Qué follón!** (What a ruckus or orgy!)
3. (Peru) **¡Qué laberinto!** (What a maze or labyrinth!)
4. (Argentina) **¡Qué quilombo! ¡Qué burdel!** (What a house of prostitution! [Both mean the same thing.])
5. (S. Cone) **¡Qué despelote!** (What an unballing!)
6. (Costa Rica) **¡Qué zambrote!** (What a Moorish party!)

The most common expression, however, is **¡Qué lío!** (What a bundle or tie-up!), which is used almost everywhere that Spanish is spoken.

el filo (blade, file) hunger, appetite ◀ Mex, CR, ES, Ven ▶
Ese cipote mantiene un gran filo para comer. That youngster keeps up his appetite.

hacerle agua la boca (to make the mouth water) to have one's mouth watering (Sp: **hacerle la boca agua**) ◀ L. Am. ▶
¿Hiciste empanadas, mi amor? Se me hace agua la boca. (L. Am.) You made empanadas, my darling? My mouth is watering.
Se me hace la boca agua. (Sp) My mouth is watering.

el malón surprise party, when a group of friends unexpectedly shows up at someone's house with food and drinks ◀ Ch ▶

matar (to kill) to finish off or up ◀ Mex, Cuba ▶
¿Matemos la ensalada? Shall we kill (finish off) the salad?

meter (to put in) to swallow, eat or drink ◀ Sp ▶

Me metí cuatro cañas y dos bocadillos en quince minutos. I wolfed down four beers and two sandwiches in fifteen minutes.

¿Qué le pongo? What shall I serve (put before) you? ◀ Sp ▶

ser para chuparse los dedos (to be to suck one's fingers) to be delicious ◀ L. Am., Sp ▶
Este postre es para chuparse los dedos. This dessert is finger-lickin' good.

la soda (soda) café that sells reasonably priced food ◀ CR ▶

tener buena cuchara (to have a good spoon) to be a good cook ◀ CR, Col ▶

tener mano de monja (to have a nun's hand) to be a good cook, have the gourmet touch ◀ Ch ▶

tomar once (to take eleven) to have tea, a snack in the afternoon ◀ Ch ▶

beer

la birra beer ◀ Hond, CR, DR, Col, Ven, Sp ▶
la birria beer ◀ Mex, G, Nic, PR ▶

la caña (cane) beer ◀Sp▶

la cerva short for **cerveza** ◀Cuba▶

la chela (blond, light) light-colored beer ◀Mex, ES, Ec, Peru, Bol▶
Vamos a tomar una chela. Let's have a beer.

la cheve beer ◀Mex, G, ES▶

de barril (from the barrel) draft (beer) ◀L. Am.▶
Una cerveza, por favor. De barril. A beer, please. Make it draft.

la fría (cold one) beer ◀G, Cuba, PR, Col▶

eating

echarle algo al buche (al pico) (to put something in one's craw [beak]) to eat (Sp: also, **llenar el buche**) ◀Mex, G, Cuba, DR, Col, U, Sp▶

iriar to eat (from an African language) ◀Cuba▶

jamar to eat (Peru: **jamear**; Nic: **jambar**) ◀Cuba, CR, Ec▶

manyar to eat (from Italian) ◀Peru, S. Cone▶

papear (to potato) to eat ◀Mex, C. Am., Cuba, DR, PR, Peru, Ven, Sp▶

expressions to say while eating or drinking

A comer se ha dicho. (To eat it has been said.) Let's eat. ◀L. Am., Sp▶

¡Arriba, abajo, al centro y p'adentro! (Up, down, to the center, and inside!) Down the hatch! Sometimes this is just said as, **¡Al centro y p'adentro!** (toast said before drinking) ◀L. Am., Sp▶

¡Chin chin! (imitating the sound of glass clinking) Cheers! ◀parts of L. Am., Sp▶
¡Chin chin y que seas muy feliz! Cheers and may you be very happy.

Comida hecha, amistad deshecha. (Meal finished, friendship ended.) said when someone eats and runs ◀most of L. Am., Sp▶

¡Fondo blanco! (White bottom [of glass]!) Bottoms up! ◀most of L. Am.▶

¡Llégale a la papa! (Go to the potato!) Eat! ◀Mex, Col▶

¡Para los (las) que amamos! For those whom we love! (a toast) ◀most of L. Am.▶

¡Qué delicia! (What a delight!) How delicious! ◀most of L. Am.▶

Retaca la buchaca. (Stuff your craw.) Eat your fill. ◀Mex▶

¡Salud! (Health!) To your health! Gesundheit! (said as a toast or after a sneeze) (Mex: also, **¡Salucitas!**) ◀L. Am., Sp▶

Ya maté a lo que me estaba matando. (I already killed what was killing me [hunger].) I'm full. ◀ES, Col▶

Yo soy como (Juan) Orozco; cuando como no conozco. (I'm like [Juan] Orozco; when I'm eating I don't recognize people.) said of someone who is too absorbed in eating ◀Mex, ES▶

glutton

comilón, comilona gluttonous ◀L. Am., Sp▶

el cuarto bate big eater ◀Cuba, DR, PR▶

el dragón, la draga (probably from **tragón**, big swallow) big eater, glutton ◀DR, PR▶
Tan flaca que es Luisa y eso que es una draga, siempre se sirve dos veces. As skinny as Luisa is, she happens to be a glutton and always takes two helpings.

hartón, hartona gluttonous ◀Mex, C. Am.▶

jamalichye gluttonous ◀Cuba▶

la piraña (piranha, fish that devours its prey) person who eats a lot ◀Mex, Col▶

tener buen diente (to have good tooth) to be a big eater ◀Mex, DR, PR, S. Cone, Sp▶
Ricardo tiene buen diente. Se comió dos hamburguesas doble carne y un batido de fresa. Ricardo is a glutton. He had two double-patty hamburgers and a strawberry shake.

el/la tragaldabas (door hinge gobbler) glutton, guzzler ◀Mex, Col▶

el tragón, la tragona big eater ◀Mex▶
Nicole es tragona; le encanta comer. Nicole is a big eater; she loves to eat.

having a drink

la alternadora (alternator) girl who acts as hostess at bars to be invited for drinks ◀ Arg ▶

brindar por las otras (cervezas que vienen) to toast the others (the other beers to come) ◀ ES, Mex, Col ▶
Brindemos por las otras (cervezas que vienen). Let's drink to the drinks we're going to have.

chupar to drink alcohol (slightly vulgar in C. Am.) ◀ L. Am., Sp ▶

darse un cañangazo to drink a strong alcoholic beverage ◀ Cuba ▶

darse un palo, palito to have an alcoholic drink ◀ Cuba, DR ▶
Vamos a darnos unos palitos para celebrar tu cumpleaños. Let's have ourselves a few slugs to celebrate your birthday.

echar un palo (to throw a stick) to have an alcoholic drink (in many places, to have sex) ◀ Ven ▶

empinar el codo (to raise one's elbow) to have a drink, wet one's whistle, have a swig ◀ L. Am., Sp ▶

el glu-glú (onomatopoeia, to sound like glug-glug or like pouring from a bottle) boozing, alcohol ◀ Mex, Col ▶

libar (to have a libation) to drink ◀ Mex, ES, Col ▶

pistear to drink (alcohol) (used mainly in northern Mex) ◀ Mex ▶

tomar una copa to have a drink (wine glass) ◀ L. Am., Sp ▶
Tomamos una copa en la Torre Latinoamericana. We're having a drink at the Torre Latinoamericana.

hungry

andar con el diente largo (to go with the long tooth) to be dying of hunger ◀ Ch ▶

andar (estar) muerto(-a) de hambre (to be dead of hunger) to be starving to death ◀ Mex, DR, PR, S. Cone, Sp ▶
¿Está lista la cena? Estoy muerto de hambre. Is supper ready? I'm starving to death.

cruzado(-a) (crossed) very hungry ◀ Cuba ▶

estar que ladra (to be barking) to be hungry ◀ Col ▶

partido(-a) (broken) very hungry ◀ Cuba, Col ▶

tener hambre de león to be hungry as a lion ◀ Mex ▶

traer la tripa amarrada (to bring the gut tied) to be faint with hunger ◀ Mex, Col ▶

pigging out

batear (to bat) to eat a lot ◀ Cuba ▶

comer como chancho (to eat like a pig) to eat fast and in a sloppy way ◀ ES, Nic, S. Cone ▶

comer como niño Dios (to eat like a child of God, meaning a child from the orphanage) to eat fast, wolf down food hungrily (or can mean the opposite, to eat with too much care as though from the orphanage) ◀ Mex, ES, Nic ▶

forrarse (to make a lining for oneself) to stuff oneself (with food) ◀ ES, Nic, Sp ▶
Enrique se forró de pollo en salsa de mole en el almuerzo. Enrique stuffed himself with chicken in mole sauce at lunch.

fututear to eat rapidly ◀ DR ▶
Oye, no me dejaron ni un chin de pizza. Se la fututearon completica. Listen, they didn't leave me a crumb of pizza. They gobbled up every last bit of it.

ponerse hasta el gorro (to put oneself up to one's cap) to eat and drink one's fill ◀ Mex, Sp ▶
Pablo se puso hasta el gorro en la fiesta. Pablo pigged out to the max at the party.
Con esta botella de tequila se pusieron hasta el gorro. With this bottle of tequila they drank themselves silly.

types of drinks

el chesco (shortened form of **refresco**) soft drink ◀ Mex ▶

el chupe small alcoholic drink ◀ Mex ▶

el chupito small alcoholic drink ◀ Sp ▶

el copete cocktail, alcoholic drink ◀ Ch ▶

la del estribo (the one of the stirrup) one for the road (usually referring to a drink) ◀ Mex, ES, S. Cone ▶
¡Echemos la del estribo! Let's have one for the road!

el farolazo drink (alcoholic) ◀ Mex, ES, Nic, CR ▶
Echemos un farolazo. Let's have a drink.

el piquete shot of alcohol put in coffee ◀ Mex, ES ▶

el tapis alcoholic drink ◀ CR, ES ▶

el trago (swallow) drink of any kind, but often refers to a cocktail, alcoholic drink ◀ L. Am., Sp ▶
Estoy cansada, necesito un trago. I'm tired. I need a drink.

types of foods

las boquitas (little mouths) appetizers ◀ ES ▶

la botana appetizer(s) ◀ Mex ▶

el casado (married man) plate of rice, beans, meat or fish, and salad ◀ CR ▶

la chuchería (from chuches, candy) fast food, junk food ◀ ES, DR, PR, Sp ▶
Me llené con puras chucherías y ahora no tengo hambre. I filled up on junk food and now I'm not hungry.

el chupe dish ◀ Pan, Ec, Peru, Bol, Arg, Ch ▶
El chupe de camarones es delicioso. The shrimp dish is delicious.

la comida chatarra (scrap-metal food) junk food, fast food ◀ Mex, Col, Ch ▶

las cosas para picar (things to pick at) appetizers ◀ Ch, Sp ▶

las croquetas de ave(rigua) (croquettes of ave, poultry, meaning averigua, find out what) mystery meat ◀ Cuba ▶

la dona doughnut (from English) ◀ Mex, C. Am., DR ▶

la jama food ◀ Cuba, CR, PR, Ec, Peru ▶

la iria, el iriampo food (from an African language) ◀ Cuba ▶

la papa (potato) food, especially used for children ◀ Mex, Cuba, DR, Col, Ch ▶
¡Vamos a la papa! Let's chow down!

el papeo (potato) food ◀ Mex, Cuba, DR, PR, Peru, Sp ▶

Es la hora del papeo. ¿Qué quieren comer? It's chow time. What do you want to eat?

los pasa-palos (drink-passers) appetizers, food taken with drinks (**palos**) ◀ Ven ▶

las picadas (pickings) appetizers ◀ Arg ▶

la(s) porquería(s) (pig stuff) junk, trash; junk food ◀ L. Am., Sp ▶
¿Cómo puedes comer esas porquerías? How can you eat that junk?

el recalentado (reheated) leftovers ◀ Mex, ES, Col ▶

el tentempié (tente en pie) (keep you on your feet) midmorning snack (Cuba: usually a coffee with milk) ◀ Mex, DR, Col ▶
Oigan, paremos de trabajar un rato. Es hora de un tentempié. Hey, guys! Let's stop working awhile. It's time to have a snack.

forgetfulness

borrar a algo (alguien) del mapa (to wipe something [someone] off the map) to forget about something or someone ◀ Mex, ES, DR, S. Cone, Sp ▶
Borra eso del mapa. Wash your hands of all that.
Después de lo que me hizo, lo voy a borrar del mapa. After what he did to me, I'm going to erase him from my mind.

estar como una regadera (to be like a watering can) to feel very forgetful, have one's mind like a sieve ◀ Sp ▶

írsele a alguien el santo al cielo (to have one's saint go to heaven) to forget something one was going to do or say (despite good intentions) ◀ most of L. Am., Sp ▶
Iba a trabajar esta mañana, pero se me fue el santo al cielo. I was going to work this morning, but my good intentions went all to heck.

írsele por alto   to go over one's head; to forget ◀ Mex, CR, ES, U ▶
Se me fue por alto la reunión. The meeting totally slipped my mind.

pajarón, pajarona   (big bird) absentminded, forgetful ◀ U, Ch ▶
Perdí mi cartera otra vez. Soy tan pajarona. I lost my wallet again. I'm such an absentminded professor.

pasar por alto   to go over one's head; to forget or not realize; to miss ◀ Mex, ES, DR, PR, S. Cone, Sp ▶

---

frequency

See also "time."

hasta en la sopa   (even in the soup) everywhere ◀ L. Am., Sp ▶
Felipe, ¿otra vez nos encontramos? Me sales hasta en la sopa. Felipe, we bump into each other again? You seem to be everywhere.

ser como arroz blanco   (to be like white rice) to be everywhere ◀ most of L. Am. ▶
Eres como arroz blanco; te veo hasta en la sopa. You really get around; we've got to stop meeting like this.

hasta en la sopa

often

a cada rato   frequently ◀ L. Am., Sp ▶
Me pides la hora a cada rato. ¿Por qué no llevas reloj? You keep asking me what time it is all the time. Why don't you wear a watch?

cada nada   (every nothing) constantly ◀ ES, Nic, CR, Col ▶

rarely, once in a blue moon

cada muerte de un obispo   (each time a bishop dies) once in a blue moon ◀ Col, S. Cone ▶

de higos a brevas   (from figs to early figs) once in a blue moon ◀ Sp ▶

de Pascuas a Ramos   once in a blue moon ◀ most of L. Am., Sp ▶

de uvas a peras   (from grapes to pears) once in a blue moon ◀ most of L. Am., Sp ▶

en la cola de un venado   (on the tail of a deer) not often ◀ Nic ▶

---

friendship

See also "affection," "help."

los amigos (las amigas) del alma   (friends of the soul) buddies, pals ◀ L. Am., Sp ▶
Juana y yo nos llevamos muy bien. Somos amigas del alma. Juana and I get along very well. We are bosom buddies.

la comay (comadre)   (comother of one's child) close female friend ◀ PR ▶

cortar   to cut off (a relationship) ◀ Mex, G, U, Sp ▶
Corté a Mario. Me tenía cansado con sus problemas. I dropped Mario. I was sick and tired of hearing about his problems.

Cuando hay higos, hay amigos; cuando hay brevas... las huevas. (When there are figs, there are friends; when there are early figs [first annual crop of figs] . . . balls [meaning no one cares about you].) Prosperity makes friends, adversity tries them. (vulgar) ◀ Nic, Ch ▶

el/la entrador(-a) (enterer) charmer, people person, person who easily becomes part of a new group, gets everything easily; CR, ES: new love, someone brave and bold in romance ◀ CR, ES, Col, S. Cone ▶

el hermanazo brotherhood, referring to close friendship ◀ Col ▶

juntos pero no revueltos (together but not mixed) together but not bosom buddies or romantically involved ◀ L. Am., Sp ▶
Pablo y Silvia son sólo amigos, juntos pero no revueltos. Pablo and Silvia are just friends, not bosom buddies or romantically involved.

llevarse bien (con alguien) to get along well (with someone) ◀ L. Am., Sp ▶
Me llevo muy bien con mis suegros. I get along very well with my in-laws.

connections and influence

el/la acomodado(-a) (made comfortable) person who benefits from having an influence with powerful people, person with an "in" with the boss or politicians ◀ U, Arg ▶
Juan es un acomodado. Juan has an "in" with the powers that be.

el acomodo connection in government, business, or with powerful people ◀ U, Arg ▶
Cecilia entró a trabajar en ese banco porque tiene un buen acomodo. Cecilia got a job at that bank because she has connections.

agarrarse a los faldones de alguien to cling to someone's skirts, accept his or her protection or help ◀ Mex, Sp ▶

arrimarse a la sombra de alguien (to put oneself in someone's shade) to look for protection from someone ◀ ES, U, Ch ▶

Me arrimé a la sombra del señor García y él me ayudó. I got close to Mr. García and he helped me.

el conecte connection ◀ Mex, ES, Nic ▶
Tengo un buen conecte en el gobierno. I have good connections in the government.

la cuña (prop, wedge) connection (social, political, etc.) ◀ S. Cone ▶
Aquí todo se arregla con cuñas. Everything is arranged through connections here.
Tiene cuñas allí. He (She) has connections there.

enchufar (to plug in) to have connections (ES: **enchuflar**) ◀ Mex, Sp ▶

estar enchufado(-a) (to be plugged in) to have connections ◀ Mex, Sp ▶
Mi tío está enchufado en el gobierno. My uncle has an "in" with the government.

hacer una gauchada (from **gaucho**, cowboy) to do an immense favor ◀ S. Cone ▶
Gracias por la gauchada, che. Thanks for the big favor.

la movida (the moved one) influential friend ◀ Ch ▶
Miguel tiene una movida en el gobierno. Miguel has influence with the government.

la muñeca (doll, wrist) connections, pull ◀ Peru, S. Cone ▶

muñequear (to wrist) to use connections, pull ◀ Peru, S. Cone ▶

la palanca (bar, lever) someone who helps someone, uses his or her influence to their benefit ◀ Mex, ES, Nic, CR, Cuba, Col, Ven, Peru, U, Arg ▶
Tiene muy buenas palancas; por eso consiguió el trabajo. He has very influential friends; that's how he got the job.

palanquear (to move levers) to help, help get a job (Ch: also, to pick on) ◀ ES, Col, Peru, S. Cone ▶

pegado(-a) a las faldas (glued to the skirts) clinging to the skirt ◀ Sp ▶

tener un enchufe (to have a plug) to have a connection, influential friend or acquaintance ◀ DR, PR, Col, Sp ▶
Tiene un enchufe en esa empresa; seguro que le dan el trabajo. He has a connection at that company; they'll give him the job for sure.

Mi abogado es mi enchufe con mi ex-esposa. My lawyer is my connection with my ex-wife.

tener santos en la corte (to have saints at court) to have connections ◀ Ch, parts of Sp ▶
Rosa recibe sus papeles pronto porque tiene santos en la corte. Rosa gets her papers quickly because she has friends in high places.

tener un tío en las Indias (to have an uncle in the [West] Indies) to count on the favor of someone wealthy or influential ◀ Sp ▶

groups of friends

la barra (bar) group of friends ◀ U, Arg ▶
Anoche fui al cine con mi barra. Last night I went to the movies with my group.

la basca, basquilla group of good friends ◀ Sp ▶
Los sábados salgo con la basca del barrio. I go out on Saturdays with the neighborhood crowd.

el combo, el parche group of friends ◀ Col ▶

el panal (honeycomb) long-term group of friends ◀ Ven, DR ▶

la peña (cliff) group of friends ◀ Sp ▶

pal, buddy

la cámara friend ◀ Col ▶

el/la cole (short for **colega**) colleague, friend, pal ◀ Mex, Sp ▶

el compa close male friend (from **compadre**) (Ch: **cumpa**) ◀ L. Am. ▶

el compi (short for **compinche**) pal ◀ Mex, Peru ▶

el compiche, cómplice (accomplice) friend ◀ Col, G, U ▶

el compinche (accomplice) friend, pal ◀ Mex, G, Nic, DR, PR, Col, Ven, Ec, S. Cone ▶
Soy bien compinche contigo. I'm really close friends with you.

el/la cuate(-a) good friend, pal ◀ Mex, C. Am. ▶
Paco es un buen cuate. Paco is a good pal.

el/la encubridor(a) (cover-upper) good old buddy, pal (ES: someone who covers for you) ◀ ES, Nic ▶

el/la hermano(-a) carnal(a) blood brother (sister), meaning close friend ◀ Mex, G, DR ▶

la llave (key) friend, connection (DR: **enllave**) ◀ Col, Ven ▶
Hola, mi llave, ¿qué tal? Hi, old buddy (for men)/my dear (for women), how's it going?

mi pana-burda my dear pal, my special buddy ◀ Ven ▶

mi yunta (yoke, as of oxen) my best friend (used by youth; Ch: only used by men) ◀ Mex, Cuba, Ec, Peru, Ch ▶
Tenía que traer a mi yunta para divertirme. I had to bring my best bud to have a good time.

el/la ñero(-a), ñis (short for **compañero[-a]**) buddy, pal ◀ Mex, Col ▶

el/la paisa short for **paisano** ◀ Mex, Col, G ▶
Mucho gusto, paisa. ¿Somos de la misma ciudad? Glad to meet you (fellow countryman or countrywoman). Are we from the same city?

el/la pana (male or female) friend, buddy, pal (from **panal**, honeycomb) ◀ DR, PR, Col, Ven, Ec ▶
Oye, mi pana, ¿qui úbo? Hey, my friend, what's happening?

el/la parcero(-a) friend, member of a certain group ◀ Col, Ec, Peru ▶

el/la socio(-a) (associate, member) friend, pal, often used in direct address (Cuba: masculine form only) ◀ Mex, Cuba, Col, Ch ▶

el vale male friend, guy (probably short for **valedor**, defender) ◀ chicano, Mex, Ven ▶

el valedor (defender) casual drinking buddy ◀ Mex, G, Col, Ven ▶

terms of endearment or address

bróder (from English "brother") friend, pal (PR: **bródel**) ◀ Ven, ES, Nic ▶

che friend, pal, used in direct address (Ch: an Argentinian) ◀ U, Arg ▶
¡Hola, che! (Arg) Hi, friend!
Vino un che a la fiesta. (Ch) An Argentinian came to the party.

chico(-a) (used in direct address) friend, pal ◀ Caribbean ▶
No es para tanto, chico. Things aren't really that bad, my dear!

chulis darling, my dear (between women) ◀ Mex, ES ▶

hombre (man) term of address for either a man or a woman ◀ L. Am., Sp ▶

macho term of endearment among males ◀ CR, Sp ▶
Venga, macho, invítame a una copa. (Sp) Hey, stud! Come here and invite me for a drink.

el/la mano(-a), manito(-a) forms of **hermano(-a)**, brother (sister), used for a close friend ◀ Mex, C. Am., DR, Col ▶
Hola, mana, ¿qué has hecho? Hi (dear). What have you been up to?

mi lic short for **mi licenciado**, a term of respect often used in jest ◀ Mex ▶

mi loco(-a) (my crazy one) my friend ◀ DR, Ec ▶
Hola, mi loco, ¿qué tal? Hey, fool, how ya doin'?

mi ñeco my friend ◀ Ec ▶

tío(-a) (uncle [aunt]) term of affection ◀ Col ▶

to be close

comer en el mismo plato (to eat out of the same plate) to be on very friendly terms ◀ Mex, G, ES, Ch ▶

comer en el mismo plato

ser uña y carne (to be fingernail and flesh) to be very close, bosom buddies ◀ L. Am., Sp ▶

ser uña y mugre (to be fingernail and dirt) to be tight (friends), like two peas in a pod ◀ Mex, Col, Ch ▶

fun

See also "dance," "invitations," "party."

A rumbear (tomar, tirar, etc.)... que el mundo se va a acabar. (Let's rumba [drink, have sex, etc.] ... since the world is going to end.) Hey, let's have a good time (drink, make love, etc.) because life is short. ◀ Ven ▶

¡Arriba el son! (Up with son [Cuban music]!) expression used to help create a festive mood ◀ Mex, Col ▶

la cascarita informal ball game ◀ Mex ▶
Se echaron una cascarita en la calle. They started a pickup ball game in the street.

la descarga (discharge, unloading) good time or jam session ◀ PR, Col, Cuba ▶

descargar (to discharge, unload) to jam (play music) ◀ Cuba, PR ▶

estar de coña to be joking ◀ Sp ▶

gufeao(-a) funny, amusing (from **gufón**, clown) ◀ PR ▶
Esa película está bien gufeá. Te la recomiendo. That movie is a laugh a minute. I highly recommend it.

hacer el viacrucis (to do the stations of the cross, a religious event) to go from bar to bar ◀ Sp ▶

irle a alguien el rollo (to have one's roll [probably of money] gone) to be into drugs, music, bars ◀ Sp ▶

jugar a taca-taca (to play bang-bang) to play an electronic game ◀ Peru, Bol, Ch ▶

la movida the action, the scene, fun ◀ most of L. Am., Sp ▶

la peli short for **película** ◄ Mex, DR, Sp ►

la película verde erotic (green) movie
◄ U, Arg, Sp ►

la puntada clever or cutting remark or something unusual and amusing that someone does; also **botarse la puntada**
◄ Mex, ES ►
Qué gran puntada la de cantar en la fiesta. What a hoot it was to do that singing at the party.

quitar lo bailado to take away what has been enjoyed (danced) ◄ L. Am., Sp ►
No se puede quitar lo bailado. The fun we have today nobody can take away from us.
Mañana tengo un examen y estoy aquí con este chico tan guapo. Bueno, ¡que me quiten lo bailado! Tomorrow I have an exam and here I am with this super handsome guy. Well, let them try to take what I'm enjoying away from me!

el relajo joke, diversion; uproar or confusion ◄ Mex, G, ES, Nic, DR, PR, Col, U, Sp ►

sonsacar to distract someone or get them to go out instead of doing their work ◄ Mex, G, ES, DR, PR ►
Ella es muy tranquila. Lo que pasa es que su hermana la sonsaca para que vaya a las discotecas. She is very quiet. What happens is that her sister gets her to go out dancing.
Iba a estudiar, pero pasaron unas amigas y me sonsacaron. I was going to study, but some friends came by and dragged me out for some fun.

trasnochar (to cross the night) to stay out or up late at night ◄ L. Am., Sp ►

el vacilón funny comment used to tease repeatedly ◄ Ven ►

amusing person

ser cachondo(-a) to be amusing, funny (vulgar) (note: **estar cachondo** means to be horny) ◄ Mex, Sp ►
Vendrá gente muy cachonda y lo pasaremos bien. (Mex) Some wild and crazy people will be coming and we'll have a good time.
Jaime es un cachondo total. (Sp) Jaime is a real wild man.

ser como payaso de circo (to be like a circus clown) to be silly ◄ Mex, ES ►

ser un vacilón

ser un plato (to be a dish) to be funny, amusing, a real character ◄ S. Cone ►
Es un plato ese tipo. That guy is a real character.

ser un rodeo (to be a rodeo) to be a cutup, amusing person ◄ G, Col ►

ser un vacilón to be a comic, entertaining person ◄ Mex, ES, CR, DR, PR, Sp ►
José es un vacilón, siempre contando chistes. José is a clown, always telling jokes.

el/la vacilador(-a) someone who enjoys life without working hard, someone who jokes or makes fun of others; also, someone who deceives others
◄ Mex, G, Cuba, ES, Col ►
No lo creas. ¡Qué vacilador! Don't believe him. What a nut!

bars, clubs

el antro dive, seedy bar or club ◄ Mex, U, Arg, Sp ►

el boliche nightclub for dancing; dive
◄ U, Arg ►
El viernes voy con los amigos a un boliche. Friday I'm going with some friends to a club.

el garito bar (usually small) (S. Cone: a place to gamble) ◄ Sp ►

la senda de elefantes (elephant paths) areas in a city where there are a lot of bars and one comes out **trompa** (trunk or drunk) ◄ Sp ►

el tugurio dive, bar (Col, CR: slum) ◄ DR, Ch ►

gadabout

la pata de perro (pata'eperro) (dog foot) gadabout, wanderer, person on the go, out and about ◀ Mex, Nic, DR, Peru, Bol, Arg, Ch ▶

el perrillo de todas bodas (little dog of all weddings) person who likes to be at all social events and parties ◀ Mex, Sp ▶

going out on the town

emparrandarse to go out on the town, party ◀ Mex, G, Col ▶

ir de juerga to go out on the town, party ◀ L. Am., Sp ▶
Anoche fui de juerga y ahora estoy muy cansada. Last night I went out on the town and now I'm very tired.

ir de parche to go out on the town ◀ Col ▶

ir de parranda to go out on the town, party ◀ L. Am., Sp ▶

irse de cachondeo to go out on the town (Mex: may imply to be on the prowl) ◀ Sp ▶
Se fueron de cachondeo y no llegaron hasta muy tarde. They went out on the town and didn't get back until very late.

irse (andar) de farra to go out on the town (Para, U, Arg: also, **farrear**) ◀ Col, Ec, S. Cone, Sp ▶
Me voy de farra esta noche. (Sp) I'm going out for a good time tonight.
A Lucy le gusta farrear. (Arg) Lucy likes to party.

irse (salir) de marcha to go out and have a good time ◀ Sp ▶

irse de rumba to go out for a good time ◀ Mex, Cuba ▶

having a good time

darse la buena (gran) vida (to give oneself the good [great] life) to live it up, enjoy oneself (Sp: **darse la vida padre**) ◀ Mex, DR, PR, S. Cone ▶
Yo quiero ganarme el premio de la lotería para darme la buena vida y no tener que trabajar. I want to win the prize in the lottery so I can live it up and won't have to work.

disfrutar a lo loco (to enjoy like crazy) to have a great time, have the time of one's life ◀ U, Arg ▶

divertirse a sus anchas (to enjoy oneself to one's widths) to enjoy oneself as much as possible ◀ L. Am., Sp ▶

echar relajo (to throw off or make a rumpus) to have a blast ◀ Mex, ES, Col ▶
Anoche echamos mucho relajo en la fiesta. Last night we had a blast at the party.

gozar a millón (to enjoy by million) to have a great time ◀ Col ▶

pasarla de peluche (to spend it like a stuffed toy) to have a great time ◀ Mex, ES ▶
¿Cómo te fue en la fiesta? —La pasamos de peluche. How'd it go at the party? —We had a great time.

pasarlo(-a) bien to have a good time ◀ L. Am., Sp ▶

pasarlo bomba (to spend it bomb) to have a good time ◀ Arg, Ch, Sp ▶
Siempre lo pasamos bomba aquí. We always have a blast here.

pasarlo caballo (regio) (to spend it horse [regal]) to have a great time, a blast ◀ Ch ▶

pasarlo chancho (to spend it pig) to have a great time, a blast ◀ Ch, Arg ▶

pasarlo en grande (to pass or spend it big) to have a great time (U, Arg: **pasarlo a lo grande**) ◀ U, Arg, Sp ▶

pasarlo pipa (to spend it pipe) to have a great time ◀ Sp ▶

pegarse la vida padre (to stick or fasten to oneself the father life) to live it up ◀ Sp ▶

tener un guiso (to have a stew) to have a party ◀ PR ▶

joking around

bachatear to relax, joke around ◀ PR ▶

bufear to clown around, have a good time; to tease, like **vacilar** ◀ DR, Col ▶

gufear to joke around, have a good time ◀ PR ▶

vacilar (to vacillate, go back and forth) to joke around, have a good time; to

Say it with slang!

Using last names for subtle criticism

Chileans sometimes spice up their descriptions of people by the subtle use of puns on common last names such as Miranda, Vivaceta, or Poblete. Someone sees several young guys watching a concert and asks, **¿Serán de la familia Miranda?** (Could they be from the Watcher family?) This means they are suspected of being gate crashers, those who "watch" (**mirar**) but don't pay. A new acquaintance is described as one of the Vivaceta even though that's not his last name because **una persona viva** is someone who takes advantage of others at the first opportunity. And if you are told that a particular woman is one of the Pobletes, despite all her talk about designer clothes, you'll know that she probably doesn't have much money at all since Poblete sounds a lot like **pobrete** (poor thing).

put someone on, tease ◀ Mex, C. Am., Col, Ven, Ec, Peru, Sp ▶
Nunca sé cuando habla en serio; siempre está vacilando. I never know when he's serious about what he's saying; he's always kidding around.
¡Vamos a vacilar! Let's enjoy ourselves!

vacilar con (alguien) to fool around with, have fun with (someone) ◀ Mex, G, Cuba, DR, Col, Pan ▶

practical jokes

la cachada trick, practical joke ◀ U, Arg ▶
Fernando me hizo una buena cachada. Fernando played a good practical joke on me.

la cargada (loaded one) joke, trick ◀ U, Arg ▶

la vacilada joke, trick ◀ Mex ▶

silliness

la bayuncada remark out of context; antic ◀ ES ▶
Como salgo siempre con bayuncadas, no me dieron el trabajo. Since I always come out with weird comments, they didn't give me the job.

el bufeo good time, joking around ◀ Mex, DR ▶

Jorgito, deja el bufeo que estoy hablando en serio. Jorgito, stop clowning around because I'm serious about what I'm saying.

la cantinflada (cantinflear) (a cantinflas thing, to cantinflas) nonsense or hot air (to speak a lot of nonsense or hot air without saying anything, the way the Mexican actor Cantinflas did in his satirical movies) ◀ L. Am. ▶

la guachafita humorous atmosphere, silliness, goofing around ◀ Ven ▶
La maestra les pidió a los alumnos que dejaran la guachafita. The teacher asked the students to stop goofing around.

el gufeo something fun or amusing ◀ PR ▶

la payasada (clown action) silly thing or action ◀ L. Am., Sp ▶

taking time off

See also "rest."

el día sándwich (sandwich day) day off between a weekend and a holiday ◀ Bol, S. Cone ▶
Este mes tenemos un día sándwich. Iré a la playa. This month we have a day off between the weekend and the holiday. I'll go to the beach.

hacer puente (to make bridge) to take a long weekend by taking a day off before or after a holiday ◀ Mex, DR, Sp ▶

San Lunes (Saint Monday) said when someone stays home from work after partying on the weekend as though Monday were a holiday ◀ Ch ▶

---

good

See also "good character," "perfection."

a las mil maravillas (to the thousand marvels) very good, excellent, perfectly ◀ L. Am., Sp ▶

buena onda (good sound wave) good deal or thing; good idea ◀ L. Am., Sp ▶
Fernando es muy buena onda. Fernando is a good guy.

chivo(-a) (goat) pretty, elegant, attractive (CR: **chiva** only, no masculine form) ◀ CR, ES ▶
una blusa chiva an elegant blouse
Bien chivo me quedó el vestido. The dress looked smart on me.
¡Qué chivo(-a)! How classy!

como los ángeles (like the angels) very good, excellent ◀ Mex, DR, Sp ▶

como una rosa (like a rose) perfectly, very good ◀ Sp ▶

con el pie derecho (with the right foot) in the right way, well ◀ Mex ▶

cuadrado(-a) (square) complete, perfect ◀ Mex ▶

entero(-a) (complete) pretty; good ◀ Mex, DR, PR, Col ▶

estar de buenas pulgas (to be of good fleas) to be in a good mood; also, **andar de** or **tener** ◀ CR, ES, Col, Arg, Ch, Sp ▶
Hoy anda de buenas pulgas. Today he (she) is in a good mood.

la flor y nata (flower and cream) the cream of the crop ◀ L. Am., Sp ▶

legal (legal) good, correct, right; good person ◀ Col, Mex, G, CR, DR, Ec, Ch, Sp ▶
Lo que dice Juan está legal. What Juan says is right.

mamey (a fruit) good, of quality ◀ Mex, Cuba, Col ▶
La rubia ésa está mamey. That blond is classy.

perderse de vista (to be lost from view) to be very superior; to be astute or clever (people or things) ◀ Sp ▶

pipiris nais highfalutin, chic (**nais** is from the English "nice") ◀ Mex, ES ▶

popis high-class (adj.) ◀ Mex, Col ▶

¡Qué amoroso(-a)! How sweet! How charmingly cute! (used by women) ◀ S. Cone ▶

¡Qué emoción! (What emotion!) expression of amazement, similar to How wonderful! ◀ Mex, DR, PR, Col, S. Cone ▶

¡Qué nota! (What a note!) How nice! ◀ Mex, Col ▶

recanchero(-a) original and charismatic (**re-** used to emphasize) ◀ U, Arg ▶

rico(-a) (rich) delicious (food); hot, sexy (Ch: **¡Qué rico!** is used for agreement) ◀ Mex, Col, Ch ▶

saber a gloria (to taste like glory) to be very pleasant ◀ Mex, CR, DR, Sp ▶

ser canela fina (to be fine cinnamon) to be of great worth, be fine (Peru: used mainly for girls or women) ◀ Mex, G, ES, Peru, Sp ▶

ser como Santa Elena, cada día más buena to be like Saint Helen, better every day ◀ ES ▶
¿Cómo estás? —Aquí como Santa Elena, cada día más buena. How are you? —Here just like Saint Helen, better every day.

ser mano de santo (to be the hand of a saint) to work like a charm ◀ Sp ▶

ser una obra maestra (to be a masterpiece) to be great, wonderful ◀ L. Am., Sp ▶

ser la octava maravilla to be the eighth wonder (of the world), said of things ◀ Mex, Peru, Bol, S. Cone, Sp ▶

servir lo mismo para un fregado que para un barrido (to serve for a scrubbing as for a sweeping) to be all-purpose; to serve for contrary uses ◀ Cuba, Sp ▶

suave (soft) good, nice, easy, pleasant (people and things) ◀ Mex, Cuba, Col ▶

tener buena sombra (to have good shade) to be pleasant, a good influence; to be lucky ◀ ES, Sp ▶

tener duende (to have elf) to have charm, be enchanting, mesmerizing (said of people or places that generate their own special attractive atmosphere) ◀ Peru, Sp ▶

tirar rostro (to throw face) to make a good impression ◀ ES ▶
En este carro andas tirando rostro aquí. In this car you're making a good impression here.
Prestáme tu carro para ir a tirar rostro en el colegio. Lend me your car so I can impress them at school.

fitting, suiting perfectly

bajado(-a) del cielo (brought down from heaven) perfect, excellent ◀ Mex, ES, DR, PR, Sp ▶

como anillo al dedo (like a ring on the finger) fitting, opportune, or appropriate ◀ L. Am., Sp ▶

como Dios manda (as God commands) in the proper way, perfectly, as it should be ◀ L. Am., Sp ▶
Lo vamos a hacer como Dios manda. We're going to do it good and proper (as it should be done).

de molde (of mold, form) fitting, perfectly ◀ Sp ▶

great, cool, awesome

a la pinta (to the spot) super, awesome ◀ Ch ▶

a toda madre (at all mother) full-blast, far-out, fantastic ◀ Mex, G, ES, Col ▶

a todas margaritas (at all daisies) fantastic, great ◀ Mex, ES ▶
Eres (Me caes) a todas margaritas. You're the best.

a todo dar (at all giving) great ◀ Mex, ES ▶

alucinante impressive, awesome ◀ Sp ▶

arrecho(-a) (sexually aroused, horny) good, well done (referring to some project or work), cool ◀ ES, Ven ▶
Los efectos especiales en esa película fueron arrechísimos. The special effects in that movie were awesome.

asombroso(-a) awesome ◀ Mex, ES ▶

bacán super, great ◀ Cuba, Col, Ec, Peru, S. Cone ▶
Es superbacán. It's super cool.

bacano(-a) good, excellent, generous ◀ DR, Col ▶

buena nota (good note) all right, good, great, cool (people or things) (Ven: also, high on drugs) ◀ CR, Ven ▶
¡Eres tan buena nota! You are so cool!

carga good, great ◀ CR ▶
¡Qué carga! Me saqué un 10 en el examen. How fabulous! I got an A (a 10) on the exam.
Manuel sí es carga. Me ayudó mucho. Manuel is really great. He helped me a lot.

chachi interesting, good, super ◀ Sp ▶

chévere great, fantastic ◀ most of L. Am.; most common in Caribbean, Col, Ven ▶
¿Vamos a un concierto de Carlos Vives? ¡Qué chévere! Es cheverísimo. We're going to a Carlos Vives concert? How cool! He's really awesome.

chicho(-a) good, nice, great ◀ Mex ▶
Se cree muy chicho. He thinks he's really cool.

chido(-a) great, super (perhaps from **chingón** or from **chic**) ◀ chicano, Mex, ES ▶
¿Qué es lo chido? Lo que vale la pena, lo divertido, lo congruente con la moda. What is considered "in"? Whatever is worth the trouble, whatever is fun, whatever is in step with the latest fad.

chido-uan (chido-one) super cool, super nice ◀ Mex ▶

chimba cool, super (also, female organ) ◀ Col ▶
¿Vas a salir con Tomás? ¡Qué chimba! You're going out with Tomás? How cool!
Mira el carro nuevo de Pedro; está la chimba. Look at Pedro's new car; it's the greatest.

cojonudo(-a) very good or admirable (vulgar) ◀ Sp ▶
Esa comida fue cojonuda. That meal was damn incredible.

dabuten, dabuti very good, great ◀ Sp ▶

de cine good, super (used like **de película**) ◀ Sp ▶

de miedo (scary, frightening) awesome, super ◀ Ch, Sp ▶
Me lo pasé de miedo en tu fiesta. I had a fantastic time at your party.

de película (like in a movie) great, fantastic ◀ Mex, DR, PR, C. Am., S. Cone, Sp ▶
Hola, Marisa. ¿Qué onda con los chavos? —De película. Hi, Marisa. How's it going with the guys? —Like a dream!

de pelos (of hairs) great, fantastic, good (like **de película**) ◀ Mex ▶

de peluche (used instead of **de película**; peluche means plush, like the fabric of stuffed toys) fantastic ◀ Mex, ES, DR, Col ▶

de perlas (of pearls) perfectly, great; often used with **caer** or **venir** ◀ most of L. Am., Sp ▶
Este dinero me vino de perlas. This money is great for me.
Esa blusa te cae de perlas. That blouse suits you to a "T."

de pinga, de pinguísima (of the male organ) great, exciting, fantastic (vulgar) ◀ Ven, DR ▶
¿'Ta la vaina? —¡De pinga, mi pana! How's life? —Havin' one hell of a good time, pal!

del carajo (of the male organ) super, fantastic, great(ly) (vulgar) ◀ DR, PR, Col, Ven ▶
Esa muchacha es del carajo. That girl is damn fantastic.
Hay que divertirse del carajo. (PR) We have to have a damn good time.

del putas (of the whores) excellent, the best (vulgar) ◀ Col ▶
Tu nuevo Mercedes es del putas. Your new Mercedes is the max.

del uno (of the one) super, great ◀ Ch ▶

el descueve (uncaving) super, fantastic (vulgar) ◀ Ch ▶

divis-divis divine, marvelous (an exaggeratedly feminine expression that may be said ironically or in jest, like "Simply divine, dahling!") ◀ Mex ▶

fenomenal (phenomenal) great, super ◀ S. Cone, Sp ▶

filete (fillet) very good, excellent ◀ Mex, DR, PR ▶

fino(-a) (fine) great, cool, fantastic ◀ Ven ▶
'Ta fino. ¡Qué fino! It's great! How cool!

fuera de serie (out of series) extraordinary, outstanding; (n.) outstanding person ◀ L. Am., Sp ▶
Ese chico es un fuera de serie; siempre saca «excelentes» en todo. That guy is outstanding; he always gets "excellent" in everything.

guay great, super, cool (same in the feminine as in the masculine); also, **guay del Paraguay** and **ir de guay** (to act cool) ◀ Sp ▶
Adela es una chica muy guay. Es guay del Paraguay. Adela is a real cool chick. She's the coolest.

macanudo(-a) (probably from the Dominican cigar or from the Argentine liar, Sr. Macana) awesome, super ◀ Nic, S. Cone ▶

maldito(-a) (cursed) great, good ◀ Bol, Peru ▶

matador(-a) fabulous, wonderful ◀ Mex, Col, U ▶
Tiene un sentido de humor matador. He has a sense of humor to die for.

morrocotudo(-a) great, fantastic ◀ Mex, DR ▶

mortadela great, good; (n.) pretty girl ◀ Ec ▶

la muerte (death) excellent, incredible, super ◀ S. Cone ▶

ñien (good, well, variant of **bien**) good, cool ◀ Ven ▶

nítido(-a) (clear, bright) great, perfect, correct, very acceptable ◀ Pan, Caribbean ▶

nitidón, nitidona augmentative of **nítido(-a)**, great ◀ Mex, PR, Col ▶

padre, padrísimo(-a) (father, very father) fantastic, super ◀ Mex ▶
Su casa es padrísima. Their house is fantastic.
¡Qué padre! How terrific!

padrote good ◀Mex▶

pleno(-a) (full, complete) good, great, good-looking; also, high on drugs ◀Col, Ec, Para▶
Se siente bien pleno. He feels great.

por encima (on top of) very good ◀Cuba, Col▶

primordial (essential) terrific ◀Col▶

pura vida (pure life) great, nice, fantastic ◀CR▶
¡Pura vida! Riding the wave! Great! (Used as positive response in many kinds of situations.)
Esa mujer es pura vida. That woman is the most.

puta madre (mother whore) very good, great (vulgar) ◀Sp▶
Esta comida es de puta madre. This is one hell of a good meal.
Esos pantalones te sientan de puta madre. Those slacks look damn good on you.
Todo va puta madre. Everything is going damn well.

redondo(-a) (round) complete, perfect ◀U, Arg, Sp▶
El viaje salió redondo. The trip turned out like a perfect dream.

regio(-a) (regal, royal) great, beautiful, super ◀Nic, Col, Ec, S. Cone▶

salvaje (savage) affected (**cuico**) talk for fabulous, super ◀Ch▶

ser una joya (to be a jewel) to be perfect, good ◀parts of L. Am.▶

ser lo máximo to be fantastic, the greatest, the best (the maximum) ◀L. Am.▶
¡Esta música es lo máximo! This music is the best!

ser una perla (to be a pearl) to be perfect, good ◀ES, Sp▶
Esta chica es una perla; cocina muy bien. This girl is a jewel; she cooks very well.

ser una soda (to be a soda) to be terrific ◀Col▶
¡Qué lugar más simpático! —**De veras, es una soda.** What a charming place! —It's really terrific.

ser un siete (to be a seven, from high mark in school) to be the best, a ten ◀Ch▶

ser la tapa to be tops ◀CR▶
El equipo de Alajuela es la tapa. Alajuela's team is tops.

sollado(-a) (referring to a deck of a ship) good, first-class ◀Col▶

soplado(-a) good, excellent (people or things) (Cuba: also, in a hurry) ◀Cuba, Col▶
Tu nueva bici está soplada. Your new bicycle is far-out!

la taquilla (ticket window) person or thing considered very cool at the moment (a singer, TV program, etc.), fad ◀Ch▶

taquillero(-a) (box office; [adj.] sometimes meaning good box office) cool, "in" ◀S. Cone▶
actor taquillero hot (popular) actor
cosa taquillera "in" thing

el top (from English) the best ◀Ch▶

tuanis great, nice, healthy, too nice; also, a greeting among young people (ES, Nic: **tuani**) ◀G, CR▶
¿Qué tal el viaje? —**¡Tuanis!** How was the trip? —Great!

uva (grape) good ◀DR, PR▶
Esa comida te quedó uva. ¿Cómo la hiciste? Your food turned out marvelously. How did you do it?

vientos, vientísimos (**viento** instead of **bien-to**) great, super; also, **vientos huracanados** (hurricane winds) ◀Mex▶

perking things up

Esto resucita a un muerto. (This brings the dead back to life.) This livens, perks (a person, things) up. ◀U, Arg, Sp▶

ser levanta muertos (to be a raiser of the dead) to perk or liven things (or someone) up ◀Mex, Nic, U, Arg▶
Esta sopa es levanta muertos. This soup perks me right up.

"with it"

en la movida, en la onda, a la moda, actualizado(-a) "with it" ◀Mex, PR, Col, Sp▶

estar de onda to be "in," cool, "with it" (Ch: **en onda**) ◀Mex, ES, Col, U, Arg▶

hacer furor   (to make a furor) to be very much in fashion ◀ most of L. Am., Sp ▶

lo propio (y lo chimbo)   what's "in" (and what's "out") ◀ Ven ▶

good character

See also "good," "patience."

buena gente   (good people) nice, kind person or people ◀ L. Am., Sp ▶
Lola es muy buena gente. Lola is a really nice person.

cálida   nice, kind ◀ Mex, Col, G ▶

choro(-a)   (mussel) very brave, daring, admirable ◀ Bol, Ch ▶
¡Qué chora es María! Sacó adelante a su familia. What a trooper María is! She helped her family get ahead.

de pura cepa   (of pure stock) genuine (said of people) ◀ most of L. Am., Sp ▶

feliciano(-a)   tolerant, easygoing ◀ Cuba, Col ▶

madre   (mother) used like **buena gente** ◀ Col ▶

panetela   (adj.) good, kind, nice ◀ Cuba ▶
Roberto es panetela; siempre me ayuda. Roberto is kind; he always helps me out.

Pobre pero caballero.   Poor but dignified (a gentleman). (Sp: **Pobre pero honrado.**) ◀ L. Am. ▶

el santito   (little saint) good boy (sometimes said sarcastically) ◀ ES, DR, Col, U, Arg ▶

santo(-a) y bueno(-a)   (holy and good) great ◀ Mex, PR, Col ▶

ser un bacalao   (to be a codfish) to be an agreeable person ◀ Col ▶
Felipe es un bacalao; me ayudó mucho en la clase de geometría. Felipe is a pleasant guy; he helped me a lot in geometry class.

ser un caramelo   (to be a caramel) to be nice, kind, a sweet person ◀ Mex, G, Cuba, Col ▶

La nueva novia de Hernando es un caramelito. Hernando's new girlfriend is a real sweetie.

ser un dulce (un bombón)   to be a sweet (bonbon) ◀ Mex ▶
Esa niña es un dulce (bombón). That girl is a sweetheart.

ser más bueno que el pan   (to be better than bread) to be as good as gold ◀ most of L. Am., Sp ▶
Ese niño es más bueno que el pan. That boy is as good as gold.

ser un pan   (to be a loaf of bread) to be kind, not selfish ◀ Mex, Cuba, DR ▶

ser (un) pan de Dios   (to be God's bread) to be good, good-natured ◀ ES, DR, U, Ch ▶
El chofer del bus es un pan de Dios. Siempre espera que entre a la casa antes de irse. The bus driver is an angel. He always waits until I get in the house before leaving.

ser un pedazo de pan   (to be a piece of bread) to be affable, good-natured ◀ DR, PR, U, Arg, Sp ▶

el sobaco de la confianza   (the armpit of confidence) absolute trust or confidentiality ◀ Nic ▶
Te voy a hablar en el sobaco de la confianza. I'm going to talk to you in complete confidence.
Los amigos que van a estar en la cena son el sobaco de la confianza. The friends who are coming to the party are absolutely trustworthy.

tener ángel   to have that special something (charm) (ES: to be a good person) ◀ Mex, ES, Col ▶

tener buena vibración   (to have good vibration) to give good vibes, inspire confidence ◀ Mex, Sp ▶
Me encanta platicar con Elenita. Tiene buenas vibraciones. I adore talking with Elenita. She has good vibes.

tener un corazón de oro   to have a heart of gold ◀ L. Am., Sp ▶

tener madera   (to have wood) to have good or a strong character ◀ Mex, Col, Sp ▶
Elizabeth tiene mucha madera. Elizabeth is made of the right stuff.

good-byes

See also "departure."

abrirse   (to open) to break up (a relationship, business or social)   ◀ S. Cone ▶
Después de la muerte de su hijo, se abrieron. After the death of their son, they broke up.

correr   (to run) to run (someone) out, to fire   ◀ Mex, C. Am., U, Arg ▶
Lo corrieron porque no trabajaba bien. They fired him because he wasn't working well.
Los corrieron de la casa porque hacían mucha bulla. They kicked them out of the house because they made too much of a ruckus.

cortar   (to cut) to hang up (the phone)   ◀ L. Am., Sp ▶
Tengo que cortar. Mamá quiere usar el teléfono. I have to hang up. Mom wants to use the phone.

dar el boleto   (to give the ticket) to throw someone out, give them their walking papers (Sp: **dar la boleta**)   ◀ Mex, ES ▶
Mónica le dio el boleto a su novio. Mónica gave her boyfriend his walking papers.

dar pasaporte a alguien   (to give someone passport) to break off with someone   ◀ Mex, ES, Sp ▶

echar a alguien a escobazos   to throw someone out (with sweeps of a broom)   ◀ Mex, Sp ▶

enterrar a alguien   (to bury someone) to break off with someone for good   ◀ Mex, Cuba, DR, U, Arg ▶
No me hables más de Juan Carlos, que ya lo enterré con flores. Don't talk to me anymore about Juan Carlos. I've put him out of my mind for good.

hacerle la cruz a alguien   (to make the cross to someone) to write someone off   ◀ S. Cone ▶

romper con alguien   to break up with someone   ◀ L. Am., Sp ▶

¿Por qué rompiste con Felipe? Why did you break up with Felipe?

Bye.

Ahí nos vidrios.   (We'll see each other there; but **vidrios**, pieces of glass, instead of **vemos**.) See you. (Mex, Ec: also, **Los vidrios.**)   ◀ Mex, G, Hond, ES, CR, Ven, Ec, Peru ▶

¡Calabaza!   (Pumpkin!) The party's over! Time to go! (from the phrase **¡Calabaza, calabaza, cada uno** [or **cada quien**] **para su casa!**)   ◀ Ch, ES ▶

Chao, mano.   (from the Italian "ciao") Bye, friend.   ◀ Mex, DR, PR, Col ▶

Chao, pesca'o.   (Bye, fish.) comic way of saying good-bye, like See you later, alligator!   ◀ Ven ▶

Chau, chau.   (from the Italian "ciao") Bye-bye.   ◀ S. Cone ▶

Hasta que nos topemos.   Until we run into each other again.   ◀ Mex, G, ES, Col, Ec ▶

Le lukeo. (Le luqueo.)   See you.   ◀ Ec ▶

Nos wachamos.   (We'll see each other.) See you. (from the English "to watch")   ◀ chicano ▶

Que lo pase(s) bien.   (May you spend it well.) Have a good day (time). Have a good one. (said to someone who is leaving or about to leave)   ◀ L. Am., Sp ▶

Que te (le, les) vaya bien.   May all go well with you. Have a nice day. (to someone who is leaving)   ◀ L. Am., Sp ▶

Te pillo mañana.   Catch you tomorrow.   ◀ Cuba ▶

Venga.   way of ending conversation on the phone; also, often used instead of **vale**   ◀ Sp ▶

Scram!

¡Buen viaje!   (Have a good trip!) Good riddance! (for people or things)   ◀ Mex, U, Arg, Sp ▶

¡Piérdete!   (Lose yourself!) Go away! Get lost! Scram!   ◀ Sp ▶

Píntate (de colores).   (Paint yourself [in color].) Go away.   ◀ Mex, ES ▶

¡Zafa! Get out of here! ◀PR▶
¿Yo? ¿Novia de Hugo? ¡Zafa! Ese tipo es un sanano. Me? Hugo's girlfriend? Get out of here! That guy is a dope.

¡Záfate! Go away! ◀Mex, G, ES, Col▶

¡Zape! Shoo! Go away! ◀DR, PR, Col▶
¡Zape, gato! Señora, llévese a este gato, por favor, que soy alérgico. Shoo, kitty! Ma'am, take this cat out of here please. I'm allergic.

gossip

See also "conversation," "information."

andar de boca en boca to travel by word of mouth (from mouth to mouth), be common knowledge ◀L. Am., Sp▶

copuchar (to puff up cheeks) to gossip (also, **copuchear**) ◀Bol, Ch▶
Estaban allí copuchando toda la tarde. You guys were there gossiping the whole afternoon.

correrse (to be run) to be said, rumored ◀Mex, G, Cuba, Sp▶
Se corre que tiene novia. There's a rumor going around that he has a girlfriend.

copuchar

el cotorreo gab session ◀Mex, ES, DR, Col▶

estar con (tener) las antenas puestas (to be with [have] one's antenna up) to be listening (and ready for gossip) ◀Mex, DR, ES, U, Arg, Sp▶
Habla bajito que por ahí viene Elena, que siempre tiene las antenas puestas. Pipe down! Here comes Elena, and she always has her ears pricked up (for the latest gossip).

hociconear (to snout) to shoot off one's mouth ◀Ch▶

La ropa sucia se lava en casa. (Dirty clothes are washed at home.) Let's not air the dirty laundry in public. ◀Mex, ES, S. Cone, Sp▶

meter el hocico en todo to stick one's nose (literally, mouth) into everything ◀Mex, DR, Sp▶

montar un cotorreo (to set up a parroting) to start a gab session ◀Mex, ES, DR, Col▶

el radio macuto nonexistent radio station from which rumors or falsehoods are supposedly broadcast ◀Sp▶

sacar los trapos al sol (to take the rags or clothes out into the sun) to give someone the lowdown, air the dirty laundry ◀L. Am., Sp▶
Saca los trapos al sol, Matilde. ¿Qué pasó entre Juan y Julia? Out with it, Matilde. What went on between Juan and Julia?

busybody, blabbermouth

bocachón, bocachona (big mouth) with a big mouth, blabbermouth ◀U, Arg▶

el bocón, la bocona big mouth, someone who speaks indiscreetly, gossip ◀Mex, ES, Nic, CR, PR, Col, Arg▶
No seas bocón. Don't be a blabbermouth.

chambroso(-a) given to gossip ◀Mex, ES▶

chute nosy, putting one's nose into everything (G: **shute**) ◀Mex, ES▶
Jorge es bien chute; se mete en todo. Jorge is a real busybody; he sticks his nose into everybody's business.

Say it with slang!

Reverse syllables and be cool!

A bus stop in Mexico at 4:30 in the afternoon. Two students are on their way home from high school.

—Por aquí pasa el **mionca**, ¿no?
—Sí, pero hace **lorca**. Vamos a tomar algo **ofri**.

What strange words they are using: **mionca, lorca, ofri**! Could these be from an Indian language? Not at all. This is a way young people have of speaking Spanish by breaking apart common words and reversing the syllables. Look at **mion-ca, lor-ca, o-fri**, and then turn the words around to see the familiar words: **camión, calor, frío** (bus or truck, heat, cold). Be cool, and see if you can figure out this conversation between two Ecuadorean students. (A translation is given on page 264.)

—¿Qué pasa, **mopri**? ¿Cómo estás?
—¡Bacán! Voy a ver a mi **jermu**.
—Te acompaño hasta la tienda de la **esnaqui**.

---

el/la copuchento(-a) gossip ◄ Bol, Ch ►

el/la cotilla person who gossips ◄ Sp ►

el/la embelequero(-a) busybody ◄ G, Cuba ►

el hocicón, la hocicona (big mouth) loudmouth, gossip ◄ Mex, C. Am., Col, Ch ►

el/la lengua larga (long tongue) someone who reveals too much ◄ Mex, ES, CR, DR, Col, U, Arg, Sp ►
No le contés eso, que éste es un lengua larga. (ES) Don't tell him that because he has a big mouth.

las malas lenguas (bad tongues) rumormongers, gossipers ◄ L. Am., Sp ►
Dicen las malas lenguas que maltrataba a sus empleados. According to the rumor mill, he (she) mistreated his (her) employees.

el metelón, la metelona busybody ◄ Mex ►

el/la métepatas (stick-your-foot-in) busybody ◄ Sp ►

metiche nosy; busybody, buttinsky ◄ Mex, G, Nic, CR, DR, PR, Col ►

el/la metido(-a) busybody (**entrometido**) ◄ Mex, C. Am., DR, PR, Col, U, Arg ►

el/la presentado(-a) (introduced) busybody ◄ PR ►

ser un bocazas (to be a big mouth) to talk too much and say things that shouldn't be said ◄ Sp ►
Eres un bocazas. ¿Por qué le dijiste a mi padre que salgo con Mónica? You're a blabbermouth. Why did you tell my father that I'm going out with Mónica?

trompudo(-a) with a big mouth ◄ Mex, G, ES, CR, Col ►

rumors

la bola gossip, rumor ◄ G, ES, CR, Cuba, DR, U, Arg ►
¿Tú crees de verdad que ella dijo eso? A lo mejor es una bola. You really believe that she said that? It's probably just a piece of gossip.
La bola se regó por toda la oficina. The rumor went around the whole office.

el chambre gossip ◀ ES ▶
María ya viene con el chambre. Here comes María already with the gossip.

la copucha gossip ◀ Ch ▶

el cuento de viejas old wives' tale ◀ most of L. Am., Sp ▶

los chismorreos gossip ◀ most of L. Am., Sp ▶
¿Que yo salgo con Enrique? ¡Puros chismorreos! So I'm going out with Enrique? Pure gossip!

el mitote (from **mito**, myth) gossip, rumor ◀ chicano, Mex ▶

el rin rin gossip ◀ Col ▶

greetings

See also "attention: attracting someone's attention."

¿'Tá la vaina? (How's the thing?) How's everything? What's up? ◀ Ven ▶

Buenas. (Good.) Good afternoon/evening. ◀ L. Am., Sp ▶

Dichosos los ojos que te están viendo (que te ven). (Fortunate the eyes that are looking at you.) Great to see you. Also, **Dichosos los ojos.** ◀ L. Am., Sp ▶

Entre nomás. (Enter already.) C'mon in. ◀ Ch ▶

¡Estás como lo recetó el doctor! You're just what the doctor ordered! (can be a street compliment) ◀ Mex, ES, DR, Col, S. Cone ▶

¡Estás como quieres! (You are like you want to be!) You look great! ◀ Mex, ES, DR, Sp ▶

¡Ideay! interjection meaning What's happening?, How's it going?, from **¿Y de ahí?** ◀ G, ES, Nic ▶
¡Ideay! ¿Qué pasa? How's it going? What's happening?

La casa es chica, el corazón grande. (The house is small, the heart large.) My humble home is yours. Make yourself at home. (similar to the expression **Estás en tu casa.**) ◀ S. Cone ▶

¡Mera mano! phrase meaning **¡Oye tú, amigo!** Hey, pal! ◀ Col ▶

Óyeme manito. term of affection used to call a friend ◀ Mex, G, ES, Col ▶

¡Qué uvas! (What grapes!) Hi! (sounds like **¡Qui úbo!**) ◀ Mex, Ec ▶

¡Qui úbole!, ¡Qui úbo! a greeting, like **¡Hola!** ◀ most of L. Am. ▶

Ya apareció (el) peine. (Now a [the] comb showed up.) greeting for a person who has been missing, like a comb that always gets misplaced ◀ ES, Nic ▶

answering "how are you?"

See also "bad," "exhaustion," "good," "health."

Aquí nomás. ([I'm] Just here.) Nothing is new. ◀ Mex, C. Am. ▶

Aquí pasándola. (Por aquí pasándola.) (Passing it here.) Just getting along, so-so. ◀ Mex, ES, Col, U, Arg ▶
¿Qué has hecho? —Por aquí, pasándola. What have you been up to? —Same as usual, just getting along.

arrastrando la cobija (dragging the blanket) dragging along, just getting by ◀ Mex, ES, Col ▶

como las huevas (güeas) (like testicles) like crap, lousy (vulgar) ◀ Ch ▶

dos que tres (two that three) so-so, not all that great ◀ Mex, G, ES ▶
¿Cómo estás? —Por ay, dos que tres. How are you doing? —So-so, not that great.

estar como la mona (to be like the she-monkey) to be feeling really bad (physically or mentally), be under the weather ◀ U, Ch ▶

Estoy que me caigo. (I'm about to fall over.) I'm in bad shape (not well). ◀ U, Arg, Sp ▶

Más o menos. (More or less.) OK. ◀ L. Am., Sp ▶

No llueve pero gotea. (It's not raining but it's dripping.) Things are going OK, not as bad as it could be. ◀ Ch ▶

Por aquí (trabajando, estudiando). ([I'm] Just here [working, studying].) Nothing is new. ◀ L. Am., Sp ▶

Por aquí, vagando. (Just here, wandering.) I'm just goofing around. ◀ C. Am. ▶

Siempre pa'lante. (Always forward.) I'm plugging along. ◀ DR, PR, Col, Ven ▶

Tirando. (Pulling.) Hanging in, getting along. ◀ U, Arg, Sp ▶
¿Qué tal? ¿Cómo estás? —Tirando. Vamos tirando. What's up? How are you? —Hanging in there.

Todo marchando. (Everything's marching.) Everything's fine, OK. ◀ Col ▶
¿Cómo estás, Claudia? —Todo marchando. How are you, Claudia? —Everything's fine.

Todo pasando. (Everything moving along.) Everything's going fine. ◀ Ch ▶

answering the telephone

¿A ver? (To see?) phrase for answering the phone ◀ Nic, CR, Hond, Col ▶

Aló. (Hello.) common way of answering the telephone ◀ most of L. Am. ▶

Bueno. (Good.) normal way of answering the telephone ◀ Mex ▶

Diga. Dígame. (Tell. Tell me.) normal way of answering the telephone ◀ Sp ▶

¡Hola! (Hello.) normal way of answering the telephone ◀ U, Arg ▶

Oigo. (I'm hearing.) way of answering the phone ◀ Cuba ▶

¿Quién es? (Who is it?) common way of answering the phone ◀ Col, Sp ▶

asking how things are

¿Cómo está la movida? How's the action? ◀ parts of L. Am. ▶

¿Cómo le baila? (How's it dancing to you?) What's up? ◀ Ch ▶

¿Cómo lo llevas? (How do you carry it?) How are things? ◀ Mex, Sp ▶

¿Cómo te ha ido? (How has it gone for you?) How have you been? ◀ L. Am., Sp ▶

¿Cómo te va? (How's it going for you?) How are you? ◀ L. Am., Sp ▶

¿En qué patín andas? (What skate are you on?) How are things? ◀ Mex, G, Ec ▶

¿Qué bolá? What's up? ◀ Cuba ▶

¿Qué jue? What's up? ◀ Mex, Col ▶

¿Qué onda(s)? (What sound wave[s]?) What's happening? ◀ L. Am. ▶

¿Qué pasa, panita? (What's happening, old buddy? [panita means good friend, male or female]) How ya doin', my friend? ◀ Ven ▶

¿Qué pasión? variant of ¿Qué pasó? ◀ Mex ▶

¿Qué pedo? (What fart?) youth slang for ¿Qué pasa? (vulgar) ◀ Mex, ES ▶

¿Qué se teje? (What's being knitted?) How's it going? What's up? ◀ Ch ▶

¿Qué tal? How are things? ◀ L. Am., Sp ▶

¿Qué tal andas? How are things? ◀ Mex, Sp ▶

shaking hands

¡Chócala! (Hit it!) Put it here! (said in greeting before a handshake) ◀ Mex, DR, PR, Col, U, Sp ▶
¡Chócala, mi hermano! ¿Cómo estás? Put 'er there, bro'! How're you doing?

Dame. Give me. (implies Give me five.) ◀ Mex, Col ▶

Dame cinco dedos. Give me five (fingers). ◀ Mex ▶

guys, girls, kids

See also "people."

girls

la chamita girl; girlfriend ◀ Col, Ec ▶

la chavala girl (Sp: a bit old-fashioned) ◀ Mex, G, ES, Nic, CR, Sp ▶

el cuero (skin, leather) girl, woman; pretty woman (a bit vulgar, especially in Chile where it can be a come-on) ◀ ES, Col, Ec, Peru, Ch ▶
Tomás sale con un cuero de la capital. Tomás is going out with a chick from the capital.

la guial, guialcita chick, babe, woman ◀ Pan ▶

la guriza young girl ◀ U, northern Arg ▶

la jaina broad, woman ◀ chicano ▶

la jeva girl, girlfriend, woman ◀ Nic, Cuba, DR, PR, Ven, Ec ▶
¿Cómo se llama la jeva del vestido verde? What's the name of the babe in the green dress?

la mina (mine, from the Argentine Lunfardo dialect used in tangos) girl, woman (Ch: **el mino** is also used for a hunk) ◀ S. Am., especially Col, Ec, S. Cone ▶
¿Quién es esa mina? —Se llama Laura. Who's that chick? —Her name is Laura.

la pava (turkey hen) girl, woman ◀ Col, Ven ▶
Esa pava es superbuena. That chick is far-out.

la piel (skin) girl (like **cuero**) ◀ Col, Ec ▶

la potranca (female horse) pretty girl ◀ Mex, DR, Col ▶
Mi potranca y yo fuimos de compras a la tienda. My filly and I went to the store to shop.

la ruca girl, woman (Mex, G: often an older and unattractive woman) ◀ L. Am. (not S. Cone) ▶

seño short for **señorita** or **señora** (DR: used for **profesora**) ◀ Mex, G, DR, Col ▶

guys

el buay guy ◀ Pan ▶

el carambas young person, guy (Col: just anyone, not young) ◀ CR, Col ▶
Ese carambas sabe tocar la guitarra muy bien. That guy can play a guitar very well.

el chavalo guy, boy ◀ chicano, Mex, C. Am. ▶

el compadrito (little pal) young hustler, guy from mean streets ◀ Arg ▶

el gallo (rooster) man, guy (Ch: also, **galla**, gal) ◀ Cuba, DR, PR, Peru, Ch ▶

Ese gallo allí vive en mi barrio. That guy over there lives in my neighborhood.

el guri young boy ◀ U, northern Arg ▶

el maestro (teacher, master) middle-aged or older man, guy ◀ L. Am., Sp ▶

el tipo (type) guy, fellow ◀ L. Am. ▶

el vato (bato) guy, dude ◀ chicano, Mex ▶
Oye, bato, ¿por qué no vamos a echar una copa? Hey, dude, why don't we go have us a drink?

guys (girls)

el/la chamo(-a) guy (girl) (Cuba: **la chama** only) ◀ Col, Ven ▶

el/la chavo(-a) boy (girl) (Nic: **los chavos** are **los novios**, boyfriend and girlfriend) ◀ chicano, Mex, G, ES, Col ▶
No conozco a ese chavo. I don't know that boy.

el/la cipote(-a) young person ◀ G, ES, Hond, Nic ▶
¿Están aquí los cipotes? —No, están en la escuela. Are the kids here? —Nope, they're at school.

el/la loco(-a) (crazy person) guy (girl) ◀ Col, Ven, Ec ▶
¿Quién es esa loca allí? Who's that gal over there?

el/la man guy (girl) (Col: **el man** only) ◀ Col, Ec ▶

el/la ñato(-a) guy, gal (not pejorative, similar to **tipo[-a]**) ◀ Arg, Ch ▶
¿Quién es ese ñato que siempre anda por aquí? Who's that guy who's always hanging around here?
Vino la ñata ésa de la casa de enfrente. The chick from the house across the street came.

ñor, ñora short for **señor, señora** ◀ Mex, Col ▶

el/la patojo(-a) guy (girl) ◀ G, Col ▶

el/la pendex boy (girl); childish person (vulgar) ◀ Arg, Ch ▶

el/la pollo(-a) (chicken) young person (Nic, CR: **polla** is a girl) ◀ Mex, G, Cuba, CR, Col ▶
Ese muchacho está muy pollo para mí. (Col) That boy is very young for me.

el tío, la tía (uncle [aunt]) guy, fellow (gal, woman) ◀ Ch, Sp ▶

kids

el/la bicho(-a) (bug, beast) kid (Sp: implies naughtiness) ◀ ES, Sp ▶
Es un bicho; no para de tocar cosas. He's a kid; he never stops touching things.

el buqui kid, young person ◀ chicano ▶
¿Conoces el conjunto «Los bukis»? Me gusta mucho su música. Do you know the group called "The Kids"? I like their music a lot.

el/la cabro(-a) (goat) kid ◀ Peru, Ch ▶

el/la cachorro(-a) (puppy) kid ◀ chicano, Mex, Col ▶

el/la carajillo(-a) (diminutive of **carajo**, vulgar) boy (girl), adolescent, young person ◀ Nic, CR ▶
El carajillo anda en la escuela. The boy's at school right now.

el/la carajito(-a) (diminutive of **carajo**, vulgar) boy (girl), adolescent, young person ◀ DR, Ven ▶

el/la chamaco(-a) young person (also, **chamaquito[-a]**) ◀ chicano, Mex, ES, CR, Cuba, PR ▶
Los chamacos fueron al campo con sus abuelos. The young people went to the country with their grandparents.

el chango (monkey) young person (pejorative, implying ugliness) ◀ Mex ▶

el/la chavito(-a) diminutive of **chavo(-a)** ◀ chicano, Mex, G, ES ▶

el/la chibolo(-a) (ball) boy (girl), kid ◀ Peru ▶

el/la chicoco(-a) boy (girl), child ◀ Ch ▶

el/la chilpayate(-a) kid, young person ◀ Mex ▶

el chiquilín, la chiquilina kid, young person ◀ U, Arg ▶

el chiquitín, la chiquitina kid, small child ◀ most of L. Am., Sp ▶
Vamos a llevar a los chiquitines al parque. Let's take the kids to the park.

el/la chiris child ◀ G ▶

el/la escuintle(-a) twerp, insignificant person or kid, from the Náhuatl word for hairless dog (also spelled **escuincle**) ◀ Mex, parts of C. Am. ▶

¿Por qué te da miedo? Es un escuincle. Why are you afraid of him? He's just a little twerp.

el guambra kid ◀ Ec ▶

el/la güila kid, baby ◀ CR ▶

el güiro (gourd, musical instrument made of a gourd) child ◀ G ▶

el/la lolo(-a) (probably from "Lolita" by Vladimir Nabokov) teen, cool young person ◀ Ch ▶

el/la mocoso(-a) (with a runny nose) kid ◀ L. Am., Sp ▶

el/la morro(-a), morrito(-a) young person, kid (Mex: **morra** is girl) ◀ ES ▶
Su morra es muy chavalita. Your daughter is very small.

el/la nene(-a) used instead of **niño(-a)** ◀ Mex, G, PR, Col, U, Arg, Para, Sp ▶

el/la pendejo(-a) (pubic hair, vulgar and offensive in many places) kid, child ◀ Arg ▶

el/la pibe(-a) kid, young person ◀ Col, Ven, U, Arg ▶

el/la piojo(-a) chico(-a) (little flea) kid ◀ Ch ▶

happiness

como niño con juguete nuevo (like a kid with a new toy) happy, like a kid in a candy store ◀ Mex, ES, U, Arg ▶
como niño con zapatos nuevos (like a kid with new shoes) happy, like a kid in a candy store ◀ Mex, ES, DR, U, Ch, Sp ▶
copado(-a), recopado(-a) (cupped, trophied) overwhelmed (usually with joy or a positive emotion), happy, fantastic ◀ Arg ▶
¡Qué lindo regalo! Estoy copada. What a lovely gift! I'm overwhelmed.
Han llegado los nietos y los abuelos están copados. The grandchildren have arrived and their grandparents are in heaven.
¿Cómo estás, Naldo? —¡Recopado! How are you, Naldo? —Fantastic!

dar saltos de alegría

estar loco(-a) de contento (to be crazy with happiness) to be very happy, ecstatic ◀DR, Sp▶

feliz como una lombriz happy as a lark (worm) ◀most of L. Am., Sp▶

la gente del bronce (bronze, tan people) happy, carefree people ◀Sp▶

¡Juepa! expression of happiness ◀Col▶

no caber de contento (to not contain oneself with happiness) to feel very happy ◀Mex, ES, Peru, U, Arg, Sp▶
Don Alonso no cabía en sí de contento con el título de su hijo. Don Alonso could scarcely contain his excitement about his son getting his degree.

ser un cachondo mental to be happy, agreeable, funny (vulgar) ◀Sp▶

dar saltos de alegría (to give jumps of happiness) to jump for joy ◀Mex, ES, PR, U, Arg, Sp▶
Con la noticia que le dieron sobre su hija, Susana daba saltos de alegría. When they gave her the news about her daughter, Susana was jumping for joy.

en su propia salsa in your (his, her) element (sauce) ◀Mex, S. Cone, Sp▶

encantado(-a) de la vida (charmed or enchanted with life) very happy ◀L. Am., Sp▶
Los niños van a la playa a pasear. Están encantados de la vida. The children are going on an excursion to the beach. They're happy as can be.

estar (alegre) como unas castañuelas (to be happy as castanets) to be very happy ◀Mex, Sp▶

estar como unas pascuas (to be like Easter) to be very happy ◀Sp▶

estar como pez en el agua (to be like a fish in water) to enjoy comforts and conveniences, be in one's element ◀L. Am., Sp▶
Me siento muy contento; aquí estoy como pez en el agua. I feel very content; I'm really in my element here.

estar en la gloria (to be in one's glory) to be in seventh heaven, on cloud nine ◀L. Am., Sp▶

harm, hurt

See also "criticism," "deception," "hostility," "information."

caer de madre a alguien (to fall of mother) to be looked down upon (vulgar) ◀Mex▶
Le cae de madre al que no tenga valor de ir. Anybody not brave enough to go is a worthless scumbag.

chingarse (to get screwed) to suffer (vulgar) (Ch: to get frustrated or disappointed, not vulgar; Sp: to break down, as a machine) ◀Mex, ES, Col▶
Yo me chingo trabajando día y noche. I wear myself out working night and day.
Si quieres ganar la vida, tienes que chingarte. If you want to earn a living, you have to work damn hard.
Yo creía que tendría ese puesto y me chingué. (Ch) I believed that I'd get that job and I got screwed.
Mi auto se chingó. (Sp) My car went all to hell (broke down).

cocerse en su propia salsa (to cook in one's own sauce) to get caught in your own trap, stew in your own juice ◀Bol, Ch▶

comer vivo(-a) a alguien (to eat someone alive) to treat badly (Mex, Ch: to say bad things about someone) ◀ Mex, ES, DR, S. Cone, Sp ▶
Ya estoy harto de ese trabajo. Mi jefe me comió vivo solamente porque olvidé unos documentos en casa. I've had it with that job. My boss ripped me apart just because I forgot and left some documents at home.

como pujo (en vendaval) (like a push [in a windstorm]) bothered, uncomfortable, frustrated ◀ Nic ▶

darse en el queso to hit oneself in the face (the cheese) ◀ Mex ▶
Me caí y me di en el queso. I fell down and smacked myself in the chops.

darse una hostia (to give oneself the Host) to fall, have an accident (vulgar, with religious reference) ◀ Sp ▶

dejar planchado(-a) a alguien (to leave someone ironed) to leave someone unable to respond to some unforeseen act or something said ◀ Sp ▶

desbancar to push (someone) out of the way, take a job away from someone ◀ U, Arg, Sp ▶

echar leña al fuego to add fuel (wood) to the fire ◀ L. Am., Sp ▶
Es mejor callarse y no echar más leña al fuego. It's better to keep quiet and not stir things up any more than they already are.

echar mal de ojo (to throw the evil eye) to curse someone, wish ill to someone and try to cause him or her bad luck (ES: **hacer ojos**) ◀ Cuba, DR, PR, S. Cone ▶

en la malle (euphemism for **en la madre**) Oh, my God! Straight to the heart! (Right "where I live") ◀ Mex ▶

enjaretar to force (on someone) ◀ Mex, U, Arg ▶
Juan me enjaretó un trabajo horrible. Juan stuck me with a horrible job.

estar sentado (to be seated) to be dominated by a girlfriend or wife ◀ Col ▶

fajar (to wrap) to punish (U: to punch) ◀ U, Arg ▶

Lo (La) besó el diablo. (The devil kissed him or her.) He or she fell down, tripped. ◀ Mex, ES ▶

meter en un puño a alguien (to put someone in one's fist) to intimidate or oppress someone ◀ Mex, Sp ▶

pelotear to bounce (someone) around (e.g., from office to office) ◀ Cuba, Col ▶
¡Qué burocracia! Me pelotearon de una oficina a otra hasta que por fin alguien me ayudó. What bureaucracy! They bounced me around from one office to another until finally someone helped me.

pisado(-a), pisa'o(-a) (stepped on) dominated ◀ DR ▶
La mujer de Ernesto lo tiene pisa'o. Ella es la que manda en esa casa. Ernesto's wife has him under her thumb. She's the one who rules in that house.

robar el show (to steal the show) to steal the show, said when someone steals someone's thunder (Ch: also, **robar la película**) ◀ Mex, ES, S. Cone ▶

sacar el jugo (to take out the juice) to take maximum advantage, get the best (from) ◀ Mex, ES, CR, DR, PR, Col, Arg, Ch, Sp ▶
Ese patrón te saca el jugo. That boss will take you for everything you got.

sapear to meddle or get in the way ◀ CR, Cuba ▶

tirar la piedra y esconder la mano (to throw the stone and hide one's hand) to hurt someone but cover up one's action, propose an action but later deny having a part in it, be a hypocrite ◀ L. Am., Sp ▶

trepársele a la cabeza (to climb up to one's head) to take advantage of ◀ Arg ▶
Que no se te trepen a la cabeza. Don't let them take advantage of you.

venir a menos (to come to less) to deteriorate ◀ L. Am., Sp ▶
Ese hombre era rico pero ahora está venido a menos. That man was rich but now he's come down in the world.

blows

el batacazo bad blow or black and blue mark ◀ U, Arg, Sp ▶
Se dio un batacazo. He (She) got bruised (a black and blue mark).

el boyo punch, hit ◀ Arg ▶
Portáte bien o te voy a dar un boyo. Behave yourself or I'm going to give you a smack.

el cachimbazo blow (Nic: vulgar) ◀ G, CR, ES, Nic ▶

el chanclazo blow or hit with a **chancleta**, sandal (from killing bugs with the **chancleta**) ◀ Mex, Col ▶

el cocotazo blow to the head (the **coco**, coconut) ◀ chicano, Cuba, DR, PR, Col ▶
Su mamá le dio un cocotazo para callarlo. His mom gave him a little smackeroo to quiet him down.

el coñazo (blow, from **coño**, vulgar) blow or punch, impact, big fight ◀ DR, Ven ▶

el dos que tres (two that three) blow or punch ◀ ES ▶
Beto le dio un dos que tres a su sobrino porque molestaba mucho. Beto gave his nephew the old one-two because he was pestering him so much.

el estatequieto (be quiet) blow or punch, hit ◀ Mex, ES, Peru ▶
Su prima le dio un estatequieto a Lalo porque no dejaba de molestar. His cousin gave Lalo a "reason to be quiet" (a spank) because he wouldn't let her alone.

el golpe bajo low blow ◀ L. Am., Sp ▶

el manotazo blow with the hand ◀ L. Am., Sp ▶

el sopapo blow or punch ◀ L. Am., Sp ▶
Si no te callas, te doy un sopapo. If you don't quiet down, I'll hit you.

el trompazo hard blow ◀ most of L. Am., Sp ▶

el vergazo hard blow (vulgar, from **verga**) ◀ ES, Nic, CR, Col ▶
Me dejó ir un vergazo. He (She) let me have it with a good punch.

la vergueada blow (vulgar, from **verga**) ◀ ES, CR ▶

dirty tricks, cheap shots

la cabronada dirty trick, something bad done to someone ◀ Mex, G, PR, Col, Sp ▶

¿Te robaron la cartera? ¡Qué cabronada! They stole your wallet? What a cheap shot!

la cagada (shit) dirty trick, piece of crap, betrayal (vulgar) ◀ L. Am., Sp ▶
Ana me hizo una gran cagada; trató de salir con mi novio. Ana played a hell of a dirty trick on me; she tried to go out with my boyfriend.

la canallada cheap shot, evil action ◀ most of L. Am. ▶

la cochinada (pig act) dirty trick ◀ L. Am., Sp ▶
¡Qué cochinadas hacen! What dirty tricks they play!

la guarrada harmful action (somewhat vulgar) ◀ Sp ▶
Ya no es amigo mío porque me hizo una guarrada. He's not my friend anymore because he pulled a fast one on me that was real crappy.

la jalada (fregadera) (pull or jerk) dirty trick ◀ Mex ▶
Pedro me hizo una jalada (fregadera). Pedro played a dirty trick on me.

la mala pasada dirty trick (Ch: **una mala jugada**) ◀ L. Am., Sp ▶
A Salvador le hicieron una mala pasada y no le dieron su cheque. They gave Salvador a dirty deal and didn't give him his check.
Nos jugaron una mala pasada con la devaluación. They played a rotten trick on us with the devaluation.

la mariconada dirty trick ◀ Ch, Sp ▶
Mi jefe me hizo una mariconada al despedirme. (Ch) My boss played a dirty trick on me by firing me.

la putada (whore thing or action) dirty trick; piece of crap ◀ L. Am., Sp ▶
Estoy muy enojada con José. —Sí, ¡fue una putada lo que te hizo! I'm very angry at José. —Yeah, it was a piece of crap what he did to you!
Le hace muchas putadas a su hermana menor. He plays a lot of dirty tricks on his little sister.

la trastada dirty trick ◀ L. Am., Sp ▶
A mí también me han hecho algunas trastadas. They've played some dirty tricks on me, too.

finding someone's weak point

agarrarle el lado flaco (to grab his or her skinny side) to use someone's weak point, soft spot ◀ U, Arg ▶

coger la baja a alguien (to take someone's drop or fall) to find someone's weak point and take advantage of it ◀ Cuba, Col ▶

getting ahead of someone

hacerle la cama a alguien (to make the bed for someone) to get ahead of someone, take him or her by surprise, prevent someone from doing well ◀ S. Cone ▶
Me distraje y ese tipo me hizo la cama. No voy a permitirle que me haga la cama otra vez. I got distracted and that guy took me by surprise. I'm not going to let him get ahead of me again.

madrugar (to get up early) to get ahead of someone, cut off at the pass, beat to the punch ◀ L. Am., Sp ▶
Si no madrugas a ese señor, él te madruga a ti. If you don't get the better of that gentleman, he's going to get the better of you.

hitting, beating up, doing in

acabar (to finish) to do in; to frustrate or confuse someone ◀ G, Cuba ▶

la calentadita (little heating up) little "workover" (beating or sexual play) ◀ Mex, ES, Col, U ▶

capar (to neuter, castrate) to punish, to kill (figuratively) ◀ Mex, Col ▶
Me van a capar en la casa si no paso el examen. They're going to murder me at home if I don't pass the exam.

dar corte (to give cut) to cut down (hit or kill) ◀ Mex, ES ▶

dar en la madre (romper/partir la madre) (to give in the mother [to break the mother]) to hit hard, hurt someone

where he or she is vulnerable ◀ chicano, Mex, C. Am., Col ▶
Si no te callas, te voy a romper (partir) la madre. If you don't shut up, I'm going to beat the living daylights out of you.
Le dieron en la madre. They gave it to him (her) where it hurts.

dar en la torre (to give in the tower) to knock (someone's) block off, fix (someone) good, hurt someone where he or she is vulnerable ◀ Mex, C. Am. ▶
Me dieron en la torre. They knocked my block off.

dar leña (to give wood) to beat up, hit ◀ Cuba, DR, PR, Sp ▶
Ese bestia le dio mucha leña a su mujer y la tuvieron que ingresar en el hospital. That animal beat his wife senseless and they had to take her to the hospital.

dar la puntilla (to give the dagger) to finish off, be the ruin of someone ◀ Sp ▶

darle caña (to give cane, a caning) to beat up ◀ PR ▶

darle mate (to give kill) to kill off, finish ◀ Mex ▶
Vamos a darle mate al pastel. Let's finish off the cake.

descontar, sonar to hit ◀ Mex, ES ▶
Te voy a descontar un golpe. I'm going to give you an extra punch.

desmadrar (to dismother) to beat up ◀ chicano, Mex, Col ▶
Me van a desmadrar en la escuela si me ven con esta camisa rosada. They're going to give me a major beating at school if they see me with this pink shirt.

entrarle a alguien a puños y patadas (to go into someone with fists and kicks) to beat someone up ◀ ES, Pan ▶
Le entré a puños y patadas cuando me mentó la madre. I lit into him (her) with everything I had when he (she) insulted my mother.

hacer boleta to beat up, beat to a pulp ◀ Arg ▶
A ese pobre tipo lo van a hacer boleta. They're going to beat that poor guy to a pulp.

hacer charquicán (to make into dried meat or jerky) to destroy (something or someone) ◀ Ch ▶

hacer fosfatina a alguien (to make someone powder) to cause someone great harm ◀ Sp ▶

hacer migas a alguien (to make someone crumbs) to leave someone exhausted or overcome, cause stress or anxiety ◀ Mex, ES, Sp ▶

hacer morder el polvo a alguien (to make someone bite the dust) to overcome someone in a fight ◀ DR, Sp ▶

hacer polvo a alguien (to make someone dust) to cause serious damage, destroy, ruin ◀ Mex, G, ES, Cuba, DR, Col, Sp ▶
Esa comida me dejó el estómago hecho polvo. That food hit my stomach like a ton of bricks.
Me peleé con él y le dejé hecho polvo. I had a fight with him and I made mincemeat out of him.

hacer puré a alguien (to make someone a purée) to cause serious damage (physically or mentally) ◀ Mex, ES, DR, U, Arg, Sp ▶

hacer tortilla a una persona o cosa to crush or break (like eggs for an omelette, which is **tortilla** in Spain) ◀ Mex, Sp ▶
El coche lo hizo tortilla. The car flattened him like a pancake.

hacer leña del árbol caído (to make firewood from the fallen tree) to kick someone when he or she is down ◀ Ch ▶

llevar contra la pared (la tabla) (to take against the wall [board]) to act cruelly (toward someone) or ask too much (of him or her) (G: **pared** only; Ch: **poner contra la pared**) ◀ Mex, G, Cuba, U, Ch ▶

madrear to hit ◀ Mex, ES ▶

partirle a alguien la cara (to break someone's face) used as a threat, to beat someone up ◀ Mex, U, Sp ▶

pasar la cuenta (a alguien) (to pass the account [to someone]) to reprimand; to settle accounts (sometimes by killing someone) ◀ Mex, Cuba, Col, Sp ▶

poner como camote a alguien (to make someone like a sweet potato) to give someone his or her due (dressing down, beating) ◀ Mex, ES ▶

poner como dado (to put like a die—from a pair of dice—square and with spots) to scold, chew out, hurt ◀ Mex ▶
Mi papá me puso como dado cuando reprobé el año. My dad made mincemeat of me when I flunked the grade.

poner cuadrado(-a) (to make someone square) to flatten, beat to a pulp ◀ Mex, Col ▶

poner parejo to flatten, beat to a pulp ◀ Mex, ES, Col ▶

sacar canas verdes (to bring out green canas, gray hairs) to do in, give someone gray hair, make them despair ◀ L. Am. ▶
Esos niños me sacan canas verdes. Those kids are giving me gray hair.

sacudir el polvo a alguien (to shake the dust off someone) to hit or verbally assault someone ◀ Sp ▶

tirar a los leones (to throw to the lions) to leave in a tight spot ◀ Ch, Sp ▶

tratar con la punta del pie (to treat with the point of the foot) to treat someone badly, treat like dirt ◀ Ch ▶

verguear to hit, strike (vulgar, from **verga**, male organ) ◀ CR, ES, Nic ▶

ruined, messed up

camao(-a) experienced (by hard luck, from **escamado**, scaled like a fish) ◀ Cuba ▶

chingado(-a) (chinga'o[-a]) (ripped, torn, broken) screwed (vulgar) ◀ Mex, C. Am., Cuba, PR, Col ▶

descojonado(-a) (without testicles) said of someone when they have problems (vulgar); broke or not working (from **descojonar**) ◀ Mex, DR, PR, Col ▶

descoñetado(-a) trashed, messed up, badly damaged or hurt (vulgar, from **coño**) ◀ Ven ▶
Los ladrones dejaron el apartamento totalmente descoñetado. The thieves left the apartment completely trashed.

estar cagado(-a) (to be pooped) to be ruined, messed up (vulgar) ◀ S. Cone ▶

estar de la cachetada to be in a bad way, bad ◀ Mex, Col ▶

Este color está de la cachetada. This color is way bad.

estar de la chingada (to be of the chingada, a woman who has been violated) to be in deep trouble, screwed (vulgar) (Mex: also, **estar de la fregada**, less strong) ◄ Mex, G, ES, Col ►
¿Van a cancelar la reunión? ¡Esto está de la chingada! They're going to cancel the meeting? This sucks!

estar de la jodida to be very difficult, bad (somewhat vulgar) ◄ chicano, Mex, G, Col ►

estar de la patada (to be of the kick) to be in a bad way ◄ Mex, G, ES, Col, Peru ►

estar fregado(-a) (to be scrubbed) to be useless, messed up, ruined ◄ most of L. Am. ►

ir por lana y volver (salir) trasquilado(-a) (to go for wool and come back shorn) to have the tables turned on oneself ◄ DR, U, S. Cone, Sp ►

jodido(-a) (past participle of **joder**) screwed, messed up (vulgar) ◄ L. Am., Sp ►

Me lleva la chingada. (The chingada, violated woman, is taking me.) I'm screwed. (vulgar) Euphemism: **Me lleva el chile.** ◄ Mex, C. Am. ►

quedar en la página dos (to remain on page two) to break, get ruined or eliminated ◄ Cuba ►

quemado(-a) (burned) damaged (usually in reputation) (Ch: also, having bad luck) ◄ Mex, G, CR, DR, Col, S. Cone, Sp ►

ruining, messing up

arruinar el estofado (to spoil the stew) to ruin the plan, mess up the works ◄ U, Arg ►
Yo lo tenía todo arreglado y esa mujer me arruinó el estofado. I had it all set up and that woman ruined my whole plan.

cagar (to shit on) to mess (someone) up by abusing, lying to, or cheating on that person or by being unfaithful; to give (someone) the shaft (vulgar) ◄ S. Cone ►
Me cagaron en la oficina. They gave me a lot of shit at the office.

Mi marido me cagó. My husband acted like a piece of crap and cheated on me.

cagarse en la canción (to shit on the song) to ruin, destroy (vulgar) ◄ Col ►

cagarse en la olla (to shit in the pot) to ruin, destroy (vulgar) ◄ G ►

cagarse en el ventilador (to shit on the fan) to say or do something that causes a big problem (vulgar) ◄ Ch ►

chingar (to rip, tear) to exploit; to have sex (equivalent of the F-word); to break (a machine) (PR: to have sex only) (vulgar) ◄ Mex, C. Am., Cuba, Col, PR ►
Vete a chingar a otra parte. Go somewhere else to cause trouble.
No me chingues; necesito dinero. Don't fuck with me; I need money.
Se me chingó el motor del carro. My car (literally, car's motor) broke down.

cuatrapear to get all messed or mixed up; to turn out badly ◄ Mex ►
Todo se me cuatrapeó. Everything went wrong.

descachimbar to break (the reflexive, descachimbarse, means to fall) ◄ ES, Nic, CR ►

descojonar (to de-testicle) to ruin, mess up ◄ Mex, DR, PR, Col ►
¿Quién descojonó el radio, que ahora no funciona? Who screwed up the radio so it won't work now?

descoñetar to trash, mess up, ruin, hurt (vulgar, from **coño**) ◄ DR, Ven ►
Pedro se metió en un accidente y se descoñetó la cara. Pedro got into a car accident and trashed his face.

escupir al asado (to spit on the roast) to ruin a plan or situation, cause things to turn out badly ◄ Arg ►

fregar (to scrub, scour, rub [the wrong way]) to mess up, ruin, jerk around; to bother with insistent requests ◄ most of L. Am. ►
Nos fregaron otra vez. They jerked us around again.
Déjate de fregar. Get off my case.

hacer harina una cosa (to make something flour) to break something to pieces ◄ DR, PR, U, Sp ►

joder to screw, bother, trick, or bug someone; to break (something) (vulgar in some places but inoffensive in others) ◀ L. Am., Sp ▶
Se jodió el pie jugando a fútbol. He messed up his foot playing soccer.
Le encanta joder a su hermana. He loves to bug his sister.
No me jodas. Don't bother me.
Joder, ¡qué hambre tengo! (Sp) Damn, am I hungry!

no dejar piedra sobre piedra (to not leave stone upon stone) to destroy completely ◀ Mex, DR, U, Sp ▶

no dejar títere con cabeza (to not leave a puppet with a head) to destroy, blow someone away with insults, screaming ◀ S. Cone ▶
Voy a revisar todo el trabajo y si está mal, no voy a dejar títere con cabeza. I'm going to look over the whole job and if it isn't good, heads will roll.

no quedar títere con cara (cabeza) (to not have a puppet with a face [head] remaining) to be totally destroyed, often because of verbal abuse ◀ Mex, S. Cone, Sp ▶
El jefe dio su discurso y no quedó títere con cabeza. The boss gave his talk and no one was left standing.

pasearse en algo (to ride around on something) to ruin something ◀ CR, ES, Nic, Col ▶
Te paseaste en el vestido. You made a mess of that dress.

health

See also "greetings: answering 'how are you?'"

achacoso(-a) person who complains a lot about health problems or imagines he or she is sick all the time, hypochondriac ◀ Mex, DR, PR, Arg, Ch ▶
Es joven para ser tan achacoso. He's young to be such a hypochondriac.

las lagartijas (lizards) push-ups ◀ G, DR, Col ▶

el/la matasanos (healthy people–killer) doctor ◀ most of L. Am., Sp ▶

¡Jesús! Gesundheit!, said after a sneeze ◀ L. Am., Sp ▶

¡Jesús, María y José! Gesundheit!, said after three sneezes ◀ parts of L. Am., Sp ▶

la mano de santa (saint's hand) effective remedy ◀ Sp ▶

pescar un resfriado to catch (fish for) a cold (also, **resfrío**) ◀ Mex, G, Ch, Sp ▶

¡Salud! (Health!) To your health! Gesundheit!, said as a toast or after a sneeze (Mex: also, **¡Salucitas!**) ◀ L. Am., Sp ▶

vivito(-a) y coleando living and breathing (wagging its tail) ◀ L. Am., Sp ▶

in good shape

en (buena) forma in (good) shape ◀ L. Am., Sp ▶
Don César está en buena forma para su edad. Don César is in good shape for his age.

estar hecho(-a) un pimpollo to look good (like a sprout, young thing) ◀ Mex, ES, DR, Sp ▶

sano(-a) como una manzana (healthy as an apple) very well, healthy ◀ Sp ▶
Hola, Verónica. ¿Cómo estás? —Sana como una manzana. Hi, Verónica. How are you? —Fit as a fiddle.

sentirse en plena forma (to feel in full form) to feel your best, in great condition ◀ Mex, Sp ▶

tener mucha cuerda (to have a lot of cord) to look very healthy ◀ Mex, Sp ▶

help

See also "friendship."

acolitar to help ◀ Ec ▶
Cuídame el changarro. (Take care of my stand [at a market].) Take my place for a few minutes. ◀ Mex, ES ▶

Say it with slang!

Techno-talk

Electronics and technology have entered the world of slang, as we can see from this literal translation of a conversation in Spanish:

María Elena: Plug yourself in, Mario! Put up your antenna. You have a face like a telephone with a busy signal.

Mario: What? Sorry. My wires have gotten crossed with a problem at work. My boss blew a fuse and insulted me in front of everyone.

María Elena: Well, forget it, man. Put in your batteries because we have to race at full machine to get to our appointment.

The original conversation follows. Can you understand the gist of it?

María Elena: ¡Enchúfate, Mario! Levanta la antena. Tienes una cara de teléfono ocupado.

Mario: ¿Cómo? Perdón. Se me han cruzado los cables con un problema en el trabajo. A mi jefe se le fundieron los fusibles y me insultó delante de todos.

María Elena: Pues, olvídalo, hombre. Ponte las pillas porque tenemos que correr a toda máquina para llegar a nuestra cita.

Eso está hecho. (That's done.) That's for certain. It's a sure thing. (used for promises) ◀ Sp ▶
¿Quieres que te pinte la casa este verano? Eso está hecho. Do you want me to paint your house this summer? It's a sure thing.

Estoy a sus órdenes. I am at your service. ◀ L. Am., Sp ▶

Más ven cuatro ojos que dos. Four eyes are (see) better than two. ◀ L. Am., Sp ▶

meter a alguien con cuchara una cosa to spoon-feed something to someone ◀ Mex, Sp ▶

perder el culo (to lose one's ass) to do the impossible (for someone) (vulgar) ◀ Sp ▶
Jaime perdió el culo por esa chica y dejó los estudios. Jaime busted a gut for that girl and gave up (left) his studies.

ser flor de estufa (to be a flower on the stove) to be overprotected, not allowed to grow or be independent ◀ Sp ▶

¡Sóbate! (Rub yourself!) expression said to a person who falls or gets a bump, meaning rub the hurt area (used like oopsy-daisy!) ◀ DR, Ven ▶

defending or backing someone up

apañar (to cover with flannel) to protect or cover for someone (who is breaking some kind of rule) ◀ ES, Nic ▶
Sí, chica, voy a apañarte si el jefe pregunta dónde estás. Yeah, I'll cover for you if the boss asks where you are.

dar cuartel (to give quarters) to help someone ◀ Mex, Sp ▶

defender a capa y espada (to defend with cape and sword) to always back someone up, take care of; to defend vehemently (e.g., a point of view) ◀ L. Am., Sp ▶
Defendió esa opinión a capa y espada. He (She) defended that opinion to the hilt.

echar un capote (echar la capa) (to throw a cape, as at a bullfight) to intervene on behalf of someone ◀ Sp ▶
Gracias por echarme un capote porque yo no sabía qué decirle. Thanks for helping me out because I didn't know what to say to him.

meter las manos al fuego por alguien (to put one's hands in the fire for someone) to vouch for someone ◀ Mex, ES, DR, Peru, S. Cone ▶
Yolanda es una buena amiga. Meto las manos al fuego por ella. Yolanda is a good friend. I vouch for her.

romper una lanza (to break a spear) to defend another person absolutely, to the hilt (Ch: **romper lanzas**) ◀ Peru, Ch, Sp ▶

sacar la cara por alguien (to bring or take out one's face for someone) to go to bat for someone, defend that person openly ◀ Mex, S. Cone, Sp ▶
El único que sacó la cara por mí cuando me peleé con mi jefe fue Tomás; los demás no dijeron nada. The only one who went to bat for me when I had a fight with my boss was Tomás; the others didn't say anything.

doing a favor

dar una mano to give (someone) a hand; also, **echar una mano** (Sp: **echar** only) ◀ Mex, G, Cuba, DR, PR, S. Cone, Sp ▶

echar una manopla to lend (put in) a big helping hand ◀ Mex, Col ▶

hacer un catorce, hacer un cuatro (to make a fourteen, to make a four) to do (someone) a favor ◀ Col ▶

hacer la media (to do the half) to go with (someone), accompany ◀ Cuba ▶
Te haré la media hasta la esquina. I'll go with you up to the corner.

hacer la pala (to make the shovel) to help ◀ G, Cuba ▶

hacer un paro (to make a stop) to do (someone) a favor ◀ Mex, parts of C. Am. ▶
Hazme un paro, mano. Do me a favor, bro'.

hacer una segunda (to do a second) to do a favor, help out ◀ Ven ▶
Mi prima me hizo una segunda. My cousin did me a favor.

la paleta (small shovel, lollipop) one who does favors, helps out ◀ Ch ▶

sacar las castañas del fuego (to take the chestnuts out of the fire) to help someone else out at one's own expense ◀ U, Arg, Sp ▶

favors

la paleteada (a lot of shovels or lollipops) favor ◀ Ch ▶

la valona favor ◀ Mex ▶

la volada favor; **de volada** as a favor ◀ Mex, G ▶

hesitation words

Bueno... (Good.) Uh ..., Well ... ◀ L. Am., Sp ▶

¿Cómo diré? How shall I put it (say this)? ◀ most of L. Am. (not S. Cone) ▶

¿Cómo (lo) diría? How should I put it (say this)? ◀ L. Am., Sp ▶

Este... Uh ..., Well ... ◀ L. Am., Sp ▶

O sea... That is ... ◀ L. Am., Sp ▶

Pues... Uh ..., Well ... ◀ L. Am., Sp ▶

hostility

See also "anger," "annoyance," "criticism," "harm, hurt," "insults."

tener cara de poco amigos (to have face of few friends) to look hostile, unwelcoming, or unfriendly ◀ Mex, U, Ch ▶

No compro nada en esa tienda porque los dependientes tienen cara de pocos amigos. I don't buy anything at that store because the clerks look like sourpusses.

giving someone the cold shoulder

dar a alguien con la puerta en las narices (to slam the door on someone) to refuse someone something ◀ Mex, ES, S. Cone, Sp ▶
Fui al consulado para pedir los documentos, pero me dieron con la puerta en las narices. I went to the consulate to ask for the documents, but they refused me.

dar hielo (to give ice) to treat coldly, not pay attention to someone, give the cold shoulder (DR: **hacer el hielo;** Ch: **poner al hielo;** Mex: **hacer a alguien la ley del hielo**) ◀ Mex, Cuba, DR, Ch ▶
Yo fui a saludarlo muy simpática y el tipo me hizo un hielo... yo no sé qué le hice. (DR) I went up to greet him very nicely and the guy gave me the cold shoulder . . . I don't know what I did to him.

ningunear to treat (someone) badly, as a nobody ◀ Mex, ES, Nic ▶

no dar calce (to not give wedge) to not give an opportunity or opening (entree) to ◀ Arg ▶
Quise hablar, pero Enrique no me dio calce; siguió hablando. I tried to speak up, but Enrique didn't give me a chance; he kept on talking.
La invité a una fiesta pero no me dio calce. I invited her to a party but she didn't give me a chance.

no darle a alguien vela (no tener vela) en el entierro (to not give someone [not have] a candle at a funeral) to not give someone authority or a reason to participate (to not have a reason to participate) ◀ Mex, DR, S. Cone, Sp ▶
Mejor no opines, que nadie te dio vela en este entierro. Better not give your opinion; nobody gave you any say in this matter.
Ni hables porque no tienes vela en el entierro. Don't even talk because you don't have any say here.

like cats and dogs, oil and water

andar como perro y gato (to walk like dog and cat) to be enemies (also, **ser como perro y gato;** Sp: also, **como el perro y el gato**) ◀ Mex, DR, ES, U, Ch, Sp ▶

como el aceite y el vinagre (like oil and vinegar) said of two people who don't get along ◀ Mex, Caribbean, Col, U, Arg ▶

como el agua y el aceite (like water and oil) said of two people who don't get along, don't mix ◀ Mex, G, ES, Ch ▶
Juan y su hermano son como el agua y el aceite; no se llevan bien. Juan and his brother are like oil and water; they don't get along.

como perros y gatos (like dogs and cats) like enemies ◀ Mex, ES, Peru, Ch ▶

No se entienden ni se enteran. (They don't understand each other or find out anything.) They don't get along. ◀ Col, Sp ▶

peleados(-as) angry at each other, treating each other as enemies ◀ L. Am., Sp ▶
María y José están peleados; ya no se hablan. María and José are angry at each other after a fight; they aren't speaking to each other anymore.

violently, pitilessly

a sangre y fuego (by blood and fire) violently ◀ Mex, Sp ▶

al duro y sin guante (hard and without a glove) pitilessly, without mercy ◀ Mex, Cuba ▶

por la tremenda (by the tremendous) violently or without respect ◀ Sp ▶

impossibility

buscar chichis a las culebras (to look for breasts on a snake) to look for the impossible ◀ Mex ▶

la cuadratura del círculo (the square-ness of the circle) the impossibility or overcomplication of something ◀ Mex, Sp ▶

pedir la luna (to ask for the moon) to ask for something in vain ◀ L. Am., Sp ▶

pedir peras al olmo (to ask the elm tree for pears) to ask for something in vain ◀ L. Am., Sp ▶
¿A Juan le pediste dinero? Es como pedir peras al olmo, que él nunca tiene nada. You asked Juan for money? That's like asking for blood from a turnip; he never has anything.

pedirle cobija al frío (to ask the cold for a blanket) to ask for the impossible ◀ Mex, ES ▶

pedirle comida al hambre (to ask hunger for food) to ask for the impossible ◀ Mex, ES ▶

sacar agua de las piedras (to get water from stones) to get something from an improbable source ◀ Mex, Sp ▶

---

inactivity

See also "laziness."

apalancarse to stay in one place without moving ◀ Sp ▶
Me apalanqué en su casa y no salimos por la noche. I settled down at their (his, her) house and we didn't go out in the evening.
No te apalanques en el sillón; ponte a hacer las tareas. Don't get settled down in the easy chair; start doing your chores.

el/la aviador(-a) (aviator) said of someone who is paid for a job but doesn't really work ◀ Mex ▶
El jefe tiene de aviadores a dos primos suyos. The boss has two of his cousins on the payroll for doing nothing.

con los brazos cruzados (with arms crossed) idle, doing nothing (also, **de brazos cruzados**) ◀ L. Am., Sp ▶
En vez de ayudarme, Pablo se queda allí con los brazos cruzados. Instead of helping me, Pablo's there twiddling his thumbs.

flotar (to float) to be lazy, goof off ◀ Cuba ▶

medir calles (to measure streets) to hang out in the street ◀ ES, CR ▶

no dar un golpe (to not give a hit) to be lazy, do nothing (Sp: **no dar golpe**) ◀ Mex, DR, Sp ▶
El esposo de Alejandra no da un golpe. Ella lo hace todo en esa casa. Alejandra's husband doesn't lift a finger to do anything. She does everything in that house.

no disparar un chícharo (to not fire a [dried] pea) to not work, do nothing ◀ Cuba ▶

no mover un dedo to not lift (move) a finger ◀ L. Am., Sp ▶
Ni siquiera movió un dedo para ayudarme con la computadora. He (She) didn't even lift a finger to help me with the computer.

pelársela to do nothing (vulgar, **la** refers to **la verga**, male organ) (CR: to fail, end up badly) ◀ Mex, G, ES ▶

pegársele a alguien la silla (el asiento) (to have the seat stuck to one) to stay somewhere for a long time ◀ U, Sp ▶

pintando varillas (painting little bars) unemployed, out of work ◀ Col ▶
Hace dos meses que estoy pintando varillas. I've been out of work for two months.

quedarse ruqueando en la caleta to hang out at home ◀ Ec ▶
¿Qué hiciste hoy? —Nada. Me quedé ruqueando en la caleta. What did you do today? —Nothing. I just hung out at home.

tocarse las narices (los cojones) (to touch one's nose [testicles]) to goof off, not do anything (vulgar) ◀ Sp ▶

---

inattention

See also "lack of knowledge."

¡Que no te enteras, Contreras! (So you don't find out, Contreras!) phrase reproaching someone for being distracted and not listening ◀ Sp ▶

daydreaming, tuning out

desconectar (to disconnect) to avoid reality, relax, tune out ◀ Mex, Cuba, DR, Col, Sp ▶
Cuando no me interesa la lección, desconecto. When I'm not interested in the lesson, I tune out.

entrarle una cosa por un oído y salirle por el otro to have something go in one ear and out the other ◀ L. Am., Sp ▶
Por un oído le entra y por el otro le sale. It goes in one ear and out the other.

estar en ele olo (como chico zapote) to be completely out of it (like the sapodilla fruit), in the dark, daydreaming ◀ Nic ▶
En la clase de esta mañana, Silvia quedó (estaba) en ele olo. No entendió nada. In class this morning, Silvia was completely out of it. She didn't understand anything.

estar en la higuera (to be in the fig tree) to be distracted, daydreaming ◀ Sp ▶

estar en la luna (de Valencia) (to be in the moon [of Valencia]) to be distracted, daydreaming ◀ L. Am., Sp ▶
Sería buen astronauta, ¿verdad? Porque siempre estoy en la luna. I'd be a good astronaut, wouldn't I? Because I always have my head in the clouds (I'm always daydreaming).

estar en las nubes (to be in the clouds) to be daydreaming ◀ L. Am., Sp ▶

hacer castillos en el aire to build castles in the air ◀ Mex, S. Cone, Sp ▶

tener la mente en blanco to be daydreaming, have one's mind blank (ES, Ch, Sp: **quedarse** or **estar con la mente en blanco**) ◀ Mex, G, DR, Col, U, Arg ▶

volado(-a) (blown up high or flown away) daydreaming ◀ Mex, Col ▶

not seeing, ignoring

hacer la vista gorda (to do the fat look) to ignore, overlook ◀ L. Am., Sp ▶
Ana llegó tarde, pero el jefe hizo la vista gorda. Ana came late, but the boss overlooked it.

hacerse de la vista choncha to ignore, overlook ◀ Mex ▶
Estaban jugando, pero la maestra se hizo de la vista choncha. They were playing, but the teacher ignored them (overlooked it).

no ver ni gorda to not see anything ◀ Sp ▶

no ver ni tres en un burro (to not even see three on a burro) to not see anything ◀ Sp ▶

without thinking, foolishly

See also "randomness: willy-nilly, without a plan, haphazardly."

a lo loco (crazily) like crazy, without thinking (Ch: **a la loca**) ◀ Mex, ES, DR, PR, U, Arg, Sp ▶
Por estar hablando a lo loco, le conté a Ana de la fiesta sorpresa. Because I was talking without thinking (like crazy), I told Ana about the surprise party.

a lo tonto like crazy, without thinking (also, **a lo tarugo, a lo pendejo**) ◀ chicano, Mex, ES ▶

a tontas y a locas recklessly, like crazy, without thought ◀ most of L. Am., Sp ▶
César hablaba a tontas y a locas de su jefe. César was talking like crazy (without thinking) about his boss.

incompetence

See also "stupidity."

a la brava without refinement, sloppily, using force (also, **a la mala**, more common) ◀ Mex, G, ES, Sp ▶
José abrió la puerta sin utilizar la llave; la abrió a la brava. José opened the door without using the key; he opened it by force.

ahogarse en un vaso de agua (to drown in a glass of water) to be incompetent ◀ L. Am., Sp ▶

131

cafre stupid, incompetent ◀ Mex, Cuba, PR, Col ▶

Maneja el coche como cafre. He (She) drives the car like a maniac (incompetently).

empezar la casa por el tejado (to begin the house with the roof, a traditional proverb) to put the cart before the horse (U: ... **por el techo**) ◀ Sp ▶

hacer algo a lo bestia to do something abruptly, badly (like a beast) ◀ Mex, PR, U, Arg, Sp ▶

hacer algo con el culo to do something badly (with the ass) (vulgar) ◀ Mex, PR, Sp ▶

La última película de Travolta la hicieron con el culo. ¡Es un clavo! Travolta's last film was half-assed. It's a dud!

el maestro Chasquila (Master Chasquila) someone who can do a lot of things but none of them very well, jack-of-all-trades (and master of none) ◀ Ch ▶

no dar pie con bola (to not hit the ball with one's foot) to not be correct; to make a mess of things, not do things right ◀ Mex, DR, PR, Sp ▶

Es la tercera vez que se me quedan las llaves dentro del carro. Estoy que no doy pie con bola. This is the third time I've left the keys in the car. I can't seem to do anything right.

no saber dónde se tiene la mano derecha (to not know where one's right hand is) to be inept, of little talent (U: ... **se tiene la nariz**) ◀ Sp ▶

ser un manazas to be a klutz (ES: thief, like **manitas**) ◀ Sp ▶

Felipe intentó arreglar el asunto y lo estropeó más. Es un manazas. Felipe tried to fix things and messed them up more. He's a klutz.

ser una maraca sin palo (to be a maraca, the musical instrument, without a handle or stick) to be an incompetent person ◀ Col ▶

En la clase de química soy una maraca sin palo: el más cafre de todos. In chemistry class I'm a real ding-a-ling, the most klutzy of them all.

ser paleta (to be a little shovel) to be backward, slow, a bit inept ◀ Sp ▶

Soy muy paleta para pedir libros por Internet. I'm very slow in ordering books on the Internet.

Soy un poco paleta para pelar la naranja con tenedor y cuchillo. I'm a bit klutzy at peeling the orange with a fork and knife.

ser un zafio to be a blunderer ◀ Sp ▶

tener manos de hacha (to have hachet hands) to be clumsy, a klutz; describing someone who breaks everything like a bull in a china shop ◀ Ch ▶

venirle grande (to come to him or her very big) to be excessive (for one's size or merit); to be too much for someone ◀ Mex, Sp ▶

Con la poca experiencia que Dolores tiene en negocios, ese trabajo le viene grande. With the little bit of experience Dolores has in business, that job is too much for her.

el/la zurdo(-a) (left-handed) someone who is slow or inept at a certain activity ◀ Mex, Cuba, Col ▶

incomprehension

See also "lack of knowledge."

estar en chino to be incomprehensible (in Chinese) ◀ Mex, CR, DR, Col, Peru, Bol, Arg, Ch, Sp ▶

Este libro parece que está en chino. No entiendo ni jota. This book looks like it's in Greek. I don't understand squat.

no tener por donde agarrarlo (to have no place to hang onto) to be difficult to comprehend (Sp: ... **cogerlo**) ◀ Mex, DR, PR, U, Ch, Sp ▶

not getting it

estar (quedarse) a dos velas (to be [remain] at two sails) to not understand something ◀ Mex, Sp ▶

estar (quedarse) detrás del palo (to be [remain] behind the tree) to not understand anything ◀ ES, CR ▶

estar (quedarse) en blanco (to be [remain] blank) to draw a blank, not know the day's lesson or answer to a question ◀ L. Am., Sp ▶
Me sabía muy bien la lección pero cuando me la preguntó el profesor, me puse tan nervioso que me quedé en blanco. I knew the lesson well but when the teacher asked me about it, I got so nervous I drew a blank.

no agarrar la onda (to not seize the sound wave) to not get it or get with it ◀ Mex, G, ES, U, Arg ▶

no dar con ello to not get it ◀ Sp ▶
No doy con ello; es muy difícil. I don't get it; it's very difficult.

no entender ni jota (ni papa) (to not understand a jot [potato]) to not understand anything ◀ L. Am., Sp ▶

What?

¿Cómo? (What? How?) Excuse me? What (did you say)? ◀ L. Am., Sp ▶

¿Mande? Excuse me? What (did you say)? ◀ Mex ▶

¿Y eso? (And that?) What does that mean? What's that all about? ◀ L. Am., Sp ▶

independence

no casarse con nadie (to not marry anyone) to keep one's own opinions or attitudes independently ◀ L. Am., Sp ▶

no dar el brazo a torcer (to not give one's arm to twist) to be stubborn or persistent and not give in ◀ L. Am., Sp ▶
En esa cuestión, yo no quería dar mi brazo a torcer. On that point, I didn't want to give in.

no pintar nada (to not paint anything) to not care, not get involved ◀ Sp ▶
Yo no pinto nada en la fiesta de Juan porque casi no lo conozco. Yo ahí no pinto nada. I'm not getting involved in Juan's party

because I hardly know him. I'm not getting involved in that.

no tener arte ni parte (to have neither art nor part) to have no part in, nothing to do with ◀ L. Am., Sp ▶

alone

a secas (dry) only; alone, and that's all ◀ Mex, Ch, Sp ▶
La carta no llegó porque no llevaba la dirección. Llevaba un nombre a secas. The letter didn't arrive because it didn't have an address. It had a name and that's it.

Cada quien se rasque con sus propias uñas. (Each person should scratch himself or herself with his or her own fingernails.) Everyone for himself or herself, being alone or without support. ◀ Mex, ES, Ch ▶

sin padre ni madre, ni perro que me ladre (without father or mother or dog that barks for me) alone, independent, or without support ◀ Mex, PR, Arg, Ch, Sp ▶

solano(-a) alone, used instead of **solo(-a)** ◀ chicano, Mex, Cuba, Col, U, Arg ▶
¿Ya no sales con Carmen? Siempre te veo solano. You're not going out with Carmen anymore? I always see you all by your lonesome.

solapiao(-a) alone, used instead of **solo(-a)** ◀ Col ▶

indifference

See also "lack of worry."

chollado(-a) not caring about anything ◀ ES ▶
Estás chollado ya; no te importa nada. You're indifferent to everything now; you don't care about anything.

como si nada (as if nothing) just like that, without giving the matter any importance, like you don't have a care in the world ◀ L. Am., Sp ▶

echar en saco roto

dar igual, dar lo mismo (to give the same) to be indifferent ◄ L. Am., Sp ▶
Me da igual (lo mismo) ir a la fiesta que no ir. Going to the party or not is all the same to me.

echar en saco roto (to put into a broken or torn sack) to disregard completely (what someone says) ◄ L. Am., Sp ▶
Echaron mis consejos en saco roto. They completely disregarded my advice.

No me vuelve loco(-a). (It doesn't drive me crazy.) It doesn't do a thing for me. ◄ Ch ▶

pasar (to pass) to be indifferent, not suffer or change because of something ◄ Sp ▶
Yo paso de todo. I don't care about anything.

el/la pasota someone who doesn't care about anything, slacker ◄ Sp ▶
Juan es un pasota, como muchos de sus amigos. No les importa nada. Juan is a slacker, like a lot of his friends. They don't care about anything.

resbalarle algo a alguien (to slide off someone) to be indifferent, to roll off one's back ◄ Mex, DR, PR, Sp ▶

el valemadrismo (from the expression me vale madre; Es, Nic: **valevergismo** [vulgar]) attitude of indifference, slacker attitude ◄ Mex, Col ▶

to not matter, be unimportant

importarle tres cojones (to matter three testicles) to not matter (vulgar) ◄ Sp ▶

importarle un comino (to matter a cumin seed) to be unimportant ◄ Mex, ES, Col, Peru, Ch, Sp ▶

importarle un pepino (to matter a cucumber) to be unimportant ◄ L. Am., Sp ▶
Como si el asunto les importara un pepino. As if they gave a fig about the matter.

importarle un pimiento (to matter a pepper) to be unimportant ◄ U, Sp ▶

importarle un pito (un bledo) (to matter a whistle [a pigweed]) to be of no importance, not worth worrying about (DR, PR: **pito** only) ◄ Mex, DR, PR, Arg, Ch, Sp ▶
Me importa un pito que no me invites a tu fiesta. I don't give a darn that you may not invite me to your party.

importarle un rábano (to matter a radish) to be unimportant ◄ Mex, ES, U, Ch, Sp ▶
Me importa un rábano si te gusta o no te gusta. I don't give a hoot whether you like it or not.

importarle/valerle madre (to matter mother) to not matter (vulgar) ◄ Mex, most of C. Am. ▶
Les vale madre lo que opinen los demás. They don't give a damn what other people think.

ni ir ni venirle (without it coming or going) without it mattering (to someone) ◄ Mex, S. Cone, Sp ▶
El asunto de la campaña electoral ni me va ni me viene. To me, the whole matter of the election campaign is neither here nor there.

no importar un carajo (to not matter a male organ) to not give a damn (vulgar) ◄ PR, U, Arg ▶
Todo les importa un carajo. They don't give a damn about anything.

pelársela to be indifferent (vulgar, **la** refers to **la verga**, male organ) (CR: to fail, end up badly) ◄ Mex, G, ES ▶

Say it with slang!

Walking on eggs

In English you can "egg someone on" or tell him he has "egg on his face," but in Spanish you have to be careful about how you use the word **huevos** (eggs). For instance, you wouldn't want to say to a Mexican man, **No tienes huevos.** Literally you would be saying, "You don't have any eggs," but because the word **huevos** also means "testicles," you could be calling into question the fellow's courage and even his manhood. Some Mexicans are so sensitive about this subject that if they need eggs at the grocery store, they ask for a dozen **blanquillos** (little white ones) and avoid the word **huevos** altogether. Actually, in many parts of Latin America, people with lots of courage (women as well as men) are said to have their eggs (balls) well placed; for example, **Rosa es líder del sindicato y tiene los huevos bien puestos** (Rosa is head of the union and she's very brave).

On the other hand, the word **huevón** (big egg) and its feminine form **huevona** are insults. Literally, they mean someone with huge or oversized testicles since the **-ón/-ona** endings are augmentatives and imply increased size—the opposite of diminutive endings like **-ito(-a)** or **-illo(-a)**. In Mexico and some parts of Central America, **huevón** or **huevona** means lazy and worthless, but in the Southern Cone it means stupid. Of course, as with so many insults, these words are often used in an affectionate way among friends; for example, **¡No seas huevón, 'mano, y ven conmigo!** (Don't be a lazy dope, bro', and come with me!) In that case you're being a "good egg" and not insulting anyone!

Me pela lo que digas. Me la pela. I don't give a damn about what you say. I don't give a damn.

valerle huevo (to be worth egg, meaning testicle) to not care, not give a damn (vulgar) ◀ Col ▶

valerle pinga (verga) (to be worth male organ) to not care, not give a damn (vulgar) (ES: **verga** only) ◀ Nic, Ven ▶

Me vale pinga (verga) no aprobar el examen. I don't give a damn about not passing the exam.

Who cares? I don't care. I don't give a damn.

Concha. (seashell; S. Cone, female organ [vulgar]) Who cares? (I don't give a damn.) ◀ Mex, Col ▶

Me la suda. I don't give a damn. (vulgar) ◀ Mex, Sp ▶

Me vale. I don't give a damn. (Used instead of **Me vale madre** or **verga** [vulgar].) ◀ Mex, ES, Col ▶

¡Qué culos! (What asses!) Who gives a damn! (vulgar) ◄ Cuba, Col ►
¡Qué culos! Vámonos a la fiesta. Who gives a damn! Let's go to the party.

¿Qué más da? (What more does it give?) Who cares? ◄ L. Am. (not S. Cone) ►

Que siga rodando la bola. (Let the ball keep rolling.) Let things happen as they may. ◄ ES ►

information

See also "conversation,"
"knowledge, understanding."

catar el melón (to inspect the melon) to sound or feel someone or something out ◄ Sp ►

opening up,
spilling the beans

caerse el casete (to have the cassette fall) to have a secret revealed ◄ Ch ►

¡Canta, pajarito! (Sing, little bird) Confess! Tell the truth! 'Fess up! ◄ Nic, Ch ►

Canta. (Sing.) Tell me, do tell. ◄ Sp ►

dejar la escoba (to leave the broom) to disclose information that is shocking or embarrassing ◄ Bol, Ch ►

desembuchar (to disgorge) to unload (problems, secrets) like **desahogar** ◄ Mex, ES, Ch ►
¡Desembucha! Spit it out!

despegar la boca (to unstick the mouth) to talk ◄ Mex, Sp ►

destaparse (to uncork oneself) to open up, tell something ◄ L. Am. ►
Destápate, cariño. ¿Qué pasó? Open up, honey. What happened?

echar de cabeza to publicly reveal someone's secrets ◄ Mex ►

Lola me echó de cabeza con Irma de algo que yo le platiqué de mi trabajo. Lola let the cat out of the bag and told Irma something I told her about my work.

no tener pelos en la lengua (to not have hair on the tongue [hair implies animals, or more primitive forms, that do not have language]) to talk clearly, without mincing words ◄ L. Am., Sp ►

soltar la cuerda (to let go of or loosen the cord) to confess, implicate someone in something ◄ Mex, Sp ►

soltar la lengua (to loosen the tongue) to open up, spill the beans ◄ DR, S. Cone ►

Súbete a la micro. (Step up to the microphone.) Join in the conversation. ◄ Ch ►

rat, tattle-tale, spy

el chivato traitor, fink, person who rats on others (Cuba, DR: also, **chiva**) ◄ Mex, Cuba, DR, Sp ►
Si mi hermano se entera de que llegue tarde, estoy frita. Es un chivato y seguro me chivatea con papi. If my brother finds out I'm coming late, I'm toast. He's a fink, and for sure he'll fink on me to Dad.

el/la oreja (ear) spy, informer ◄ Mex, ES, Nic ►

el rata (rat) informer, fink ◄ PR, Col ►

el sapo (frog, toad) informer, stool pigeon, fink (used like **soplón**) (Col: also, **rana;** Peru: **ranear**) ◄ Nic, CR, Col, Ven, Ec, Ch ►

el soplón, la soplona informer, tattle-tale, rat; someone who whispers the answer to someone taking a test ◄ L. Am., Sp ►
Fue expulsada por soplona. She was expelled for cheating (being a cheater).

squealing,
ratting on, informing

cantar (to sing) to denounce, inform ◄ L. Am., Sp ►

cantar (soltar) la pepa (to sing [release] the pit or stone) to inform on someone, squeal, rat on, especially to police ◄ Ch ►

sapear to tell on someone, squeal (Ch, Peru: to spy on) ◀ CR, Col, Ven ▶
No me vayas a sapear a la maestra. Don't tell the teacher on me.

señalar a alguien con el dedo; poner el dedo a alguien to point the finger at someone ◀ Mex, ES, Peru, Ch, Sp ▶
Le puso el dedo al narcotraficante. He (She) signaled out the drug dealer.

soplar (to blow) to squeal, tell or inform on someone, tattle; to whisper the answer to someone taking a test ◀ L. Am., Sp ▶

---

innocence

¡A mí que me registren! Search me! Check me out! (I'm innocent.) ◀ Mex, S. Cone, Sp ▶

como patos cagados (like shit-upon ducks) easy to capture or kill, like sitting ducks ◀ Nic ▶

estar muy verde (to be very green) to be innocent, immature, not socially active ◀ S. Cone, Sp ▶

la fresa (strawberry) young woman who is innocent but also a bit disdainful or spoiled, usually living with her parents ◀ most of L. Am., Sp ▶
Su hermana es una fresa; sus papás la miman mucho. His sister is an innocent young thing; her (their) parents spoil her a lot.

el manzano young person who is innocent, not very active socially ◀ Col ▶

Mírame esta cara. (Look at this face.) phrase implying that the other person is innocent or unaware of one's merits ◀ Mex, Sp ▶

la niña fresa naive, conservative girl (virgin) ◀ Mex ▶

el/la zanahorio(-a) (carrot) young person who is innocent, not socially active or "with it" (Ven, Ec: also, a health nut who doesn't smoke, drink, etc.) ◀ Col, Ven, Ec ▶

gullibility

caer como un gil (como un angelito) (to fall like a fool [like a little angel]) to be taken in, tricked, duped ◀ Bol, S. Cone ▶

caer en la trampa (en la red) to fall into the trap (the net) (Ch: **trampa** only) ◀ Mex, ES, DR, S. Cone, Sp ▶

caído(-a) del nido (fallen out of the nest) wet behind the ears, naive, clueless ◀ L. Am. ▶
Te lo expliqué cien veces, pero ni cuenta te diste. Pareces como caído del nido. I explained it to you a hundred times, but you didn't get it. You seem clueless.

caído(-a) del zarzo (fallen out of the attic) foolish, clueless ◀ Col ▶

comulgar con ruedas de molinos (to commune with windmills) to believe the most unlikely things ◀ Sp ▶

tragar el anzuelo (to swallow the hook) to be deceived ◀ Mex, ES, DR, S. Cone, Sp ▶

tragar(se) algo to believe (swallow) something ◀ L. Am., Sp ▶
No voy a tragar ese cuento. No me lo trago. I'm not swallowing that story. I'm not swallowing it.

tragarse la píldora (to swallow the pill) to believe a lie, fall for something (Sp: also, **tragarse la bola**, to swallow the ball) ◀ Mex, U, Ch, Sp ▶

holding the bag, stuck with the blame or responsibility

pagar el pato (los patos) (to pay for the duck[s]) to pay for something unfairly (when someone else has done it), to be left holding the bag ◀ Mex, Nic, S. Cone, Sp ▶

pagar los platos rotos (to pay for the broken plates) to pay for something unfairly (when someone else was responsible), be left holding the bag, be the fall guy (CR: **pagar los elotes**) ◀ L. Am., Sp ▶
Ellos causaron el problema, pero yo pagué los platos rotos. They caused the problem, but I was left holding the bag.

pagar los vidrios rotos (to pay for the broken windows) to pay for something unfairly (when someone else has done it) ◀ Mex, Sp ▶

insignificance

don Nadie (Sir Nobody) unimportant person, with little influence or power ◀ L. Am., Sp ▶

ser una bacteria en el horizonte (to be a bacterium on the horizon) to be of no consequence ◀ Sp ▶

ser el último mono (to be the last monkey) to be insignificant, not count (people) ◀ Sp ▶
Parece que soy el último mono en esta oficina. Seems like I'm the least important person in this office.

insults

See also "anger," "annoyance," "criticism."

hay que joderse (jorobarse) expression of opposition, something like "screw you" but not as strong (vulgar) ◀ DR, PR, Sp ▶

el ñero Mataratas (comrade rat-killer) dirty Dan or any name of disrespect ◀ Mex, Col ▶

bitching, cursing, swearing

decir madres (to say mothers) to say crude or stupid things, insults ◀ Mex, Col ▶

echar madres (to throw mothers) to curse, swear at (Col: also, **echar la madre**) ◀ chicano, Mex, Col ▶

pagar los vidrios rotos

hijueputear used like **putear** (vulgar) ◀ ES, CR, Col ▶

madrear to offend with bad language, swear at ◀ CR ▶

mentar la madre (to mention the mother) to insult someone by suggesting the moral impurity of his or her mother (usually this means calling someone an **hijo de puta**) (Ch: **sacar la madre**; Sp: **mentar a la madre**) ◀ Mex, C. Am., Col ▶

putear, echar puteadas to insult with offensive names (vulgar) ◀ L. Am. ▶
Ayer fui a un partido de fútbol con Jesús. Primera y última vez, porque estaba puteando al árbitro y yo me sentía mal. Yesterday I went to a soccer game with Jesús. First and last time because he was swearing at the referee and I felt bad.

rayársela used like **mentar la madre** ◀ Mex ▶
Me la rayaron. They insulted me big-time.

telling someone to get lost

Note: Get lost! Go to the devil! There are all sorts of ways to express these ideas in Spanish, as in English. The expressions in this and the following section can be used as direct insults with the verbs **ir** or **andar**. If you hear these (and we hope that they will not be directed toward you!), they will very often be in the **tú** form: **Vete a paseo (por un tubo, al demonio**, and so on). The **usted** form would be **Váyase...** You might also hear them with the verb **andar**, especially in Spain or the Southern Cone.

Mandar a alguien... (To send someone . . .)

a bañarse (to take a bath) ◀ ES, Nic, Peru, Bol, Ch ▶

a buscar berros (to find watercress) ◀ Sp ▶

a freír buñuelos (to fry doughnuts) ◀ Mex, Sp ▶

a freír espárragos (to fry asparagus) ◀ Mex, ES, PR, Ch, Sp ▶
Cuando Estela le pidió un aumento de sueldo a su jefe, éste la mandó a freír espárragos. When Estela asked her boss for a raise, he told her to get lost.
Vete a freír espárragos. Get lost.

a freír papas (to fry potatoes) ◀ PR ▶

a la goma (to the rubber, as far as rubber expands) ◀ Mex ▶

a hacer gárgaras (to gargle) ◀ Sp ▶

a hacer puñetas (to masturbate; vulgar, but not considered very vulgar in Sp) ◀ PR, Sp ▶
Me quería cobrar dos mil pesetas de esa radio y lo mandé a hacer puñetas. He wanted to charge me two thousand pesetas for that radio and I told him to go to the devil.

a paseo (to take a walk) ◀ Col, Sp ▶

a tirar piedras al río (to throw stones in the river) ◀ Col ▶

por un tubo (through a pipe) to get rid of someone, ignore them; to dump (a friend or sweetheart) ◀ Mex, ES, Col ▶
¿Cómo estás, Juan? —Mal. Mi novia me mandó por un tubo. How are you, Juan? —Bad. My girlfriend dumped me.

telling someone to go to hell (the devil)

Mandar a alguien... (To send someone . . .)

al carajo (to the male organ, vulgar) ◀ L. Am., Sp ▶

a la chingada (to the **chingada**, a violated woman, vulgar) ◀ Mex, C. Am. ▶
Mi jefe me mandó a la chingada. My boss told me to go to hell.

a la chucha (to the female organ, vulgar) ◀ Ch ▶

al cuerno, a la eme (to the horn; to the "m," which stands for **mierda**, shit) ◀ Mex, ES, DR, PR, Peru, S. Cone, Sp ▶

al demonio (to the devil) ◀ Mex, G, Col, ES ▶

a la jodida (used like **a la chingada** but only slightly vulgar) ◀ chicano, Mex, G ▶
Cuando traté de explicarle la situación, no quiso escuchar. Me mandó a la jodida. When I tried to explain the situation, he refused to listen. He told me to go to the devil.

a la mierda (to shit, vulgar) ◀ L. Am., Sp ▶
¡Vete a la mierda! Go to hell!

a la porra (to the pot) ◀ L. Am., Sp ▶

a la verga (to the male organ, vulgar) ◀ ES, Nic, Ven ▶

vulgar words to tell someone off or describe someone nasty

Note: The expressions in this section are direct insults, but they may also be used in the third person to describe someone. In such cases, the **tú** form is changed to the third person; e.g., **Ese coño de su madre nunca hace nada. ¡La puta que lo parió! Tenía que ser de alquilar, como su madre.**

el cabrón, la cabrona (big goat) son of a bitch (bitch) (vulgar) ◀ most of L. Am. (not S. Cone) ▶

el/la ca'e pija (cara de pija) dickface, dope (vulgar) ◀ Hond ▶

el/la ca'e verga (cara de verga) dickface, dope (vulgar) ◀ Hond, ES ▶

el/la cara de culo (ass face) asshole (vulgar) ◀ ES, Arg, Sp ▶

el cerote (turd) asshole (vulgar) ◀ C. Am. ▶

¡Chorro de mierda! (Squirt of shit!) Piece of shit! ◄ ES, DR, PR ►

la concha de tu madre (your mother's shell, referring to female organ) son of a bitch (to friend or foe, as an insult or term of endearment, vulgar) ◄ S. Cone ►

el coño de tu madre (your mother's female organ) real son of a bitch (vulgar) ◄ Ven, DR, PR ►

Dale saludo a la más vieja de tu casa. (Give a greeting to the oldest woman in your house.) insult equivalent to **¡Tu madre!** ◄ chicano ►

el/la hijo(-a) de la chingada (son [daughter] of the violated woman) son of a bitch (bitch) (vulgar) ◄ Mex, C. Am. ► **¿Qué te hizo el hijo de la chingada?** What did the son of a bitch do to you?

el/la hijo(-a) de la gran puta (son [daughter] of the big whore) son of a bitch (bitch) (vulgar) ◄ L. Am., Sp ►

el/la hijo(-a) de mil demonios (de mil desgracias) (son [daughter] of a thousand demons [of a thousand misfortunes]) used in ES instead of a harsher expression ◄ ES ► **Vete al carajo, hijo de sesenta mil demonios.** Go to hell, you SOB.

el/la hijo(-a) de puta (son [daughter] of a whore) son of a bitch (bitch) (L. Am.: also, **hijueputa**; Sp: also, **hijoputa**) (vulgar) ◄ L. Am., Sp ►

el/la hijo(-a) de su SOB (bitch) (somewhat vulgar, euphemism for **hijo[-a] de su puta madre**) ◄ most of L. Am., Sp ►

el hijuemilpesos euphemism for **hijo de puta** ◄ ES, CR ►

¡La madre que te parió! (The mother who gave birth to you!) expression of anger, indignation (vulgar) ◄ Mex, ES, DR, PR, Arg, Sp ►

¡La puta que te parió! (The whore who gave birth to you!) You son of a bitch! (vulgar) ◄ S. Cone, Sp ►

¡Me cago en tu madre (en la madre que te parió, en tus muertos)! I shit on your mother (that gave birth to you, on your dead)! (Sp: also, **cagarse en su padre**) (vulgar) ◄ PR, Sp ►

Ese profesor me ha vuelto a suspender. ¡Me cago en su madre (padre)! That teacher has flunked me again. Fuck him!

¡Métetelo donde te quepa (por el culo)! (Arg, U: **donde no te da el sol,** where the sun doesn't shine) (Put it where it fits [up your ass]!) angry rejection, like Up yours! (vulgar) ◄ Mex, ES, DR, PR, Ch, Sp ►

narices (noses) dickens, often a euphemism for **cojones** ◄ Sp ► **¡Tócame las narices/los cojones!** vulgar insult **¡Tócate las narices!** expression of anger or surprise

¡Pa'joderte! Screw you! (vulgar) ◄ Mex, Col ►

pelotudo(-a) (big-balled) jerk (bitch), schmuck (often accompanied by a gesture with hands up as though holding two balls; similar to **huevón** in Mex and Ch or **Le pesan** in Nic, vulgar) ◄ S. Cone ►

pinche cabrón insult similar to rotten bastard (vulgar) ◄ Mex ►

pisado(-a) (stepped on) insult similar to **cabrón** ◄ G ►

Tenías que ser de alquilar, como tu madre, ¡huevón! (You must have been rented out, like your mother, stupid!) You are useless, you son of a bitch! ◄ Ven ►

¡Tu abuela! (¡Tu padre!) (Your grandmother! [Your father!]) expression of anger ◄ ES, DR, Sp ►

¡Tu madre! (Your mother!) insult impugning the honor of one's mother, often accompanied by a gesture with the fist of one hand raised and clenched (vulgar) ◄ Mex, C. Am. ►

intelligence

See also "competence."

la chispa (spark) smarts, intelligence, astuteness ◄ Mex, ES, CR, DR, Col ►

Julio tiene chispa para trabajar (para los negocios). Julio es muy chispa. Julio is good at work (astute in business). Julio is very sharp.

la jaiba (crayfish) astuteness, especially of people in the country who are wiser than they may appear ◀ PR ▶

no chuparse el dedo (to not suck one's thumb) to not be naive or easily deceived ◀ Mex, DR, PR, ES, S. Cone, Sp ▶
Yo no me chupo el dedo. Eso es pura mentira. You can't pull the wool over my eyes. That's a lie.

clever, smart

abusado(-a) (abused) sharp, clever ◀ Mex ▶
Paco es muy abusado, abusadísimo. Paco is very clever, extremely sharp.

avispado(-a) (wasped) alert, smart, clever ◀ L. Am. (not S. Cone), Sp ▶

buzo (diver) smart, alert, on the ball ◀ Mex, G, Hond, ES ▶
Si te pones buzo, lo logras. If you're on the ball, you'll manage (achieve) it.
Ya se puso buzo para los negocios. He (She) became sharp at business.

fino(-a) como un coral (fine as a coral) astute, wise, bright as a dollar ◀ Sp ▶

el listón, la listona (big clever) a real smartie ◀ Mex, Col ▶
Juan es un listón. Juan is a real smartie.

más listo(-a) que el hambre (more clever than hunger) bright, quick-witted ◀ Sp ▶

más listo(-a) que un rayo (el relámpago) (more clever than lightning) smart, sharp as a tack ◀ ES ▶
¡Qué buena solución! Eres más listo que un rayo. What a good solution! You're sharp as a tack.

picudo(-a) well connected and clever ◀ Mex, ES ▶
Juan es muy picudo, por eso le promovieron. Juan is very well connected and clever; that's why they promoted him.

pillo(-a) sharp, alert, clever ◀ Mex, Hond, CR, Col, Peru, S. Cone, Sp ▶

pipa (small coconut) intelligent (Col: pepa) ◀ CR ▶

Fernando es muy pipa. (CR) Fernando is very clever.
¡Qué pepa! (Col) How smart!

el/la profe smart person (said in jest, short for **profesor[a]**) ◀ chicano, Mex ▶

el/la sabe de letras (letter-knower) intelligent person, egghead ◀ Mex, DR, Col ▶

ser (un) coco (to be a coconut) to be smart, intelligent (feminine is also **coco**) ◀ L. Am. (not S. Cone) ▶
Marisa es bien coco. Pedro es un coco. Marisa is a smart cookie. Pedro is a smart cookie.

ser un durote (to be very hard) to be sharp, have a lot of smarts ◀ Col ▶
Emilio es un durote. No estudia y siempre sale bien en todas sus clases. Emilio's really sharp. He doesn't study and always does well in all his classes.

tener buen coco (to have a good coconut, head) to be smart (Mex: more common, **ser coco**) ◀ Mex, Ch ▶

tener mucho coco (to have a lot of coconut) to be smart ◀ Sp ▶
Anita tiene mucho coco. Anita is very smart.

zorro(-a) (fox) sly, clever like a fox (Ch: masculine form only) ◀ L. Am., Sp ▶

interruption

butting in

cortar el hilo (to cut the thread) to interrupt a conversation or other thing (Ch: also, to interrupt one's train of thought) ◀ Mex, DR, S. Cone ▶

cortar la nota (to cut off one's news or note) to dampen one's spirits, knock someone out of kilter; to interrupt ◀ Ec ▶

meter baza (to play a card trick) to butt into someone's conversation ◀ Ch, Sp ▶

meter la cuchara (to put in the spoon) to butt into someone else's business ◄ L. Am., Sp ►
Y ¿quién es usted para meter la cuchara? And who are you to butt in?
Metí la cuchara para decirles la verdad. I butt in to tell them the truth.

Pasáme el mate. (Pass me the mate tea.) Let me get a word in. ◄ Arg ►

Préstame la guitarra. (Lend me the guitar.) Let me get a word in. ◄ ES ►

stopping someone or something

Córtala. (Cut it.) Cut it out. ◄ S. Cone ►

parar(se) en seco (to stop someone [oneself] dry) to stop in one's tracks or stop someone cold ◄ Mex, ES, Col, U, Ch ►
Cuando Yoli me vio, se paró en seco. When Yoli saw me, she stopped in her tracks.

pararle el carro a (to stop his or her cart) to firmly prevent someone from doing something, put one's foot down ◄ S. Cone, Sp ►
Habló de vender el negocio, pero yo le paré el carro. He (She) wanted to sell the business, but I put my foot down.
Mateo quería irse de la casa, pero le dije, «¡Para el carro!» Mateo wanted to leave the house (leave home), but I said to him, "Hold your horses!"

poner freno a algo (to put the brake on something) to put a stop to something ◄ most of L. Am., Sp ►

invitations

See also "dance," "fun," "party."

agarrar viaje (to grab a journey) to accept an invitation or proposal ◄ U, Arg ►
Me propuso un negocio y agarré viaje. He (She) proposed an enterprise to me and I went for it.

rajarse to treat, pay the check ◄ Hond, CR, Pan ►

going dutch

a escote dutch treat (each person pays for himself or herself) ◄ Sp ►

a la americana (American style) dutch treat ◄ Mex ►
Siempre salimos a la americana. We always go dutch.

a la inglesa (English style) dutch treat ◄ Peru, Bol, Arg, Ch ►

hacer serrucho to split a bill, go dutch ◄ DR, PR ►

miti-miti (half-half) halves on a bill, dutch treat (Ch: also, **miti-mota**; ES: **mita' mita'**; Nic: **mitimita**) ◄ S. Cone ►
Vamos miti-miti con la cuenta. Let's split the bill (like the old expression "go halfsies").

knowledge, understanding

See also "thinking."

jugar a cartas vistas (to play with cards that can be seen) to do something openly or to do something with knowledge that others don't have (referring to cards out on the table or cards in one's hand) ◄ Sp ►

saber de qué pie cojea (to know what foot someone is limping on) to know what's going on with someone or some situation, know how the cookie crumbles, know what someone's weak point is ◄ L. Am., Sp ►

¿Te fijas? (Do you notice?) See? Get it? (like **¿Cachas?**, page 143) ◄ Ch ►

¿Viste? (Did you see?) See? ◄ L. Am. ►

being correct

dar en el clavo to hit the nail on the head, figure out or be right about something ◄ L. Am., Sp ►
¡Eso es! Diste en el clavo. That's right! You hit the nail on the head.

dar la patada a la lata (to kick the can) to be right ◀ Cuba ▶

tocar la flauta (to play the flute) to be right, guess correctly ◀ Cuba ▶

catching the drift, finding out

agarrar el hilo (to grasp the thread) to get the point ◀ Mex, ES, Col, Ch ▶

agarrar la onda (to grasp the sound wave) to get it, get with it ◀ Mex, G, ES, Col, Ch ▶

Ahora caigo. Now I get it (fall). ◀ L. Am., Sp ▶
Ahora caigo. Quieres romper conmigo. Now I get it. You want to break up with me.

cachar to catch the drift, get it (Ch, Peru: also, to have sex) ◀ most of L. Am. ▶
¿Cacha el mote? (Ch) Catch the drift? ¿Cachas? (¿Cachaste?) —No cacho, amigo. Get it? (Did you get it?) —I don't get it, pal.

caer en el chiste (to fall into the joke) to figure out the reason that someone is saying or doing something ◀ Mex, Sp ▶

caer en la cuenta (to fall into the account) to become aware of something or finally "get it" ◀ Mex, DR, PR, U, Arg, Sp ▶
Cuando vi su foto, caí en la cuenta de que lo conocía desde hacía muchos años. When I saw his photo, it dawned on me (I figured out) that I had known him for many years.

caer el veinte (to have the twenty [meaning twenty-cent coin] fall, as into the telephone) to get it, understand ◀ Mex ▶
Ya me cayó el veinte. Now I get the message.

caerse de la mata (to fall out of the bush or shrub) to find out something everyone else already knows, wise up ◀ Cuba, DR, PR, Col ▶
¿Te caíste de la mata? Did you (finally) wise up?

caerse del mecate (to fall off the cord) to realize one has been deceived, wise up ◀ Mex ▶

captar la onda (to capture the sound wave) to understand something insinuated ◀ Mex, DR ▶

descubrirse el pastel

descubrirse el pastel (to discover the cake) to have a secret revealed ◀ Mex, S. Cone, Sp ▶
Ayer se descubrió el pastel. Ahora todo el mundo lo sabe. Yesterday the lid was blown off the story. Now everyone knows.

morder (to bite) to understand ◀ Ec ▶

ponerse al hilo (en onda) to get with it, become aware ◀ Mex, Hond, ES, CR, Col ▶
Pongámonos al hilo. Let's get with it.

quedarse con la copla (to remain or end up with the verse, stanza) to realize what someone was trying to do secretively, find out ◀ Sp ▶

knowing or having knowledge

conocer a alguien desde su (la) cuna to know someone from infancy (from their cradle) ◀ most of L. Am., Sp ▶

conocer como la palma de la mano to know like the back (palm) of one's hand ◀ L. Am., Sp ▶
Conozco la capital como la palma de la mano. I know the capital like the back of my hand.

empaparse en algo (to get wet in something) to inform oneself about something ◀ Mex, G, ES, Cuba, DR, PR, Col, U, Arg ▶
Necesito empaparme en el asunto. I need to learn about the matter (to immerse myself).

estar en el ajo (to be in the garlic) to be in the know ◀ Mex, Sp ▶

Say it with slang!

Latin hospitality

Latin hospitality is famous the world over. In many places in Latin America, guests who enter someone's house for the first time are greeted with a humble and welcoming phrase: **La casa es chica, el corazón grande.** (The house is small, the heart large.) Mexicans, particularly, delight foreign visitors with their warmth and openness when they offer them their home in the standard greeting of welcome: **Mi casa es tu casa** (My house is your house) or **Estás en tu casa** (You are in your own home). In the city of Leon, Guanajuato, however, there is a saying that outdoes this generosity. When a large group of people come to visit, the host insists that it will be no problem for them all to stay because **De la puerta hasta el rincón, ¡toda mi casa es un colchón!** (From the door to the corner, my whole house is just one mattress!)

estar puesto(-a) (to be put, turned on) to have a lot of knowledge (about something) or a talent for it ◀ Mex, Sp ▶ **Está muy puesto en matemáticas.** He (She) is very savvy about math.

saber al dedillo (to know to the little finger) to know to a "T," have knowledge at one's fingertips ◀ Mex, Sp ▶

saber de buena fuente to know from a good source ◀ Mex, Peru, Bol, S. Cone ▶

saber de buena tinta una cosa (to know something from good ink) to know something from a reliable source, have it on good authority ◀ L. Am., Sp ▶

saber dónde le aprieta el zapato (to know where the shoe is too tight) to know what is suitable or appropriate for one ◀ L. Am., Sp ▶

saberse la cartilla (to know the primer) to know the score; to have gotten instructions on how to behave or what to do (also, Mex, Sp: **tener aprendida la cartilla**) ◀ PR, Sp ▶

sabiondo(-a) (sabihondo[-a]) know-it-all ◀ Mex, G, DR, PR, Col, S. Cone ▶

Ella se cree que tiene todas las respuestas. Se las da de sabihonda. She thinks she has all the answers. She acts like a know-it-all.

tener clara la película (to have the movie or film clear) to have a clear picture of some situation, understand it in full ◀ Peru, S. Cone, Sp ▶

you know

pa' (para) que sepas just so you know ◀ L. Am., Sp ▶

sae (sa, tusa, tusabe) used like **tú sabes,** for emphasis ◀ PR ▶ **A mí no me interesan las cosas materiales, sae. Lo mío es lo espiritual.** I'm not interested in material things, you know. My thing is spirituality.

Ya sábanas (sabadabas). Ya sabes. ◀ Mex, Col ▶ **Ya sábanas; paquetes de hilo. (Ya sabes, ¿p'a qué te digo?)** You know what I mean; why should I tell you?

ya tú sabe' you know (already) ◀ Caribbean ▶

lack of knowledge

See also "inattention," "incompetence," "stupidity."

conocido(-a) en su casa (known in his or her own home) unknown person, describing someone who goes to a party or meeting and no one knows who he or she is (used ironically, as if to say, "Well, at least he must be known in his own home!") (Sp: **A ése no lo conocen, ni en su casa.** Mex: **Lo conocen en su casa.**) ◀ Ch ▶

estar en pañales (to be in diapers) to have little or no knowledge of something ◀ L. Am., Sp ▶

guillado(-a) not understanding or ignorant (of something) or not wanting to tell it ◀ Cuba, DR ▶

no saber de la misa la mitad (to not know half the mass) to not know something ◀ U, Sp ▶

no saber ni papa (to not know potato) to know nothing ◀ Mex, ES, DR, PR, U, Ch, Sp ▶
Ojalá no me pregunten en la clase de historia porque no sé ni papa de la Revolución Mexicana. I hope they don't ask me any questions in history class because I don't know beans about the Mexican Revolution.

in the dark, unaware

estar detrás del palo (to be behind the tree) to be uninformed, in the dark ◀ Cuba ▶

estar en ayunas (to be fasting) to be in the dark, unaware (Mex: also said of a woman who has just had a baby and stays at home for a while) ◀ Mex, S. Cone, Sp ▶
María estaba en ayunas. Pues no había caído. María was completely in the dark. She hadn't figured it out.

estar fuera de bola (to be out of the ball) to be in the dark ◀ Cuba ▶

quedarse a oscuras (to be left in the dark) to not understand ◀ Mex, Ch, Sp ▶

lack of worry

See also "indifference."

reírse de los peces de colores (to laugh at colored fish) to not worry about something, not take seriously the consequences of one's or another's action, let it roll off like water off a duck's back ◀ CR, Cuba, S. Cone ▶
Pase lo que pase, me río de los peces de colores. Whatever happens, I let it roll off my back.

sacarse/quitarse un peso de encima (to take a weight off oneself) to take a load off; to sit down ◀ Mex, DR, PR, S. Cone, Sp ▶
Te sacaste un peso de encima cuando terminaste tu trabajo. You took a load off when you finished your work.

suave y sin sudar (soft and without sweating) calmly ◀ Col ▶

tomar a coña algo (to take something at **coña**, a word referring to the female organ) to not take something seriously (vulgar) ◀ Sp ▶

tomar algo con soda (to take something with soda) to take something calmly ◀ Ch ▶
Esas cosas, hay que tomarlas con soda. You have to take those things calmly.

calm

cul calm in any situation (from the English "cool") ◀ Mex, DR ▶

fresco(-a) (fresh) not worried, cool as a cucumber ◀ Mex, Col, Ch, Sp ▶
Tiene un examen mañana, pero está tan fresca. She has a test tomorrow, but she's cool as a cucumber.

laxo(-a) not worried, laid back ◀ Col ▶
Mañana Alfonso tiene que dar una conferencia y no ha hecho nada para prepararse. ¡Qué laxo! Tomorrow Alfonso has to give a talk and he hasn't done anything to prepare. He's so laid back!

ser más (tan) fresco(-a) que una lechuga (to be more [as] fresh as a lettuce) to be very brazen, bold, cool as a cucumber, fresh as a daisy ◀ L. Am., Sp ▶

todo fresas (all strawberries) calm, not worried ◀ Col ▶
Yo estaba muy nerviosa por el examen, pero los otros estudiantes parecían todo fresas. I was very nervous about the test, but the other students seemed cool as cucumbers.

No problem.

No es para tanto. (It's not for so much.) It's not as bad as all that. ◀ L. Am., Sp ▶

No hay bronca. (There's no dispute.) No problem. ◀ Mex, ES ▶

No hay casco. (There's no helmet.) Forget it, let it go. ◀ G, PR ▶

No hay tos. (There's no cough.) variant of **No hay problema.** ◀ Mex, ES ▶

No te comas un cable. (Don't eat a cable.) Don't worry. Don't have a cow. ◀ PR, Col ▶

No te pongas cerril. (Don't put wax on yourself.) Don't get rigid, uptight. ◀ Sp ▶

No te rompas la cabeza. (Don't break your head.) Don't worry about it. ◀ L. Am., Sp ▶

Suave. (Smooth, soft.) Chill out. Easy does it. ◀ Ch, DR, Ven ▶

Tranquilo(-a). (Tranquil.) No problem, relax. (very common in Col; Sp: also, **tranqui** for short and **de tranqui**, calmly) ◀ Mex, DR, Col, Ven, S. Cone, Sp ▶
Tranquilo, tranquilo. No hay problema. Keep your cool. (Relax.) There's no problem.
Tranqui. (Sp) Relax. Chill out.
Comimos de tranqui. (Sp) We ate in peace.

taking things easy

bajar el volumen (to lower the volume) to take it easy, cool down ◀ Mex, Col ▶

llevarla suave to take it easy, calmly (Pan, Cuba: **cogerlo suave**) ◀ ES, CR, Col, U ▶
Llévala suave, que no hay prisa. (ES) Take it easy; there's no hurry.
Cógelo suave, que no vale la pena. (Cuba) Keep your cool; it's not worth worrying about.

pasarlo piola (to pass it string, from "piola" in Italian, string or cord) to take it easy, keep cool or mellow about a problem ◀ S. Cone ▶

mearse de la risa

laughter

la pavera (from **pavo**, turkey) silly giggling, childish nonsense ◀ DR, PR ▶
Tienen pavera. They're always giggling.

el pelón, la pelona (bald) someone who can't make a joke or laughs at things that are not funny ◀ PR ▶

dying of laughter

cagarse de la risa (to shit from laughter) to die laughing (also, **cagado de la risa**) (vulgar) ◄ Mex, ES, Ven, S. Cone ►

descojonarse de risa (to de-testicle oneself with laughter) to laugh uncontrollably (vulgar) ◄ Sp ►

estar muerto(-a) de risa to be dying of laughter ◄ L. Am., Sp ►
¡Qué chistoso! ¡Estaba muerta de risa! How funny! I was dying of laughter.

mearse de (la) risa to wet one's pants with laughter (also, **meado de la risa**) ◄ Mex, DR, S. Cone, Sp ►
Cuando vi ese programa, estaba meado de la risa. When I saw that show, I wet my pants laughing.

morirse de risa to die of laughter ◄ L. Am., Sp ►

partirse de risa to break up with laughter ◄ DR, PR, Sp ►

pelao(-a) como un guineo (peeled as a banana) dying of laughter ◄ PR, Col ►

reventar de risa to crack up with laughter ◄ DR, Sp ►

troncharse de risa to break up laughing, crack up ◄ ES, Sp ►

smiling

mostrar los dientes (to show teeth) to smile; also, to threaten ◄ L. Am. ►

pelar los dientes (to peel the teeth) to smile or make smile ◄ Mex, ES, Nic, CR, Col, Ec ►
Vos sólo pelando los dientes pasas. (ES) You're always smiling.
Tus palabras me pelan los dientes. (Mex) Your words make me smile.

laziness

See also "inactivity."

el achantazón lack of spirit, being without the desire to do anything ◄ CR ►

dejamestad ("let me be"-ness, sounding like **déjame estar**) laziness, boredom ◄ Col ►

la flojera laziness, lack of spirit ◄ Mex, ES, Nic, CR, DR, PR, Col, Ch ►

Que lo haga Rita. Let George (literally Rita, meaning someone else) do it. ◄ Sp ►

la sopa boba (crazy or foolish soup) life lived at others' expense, without working ◄ Sp ►

goofing off

achancharse (to become like a pig) to be lazy, slack off, loaf around ◄ Arg ►

aplanarse to be lazy, not want to work (also, **aplanado[-a]**) ◄ CR, Col ►

huevear (to egg around) to goof off, mess around (vulgar) ◄ Ch ►

jorochar to fool around, goof around ◄ Col ►

majasear to goof off ◄ Cuba ►

slackers

el/la achanchado(-a) (pigged out) slacker, loafer, underachiever ◄ Arg ►
Mirá a Mariano. Ya casi ni trabaja. Está totalmente achanchado. Just look at Mariano. He hardly works anymore. He's a total slacker.
Ese muchacho no te conviene; es un achanchado. That boy is no good for you; he's a slacker.

el/la achantado(-a) (hidden, lying low, submitting) person with no ambition, loser, slacker ◄ Hond, Nic, CR, Ven ►

aplatanado(-a) lazy, slow (Sp: sleepy) ◄ Mex, DR, PR, Sp ►
¡Qué aburrimiento! Me pasé todo el fin de semana aplatanado en casa. How boring (What boredom)! I spent the whole weekend lazing around at home.

atenido(-a) lazy, letting others do things ◄ Mex, ES, CR ►
Ese cipote es muy atenido; no le gusta hacer nada. (ES) That kid is very lazy; he doesn't like to do anything.

el bacalao (codfish) lazy person ◄ PR ►
En la parada de guaguas siempre está ese bacalao pidiendo chavos. At the bus stop there's always that bum asking for money.

calzonudo(-a) (in oversized pants) lazy (like **huevón**) ◀ ES, CR, Col, Ch ▶

flojo(-a) (loose, slack) lazy, slow, with no spirit; (n.) slacker, couch potato (CR: cowardly, weak; ES: often means gullible, as in **No seas flojo, que vos todo lo creás.** Don't be gullible; you believe everything.) ◀ Mex, ES, CR, DR, PR, Col, Ch ▶

el huevón, la huevona (big egg, meaning with large, heavy testicles) lazy, useless person, lazy bum (vulgar) (note: in many countries, such as the S. Cone and CR, this word means idiot; see "stupidity") ◀ Mex, C. Am. (not CR, Cuba, Ven) ▶

No quiero trabajar con Marcos. Es un huevón. I don't want to work with Marcos. He's a lazy bum.

majá (majado[-a]) lazy ◀ Cuba ▶
Qué majá me ha salido tu hermano. How lazy your brother has turned out.

el/la pasota someone who doesn't care about anything, slacker ◀ Sp ▶
Juan es un pasota, como muchos de sus amigos. Juan is a slacker, like a lot of his friends.

el/la vago(-a) slacker, drifter; can also be a drug addict or alcoholic ◀ Mex, ES, Col, Peru, Bol, S. Cone ▶

el/la zángano(-a) (drone) lazybones, slacker ◀ Mex, G, Nic, CR, Col, S. Cone ▶

Test your slang power!

Learning and education

Relevant categories: completeness, education, failure, flattery, intelligence, knowledge, lack of knowledge

How much Spanish "slanguage" do you know related to this topic? Test yourself by completing the exercises. Answers and rating scale are on page 263. (If you don't do very well, read through the categories listed above and try again. The items in each exercise occur in the same order as the categories.)

A. Something's missing. *Select the appropriate word to complete the sentence.*

1. At this university there is something for everyone. **En esta universidad hay de todo como en (escuela / tienda / botica)** _____.

2. You didn't have to tell it to every living soul. **No lo tenías que contar a cada hijo de (vecino / padre / ciudadano)** _____.

3. That speaker describes each topic in great detail. **Esa conferenciante describe cada tema con (letras / pelos / comas)** _____ **y señales.**

4. One of my classmates used a cheat sheet during the test. **Uno de mis compañeros de clase usó (un micro / un acordeón / una llave)** _____ **durante el examen.**

5. My cousin is always studying. He's a bookworm. **Mi primo siempre está estudiando. Es (un ratón / una serpiente / una araña)** _____ **de biblioteca.**

6. In Spain, a "pumpkin" is a very bad grade. **En España, una (bala / naranja / calabaza)** _____ **es una nota muy mala.**

7. Eusebio always gets an "in" with the powers that be. **Eusebio siempre se arrima (a la estrella / al sol / al fuego)** _____ **que más calienta.**

8. You don't want to show me your notes, right? Now I get it! **No quieres mostrarme tus apuntes, ¿verdad? ¡Ahora (brinco / caigo / vuelo)** _____!

9. My friend, you hit the nail on the head this time. **Amiga mía, diste en el (clavo / gancho / punto)** _____ **esta vez.**

10. Everyone in the Juárez family is brilliant. They are really sharp. **En la familia Juárez todos son brillantes. Tienen (pimienta / chispa / ola)** _____.

B. Pick a letter! *Choose the letter of the word or phrase that best completes each sentence. Write it in the blank.*

11. _____ In Mexico, to say "Yesterday I played hooky," you can say: **Ayer me fui de**
    a. **bosque.**
    b. **campanas.**
    c. **plano.**
    d. **pinta.**

12. _____ Tonight we are going to study like crazy. **Esta noche vamos a estudiar hasta más no**
    a. **saber.**
    b. **creer.**
    c. **poder.**
    d. **dormir.**

13. _____ To get ahead, you have to burn the midnight oil. **Para salir adelante, tienes que quemarte**
    a. **los ojos.**
    b. **la cabeza.**
    c. **las pestañas.**
    d. **la estufa.**

14. _____ If a Mexican says **Mi hermano tronó como ejote** (literally, snapped like a peapod), he means that his brother
    a. made a scene.
    b. won major honors.
    c. failed miserably.
    d. lost his temper.

15. _____ In Bolivia, Peru, and the Southern Cone, a brownnoser or suck-up is called a **chupamedias** (stocking sucker). In Mexico a person like this is called a
   a. **barbero.**
   b. **cartero.**
   c. **carpintero.**
   d. **plomero.**

16. _____ We know the lesson to the letter. **Sabemos la lección**
   a. **hasta atrás.**
   b. **al dedillo.**
   c. **con calma.**
   d. **para eternidad.**

17. _____ At last! Now we know our lab assistant's weak spot. **¡Por fin! Ahora sabemos de qué _____ cojea el ayudante de nuestro laboratorio.**
   a. **zapato**
   b. **muleta**
   c. **oreja**
   d. **pie**

18. _____ Those students don't know beans about World War II. **Esos estudiantes no saben ni _____ de la Segunda Guerra Mundial.**
   a. **menudo**
   b. **lechuga**
   c. **papa**
   d. **sal**

19. _____ In Mexico, someone who is sharp as a tack is often called **muy abusado (abusada),** but in Spain he or she may be described as **más listo (lista) que**
   a. **el hambre.**
   b. **el cuchillo.**
   c. **un huracán.**
   d. **una maestra.**

20. _____ In most of Latin America, a person who is considered a real brain may be referred to as
   a. **una guayaba.**
   b. **una manzana.**
   c. **un plátano.**
   d. **un coco.**

likes and dislikes

antojado(-a) (antojao[-a]) intent on; (n.) person who wants something ◀ Mex, G, PR, Col ▶

caerle bien (mal) una persona (to fall well [badly] on someone) to be likeable (not likeable, used like **gustar**) ◀ L. Am., Sp ▶
Esteban es muy antipático; me cae muy mal. Esteban is very unlikeable; I don't like him.
Creo que no le caigo bien a la maestra. I don't think the teacher likes me.

Como quiera(s). As you like. If you want. ◀ L. Am., Sp ▶
¿Comamos en aquel restaurán? —Como quieras. Shall we eat at that restaurant? —If you want.

de buena (mala) gana gladly (grudgingly) ◀ L. Am., Sp ▶

de mil amores (of a thousand loves) with pleasure ◀ Mex, ES, DR, S. Cone, Sp ▶
Haré lo que me pides de mil amores. I'll do what you ask with pleasure.

más que la cresta (more than the crest) very badly, a lot (used for wants, desires) ◀ Ch ▶

para puro paladar curtivo (only for the finest palate) for gourmets ◀ Mex ▶

por las buenas o por las malas (for the good or for the bad) one way or another, by force or voluntarily (Pan: **a la buena o a la mala**) ◀ L. Am., Sp ▶
Vas a acompañarme al concierto por las buenas o por las malas. You're going with me to the concert whether you want to or not.

¿Qué te parece (si...)? How does it seem to you (if . . .)? How about (if . . .)? How do you like . . . ? ◀ L. Am., Sp ▶
¿Qué te parece la música? How do you like the music?

el sueño dorado (golden dream) heart's desire, dream ◀ L. Am., Sp ▶

tener buena (mala) barra a alguien (to have a good [bad] bar for someone) to like (dislike) someone ◀ Peru, Ch ▶

disliking

caerle de la patada (pedrada) (to fall on someone like the kick [blow with a stone]) to be a pain, not be tolerable to (used like **gustar**) ◀ Mex, Ch ▶
Su mamá me cae de la patada. I can't stand his mom.

caerle (como una) bala (to fall on someone like a bullet) to be a pain, not be tolerable to ◀ CR ▶

caerle como piedra (plomo) (to fall on someone like stone [lead]) to be a pain, not tolerable to ◀ S. Cone ▶

caerle en el hígado (to fall to one's liver) to be intolerable, distasteful to (also, **caerle en los huevos**, vulgar) ◀ Mex, ES ▶
Me cae en el hígado ir a trabajar lejos. I hate working far away.

caerle gordo(-a) (to fall fat on someone) to be a pain, be intolerable to (also, **caerle pesado[-a]**) ◀ L. Am., Sp ▶
Ese hombre me cae gordo. That man is a pain in the neck. (I don't like that man.)

darle palo (to give someone stick) to be disagreeable to, not want to ◀ Sp ▶
Me da palo salir con él, pero tengo que ir. I hate going out with him (Going out with him is a pain), but I have to go.

echar para atrás to put off ◀ Sp ▶
Ese olor a ajo me echa para atrás. That garlic smell puts me off.
Sólo con verlo te echa para atrás. Just seeing him puts you off.

no bancar to dislike (used like **gustar**) ◀ U, Arg ▶
No me bancan esas muchachas tan creídas. I can't stand those stuck-up girls.

no pasar a alguien (to not pass someone) to not like someone, not be able to stand someone ◀ Mex, ES, DR, S. Cone ▶
La empleada de esa tienda no me pasa. I don't like the clerk in that store.

no poder ver a alguien ni en pintura (to not be able to see someone even in a painting) to not be able to stand the

sight of someone (CR, Arg, Sp: also, **ni pintado**) ◀ Mex, ES, DR, PR, Ch, U, Sp ▶
Matilde es tan orgullosa. No puedo verla ni en pintura. Matilde is so conceited. I can't stand the sight of her.

no tragar (to not swallow) to not stand ◀ Mex, G, ES, DR, S. Cone, Sp ▶
No trago a esos chicos. I can't stand those guys.
A Carlos lo masco pero no lo trago. I deal with (literally, chew) Carlos but I don't want him as a friend.

repatear (to rekick) to repel, bother; to dislike ◀ Mex, Sp ▶
Me repatea esta música. This music sucks (bothers me).

revolver a alguien las tripas (el estómago) (to have one's intestines [stomach] turn) to cause disgust, repugnance ◀ Mex, ES, DR, Cuba, S. Cone, Sp ▶

(no) ser plato del gusto de alguien to (not) be one's cup of tea (preferred dish) ◀ Sp ▶

traerlo (tenerlo) entre ojos (to bring it between the eyes) to have a grudge against someone, dislike ◀ Mex, Ch ▶
Me trae entre ojos. He (She) has a grudge against me.
Lo traigo entre ojos. I have a grudge against him.

doing whatever you please

See also "reasons."

darle a alguien el punto (to give oneself the point) to feel like (doing something), get in a mood (**punto** means attitude, state of mind, mood) ◀ Sp ▶
El otro día me dio el punto y mandé a mi jefe a freír espárragos. The other day I got in a mood and told my boss to go jump in the lake.

darle a alguien la real gana (to give oneself the royal desire) to want to do something with or without a reason; to do exactly what one pleases ◀ Mex, S. Cone, Sp ▶
Alberto siempre hace lo que le da la real gana. Alberto always does exactly what he pleases.

darle a alguien la regalada gana (to give oneself the gifted desire) to want to do something with or without a reason; to do whatever one pleases ◀ Mex, ES ▶

hacer de las suyas (to do your own) to do whatever you please ◀ Mex, ES, DR, PR, S. Cone ▶

hacer su regalada gana (to do one's gifted desire) to do whatever one pleases, often describing a whim ◀ Mex, ES ▶

(no) salirle a alguien algo de los cojones (huevos) (to [not] come from one's testicles) to [not] be in the mood, [not] feel like (vulgar) (Sp: also, **de las narices,** not vulgar) ◀ PR, Sp ▶
No me sale de los cojones cortarme el pelo y no lo haré. I don't freaking feel like cutting my hair and I won't do it.
¿Por qué no quieres preparar el café? —Porque no me sale de los huevos. Why don't you want to make the coffee? —Because I don't freaking feel like it.

salirse con la suya to get one's way ◀ L. Am., Sp ▶
Mi hermana siempre se sale con la suya. My sister always gets her way.

liking

apetecerle (to provoke a desire or yearning, be appealing or appetizing) to like or feel like ◀ Sp ▶
Me apetece bailar. I feel like dancing.

chiflar to be crazy about, love ◀ Mex, Sp ▶
Me chifla bailar. I love to dance.

cuadrar (to square) to suit; to agree with ◀ L. Am. ▶
No me cuadra el color de este vestido. I don't like the color of this dress (it doesn't look good on me).

hacer tilín (to make a ringing sound, as of a bell) to be appealing; to like a little (functions like **gustar**) ◀ Ch, Sp ▶
Juan me hace tilín. I kind of like Juan.

latir (to beat) to like ◀ Mex ▶
Me late mucho ese programa. I really like that show.

molar (functions like **gustar**) to please, be pleasing; **molar cantidad**, to be very pleasing to; to rock ◀ Sp ▶
Juan me mola. Nos mola cantidad tocar música juntos. I like Juan. We really like to play music together.
Esta canción mola cantidad. This song really rocks.

provocarle algo a alguien (to have something provoke a desire in someone) to feel like having something ◀ Col ▶
¿Te provoca un tinto (café)? Do you feel like having a coffee?

Yuck!

¡Fuchi! (¡Fúchila!) Yuck!, expression of disgust ◀ Mex, ES, Col ▶

¡Huaca! (¡Huácala!) Yuck!, expression of distaste; also, **guaca, waca** ◀ Mex, G, ES, DR, Col ▶
¡Huácala! Esta carne está casi cruda. Yuck! This meat is almost raw.

¡Úchala! Yuck!, expression of repugnance ◀ Mex ▶

yucky, disgusting

See also "bad."

imbancable (unbankable) unbearable, intolerable ◀ U, Arg ▶
Esta comida es imbancable. This food is disgusting.
¡No te pongas imbancable! Don't be impossible!

mafufo(-a) yucky, gross, weird (originally used to mean marijuana) ◀ Mex ▶

ser un asco to be something disgusting; to be worthless ◀ Mex, U, Arg, Sp ▶

luck

See also "opportunity."

por poco (by little) by a miracle, by a hair ◀ L. Am., Sp ▶

Choqué el carro. Por poco me mato. I crashed the car. It was a miracle I wasn't killed. (I was nearly killed.)

quedar bien (mal) parado(-a) (to end up standing well [badly]) to have good (bad) luck in something, come out well (badly) ◀ L. Am., Sp ▶

salir bien (mal) parado(-a) (to come out standing well [badly]) to come out well (badly), be lucky (unlucky) ◀ L. Am., Sp ▶

bad luck

See also "error," "failure."

Desgraciado en el juego, afortunado en amores. (Unlucky in a game or gambling, lucky with love.) said to console someone who has lost a game or at gambling ◀ Mex, ES, S. Cone, Sp ▶

estrellado(-a) (seeing stars) with bad luck ◀ Mex, ES, S. Cone ▶
Unos nacen con estrella y otros estrellados. Some people are born with a lucky star and some are born seeing stars (with bad luck).

el gafe jinx ◀ Sp ▶
Siempre que va Juan en el coche nos pasa algo. Es un gafe. Every time Juan goes in the car with us something happens. He's a jinx.
Soy gafe. I'm a jinx.

irle a alguien como en feria (to go as in a fair for someone) to go badly for someone ◀ Mex, ES ▶

irle a alguien como los perros en misa (to go like dogs in mass for someone) to go badly for someone ◀ Sp ▶

Las desgracias nunca vienen solas. Bad things never come alone (one at a time). ◀ L. Am., Sp ▶

levantarse con el pie izquierdo (to get up with the left foot) to get up on the wrong side of the bed (have a day of bad luck or be in a bad mood) ◀ L. Am., Sp ▶
Hoy me levanté con el pie izquierdo. Primero perdí las llaves y después peleé con mi esposa. Today I got up on the wrong side of the bed. First I lost my keys and then I had a fight with my wife.

llover sobre mojado (to rain over the wetness) to have one bad thing happen after another; also, to be repetitive or superfluous ◀ L. Am., Sp ▶
Llueve sobre mojado: otra vez subieron los precios. It never rains but it pours: they raised the prices again.

martes 13, jueves 13 Tuesday the 13th, Thursday the 13th (considered unlucky days in Spanish-speaking countries) (U, Ch: only **martes 13**) ◀ L. Am., Sp ▶

pando(-a) unlucky ◀ ES ▶

la pandura bad luck ◀ ES ▶
Qué pandura trae Oscar; no le sale nada. ¡Qué pandura suya! What bad luck Oscar has; nothing turns out well for him. What bad luck (of his)!

Parió la mula. (The mule gave birth.) phrase meaning that things turned out badly or something unexpected happened ◀ ES, Col ▶
Todo andaba sobre ruedas hasta enero; después, parió la mula. Everything was going great until January; then it hit the fan.

salado(-a) (salty) unlucky (Sp: kind, nice) ◀ Mex, C. Am., PR, Cuba, DR, Col, Ven, Peru, Bol, Ch, U ▶
¡Qué hombre más salado! Primero perdió su empleo y después le robaron el carro. What an unlucky man! First he lost his job and then they stole his car.

salarse (to be salted) to be unlucky ◀ Mex, G, Cuba, DR, Col, CR ▶
Ya me he salado: primero se me jodió la computadora y perdí todos los archivos. Después se canceló una reunión importante. I've been really unlucky: first the computer broke down and I lost all my files. Then an important meeting was canceled.

salir con su domingo siete (to turn out with his or her Sunday the 7th) to have bad luck, usually meaning to be pregnant; Sunday the 7th is an unlucky day (CR, U, Arg: to say stupid things; Ch: both meanings) ◀ Mex, ES, S. Cone ▶
¿Has oído la noticia? Esperanza salió con su domingo siete. Y su novio se ha esfumado. (ES) Have you heard the news? Esperanza got pregnant. And her boyfriend has disappeared into thin air.
Salió con su domingo siete cuando empezó a contar chistes colorados en el velo-rio. (S. Cone) He lost it and said a bunch of nonsense when he started telling dirty jokes at the wake.

salir el tiro por la culata (to have the shot go out the butt of the rifle) to backfire, have an opposite result from what was expected ◀ L. Am., Sp ▶

ser más desgraciado(-a) que el Pupas to be very unlucky; also, **ser el pupas** ◀ Sp ▶

tener mala leche (to have bad milk) to be unlucky ◀ G, ES, Col, Ven, Peru ▶
Tengo muy mala leche. ¿Por qué me escogieron a mí? I have very bad luck. Why did they choose me?

tener mala pata (to have bad foot) to have bad luck ◀ Mex, G, ES, CR, DR, PR, Ven, S. Cone, Sp ▶
¡Qué mala pata (tiene)! Todo le sale mal. What bad luck (he or she has)! Everything turns out badly for him (her).
Dicen que perdieron las elecciones porque tuvieron mala pata. They say they lost the elections because they had bad luck.

tener el santo de espaldas (to have one's saint turning his back on one) to have bad luck ◀ Mex, ES, Sp ▶

Todo me sale torcido (al revés). (Everything turns out twisted [backwards] for me.) Everything turns out badly for me. (S. Cone: **al revés** only) ◀ ES, Nic, CR, Sp ▶

Voló la paloma. (The dove flew off.) said when something escapes unexpectedly from one's grasp ◀ Mex, ES ▶

betting

chiviar to gamble, play dice ◀ Mex, C. Am. ▶

el chivo (kid goat) die; dice game ◀ Mex, G, Hond, ES ▶

jugarse la pasta to bet one's money ◀ Sp ▶

jugarse el todo por el todo (to bet all for all) to bet everything at once, put all your eggs in one basket ◀ L. Am., Sp ▶
Decidieron jugarse el todo por el todo cuando compraron el negocio. They decided to put all their eggs in one basket when they bought the business.

jugársela (to bet it) to take a risk ◀ Mex, G, CR, DR, S. Cone, Sp ▶

jugársela fría (to bet it cold) to take a risk ◀ Col ▶
Te la jugaste fría, hombre. You took a big risk, man.

jugárselo todo a una carta to bet everything on one card, put all your eggs in one basket ◀ Mex, S. Cone, Sp ▶

poner toda la carne en el asador (to put all the meat on the spit) to put all one's eggs in one basket ◀ Mex, Sp ▶

good luck

See also "success."

caer parado(-a) (to fall standing up) to get out of a bad situation with no harmful consequences, land on one's feet, emerge unscathed ◀ ES, DR, S. Cone ▶
En la oficina Mario metió una gran pata pero pudo solucionar el problema. ¡Qué suerte! Cayó parado. At work Mario made a big mistake but managed to solve the problem. What luck! He landed on his feet.

la chiva (female goat) good luck ◀ Bol ▶

el/la chivero(-a) lucky (person) ◀ Mex, PR ▶

con buen pie (with good foot) happily, with good fortune ◀ Mex, DR, PR, Ch ▶

dar un palo (to give a stick) to get something really good, maybe too good for one (e.g., a very good-looking boyfriend or girlfriend) ◀ DR ▶
¿Viste que Laura es la novia de Humberto? —¿Ese tipo tan tonto? La verdad es que él dio un palo. Did you see that Laura is Humberto's girlfriend? —That stupid guy? The truth is that he really lucked out getting her.

de carambola (billiard term referring to a lucky play) by a lucky chance ◀ ES, Nic, DR, Ch ▶

de chepa luckily, by pure luck or chance ◀ CR, DR, PR, Col ▶
Encontré tu casa de pura chepa pues tenía la dirección equivocada. I found your house by pure chance because I had the wrong address.

de chivo (of kid goat) luckily ◀ PR ▶

de perillas (of little pears) timely or opportune ◀ S. Cone, Sp ▶

Ese libro me vino de perillas. That book came to me at a very good time.
El dinero me cae de perillas. The money is really opportune.

lechero(-a) lucky, as in **tener leche** (ES: **lechudo** is more common; Ec: **lechoso[-a]**) ◀ ES, Nic, CR, Col, Peru ▶

lechudo(-a) lucky, lucky stiff, as in **tener leche** (Ven: **lechu'o**) ◀ ES, Ven ▶
¡Qué lechudo! Le dieron el trabajo. Tiene leche. What a lucky stiff! They gave him the job. He's lucky.

nacer con el pie derecho (to be born with the right foot) to be born lucky (Ch: also, **amanecer con...**) ◀ Mex, ES, S. Cone ▶

nacer de pie (to be born standing) to be born lucky ◀ DR, U, Ch, Sp ▶

por chiripa (by a fluke, from a term in billiards) by luck, by chance (ES, DR, Ven, U, Arg: **de chiripa**) ◀ Hond, Nic, CR, DR, Col, Ch, Sp ▶

¡Qué leche! (What milk!) What luck! (a bit vulgar in Sp) ◀ Mex, G, PR, Col, Sp ▶
Qué leche que tienes; ¿te tocó la lotería y es la primera vez que jugabas? What luck you have; you won the lottery and it's the first time you've played?

¡Qué dicha! (What bliss!) What luck! ◀ Nic, G, CR ▶

rayado(-a) lucky ◀ Mex, G, ES ▶

rayarse to luck out, often by getting something good ◀ chicano, Mex, G, ES, Peru ▶
Te rayaste con la grabadora, hombre. You lucked out with the cassette player, man.

tener el santo de cara (to have one's saint facing one) to have good luck ◀ ES, Sp ▶

tener estrella (to have a star) to be lucky and easily accepted by people ◀ Mex, Sp ▶

tener leche (to have milk) to be lucky (a bit vulgar in Sp) ◀ PR, Col, Ec, Ch, Sp ▶
Le salieron en el examen sólo los temas que había estudiado. ¡Tiene una leche! Only the topics he had studied turned up on the exam. He's so lucky!

tener más vidas que un gato to have more lives than a cat ◀ Mex, ES, U, Ch, Sp ▶

tener mucha chorra to have good luck
◀ Sp ▶

tener mucho culo (to have a lot of ass) to be very lucky (vulgar) ◀ U, Arg ▶

tener siete vidas como los gatos (como el gato) to have seven lives like a cat ◀ L. Am., Sp ▶

tocarle a alguien la lotería (to win the lottery) to have a windfall, luck out (also, **caerle, sacar...**) ◀ Mex, Cuba, S. Cone, Sp ▶
Le tocó la lotería de tener un nombre único, interesante. He (She) lucked out having a unique, interesting name.

¡La vida me sonríe! (Life is smiling on me!) What a stroke of luck! ◀ L. Am., Sp ▶

¡La vida me sonríe!

mess, fuss, disorder

See also "disagreement," "problems."

mess, confusion

el barullo noisy fuss or mess, uproar ◀ CR, U, Arg, Sp ▶
Por favor, ¡no armen tanto barullo! Please, don't make such a hullabaloo!

el berenjenal (eggplant patch) mess, disorder, fix ◀ Mex, PR, S. Cone, Sp ▶
Te has metido en un berenjenal al aceptar su propuesta. You've gotten into a mess by accepting his (her, their) offer.

el burdel (bordello) mess ◀ U, Arg ▶

la burundanga something confusing, mess ◀ Mex, PR, Cuba ▶
Mañana tengo que pagar los impuestos y estoy muy desorganizada. ¡Qué burundanga! Tomorrow I have to pay taxes and I'm very disorganized. What a confusing mess!

el camote (sweet potato) mess, trouble (CR: also, fight or fit) ◀ Mex ▶
No tenía los papeles que necesitaba y me metí en un camote. I didn't have the papers that I needed and I got into a bind.

Resolver el problema de la inmigración es un camote. Solving the immigration problem is a mess.

el cirio (candle) upheaval; mess ◀ Sp ▶
Vaya cirio se montó cuando se salió el agua de la lavadora. What a mess there was when the water came out of the washing machine.

el desmadre (dismother) mess, confusion ◀ chicano, Mex, C. Am., Ec, Sp ▶
Había siempre un desmadre en esa casa. There was always a mess in that house.
Fue un desmadre total. It was a total disaster.

el despelote disorder, mess ◀ L. Am., Sp ▶
No me gustan los conciertos rock por el despelote que se forma. (Sp) I don't like rock concerts because of all the ruckus people make at them.

el follón mess, confusion (a bit vulgar but very commonly used) ◀ Sp ▶
¡Qué follón! What a mess!

el gazpacho (cold vegetable soup) mess, mixup ◀ Sp ▶

el jaleo tumult, fuss; lots of people ◀ Mex, Arg, Ch, Sp ▶
Había un jaleo impresionante en la calle. There was quite a hoopla in the street.

el laberinto (labyrinth) mess ◀ Peru ▶

el lío (bundle) mess ◀ L. Am., Sp ▶

el marrón (chestnut) mess, bad situation, embarrassing situation ◀ Sp ▶

el menjurje (mixture, potion) mess, confusion (Ch, Sp: **menjunje** is more common) ◀ Mex, ES, CR, Col, Sp ▶

el merequetengue disorder, confusion, mess ◀ Col ▶

la mescolanza confusion, mess ◀ Mex, G, Col, S. Cone ▶

el mitote party; mess ◀ chicano, Mex ▶

la pelotera (ballplayer; brawl) mess ◀ Ch ▶

el potaje (stew) complicated or difficult situation ◀ Cuba ▶

el quilombo (bordello) mess ◀ U, Arg ▶
¡Qué quilombo! Todo nos salió mal. What a mess! Everything turned out badly for us.

el reguero (stream, sprinkle) mess, disorder ◀ Mex, DR, PR, Col ▶
Por favor, no veas el reguero que tiene el cuarto. Please, don't look at the mess in the room.

el revoltijo disorder, mess ◀ Mex, S. Cone ▶

el revolú disorder, mess, brawl ◀ DR, PR, Col ▶
Se formó un revolú porque ninguno de los dos equipos aceptaron la decisión del referee. There was a brawl because neither of the teams accepted the referee's decision.

el revoluto disorder ◀ Col ▶

el sal pa'fuera (go outside) commotion, mess ◀ PR ▶
Cuando gritaron «¡Fuego!», se armó un sal pa'fuera dentro del cine. When they yelled "Fire!," there was a big commotion inside the movie theater.

la sopa de letras (alphabet soup, referring to something spoken or written) confusion ◀ Mex, Col ▶
Este poema es una sopa de letras. No lo entiendo. This poem is like alphabet soup. I don't understand it.

la tirijala (tira y jala) (pull and pull) mess, confusion ◀ DR, PR ▶

el traqueteo (banging, creaking) intense activity, mess, transaction (Col: refers to drug dealing) ◀ Mex, G, ES, DR, PR, Col ▶

¿Cuál es el traqueteo que tienen esos dos? A mí me huele bien feo. What's the deal with those two? It looks (literally, smells) ugly to me.
Deja el traqueteo, que vamos a llegar tarde. Stop messing around—we're going to be late.
¿Cuál es el traqueteo? What's up? (greeting, but implies immoral activity in Caribbean and Col)

el zambrote (Moorish party) mess ◀ CR ▶

el zaperoco mess, mixup ◀ PR, Ven ▶
¡Qué zaperoco tenemos! What a mess we have!

messy

anárquico(-a) (anarchical) disorganized ◀ DR, PR, Col ▶

cochambroso(-a) messy, like a slob, in ruins; dirty (usually referring to mind, with reference to sex, except in Sp) ◀ Mex, DR, PR, ES, Col, Sp ▶
Mi amiga tiene la mente bien cochambrosa. My friend has a very dirty mind.

descachimbado(-a) slovenly, untidy (ES: also, broken or messed up) (vulgar) ◀ ES, Nic ▶

deschavado(-a) messy ◀ ES, CR ▶
Mi casa está deschavada. My house is messy.

despelotado(-a) disorganized, messy ◀ S. Cone ▶

estar más liado(-a) que la pata de un romano (de una momia) (to be more entangled than the foot of a Roman [of a mummy]) to be a very messy or tangled situation, a can of worms ◀ Sp ▶

to'tirao (todo tirado) (everything thrown) messy, disorderly ◀ PR ▶

raising a fuss, causing a stir or uproar

alborotar las avispas (el panal) (to stir up the wasps [honeycomb]) to upset the apple cart, get people riled up

(Mex, Ch, Sp: also, **alborotar el gallinero**) ◀ Mex, ES, CR, Ch, Sp ▶
Juana siempre anda alborotando las avispas. Juana is always stirring up trouble.

armar un cristo (to arm a Christ) to create a big mess or problem ◀ Sp ▶

armar un escándalo (to make a scandal) to make a fuss ◀ L. Am., Sp ▶

armar gresca (to make a din or brawl) to cause a big fuss ◀ S. Cone, Sp ▶

armar un jaleo to make a fuss, commotion ◀ Mex, Sp ▶

armar la de San Quentín (to make that of Saint Quentín) to cause a fuss (Mex: **un sanquentín**; also, **armarle un sanquentín**, to give hell to) ◀ Mex, Ch, Sp ▶
El papá de la novia le armó un sanquintín al novio. (Mex) The bride's father gave the groom hell.

armar mitote (to make a big myth) to create a fuss ◀ Mex ▶

armar un molote (to set up a bunch) to cause a huge mess ◀ ES, Nic, DR ▶

armar un revuelo to make a commotion, cause a scene ◀ U, Arg, Sp ▶

armar el taco (to make the swear word) to cause a fuss; also, to triumph, cause admiration ◀ Sp ▶

armarse la gorda (to make the fat one) to have a ruckus or upheaval created, to have all hell break loose ◀ L. Am., Sp ▶
Cuando supo que su novio salía con su mejor amiga, se armó la gorda. When she found out that her boyfriend was going out with her best friend, all hell broke loose.

enquilombar (to put in a whorehouse, from **quilombo**, bordello) to make a mess or problem ◀ Arg ▶

haber (armarse) una de todos los diablos (to have [make] one of all the devils) to have a big problem or upheaval, have a devil of a mess ◀ L. Am., Sp ▶

hacer un tango (to do a tango) to put on a show, cause a scene, have a fit ◀ Mex, Col ▶

Hizo un tango porque no lo dejaron entrar en la discoteca porque no llevaba identificación. He made a scene because they wouldn't let him in the disco because he didn't have ID.
El niño hizo un tango en McDonald's. The boy had a fit in McDonald's.

hacer teatro (to make theater) to act in a theatrical way ◀ Mex, ES, Peru, Arg, Ch, Sp ▶
Deja de estar llorando; no estés haciendo teatro. Stop crying; don't act so melodramatic.

montar un cirio (to put on a candle) to raise a fuss, do something that gets attention ◀ Sp ▶

montar un numerito (to put on a little number) to do something rowdy, something that gets attention ◀ Mex, ES, DR, Sp ▶

montar un número (to put on a number) to behave badly or do something wrong; to have a fit ◀ Mex, Cuba, DR ▶

revolver el gallinero (to stir up the chicken coop) to cause a big fuss or stir (trouble) ◀ Ch ▶

revolverla (to stir it) to stir things up, rock the boat ◀ Ch ▶

topsy-turvy, with no order

no tener pies ni cabeza (to have neither feet nor head) to have no order or logic ◀ L. Am., Sp ▶

patas pa'arriba, patas arriba (paws up in the air) topsy-turvy, disorganized ◀ ES, Nic, DR, PR, S. Cone, Sp ▶
El terremoto puso el mundo patas arriba. The earthquake turned the world upside down.

poner pies con cabezas las cosas (to put things feet with heads) to confuse things or mix them up ◀ Sp ▶

sin ton ni son (without tone or sound) without rhyme or reason ◀ L. Am., Sp ▶
Esa novela es absurda. Sin ton ni son. That novel is absurd. Without rhyme or reason.

Say it with slang!

Let's face it!

We often talk about someone "losing face" over a serious embarrassment or point of honor, but in Spanish a "de-faced person," **un descarado** or **una descarada**, is someone shameless or insolent, a total jerk. In Mexico, however, if one talks about people "seeing his (her) face," it means they are cheating or taking advantage; for example, **En esa tienda le vieron la cara a Rodolfo.** Literally, this means: In that store, they saw Rodolfo's face. But in reality there is something missing that is understood by all: **Le vieron la cara... de pendejo.** (They saw he had the face of a fool.) So the actual meaning is: In that store they took advantage of Rodolfo. In Mexico and El Salvador, a person with a nasty or sour look is said to have **una cara de limón** (a face of a lemon). In Argentina and Uruguay, that same person can be described, somewhat picturesquely, as having **una cara de culo,** or "ass face." (This becomes **cara de poto** in Chile, as Chileans have their own word for that part of the anatomy.)

money

See also "wealth and poverty."

apretarse el cinturón   to tighten one's belt (economically) (Mex: also, **amarrarse el cinturón**) ◀ Mex, DR, PR, S. Cone, Sp ▶
Con esta crisis económica, todos tenemos que apretarnos el cinturón. With this economic crisis, we all have to tighten our belts.

Cantó Gardel.   (Gardel [the famous classic tango singer] sang.) Payday. Now we get paid. ◀ Ch ▶

el/la chivero(-a)   person who buys things in the United States and sells them in Mexico ◀ Mex ▶

creer que el dinero se encuentra debajo de las piedras   (to believe that money is found underneath rocks) to think that money is easy to get, that money grows on trees ◀ U, Sp ▶

el sablazo   (blow with a saber) loan (Ch: bad loan scam) ◀ Mex, Ch ▶
No tengo dinero. Voy a tirarle un sablazo a mi hermano. I don't have any money. I'm going to hit up my brother for a loan.

venderse como pan caliente   (to sell like hot bread) to sell very well, sell like hot cakes ◀ DR, PR, Ch ▶

vender la pomada   (to sell the ointment) to do a hard sell, sell snake oil ◀ Peru, Ch ▶

bribes

el acomodo   bribe ◀ Arg ▶
Juan recibió un acomodo cuando trabajaba en la aduana. Juan took a bribe when he worked at the customs office.

el chayote   (vegetable with prickly skin) bribe ◀ Mex ▶

la coima   bribe (also, **el coimero,** person on the take, accepting bribes) ◀ Peru, S. Cone ▶

la mordida bribe ◄ Mex, G, Nic, Pan ►

pistear to bribe (Mex: to drink) ◄ G, ES ►

cheap, bargain

a precio cómodo (at a comfortable price) cheap(ly) ◄ Nic, Peru ►

a precio de huevo (for the price of an egg) dirt cheap ◄ Ch ►

estar por los suelos (to be on the floor) to be dirt cheap (things) ◄ ES, Ch, Sp ►
En esa tienda todo está por los suelos ahora. In that store everything is dirt cheap now.

ser un chollo to be a bargain ◄ Sp ►

tirado(-a) (thrown away) cheap, a steal (at such a good price), used with **ser** or **estar** ◄ U, Arg, Sp ►

expensive

el afano total rip-off ◄ Arg ►
Este suéter cuesta carísimo; es un afano total. This sweater is really expensive; it's a total rip-off.

costar un huevo y la mitad de otro (to cost an egg, meaning testicle, and a half) to cost a fortune or a lot of effort (vulgar) (S. Cone: **costar un huevo**) ◄ Mex, G, ES, Sp ►
Este coche costó un huevo. This car cost a fortune.

costar más que un hijo tonto (to cost more than a foolish son) said when someone keeps showing up to eat or costs someone money excessively (Arg: ... **bobo**) ◄ Mex, U, Sp ►

costar un ojo de la cara (to cost an eye of the face) to cost a fortune ◄ L. Am., Sp ►

costar un pastón to cost a fortune (augmentative of **pasta**, meaning money) ◄ Sp ►
Esta moto me costó un pastón. This motorcycle cost me a fortune.

estar por las nubes (to be in the clouds) to be sky-high, very expensive ◄ Mex, ES, DR, S. Cone, Sp ►

¡Híjole! La gasolina está por las nubes ahora. Wow! Gasoline prices are sky-high now.

salado(-a) (salty) pricey ◄ S. Cone ►

ser una pasada (to be a past) to be expensive, overpriced ◄ Sp ►

valer un imperio (un mundo, un Potosí) (to be worth an empire [a world, a Potosí, from the silver-mining area in Peru]) to be worth a fortune (Peru: also, **valer un Perú**) ◄ Mex, DR, Peru, Sp ►

valer su peso en oro (to be worth its weight in gold) to be worth a fortune ◄ Mex, DR, Sp ►

free, costing nothing

de balde free of charge ◄ L. Am., Sp ►
Este viaje me ha salido de balde. This trip was free for me.

de choto for free ◄ ES ►
No voy a trabajar de choto. I'm not going to work for nothing.

de hoquis for free ◄ Mex ►

de yapa for free ◄ S. Cone ►

gratarola for free (U: **gratirola**) ◄ Arg ►

pool, kitty

la coperacha pool of money used to buy something collectively ◄ Mex, G, ES ►
Para comprar la comida hacemos una coperacha entre todos. To buy the food, everyone puts money in a kitty.

hacer una vaca (echar la vaca) (to make a cow [throw the cow]) to chip in, pool money for a common cause (Mex: **hacer una vaquita**) ◄ G, Nic, Ven, Para, Arg, Ch ►

prestar pa' la orquesta (to loan for the orchestra) to chip in for some cooperative event ◄ Mex, Col ►

el serrucho pool of money to buy something collectively ◄ DR, PR ►
Señores, es un serrucho: cada uno pone quince pesos. People, it's a collective effort; everyone puts fifteen pesos (in the kitty).
Hay que hacer un serrucho. We have to take up a collection.

spending

aflojar el billete (to loosen the bill) used like **aflojar la bolsa**, to loosen up and spend money ◄ Mex, Ch ►
Para salir de ese apuro, tuvo que aflojar el billete. To get out of that jam, he (she) had to loosen up and spend money.

aflojar la bolsa to loosen the purse strings ◄ Mex, Sp ►

bajarse de la mula (to get off the mule) to give something in exchange for a favor, pay up ◄ Ven ►
Oye, amigo, me debes veinte bolos. ¡Bájate de la mula! Hey, pal, you owe me twenty bucks. Pay up!

caer con (to fall with) to pay up ◄ Mex ►
Cáele con la lana. Fork over the dough.

echar/tirar la casa por la ventana (to throw the house out the window) to spend lavishly, blow the works ◄ L. Am., Sp ►
Para los quince años de Rocío, doña Ana tiró la casa por la ventana. Fue una fiesta a todo dar. For Rocío's fifteenth birthday, Doña Ana blew the works. It was a real bash.

largar los mangos (to distance the mangos, Lunfardo for money) to spend money ◄ U, Arg ►

pagar el piso (to pay for the floor) to pick up the tab for a meal after one receives the first paycheck in a new job or to invite people out when one is new; also, to get the worst of the lot (hours, parking place, etc.) because of lack of seniority ◄ S. Cone ►

pagar por sustos (to pay in frights) to buy something on credit ◄ ES ►
Mi esposo compró el carro hace un año y todavía estamos pagando por sustos. My husband bought the car a year ago and we're still paying on credit.

rascarse el bolsillo (to scratch the pocket) to spend money against one's will, without really wanting to (also, old-fashioned, **rascarse la faltriquera**) ◄ Sp ►

words for money

a tocateja in cash ◄ Sp ►
el billullo (big bill) lots of money ◄ Ch ►

las campanitas de la catedral (little bells in the cathedral) lovely cash (from the tinkling sound of money jingling in one's pockets) ◄ Mex, Col ►

la chaucha small change, just pennies ◄ Ch ►

el chavo peso or dollar ◄ Cuba, PR ►
¿Tú tienes chavos? Se me quedó la cartera en casa. Do you have any money? I left my wallet at home.

el chele cent ◄ DR, Sp ►
Lo siento. No tengo ni un chele encima. I'm sorry. I don't have a penny on me.

el chen chen money, dough ◄ Pan ►
Ese viejo siempre tiene chen chen. That guy always has dough.

el chucho peso ◄ Mex, Col ►

los dolores (pains) used for **dólares** ◄ ES, Cuba, DR ►
Ahora yo no tengo dolores. Right now I don't have any greenbacks.

el duro five pesetas ◄ Sp ►

la feria (fair or day off) money ◄ Mex, C. Am. ►
No tengo feria. I don't have any money.

la gorda (fat one) ten-cent coin ◄ Sp ►
Está sin una gorda. He (She) doesn't have a dime.

la guita money ◄ Ec, Peru, S. Cone, Sp ►
la harina (wheat) money ◄ CR, Ec ►
el kilo (kilo) a million pesetas ◄ Sp ►
la lana (wool) money ◄ Mex, C. Am., Cuba, Peru ►
Esos señores tienen mucha lana. Son los dueños de unos boutiques exclusivos. Those people have a lot of dough. They own some exclusive boutiques.

la lechuga (lettuce) dollar (Sp: a thousand pesetas) ◄ Cuba ►

la luca a thousand pesos or units of money ◄ Ec, Peru, Bol, S. Cone ►

la luz (light) money (also: **morlacos, ojos**) ◄ Mex ►

el maíz (corn) money ◄ Cuba ►

el mango (mango) money, dough ◄ U, Arg ►

la pachocha dough, money (used instead of **papel**, referring to paper money) ◄ Mex, Col ►

la pasta (pasta, dough) money ◄ Cuba, Sp ►

la pasta gansa (goose pasta, dough) a lot of money, fortune ◄ Sp ►

la perra (female dog) ten-cent coin ◄ Sp ►
No tiene ni una perra. He (She) doesn't have a dime.

el pisto money ◄ G, ES, Nic, CR ►

la plata (silver) money ◄ L. Am. ►

el platal a lot of money (**plata**) ◄ ES, CR, Col ►

la pura papa (the pure potato) cash (ES: also, used jokingly in reference to rich people: **Allí está la papa.**) ◄ ES, Col ►
Aquí está la pura papa. Here's the cash.

el talego a thousand pesetas ◄ Sp ►

---

nakedness

---

chulón, chulona naked ◄ ES ►
La niña se quitó la ropa y anda chulona. The little girl took off her clothes and is walking around in her birthday suit.

despelotarse to take off one's clothes (vulgar) ◄ PR, Arg, U, Sp ►
Se despelotaron en la playa. They took off their clothes at the beach.

el despelote nakedness, removal of clothes (vulgar) ◄ PR, Sp ►
En esa película hay mucho despelote. There's a lot of undressing in that film.

en bolas (in balls) naked (vulgar) ◄ Nic, U, Arg, Sp ►

en carnes (in flesh) naked ◄ Sp ►

en cuernavaca naked (**en cueros;** Cuernavaca is a city.) ◄ Mex, Col ►

en cueros (in skins) naked ◄ Mex, G, DR, Sp ►
Miguelito se puso en cueros en la playa. Miguelito got naked at the beach.

en pelota (in ball) naked (vulgar) ◄ G, Nic, DR, PR, S. Cone ►

en pelotas (in balls) naked (vulgar) ◄ Mex, DR, PR, Col, S. Cone, Sp ►
Toca la puerta antes de entrar, que a don Bartolo le gusta andar en pelotas por la casa. Knock on the door before you go in; Don Bartolo likes to go around the house naked.

---

negation

Ahí muere. (It dies there.) No way. Absolutely not, period. (Ch: **Ahí murió el payaso.** The clown died there.) ◄ Mex, ES ►

chale used as negative ◄ chicano, Mex ►

De ninguna manguera (como dijo el bombero). (No hose [as the fireman said]. **Manguera** sounds like **manera,** way.) Absolutely not. ◄ Mex , ES ►

hacer tapa (to make a top, accompanied by a gesture, very common, somewhat vulgar) to say no to something ◄ Ch ►
La invité pero me hizo tapa. I invited her but she turned me down.

Nacaradas conchas. (Mother-of-pearl shells. **Naca** sounds like **nada.**) Nothing. No way. ◄ Nic ►

Me hizo tapa.

Nada de eso. (None of that.) Not at all. ◀ L. Am., Sp ▶

Nada, pescadito mojado. (Swim, little wet fish, with a pun on **nada** meaning both nothing and swim.) Zero, nothing. ◀ Mex, Col ▶

Naranjas. (Oranges.) No. No way. ◀ chicano, Mex, G, ES, Col, Sp ▶
¿Me prestas mil pesos? —Naranjas. No tengo nada. Will you lend me a thousand pesos? —No way. I don't have anything.

¡Naranjas de la China! (Oranges from China!) Nothing doing! ◀ Sp ▶

Nel. Nel, pastel. (No. No, cake.) No. No way. ◀ chicano, Mex, G, ES, Nic ▶
Paco, ¿me prestas dinero para ir al cine? —¡Nel, pastel! No tengo ni cinco. Paco, will you lend me money to go to the movies? —No way, José. I don't have a dime.

Ni a la de tres. (Not even by that of three.) No way. ◀ Sp ▶
No hay manera de que nos tomen en serio ni a la de tres. No way they'll take us seriously.
Aquí no llueve ni a la de tres. It doesn't rain here at all.

Ni a la fuerza. (Not even by force.) Not on your life, no way. ◀ L. Am. ▶

Ni a huevos. (Not even by eggs, meaning testicles.) No damn way. (vulgar) ◀ Mex, ES ▶
No me hacen ir ni a huevos. No damn way they can make me go.

Ni a palos. (Not even with blows of a stick.) No way. ◀ L. Am., Sp ▶
Ni a palos lo iba a soltar. No way was he (she) going to let go of it.

Ni a putas. (Not even by prostitutes.) No damn way. (vulgar) ◀ ES, CR, Col ▶

Ni a tiros. (Not even by gunshots.) Not a chance. ◀ Mex, Sp ▶

Ni cagando. (Not even shitting.) Not on your life. No damn way. (vulgar) ◀ Col, Arg, Ch ▶

Ni chicles. (Not even chewing gum.) No. No way. ◀ Mex ▶

Ni cojones. (Not even testicles.) No. No damn way. Nothing. (vulgar) ◀ Cuba, Col ▶

Ni de coña. (Not even as a joke.) No damn way. (vulgar) ◀ Sp ▶
Yo no trabajo con ese explotador, ¡ni de coña! I'm not working with that exploiter, no damn way!

Ni de vaina. (Not even as a husk.) No. No way. ◀ Nic, Col, Ven ▶

Ni ebrio(-a) ni dormido(-a). (Neither drunk nor asleep.) No way. ◀ Mex, Col ▶
¿Vas a la fiesta de Martín? —Ni ebria ni dormida. Are you going to Martín's party? —No way. Not for love nor money.

Ni en sueños. (Not even dreaming.) No way. ◀ L. Am., Sp ▶
¿Qué tal si Enrique te invita a pasar el día en la playa? —¡Ni en sueños lo haría! What if Enrique invites you to spend the day on the beach? —Not even in his dreams!

Ni gorda. (Not even a fat one [coin of little value].) Nothing. ◀ Sp ▶

Ni gota. (Not even a drop.) Nothing. ◀ Mex, ES, DR, U, Ch, Sp ▶

Ni hablar. Don't even think (talk) about it. No way. Out of the question! ◀ L. Am., Sp ▶

Ni hablar del peluquín. (Don't even talk about the toupée.) Enough said. ◀ ES, Peru, Ch, Sp ▶

Ni hostia. (Not even Host, religious reference.) No, nothing. (vulgar) ◀ Cuba, Sp ▶

Ni jota. (Not a jot.) No, nothing. ◀ L. Am., Sp ▶
De biología no entiendo ni jota. I don't understand beans about biology.

Ni loco(-a). (Not even crazy.) No way. ◀ Mex, ES, Peru, Bol, S. Cone, Sp ▶
¿Me prestas tu carro? —Ni loca. Will you loan me your car? —No way.
Ni loco que fuera lo haría. No way I'd do it.

Ni madre. (Not even mother.) No. No way. (vulgar) ◀ Mex, C. Am., Col ▶

Ni maíz. (Not even corn.) Nothing. ◀ Mex ▶
No entendí ni maíz. I didn't understand squat.

Ni mierda. (Not even shit.) No, nothing. (vulgar) ◀ Mex, G, ES, Nic, Arg, Ch ▶

No me dieron ni mierda por la bicicleta. They didn't give me a damn thing for the bicycle.

Ni mocho. No, no way (used instead of **Ni modo**). ◄ Mex, ES ►

Ni módulo (como dijo el astronauta). (No module [as the astronaut said]. **Módulo** sounds like **modo**, way.) No way, José. ◄ Mex ►

Ni pa'l carajo. (Not even to male organ.) No damn way. (vulgar) ◄ PR, Col ►

Ni papa(s). (Not even potato[es].) No, nothing. ◄ Mex, C. Am., Col ►

Ni pelotas. (Not even balls.) No way, not at all (vulgar). ◄ Col, Ch ►

Ni pensarlo. Don't even think about it. ◄ L. Am., Sp ►

ni pizca de (not even a pinch of) not even a shred of ◄ Mex, C. Am., DR, Col, Arg, Ch ►
No tiene ni pizca de educación. He (She) has no manners whatsoever.

Ni por asomo. (Not even by conjecture.) No way, not by a longshot. ◄ DR, S. Cone, Sp ►
¿Yo hacer semejante cosa? No, hombre, ni por asomo. Me do such a thing? No, man, not by a longshot.

Ni por el forro. (Not even by the lining.) Nothing, not at all. ◄ U, Sp ►
Hugo no entendía de números ni por el forro; nunca había pasado ningún examen de matemáticas. Hugo didn't understand diddly about numbers; he'd never passed any math test.

Ni puel putas. (Not even by prostitutes.) No freaking way. (vulgar) ◄ Col ►

Ni soñarlo. Don't even dream about it. ◄ L. Am., Sp ►

Ni torta. (Not even cake.) Nothing. ◄ Sp ►
Con estas gafas no veo ni torta. I can't see squat with these glasses.

¡Nones! No! ◄ Mex, Col ►

Punto acabado. (Punto final.) (Finished period.) Absolutely not, period. ◄ Mex, U, Arg ►

todo lo contrario (all the contrary) just the opposite ◄ L. Am., Sp ►

news

See also "gossip," "greetings," "information."

estar al corriente de (to be at the running total of) to be up to date on ◄ L. Am., Sp ►

news flash, piece of news

el bajón de baterías (big down of drums) arrival of bad news ◄ Nic ►

la bomba, el bombazo (bomb) surprising piece of news, news flash ◄ Mex, G, ES, DR, Sp ►
El asunto de Juan y Teresa ha sido una bomba; nadie sabía que salían juntos. The thing about Juan and Teresa was a bombshell; no one knew that they were going out together.
Agárrate, que tengo un bombazo. ¿Adivina quién salió embarazada? Hang on—I've got a news flash. Guess who got pregnant?

la gaceta piece of news ◄ Col ►
Tengo una gaceta: Julio se va a casar. I've got a news flash: Julio is getting married.

la(s) nota(s) news ◄ L. Am. ►

What's new?

¿Qué me cuentas? (What do you tell me?) What's happening? ◄ L. Am., Sp ►

¿Qué notas me cuentas? (What notes are you telling me?) What news can you tell me? ◄ most of L. Am. ►

Y de la vida, ¿qué más? (And of life, what more?) What else is happening in your life? ◄ Caribbean ►

opportunity

See also "luck."

el chance   chance (from English) ◀Mex, C. Am., Caribbean, Col, Ven, S. Cone▶
Dame otro chance; te prometo que esta vez no te voy a fallar. Give me another chance; I promise you that this time I won't let you down.

la chanza   break, chance (from the English "chance") ◀chicano, Mex, Col▶

el chollo   great chance or advantage; something very cheap ◀Sp▶

giving or taking an opportunity

agarrar su patín   (to grab your skate) to find your path (opportunity) in life ◀Mex, ES▶

cerrarle una puerta y abrirle otra   to have one door (opportunity) close and another open ◀Mex, ES, Sp▶

La luz d'alante (de adelante) es la que alumbra.   (The light in front of you is what shines.) A bird in the hand is worth two in the bush. Take what's right in front of you when you have the chance. (said by someone who offers you something to eat or drink, for instance, or when a job presents itself) ◀PR▶

pescar en río revuelto   (to fish in a turbulent river) to take advantage of confusion or disorder and profit from it ◀Mex, DR, Sp▶

poner una vela a San Miguel (a Dios) y otra al diablo   (to light one candle for Saint Michael [for God] and one for the devil) to try to keep one's options open to profit from either of two people or groups ◀DR, PR, Sp▶

ponerle algo en (una) charola de plata   (to put something on a silver platter for someone) to give someone a great op-

portunity (S. Cone: **en bandeja de plata**) ◀Mex, ES, Bol, S. Cone▶

sacar el jugo   (to take out the juice) to take maximum advantage, get the best (from) ◀Mex, ES, CR, DR, PR, Col, Arg, Ch, Sp▶
Diego le sacó el jugo a la fiesta. Diego enjoyed himself to the max at the party.

sacar partido   (to take out game) to take maximum advantage, get or make the most of ◀S. Cone, Sp▶
Le sacó partido a este juguete. (Sp) He (She) enjoyed this toy to the max.
Tenemos que sacarle partido a lo poco que tenemos. We have to make the most of what little we have.

venir a alguien en bandeja   (to come to someone on a tray) to come without effort ◀U, Ch, Sp▶
¡Qué suerte! Este puesto me vino en bandeja. What luck! This job was handed to me on a silver platter.

ya tener una pata allí   (to now have a paw in there) to have earned a place somewhere, have a foot in the door ◀Mex▶

missing the boat

dejarle a alguien el tren   (to have the train leave you) to lose out; often, to be left a spinster (Mex: **irse el tren**) ◀CR, DR, Col, Ch▶
A Elvira la dejó el tren. (CR) Elvira was left an old maid.

Pasó la vieja.   (The old lady went by.) said to mean that someone missed out on something by acting too slowly or forgetting it, missed the boat ◀Ch▶

perder el (último) tren   (to miss the [last] train) to miss the boat, lose out ◀Mex, ES, DR, Arg, Ch, Sp▶
Tomás perdió el tren cuando no aceptó el empleo en la nueva compañía. Tomás missed the boat when he didn't accept the job at the new company.

quedarse en el aparato   (to be left on the phone receiver) to be left behind in life, miss the boat, be a loser ◀Ven▶

quedarse para vestir santos   (to stay behind to dress [statues of] saints) to be left behind, usually meaning to be

an old maid (also, less commonly, **vestir imágenes**) ◀ L. Am., Sp ▶
Ramona cumplió cuarenta y dos años el jueves. —¿Y todavía soltera? —Bueno, ésa se quedó para vestir santos. Ramona turned forty-two years old on Thursday. —And still single? —Well, she was left an old maid.

ordinariness

achatado(-a) (pug-nosed, with nose cut off) mediocre, blah, without personality ◀ Arg ▶
A Marianita no le gusta ni ir al cine; es tan achatada. Marianita doesn't even like to go to the movies; she's so lackluster.

corriente y moliente everyday, normal ◀ Mex, Sp ▶
Aunque es un actor famoso, es una persona corriente y moliente. Even though he's a famous actor, he's a regular guy.

de tres al cuarto (from three to fourth) so-so, phrase denoting the small value or esteem of something ◀ Sp ▶

¿Dónde va Vicente? Donde va (toda) la gente. (Where is Vicente going? Wherever everyone else goes.) phrase

Pasó la vieja.

expressing the lack of initiative of someone or saying that he or she is just a follower ◀ Mex, ES, DR, Ch, Sp ▶

irse con el viento que corre to go with the prevailing wind (opinions, ideas) ◀ Mex, Sp ▶

ni fu ni fa neither good nor bad, expression of indifference ◀ L. Am., Sp ▶
—¿Te gustó el concierto de Luis Miguel? —Ni fu ni fa, fue idéntico al del año pasado. Did you like the Luis Miguel concert? —It was no great shakes—the same as last year.
¿Qué tal? ¿Cómo estás? —Ni fu ni fa. What's up? How are you? —So-so. OK.

ni muy muy ni tan tan (not very very nor so-so) mediocre, blah ◀ Mex, ES, Nic, DR, Col, U, Arg ▶

no ser nada (cosa) del otro jueves (to not be a thing of next Thursday) to not be extraordinary ◀ Sp ▶
Es guapo, pero no es cosa del otro jueves. He's good-looking, but nothing to write home about.

no ser nada del otro mundo (to not be something from the other world) to be nothing to write home about, not rare ◀ Mex, ES, DR, PR, S. Cone, Sp ▶

no tener chiste (to not have any joke) to be blah, unappetizing; to be senseless or useless ◀ Mex, ES, Col, Peru, Bol ▶
Esa novela no tiene chiste. That novel is mediocre.

ordinario(-a) common, low-class, tacky (Ch: also, **ordaca**) ◀ L. Am., Sp ▶
Es más ordinario que un yogurt de yuca. (CR) It's plainer than a yogurt made of yucca (a starchy tuber).

pasable (passable) tolerable, so-so ◀ Mex, S. Cone ▶
La película de anoche era pasable. The movie last night was so-so.

ser de corto alcance (to be of short reach) to be narrow-minded, conventional ◀ Ch ▶

ser del montón (to be of the heap) to be common or mediocre ◀ L. Am., Sp ▶
Esa maestra es del montón. That teacher is no great shakes.

sin chiste (without joke) blah, unappetizing ◀ Mex, Col, Peru, Bol ▶

Say it with slang!

Amphibians for various occasions

Amphibians are used in Spanish slang for various reasons. In many places, to refer to a very improbable event in the future you can say that something will happen "when a frog (with its smooth hairless skin) becomes hairy": **Eso pasará cuando la rana eche pelos.** The word for "toad," **sapo,** has different meanings depending on the region. In several Latin American countries, **un sapo** is a stool pigeon or informer, perhaps because of its croaking voice, and the verb **sapear** means to squeal on someone. In Chile a **sapo** is a person who observes or spies on others (maybe because of its large, protruding eyes), and the verb **sapear** means "to spy on." In Mexico and some other places, the repeated voices of frogs in a chorus are mimicked in the phrase, **¡Iguanas ranas!** (Iguanas frogs!, with **iguanas** being a play on **iguales**), which is used to second someone's choice or opinion: "Me too!" or "The same for me!"

party

See also "dance," "fun."

party, dance, bash

la bachata (a type of music) party ◀ DR, Col ▶

el bailongo dance, dancing party ◀ U, Arg ▶
¡Vamos ya al bailongo! Let's go to the dance now!

el bailorio party, dance ◀ Ec ▶

el bayú party, get-together ◀ PR ▶
Tremendo bayú se armó en casa de René anoche. ¿Por qué no fuiste? There was a great party at René's house last night. Why didn't you go?

el bembé party ◀ Caribbean ▶
Sin planearlo llegaron los muchachos y se formó un bembé de apaga y vámonos. The guys (and girls) showed up on the spur of the moment (literally, without planning) and there was an all-out bash.

el bonche party, celebration; also, mess or disorder ◀ Mex, DR, ES, Nic, Ven, Bol ▶
Ana tiene un bonchecito en su casa esta noche. (DR) Ana's having a little party at her house tonight.

el carnaval fun time (like carnival, Mardi Gras; ES: a big street dance) ◀ Mex, ES, CR, Col ▶

la charanga party, dance ◀ ES, CR, Col ▶

la charanguiada party, dance (ES: also, charanguiar) ◀ ES, Col ▶

el corillo group, social gathering; corillo bacanal, party ◀ PR ▶
Vamos a la fiesta con el corillo de Luis, que son unos muchachos cheverísimos. Let's go to the party with Luis's group; they're a great bunch of guys (and girls).

la despedida de soltera send-off party for the bride before her wedding ◀ L. Am., Sp ▶

el fandango (flamenco dance) party ◀ U, Arg ▶

la fanfarria party ◀ Mex, Col ▶

la farra party ◀ Ec, S. Cone, Sp ▶

la festichola fantastic party ◀ U, Arg ▶

el güiro (gourd instrument) party ◀ Cuba ▶

la jarana party ◀ Mex, Peru, U, Arg, Sp ▶
Me voy de jarana esta noche. I'm going out partying tonight.

la minga thank-you party for workers ◀ Ch ▶

el motivito party among friends ◀ Cuba ▶

la pachanga, el pachangón party (ES, CR: also, **pachanguear**) ◀ Mex, G, Hond, ES, Nic, CR, Cuba, Ven, Para, U, Arg ▶
Este sábado habrá una pachanga en casa de Eduardo. This Saturday there'll be a party at Eduardo's house.

la quedada get-together ◀ Sp ▶

el reventón (de primera) (a blowout [of first]) a (first-class) bash ◀ Mex, C. Am. ▶
Fuimos a un reventón de primera el viernes. We went to a first-class bash on Friday.

el rumbón (augmentative of **rumba**) spontaneous party ◀ PR, Col ▶

el vacilón party, fun, diversion (CR: also, **la vacilada**) ◀ Mex, ES, CR, DR, PR ▶
Tenemos que planear desde ahora el vacilón para las navidades. We have to start planning the Christmas party now.

party lover

jaranero(-a) party-loving, party animal ◀ Sp ▶
Es un chico muy jaranero. He's a party-loving guy.

el/la parrandista, fiestero(-a) party lover ◀ Mex, Col ▶

el/la patialegre party lover ◀ Col ▶

patience

See also "resignation."

aguantar el chaparrón (to put up with the rain shower) to get through some-

thing difficult but necessary, take your medicine, face the music ◀ S. Cone, Sp ▶

aguantar el nublado (el nubarrón) (to put up with the cloudiness) to wait patiently until someone (usually a superior) is no longer angry, wait it out ◀ Sp ▶

barajárselas (to shuffle them) to keep trying (to solve a problem, for instance) ◀ Mex, ES, Arg, Ch ▶

dar tiempo al tiempo (to give time to time) to be patient, wait for an opportunity ◀ Mex, ES, DR, PR, Ch ▶
Dale tiempo al tiempo y verás cómo se resuelven las cosas. Give it some time and you'll see that things will work out.

people

See also "bad character,"
"good character," "guys, girls, kids."

babies

la chancleta (sandal) recently born female baby, said with affection ◀ DR, PR, S. Cone ▶
¡Qué lindo! ¡Fue una chancleta! How lovely! It was a little girl!

aguantar el chaparrón

el/la chichí baby (Col: peepee) ◀ Mex, ES, Hond, CR, DR ▶
¿Dónde está mi chichí? Where's my baby?

la criatura (creature) baby ◀ L. Am., Sp ▶

la guagua baby ◀ Ec, Peru, Bol, Ch ▶
¡Qué bonita guagua! How pretty the baby is!

cliques, groups

la piña (pineapple) clique, select group, two or more people who act as one ◀ CR, Cuba, Sp ▶
Tengo un problema en el trabajo. Se formaron piñas allí. I have a problem at work. There are cliques there.
Los trabajadores hicieron piña para exigir sus derechos. (Sp) The workers got together in a group to demand their rights.
Están hechos una piña. (CR) They've become very close (formed a pair or group).

la rosca (doughnut) circle, closed group ◀ Col, U, Arg ▶
Si no estás en esa rosca, para ellos no estás en na'a. If you're not in that clique, to them you're nobody.

country person, hick

el/la guajiro(-a) country person, simple person from rural area ◀ Cuba, Col ▶

el/la jíbaro(-a) (country person) ignorant person, someone afraid to speak ◀ PR ▶
No seas jíbaro. Ve y habla con ella. Don't act like a country bumpkin. Go talk to her.

el/la jincho(-a) country person, simple person who doesn't know all the sophisticated urban ways ◀ ES, Nic ▶
Bueno, amigos, ustedes saben que soy jincha y no conozco los lugares aquí. Well, guys (friends), you know I'm a country bumpkin and don't know places [to go] here.

parcelero(-a) ridiculous, uneducated ◀ PR, Col ▶

el/la payuco(-a) person from a rural area who doesn't know the ways of the city, country bumpkin ◀ U ▶

el/la primo(-a) (cousin) naive person, hick ◀ Mex, Sp ▶

ser más del campo que las amapolas (to be more from the country than poppies) to be a hick ◀ Sp ▶

crowds

el bululú noisy, moving crowd ◀ Ven ▶

el carajal crowd, horde (vulgar) ◀ Mex ▶

la chamacada group of young people ◀ Mex ▶
Había una chamacada en la calle. There was a group of kids in the street.

el cochambre (grease, dirt) crowd (pejorative) ◀ Col ▶
Había mucha gente en la plaza: ¡qué cochambre! There were a lot of people in the plaza—what a mob!

el cojonal crowd, horde (vulgar) ◀ PR ▶

medio mundo (half the world) a lot of people ◀ L. Am., Sp ▶
Esa noticia la sabe medio mundo. A lot of people know that news.

el molote tumult; crowd ◀ G, ES, Nic, CR, Cuba, DR ▶
Vamos a salir del partido un poco antes para evitar el molote. Let's leave the game a little early to avoid the crowd.

la muchachada group of young people ◀ Mex, ES, CR, DR ▶
Allí está toda la muchachada. There's the whole gang (of kids).

la pacotilla gang, crowd ◀ G, ES, Nic, Ec ▶
Era una pacotilla de vagos la que llegó. A bunch of slackers showed up.

la panda band, gang (Sp: panda, pandilla, a bit old-fashioned; Mex: pandilla or banda) ◀ Col, Sp ▶
Es una panda de gilipollas. (Sp) They're a bunch of idiots.

la patota (great big foot) bunch of people ◀ S. Cone ▶

la pelusa (fuzz) the masses, hordes ◀ chicano, Mex ▶

el reguero de gente (stream of people) crowd ◀ Mex, DR, PR ▶

family

los cochos parents (Ec, Col: cuchos) ◀ Peru ▶

el/la guacho(-a) orphan, fatherless child, single person (e.g., at a party); can be a term of endearment ◀ Arg, Ch ▶
Es guacho; su padre nunca se casó con su madre. He's a fatherless (illegitimate) child; his father never married his mother.
Tengo un calcetín guacho después del lavado. I have a single sock after doing the wash.
Guachita, hazme un gran favor. Honey, do me a big favor.

el/la hijo(-a) natural (natural child) illegitimate child ◀ L. Am., Sp ▶

la jamona old maid ◀ CR, PR ▶

los jamones (hams) parents ◀ Col, Ec ▶

el/la jefe(-a) (boss) husband (wife) ◀ L. Am., Sp ▶

los jefes (bosses) parents ◀ parts of L. Am., such as Mex, S. Cone ▶
Mis jefes no están aquí. My parents aren't here.
Mi jefecita dice que no. My mom says no.

maruja homebody, describing someone who likes to stay home and take care of the house (clean, etc.); same in the masculine as in the feminine ◀ Sp ▶
Mi esposo y yo somos muy marujas; los fines de semana nos quedamos en casa. My husband and I are homebodies; we stay home on weekends.

el ministerio de guerra (war department) my wife (said by a man ironically) ◀ Mex ▶

parecer que alguien está empollando huevos (to seem like someone is nesting eggs) to seem like a homebody ◀ Sp ▶

la Santa Inquisición (the Holy Inquisition) your (inquiring) wife ◀ Mex, Col ▶

el tata father (variant in some rural areas of DR, Col, Ven, Ch: **taita**); also, grandfather ◀ L. Am. ▶

los tatas parents, father and mother; also, grandparents ◀ most of L. Am. ▶
¿De dónde vinieron tus tatas? Where did your grandparents (or parents) come from?

el trauco (mythological figure of the island of Chiloé) unknown father ◀ Ch ▶
hijo(-a) del trauco, fatherless child

los vegetales (vegetables) parents ◀ Ec ▶
Adelante. Mis vegetales no están en casa. Come on in. My parents aren't home.

los veteranos (veterans) parents ◀ U, Arg ▶

el/la viejo(-a) (old one) father (mother); also, term of endearment ◀ Mex, G, ES, Cuba, Col, S. Cone, Sp ▶
Mis viejos no me permiten salir de noche. My folks won't let me go out at night.

el/la viejo(-a) (old one) husband (wife), partner ◀ L. Am., Sp ▶
Momento. Déjame preguntarle a mi viejo. Just a minute. Let me ask my husband (common and not as pejorative as "old man").

geeks, nerds

el ganso (goose) turkey, geek, introvert (Ch: also, **gansa** and **pavo[-a]**) ◀ S. Cone, PR ▶
¡Qué ganso! (Ch) What a geek!

el nerdo nerd ◀ parts of L. Am. ▶

el verde (green) very studious person, nerd ◀ CR ▶

goody-goody, too religious

el/la mocho(-a) overly religious in appearances, always in church ◀ Mex ▶
Tú eres una mocha. You're a real church lady.

el/la pechoño(-a) very religious person (always pounding his or her chest, **pecho,** saying things like **¡Ay, de mí!**) ◀ Ch ▶

el santurrón, la santurrona goody-two-shoes, goody-goody (parts of the Americas: **santulón, santulona**) ◀ Mex, ES, Nic, DR, Col, S. Cone ▶
¿Qué quiere ese santurrón de tu primo? What's that goody-goody of a cousin of yours want?

homosexuals

Note: Some of the following words for homosexuals are pejorative.

¿Andas con Mari? expression that insinuates that someone is a **maricón,** homosexual ◀ Mex ▶

"It's scarcely comprehensible the state of disillusionment that so many false, devious, corrupt politicians have led us to, manipulating the hopes of the people." "That's right . . . Ideally we should be able to count on leaders like those of days past: upright, clean, honest . . ." "Oh, get serious (literally, don't screw around, be annoying)! I don't want anything to do with those party-pooping goody-goodies!" (**Santulón,** see page 171.)

la arepera   lesbian; also, prostitute ◀ Col ▶

el bugarrón   male homosexual who acts masculine and likes straight guys ◀ PR, Cuba ▶

la cachapa   (corn bread) lesbian ◀ G ▶

la cachapera   (from **cachapa,** corn bread) lesbian, bisexual woman ◀ PR, Ven ▶

el chuparosa, flor   (hummingbird, flower) homosexual ◀ chicano, Mex ▶

el cola   (tail) gay, homosexual (pejorative) ◀ Ch ▶

de la otra banqueta   (from the other sidewalk) homosexual ◀ Mex, G ▶

del otro barrio   (from the other neighborhood) homosexual ◀ ES ▶
Mi vecino es del otro barrio. My neighbor is gay.

del otro Laredo   homosexual (probably from **del otro lado**) ◀ Mex, ES ▶

del otro lado (bando)   (from the other side [band]) homosexual ◀ chicano, Mex, G, ES, DR, Col, U, Ch ▶
Carmen se la pasa invitando a Julio a salir; parece que no sabe que es del otro lado. Carmen keeps inviting Julio to go out; it looks like she doesn't know he's gay.

el hueco   (hollow, hole) homosexual (vulgar, pejorative) ◀ G, Ch ▶

joto(-a)   effeminate man, homosexual (vulgar) (feminine form is used among chicanos for lesbian) ◀ chicano, Mex, ES ▶
película jota, lesbian film

jugar en los dos bandos   (to play in both bands or groups) to be bisexual, swing both ways ◀ Mex, Cuba, DR, PR, Col, U ▶

jugar para el otro equipo (to play for the other team) to be homosexual ◀ L. Am. ▶

¡**No me digas! ¿Jaime juega para el otro equipo?** Don't tell me! Jaime is gay?

el marica sissy; euphemism for **maricón** ◀ L. Am., Sp ▶

el maricón homosexual ◀ L. Am., Sp ▶

la mariconada attitude or act of being effeminate or gay ◀ L. Am., Sp ▶

la marimacho/la marimacha lesbian; tomboy (Mex, Col: **marimacha** means tomboy) (**marimacho** is used in G, Ch and PR) ◀ Mex, G, DR, PR, Col, Ch, Sp ▶

el mariposa (butterfly) homosexual ◀ Mex, ES, Nic, Pan, Col, U, Sp ▶

el mariposo, el mariposón (big or male butterfly) homosexual (pejorative) ◀ chicano, Mex, DR, Col, Ch, Sp ▶

el mariquita sissy; also, euphemism for **maricón** ◀ chicano, Mex, Cuba, DR, PR, Col, Ch, Sp ▶

el pájaro (bird) effeminate, homosexual ◀ chicano, CR, Cuba, DR ▶

el pato (duck) sissy; homosexual ◀ Nic, PR, Cuba ▶

el patojo homosexual, gay (G: **patán**) ◀ Mex, Col ▶

el puto homosexual (vulgar, pejorative) ◀ Mex, U, Arg ▶

un bar de putos, gay bar

ser de la izquierda (to be of the left) to be homosexual or lesbian ◀ Col ▶

ser de la otra acera (to be of the other sidewalk or row of houses on the other side) to be homosexual (Sp: also, **de la acera de enfrente**) ◀ Mex, Sp ▶

la tortillera (tortilla maker) lesbian ◀ Mex, C. Am., Cuba, DR, Col, S. Cone, Sp ▶

el volteado (turned) homosexual; pervert (vulgar, pejorative) ◀ Mex, Col, ES ▶

macho man

el compadrón (big pal) arrogant macho man ◀ U, Arg ▶

el guapo (attractive, gorgeous) arrogant braggart, macho man ◀ U, Arg ▶

el machote macho man, male chauvinist pig ◀ Mex, Col, ES ▶

people from certain places

agringado(-a) having become like a gringo ◀ chicano, Mex, G, DR, Col ▶

Marcos ha venido bien agringado; ya no quiere comer la comida de nosotros. Marcos came back acting like a gringo; he doesn't want to eat our food anymore.

aplatanado(-a) having become like a native ◀ Cuba ▶

el/la baquiano(-a) person who seems to be from the neighborhood, local yokel ◀ S. Cone ▶

Pregúntale a ese baquiano la dirección. Debe ser de estos lugares. Ask that local yokel for the address. He must be from around here.

el chapín, la chapina Guatemalan ◀ most of L. Am. ▶

¿Cómo se llama el chapín? What's the Guatemalan guy's name?

el/la chilango(-a) person from Mexico City ◀ Mex ▶

¿Dónde está el Castillo de Chapultepec? —No eres chilanga, ¿verdad? Where is Chapultepec Castle? —You're not from the capital, are you?

el/la guanaco(-a) Salvadoran ◀ C. Am., DR ▶

la mancha de plátano (banana stain) quality of being a real native of Puerto Rico ◀ PR, Sp ▶

Mucha gente cree que soy de México, pero soy puertorriqueño. ¿Tú no me ves la mancha de plátano? Many people think I'm from Mexico, but I'm Puerto Rican. Can't you see my Puerto Ricanness?

mojado(-a) (wet) wetback, illegal(ly) (pejorative, meaning wet from crossing the Rio Grande) ◀ chicano, Mex, G, ES, Col ▶

Don Fernando se vino mojado hace treinta años. Don Fernando came illegally thirty years ago.

el/la nica Nicaraguan, short for **nicaragüense** ◀ L. Am. ▶

el/la pocho(-a)   someone of Mexican descent, usually those living in the United States (from the Ópata Indian potzico, to cut or pull up grass; the Sonoran community called those who left pochis, uprooted grass) ◄chicano, Mex, ES►

el/la tico(-a)   Costa Rican ◄L. Am.►

yuma   foreign(er) ◄Cuba►

personal reference

ciertas hierbas   (certain herbs) a certain someone (used jokingly to avoid naming a person) ◄Col►
Ciertas hierbas no limpió su cuarto. A certain someone didn't clean up his (her) room.

el mismo (la misma) que viste y calza   (the same who dresses and is shod) yours truly ◄L. Am., Sp►

mi (el/la) menda   I, me (used in third person to refer to oneself) ◄Sp►
El (La/Mi) menda no va a fregar los platos. (meaning: Yo no voy a fregar los platos.) I'm not going to wash the dishes.

Miguel(ito)/Tiburcio   me/you (para Miguel/para Tiburcio, meaning para mí/ para ti, for or to me, in my opinion/for or to you) ◄Mex, ES, Col►
Estos dulces son para Miguel y Tiburcio. These sweets are for me and you.
Para Miguelito, es muy caro. In my opinion, it's very expensive.

yo que tú   (I that you) if I were you ◄L. Am., Sp►
Yo que tú, no lo compraría. If I were you, I wouldn't buy it.

so-and-so

el/la carajo(-a)   (male organ) unknown person (pejorative) (ES: used like tonto but can be used for unknown person without being too strong; also, carajito for affection) ◄ES, Nic, CR, DR, Col►
¿Quién es ese carajo (esa caraja) que va por allá? (CR) Who's that guy (girl) going that way?
¡Cuidado, carajo! (ES) Be careful, you jerk!

el/la fulano(-a), fulano(-a) de tal   so-and-so (to refer to someone you don't know), John or Jane Doe ◄L. Am., Sp►

Fulano, Mengano y Zutano   so-and-so and his brothers; Tom, Dick, and Harry (expression used to name unknown people) ◄L. Am., Sp►

mandujano   so-and-so; extension of fulano, mengano, zutano ◄Mex►

el/la menda   so-and-so (to refer to someone you don't know) ◄Sp►

perfection

See also "competence," "good."

la persona tiliche   (thing person) perfect person, person who has everything: looks, money, position, etc. ◄Nic►

poner los puntos sobre las íes   to dot the "i"s (and cross the "t"s) ◄Mex, G, DR, S. Cone►
Hablé con los estudiantes claramente y les puse los puntos sobre las íes. I talked clearly to the students and explained things in detail.

Sal quiere el huevo.   (The egg wants salt.) said when someone wants to be praised for something or to mean that a business is close to coming to perfection ◄DR, PR►

correctly, accurately

al pie de la letra   (to the foot of the letter) exactly, to the letter ◄L. Am., Sp►
Vamos a hacer todo al pie de la letra. We're going to do everything just so.

con puntos y comas   (with periods and commas) meticulously ◄Mex, DR, U, Arg, Sp►
A mi tía le gusta hacer las cosas con puntos y comas. My aunt likes to do things just so.

por la goma   (by the rubber) correct ◄PR►

por el librito   (by the little book) right, well done ◄DR►
La asistente de la doctora Ramos es muy eficiente. Hace todo por el librito. Dr. Ra-

mos's assistant is very efficient. She does everything very meticulously.

por el libro (la libreta) (by the book [the notebook]) right, good, well done, perfect ◀ Col ▶

sin faltar una coma (jota) (without missing a comma [jot]) with accuracy ◀ Mex, DR, Sp ▶

finishing touch

dar la última pincelada (to give the last brush stroke) to put on the finishing touch, to perfect ◀ Sp ▶

la manito de gato (little cat's hand) touch-up, quick once-over to help someone look good ◀ Ch ▶

el último toque finishing (last) touch ◀ Mex, U, Ch, Sp ▶

just right

a carta cabal exactly, right; irreproachably or impeccably ◀ Mex, DR, Arg, Ch, Sp ▶

a pedir de boca (at the mouth's asking) exactly as one wishes, just right or perfect ◀ L. Am., Sp ▶
¡Qué bien! Nos ha salido a pedir de boca. How nice! It came out exactly as we wanted.

al pelo (to the hair) exactly, as one wishes ◀ Mex, G, ES, DR, Ven, S. Cone ▶
La bici le cae al pelo. The bike is just right for him (her).

persistence

darle con el palo al gato (to hit the cat with the stick) to keep on trying to do something that isn't working out well, beat a dead horse; to get the runaround ◀ Ch ▶

echar pa'lante (to throw forward) to move on, keep going after confronting a problem ◀ Col, DR, PR, Ch, Ven ▶
La situación es muy difícil, pero hay que echar pa'lante. The situation is very difficult,

but we (you, they, etc.) have to keep plugging along (going forward).
Echemos pa'lante porque p'atrás no cunde. Let's move forward because there's no going back.

emperrarse to persist doggedly ◀ U, Ch, Sp ▶

no dejar (ni) a sol ni a sombra a alguien (to not leave someone in the sun or the shade) to hound, pursue someone at all hours and in all places ◀ L. Am., Sp ▶

seguir en sus trece (to keep in one's thirteen) to persist in an opinion or in doing something (Ch: also, **ponerse en sus trece**) ◀ Ch, Sp ▶

To'el tiempo pa'lante. (All the time forward.) Onward and upward. ◀ Caribbean ▶

persuasion

See also "deception," "flattery."

cepillar (to brush) to flatter in order to get something, butter up, suck up to ◀ Nic, Bol ▶

chamullar to talk at length trying to persuade (Peru, Ch: **chamullo**, story, fib) ◀ Peru, Arg, Ch ▶

comer el coco a alguien (to eat someone's coconut, meaning head) to influence or convince someone ◀ DR, PR, Sp ▶
Le comieron el coco a Paula e ingresó en esa secta. They brainwashed (convinced) Paula and she joined that cult.
Para de comerme el coco y déjame en paz. Stop hammering away at me and leave me in peace.

cuentiar to sweet-talk; to butter up (CR: **cuentear**) ◀ Mex, G, ES, CR, Col ▶
Ese hombre me estaba cuentiando, pero no le hice caso... lo mandé a volar. That man was sweet-talking me, but I didn't pay him any attention... I told him to get lost (literally, told him to fly off).

dar carreta to feed someone a line, flatter, deceive (also, **agarrar carreta**) ◀ ES ▶
No me des carreta, que no te creo. Don't put me on (try to feed me a line); I don't believe you.

dar coba (to give flattery, tales) to flatter, usually to gain something, butter up, suck up ◀ most of L. Am., Sp ▶
A Rolando lo nombraron vice presidente del banco y lo único que sabe hacer es dar coba al presidente. They made Rolando vice president of the bank, and all he knows how to do is suck up to the president.

dar cuerda (to give string) to string someone along, often in a provocative or annoying way or to butter up, sweet-talk ◀ L. Am., Sp ▶
Carlos me iba dando cuerda para que le contara lo que realmente pasó. Carlos was buttering me up so that I would tell him what really happened.
Deja de darle cuerda a Luis, que tú sabes como se pone. Stop jive-talking Luis; you know how he gets.

duro(-a) (hard) hard to convince, pigheaded ◀ Mex, G, Ch ▶

duro(-a) de pelar (hard to peel) difficult to convince or get (CR: someone who waits a long time before getting married) ◀ U, Sp ▶
Felipe es duro de pelar. Felipe is hard to convince (not easily influenced).

echar carreta (to throw cart) to sweet-talk, butter up ◀ Col ▶

echar el cuento (to throw the story) to sweet-talk, butter up ◀ CR, Col ▶

echar un rollo (to throw a roll) to sling the bull, sweet-talk ◀ Mex, ES, Col, Ven ▶

enrollarse (to get rolled up) to sling the bull, talk at length, string along with talk or flattery (like **dar cuerda, ser yoyo**) ◀ ES, Sp ▶
Miguel, ¡no se enrolle tanto! (Sp) Miguel, don't sling the bull!
Felipe vio a una amiga y se enrolló con ella. Felipe saw a friend and started a long conversation with her.

enyoyarse to butter someone up hoping to get something (a yoyo rolls up, and so this refers to the expression en-rollarse, which is used similarly) ◀ ES, Col ▶
Raúl se enyoyó con el jefe, regalándole cosas. Raúl buttered up the boss, giving him presents.

el/la grupiento(-a) (grouper) person who sells himself or herself well, smooth talker ◀ Ch ▶

hacer la pelota (pelotilla) a alguien (to make the ball to someone) to flatter someone to obtain something, butter up (also, **hacer la rosca**) ◀ Sp ▶
Ese tío le hace la pelota al jefe. That guy is buttering up the boss.

jalar mecate (to pull cord, like **enrollar** or **dar cuerda**) to flatter, suck up to ◀ Ven ▶

la muela (molar, tooth) talk, chat, often with idea of persuading or sweet-talking (DR: **dar muela, muelear;** Cuba: **bajar una muela**) ◀ Cuba, DR, Col ▶
Deja de darle muela a esa muchacha, que tiene novio. (DR) Stop sweet-talking that girl; she has a boyfriend.
Yo no quería ir a la recepción pero Lourdes me bajó una muela y terminé diciendo que iría. (Cuba) I didn't want to go to the reception, but Lourdes convinced me and I ended up saying I would go.
Tienes buena muela. (Cuba) You're a good talker.

palabrear to try to persuade, talk a lot ◀ ES, CR, Ch ▶
A este tipo le gusta palabrear. That guy likes to jive.

ponerles la mosca detrás de las orejas (to put the fly behind their ears) to tell people something with the intent of changing their minds or moving them to action, put a bug in their ears ◀ Sp ▶

rapear, montar el rapeo, montar rancho to sweet-talk (a woman) ◀ PR ▶
Deja el rapeo, que tengo novio. Cut out the sweet-talk; I have a boyfriend.

el rapero smooth talker (with women) ◀ PR, Col ▶

ser yoyo to be a suck-up (yoyo), related to **enrollar** because a yoyo rolls upward (CR: **yuyo**) ◀ ES, Col ▶
No seas yoyo. Don't be a suck-up.

tallar (to carve, engrave) to sweet-talk, talk with wit and charm ◀ Cuba, Ch ▶

tener en el bote (to have in the boat) to sweet-talk or pick up, to convince ◀ Sp ▶

physical characteristics

See also "body."

más planchado(-a) que un sapo en la carretera (more ironed than a toad in the road) with no wrinkles ◀ PR, Col ▶

mechudo(-a) with hair uncombed or very long (pejorative) ◀ Mex, ES, Nic, CR, Col ▶
Qué mechudo anda ese cipote. (ES) How long (messy) that kid's hair is.

por la (su) pinta (by the[ir] spot) because of their appearance (e.g., because of some signal or because of family resemblance) (Sp: also, **sacar a alguien por la pinta**) ◀ L. Am., Sp ▶
Descubrí que era tu hermano por la pinta. I discovered that he was your brother because of family resemblance.
Por su pinta se conoce. You can recognize him (her) by his (her) appearance.

mechudo

ser más sordo(-a) que una tapia (to be more deaf than a wall) to be deaf as a doornail ◀ Ch, Sp ▶

ser un poste (to be a post) to be deaf; to be slow, dim-witted ◀ Sp ▶

tener pinta (de) (to have spot [of]) to look (like) ◀ L. Am., Sp ▶
Ese cocido tiene buena pinta. (Sp) That stew looks good.
Ese fulano tiene pinta de narcotraficante. That guy looks like a drug dealer.

distinctive traits

chato(-a) pug-nosed ◀ Mex, C. Am., DR, Col ▶

chino(-a) curly haired ◀ Mex, C. Am. ▶

Parece Volkswagen con las puertas abiertas. (He or she looks like a Volkswagen with the doors open.) having very large ears ◀ parts of L. Am. ▶

pitudo(-a) with a very high voice, like a pito, whistle ◀ ES, CR ▶

radar (radar) with big ears ◀ Mex, Col ▶

hair, skin, eye color

el/la bolillo(-a) (bread roll) anglo ◀ chicano, Mex ▶
Usted no parece chicana; parece bolilla. You don't look chicano; you look anglo.

el/la carmelita mulatto ◀ Cuba, Col ▶

catire(-a) fair-headed or fair-complexioned (Ec: **catiro[-a]**) ◀ Ven, Bol, Col, Peru ▶

chele blue-eyed, fair-complexioned (also, green-eyed) (from the Mayan word "chel," blue). In Nic the feminine is **chela**. ◀ ES, Nic, CR ▶

chelo(-a) fair, blue-eyed (from the Mayan word "chel," blue) ◀ Mex ▶
Los amigos de Silvia temen que ella se enamore de un chelo en Tejas y luego no vuelva a su país. Silvia's friends are afraid that she'll fall in love with a blue-eyed (fair) guy in Texas and then won't go back to her country.

güero(-a) blond, fair ◀ Mex, C. Am. ▶
Hola, güera, ¿qué tal? Hi, (blondie), what's up?

jincho(-a) very white ◄ PR ►
Es hora de que vayas a la playa. Estás jincho. It's time for you to go to the beach. You're very white.

mono(-a) blond or with light brown hair ◄ Col ►

moreno(-a) (dark-complexioned) black (person) ◄ chicano, Mex, G, ES, Cuba, DR, Col ►

morocho(-a) brunette ◄ U, Arg ►

prieto(-a) black or dark (person) (can also be a nickname of endearment) ◄ Mex, G, ES, Cuba, DR, PR ►
Llegaste prieta de la playa. Ten cuidado con el sol. You came back from the beach very brown. Be careful of the sun.

height, size

chaparro(-a) short of stature ◄ Mex, C. Am., parts of Caribbean, Col ►
Ernesto es muy chaparro; todas sus hermanas son más altas que él. Ernesto is very short; all of his sisters are taller than he is.

chiquitico(-a) very, very tiny ◄ CR, Col, Ven ►

enano(-a) (dwarf) short or small ◄ Mex, G, Col, Ch, Sp ►

más largo(-a) que la esperanza del pobre (longer than the hope of the poor person) very tall ◄ PR ►

palancón, palancona very tall (from **palanca**, a lever or stick) ◄ most of L. Am., Sp ►

parecer siete pisos to seem or look very tall (seven stories) ◄ Florida, Col ►

peque short for **pequeño(-a)** (a bit old-fashioned in Sp) ◄ L. Am., Sp ►
Cuando era peque, me gustaba mucho la película «La sirenita». When I was little, I really liked the movie "The Little Mermaid."

petizo(-a) short, small ◄ S. Cone ►

el tablazo (blow given with a board) straight-up-and-down guy (with no hips) ◄ Col ►

wearing glasses

chicato(-a) wearing glasses, blind (as a bat) ◄ Peru, U, Arg ►

el/la cuatro-pepas (four-seeds) person with glasses, four-eyes ◄ Ven ►

el/la cuatrojos (four-eyes) person with glasses ◄ Mex, Cuba, DR, PR, Col, S. Cone ►
Me puse lentes de contacto para que no me dijeran cuatrojos. I put on contact lenses so they wouldn't call me four-eyes.

el/la gafudo(-a) (big glasses-wearer) person with glasses (Sp: **gafas**), four-eyes ◄ Sp ►

weight

el bacalao (codfish) very thin, skinny person, string bean ◄ Florida, PR, Col, U ►
No sé qué se cree esa tipa si no es más que un bacalao. ¡Parece anoréxica! I don't know why that girl thinks she's hot stuff when she's nothing but a beanpole. She looks anorexic!

la ballena (whale) very corpulent person ◄ Mex, G, ES, Col ►
Este vestido será para una ballena. This dress must be for a cow.

el botero large or robust person (from the Colombian artist Fernando Botero, whose figures are rotund) ◄ Col ►

cuadrado (square) corpulent, with a nice build (man) ◄ Mex, G, ES, Sp ►
Hace mucho deporte y está cuadrado. He plays a lot of sports and has a nice build.

entradito(-a) en carnes (a little bit entered into flesh) a little bit heavy, pleasingly plump (euphemism) ◄ DR, S. Cone, Sp ►

el estantillo (small post or pillar) skinny person ◄ Col ►
No me gusta hablar mal de nadie, pero Susana ha bajado de peso, ¿no? ¡Qué estantillo! I don't like to speak badly of anyone, but Susana has lost weight, hasn't she? What a string bean!

la foca (vaca) (seal [cow]) fat person ◄ U, Arg, Sp ►

el fósforo (matchstick) string bean, skinny person ◄ Col ►

jalao(-a) (pulled) skinny ◄ ES, PR ►

el palo de escoba (broomstick) person who is too skinny ◄ L. Am. ►
Es tan flaco el profesor. Es un palo de escoba. The professor is so skinny. He's thin as a rail.

Say it with slang!

Monkeying around with idioms

Monkeys have certain endearing qualities, and maybe that's why the word **mono(-a)** (monkey) means "cute" in Spain and most of Latin America, as in **Esas chaquetas son muy monas.** (Those jackets are very cute.) Something really nice or an attractive and well-behaved child is **una monada** (a monkey thing): **Tu hijo es una monada.** (Your son is a darling.) When Mexicans think someone is looking at them strangely, they might say: **¿Tengo monos en la cara?** (Why are you looking at me like that? Literally, Do I have monkeys on my face?) When Cubans feel chilly, they are liable to say: **Chifla el mono.** (It's cold out. Literally, The monkey is whistling.) But who can explain why Argentinians, Chileans, and Cubans describe someone who is very drunk by saying **anda con la mona** (he or she is walking with the she-monkey)?

Los gorilas (gorillas) are big, rough guys in Guatemala and Mexico: **No quiero jugar contra ese equipo; los jugadores son unos gorilas.** (I don't want to play against that team; the players are big bruisers.) In Venezuela, however, the reflexive verb **engorilarse** (to become gorilla) means to go mad and lose control: **Mi jefe se engoriló cuando llegué tarde.** (My boss went ballistic when I arrived late.)

salirse por el cuello de la camisa (to go out by the neck of the shirt) to be very skinny ◀ Sp ▶

places

la capirucha good old capital (Mex: Mexico City; ES: San Salvador) ◀ Mex, ES ▶

donde (where) in the home of, where someone is ◀ L. Am. ▶

La fiesta fue donde Susana y Naldo. The party was at Susana and Naldo's house.

Gringolandia (Gringoland) the United States ◀ L. Am. ▶

jungla, monte y pasto (jungle, brush, and pasture) the countryside ◀ PR ▶

México es un pañuelo. (Mexico is a handkerchief.) Mexico is a small world. ◀ Mex ▶

Nicaragua es un ranchón (una hacienda). Nicaragua is a small world (ranch). (Everybody knows each other in Nicaragua.) Another place can be substituted, e.g., **El mundo es un ranchón.** ◀ Nic ▶

yumático(-a) United States ◀ Cuba ▶

praise

a bombo y platillo (at drum and saucer) with a lot of fanfare; said when news is broadcast far and wide ◀ Mex, DR, PR, Sp ▶

dar bombo a alguien (to give drum, fanfare) to praise someone with exaggeration ◀ Mex, DR ▶
Yo no sé por qué le dan tanto bombo a esa cantante... ¡tan mal que canta! I don't know why they praise that singer so highly . . . she sings so badly!

echar flores (to throw flowers) to compliment ◀ L. Am., Sp ▶
¡Qué flores me está echando! What nice compliments you're giving me!

Favor que usted me hace. (Favor that you do me.) How nice of you to say so. ◀ L. Am., Sp ▶

piropear to compliment ◀ L. Am., Sp ▶

poner en el cielo (to put to the sky) to praise highly ◀ Mex, DR, Sp ▶

poner en los cuernos de la luna (to put on the horns of the moon) to praise (someone or something) a great deal ◀ Peru, Ch ▶

pride

See also "boasts."

looking down on

limpiarse el culo con algo (to wipe one's ass with something) to disdain something (vulgar) ◀ Mex, PR ▶

mirar a alguien por encima del hombro (literally, over one's shoulder) to look down one's nose at someone ◀ L. Am., Sp ▶

tener a menos (to hold for less) to disdain ◀ Sp ▶

tener en poco a una persona o cosa (to hold someone or something in small) to have little regard for someone or something ◀ Sp ▶

putting on airs, being full of oneself

darse coba (to give oneself flattery) to brag, put on airs ◀ Mex, DR, CR, Sp ▶
Ese tipo es un engreído; todo el día se la pasa dándose coba. That guy is stuck-up; he spends all day tooting his own horn.

darse lija (to give oneself sandpaper) to put on airs ◀ CR, Cuba, PR ▶

darse paquete (to give oneself package) to put on airs ◀ Mex, G ▶
Lucy se da mucho paquete desde que se sacó la lotería. Lucy is really full of herself since she won the lottery.

darse taco (to give oneself taco or plug) to put on airs ◀ Mex, Hond, CR ▶

dárselas de... (to give them to oneself as . . .) to pretend to be or act like . . . (also, **picarse de...**) ◀ L. Am., Sp ▶
Se las da de culta, pero no lo es. She acts like she's well educated (cultured), but she isn't.

hacerse de(l) rogar (to make oneself begged) to play hard to get, like to be begged (Mex, ES, Pan, Col: **del**; DR, Ch, Sp: **de**) ◀ Mex, ES, Pan, DR, Col, S. Cone, Sp ▶
A mi hermana le gusta hacerse de(l) rogar. My sister likes to play hard to get.

hacerse el musiú (to become the monsieur or gentleman) to act in an unconcerned or condescending manner, be uppity ◀ Ven ▶
Le pregunté sobre la plata que me debía y él se hizo el musiú. I asked him about the money he owed me and he acted very uppity.

las ínfulas airs ◀ S. Am., Sp ▶
Hablaba con grandes ínfulas de su amistad con el presidente. Iba llena de ínfulas. (Se daba muchas ínfulas.) She was putting on

airs about her friendship with the president. She went around with her head swollen up.

tener la cabeza llena de humos   (to have the head full of smokes/vapors) to be full of oneself, have one's head swollen ◀ Florida, Mex, ES, DR, Col, U, Arg ▶

tener muchos humos   (to have many smokes/vapors) to be full of oneself ◀ ES, PR, U, Arg, Sp ▶

stuck-up

el/la acartonado(-a)   (cardboard-like) stiff, unsociable person; pretentious person ◀ Arg ▶
Ese señor ni saluda, es un acartonado. That guy doesn't even say hello; he's very stand-offish.
Esa señora tan paqueta es una acartonada; desprecia a todos. That nicely dressed lady is a snob; she looks down on everyone.

el/la agrandado(-a)   (made larger) conceited, self-important, person with a big ego ◀ ES, U, Arg ▶
Ese tipo es un agrandado; vive diciendo pavadas y haciéndose el importante. That guy is a big snob; he goes around talking nonsense and acting like he's important.

el/la alzado(-a)   (raised up) pretentious, arrogant person ◀ Mex, U, Arg ▶
Esmeralda es una alzada; no le viene nadie bien. Esmeralda is a snob; she doesn't like anybody.

burguesito(-a)   (bourgeois) pretentious, snooty ◀ Mex, G, Col, U, Arg ▶

copetudo(-a)   (crested, referring to the copete, crest or crown) highfalutin, stuck-up ◀ ES, S. Cone ▶
Esa mujer es muy copetuda; se cree la muy muy. That woman is really stuck-up; she thinks she's hot stuff.

creído(-a)   (believed) stuck-up ◀ Mex, G, ES, Arg, Ch, Sp ▶

cuico(-a)   ostentatious, snobbish ◀ Ch ▶

engrupido(-a)   (grouped up) pretentious, a bit snobbish ◀ U, Arg ▶

esnob   snobbish ◀ L. Am., Sp ▶

estirado(-a)   (stretched out) uptight, snobbish (Nic: implies upper class or high society) ◀ ES, Nic, CR, S. Cone, Sp ▶

Es buena persona aunque un poco estirada. She's a good person although a bit snobbish.

fantasioso(-a)   stuck-up ◀ L. Am., Sp ▶

el/la fantoche(-a)   (puppet) presumptuous or ridiculous person; show-off (CR: person who is ridiculous, usually because of dress, not a show-off) ◀ Mex, ES, CR, DR, Sp ▶
Ese joven es un fantoche; se cree la gran cosa. That young guy is so stuck-up; he thinks he's hot stuff.

fifí   affected (adj.) ◀ G, Col ▶

finolis   exaggeratedly refined, uppity ◀ Sp ▶

fufurufo(-a)   stuck-up ◀ most of L. Am. (not Peru, Bol, Ch) ▶
Felipe es muy amable, pero su esposa es bien fufurufa. Felipe is very nice, but his wife is very stuck-up.

jaibón, jaibona   (from English "high-born") snob (often said ironically) ◀ Ch ▶

pepepato(-a)   pretentious, arrogant ◀ Ch ▶

pituco(-a)   affected, snobbish (Peru: wealthy) ◀ S. Cone ▶

popoff (popis)   posh, upper-class, snooty (can go with gesture of index finger under the nose and moving up) ◀ Mex, DR ▶
Ese chico es muy popoff y no me gusta salir con él. That guy is very snooty and I don't like to go out with him.

quebrado(-a)   (broken) stuck-up, snobbish ◀ Ch ▶

sifrinito(-a)   snobbish, pretentious ◀ Ven ▶

siútico(-a)   affected, pretentious ◀ Ch ▶

sobrado(-a)   (more than enough, excessive) stuck-up ◀ Peru, Ch ▶

el/la tiquis miquis   fussy or high-class person, not easily pleased ◀ PR, Sp ▶
A la prima de Roberto no le gusta nada de lo que hacemos. Es una tiquis-miquis. Roberto's cousin doesn't like anything we do. She's a snob.

thinking you're hot stuff, God's gift

creerse (to believe oneself) to feel superior (without reason), be proud or pretentious, stuck-up ◀ L. Am., Sp ▶
Juanita se cree mucho. Juanita is very stuck-up.
No te creas. Don't kid yourself. Don't be so full of yourself.

creerse el choro de la playa (to think one is the mussel on the beach) to think one is a big shot ◀ Ch ▶

creerse la divina garza (to think one is the divine heron) to think one is hot stuff ◀ most of L. Am. ▶
Elena se cree la divina garza. Es muy egoísta. Elena thinks she's God's gift to humanity. She's very selfish.

creerse la divina pomada (to think one is the divine cream) to think one is hot stuff ◀ L. Am. ▶

creerse la gran caca (to think one is the great poop) to think one is a big deal (vulgar) ◀ chicano, Mex, G, Col ▶

creerse la gran cosa (to think one is the big thing) to think one is a big deal, hot stuff (also, **cosota**) ◀ Mex, G, DR, Arg, Sp ▶
No soporto a Raquel. Es una engreída; se cree la gran cosota. I can't stand Raquel. She's very conceited; she thinks she's hot stuff.

creerse la gran mierda (to think one is the great shit) to think one is hot shit (vulgar) ◀ G, DR ▶

creerse el hoyo del queque (to think one is the hole in the center of the cake) to have a very high opinion of oneself, think one is the center of the universe ◀ Ch ▶

creerse la mamacita peluda (la maravilla peluda, la mamacita de Tarzán) (to think one is the hairy little mother [the hairy marvel, the little mother of Tarzan]) to think one is God's gift ◀ Nic ▶

creerse el (la) muy muy (to think one is the very very) to think one is hot stuff ◀ Mex, C. Am., Col ▶

creerse el ombligo del mundo (to think one is the belly button of the world) to think one is hot stuff ◀ Sp ▶

creerse la última chupada del mango (to think one is the last suck on the mango) to think one is hot stuff (S. Cone: **del mate**, of the **mate**, a strong tea) ◀ Mex ▶

creerse la última Coca-Cola en el desierto (to think one is the last Coca-Cola in the desert) to think one is hot stuff, God's gift ◀ Mex, ES, Nic, Pan, DR, PR, Col ▶
Carmen se ve muy bonita, ¿no? Su vestido es de París. —¡Pero es tan engreída! Se cree la última Coca-Cola en el desierto. Carmen looks very pretty, doesn't she? Her dress is from Paris. —But she's so stuck-up! She thinks she's God's gift.

No tiene agua para beber y quiere bañarse. (He or she doesn't have water to drink and wants to take a bath.) said of someone who wants to be more than he or she can be ◀ Mex ▶

parecer que se ha tragado un palo de escoba (to look like one has swallowed a broomstick) to be hard to deal with, uppity, or arrogant ◀ Mex, Sp ▶
La recepcionista que trabaja allí parece que se ha tragado un palo de escoba. ¡Qué arrogante! The receptionist who works there looks very stuck-up. How arrogant!

quebrarse (to get broken) to turn one's nose up at others, act like a snob ◀ Ch ▶

problems

See also "difficulty," "embarrassment," "mess, fuss, disorder."

clavado(-a) (nailed) stuck ◀ Mex, Col, U, Arg ▶
Estoy clavada aquí, cocinando. I'm stuck here, cooking.
Nos tienen clavados estudiando. They have us stuck studying.

darse con la cabeza en la pared (to bang your head against the wall) to be frustrated because of wasted effort ◀ DR, Ch ▶

la embarrada (mud plaster [for walls]) embarrassment, problem ◀ Mex, Col, S. Cone ▶

¡Qué embarrada! Se me olvidó mandar el cheque. (Col) How embarrassing! I forgot to mail the check.

Después del discurso del presidente, quedó la embarrada. (Ch) After the president's speech, the problem (embarrassing situation) remained.

embarrado(-a) (mud plaster for walls) stained (like having covered oneself with mud), involved in shady business, trouble ◀ Mex, G, ES, CR, U, Arg ▶

Ese señor está bien embarrado en malos negocios. That man is really tainted by shady business deals.

quemarse (to be burned, burn oneself) to get involved in a problem; blow it; discredit oneself (Cuba: also, to reveal one's true self) ◀ Mex, Cuba, DR, Col, S. Cone ▶

Ese hombre llegaba a las reuniones de infiltrado, pero se quemó. (Cuba) That man came to the meetings as an infiltrator (spy), but he revealed his true identity.

Te quemaste. You blew it.

¡Pobre Ramón! Se quemó ante todos sus amigos. Poor Ramón! He discredited himself in front of all his friends.

salir por la ventana (to take off through the window) to get out of a place or business in a disgraceful way ◀ Sp ▶

tener mal rollo (con alguien) to lead a bad life (with someone) ◀ Sp ▶

Tiene mal rollo con su mujer. He has a bad life with his wife.

traer cola (coleta) (to bring a tail [pigtail]) to bring serious consequences (used for things) ◀ Mex, U, Arg, Sp ▶

disaster

caérsele a alguien la casa encima (to have the house fall on one) to have something terrible happen ◀ Mex, DR, S. Cone, Sp ▶

caérsele a alguien el mundo encima (to have the world fall on one) to have something terrible happen, have the world crumbling around one ◀ Mex, ES, DR, PR, S. Cone, Sp ▶

¡Pobre doña Altagracia! Se le está cayendo el mundo encima. Primero murió don Danilo y ahora se le enfermó Altagracita. Poor Doña Altagracia! Her world is crumbling around her. First Don Danilo died and now little Altagracita is sick.

irse todo en humo to have everything go up in smoke ◀ Sp ▶

Esperaba que volviera con ella, pero se fue todo en humo. He was hoping to get back together with her, but everything went up in smoke.

expressions about problems

a pesar de los pesares (in spite of the sorrows) in spite of everything ◀ L. Am., Sp ▶

A pesar de los pesares, todavía tenemos esperanza. In spite of everything, we still have hope.

Apaga y vámonos. (Turn off and let's go.) said when something comes to an end or something crazy or scandalous happens ◀ Mex, DR, Sp ▶

¿Adivina quien llegó? ¡Felipe, borracho! —Apaga y vámonos que siempre se pone pesado cuando está así. Guess who came? Felipe, drunk! —Let's beat it because he's always a drag when he's like that.

¡Lo que faltaba para el duro! (What was missing for the hard one!) That's all we needed! ◀ Sp ▶

¡Nadie lo (la) salva! (No one saves him [her, it]!) Nothing can be done. It's a hopeless case. ◀ Mex, U ▶

no tener remedio (to have no remedy) to be hopeless, beyond help ◀ L. Am., Sp ▶

¡Qué caso! No tiene remedio. What a case! It's hopeless.

Nunca falta un pelo en la sopa. (There's always a hair in the soup.) There's always a hitch, problem. ◀ L. Am. ▶

Quedó la escoba (la crema). (The broom [cream] stayed behind.) It was a total disaster. ◀ Ch ▶

Se jodió el invento. (The invention or TV broke.) expression used when something goes wrong or is not obtained ◀ Sp ▶

Son palabras mayores. (They are major words.) There's something very serious or difficult that has to be talked about. ◀ Mex, ES, Nic, DR, Peru, S. Cone ▶

tapando el sol con un dedo (covering the sun with a finger) covering things up, trying to keep up appearances ◀ Mex, ES, Nic, Pan, Ven, Col, Ch ▶

from bad to worse

embarretinar(se) to get complicated ◀ Cuba ▶
La cosa empezó a embarretinarse. Things began to get complicated.

entrar bizco y salir cojo (to come in cross-eyed and leave crippled) to have things go from bad to worse ◀ parts of L. Am. ▶
Entré bizco y salí cojo. Things went from bad to worse for me.

escapar del trueno y dar con el relámpago (to escape the thunder and face or get hit by the lightning) to go from the frying pan to the fire ◀ PR, Sp ▶
Después del huracán hubo una inundación. Escapamos del trueno y dimos con el relámpago. After the hurricane there was a flood. We went from the frying pan to the fire.

huir del fuego y caer en las brasas (to flee the fire and fall into the coals) to go from the frying pan to the fire ◀ L. Am., Sp ▶

para acabarla de joder (to finish screwing it up) to make matters worse (vulgar) ◀ chicano, Mex, G, ES, DR, PR, Col, Sp ▶

para colmo; para colmo de desgracias (de males) (for the culmination of misfortunes) to top it all off, on top of everything else ◀ L. Am., Sp ▶

ponerse al rojo vivo to get red hot (a situation), heat up ◀ Mex, ES, DR, PR, Col ▶

sacar (apagar) un fuego con otro fuego (to take out [put out] one fire with another fire) to forget one bad thing because of another bad thing ◀ Mex, Sp ▶

salir de Guatemala para entrar en Guatepeor to go from the frying pan (from Guatemala [meaning "bad"]) into the fire (Guatepeor [meaning "worse"]) ◀ Mex, DR, Col, ES, S. Cone, Sp ▶

tocar fondo to touch bottom, hit rock bottom; to get to the bottom of something ◀ L. Am., Sp ▶
Parece que la economía ha tocado fondo. It looks like the economy has hit rock bottom.
Tenemos que investigar la situación hasta tocar fondo. We have to investigate the situation until we get to the bottom of it.

Un clavo saca otro clavo. (One nail takes out another nail.) One problem overshadows another, making it less important. ◀ Mex, ES, DR, PR, S. Cone, Sp ▶

having a tough time

estar vergueado(-a) to be really down and out (vulgar, from **verga**) ◀ Nic ▶

irse por un tubo (to go through a pipe) to get through something tough ◀ Ch ▶

pasar las de Caín (to spend those of Caín) to have a rough time, often financially ◀ Mex, CR, DR, PR, S. Cone, Sp ▶
Pasamos las de Caín anoche, pues mamá se enfermó y tuvimos que llevarla al hospital. We had a tough time last night because Mom got sick and we had to take her to the hospital.

pasarlas negras (canutas) (to spend them blacks [tubes]) to have a rough time (Mex, U, Arg: **negras** only) ◀ Mex, S. Cone, Sp ▶
Las pasé negras con todos los niños allí a la vez. I had a tough time with all the kids there at once.

pasarlas putas (to spend them prostitutes) to have a hell of a time (vulgar) ◀ Mex, Sp ▶

quedarse en la estacada (to end up in the stockade) to come out of a business badly; to have been gotten the better of in a dispute ◀ Ch, Sp ▶

verla peluda (to see it hairy) to see or find oneself in a jam, pinch ◀ Mex, ES, CR, Col ▶

verse a palitos (to see oneself with little sticks) to find oneself in a jam ◀ ES, CR ▶

vérselas negras (to see them black) to have a problem, have trouble ◀ Mex, ES, S. Cone ▶
Me las vi negras con el jefe porque no le gustó el trabajo que hice. I had a devil of a time with the boss because he didn't like the work I did.

estar metido en un rollo

in hot water, up the creek

colgado(-a) del cuello (hung by the neck) in a bad situation, usually economic ◀ Mex, ES ▶

con la soga al cuello (with the noose at the neck) at risk, in a bad position or situation ◀ L. Am., Sp ▶

en las astas del toro (at the horns of the bull) in a dangerous position (usually used with **dejar**) ◀ Mex, Sp ▶
Nos dejaron en las astas del toro. They left us up the creek without a paddle.

en la estacada (in the stockade) in danger, holding the bag (usually used with **dejar**) ◀ Bol, Ch, Sp ▶
En los momentos difíciles nunca me dejó en la estacada. At the most difficult times, he (she) never left me in the lurch.

entre la espada y la pared (between the sword and the wall) between a rock and a hard place, without the possibility of escape ◀ L. Am., Sp ▶
¡Qué dilema! Estoy entre la espada y la pared. What a dilemma! I'm between a rock and a hard place.

estar donde las papas queman (to be where the potatoes get burned) to be where the action is, in the eye of the storm, where it's at ◀ Ch ▶

estar en la olla (to be in the pot) to be in hot water, in trouble ◀ parts of L. Am. ▶
Si no llego a la entrevista a las once, estaré en la olla. If I don't get to the interview at 11:00, I'll be in hot water.

estar frito(-a) (to be fried) to be toast, sunk, in trouble ◀ L. Am., Sp ▶
Si no encuentras los papeles, estás frita. If you don't find the papers, you're toast.

estar metido(-a) en un rollo (to be put in a roll) to be involved or stuck in a problem ◀ Mex, G, Nic, Col, Ven, Ec, Sp ▶
Tengo un gran problema. De veras, estoy metida en un rollo. I have a big problem. I'm in a real bind.

meterse en la boca del lobo (to put oneself in the wolf's mouth) to expose oneself to unnecessary danger ◀ Mex, ES, DR, S. Cone, Sp ▶
Estás loco si vas allí. ¿Te quieres meter en la boca del lobo? You're crazy if you go there. Do you want to go into the lion's den (get into a dangerous position)?

meterse en camisa de once varas (to put oneself in a shirt of eleven rods) to bite off more than one can chew; to get mixed up in something unnecessarily ◀ L. Am., Sp ▶

meterse en Honduras (to put oneself into Honduras, meaning the country and also "the depths," literal meaning of Honduras) to get into deep trouble ◀ Mex, Ch ▶

pender de un hilo to hang from a thread ◀ L. Am., Sp ▶

sonado(-a) (sounded, rung) in big trouble ◀ S. Cone ▶
Alberto está sonado. Su novia lo vio con otra chica. Alberto is in big trouble. His girlfriend saw him with another girl.

tener la vida en un hilo (to have one's life by a thread) to be in great danger ◀ Mex, ES, DR, S. Cone, Sp ▶

saving one's skin

salvar el pellejo to save one's skin ◀ L. Am., Sp ▶

salvarse en el anca de una pulga (to be saved on the rear end of a flea) to be saved at the last minute, have a close call ◀ U ▶

salvarse en tablitas (to be saved on little boards) to be saved by a miracle, get out of danger or a difficult task ◀ Cuba, DR, Col ▶

salvarse por un pelo (to be saved by a hair) to be saved by the bell, escape by a hair (Peru: **salvarse por los pelos**) ◀ Mex, ES, Peru, S. Cone, Sp ▶
El preso se salvó de la pena de muerte por un pelo. The prisoner escaped the death penalty by a hair.

thorny problem or situation

el atado (tied-up package) thorny problem or situation ◀ Ch ▶

el atolladero mess, quagmire, bad situation ◀ ES, CR, Ch, Sp ▶

el ay de mí (oh my goodness) real worry, thorn in the flesh ◀ Nic ▶

el bache (pothole) disappointment, obstacle, something that gets in the way of success ◀ Mex, DR, ES ▶

el callejón sin salida dead end; problem or conflict that is difficult or impossible to resolve ◀ L. Am., Sp ▶
No sé qué hacer; estoy en un callejón sin salida. I don't know what to do; I'm in a dead-end situation.

el cangrejo (crab) hard case, tough nut to crack, problem; unsolved crime ◀ CR, Ven ▶
Mi esposo dice que no. ¡Qué cangrejo! My husband says no. What a hard case!

carros y carretas (cars and carts) obstacles or problems that one puts up with patiently ◀ Mex, Sp ▶

el clavo (nail) problem, embarrassment ◀ G, Nic, ES, CR, S. Cone ▶
Tengo un clavo, un problema muy grande. I have a problem, a very big problem.
¡Qué clavo! How embarrassing!
Mi auto es un clavo: necesita muchos arreglos. My car is a problem; it needs a lot of repairs.

la drama, el dramón problem, difficult situation ◀ S. Cone ▶

la onda gruesa (thick sound wave) heavy (difficult, scary, dangerous) thing, situation ◀ Mex, ES, Col ▶

pasar de castaño oscuro (to get darker than chestnut) to be too serious or troublesome (things) ◀ DR, PR, S. Cone, Sp ▶
Tus problemas han pasado de castaño oscuro. Your problems have gotten very serious.

el pasme problem, embarrassment, stupefaction ◀ PR ▶

la patata caliente (hot potato) very delicate matter ◀ Mex, Sp ▶

el pedo (fart) problem (vulgar) ◀ chicano, Mex, G, Hond, ES, Ven ▶
Después del juego, se armó un gran pedo. After the game, there was a big stink.
Yo no tengo la culpa. Ése no es mi pedo. It's not my fault. That's not my problem.

el rocheo problem, mental conflict, something bad or boring ◀ PR ▶
¡Qué rocheo! Tengo que estudiar pero quiero ir a la discoteca. What a drag! I have to study but I want to go to the disco.

ser un problema mayúsculo to be a major (capital letter) problem ◀ L. Am. ▶
Aquí el tráfico es un problema mayúsculo. The traffic here is a mega problem.

el tejemaneje (knack) problem, bad business, scheme (Sp: **tequemaneje**) ◀ Mex, DR, PR, Ch, Sp ▶
No sé que tequemanejes te traes ni quiero saberlos. (Sp) I don't know what shenanigans you're up to (bringing here) nor do I want to know.

la vaina (husk) problem, mess (all-purpose word for any thing, situation, etc., slightly vulgar) ◀ Nic, G, CR, Pan, DR, PR, Col, Ven ▶
¡Qué vaina! Dejamos los pasaportes en el hotel. What a pain! We left the passports in the hotel.

trying to solve a problem

agarrarse a un clavo ardiendo (to cling to a burning nail) to clutch at straws ◀ L. Am., Sp ▶

Say it with slang!

People can be beastly!

In Latin America, the word **bestia** (beast) is an insult, implying that someone is a rude boor with no manners; for example, **¡Bestia! No me hables así.** (Beast! Don't talk to me like that.) In Spain and many parts of Latin America, to do something **a lo bestia** (literally, in a beastly manner) means to do it crudely or abruptly. For example, **Tu amigo hizo la silla pero a lo bestia.** (Your friend made the chair but in a rough and ready way.)

Worse than being a boor is being an ignorant boor and proud of it. In Mexico and Colombia that concept is expressed with a combination of **analfa-** (from **analfabeto[-a]**, the word for illiterate) and **-bestia**, giving us the word **analfabestia. Ese tipo es analfabestia y no me interesa para nada.** (That guy is a redneck and doesn't interest me at all.)

Because slang is so fluid, it shouldn't surprise us to find out that the adjective **bestial** (beastly) has two directly opposite meanings. In Mexico it usually means awful, beastly, in the sense you would expect, **un libro horrible, bestial** (a horrible, trashy book). In Spain and some parts of the Caribbean and South America, **bestial** can mean tremendously good, marvelous, **una fiesta fantástica, bestial** (a fantastic, awesome party).

bajar a todos los santos (to get all the saints down—as if to pray to all of them at once) to try everything in times of trouble ◀ Mex, ES ▶
¡Qué problema más grande! Vamos a bajar a todos los santos para tratar de resolverlo. What a big problem! We're going to go all out to try to solve it.

desnudar a un santo para vestir a otro (to strip one statue of a saint naked to dress another) to move something unnecessarily or take something from one person and give it to another when both need it, take from Peter to pay Paul ◀ S. Cone ▶

jugar la última carta (to play the last card) to go to the last resort, play one's last trick ◀ Mex, Arg, U, Sp ▶

El presidente del sindicato estaba listo para jugar su última carta. The president of the union was ready to play his last trick.

quemar el último cartucho (to burn the last cartridge) to go to the last resort, play one's last trick ◀ L. Am., Sp ▶

sacarle a alguien de un apuro to get someone out of a jam ◀ L. Am., Sp ▶
Me sacaste de un apuro ayer. ¡Gracias! You got me out of a jam yesterday. Thanks!

tocar muchas teclas (to touch many keys) to go to everyone or do everything to solve a problem ◀ U, Arg, Sp ▶
Tuve que tocar muchas teclas para conseguir el permiso. I had to push a lot of buttons to get the permit.

pushiness

See also "bad character," "selfishness."

entrar (andar) como Pedro por su casa (to enter [walk around] like Pedro in his house) to feel or make oneself at home (Mex: **Juan** instead of **Pedro**) ◄ Mex, DR, Peru, Bol, Arg, Ch, Sp ►
El vecino andaba aquí como Pedro por su casa. The neighbor made himself at home here.

meter el pie (to stick one's foot in) to get into a house, business ◄ Mex, Sp ►

el tigre (tiger) aggressive person (DR: also, stud or streetwise guy) ◄ Mex, G, DR, Col ►

gate crashing

el cacheteo party crashing ◄ PR, Ch ►

el/la colado(-a) (passed through a sieve) party or gate crasher, someone who shows up uninvited or gets in somewhere ◄ L. Am., Sp ►

colarse (to be filtered or strained) to cut in line, squeeze in or through ◄ L. Am., Sp ►
Como no tenían boletos, se colaron en el concierto. Since they didn't have tickets, they crashed the concert.
Se coló al estadio y no pagó la entrada. He (She) sneaked into the stadium and didn't pay the entrance fee.

el/la colevaca someone who sneaks into a place, gate crasher ◄ Nic ►

nerve, chutzpah

la concha (shell) shamelessness, insolence, nerve ◄ Mex, Nic, Pan, Ec, Peru ►
¡Qué concha la tuya… me debes plata y no me has pagado! What nerve you have … you owe me money and you haven't paid me!

la jeta/la cara (face) nerve, pushiness ◄ Sp ►
Esa chica tiene mucha jeta. That girl has a lot of nerve.

el morro/el rostro (face) brazenness, nerve ◄ Sp ►
¡Qué morro! Mirabel no te ha llamado para invitarte a su fiesta. What nerve! Mirabel hasn't called you to invite you to her party.

nervy, pushy, shameless

el/la cara de palo (stick face) person with a lot of nerve, chutzpah ◄ Ch ►

el/la cara dura (hard face) person with a lot of nerve, chutzpah; someone who doesn't pay attention to criticism (U: also, **cara rota**) ◄ ES, PR, S. Cone ►
Miguel es un cara dura. A pesar de haber tratado mal a su suegro, ahora vive en su casa y usa su auto. Miguel has a lot of chutzpah. In spite of having treated his father-in-law badly, he now lives in his house and uses his car.

el/la cara'e barro (clay face) person with a lot of nerve, chutzpah; someone who doesn't pay attention to criticism ◄ CR ►

la conchuda (big hard shell) pushy female ◄ Nic, Ec, Peru, Bol ►

fresco(-a) (fresh) shameless, unaffected by criticism ◄ Ch, Sp ►
Es una fresca. Le dejé un libro y aún no me lo ha devuelto. She's shameless. I left a book for her and she still hasn't returned it to me.
Es un fresco; se ha ido sin pagar. He's shameless; he's left without paying.

no tener cara (to have no face) to have no shame, be shameless ◄ Mex, Col, ES ►

el/la patudo(-a) ([ugly] bigfoot) pushy or nervy person ◄ S. Cone ►

tener cara de cemento armado (to have the face of fixed cement) to have a lot of nerve, brazenness ◄ Sp ►

tener mucha cara (mucho rostro, mucho morro, mucha jeta) to have a lot of nerve (face), be an opportunist ◄ Sp ►
Carmen tiene un morro que se lo pisa.
—Sí, tiene mucha cara. Carmen has so

much nerve (literally, so much face she steps on it). —Yes, she has a lot of chutzpah.
Juan tiene mucho rostro. Habla mal de Rosa pero sale con ella. Juan has a lot of nerve. He speaks badly of Rosa but goes out with her.

zafado(-a) sassy, fresh, disrespectful ◀ PR, Col ▶
Ten cuidado con lo que dices, que andas zafadito hoy. Be careful what you say; you're a little sassy today.

What nerve!

Le da la mano y se agarra hasta el codo. (You give him or her a hand and he or she takes even the elbow.) Give him (her) an inch and he'll (she'll) take a mile. (Mex: **... y se toma el pie**) ◀ ES, S. Cone, Sp ▶

Le da el pie y le toma la mano. You give him or her an inch (your foot) and he or she takes a mile (your hand). (Mex: more common, **Le das la mano y se toma el pie.** Also, **Te dan la mano y quieres el pie.**) ◀ L. Am., Sp ▶

¡Qué cojones! (What testicles!) What nerve! (vulgar) ◀ PR ▶

¡Qué descaro! What nerve (brazenness)! ◀ L. Am., Sp ▶

¡Qué huevotes! (What big eggs, or testicles!) What nerve! (vulgar) (G: **¡Qué huevos!**) ◀ Mex, ES ▶

Te dan pon y ya quieres guiar. They give you a ride and you already want to steer (meaning take over). ◀ PR ▶

---

quantity

---

a little

el cachito (little catch) little bit (Ch: also, short while) ◀ Mex, G, ES, S. Cone, Sp ▶
Dame un cachito de canela, porfa. Give me a little bit of cinnamon, please.
Espera un cachito. (Ch) Wait a bit.

el chin chin little bit ◀ DR ▶
No tengo mucha hambre. Sólo quiero un chin chin de arroz. I'm not very hungry. I just want a little rice.

Gran puñado son tres moscas. (Three flies are a big fistful.) expression pointing out the numerical scarcity of people or things ◀ DR ▶

el pellizco (pinch) pinch, small adjustment, tweaking ◀ L. Am., Sp ▶

el pelo, pelito (hair) little bit ◀ L. Am., Sp ▶
Sólo un pelito. Just a tad.

por un pelo (by a hair) by a little bit ◀ DR, PR, S. Cone, Sp ▶
Evitamos un accidente por un pelo. We avoided an accident by a hair.

el toque (touch) little bit ◀ CR, Col, Sp ▶

y pico and a bit, small amount (used for time and money except in Ch, where **pico** is vulgar and refers to the male organ) ◀ L. Am., Sp ▶
Son las tres y pico. It's a bit after three.

a lot

a montones (in heaps) abundantly, in big quantities ◀ Mex, DR, PR, Ch, Sp ▶
Había comida a montones. There was a ton of food.

a rolete in great quantities, in droves, tons, or bunches ◀ Arg, U ▶
Estoy agotada porque tuve visitas a rolete. I'm exhausted because I had droves of visitors.

la barbaridad (barbarity) large amount ◀ L. Am., Sp ▶
Fuimos a Miami y compramos una barbaridad de cosas. We went to Miami and bought a whole bunch of things.

la biblia en verso (the Bible in verse) huge amount ◀ Sp ▶
De esa materia, Julia sabe la biblia en verso. Julia knows a ton about that subject.

el bonche bunch, group (from English) ◀ Mex, PR ▶
Tengo un bonche de ropita que ya no le queda a mi hija. I have a bunch of clothes that my daughter can no longer wear.

burda a lot, great deal (of) (invariable) ◀Ven▶
Ese tipo tiene burda plata (burda dinero). That guy has a lot of money.

el cachimbal bunch of things or people together (Hond, Nic: **cachimbo**) ◀ES, CR▶
Hubo un cachimbal de personas en la plaza. There was a horde of people in the square.

cantidad a lot (used as an adverb in slang) ◀Mex, ES, Ch, Sp▶
Mola cantidad. (Sp) It really rocks.
He comido cantidad. I've eaten a lot.

el chingo large amount (vulgar) ◀Mex, C. Am.▶
Había (un) chingo de gente allí. There was a slew of people there.

el chorro (stream) large amount ◀Mex, ES▶
Gastó un chorro de dinero. He spent gobs of money.
Falta un chorro para las elecciones. There's a ton of time before the elections.

chorrocientos(-as) many, an uncountable number ◀Mex, ES▶
¿Cuánto vale? Umm… como chorrocientos. How much is it? Hmmm . . . about a gazillion.

ciento y la madre (one hundred and the mother) abundance of people ◀Sp▶

como sardina en lata like sardines in a can, crowded or packed (Sp: also, **como una lata de sardinas**) ◀Mex, G, DR, PR, Col, S. Cone, Sp▶
La gente iba en el autobús como sardina en lata. People were riding in the bus like sardines in a can.

cuchucientos(-as) (mil) a gazillion, uncountable number ◀PR▶

demasié short for **demasiado**, too much ◀Sp▶

en paleta (on a little shovel) abundantly ◀Nic, G▶

en puta (in prostitute) in abundance (vulgar) ◀ES, Nic, CR▶
Aquel hombre tiene plata en puta. That guy has a shitload of money.

ene (n.) many, a great number, a lot ◀Ch▶
¡Por Dios! Tienen ene libros aquí. Good grief! You have a lot of books here.

No sé, amigo, estos días te quejas ene. I don't know, pal; these days you complain a lot.

el fracatán many, large amount ◀DR, PR▶
El premio de la lotería este fin de semana es de un fracatán de pesos. The lottery prize this weekend is for heaps of money.

mazo many, large amount ◀Sp▶
Tocó mazo (de) canciones. He (She) played a lot of songs.

el mogollón disorder, exaggeration, abundance; **mogollón de**, a lot of ◀Sp▶
Había un mogollón de gente en la fiesta. There were zillions of people at the party.
Me alucina mogollón. I like him (her) a lot.

el montón (heap) a lot (of) (also, **montones**) ◀L. Am., Sp▶
Hicimos un montón de comida para la fiesta. We made a ton of food for the party.

para dar y regalar (to give and give as a present) in abundance ◀Mex, Ch, Sp▶

para dar y tomar (to give and take) in abundance ◀Mex, Sp▶
Tienen tanto dinero como para dar y tomar. They have money to burn.

para tirar pá (para) arriba (to throw up in the air) in abundance ◀S. Cone▶

por un tubo (through a pipe) abundantly ◀DR, Sp▶
En esa fiesta había bebidas por un tubo. At that party there were tons of drinks.
Gracias, pero ya no quiero más. Comí torta por un tubo. Thanks, but I don't want any more. I ate a ton of cake.

sapotocientos(-as) (mil) a gazillion, uncountable number ◀G▶

sendo(-a) big, great ◀Mex, C. Am.▶
Se sirvieron sendos platos de menudo. They served themselves great plates of tripe soup.

sepetecientos(-as) many, an uncountable number ◀Mex, DR, PR, Col▶
Te lo he dicho sepetecientas veces: ¡No voy! I've told you a zillion times: I'm not going!

sobrar (haber) tela que cortar (to have extra material to cut) to have plenty of material to deal with an issue ◀Mex, DR, PR▶

Todavía hay mucha tela que cortar sobre esta materia, según la maestra. There's still a lot of material to deal with on this topic, according to the teacher.

la tracalada large quantity; crowd ◄ Mex, Ch ►

quiet

achantar to quiet ◄ Sp ►

achantarse to comply, be quiet about something ◄ Sp ►
Se achantó en la reunión y no dijo nada. He (She) remained quiet at the meeting and didn't say anything.

camuflar la onda (to camouflage the sound wave, thing) to keep a secret ◄ Ec, Col ►
Es una fiesta sorpresa. Hay que camuflar la onda. It's a surprise party. We have to keep a lid on it.

cerrado(-a) (closed) not admitting anything, taciturn (Sp: also, introverted) ◄ G, Col, U, Arg, Sp ►
A Teresita le cuesta hacer amigos porque es muy cerrada. It's hard for Teresita to make friends because she's very introverted.

cerrar el pico (to close the beak) to be quiet ◄ Mex, DR, PR, U, Arg, Sp ►
Cierra el pico, que los niños están escuchando. Shut up (Close your mouth); the children are listening.

cortante (cutting) abrupt, giving short answers only ◄ Mex, G, ES, Col, Arg, Ch, Sp ►
Estaba hablando con ella, pero es bien cortante. I was talking to her, but she's very abrupt.

cortar el rollo (to cut the roll) to cut the jive, talk ◄ Mex, Sp ►
Corta el rollo y págame lo que me debes. Cut the jive and pay me what you owe me.

desmayar (to faint) to keep quiet; to stop (talking or doing something) ◄ G, Cuba ►
Desmaya, niño. Olvídalo. Quiet (child). Forget it.

doblar el pico (to fold up the beak) to keep quiet, shut up ◄ Mex, ES ►
No le gustó lo que le dije y rápido dobló el pico. He (She) didn't like what I said and quickly shut up.

morderse la lengua to bite one's tongue, avoid saying something ◄ L. Am., Sp ►

morir pollo (to die chicken) to keep quiet, keep one's lips sealed ◄ Ch ►

multiplicarse por cero (to multiply oneself by zero) to keep quiet ◄ Sp ►
Si no te gusta, multiplícate por cero. If you don't like it, shut up.

no decir «esta boca es mía» (to not even say "this mouth is mine") to not say a word ◄ L. Am., Sp ►

no decir ni mu (to not even say **mu**) to not say a word ◄ U, Arg, Sp ►
De esto ni mu, ¿entiendes? —Calladita como una tumba. Don't say a word about this, understand? —Mum's the word (literally, Quiet as a tomb).

no decir ni pío (to not even say **pío**, peep) to not say a word ◄ Mex, DR, PR, Ch, Sp ►

No se lo sacarán ni con pinzas. They won't get it out of him (her, them) even with tweezers. (referring to information from someone who is reserved or who clams up) ◄ Mex, DR, S. Cone, Sp ►

Pasó un ángel. (An angel passed by.) said when there is silence in a conversation (also, **pasa un ángel**) ◄ S. Cone, Sp ►

poner un candado a la boca (to put a lock on one's mouth) to keep a secret or keep quiet ◄ Mex, DR, U, Arg, Sp ►
Ponte un candado a la boca. Keep your lips sealed.

poner un zíper en la boca to zip up one's mouth, keep quiet (U: **poner un cierre...**) ◄ Mex, ES ►

ponerse un bozal (un zíper) to be quiet ◄ ES, CR, Col ►

por lo bajini (bajo) (by the low) in secret ◄ Sp ►

quedarse como en misa (to be left as in mass) to be quiet ◄ CR, Col, U ►

poner un zíper en la boca
(See page 191.)

quedarse pa'adentro (to stay inside) to be left speechless ◀ Ch ▶

sin co short for **sin comentarios**, without comment ◀ Mex, Col ▶

Shh! Keep quiet.

¡Chis! Shh! ◀ Mex, Col ▶

¡Corta! ¡Corta! (Cut! Cut!) Be quiet! Stop! Cut it out! ◀ Mex, PR ▶

¡Córtala! (Cut it!) Quiet! ◀ Mex, ES, S. Cone ▶

En boca cerrada no entran moscas. (In a closed mouth flies don't enter.) Talking can get you into trouble. Loose lips sink ships. ◀ L. Am., Sp ▶

randomness

See also "inattention: without thinking, foolishly."

a diestra y siniestra (right and left) helter-skelter ◀ L. Am., Sp ▶

a lo que salga (with whatever comes up) without knowing or caring about the result ◀ Mex, ES, DR, PR, U, Arg, Sp ▶
Yo prefiero los viajes organizados pero a Víctor le encanta la aventura, así que nos vamos a México a lo que salga. I prefer organized tours but Víctor likes adventure, so

we're going to Mexico and we'll take what comes.

salga pato o gallareta (whether a duck or wild turkey turns up) whatever may happen, come what may ◀ DR ▶

tomar el rábano por las hojas (to grab the radish by the leaves) to start something without any method or planning, jump in any which way ◀ Nic, Peru ▶

willy-nilly, without a plan, haphazardly

a la que te criaste (in the way you were brought up) as well as possible, with a hope and a prayer ◀ Ch ▶
Los niños terminaron el trabajo a lo que te criaste. The children finished the work as well as possible, in a haphazard way.

a troche y moche (trochemoche) willy-nilly, pell-mell ◀ parts of L. Am., Sp ▶

a la zumba marumba spontaneously, without advanced plans, any which way ◀ Nic ▶
Decidí hacer una fiesta esta noche a la zumba marumba. I decided to have a party tonight on the spur of the moment.

al garete with no fixed direction or destination (**ir, andar al garete**) ◀ Mex, CR, DR, Ch ▶
El muchacho andaba al garete. The boy was going along with no fixed direction.

al tuntún haphazardly, without thinking or knowing about a subject, without a plan ◀ S. Cone, Sp ▶
Siempre hace las cosas al tuntún, sin pensar. He (She) always does things haphazardly, without thinking.

por hache o por be (by "h" or by "b") one way or another ◀ DR, Sp ▶

readiness

estar al pie del cañón (to be at the foot of the cannon) to be always at one's post, ready and waiting, on one's toes ◀ Mex, ES, S. Cone, Sp ▶

Si necesitas algo, llámame. Aquí estaré al pie del cañón. If you need something, call me. I'll be here ready and waiting.

estar listo como el pisto (to be ready as money) to be ready ◀ ES ▶

estar puesto(-a) (to be put, turned on) to be ready ◀ Mex, U ▶

Estoy bien puesta para irme a Hawai mañana. I'm really ready to go to Hawaii tomorrow.

reasons

See also "likes and dislikes: doing whatever you please"

¿A son de qué? For what reason? (Mex, U: **¿Al son...?**) ◀ Mex, DR, U, Ch, Sp ▶

¿A son de qué tenías que contarle que viste a su novio en la playa? For what reason did you have to tell her that you saw her boyfriend at the beach?

la madre del cordero (the mother of the lamb) the real reason for something ◀ Peru, S. Cone, Sp ▶

por gusto, de puro gusto for the fun of it, as a whim ◀ L. Am., Sp ▶

por pitos o por flautas (for fifes or for flutes) for one reason or another ◀ Mex, Ch, Sp ▶

por las puras alverjas (because of pure green peas) just for the heck of it, for no reason at all ◀ Peru, Ch ▶

por un «quítame allá esas pajas» (for a "take away from me those straws") for nothing, for no reason at all ◀ Mex, Nic, Ch, Sp ▶

por real decreto (by royal decree) because that's how it is, it's not to be appealed ◀ most of L. Am., Sp ▶

por su cara bonita (because of his or her pretty face) for no good reason, usually meaning that something may

come about undeservedly (more common in Sp than **por su linda cara**) ◀ Mex, ES, Ch, Sp ▶

¿Crees que por tu cara bonita vas a aprobar el examen? Do you think you're going to pass the test because of your good looks?

por su linda cara (because of his or her handsome face) for no good reason, usually meaning that something may come about undeservedly ◀ Mex, DR, S. Cone, Sp ▶

porque la abuela fuma (because his [her, your, my, etc.] grandmother smokes) for no good reason, meaning that someone is inventing an excuse for something ◀ Sp ▶

Le pegó la depresión porque la abuela fuma. He (She) is depressed because his (her) grandma smokes (there is no real reason).

porque voló la mosca (because the fly flew away) just for the heck of it, for no reason at all ◀ Mex, Col ▶

rejection

See also "insults."

expressions of rejection

A otra cosa, mariposa. (To another thing, butterfly.) That's that, forget it. (also used for changing the topic) ◀ Mex, DR, Sp ▶

Contigo ni a China me voy. (I'm not even going to China with you.) I want nothing to do with you. ◀ Mex, ES, Col ▶

Contigo ni a la vuelta de la esquina. (I'm not even going down to the corner with you.) I want nothing to do with you. ◀ S. Cone ▶

Contigo ni el saludo. (With you not even the greeting.) used humorously after being refused when an invitation was made, meaning that the other person is being unfriendly ◀ Mex, G, ES, Col ▶

¡De eso nada, monada! (Of that nothing, monkey (cute) face!) mild expression of rejection ◀Sp▶

¡Toma! (Take!) interjection implying that something is unimportant or not new; also, Take that! (as punishment, for instance) ◀Sp▶

¡Toma castaña! (¡Toma del frasco, Carrasco!) (Take chestnut! [Take from the flask, Carrasco!]) Take that! (in a discussion) So what? (when something has happened that doesn't affect one directly) ◀Sp▶

¡Un rábano! (A radish!) expression of rejecting or declining something ◀Mex, Sp▶

standing up, being stood up

la cañona standing up of someone, used like **bomba** ◀DR, PR▶

dar calabazas (ayotes) (to give pumpkins [squash]) to jilt; to stand (someone) up (Sp: also, to fail someone [on an exam]; C. Am.: also, to make jealous) ◀L. Am., Sp▶
Pobre Martín. Su novia le dio calabazas. Poor Martín. His girlfriend jilted him.

dar (un) plantón (to give [a] planting) to stand (someone) up; also, **plante** (Arg, Ch: **pegarse un plantón**) ◀L. Am., Sp▶
Me dio un plantón porque le surgió un problema en el último momento. He (She) stood me up because something came up at the last minute.
No me des plantón. Don't stand me up.

dejar (estar) colgado(-a) (to leave [be] hung, suspended) to leave (be) hanging or stood up ◀Mex, ES, U, Arg, Sp▶
Mi novio me dejó colgada antes de la boda. My fiancé stood me up before the wedding.
Me dejó colgado en la puerta del cine. She left me waiting at the door of the movie theater.
Cerraron la puerta y me quedé fuera colgada. They closed the door and left me hanging there outside.
Estaba colgada al teléfono. (ES) She was stuck on the phone.

dejar con los churquitos (colochos) hechos (to leave [someone] with their curls done) to stand up, leave waiting ◀C. Am., Caribbean▶
¡Otra vez me dejó con los churquitos hechos! He (She) stood me up again!
No me dejes con los colochos hechos. Don't stand me up.

dejar pegado(-a) (arrollado[-a]) (to leave stuck [rolled up or overwhelmed]) to stand up, abandon ◀PR, Col▶
Me dejaron pegado en la fiesta. They left me at the party.

dejar pelando papas (to leave [someone] peeling potatoes) to leave waiting, stand up ◀ES, Ven▶

dejar plantado(-a) (to leave [someone] planted) to stand up ◀L. Am., Sp▶
No me dejes plantada. Don't stand me up.

estar de plantón (to be planted) to be stuck somewhere for a while, stood up ◀Mex, ES, Ch, Sp▶

el plantón (planting) standing up (of someone); also, someone who stands someone else up ◀L. Am., Sp▶

quedar como semáforo (to wind up like a traffic light) to be stood up, left hanging ◀Nic▶

dejar plantado

quedar en un quedar (to be left in a being-left-in state) to be stood up, left hanging ◀ Nic ▶

quedarse con los crespos hechos (to be left with one's curls all made) to be stood up, left hanging ◀ ES, Peru, Bol, Ch ▶

quedarse con el moño hecho (to be left with one's bun or hair all done up) to be stood up, left hanging ◀ DR ▶

quedarse tirado(-a) (to be left cast off) to be left (somewhere); to be stood up; to lose everything ◀ Mex, U, Arg, Sp ▶

tirar bomba (to throw a bomb) to stand (someone) up ◀ Caribbean ▶
No vuelvo a hacer planes con Víctor. Es la segunda vez que me tira bomba y me quedo sin hacer nada. I'm not going to make plans with Víctor again. This is the second time he's stood me up and left me (literally, I'm left) with nothing to do.

Say it with slang!

Don't be gross—euphemisms to the rescue!

English speakers sometimes soften strong language with euphemisms; they say "Darn it!" instead of "Damn it!" and "Jeez" instead of "Jesus." Spanish speakers do the same thing.

It's common to substitute **¡Miércoles!** (Wednesday!) for **¡Mierda!** (Shit!), **jorobar** (to hump) for **joder** (to screw but with the general meaning of "to bother"), and **¡Caray!**, **¡Caramba!**, or **¡Caracoles!** (literally, Snails!) for the more vulgar word **¡Carajo!** (literally referring to the male organ but used with the meaning of "Damn!" or "Hell!"). So, you can say: **¡Miércoles! No me jorobes más con ese asunto. ¡Caramba!** (Darn it! Don't screw around with me anymore about that business. The heck with it!) and get the sweet relief of *almost* letting loose with some major swear words but without offending anyone.

Every country has a few very strong words with the power to shock and offend. In Spain, a big one is **¡Hostias!** (literally, Hosts!, but with a hint of sacrilege because of the importance of religion in Spanish history and culture). A common euphemism for this word is **¡Ostras!** (Oysters!), and the effect is similar to saying "Gosh darn it" instead of "Goddamn it." In Mexico the strongest words are **chingar** (the F-word) and **chingada** (she who has been "violated," to put it euphemistically). Many and varied are the euphemisms for these terms: **¡Chin!**, **¡Chispas!** (Sparks!), or **¡Ay, Chihuahua!** to name just a few. And just as in English you may want to refer to some real jerks as "a couple of SOBs," you can refer to them in Mexico as **hijos de la guayaba** (literally, sons of the guava fruit) and every Mexican will know exactly what you mean! (See also Say it with slang! "Where is the powder room?," page 215.)

repetition

dale que dale phrase that expresses repetition ◄ L. Am., Sp ►
Aquí estoy, dale que dale a la cocina. Here I am, working away in the kitchen.
Ya me cansé de que siempre estés dale que dale al piano. I'm tired of you always banging away at the piano.

repetirlo hasta el cansancio (hasta el agotamiento) (to repeat it until tiredness [exhaustion]) to keep saying something again and again, go on and on, repeat ad nauseam (DR, PR, Ch: **cansancio** only) ◄ DR, PR, S. Cone, Sp ►

Y dale la burra al trigo. (And let the donkey keep at the wheat.) said when someone keeps repeating the same thing ◄ Mex, ES, Col ►
Y dale la burra al trigo. Siempre con lo mismo. Same old story. Always with the same thing.

requests

acho word used to introduce a request, short form of **muchacho**; can also begin a conversation ◄ PR ►
Acho 'mano, ¡cuánto tiempo que no te veía! Hey, bro', I haven't seen you in a long time!
Acho, ¿me prestas ese lápiz? Hey, will you lend me that pencil?

En pedir no hay engaño. (There is no deceit in asking.) No harm in asking. ◄ Ch ►

hacer un disparo a alguien (to fire a shot at someone) to ask someone for something blatantly, without mincing words ◄ Cuba ►

¿Qué querétanos? variant of **¿Qué quieres?** ◄ Mex ►

tener el santo de cabeza (to have the saint on its head) to ask for something until you get it ◄ Mex ►

please

Pero bendito... (But blessed one . . .) But please . . . ◄ PR, Col ►
¡Pero bendito! Déjame ir contigo. But please! Let me go with you.

por favorciano pretty please (**por favorciano, mi amorciano**) ◄ Mex, Col ►

porfa (short for **por favor**) please ◄ most of L. Am., Sp ►

resignation

See also "patience."

el/la agachado(-a) (bent over) submissive person ◄ Mex ►
Lo acepta todo, es un agachado. He accepts everything; he's a doormat.

expressions of resignation

Atente a pan y no comas queso. (Rely on bread and don't eat cheese.) Be content with one thing and don't wish for something else. ◄ Mex, PR ►

Comer y callar. (Eat and be quiet.) said when someone is benefiting from someone else and should not speak against them, beggars can't be choosers ◄ most of L. Am., Sp ►

Como dijo Herodes, te jodes. (As Herod said, you're screwed.) phrase of resignation (vulgar); Mex: also, **Como dijo Herodes, te chingas y te jodes.** (vulgar) ◄ Mex, DR, Sp ►

¿Diay? But what can one do? ◄ CR ►

El que las hace las paga. (He who makes them pays for them.) You have to accept the consequences of an action. ◀ Mex, ES, DR, PR, S. Cone ▶
Ya era tiempo que le pasara eso, porque el que las hace las paga. It was about time that happened (to him, her, you), because when you make your bed you have to lie in it.

El que pone el baile que pague la marimba. (Let the host of the dance pay for the music.) The one who thinks up an idea should take care of implementing it. ◀ ES, Nic ▶

Hay que joderse. You have to put yourself out, put up with hard times. (vulgar) ◀ Mex, ES, Sp ▶
En este país hay que joderse para ganarse la vida. In this country you have to kill yourself to earn a living.

Menos da una piedra. (A stone gives less.) phrase urging someone to accept what little they have obtained ◀ Sp ▶

No hay más narices (cojones). (There are no other noses [testicles].) There's no alternative. (vulgar with **cojones**) ◀ Sp ▶

Peor es chile y agua lejos. (Worse is chili and water far away.) Things could be worse. ◀ Mex ▶

Peor es nada. (Worse is nothing.) phrase meaning one should be satisfied with what one has ◀ L. Am., Sp ▶

¡Qué remedio! (What a remedy!) phrase of resignation meaning there is no alternative ◀ L. Am., Sp ▶

Santo que no me quiere, basta con no rezarle. (Saint that doesn't like me, it's enough not to pray to him.) There's no need to bother with someone who doesn't care about me. ◀ parts of L. Am. ▶

putting up with something

arremangarse to submit, give in ◀ Arg ▶
Ni modo. Tuve que aguantar ese regaño. Me tuve que arremangar. No way. I had to accept being dumped on (literally, that dressing-down, scolding). I had to put up with it.

arrugarse (to wrinkle up, get wrinkled) to accept or put up with something ◀ U, Arg ▶
Me la tuve que tragar; tuve que arrugarme. I had to swallow it; I had to put up with it.

bancar(se) to cope or put up with (Arg: also, to bankroll, support financially) ◀ U, Arg ▶
Hay que bancarse las malas rachas. You have to put up with the bad times.

comerse el buey (to eat up the ox) to put up with something you don't like ◀ Ch ▶
La atienden a ella y nosotros tenemos que comernos el buey. They're waiting on her and we have to put up with it.

morder el cordobán (la soga) (to bite the leather [the cord]) to bite the bullet, do something one has to do ◀ Cuba ▶

tragar (to swallow) to accept, put up with ◀ Nic, DR, U, Arg, Sp ▶
No estoy de acuerdo con algunas cosas que dice el jefe, pero hay que tragárselas. I don't agree with some of the things the boss says, but I have to put up with them.

tragar camote (to swallow sweet potato) to have to put up with something quietly or to be unable to express oneself ◀ Mex ▶
El jefe me regañó y yo tragé camote. The boss bawled me out and I had to just keep quiet.

rest

aflojar la cuerda (to slacken the cord) to take a breather, loosen up discipline ◀ Mex, Sp ▶

coger un brei to take a break ◀ Cuba, DR ▶
Vamos a estudiar primero y a las cuatro cogemos un brei. First let's study and then at four we'll take a break.

coger un diez (un cinco) to take ten (five) ◀ Cuba ▶

miquear to take it easy, not work too hard ◄ PR ▶

Vamos a trabajar, que llevamos media hora miqueando. Let's get to work; we've been monkeying around for a half hour.

romance

See also "affection," "sex."

el asaltacunas (cradle assaulter) cradle robber, someone who goes out with someone much younger ◄ Mex, Sp ▶

Rolando estaba muy enamorado de Silvia, aunque sus amigos le decían asaltacunas. Rolando was very much in love with Silvia, although his friends were calling him a cradle robber.

la aventura (adventure) love affair ◄ L. Am., Sp ▶

barrer con (to sweep with) to take away from (someone), usually referring to women ◄ ES, CR, Col ▶

Fernando anda barriendo con todas las muchachas. Fernando is sweeping up all the women (taking them all).

el brete love affair ◄ PR ▶

Cada oveja con su pareja. (Every sheep with its partner.) Everyone with a partner. ◄ L. Am., Sp ▶

deshojando la margarita (taking off the petals from the daisy) worrying "Does he/she love me or not?" ◄ L. Am., Sp ▶

echar una canita al aire (to throw a gray hair in the air) to have an affair, let one's hair down ◄ Mex, ES, DR, PR, S. Cone, Sp ▶

Gato viejo, ratón tierno. (Old cat, young mouse.) phrase meaning that old geezers like sweet young things (Ch: also, **Buey viejo, pasto tierno.** Old ox, fresh grass.) ◄ Mex, ES, Ch ▶

hacer un gancho (to make a hook) to set up a blind date; also, to punch ◄ S. Cone, Sp ▶

el mamitón guy who likes to be seen with girls ◄ PR ▶

la media naranja (half orange) spouse, sweetheart (male or female), soul mate ◄ L. Am., Sp ▶

Hola, Pilar. ¿Qué tal? ¿Cómo está la media naranja? Hi, Pilar. What's up? How's your better half?

no comerse una rosca (to not eat a doughnut) to not find anyone to pick up, not have luck with the opposite sex ◄ Sp ▶

Fui a la discoteca pero no me comí una rosca. I went to the disco but I wasn't able to hook up with any girls (guys).

pescar (un marido, etc.) (to fish) to trap (a husband, etc.) ◄ Mex, ES, Cuba, Col, S. Cone, Sp ▶

el picaflor (hummingbird) playboy ◄ Nic, R, Col, Arg, Ch ▶

sufrir un ataque de cuernos (to suffer an attack of horns) to be very jealous and react violently ◄ Sp ▶

Jaime sufrió un ataque de cuernos cuando vio a Cristina y Pedro en el cine. Jaime had an attack of jealousy when he saw Cristina and Pedro at the movies.

Gato viejo, ratón tierno.

tener un ligue   to have a date, relationship (Sp: superficial love affair) ◄ Mex, ES, Cuba, Sp ►

being a fifth wheel

cargar el arpa   (to carry the harp) to go along with a couple on a date, be a fifth wheel ◄ Mex, Ec ►

poner gorro a alguien   (to put the cap on someone) said of lovers who make out in someone else's presence ◄ Mex, DR ►
No me gusta salir con Rosa y Pepe porque me ponen gorro. Siempre andan besuqueándose. I don't like to go out with Rosa and Pepe because they treat me like a fifth wheel. They're always smooching.

tocar el violín   (to play the violin) to go out with a couple and have the feeling they really want to be alone, be a fifth wheel (Ec: **violinista**, fifth wheel) ◄ U, Ch ►

flirting

dar entrada   (to give entrance) to flirt ◄ Mex ►

hacer ojitos   (to make little eyes) to flirt ◄ L. Am., Sp ►
Siempre te está haciendo ojitos en clase. He's (She's) always making eyes at you in class.

miquear   to flirt, draw attention ◄ G ►

going steady, getting engaged or married

ahorcarse   (to hang oneself) to get married (like **echarse la soga al cuello**) ◄ Mex, CR, U ►

amarrado(-a)   (tied) married ◄ chicano, Mex, G, ES, DR, Col ►

andar (estar) de novios   to be engaged; also, to go steady in a serious way ◄ L. Am. ►
Felipe y Carmen andan de novios. Felipe and Carmen are going steady (engaged).

casarse de penalti   (to get married as a penalty) to have a shotgun wedding ◄ Mex, Col, Sp ►

casarse por detrás de la iglesia   (to get married behind the church) to go off together without getting married (Ch: **detrás de la puerta**, behind the door; ES: **detrás del palo**, behind the tree) ◄ U ►

casarse por el sindicato de las prisas   (to get married by the syndicate of haste) to get married hastily because the woman is pregnant ◄ Sp ►

cuadrado(-a)   (square) hooked up with, going steady with ◄ Col ►
Juan está cuadrado con Marisa; llevan un año cuadrados. Juan is going steady with Marisa; they've been going together for a year.

echarse la soga al cuello   (to put the rope around one's neck) to get into trouble or debt; in L. Am., very commonly means to get married, but this is not as true in Sp (Ch, Sp: also, **ponerle la soga al cuello**, to get someone into trouble) ◄ Mex, G, CR, DR, PR, Col, Ch, Sp ►

empatar(se)   to pair up, get together; to obtain or get ◄ Mex, CR, Cuba, Col, Ven ►
Silvia y Pablo se empataron en febrero. Silvia and Pedro got together (paired up) in February.

engancharse   to hook up with, hook someone up with; to be in love ◄ Mex, ES, CR, Col ►
Engánchame con aquélla. Hook me up with her over there (introduce me).
Juan y María están enganchados. Juan and María are an item (couple).

estar empatados   (to be tied) to be a couple ◄ Mex, PR, Ven ►

el matricidio   (matricide) matrimony, used in jest ◄ CR ►

pololear   (to buzz around like a bee) to go steady with someone ◄ Ch ►

ser un buen partido   to be a good match (for marriage) ◄ L. Am., Sp ►
Debes casarte con Julián. Es un buen partido. You should marry Julián. He's a good match.

ser la pierna de alguien   (to be someone's leg) to be someone's main squeeze, be going out with that person ◄ Ch ►

in love

asfixiado(-a) (asphyxiated) in love ◀DR▶
Creo que esos dos se casan pronto. Están asfixiados. I think those two will get married soon. They're a hot item.

colgado(-a) (hung, suspended) in love ◀Mex, G, Sp▶

colgarse to fall in love ◀Mex, G, Sp▶

enchulado(-a) in love ◀PR▶
Nena, tan enchulado que está Roberto y tú lo tratas tan mal. Girl, Roberto is so in love and you treat him so badly.

enculado(-a) in love; enthusiastic (slightly vulgar) ◀Mex, C. Am.▶
Estás enculado ya de esa bicha. (ES) You're in love with that girl now.

encularse to fall in love (slightly vulgar) ◀Mex, ES, CR▶
Julio se enculó de la Rosa. (ES) Julio fell in love with Rosa.

enguayabado(-a) madly in love ◀Ven▶

enpiernado(-a) (legged-in) sexually captivated by someone ◀Ven▶

estar camote con (to be sweet potato with) to be madly in love with, often referring to puppy love (CR: also, **estar encamotado[-a]**) ◀CR, Bol, Ch▶

estar metido(-a) to be in love ◀U, Arg▶

flecharle (to strike with an arrow) to feel love at first sight ◀Mex, ES, DR, Col, S. Cone▶
Me flechó. Estoy enamorada. It was love at first sight. I'm in love.

Huy, ¡qué flechazo! (Oh, what a shot of the arrow!) said when people fall in love at first sight (referring to Cupid's arrow) ◀Mex, Col, DR, U, Arg, Sp▶

quedar flechado(-a) to end up hit by an arrow (that is, Cupid's), be in love ◀Mex, G, DR, S. Cone▶

traer azorrillado(-a) to have (someone) helplessly in love (skunked) ◀Mex▶

traer de una ala (to bring by a wing) to have (someone) helplessly in love ◀Mex▶

tragarse de alguien (to swallow someone) to have a crush on someone ◀Col▶
Me tragué de Juan de una forma tan horrible que no podía dormir ni comer. Estoy tragada de él. I had such a horrible crush on Juan that I couldn't sleep or eat. I have a crush on him.

picking someone up, putting on the moves

abordar (to board) to make a pass (at someone of the opposite sex) ◀Mex▶

andar tras sus huesos (to go after his or her bones) to be on the prowl, out to get (a lover) ◀Mex, ES▶

cargar (to load) to tease, make fun of; also, to make a pass at, hit on, come on to ◀U▶
Me cargó toda la noche. He hit on me all evening.

echar bala (to throw bullet) to make amorous conquests, put on the moves ◀Cuba▶

echar (lanzar) los perros (to throw on the dogs) to call out the cavalry, go all out to win (C. Am.: **echar los perros** more common than **lanzar**; both are used in Mex) Also, **lanzar los canes.** ◀Mex, C. Am., Col, Ven▶
Le eché los perros a esa chica. I went all out for that girl (did everything possible to get or win her).

echar el ruco (to throw the horse) to go all out to win (someone), used like **echar los perros** ◀CR▶

lanzar los doberman (to throw on the dobermans) to call out the cavalry, go all out to win ◀Mex, Col▶

levantarse a alguien to pick up (someone of the opposite sex) ◀Mex, G, ES, DR, PR, Col, U, Arg▶
Ese tipo sí tiene suerte. Acaba de llegar a la fiesta y ya se levantó a esa rubia. That guy is really lucky. He just got to the party and he already picked up that blond.
Me voy a levantar a ese muchacho. I'm going to pick up that guy.

el levante pickup, date (G: short-term lover); **hacer un levante** to pick someone up ◀Mex, G, DR, PR, Col▶
Intenté hacer un levante en la playa. I tried to pick someone up at the beach.

ligar to make amorous conquests, pick up (e.g., someone of the opposite sex);

ÉL INSISTE EN ECHARME EL RUCO PERO CREO QUE SOMOS INCOMPATIBLES.

"He's calling out the cavalry to win my heart, but I think we're incompatible."

to obtain, get ◀Mex, ES, Cuba, PR, Col, S. Cone, Sp▶
Se la ligó durante las fiestas. He hooked up with her during the holidays.
Ligué un avión a México. I got a plane to Mexico.
El maestro se la pasa ligando con las estudiantes. The teacher keeps picking up female students.
Ésos ya ligaron. Those two are hooked up together (going out together) now.

el ligón pickup, date; guy who flirts and is successful with women ◀Col, Sp▶
Es un ligón. Cada semana sale con una chica distinta. (Sp) He's a hustler. Every week he goes out with a different girl.

llevarle la carga (to carry the cargo for someone) to make a pass at, hit on, be coming on to someone sexually ◀U, Arg▶
Ese muchacho siempre le lleva la carga a la más bonita. That guy always puts the moves on the prettiest girl.

tirar/echar los tejos to seduce, make passes ◀Sp▶

Seguro que le gustas a Alberto porque siempre te está tirando los tejos. Alberto must like you because he's always making passes at you.

vacilar a alguien to look at someone with lascivious intentions; to try to pick up ◀ES, Cuba, Col, Ec▶
Estás vacilando a esa chama, ¿no? You're hitting on that girl, right?
Vamos a vacilar a aquella chava. Let's go put the moves on that girl.

sweetheart

el/la cabro(-a) (goat) boyfriend (girlfriend, woman) (note: **cabra** can mean woman in CR, but in ES it's used instead of **cabrona**, bitch) ◀CR▶

la chichi girl, girlfriend ◀Pan▶

el/la cuadre boyfriend (girlfriend) ◀Col▶
Luis es mi cuadre. Luis is my main squeeze.

el/la empate (tied game, equal score) girlfriend (boyfriend), partner, companion ◀Ven, Nic▶

el/la filito(-a) (little blade, file) lover, boyfriend (girlfriend) ◀ Arg ▶
Me parece que tu hija tiene por ahí su filito. It looks like your daughter has a boyfriend there.

el jevo boy; boyfriend ◀ Cuba, DR, PR, Ec ▶

la movida (moved one) romance, prospect ◀ Ch ▶
Mi hermano tiene una nueva movida. Está muy enamorado. My brother has a new love. He's really in love.

el/la pasa rato (pastime) boyfriend or girlfriend who's just OK for now; also, in the feminine, slut ◀ Mex, DR, Col, ES ▶

el/la peoresnada (worse is nothing) phrase used to describe a boyfriend or girlfriend (sometimes chosen because there was no one better, said in jest) ◀ Mex, ES, Col, Peru, Bol, S. Cone ▶

el/la pololo(-a) (bumblebee) sweetheart, steady boyfriend (girlfriend) ◀ Ch ▶

el/la primerísimo(-a) (very first) sweetheart ◀ Col ▶
¿Cómo se llama tu primerísimo? What's the name of your main squeeze?

el príncipe azul (blue prince) prince charming, ideal man ◀ L. Am., Sp ▶

sadness

achicopalarse to be sad, depressed ◀ Mex, ES, Nic ▶
No te achicopales, que ya lo vamos a hacer. Don't let yourself get down; we're going to do it.

ahuevarse to be sad or feel put down (also, **ahuevado[-a]**) ◀ ES, CR ▶
Lilián se ahuevó con lo que le dijo. Lilián felt down about what he (she) told her.
Te miro bien ahuevado. You look really down (to me).

aplatanarse to get beaten down by troubles, beaten down (also, **aplatanado[-a]**) ◀ Mex, Col ▶

bajarse los humos (to lower one's airs/vapors) to become disillusioned, lose hope or interest ◀ ES, CR ▶

el bajón (big down) bad feeling, downer (including one caused by drugs), bummer ◀ Mex, ES, DR, PR, S. Cone, Sp ▶
¡Qué bajón! What a bummer!

bajoneado(-a) down and depressed ◀ S. Cone ▶

caérsele a alguien el alma a los pies (to have one's soul fall to one's feet) to lose heart ◀ DR, U, Ch, Sp ▶
Cuando vi que había vuelto a beber, se me cayó el alma a los pies. (Sp) When I saw that he (she) had gone back to drinking, my heart sank.

el/la caralarga (long face) person with a sad appearance, sad sack ◀ Mex, ES, DR, Col, U, Ch, Sp ▶

cebollita (little onion) making women cry ◀ Col ▶

la depre (short for **depresión**) depression ◀ L. Am., Sp ▶
Tengo una depre que no me deja pensar en nada. I'm so depressed I can't think about anything.

estar hecho(-a) pelota (to be made into a ball) to be all broken up and sad about something (a death or loss) ◀ U, Arg ▶

el gozo en un pozo (the enjoyment in a well or pit) said when one's hopes for something have been dashed ◀ Mex, Sp ▶

La procesión va por dentro. (The procession goes on the inside.) said when one feels pain or sadness but covers it up (Mex: also, **Las penas se llevan por dentro.**) ◀ Mex, S. Cone, Sp ▶

moqueado(-a) (sniveling, with a runny nose) sad ◀ Col, U, Arg ▶

pasar muchas navidades y sin nochebuena (to have a lot of Christmases with no Christmas Eve celebrations) describing a bitter person ◀ PR, Col ▶

rocharse, rochearse to be upset or depressed ◀ PR ▶

Se me cayó un imperio. (An empire fell on me.) I lost my illusions, hopes. (said by someone who feels down or disheartened) ◀ Col ▶

crying

atacarse to begin to cry ◀ CR, Col ▶

llorar a mares to cry a sea (of tears), cry buckets ◀ Mex, ES, S. Cone, Sp ▶

llorar a moco tendido (to cry with a lot of mucus) to cry like a baby ◀ L. Am., Sp ▶

miquiar to cry (Col, PR: to monkey around) ◀ CR ▶

moquiar to cry, snivel (Peru: **moquear**) ◀ Mex, ES, U, Arg ▶
La niña ya está moquiando otra vez. The girl's sniveling again.

selfishness

See also "bad character," "pushiness."

agandallar to take over, snatch ◀ Mex ▶

Al nopal lo van a ver sólo cuando tiene tunas. (They only go to see the nopal cactus when it has **tunas**, fruits.) saying that means people will call on others only when they are prosperous or doing well ◀ Mex ▶

alzarse con el santo y la limosna (to make off with the saint and the alms) to take everything, one's own and others' (CR: **quedarse sin el santo y sin la limosna**, to be left with nothing, often when two things were possible and neither was obtained) ◀ CR, DR, PR ▶

basto(-a) selfish ◀ ES ▶

hacer perro muerto (to do the dead dog) to run off without paying the bill ◀ Ch ▶

hacerse el vivo (to become the live one) to advance, get ahead, be clever at taking advantage of others ◀ L. Am., Sp ▶

meter la mano hasta el codo en una cosa (to put one's hand up to the elbow in something) to take something selfishly ◀ most of L. Am., Sp ▶

pasarse de listo(-a) (vivo[-a]) (to pass oneself as clever, be overly clever) to try to show oneself (erroneously) to be smarter than others (Mex: also, **pasarse de víbora**, instead of **vivo**) ◀ L. Am., Sp ▶
¡Te pasaste de listo! You thought you were clever (but weren't so clever after all)!

ponerse las botas (to put on one's boots) to indulge in something (food, sex, etc.) or partake of it; to make a killing (financially, sometimes to others' detriment) (Ch: second meaning only) ◀ U, Ch, Sp ▶
Me puse las botas en esa cena. Comí de todo. I really pigged out (indulged myself) at that dinner. I ate some of everything.

ser muy vivo(-a) (to be very clever) to be a go-getter, very good at getting ahead ◀ L. Am., Sp ▶

vivaracho(-a) sharp, astute; fresh ◀ S. Cone, Sp ▶

vivazo(-a) astute, like **vivo**, implying that one takes advantage of others a bit ◀ ES, CR, Col ▶

vivir de panza (to live by the belly) to enjoy life without working ◀ Cuba, Col ▶

opportunistic, sponge, mooch

el/la abusador(-a) opportunist, mooch ◀ S. Cone ▶

el/la abusivo(-a) (abusive) someone who takes advantage of others, mooch ◀ Mex, C. Am. ▶

el abusón, la abusona someone who takes advantage of others, sponge ◀ Mex, Sp ▶

aprovechado(-a) opportunistic (S. Cone: **aprovechador[-a]**) ◀ L. Am., Sp ▶

arrimado(-a) opportunistic (from **arrimarse al sol que más calienta**) ◀ Mex, G, Nic, DR, PR, Col ▶

bolsear (to purse) to mooch, freeload (Mex, C. Am.: to pick pockets); also, **el bolsero**, freeloader ◀ Ch ▶

el buitre (vulture) opportunist ◀ Mex, PR, Col, Ven, U, Arg, Sp ▶

Say it with slang!

Food for love

Food terms appear frequently in slang connected with love, sex, and romance. Mexican men like to **echar un taco de ojo** (take a look, literally "throw an eye-taco") at the women passing by in hopes of seeing a real doll, a **bizcocho** (cookie, biscuit), especially if she happens to be endowed with **una pechuga almendrada** (an attractive bust, literally, "chicken breast almondine"). The men might then be inspired to give a **piropo** (street compliment) such as: **¡Qué bombón y yo con diabetes!** (What a piece of candy and here I am with diabetes!)

Hispanic women, of course, like to do some looking around too, and in Spain, Mexico, Chile, and Uruguay, they may discuss which of the men passing by strike them as **potable** (appealing, literally potable, good for drinking). If an Argentinian woman sees a good-looking male, she could well comment to her girlfriend, **¡Qué churro más bárbaro!** (What a gorgeous fritter! A **churro** is a cylindrical fried pastry.)

When it comes to sex, food terms are popular too, such as **pastelear** (caking), which means petting in Mexico, **jamón** (ham), which means a French kiss in Venezuela, and many others.

---

el buscón, la buscona (searcher) opportunist ◀ Mex, DR, PR, Col, Sp ▶
Cerca del departamento de tránsito, hay unos buscones que por unos pesos te renuevan la licencia de conducir. Near the transportation department, there are some opportunists who will renew your driver's license for a few pesos.

el/la cachetero(-a) (small dagger) opportunist, freeloader ◀ PR, Col ▶
Ese Julio es un cachetero. Llegó sin invitación a la fiesta y encima se bebió todas las cervezas. That Julio is an opportunist. He came to the party without an invitation and on top of that he drank all the beers.

cuervear (to crow) to take advantage of others financially, get others to pay your way; also, **el cuervo**, sponge ◀ U, Arg ▶
Siempre cuervea a la hora de la fiesta. He (She) always mooches when there's a party.

de gorra (by the cap) free, at someone else's expense ◀ Mex, ES, CR, Sp ▶

Siempre como de gorra aquí. I always mooch food here.
Entró de gorra al cine. He (She) got into the movies free.
No quiero vivir de gorra. I don't want to live off other people.

El muerto al hoyo y el vivo al bollo. (The dead person in the hole and the opportunist at the widow.) (vulgar in some places) ◀ Mex, ES, CR, Ch, Sp ▶

encajarse to sponge, take advantage ◀ Mex ▶
Cada vez que lo invito, se encaja y trae a varios amigos. Every time I invite him, he takes advantage and brings several friends.
Esos comerciantes se encajan con sus clientes. Those businesspeople are taking advantage of their customers.

el ganso (goose) freeloader ◀ PR, Col ▶
Mario es un ganso. Entró al concierto sin pagar. Mario is a freeloader. He got into the concert without paying.

gorrear to sponge, not pay for things (Sp: also, **gorronear**) ◄ Mex, Col, Sp ►
Siempre está gorreando tabaco a los amigos. Es un gorrón. He always bums tobacco from his friends. He's a sponge.
Paco siempre dice que no tiene dinero y va gorreando todo el día. Paco always says he doesn't have money and mooches all day.
Ella siempre me gorrea comida. She always hits me up for food.

el gorrón, la gorrona sponge, mooch (Col: **gorrero[-a]**) ◄ Mex, C. Am., Peru, Sp ►

guevero(-a) opportunistic ◄ Col ►

hacer un sinpa (to do a no-pay, from **sin pagar**) to leave without paying ◄ Sp ►
Rolando hizo un sinpa en el bar. Rolando left the bar without paying.

ir de gorra, de gorrón to go (somewhere) without having to pay, crash ◄ Mex, ES ►

el/la jeta (face) sponge ◄ Sp ►
Es un jeta. Siempre dice que no tiene dinero para que lo inviten. He's a sponge. He always says he doesn't have money so that people will treat him.

lanzado(-a) (thrown) referring to someone who takes advantage of others or is aggressive, bold ◄ Mex, Col, Arg, Ch, Sp ►

machetear (to machete) to mooch off others ◄ S. Cone ►

el mamón, la mamona (sucker, like a suckling baby) person who takes advantage of others ◄ Sp ►
Vaya mamón, se ha ido sin pagar. What a mooch; he left without paying.

el/la paracaidista (parachutist) freeloader, party crasher (also, less common, someone who jumps into a discussion but doesn't know anything about the topic) ◄ Nic, CR, DR, Ec, Peru, S. Cone ►

pegar la gorra (to glue or fasten the cap) to eat at someone else's house, sponge ◄ Cuba ►

pegarle en la pera (to hit someone in the pear) to freeload a meal from someone ◄ Ch ►

el/la piola sponge, someone who wants a free ride ◄ Arg ►

el/la piraña (piranha) shark; astute in business, taking advantage of others ◄ ES, CR, Col ►
No le compres a ése, que es muy piraña. Don't buy from him; he's a shark.

el pulpo (octopus) very aggressive or selfish person ◄ G ►

el/la relambío(-a) sponge; also, mediocre (person) ◄ Cuba, DR ►
¿Alguien invitó a Rosita o vino de relambía? Did someone invite Rosita or did she crash?
Ese muchacho tiene cara de relambío. That guy looks like a mooch.

el remo (oar) sponge (also, **remar**, to sponge) ◄ Ec ►

ventajoso(-a) opportunistic (from **ventaja**, advantage) ◄ Mex ►
No seas ventajoso. Don't take advantage.

stingy

agarrado(-a) (grabbed) stingy, tightfisted ◄ most of L. Am., Sp ►
No me quiso llevar a cenar porque es bien agarrado. He refused to take me to dinner because he's very stingy.
Ese señor es más agarrado que la hiedra de la roca. That man is stingier (literally, tighter) than the ivy on the rock.

el amarrete (one who ties things up) miser, stingy person ◄ Bol, S. Cone ►

el/la caleta (cove, bay, place where objects get collected by being washed up to shore) stingy person who never invites anyone and hides things so as not to have to share them, tightwad ◄ Ven ►

caminar con los codos (to walk with one's elbows) to be stingy ◄ Cuba, DR, PR ►

codo(-a) (elbow) stingy (ES: invariable as an adj.) ◄ chicano, Mex, G, Hond, ES, Nic, DR, PR ►
Paula es bien codo; tiene dinero pero nunca quiere gastarlo. (ES) Paula is very stingy; she has money but she never wants to spend it.
Marcos no puso dinero para la colecta; es un codo. Marcos didn't put any money in the kitty; he's a tightwad.

¡Qué codo!
(See page 205.)

cutre stingy ◀ Sp ▶
No seas tan cutre y paga de una vez. Don't be so stingy; just pay.

duro(-a) (hard) stingy ◀ Cuba, ES, Pan, Peru ▶

duro(-a) de codo (hard of the elbow) stingy ◀ DR ▶

ir a la pela to be stingy (**pela** is short for **peseta**) ◀ Sp ▶

el/la maceta (flower pot) tightwad ◀ PR ▶
Andrés es un maceta. No invita ni a su novia; siempre hay que hacer serrucho. Andrés is a cheapskate. He never even treats his girlfriend; they always have to go dutch.

más duro(-a) que el cemento (harder than cement) stingy (Col: **duro[-a] como cemento**) ◀ PR ▶
Elena es más dura que el cemento. No comparte nada con nadie. Elena is as stingy as can be. She doesn't share anything with anyone.

no comer un huevo por no perder la cáscara (to not eat an egg so as not to lose or waste the shell) to be miserly, especially with food ◀ Mex, ES, Peru, U, Arg ▶

no comer plátano por no tirar la cáscara (to not eat a banana so as not to throw out the peel) to be miserly, especially with food ◀ Mex ▶

no dar ni los «Buenos días» (to not even give a "Good day") to not even give (someone) the time of day ◀ Mex, ES, DR, PR, U, Arg, Sp ▶

no dar ni la hora to not even give (someone) the time of day ◀ Mex, ES, S. Cone, Sp ▶
Vi a Marcelo en la universidad, pero no me dio ni la hora. I saw Marcelo at the university, but he didn't even give me the time of day.

pichicato(-a) (from the Italian "pizzicato," pinch) stingy ◀ Mex, Nic ▶
Es tacaño el señor, bien pichicato. The man is stingy, a real penny-pincher.

poco espléndido(-a) (not very splendid) tightfisted, stingy ◀ ES, DR, Ven, Sp ▶

requeñequero(-a) stingy ◀ Col ▶

tener mano de guagua (to have a baby's hand) to be very tight with money, like the tight fist a baby makes when grabbing someone's finger ◀ Ch ▶

Test your slang power!

Sex, love, and romance

Relevant categories: affection, attractiveness, friendship, romance, sex

How much Spanish "slanguage" do you know related to this topic? Test yourself by completing the exercises. Answers and rating scale are on page 263. (If you don't do very well, read through the categories listed above and try again. The items in each exercise occur in the same order as the categories.)

A. Something's missing. *Select the appropriate word to complete the sentence.*

1. My friend is the youngest child of his family and all his sisters give in to whatever he wants. **Mi amigo es el menor de su familia y todas sus hermanas le (alcahuetean / muñequean / romancean) _____ todo.**

2. The girls think that Ricky Martin is drop-dead gorgeous. **Las niñas creen que Ricky Martin está para (ponerlo en bolsa / comérselo / mirarlo) _____.**

3. A common street compliment in Spain and Latin America is "What curves and me without a brake!" **Un piropo común en España y Latinoamérica es «¡Qué curvas y yo sin (pedal / volante / freno) _____!»**

4. All my bosom buddies live far away. **Todos mis amigos (corazonados / de la silla / del alma) _____ viven lejos.**

5. The two boys are close friends, completely inseparable. **Los dos muchachos son buenísimos amigos, uña y (carne / flor / sangre) _____.**

6. I'm going out with my sister and her boyfriend. Another night as a fifth wheel! **Salgo con mi hermana y su novio. ¡Otra noche cargando (el tambor / el arpa / la guitarra) _____!**

7. Where is your better half (spouse, the love of your life)? **¿Dónde está tu (techo superior / alta falta / media naranja) _____?**

8. My cousin decided to go all out to win Graciela. **Mi primo decidió echarle los (perros / burros / motores)** _____ **a Graciela.**

9. Unfortunately, my aunt is cheating on my uncle. **Desgraciadamente, mi tía le está poniendo los (seguros / cuernos / collares)** _____ **a mi tío.**

10. That couple went home and had a quickie during lunch hour. **Ese matrimonio volvió a casa y echó un (baile / polvo / jabón)** _____ **durante la hora del almuerzo.**

B. Pick a letter! *Choose the letter of the word or phrase that best completes each sentence. Write it in the blank.*

11. _____ Her husband is so crazy about her that he sends her smooches on the telephone. **Su marido está tan loco por ella que le manda** _____ **por teléfono.**
    a. **pequeñitos**
    b. **detalles**
    c. **besotes**
    d. **corazones**

12. _____ One common term of endearment for a woman is **luz de mi vida** (light of my life); another very common word that literally means "fat" but can also mean "darling" or "sweetie" is
    a. **jícama.**
    b. **gorda.**
    c. **taquita.**
    d. **cuadra.**

13. _____ Spaniards say that someone has **gancho** (hook) when he or she has sex appeal. Mexicans say he or she has
    a. **flor.**
    b. **aroma.**
    c. **melodía.**
    d. **pegue.**

14. _____ My new neighbor is a hunk. (Latin America) **Mi nuevo vecino es**
    a. **una pera.**
    b. **una sandía.**
    c. **un mango.**
    d. **un melón.**

15. _____ For affection or friendship, Cubans often call each other **chico** or **chica**, and Uruguayans, Argentinians, Bolivians, and some

208

Paraguayans say **che** to each other. In the same way, Mexicans call each other
a. **mano** or **mana.**
b. **ramo** or **rama.**
c. **tenedor.**
d. **frijol.**

16. _____ My mother's friend has connections in that company. (many parts of Latin America) **El amigo de mi mamá tiene _____ en esa compañía.**
a. **cadenas**
b. **anillos**
c. **palancas**
d. **billetes**

17. _____ It was love at first sight. **Fue un**
a. **primerizo.**
b. **flechazo.**
c. **torbellino.**
d. **levante.**

18. _____ Amalia is looking for her Prince Charming. **Amalia está buscando a su príncipe**
a. **dorado.**
b. **verde.**
c. **azul.**
d. **violeta.**

19. _____ If in Spain they say that someone **es de la otra acera** (is from across the street, or literally, "the other sidewalk") or in Latin America that he or she **juega para el otro equipo** (plays for the other team), then they are referring to someone who is
a. **extranjero(-a).**
b. **intelectual.**
c. **homosexual.**
d. **intuitivo(-a).**

20. _____ One of the most common verbs in Spain and some other regions means "to take or grab," but in most of Latin America it is vulgar and means "to have sex." This verb is
a. **recibir.**
b. **tomar.**
c. **aceptar.**
d. **coger.**

sex

See also "affection," "romance."

acabar (to finish) to come sexually (vulgar) ◄ Mex, C. Am., S. Cone ►

afilar con (to sharpen with) to be fooling around sexually with, making passes at ◄ Arg ►
Tu marido está afilando con la vecina. Your husband is fooling around with the neighbor.

aflojar la torta (to loosen the cake, slang for female organ) to give in and have sex (a woman) (vulgar) ◄ Mex ►

apretada (tight) tight-assed, proud, prissy (woman) ◄ Mex, Col, ES ►

el/la birriondo(-a) dirty old man (woman) ◄ Mex, G, ES ►

el bullín hotel where people go to have sex ◄ U, Arg ►

el chulo man who lives off women (Ch: lout) ◄ Pan, DR, PR, Col, Ven, Sp ►

comer el sanduche antes del recreo (to eat the sandwich before recess) to enjoy something before it should be enjoyed, usually with a sexual overtone ◄ PR ►
¡No me digas! ¿Se comió el sanduche antes del recreo? Don't tell me! They jumped the gun (started the honeymoon before the wedding)?

comer la torta antes de la fiesta (to eat the cake before the party) to enjoy something before it should be enjoyed, usually with a sexual overtone ◄ ES ►

correrse to come (sexually) (vulgar) ◄ Sp ►

la cosa (thing) can be a euphemism for male or female organ ◄ parts of L. Am., Sp ►

el culito (small ass) girl, woman (vulgar, like piece of ass) (Mex, Ven: hot chick) ◄ Mex, G, Ven ►

dar cabida (to give space, make room) to tease a man sexually, said of women ◄ Mex, ES ►

IMPOTENCIA AFECTA A NACIONALES...

COMPRENDELO MUJER... ESTO TIENE QUE VER CON NUESTRA ACHANTAZÓN CON LA SELE... NUESTRA DESMOTIVACIÓN CON LA POLÍTICA...

Impotence affects the country's citizens . . .
"You have to understand, (wife) . . . This has to do with our (national) low spirits about the **sele** (short for **selección**: national soccer selection), our apathy about politics . . ."

dar jamón (to give ham) to exhibit part of one's body, sometimes to tease sexually ◀ Mex, Cuba ▶

donde te dicen hijito sin conocerte (where they call you my son without knowing you) bordello, house of prostitution ◀ parts of L. Am., Sp ▶

el gallinazo womanizing ◀ Mex, Col ▶

loca (crazy) effeminate (Ch: homosexual) ◀ CR, Cuba, DR, Col, Ch ▶

machango describing a masculine woman ◀ Cuba ▶

no ser de piedra (to not be of stone) to be vulnerable to sexual provocation ◀ L. Am., Sp ▶

partes (parts) euphemism meaning private parts ◀ most of L. Am., Sp ▶

partido (split, broken) effeminate (adj.) ◀ Cuba, DR, PR ▶

la pitopausia male menopause ◀ Mex, Sp ▶

la porno short for **pornografía** ◀ L. Am., Sp ▶

el sombrero (el gorro) (hat [cap]) condom ◀ G, ES, DR, PR, Col ▶

tener un rollo con alguien to have an affair (literally, roll) with someone (ES: to have a disagreement) ◀ Sp ▶
Tuve un rollo con mi terapista. I had a fling with my therapist.

venir(se) to come sexually (vulgar) ◀ Mex, Cuba, DR, PR ▶

verde (green) natural, referring to sex ◀ parts of L. Am., Sp ▶

cheating or illicit sex

agarrar a alguien en la maturranga (to grab someone in trickery) to catch someone in the act of having illicit sex ◀ Nic, CR, Ch ▶

el/la cornudo(-a) cuckold ◀ L. Am., Sp ▶

el decorado (decorated one) man whose wife is decorating him with horns (**cachos**) by being unfaithful ◀ Ch ▶

golfo(-a) living a disorganized life or being dishonest sexually (Mex: mas-

ponerle los cuernos a alguien

culine form means tramp; ES: feminine form only is used, meaning loose woman, tramp) ◀ Mex, ES, Sp ▶
Sale por la noche cada día y con un chico distinto. Es bastante golfa. (Sp) She goes out every night with a different guy. She's a bit of a tramp.
Vi a un par de golfos en la calle. (Mex) I saw a couple of bums in the street.

hacerle a alguien de chivo los tamales (to make someone's tamales out of kid goat meat) to deceive one's mate ◀ Mex, ES ▶

pegarle en la nuca (to hit someone in the back of the neck) to have an affair with someone's partner (often accompanied by the gesture of hitting the back of the neck with the edge of one's hand) ◀ Ch ▶

poner el gorro, gorrear (to put on the cap) to cheat on (especially in love), be unfaithful to ◀ Ch ▶

ponerle los cachos a alguien (to put the horns on someone) to be unfaithful to someone (a significant other) ◀ C. Am., Col, Ec ▶

ponerle los cuernos a alguien (to put the horns on someone) to cheat on one's significant other ◀ L. Am., Sp ▶
Ese señor le pone los cuernos a su esposa. That man is cheating on his wife.

rayar la pintura a alguien (to scratch someone's paint job) to deceive one's mate ◀ Cuba ▶

el segundo frente (second front) mistress, lover of a married man ◀ Mex, ES, Ven ▶

tener cuernos to have horns, like a cuckold, meaning that a person's spouse or sweetheart is cheating on him or her (CR: **tener cachones**) ◀ S. Cone ▶

easy woman

la bataclana woman who acts on the stage wearing very little clothing; vulgar-looking woman wearing scanty or cheap-looking clothing; floozie ◀ S. Cone ▶
Mirá esa mina mal vestida; parece una bataclana. Look at that badly dressed girl; she looks like a floozie.

la casquivana easy woman ◀ G ▶

la coscolina loose woman ◀ Mex ▶

el cuero easy woman (vulgar) ◀ Cuba, DR, PR, Col ▶
En la escuela Martica tiene fama de cuero. At school Martica has a reputation for being easy.

fácil easy (woman) ◀ L. Am., Sp ▶
Esa mujer es bastante fácil. That woman is rather easy.

el fosforito (little match) describing a girl that is easy to win ◀ Col ▶
Marcela es un fosforito; sale con todo el mundo. Marcela is an easy woman; she goes out with everyone.

la golfita easy woman ◀ Mex, Col ▶

la guarra hussy, loose woman ◀ Sp ▶

la loca (crazy person) floozie, woman who likes sex ◀ Mex, DR, Col, Ec, U, Arg ▶

la mujer de mal vivir (woman who lives badly) prostitute (Sp: **de mala vida**) ◀ L. Am., Sp ▶

la pava (turkey) easy woman ◀ G ▶

la pierde tiempo (time waster) floozie ◀ Mex ▶

ser más puta que las gallinas to be more of a slut than the hens are (vulgar) ◀ Mex, ES, PR, S. Cone, Sp ▶

ser un putón verbenero (to be a whore of the evening) to be a real slut (vulgar) ◀ Sp ▶

la tíguera (tigress) clever bitch, heartbreaker, sleazy gal ◀ DR ▶

la viuda verde (mujer rabo verde) (green widow [woman with a green tail]) dirty old woman ◀ chicano, Mex ▶

female body parts

Note: The following are vulgar words for the female organ.

el bizcocho (biscuit) ◀ chicano, Mex ▶

el bollo (bread roll) ◀ ES, Nic, Cuba, PR, Col ▶

el chocho (round sweet) (PR: **la chocha**) ◀ Mex, Nic, Cuba, Sp ▶

la concha (shell) ◀ S. Cone ▶

la cuca (sedge; a sweet) ◀ G, ES, DR, Col, Ven ▶

la panocha (kind of candy) ◀ chicano, Mex, ES, CR, Col ▶

la papaya (papaya) ◀ Mex, Nic, Cuba, Col ▶

la torta (cake) ◀ Mex, G, ES ▶

going without sex

a dieta (on a diet) going without sex ◀ Mex, G, ES, Cuba, Sp ▶

arrollado(-a) (rolled up, overwhelmed) going without sex (also: **arrolladera**, time without sex) ◀ PR ▶
Desde que me dejó Patricia, estoy arrolla'o. Since Patricia left me, I've had a dry spell (without sex).

having sex

apañar (to seize) to have sex (vulgar) ◀ Mex ▶

chichar to have sex (vulgar) ◀ PR ▶

chingar (to rip, tear) to exploit; to have sex (equivalent of the F-word); to break (a machine) (PR: to have sex only) (vulgar) ◀ Mex, C. Am., PR, Cuba, Col ▶

clavar (to nail) to have sex (U: **clavarse**; Mex: **clavado** can mean in love) ◀ Mex, G, ES, Cuba, PR, Col, U ▶

coger (to take, catch, grab) to have sex (vulgar; CR, Cuba: also, to take, as in Sp—that is, the use is not exclusively referring to sex) ◀ L. Am. (not Ch) ▶

culear to have sex (vulgar) ◀ ES, Nic, CR, Ec, Ch ▶

echar un casquete (to throw a cap) to have sex (a bit vulgar) ◀ Sp ▶

echar un palo (to throw a stick) to have sex (vulgar; also, **palito**) ◀ Mex, G, ES, Cuba ▶

echarse a alguien (to throw oneself at someone) to have sex with someone ◀ Mex, G, Cuba ▶

echar(se) un polvo (to throw oneself powder or dust) to have sex (vulgar; also, **un polvito**) ◀ L. Am., Sp ▶
Ése se echa un polvo cada día con una chica distinta. That guy has sex every day with a different girl.

encamarse con (to get in bed with) to go to bed and make love with ◀ S. Cone ▶

enchufar (to connect, plug in) to get laid, get lucky, have sex ◀ Mex, Col ▶

follar to have sex, equivalent of the F-word (vulgar) ◀ Sp ▶

hacer cuchi-cuchi to make out, have sex (G: to sleep) ◀ Mex, Cuba, Col ▶

inaugurar el pastel (to inaugurate the cake) to have sex with a virgin ◀ Mex, Col ▶

joder to screw ◀ L. Am., Sp ▶

jorobar euphemism for **joder** ◀ Mex, G, CR, Cuba, DR, PR ▶

jugar al balero (to play cup and ball, a children's game) to have sex ◀ Mex, Col ▶

parchar (to put a patch on) to have sex ◀ Mex, ES ▶

pegarse la gran picada (to stick to oneself the big pickings) to have sex ◀ Nic ▶

pisar (to step on) to have sex (vulgar) ◀ Mex, G, ES, Nic, CR, Cuba ▶

soplarse (to make love to a virgin; vulgar) ◀ Mex ▶
Ya se la soplaron. They've "deflowered" her now. (vulgar in Spanish)

tirarse a alguien (to throw oneself at someone) to have sex (vulgar) ◀ Mex, C. Am., DR, PR, Col, Ven, Ec, Peru, Arg, Ch, Sp ▶
Pablo se tiró a tres mujeres de su colonia. Pablo had sex with three women in his neighborhood.

tumbarse (to fell, knock down) to make love ◀ Bol, U ▶

hot, interested in sex

acelerado fast (not waiting an appropriate time before pressing for sex) ◀ Mex, G, ES, Sp ▶
Salí con Fernando por primera y última vez. ¡Qué acelerado! I went out with Fernando for the first and last time. He's so fast!

alzado(-a) (raised up) in heat, horny ◀ Mex, U, Arg ▶
Ese hombre está alzado; quiere ligarse. That guy is horny; he wants to find a woman.
Tu gata está alzada, lista para aparearse. Your cat is in heat, ready to be mated.

al rojo vivo red hot (passions) ◀ Mex, Sp ▶

cabreado(-a) horny; angry ◀ Mex, CR, Col, Sp ▶

calentar(se) to heat up (become heated) with anger or sexual desire; to anger (become angry); to turn on (often has sexual overtones) ◀ L. Am., Sp ▶
Esa mujer me calienta mucho. That woman really turns me on.

el calentón, la calentona (big hot one) person who is easily aroused sexually; hothead ◀ U, Arg ▶

caliente (hot) fast (sexually), passionate, excited ◀ L. Am., Sp ▶

estar buenísima (to be very good) to be very hot, good in bed (said about women) (Sp: to be very beautiful) ◀ Mex, ES, DR, PR, Ven, Ch ▶
Esa chica está buenísima. That girl is a hot number.

estar cachondo(-a) to be horny, sexually excited, hot (vulgar) (also, **poner a alguien cachondo**) ◀ Mex, ES, Sp ▶
Está muy cachondo. He's very horny.
Me pones siempre muy cachondo. You always make me hot.
Le gustan los bailes cachondos. He (She) likes sexy dances.

estar como agua pa' chocolate (to be like water for chocolate) to be very hot with anger or passion ◀ Mex ▶

excitado(-a) aroused, excited (usually sexually) ◀ L. Am., Sp ▶

fosforón, fosforona (big match) hot ◀ CR ▶

prender to turn on ◀ Mex ▶
Ese tipo me prende. That guy turns me on.

ser un cachondo mental to be happy, agreeable, funny; also, to be obsessed with sex (vulgar) ◀ Sp ▶

tener una calentura (to have a fever) to be really excited sexually, be turned on, hot ◀ U, Arg ▶

male body parts

las bolas   balls; testicles (vulgar) ◀ S. Cone ▶

el chile   (chili pepper) male organ (vulgar) ◀ Mex, ES ▶

el chorizo   (sausage) male organ (vulgar) ◀ Mex, G, ES, Cuba, U ▶

los cojones   testicles (vulgar) ◀ parts of L. Am., Sp ▶

los coyoles   (fruits of a kind of palm tree) testicles (vulgar) ◀ C. Am. ▶

el cuero   (hide, leather) male organ (vulgar) ◀ chicano, Cuba, Col ▶

las huevas   testicles (vulgar, variant of **huevos**) ◀ Nic, Ch ▶

los huevos   (eggs) testicles (vulgar) ◀ L. Am., Sp ▶

el pájaro   (bird) male organ (vulgar) ◀ Mex, G ▶

el palo   (stick) male organ (vulgar) ◀ Mex, G, ES, CR, Cuba, DR, Col ▶

la paloma   (dove) male organ ◀ C. Am., Col, Ven, Ec, Peru, Bol ▶

la penca, el virote   euphemisms for male organ ◀ Nic ▶

el pico   (beak) male organ (vulgar) ◀ G, ES, CR, Ch ▶

la pija   male organ (vulgar) ◀ Hond, Nic, U, Arg ▶

la pinga   male organ (vulgar) ◀ G, CR, Cuba, DR, PR, Col ▶

la pirula   (children) male organ ◀ Arg, Sp ▶

la pistola   (pistol) male organ (vulgar) ◀ ES, CR, U ▶

el pito   (whistle, fife) male organ (vulgar) ◀ Mex, G, ES, CR, Cuba, U, Arg, Sp ▶

la polla   (young female chicken, pullet) male organ (vulgar) ◀ Sp ▶

el ripio   male organ (vulgar) ◀ DR ▶

el tolete   (billy club used by police) male organ (vulgar) ◀ DR ▶

la verga   male organ (vulgar) ◀ Mex, ES, Nic, CR, Col, Ec, U, Arg ▶

petting, foreplay, masturbation

cachondear   to make out, indulge in foreplay ◀ Mex, ES ▶

el cachondeo   (horning around) petting, foreplay ◀ Mex, ES, Sp ▶

la calentadita   (little heating up) little "workover" (beating or sexual play) ◀ Mex, ES, Col, U ▶

franelear   (to flannel) to make out, pet, indulge in foreplay ◀ U, Arg ▶

hacerse una chaqueta   to masturbate (males, vulgar) ◀ Mex ▶

hacerse una paja   (to make oneself a straw) to masturbate (vulgar; Col, Arg: **hacerse la paja**) ◀ L. Am., Sp ▶

jugar con los cinco latinos   (to play with the five Latinos, meaning fingers) to masturbate (vulgar) ◀ Cuba ▶

mamar   (to suckle) to have oral sex (vulgar) ◀ L. Am., Sp ▶

el mameluco/el mamey   oral sex (vulgar) ◀ G ▶

Manuela   (pun on **mano** meaning hand) masturbation (vulgar); **usar Manuela, hacer el amor con Manuela** ◀ Mex, G, Cuba, DR, PR, Col, Ch ▶

matar al oso   (to kill the bear) to masturbate (males, vulgar) ◀ Mex, Col ▶

meter mano   (to put hand) to touch someone with sexual intentions ◀ Mex, PR, U, Sp ▶

Intentó meterme mano en el cine. He tried to feel me up in the movie theater.

presentar armas   (to present arms) to have a hard-on (vulgar) ◀ L. Am., Sp ▶

la puñeta   hand job, masturbation (vulgar) ◀ chicano, Mex, U ▶

tirar de manoletina   to masturbate (males, vulgar) ◀ Sp ▶

pimp

el cafiche   pimp ◀ S. Cone ▶

el padrote   pimp ◀ Mex, G, ES, Col ▶

el puto   pimp (vulgar) ◀ parts of L. Am. ▶

womanizer

el barbarazo   Don Juan, someone who goes after someone else's woman ◀ Mex, PR, Col ▶

Ahí está María llorando por Juan otra vez. —Ella se lo busca andando con ese barbarazo. There's María crying about Juan again. —She brought it on herself going around with that two-timer.

el buitre (vulture) wolf, womanizer ◀ Mex, PR, Col, Ven, U, Sp ▶

el cachetero (small dagger) wolf, aggressive man (Don Juan) ◀ PR, Col ▶

el caimán (alligator) womanizer, Don Juan ◀ Mex, Col ▶

el chivo (kid goat) womanizer; man who lives off women (Nic: cuckold) ◀ C. Am., Col ▶

el coscolino dirty old man ◀ Mex, ES ▶

el don Juan Don Juan, womanizer ◀ L. Am., Sp ▶

el gavilán (hawk) wolf, Don Juan ◀ Mex, Col ▶

el león (lion) wolf, womanizer ◀ DR, PR ▶

el lobo (wolf) wolf, womanizer ◀ chicano, Mex, PR ▶

el mátalas callando (kill-them-being-quiet) discreet womanizer who appears faithful ◀ Mex, ES, DR, Col ▶

el mujeriego (mujerero) womanizer ◀ L. Am., Sp ▶

el potro (colt) guy who's always following girls around ◀ DR, Col ▶

el pulpo (octopus) wolf, womanizer, guy who likes to touch women inappropriately ◀ Mex, DR, Col, Sp ▶
Yo no bailo con ese hombre porque es un pulpo. I'm not dancing with that man because he's all hands.

el quebrador (breaker) womanizer ◀ Col ▶

el rabo verde (green tail) dirty old man ◀ Mex, C. Am., Peru ▶

el rapeador womanizer ◀ PR ▶

el tenorio womanizer, Don Juan ◀ L. Am., Sp ▶

el tiburón (shark) wolf, womanizer ◀ PR, Col, U ▶

el tigre (bárbaro) ([barbaric] tiger) wolf, womanizer ◀ U ▶

el viejo verde (viejo caliente) (green old man [hot old man]) old man who is still involved in romantic relationships ◀ L. Am., Sp ▶

---

similarity

---

como dos gotas de agua (like two drops of water) like two peas in a pod ◀ L. Am., Sp ▶
Paco y su amigo Miguelito son como dos gotas de agua. Paco and his friend Miguelito are like two peas in a pod.

Say it with slang!

Where is the powder room?

When it comes to the bathroom, every language certainly has plenty of euphemisms (rest room, powder room, the ladies, or gents). One euphemism in Spain is **Voy a visitar al señor Roca.** (I'm going to visit Mr. Rock.) Another euphemism, common in Spain and several places in Latin America, is **Tengo que cambiarle el agua a los peces (al canario, al pájaro).** (I have to change the water for the fish [canary, bird]). In general, a way to ask the question politely when the need arises is **¿Dónde están los servicios?** (Where are the services?) or, in Mexico, **¿Dónde está el excusado?** (Where is the excused place?)

215

cortado(-a) por la misma tijera (cut by the same scissors) cut from the same cloth, very similar (Sp: more common, **cortado por el mismo patrón**) ◀ Mex, ES, DR, PR, S. Cone, Sp ▶

cortado(-a) por (con) el mismo patrón (cut by [with] the same pattern) very similar ◀ Mex, Sp ▶

encontrar la horma de su zapato (to find one's shoe size; **horma** means wooden model of foot) to meet one's match ◀ Mex, ES, DR, S. Cone, Sp ▶

estar en el pellejo de otro to be in someone else's shoes (skin), to be in someone else's circumstances or situation (Mex: also, **estar en los zapatos de otro**) ◀ L. Am., Sp ▶
No me gustaría estar en tus zapatos. (Mex) I wouldn't want to be in your shoes.

refrito(-a) (refried) rehashed stories, re-runs of TV programs ◀ Mex, Ven ▶

seguir las huellas de alguien to follow in someone's footsteps ◀ Mex, Ch, Sp ▶

ser de la misma madera to be of the same nature (wood) or in the same condition ◀ Mex ▶

ser la fiel estampa de alguien (to be the faithful print of someone) to be the spitting image of someone ◀ L. Am., Sp ▶

seguir las huellas de alguien

ser la viva (fiel) imagen de alguien (to be the live [faithful] image of someone) to be the spitting image of someone ◀ L. Am., Sp ▶
Mi hermanita es mi fiel imagen, ¿no? My little sister is the spitting image of me, isn't she?

ser el vivo retrato de alguien to be the spitting image (living portrait) of someone ◀ L. Am., Sp ▶

expressions about similarity

A falta de pan, buenas son tortas. (When there is no bread, cakes are fine.) One thing is as good as another. ◀ most of L. Am., Sp ▶

De tal palo, tal astilla. (From such a tree or stick, such a splinter.) A chip off the old block, like father like son. ◀ L. Am., Sp ▶
Mario y su papá se parecen mucho, ¿no? De tal palo, tal astilla. Mario and his dad look a lot alike, don't they? He's a chip off the old block.

El cachicamo llamando el morrocoy conchudo. (The armadillo calling the box turtle hard-shelled.) said when someone complains about a quality in another person when he or she is even more guilty of having that quality, the pot calling the kettle black ◀ Ven ▶

El comal le dijo a la olla: ¡Mira qué tiznada estás! (The comal [a flat pan for cooking tortillas] said to the pot: Look how black you are!) The pot calls the kettle black, meaning that both are alike but one puts the other down (**tiznada** can also mean something like **chingada**) ◀ Mex, ES ▶

En la noche todos los gatos son pardos (negros). (At night all cats are dark-colored.) It is hard to see any difference between some things. ◀ L. Am., Sp ▶

Este disco tiene raya. (Este disco está rayado.) (This record has a scratch [is scratched].) Same old story. It's like a broken record, same thing over and

over. (DR, Ch: **está rayado,** not **tiene raya**)
◀ Mex, ES, Nic, DR, Ch ▶

Perdí el trabajo por llegar tarde. Este disco tiene raya. I lost my job because I was late. Same old story.

Pareces disco rayado, repitiendo siempre que quieres más dinero. You sound like a broken record, always repeating how you want more money.

Hijo(-a) de tigre, sale rayado(-a). (Son [Daughter] of the tiger turns out striped.) Like father, like son. ◀ Mex, CR, S. Cone ▶

Lo mismo es Chana que Juana. (Chana is the same as Juana.) There's no choice. Two of the same. ◀ Mex, ES, Nic ▶

Lo que se hereda no se roba (hurta). (What is inherited is not robbed.) This person is just like his or her father (mother, grandfather, etc.). Here's a chip off the old block. ◀ S. Cone, Sp ▶

Mono mayor. (Older monkey.) Monkey see, monkey do. ◀ Ch ▶

tal para cual made for each other, birds of a feather ◀ L. Am., Sp ▶

getting or being even

arreglo de cuentas (settling of accounts) the act of avenging oneself ◀ Mex, DR, PR, Arg, Ch, Sp ▶

estar a mano (to be at hand) to be even (with each other) ◀ Mex, ES, S. Cone ▶
Te pagué la plata y ahora estamos a mano, amigo. I paid you the money and now we're even, pal.

jugar taco a taco (to play taco for taco) to play even or fifty-fifty ◀ Nic ▶

limpiarse (to clean oneself) to pay (someone) back, be even ◀ Cuba, Col ▶
Me limpié con el favor que le hice. I paid you back with the favor I did for you.

pagar con la misma moneda (to pay with the same currency) to give tit for tat ◀ L. Am., Sp ▶

sacarse el clavo (to take the nail out of oneself) to get even ◀ CR, Col ▶

sleep

aplastar la oreja (to flatten the ear) to sleep ◀ Mex ▶

apolillar (to moth) to sleep, go to sleep (from **polilla,** moth) ◀ U, Arg ▶
Estoy cansado; me voy a apolillar. I'm tired; I'm going to go to sleep.

buscar los costales (to look for the sacks) to go to bed, hit the sack ◀ Col ▶
Ya es tarde. Voy a buscar los costales. It's late. I'm going to hit the sack.

clavar el pico (to nail the beak) to fall asleep ◀ Mex, CR, Col, U ▶
El niño fue a su cuarto y clavó el pico de inmediato. The child went to his room and fell immediately asleep.

dormir a lo chancho chingo (to sleep like a long-tailed pig) to sleep like a log ◀ CR ▶
Anoche dormí a lo chancho chingo. Last night I slept like a log.

dormir a cuerpo de rey to sleep like a king (like the body of a king) ◀ most of L. Am., Sp ▶
En ese hotel, se duerme a cuerpo de rey. In that hotel, you sleep like a king.

dormir como un lirón (to sleep like a dormouse) to sleep deeply ◀ Mex, DR, S. Cone, Sp ▶

dormir como un tronco to sleep like a log (trunk) (Sp: also, less commonly, **como una leña**) ◀ Mex, S. Cone, Sp ▶

dormir con los ángeles
(See page 218.)

dormir con los ángeles (to sleep with the angels) to sleep well (ES: also, **soñar con los angelitos**) ◀ Mex, ES, S. Cone ▶
Que duermas con los angelitos. Sweet dreams.

echar una pestaña (pestañeada) (to throw an eyelash) to catch some winks ◀ Mex, Ch ▶

estar en el quinto sueño (to be in the fifth sleep) to be fast asleep ◀ Mex, ES, DR ▶

hacer la rosca (to make the doughnut, e.g., rolled up like a doughnut) to sleep anywhere, although it may not be comfortable; to flatter, butter up ◀ Sp ▶

hacer tuto to go to sleep, go sleepy-bye (used mainly with children) (U, Arg: **hacer nono**) ◀ Ch ▶

irse a la cucha (to go to the doghouse) to drop into bed when you're tired ◀ U, Arg ▶

jatear to sleep ◀ Peru ▶

meterse en el sobre (to put oneself in one's envelope) to go to bed ◀ Ec, S. Cone, Sp ▶

pegársele a alguien las sábanas (to have the sheets stick to one) to oversleep ◀ Mex, ES, DR, PR, Col, Peru, S. Cone, Sp ▶
Se me pegaron las sábanas y llegué tarde al aeropuerto. I overslept and got to the airport late.

planchar la oreja (to iron one's ear) to go to bed, sleep ◀ Mex, CR, PR, Col, Ven, Ec, Sp ▶

privarse to fall into a deep sleep ◀ ES, CR ▶

sobar (to massage) to sleep ◀ Sp ▶
Me pasé el día sobando. I spent the day sleeping.

la noche toledana (Toledo night) sleepless night, night of insomnia ◀ Sp ▶

pasar la noche contando estrellas (cabritos) (to spend the night counting stars [little goats]) to be sleepless, counting sheep ◀ Mex, ES ▶
No pude dormir; pasé la noche contando estrellas. I couldn't sleep; I spent the night counting sheep.

pasar la noche en blanco (claro) (to spend the night blank [clear]) to spend a sleepless night ◀ Mex, DR, PR, S. Cone, Sp ▶

pasar la noche en vela (to spend the night on watch) to spend a sleepless night ◀ L. Am., Sp ▶

sleepy, asleep

el dormilón, la dormilona describing someone who sleeps a lot, sleepyhead ◀ L. Am., Sp ▶
¿Son las diez de la mañana ya? ¡Qué dormilón! It's already ten o'clock in the morning? What a long time I slept (literally, what a big sleeper)!

estar sopa (to be soup) to be asleep; to be stunned ◀ Sp ▶

frito(-a) (fried) asleep ◀ U, Arg, Sp ▶
Se quedó frito en la playa. He fell asleep on the beach.
Después de comer, siempre me quedo frito. After eating, I always fall asleep.

tener un muermo, estar amormado(-a) to be sleepy ◀ Sp ▶
Tengo un muermo. Estoy amormado(-a). I'm sleepy.

tener una polilla (to have a moth) to be sleepy ◀ Arg ▶

sleepless

no pegar los ojos en toda la noche to not sleep a wink (glue the eyes) the whole night (Sp: **no pegar ojo**) ◀ L. Am., Sp ▶
Tengo un problema en la oficina. No pegué los ojos en toda la noche. I have a problem at the office. I didn't sleep a wink all night.

s|owness

a paso de tortuga (at a turtle's pace) slow as a snail, at a snail's pace ◀ L. Am., Sp ▶
La construcción del nuevo hotel marcha a paso de tortuga; dudo que lo inauguren a

fin de año. The construction of the new hotel is going at a snail's pace; I doubt if they'll dedicate it by the end of the year.

a poquitos bit by bit ◀ Mex ▶

a vuelta de ruedas (at wheels' turning) slow(ly) (Ch: **a la vuelta de la rueda**) ◀ Mex, Hond, ES ▶
El tráfico está a vuelta de ruedas. The traffic is moving very slowly.

estar espeso(-a) to be slow, dull ◀ Sp ▶
Estoy muy espeso hoy. I'm very slow today.

lento(-a) pero tardado(-a) (slow but late) very slow (ironic) ◀ Mex, ES ▶
Voy a llegar pronto. Soy lenta pero tardada. I'm going to get there soon. I'm slow but late.

más lento(-a) que una caravana de cojos (slower than a caravan of limping people) as slow as a snail ◀ PR, Col ▶

más lento(-a) que un suero de brea (slower than tar plasma) as slow as molasses ◀ PR ▶

muerto(-a) (dead) slow, with no initiative ◀ Cuba, Col ▶

ser la muerte en bicicleta (to be death on a bicycle) to be as slow as a snail ◀ Florida ▶

la tortuga (turtle) slow person ◀ Mex, ES, DR, Col ▶
Siempre que salimos con Beatriz llegamos tarde porque es una tortuga. Every time we go out with Beatriz we're late because she's a slowpoke.

speed

a rienda suelta with free rein, freely or quickly ◀ Mex, DR, PR, S. Cone, Sp ▶

así como así just like that ◀ L. Am., Sp ▶
No puedo decidirme así como así. I can't decide just like that.

brotar como callampas (to grow like mushrooms) to grow like mad (U: **como hongos**) ◀ Ch ▶

meterse como la pobreza (to intrude like poverty) to appear all over and spread like wildfire ◀ Nic ▶

fast, very quickly

a toda hostia (at all Host) fast, quickly (vulgar, with religious reference) ◀ Sp ▶

a toda leche (at all milk) fast, quickly (vulgar) ◀ Sp ▶
Iba a toda leche. I (He, She) was going like a house afire.

a toda madre (at all mother) full blast ◀ Mex, G, ES, Col ▶

a toda máquina (at all machine) quickly, fast ◀ chicano, Mex, G, DR, Ch, Sp ▶

a toda marcha (at all march) very quickly ◀ Mex, Sp ▶

a toda mecha (at all wick) very quickly ◀ Mex, Sp ▶

a toda pastilla (at all pill) quickly ◀ Sp ▶
Íbamos a toda pastilla. We were going at top speed.

a todo chancho (at all pig) intensely ◀ Ch ▶

a todo dar (at all giving) fast ◀ Mex, ES ▶

a todo ful fast; at full volume ◀ Nic, CR, Col, Ch ▶

a todo gas (at all gas) fast ◀ Mex, Sp ▶

a todo lo que da (at all that it gives) going great guns, like a house afire ◀ Mex, S. Cone ▶
El partido está a todo lo que da. The game is going full blast.

a todo mamón (at all nursing from the breast) fast, like mad, like a house on fire (vulgar) ◀ Nic ▶

a todo meter (at all putting) fast, with vehemence ◀ Mex, DR, PR, Sp ▶
Salió de la clínica a todo meter. He (She) went out of the clinic at full speed.

a todo vapor (at all steam) fast, with vehemence ◀ Peru, U, Arg ▶

afanado(-a) (enthusiastically, zealously) in a hurry ◀ Col ▶

cagando leches (shitting milk) hurriedly (vulgar) ◀ Sp ▶

cayendo el muerto y soltando el llanto (the dead person falling and the scream being let out) fast, quickly ◀ Mex, ES ▶

como alma que lleva el diablo (like a soul that the devil takes) with great agitation or speed ◀ Mex, ES, CR, DR, S. Cone, Sp ▶

Oye, niño, tienes que manejar más despacio. Ayer te vi por la (Avenida) Lincoln como alma que lleva el diablo. Listen (child), you have to drive more slowly. Yesterday I saw you on Lincoln Avenue speeding like the devil.

como carreta en bajada (like a cart going downhill) fast, without much control, and no stopping it ◀ Nic ▶

Un viejo enamorado es peor que una carreta en bajada. An old man in love is worse than a cart going downhill.

como entierro de pobre (like a poor person's funeral) quickly ◀ ES, CR, Col ▶

como un rayo (like a lightning bolt) quick as lightning, lightning fast ◀ ES, Nic, CR, U, Ch, Sp ▶

Es rápido como un rayo. He's lightning fast.

de boleto on the fly, fast or while doing something else ◀ Mex ▶

de pasada on the fly, fast and while doing something else ◀ Mex, Col, ES, Ch ▶

de un plumazo at the stroke of a pen (**pluma**), quickly ◀ L. Am., Sp ▶

de una puta vez (at one whore time) at once, definitively (vulgar) ◀ Mex, ES ▶

de un tirón (at one pull) at once, all at one time ◀ Mex, ES, DR, PR, Peru, Arg, Ch, Sp ▶

Terminé el trabajo de un tirón. I finished the work in one fell swoop.

de volada quickly, on the fly or run ◀ Mex, ES, Col ▶

Eso se hace de volada. That can be done very quickly.

de volón pinpón on the fly, fast or while doing something else ◀ Mex, ES ▶

hecho(-a) la mocha (la raya) (made into the bow [the stripe]) very quickly ◀ Mex ▶

Me voy hecha la mocha. I'm going in a flash.

más rápido(-a) que ligero(-a) (more quick than fast) hurriedly, in a rush ◀ Mex, G, PR ▶

rajado(-a) (split) at breakneck speed ◀ Ch ▶

rapidingo very quick ◀ parts of L. Am. ▶

soplado(-a) (blown) quickly, fast as the wind ◀ CR, Col, Ch ▶

volado(-a) (blown up high or flown away) in a hurry ◀ Mex, Nic, Col ▶

Llegó volado al hospital. He got to the hospital in a flash.

getting a move on

¡Ale, ale! Hurry up! ◀ Mex ▶

Andando. (Walking.) Hurry up. ◀ Mex, Sp ▶

la caña (cane) effort, intensity (with **darle** or **meterle**) ◀ Sp ▶

Métele caña al acelerador, que vas muy despacio. Floor it (apply more effort to the accelerator); you're going very slowly.

Dale más caña, que no llegaremos nunca. Speed it up, or we'll never get there.

Date. (short for **Date prisa.**) Hurry up. ◀ Ven ▶

hacer algo volando to do something quickly (flying) ◀ Mex, G, ES, DR, S. Cone, Sp ▶

ir hecho(-a) bala to go rapidly (as a bullet) (Mex: also, **hecho la** or **una bala**; U, Arg: **ir como bala**) ◀ Mex, G, Ch ▶

Me infraccionaron por ir hecho la bala. They gave me a ticket for speeding (going like a bullet).

ir pisa'o(-a) (to go stepped on) to go quickly ◀ Col ▶

ir volando to go quickly (flying) ◀ Mex, G, ES, S. Cone, Sp ▶

meter chala (fierro, pata) (to put on the corn husk [iron, paw]) to step on it, accelerate ◀ Ch ▶

meter cuarta (to put horsewhip) to step on it, step on the gas ◀ Mex, Col ▶

meterle to step on it, step on the gas ◀ Mex, ES, Col ▶

¡Métele! Step on it!

meterle la chancla al pedal (to put the sandal on the pedal) to step on it, step on the gas ◀ Mex, Col ▶

meterle velocidad (to put in speed) to hurry up ◀ Mex ▶

Métele velocidad. Speed it up.

perder el culo (to lose one's ass) to move fast (vulgar) ◀ Sp ▶

Say it with slang!

The Bible in everyday expressions

Biblical characters are familiar figures in Spanish. A really old guy may be described as **más viejo que Matusalén** (older than Methuselah), and agreement can be expressed in Mexico, El Salvador, and Colombia with the phrase **¡Ya vas, Barrabás!** (Right, I agree! Literally, There you go, Barrabas!) Evil characters appear too. **Como dijo Herodes, ¡te jodes!** (As Herod said, you're screwed!—meaning that nothing can be done.) In El Salvador a nasty person can be called **puro Satanás** (a real Satan), and to state that nobody knows about something, they might say **¡Sepa Judas!** (Maybe Judas knows!) Perhaps this is because Judas is known for having a guilty secret. In Spain someone swearing a blue streak is said to be **jurando en arameo** (swearing in Aramaic, the language of Christ).

pelárselas (to peel them) to do something quickly or intensely ◀ Ch, Sp ▶

picarle (to poke at it) to hurry up, get a move on ◀ Mex, ES, Col ▶
¡Pícale! Hay que picarle duro para que terminemos ligero. Hurry up! We have to get a move on so we can finish quickly.

tupirle (to compact it) to hurry up, get a move on ◀ Mex ▶
¡Túpele! Se nos atrasa. Speed it up! We're getting behind.

volarle (to fly it) to hurry it up, take off ◀ Mex, Col ▶
¡Vuélale! Take off!

in a jiffy

en un abrir y cerrar de ojos (in an opening and closing of the eyes) in a blink of the eyes ◀ L. Am., Sp ▶

en una avemaría (in the time it takes to say Ave María) in an instant ◀ L. Am., Sp ▶

en dos monazos (in two hits) quickly ◀ ES, CR, Col ▶

en dos patadas (in two kicks) quickly ◀ Mex, ES, CR, Col, S. Cone ▶

en un dos por tres (in a two by three) quickly, in an instant ◀ Mex, ES, CR, DR, PR, Col, S. Cone ▶
Mejor envíalo por fax que llega en un dos por tres. Send it by fax instead; it'll get there on the double.

en menos que canta un gallo (in less than a cock crows) in very little time, in a jiffy ◀ L. Am., Sp ▶
Voy a terminar mis tareas en menos que canta un gallo. I'm going to finish my work in a jiffy.

en un parpadeo (in the blink of an eye) fast ◀ Mex, ES, Nic ▶
Me lo robó en un parpadeo. He (She) stole it from me in the blink of an eye.

en un santiamén (in the time it takes to say santiamén) in an instant ◀ L. Am., Sp ▶
Lo puedo hacer en un santiamén. I can do it in a jiffy.

en un zas quickly ◀ Mex, ES ▶

strength

a cal y canto (lime and stone, stone masonry) strong, tightly ◀ Mex, Sp ▶
La tienda estaba cerrado a cal y canto. The store was closed tightly.

estar como un tanque (como un tren) (to be like a tank [like a train]) to be attractive, strong, a hunk ◀ Mex, Sp ▶

estar hecho(-a) un mulo (to be made into a mule) to be very strong ◀ Sp ▶

firme como el roble (firm as the oak) hard; strong ◀ Mex, S. Cone, Sp ▶

maceta (maceteado[-a]) (flower pot [flower potted]) stacked, muscular, big (person) ◀ Ch ▶

macizo(-a) muscular, well-built (Col, ES: also, **el macizo**, big boss or big man) ◀ Mex, ES, Col, S. Cone, Sp ▶
Luis Rodrigo sólo tiene seis años pero es bien macizo. Luis Rodrigo is only six years old but he's very muscular.

para parar un tren (to stop a train) very strong ◀ Mex, ES, Sp ▶

ser de acero (bronce) (to be of steel [bronze]) to be tough, inflexible, strong ◀ Mex, U, Arg, Sp ▶

stupidity

See also "incompetence," "lack of knowledge."

cerrado(-a) (closed) with a closed mind ◀ Mex, G, ES, DR, Col, S. Cone, Sp ▶
Celia tiene una mente muy cerrada. Celia has a very closed mind.
No me gusta hablar de esos temas con Felipe porque es muy cerrado y terminamos peleados. I don't like to talk to Felipe about those topics because he's very close-minded

and we end up not speaking to each other (literally, having fought).

Deja de comer mierda. (Stop eating shit.) Stop with your foolishness, trickery. (Col: also, stop letting people treat you badly) (vulgar) ◀ Mex, DR, Col ▶

Déjate de chiquilladas. (Stop the childish behavior.) Stop the foolishness. ◀ ES, U, Arg, Sp ▶

hacer castillos de naipes (to build castles of cards) to make houses of cards, count on something one can't count on or do something in a foolish way ◀ Sp ▶

la macana stupid act ◀ Bol, U, Arg ▶

parar de decir paridas to stop saying ridiculous things (vulgar) ◀ Sp ▶

tener bonita letra (to have pretty handwriting) to not be too smart (typical Chilean irony: The only positive thing you can say about this person is that his or her handwriting is good.) ◀ Ch ▶

tener cara de chiste (to have the face of a joke) to look ridiculous ◀ Mex, Sp ▶

doing something stupid

carajear to fool around, dick around (vulgar, from **carajo**) ◀ Col ▶
Ya no vamos a carajear. We're not going to dick around anymore.

dar papaya (to give papaya) to do or say something that exposes one to ridicule; also, **Papaya servida, papaya partida.** (Papaya served, papaya cut up, meaning that someone deserves to be made fun of because of a ridiculous action or comment.) ◀ Col ▶

estar papando (cachando) moscas (to be swallowing [catching] flies) to be acting foolish, goofing off ◀ Mex, U ▶

hacer el ridículo (to make the ridiculous) to appear foolish, act like a fool ◀ L. Am., Sp ▶

macanear to say crazy or wild things that make no sense; also, to tease or make fun of ◀ U, Arg ▶
No me macanées. Me estás macaneando. Don't put me on. You're putting me on.

mensear to act foolishly, like an idiot; also, to confuse someone with silly talk ◀ Mex ▶

Ramón chocó porque iba menseando en el carro. Ramón crashed because he was acting like a fool in the car.
No lo mensées más. Don't confuse him more.

pelar cable (to peel cable) to talk nonsense ◄ Ch ▶

pendejear to behave in a foolish or stupid way (vulgar) ◄ Mex, C. Am. ▶

tontear to behave in a foolish or stupid way (Sp: also, to flirt) ◄ L. Am., Sp ▶
Iba tonteando durante media hora, pero por fin encontré la casa. (ES) I was putzing around (going along stupidly) for a half hour, but I finally found the house.
Luisa siempre está tonteando con los chicos del barrio. (Sp) Luisa is always flirting with the guys in the neighborhood.

zoncear to behave stupidly ◄ most of L. Am. (not S. Cone) ▶

fool, dope, idiot

el/la ahuevado(-a) dope ◄ Pan, Col, Peru ▶

el/la batata (sweet potato) loser, idiot ◄ Para, U, Arg ▶
Ese señor es un batata. That man is a fool.

el/la bobolóngolo(-a) fool (**bobo**) ◄ PR, Col ▶

el/la bolido(-a) (sort of ballish) somewhat stupid (probably comes from **boludo**) ◄ Arg ▶
Es un bolido. He's sort of dumb.

el/la bolsa (bag, purse) dope, empty-headed person ◄ Ven ▶

el/la boludo(-a) (big balled) lazy dope, stupid jerk, deadhead (vulgar) ◄ Nic, CR, S. Cone ▶
El gobernador es un boludo que no sabe hacer nada. The governor is a stupid jerk who doesn't know how to do anything.

el/la buenas peras (good pears) simpleton ◄ Bol, Ch ▶

el buey, güey (from "bovis": stupid, lazy [castrated] animal) loser, dummy. Often used with affection among men, a mild insult like SOB ◄ chicano, Mex, ES, PR, Col ▶
Había puros güeyes, ni una pinche vieja. There were only guys there, not a single broad.

Qué güey soy; olvidé el pasaporte. How stupid I am; I forgot my passport.
Ey, güey, pásame el martillo. Hey, pal, pass me the hammer.

el/la cabeza de chorlito (head of golden plover, a small bird) birdbrain, scatterbrain ◄ Mex, G, PR, DR, Col, S. Cone, Sp ▶

el/la cojudo(-a) idiot (Peru: strong insult) ◄ Ec, Peru ▶

el/la cretino(-a) (cretin) idiot ◄ L. Am., Sp ▶
Ese cretino no sabe nada. That idiot doesn't know anything.

el gil (la gila, el gilberto) chump, dupe, dope ◄ Mex, Cuba, Col, Ec, Peru, S. Cone ▶
No te hagas el gil. Don't act like a chump.

el/la gilipollas jerk, dope, asshole (vulgar, from **polla**) ◄ Sp ▶

el/la guajolote(-a) (turkey) fool, stupid person ◄ Mex ▶
Soy un guajolote; no pasé el examen. I'm such a turkey; I didn't pass the test.

el guanajo (turkey) idiot, fool ◄ DR ▶
Tomás le recordó a la profesora que hoy era el examen. ¡Qué guanajo! Tomás reminded the teacher that there was a test today. What a turkey!

el huevón, la huevona (big egg) idiot, fool; also used affectionately between friends (vulgar; see also "laziness") ◄ CR, PR, Col, Ec, Ch ▶

el/la lentejo(-a) (sounds like **lenteja**, lentil, or a combination of **lento**, slow, and **pendejo**, stupid) dope, idiot, fool ◄ Mex, Col, Peru ▶

el/la loco(-a) (tonto[-a]) perdido(-a) (lost fool) hopeless case, someone very stupid ◄ L. Am., Sp ▶

el/la mama'o(-a) fool ◄ PR ▶
No soporto a ese mama'o. Es un estúpido. I can't stand that fool. He's really stupid.

el melón, la melona (melon) foolish, stupid ◄ Sp ▶
No seas tan melón y piensa un poco. Don't be so foolish and think a bit.
Me quedé como un melón. I sat (stood) there like a dolt.

el/la mensolaco(-a) crazy retard ◄ Mex ▶

el merluzo (a fish called hake) dope, idiot ◀ Sp ▶
¿Aún no sabes las tablas de multiplicar? Eres un merluzo. You still don't know the multiplication tables? You're a dope.

el pedazo de alcornoque (piece of cork oak) blockhead, fool ◀ Mex, DR, G, Col, Ch, Sp ▶

pendejo(-a) (pubic hair) foolish, stupid (vulgar) ◀ Mex, C. Am., DR, PR, Col, Ven ▶

el/la pensante dope, idiot ◀ Mex, Col ▶

el petardo (detonator, firecracker) idiot ◀ Col ▶
¡Qué petardo! Salí sin apagar el horno. What an idiot! I left without turning off the oven.

el saco (mata) de huevas (bunch of testicles) dickhead, fool ◀ Ch ▶

el salmón (salmon) idiot, fool ◀ PR ▶

foolish, stupid

aguacate (avocado) foolish, stupid ◀ G, ES, CR, PR, Col ▶

aguacatón, aguacatona (big avocado) stupid ◀ ES ▶
No te metas con él, que es aguacatón. Don't get involved with him; he's stupid.

aguacatudo(-a) foolish, stupid ◀ ES, CR ▶

ahuevonado(-a) (egged up) boneheaded, hopelessly dumb ◀ Ch ▶

baboso(-a) (drooling) foolish, stupid ◀ most of L. Am. ▶

bambalán, bambalana foolish, stupid ◀ PR ▶

borde stupid, ill-mannered; **ponerse borde** to go too far ◀ Sp ▶
Se puso borde en la fiesta y empezó a gritar. He went off the deep end at the party and began to yell.

bruto(-a) (brutish) stupid; rude ◀ L. Am., Sp ▶
Es un bruto; le dijo que se había muerto su padre cuando ella estaba enferma en el hospital. He's an oaf; he told her that her father had died when she was sick in the hospital.

caído(-a) del catre (fallen from the hospital cot) not very bright, easily taken advantage of, soft in the head ◀ Ch ▶

caído(-a) de la cuna (fallen from the cradle) foolish, not right in the head (because of being dropped from the cradle), dopey or easily taken advantage of ◀ U, Arg ▶

caído(-a) del zarzo (fallen out of the attic) foolish, out of it ◀ Col ▶

cerrado(-a) (closed) stupid, dull ◀ Mex, CR, PR, Col ▶

deschavetado(-a) (headless) stupid ◀ Mex, ES, Ch ▶

dundo(-a) foolish ◀ C. Am. ▶

lelo(-a) foolish, stupid ◀ chicano, Mex, G, DR, Col, U, Arg ▶
—No sé, dije como una lela. "I don't know," I said like a fool.

maje stupid (CR: also, a common term of address to friends, male or female, pronounced **mae**) ◀ parts of Mex, G, Hond, ES, CR ▶
No seas tan maje. Don't be so stupid.
Qué maje eres, que así no se hace eso. (ES) What a jerk you are; you don't do it that way.
No te hagas el maje. Don't act like a dope.
Hola, mae, ¿qué tal? (CR) Hi, pal, how are you?

más cerrado(-a) que un huevo de gallina (un tubo de radio) (CR: **que un bombillo** [a lightbulb]) (more closed than a hen's egg [a radio tube]) very stupid ◀ Mex, PR ▶
Ese perro que tenemos es más cerrado que un bombillo. (CR) That dog of ours is really thickheaded.

memo(-a) foolish, stupid ◀ DR, PR ▶

menso(-a) stupid, foolish ◀ chicano, Mex, C. Am., DR, PR, Col, Ch ▶
Llegó el señor Hernández con la mensa de su mujer. Mr. Hernández arrived with that fool of a wife of his.

no tener dos dedos de frente (to not have two fingers' length of forehead) to be stupid, brainless ◀ L. Am., Sp ▶
¡Caramba! Parece que mi hijo no tiene dos dedos de frente. Jeez! Seems my son doesn't have the sense God gave a goose.

no tener sal en la mollera (to not have salt on the crown of the head) to not be very bright ◀ L. Am., Sp ▶

pasmado(-a) foolish, stupid ◀ Mex, C. Am., U ▶

sanano(-a) stupid, foolish ◀ PR ▶
El perrito de la esquina es bien sanano; corre delante de los carros. Un día lo van a matar. The little dog on the corner is really stupid; he runs in front of cars. One day he's going to get killed (they're going to kill him).

sato(-a) stupid, foolish (also, a mixed breed animal) ◀ PR ▶
¡Qué nena más sata! Ahora se las da de Madonna. What a silly girl! Now she's acting like she's Madonna.
Ese perrito parece un labrador pero es sato. That little dog looks like a Labrador but he's a mongrel.

ser más corto(-a) que las mangas de un chaleco (to be shorter than the sleeves of a vest) to be stupid ◀ Sp ▶

sholón, sholona foolish, stupid ◀ G ▶

tarado(-a) foolish, stupid (from **tara**, mental deficiency) ◀ Mex, C. Am., DR, Col, S. Cone, Sp ▶

tarugo(-a) stupid ◀ chicano, Mex, DR, Col, Sp ▶

tonto(-a) de capirote (idiot chief) extremely stupid, dope of dopes ◀ Mex, Peru, Sp ▶

tener cabeza de mosquito (to have a mosquito's head) to be brainless ◀ U, Arg, Sp ▶

tener la cabeza hueca (to have the head hollow) to be brainless, an airhead ◀ Mex, U, Arg, Sp ▶

tener ya dura la mollera (to have the crown of the head already hard) to no longer be able to learn (also, **tener mucha/poca mollera**, to be bright/stupid) ◀ U, Sp ▶

topado(-a) (blocked, butted up against) stupid ◀ chicano, Mex, Col ▶

torpe dim-witted, slow ◀ Mex, C. Am., Cuba, DR, PR ▶

zángano(-a) foolish, silly (see also "laziness") ◀ DR, PR, Col ▶
No seas zángano. ¡Pídele el teléfono! Don't be foolish. Ask her for her telephone number!

zonzo(-a) silly, stupid ◀ most of L. Am. (not Ch) ▶

zoquete (zoqueta) stupid, foolish ◀ chicano, Mex, DR, Col, Sp ▶
¡Qué muchacha más zoqueta! ¡No quiso salir en el show de don Francisco! What a foolish girl! She refused to go on Don Francisco's show!

nonsense, foolish talk or actions

la babosada stupidity ◀ L. Am. ▶

las chorradas stupidities, nonsense, pieces of junk ◀ Sp ▶
No me gusta lo que dijo Felipe porque son sólo unas chorradas. I don't like what Felipe said because it's only nonsense.
Hace chorradas. He (She) does stupid things.

el disparate (shot off the mark) nonsense ◀ L. Am., Sp ▶
¡Qué disparate! ¡Puros disparates! What nonsense! Pure nonsense!

la gilada stupid action typical of a **gil**, or jerk; dirty trick ◀ U, Arg ▶
Eso de sacarle el 10 por ciento de sueldo a los jugadores es una gilada. Taking 10 percent of the players' salary is a dirty trick.

las gilipolleces stupidities (slightly vulgar) ◀ Sp ▶

la huevada stupid action typical of a **huevón** or **huevona** (vulgar) ◀ Ec, Ch ▶

la huevonada stupidity, fooling or goofing around (vulgar) ◀ CR, Ven ▶
—¡Dejen la huevonada! gritó la maestra. "Stop the damn nonsense!" yelled the teacher.

la lesera nonsense ◀ Ch ▶

la mamada (sucking, nursing) nonsense, lie, fib (vulgar) ◀ Mex, ES, Col ▶
Es un buen hombre. —¡Mamadas! He's a good man. —Baloney!

la memez stupid thing or idea, idiocy ◀ Sp ▶

los negocios chuecos (crooked deals) monkey business ◀ Mex, ES, DR, Col, Ch ▶

las pamplinas (from the name of a plant) stupidities, trivia ◀ Sp ▶
Déjate de pamplinas y come, que estás muy delgada. Stop the nonsense and eat; you're very thin.

la pendejada silly or stupid thing to do; trick (vulgar) ◀Mex, C. Am.▶

las sandeces nonsense ◀Mex, G, PR, Col, S. Cone, Sp▶
No diga sandeces. Don't talk nonsense.

el telele (fit, fainting attack) foolishness (also, **ser un telele,** to be foolish) ◀ES, CR▶

silly, foolish, goofy

bayunco(-a) mischievous, with antics ◀ES▶
Mi hermano se portó bien bayunco cuando fuimos al cine. My brother acted very silly when we went to the movies.

bobo(-a) silly ◀Mex, G, Cuba, DR, PR, Col, Peru, Bol, Arg, Sp▶

casquivano(-a) feather-brained, silly ◀L. Am., Sp▶

chango (monkey) silly (person) ◀PR▶
¡Ave María! ¡Qué nene más chango! Llora por todo. Good heavens! What a silly child! He cries about everything.

gafo(-a) silly, foolish ◀Ven▶
¡Qué gafo! Ese chiste es muy viejo. How silly! That joke is very old.

ligero(-a) de cascos (light of head) frivolous, foolish (Mex: easy woman); also, **liviano(-a) de cascos** ◀L. Am., Sp▶

success

andar sobre ruedas (to go on wheels) to be going smoothly, great (also, **ir/ marchar sobre ruedas**) ◀Mex, ES, Nic, DR, PR, Col, Ch, Sp▶
Todo anda (marcha) sobre ruedas. Everything is going great.

el bacán (controller of a woman who earns money for him, from Lunfardo) successful player, achiever (also, shallow glamour boy) ◀S. Cone▶

Ese hombre es un bacán; consigue todo lo que quiere. That guy is a successful player; he gets everything he wants.

Ese arroz ya se coció. (That rice has already been cooked.) It's in the bag, said when something one has tried to get has come through (e.g., a favor). ◀Mex, ES▶

estar en la cresta de la ola (to be on the crest of a wave) to be at one's high point ◀Sp▶

flotar como el corcho en el agua (to float like cork in water) to come out well despite adverse events or problems ◀Sp▶

hacer brecha (to make an opening, breach) to achieve fame or success ◀Mex, ES, Sp▶

ir con viento en las velas (to go with wind in the sails) to be doing fine, steaming along, progressing ◀Ch▶

ir (muy) lejos to go (very) far ◀Mex, DR, Ch, Sp▶

ir viento en popa (to go wind at the stern) to go forward, full-speed ahead ◀L. Am., Sp▶
El negocio me va viento en popa. My business is going full-speed ahead.

irse arriba to go above, outdo, or excel ◀ES, CR, DR▶
Felipe se le fue arriba a José. Felipe outdid (got ahead of) José.
Este creído ya se me quiere ir arriba. This snob wants to get ahead of me.

llegar y besar (el santo) (to arrive and kiss [the saint]) phrase describing how quickly something was obtained ◀Sp▶

marchar requete bien to be going very well (in Sp, a bit old-fashioned) ◀Mex, G, Para, U, Arg, Sp▶
¿Cómo te va la vida? —Me marcha requete bien. How's life going for you? —It's going very well (for me).

salir adelante to get ahead ◀L. Am., Sp▶

tandear to win with a big advantage or lead (also, **la tandeada,** big lead or victory) ◀CR, Col▶

tomar vuelo to take flight, make progress (things) ◀Mex, DR, U, Arg▶

surprise

agarrarse (to hang on) to get ready for a shock or surprise ◀ Mex, ES, DR, PR, S. Cone, Sp ▶
Agárrate. ¿Adivina quién me llamó anoche? Hang on. Guess who called me last night?

alucinar to be surprised or impressed (Mex: to dislike, as **Alucino a mi suegra.** I dislike my mother-in-law.) ◀ Sp ▶
Alucina lo bien que habla este niño. It's surprising how well this boy talks.
Me alucinó la película. The film impressed me.
Cuando oí la noticia, aluciné en colores. When I heard the news, I was amazed.

boquiabierto(-a) (open-mouthed) amazed ◀ L. Am., Sp ▶
Susana se quedó boquiabierta cuando le dije que me había casado. Susana was dumbfounded when I told her I'd gotten married.

caer como bomba to fall like a bomb(shell); to arrive as a surprise, generally unpleasant ◀ Mex, G, ES, DR, PR, S. Cone, Sp ▶
La noticia (La comida) me cayó como bomba. The news (The food) hit me like a bombshell.

boquiabierto

caérsele a alguien la baba (to have drool falling) to be very surprised (often by something attractive) ◀ Mex, ES, S. Cone ▶
Se me cayó la baba cuando ella salió en esa minifalda (cuando vi mis calificaciones). I was very surprised when she came out in that miniskirt (when I saw my grades).
Se le cayó la baba cuando vio a ese muchacho. She was very surprised (drooling with admiration) when she saw that guy.

caído(-a) del cielo (fallen from the sky) describing a windfall, boon ◀ Mex, ES, S. Cone ▶
El dinero me vino como caído del cielo. Me cayó del cielo. The money was a real windfall. It came out of nowhere.

como caído(-a) de las nubes (like fallen from the clouds) unexpected ◀ Mex, Sp ▶

dejar a alguien frío(-a) (helado[-a]) (to leave someone cold [frozen]) (ES: also, **fresco**) to shock, surprise (Sp: also, **Me trae al fresco.**) ◀ Mex, ES, DR, U, Arg, Sp ▶
La noticia de la muerte del presidente me dejó fría. The news of the president's death left me in shock.

fuerte (strong) surprising, shocking; used as an intensifier ◀ Mex, Sp ▶
¿Lo arrestaron? ¡Qué fuerte! They arrested him? What a shock!

pasmar to dumbfound or surprise; also, to scold ◀ Mex, Col, Sp ▶

Parió la mula. (The mule gave birth.) phrase meaning that things turned out badly or something unexpected happened ◀ ES, Col ▶

quedar pasmado(-a) to be dumbfounded, surprised ◀ Mex, Col, S. Cone, Sp ▶
Me quedé pasmada cuando me dijeron que se habían divorciado. I was flabbergasted when they told me that they'd gotten a divorce.

quedarse con la cara cuadrada (to be left with the square face) to be very surprised ◀ Mex ▶
Juan se quedó con la cara cuadrada cuando me vio llegar en mi carro nuevo. Juan was stunned when he saw me arrive in my new car.

quedarse frío(-a) (helado[-a]) (to end up cold [frozen]) to be surprised, stunned; said when something turns out contrary to what one wanted or expected ◀ Mex, ES, CR, Ec, Ch, Sp ▶
Me quedé frío de lo que me dijo. I was dumbfounded by what he (she) told me.
Me quedé helada cuando me dijeron que había muerto. I was shocked when they told me that he (she) had died.

¿Y eso? (And that?) What does that mean? What's that all about? ◀ L. Am., Sp ▶

Holy smoke! Good grief!

¡A la perica! (To the parakeet!) expression of surprise ◀ ES, Nic, CR ▶
¡A la perica! Se me olvidó por completo. Good grief! I completely forgot.

¡Anda la hostia (leche, osa, puta)! (Go the Host [milk, bear, whore]!) expressions of surprise (all are vulgar and sometimes can also express annoyance) ◀ Sp ▶

¡Ave María! expression of surprise or other emotion, said mainly by people who are religious ◀ Mex, G, CR, PR, Col, Sp ▶
¡Ave María! ¡Esas cosas no se dicen! Good heavens! You can't say such things! (Literally, Those things are not said.)

¡Cámara!, ¡Camaronchas! Wow! (seeing a gorgeous person of the opposite sex, etc.) ◀ Mex ▶

¡Chale! expression of surprise, like **caray** or **caramba**; can also indicate disbelief ◀ Mex ▶
¡Chale! No te creo. Wow! I don't believe you.

¡Chanclas! (Old shoes!) expression of surprise ◀ Mex, ES ▶

¡Chanfle! Good grief! expression of surprise ◀ Mex, Col ▶

¡Chicles, muéganos y palomitas! (Chewing gum, caramel-covered candies, and popcorn!) exclamation of great surprise ◀ Mex, Col ▶

¡Chispas! (Sparks!) expression of surprise ◀ Mex, Col ▶

¡Cielo verde! (Green sky!) Holy smoke!, used to express that something is surprising or unusual ◀ PR ▶

¡Cojones! (Testicles!) common expletive used for anger, surprise ◀ Cuba, Sp ▶

¡Coño! (reference to female organ) interjection of anger, surprise, pain (vulgar, especially in L. Am.) ◀ Mex, Caribbean, Col, Sp ▶
¡Coño! ¡Qué suerte has tenido! ¡Qué guapa que estás! Damn! How lucky you've been! How beautiful you look!

¡Diablo! (Devil!) expression of surprise (Mex: more common, **¡Diablos!**) ◀ Mex, DR, PR, Col ▶

¡Dianche!, ¡Diantre! (Devil!) Holy smoke!, used instead of ¡Diablo!, ¡Demonio! to express surprise, dismay (DR: **diache**; Mex: **diantres**) ◀ Mex, DR, PR, Col ▶
¡Diantre! (¡Diache! ¡Diablo!) ¡Tú no sabes de lo que te pierdes! (DR) Holy smoke! You don't know what you're missing!
¡Diantres! (Mex) Holy moley!

¡Dios mío! (My God!) My goodness! ◀ L. Am., Sp ▶

¡Dios santo! (Holy God!) My goodness! ◀ L. Am., Sp ▶

¡Epa, Chepa! (Hey, Chepa!) interjection of surprise and disbelief ◀ Nic ▶

¡Epa, epa! interjection expressing surprise or shock ◀ Caribbean ▶

¡Hijo de Dios! (Son of God!) expression of surprise ◀ ES, CR, Col ▶

¡Híjole! expression of surprise, similar to Wow!, Darn! ◀ Mex, G, ES, Nic, Col ▶

¡Hostia(s)! (Host[s]!) a strong expletive implying religious sacrilege (vulgar) ◀ Sp ▶

¡Huy! Wow! Damn! (expression of surprise) ◀ L. Am., Sp ▶

¡Joer! from **joder**; interjection used in Sp, something like Damn!; also, less strong, **¡Jolines!** ◀ Sp ▶

¡La osa! exclamation of surprise, euphemism for **la hostia** ◀ Sp ▶

¡Manda huevo! used to indicate impossibility, opposition, surprise, the height of something (Sp: also, **manda cojones**) (vulgar) ◀ ES, CR, Col, Sp ▶
¡Manda huevo que vos no le entrés a esa hembra! (said by males, ES) Bet you can't get (win, charm) that girl!

Say it with slang!

Saints, angels, and religious references

Saints and angels abound in everyday expressions in many parts of Spain and Latin America. If you have a good intention but get sidetracked, you might say, **Se me fue el santo al cielo** (literally, My saint left me and went up to heaven). If there is a sudden silence in a conversation, a possible comment would be **Pasa un ángel.** (An angel is going by.) And to wish someone pleasant dreams, you might say, **¡Que duermas con los angelitos!** (May you sleep with the little angels!) New Testament figures also make their appearance. To show surprise or excitement, Spanish speakers from different places may exclaim, **¡Virgen santísima!** (Most holy virgin!); **¡Ave María!** (Hail, Mary!); **¡Ay, bendito!** (Oh, blessed one!); or **¡Santísima Trinidad!** (Holiest Trinity!). If you sneeze, people may say, **¡Salud!** (Health!), or they may say, **¡Jesús!** And if you sneeze a second time, **¡María!**, and a third, **¡José!** That way you have the entire Holy Family working with you against a possible virus.

Islamic as well as Christian influence is still evident in the Spanish language; after all, there were almost 800 years of Moslem rule in parts of Spain (711–1492). The important expression of hope that something will (or will not) happen, **ojalá (que)**, contains the word for Allah (**Alá**) and derives from the phrase "May Allah grant (that) . . ."; for example, **¡Ojalá que los niños estén bien!** (I hope the children are well!) But those children could be running around from one place to another, "from pillar to post," in which case you might say in present-day Spanish that they are going **de la Ceca a la Meca** (literally, from the mint to Mecca, the sacred Moslem city of pilgrimage).

¡Ostras! (Oysters!) euphemism for **¡Hostias!** ◀ Sp ▶

¡Por la flauta! (By the flute!) By heaven! ◀ Ch ▶

¡Pucha! ¡La pucha! euphemism for **¡La puta!**, equivalent to Holy smoke! ◀ L. Am. ▶

¡Púchica! Holy cow!, euphemism for puta (CR: **¡Pucha!, ¡A la pucha!**) ◀ C. Am. ▶

¡Puchis! Holy cow!, euphemism for puta ◀ G ▶

¡Puta! (Whore!) Damn! (vulgar) ◀ L. Am., Sp ▶

¡Puta madre! (Mother whore!) expression of surprise or anger (vulgar) ◀ Mex, C. Am., S. Cone ▶

¡Qué barbaridad! (What barbarity!) Good grief! ◀ L. Am., Sp ▶

¡Qué bárbaro! (How barbarous!) Good grief! ◀ L. Am., Sp ▶

¿Qué huevada (güea)? (What bunch of testicles?) What's going on? (vulgar) ◀ Ch ▶

¿Qué huevonada (verga) es ésta? (What screwup [male organ] is this?) What's happening? What's going on? (vulgar) ◀ Ven ▶

229

¡Qué vaina! (What a husk, sheath!) expression of surprise, unpleasantness, anger, annoyance, disagreement ◀G, Nic, CR, DR, Col, Ven▶

¿Qué vaina (mierda) es ésta? (What husk [shit] is this?) What's happening? What's going on? (vulgar) ◀ES, Ven▶

¡Rayos! (Lightning rays!) Good grief! (a bit old-fashioned, used to express surprise or when there is a problem) ◀most of L. Am., Sp▶
¿Qué rayos pasa? What in blazes is happening?

¡Santísima Trinidad! (Holy Trinity!) expression of surprise or fright, especially used by women ◀Mex, ES, CR, Col▶

Si no lo veo, ¡no lo creo! (If I don't see it, I don't believe it!) I can't believe my eyes! Incredible! ◀Mex, ES, S. Cone, Sp▶

¡Uff! Oh dear! Oops! ◀Mex, Col▶

¡Virgen santísima! (Holy Virgin!) expletive equivalent to Good heavens! (old-fashioned) ◀L. Am., Sp▶

¡Vóytelas! interjection of surprise ◀Mex▶

sympathy

expressions of sympathy

¡Acharà!, ¡Charà! What a shame! ◀CR▶

¡Ay, bendito! (Blessed one!) Bless my soul!, expression of sympathy ◀PR▶

Cuenta conmigo. Count on (with) me. ◀L. Am., Sp▶

Estoy con ustedes. I am with you. I feel for you. (expressing sympathy for misfortune) ◀L. Am., Sp▶

Lo (La/Le) acompaño en su dolor (en sus sentimientos). Te acompaño en tu dolor. (I accompany you in your pain.) Please accept my condolences. ◀L. Am., Sp▶

Lo siento muchísimo. (I feel it very, very much.) I am very, very sorry. ◀L. Am., Sp▶

¡Pobrecito(-a)! Poor (little) thing! ◀L. Am., Sp▶

¡Qué lástima! What a shame! ◀L. Am., Sp▶

feeling someone's pain

arrancarle a alguien el alma to tear out one's soul, feel great pain because of some past event or events ◀Mex, ES, Sp▶
Me arrancó el alma ver a esos niños trabajando. It broke my heart to see those children working.

arrancarle a alguien la vida (to tear out one's heart [life]) to feel great pain ◀Mex, ES▶

dar el pésame (to give the "it weighs on me") to express one's sympathy in times of death or misfortune ◀L. Am., Sp▶
Permítame darle el pésame, señora Moreno. Allow me to express my sympathy, Mrs. Moreno.

partirle el alma a alguien to break someone's heart (soul) ◀L. Am., Sp▶
Me parte el alma verlo tan triste. It breaks my heart to see him so sad.

rasgarle el alma a alguien (to scratch someone's soul) to hurt badly, feel pain ◀Mex, ES▶
Me rasgó el alma verla tan enferma. It tore me up to see her so sick.

tener a alguien en el alma (to have someone in one's soul) to feel for someone who is having problems, wanting to help ◀Mex, Sp▶

unsympathetic

Mírate en ese espejo. (Look at yourself in that mirror.) Let that be a lesson for you. ◀Mex, ES, DR, U, Arg▶

tener alma de acero (to have a soul of steel) to be without feelings, cold ◀Mex, ES, Sp▶

tener un corazón de piedra to have a heart of stone ◀Mex, ES, DR, S. Cone▶

technology, computers

chatear to chat on the Internet ◀parts of L. Am.▶

cliquear to click (e.g., on a key) ◀parts of L. Am.▶

la compu short for **la computadora** ◀L. Am.▶

el cuarto de discusión chat room (Mex: **el chat**) ◀L. Am., Sp▶

el email E-mail (pronounced with the sound of E-mail in English) (Florida, Sp: emilio) ◀L. Am., Sp▶

emailear to E-mail (pronounced with the sound of E-mail in English) ◀L. Am., Sp▶
Te voy a emailear unos chistes. I'm going to E-mail you some jokes.

el fax fax ◀L. Am., Sp▶

faxear to fax ◀L. Am., Sp▶
Te lo puedo faxear si quieres. I can fax it to you if you want.

hacer clic to click (e.g., on a key or a mouse) ◀L. Am., Sp▶

hacer un download (un backup) to download (back up) (a computer file) ◀L. Am., Sp▶
Laura, necesito que me hagas un backup. Laura, I need you to make me a backup.

el mouse mouse (computer, from English) ◀parts of L. Am.▶

surfear la Red (la Internet) to surf the Internet ◀parts of L. Am.▶

television and radio

la caja tonta (idiot box) television, boob tube ◀Mex, Sp▶

el culebrón (big snake) soap opera ◀CR, Ven, Bol, Arg, Ch, Sp▶

hacer zapping (to do zapping) to change the channel ◀Peru, S. Cone, Sp▶
Mi esposo prende la tele y empieza a hacer zapping. My husband turns on the TV and starts changing the channels.

la tele (short for **televisión**) television ◀L. Am., Sp▶

la teleculebra (tele-snake) TV program that tells a silly story in installments; cheesy soap opera ◀Mex, ES, Ven▶

thank-yous

chasgracias short for **muchas gracias** ◀L. Am., Sp▶

Con mucho gusto. (With great pleasure.) You're welcome. ◀CR▶

Graciela. used instead of **gracias** ◀Peru▶

¿Para qué? (For what?) You're welcome. ◀Mex▶

things

house, home, pad

la caleta house, home ◀Ec▶

el chante home, pad (ES: **chanti**; Pan: **chantín**) ◀Mex, ES, Nic, CR, Pan▶
Tengo que ir a mi chante. (CR) I have to go home.
Voy para el chantín de Gustavo. (Pan) I'm going to Gustavo's house.

la choza (hut) house, home ◀Mex, G, ES, CR, Col, U, Arg, Para▶

la cueva (cave) teenagers' word for home ◀Mex, Col▶

el gao house, home (from an African language) ◀ Cuba ▶

la home home (from English) ◀ parts of L. Am. (not S. Cone) ▶

el jato house, home ◀ Peru ▶

la ruca house, home (from the Mapuche language) ◀ Ec, Ch ▶

miscellaneous words for things

la chacra (Quechua word) country cottage ◀ Peru, Bol, S. Cone ▶

la chafa low-quality or fake item ◀ Mex, G, ES ▶

el chucho pooch, dog ◀ Mex, ES ▶

la cosa grandototota (great big thing) humongous thing ◀ Mex, ES, Nic, U, Arg ▶

el cuzco pooch, cute little dog (**cuzquito** means doggie) ◀ Arg ▶

gran cosota big deal ◀ Mex, C. Am. ▶
Para mí, el asunto del accidente es una gran cosota. To me, the accident is a big deal.

el hierro (yerro) (iron) pistol, revolver ◀ Cuba, PR ▶

la lira (lyre) guitar ◀ Mex, Col ▶

el loro (parrot) radio cassette player ◀ Sp ▶

la marca perra (dog brand) common low-quality brand in a product (blouse, computer, etc.) (Arg: also, **marca pistola** pistol brand) ◀ U, Arg ▶

el mataburros (donkey killers) dictionary ◀ Mex, CR, DR, PR, Peru, U, Arg ▶

media cosita (half a little thing) every little thing ◀ Mex, C. Am. ▶
Si me dice media cosita, lo voy a mandar a freír espárragos. If he says the slightest thing to me, I'm going to tell him to get lost.

los pelos de la cola (tail hairs) loose ends ◀ Ch ▶

la tartamuda (stutterer) machine gun, automatic weapon ◀ Mex ▶

la yapa freebie; free gift ◀ S. Cone ▶

short forms of common things

el boli (short for **bolígrafo**) pen ◀ L. Am. (not S. Cone) ▶

la mani, manifa (short for **manifestación**) demonstration ◀ Sp ▶

la migra (short for **inmigración**) U.S. INS, immigration ◀ chicano, Mex, G, ES ▶

el mono (monkey) sketch, drawing (**monos animados** are cartoons) ◀ Ch ▶

la pelu (short for **peluquería**) beauty shop, barber shop ◀ Mex, Sp ▶

el/la refri (short for **refrigerador[a]**) refrigerator (**el** in Mex, **la** in G, ES) ◀ Mex, G, ES ▶

things of little value, odds and ends

las baratijas baubles, trifles ◀ L. Am., Sp ▶

el cacharro worthless object ◀ Mex, DR, PR, Col, U, Arg, Sp ▶

los cachivaches junk, things of little value ◀ L. Am. ▶
En esa tienda sólo se venden cachivaches. In that store they sell only junk (trinkets, odds and ends).

el cachureo (horned things) odds and ends, junk ◀ Ch ▶

la cafrería useless stuff, junk (similar to **porquería**) ◀ Mex, PR ▶

la carajada (from **carajo**, male organ) thingamajig, whatchamacallit (vulgar) ◀ ES, Nic ▶

la carambada thing of little value; nonsense ◀ ES, CR, Col, Nic ▶
¡Qué carambada más cara! What an expensive piece of junk!
Deja de hablar carambadas. Stop talking nonsense.

la cháchara chatter, gab session (Mex: also, object of little value) ◀ Mex, DR, Sp ▶
Llegué tarde porque en la oficina teníamos una cháchara muy entretenida. I got here (there) late because in the office we had a very entertaining gab session.

Íbamos de cháchara y se nos pasó el tiempo volando. (Sp) We were talking away and the time flew by.
Allí venden puras cháncharas. (Mex) They sell nothing but claptrap there.

los chécheres everyday objects of all sorts ◀ CR, Col ▶

los cheles things of little value ◀ Cuba ▶

los chiches knickknacks, trinkets, small toys ◀ S. Cone ▶

la chingadera thingamajig, worthless thing, bad thing, trick, bad or swear word (vulgar) ◀ chicano, Mex, G, ES ▶
Esa chingadera, ¿qué es? What's that piece of crap?
No digas chingaderas. Don't say bad things (like that).

el chirimbolo doohickey, thingamabob ◀ Mex, Cuba, Col, U, Arg ▶

chirolas something of little worth, small change ◀ U, Arg ▶
Este vestido me costó chirolas. This dress cost me a pittance.

la chiva thing of little value ◀ Mex ▶

la chuchería (from **chuches**, candy) something of little value but cute ◀ DR, PR, Ch, U, Sp ▶
No me quiero gastar mucho dinero para el cumpleaños de Claudia; sólo le quiero comprar una chuchería. I don't want to spend a lot of money for Claudia's birthday; I just want to buy her a little trinket.

el chunche thing, thingamajig (usually masculine but in CR **chuncha** is used if the object referred to is feminine) ◀ C. Am. ▶
Dame ese chunche allí. Give me that thingamajig there.

el comosellama (the what's-its-name) thingamajig, whatchamacallit ◀ Nic, U, Arg ▶

la cuestión (issue, theme) thingamajig, whatchamacallit ◀ Nic, DR, ES, Ch ▶

los féferes things of little value ◀ Cuba, DR ▶
No me gusta salir de compras contigo porque te antojas de todos los féferes que ves. I don't like to go shopping with you because you want all the claptrap you see.

la fregadera thingamajig (slightly vulgar) ◀ chicano, Mex, G, ES, CR ▶

la guarandinga thingamajig ◀ Nic, Cuba ▶

las guarrerías (pig things) junk, pieces of crap ◀ Sp ▶

el picao thing ◀ Cuba, Col ▶

la(s) porquería(s) (pig stuff) junk, trash; junk food ◀ L. Am., Sp ▶

puras madres (pure mothers) things of little value ◀ Mex, C. Am. ▶

los tiliches things, stuff ◀ Mex, C. Am. ▶

la vaina (husk) thing (all-purpose word for any thing, situation, etc., slightly vulgar) ◀ Hond, Nic, CR, Pan, DR, PR, Col, Ven ▶
Dame esa vaina, por favor. Give me that thingamabob, please.

la vara thing ◀ CR ▶

la verga (male organ) thing, piece of crap (vulgar) ◀ Nic ▶
No me gusta esta verga (café amargo) que nos sirvieron. I don't like this crap (bitter coffee) that they served us.

thinking

See also "knowledge, understanding."

cambiar el chip (to change one's [computer] chip) to change one's way of thinking ◀ Mex, Sp ▶
Ustedes tienen que cambiar el chip si quieren tener éxito. You have to change your way of thinking if you want to succeed.

consultar con la almohada (to consult with the pillow) to sleep on it, wait and think things over (also, **hablar con la almohada**) ◀ L. Am., Sp ▶

encendérsele el bombillo (to have the lightbulb turned on) to have a brilliant idea (Mex, ES: **encendérsele el foco**; U, Arg: **encendérsele la lamparita**) ◀ Cuba, DR, PR, Col ▶
A Juana se le encendió el bombillo (el foco). Juana had a brilliant idea.

233

la mente de alcantarilla (gutter mind) dirty mind, describing someone who always thinks in crude ways ◀ Ch ▶

la tranca hangup, block, inhibition ◀ Peru, Ch ▶

trancarse (to be blocked, as with a bar) to not be able to answer (a question) or respond ◀ DR, Col, Ch ▶
Lo tenía en la punta de la lengua, pero me tranqué y me quedé callado. I had it on the tip of my tongue, but I drew a blank and kept quiet.

having a feeling or hunch

hacérsele to think, imagine ◀ most of L. Am., Sp ▶
Se me hace que el otro equipo va a ganar. I have a hunch that the other team is going to win.

latirle to foresee, have a feeling about ◀ Mex, ES, CR, Col, DR, PR, Ch ▶
Me late que no le va a ir nada bien. I have a feeling that it's not going to go well for him (her).
Me late que va a chocar. I have a feeling that he's (she's) going to crash.

ponérsele to suppose, think ◀ ES, CR, Ch ▶
A Fernando se le puso que iban a cancelar la reunión. (CR) Fernando had a feeling (suspicion) that they were going to cancel the meeting.
Se me pone que va a llover ahora. I think it's going to rain now.

la tincada hunch ◀ Ch ▶

tincarle to think, have a hunch ◀ Peru, Ch ▶
Me tinca que va a llover. I have a hunch that it's going to rain.

obsessing, fixating on

Cada loco con su tema. (Every crazy person with his or her subject.) expression usually said when someone is excessively insistent about something ◀ L. Am., Sp ▶

comerse el coco (to eat the head) to worry or be preoccupied (Sp: also, **comerse el tarro, comerse la olla**) ◀ Mex, Sp ▶

estar cachudo(-a) (to be big horn of an animal) to be obsessed (with something) ◀ Ch ▶

hacerse bocho to obsess over something ◀ U, Arg ▶

hacerse caldo de cabeza (to make oneself head broth) to obsess or mull over (something), rack one's brain ◀ Ch ▶

hacerse (un) cráneo (to make oneself [a] skull) to get illusions about or get fixated on ◀ Cuba ▶
Me hice mucho cráneo con esa muchacha. I obsessed about that girl.

hacerse pajas mentales (to do mental masturbation) to think a lot about something (vulgar) ◀ PR, Ch, Sp ▶

ir y venir en una cosa (to go and come in something) to insist on something ◀ Sp ▶

meterse algo en la cabeza (to put something in one's head) to have something fixed in one's head, get an idea and cling to it ◀ ES, Ch, Sp ▶

meterse algo entre ceja y ceja (to put something between eyebrow and eyebrow) to have something fixed in one's head, get an idea and cling to it ◀ most of L. Am., Sp ▶

straining the noggin, racking one's brain

cranear to think a lot ◀ G, Col, Ec, Ch ▶
Estoy aquí craneando, pero no veo ninguna solución. I'm here racking my brain, but I don't see any solution.

dar cráneo (cabeza) (to give cranium, skull [head]) to think a lot ◀ Mex, PR ▶

darle al coco (to give to the coconut, head) to think, study ◀ Mex, Sp ▶

darse de cabezazos (to give oneself big hits on the head) to rack one's brain ◀ Ch ▶

devanarse los sesos (to wind up one's brain) to rack one's brain ◀ Mex, Ch, Sp ▶

estrujarse el coco (to press one's coconut, or head) to think, rack one's brain ◀ Ch ▶

estrujarse el melón (to press one's melon, or head) to think ◀Sp▶

hacer cerebro (to make brain) to think (DR, PR: implies lust) ◀Nic, CR, Col▶

meter el coco (to put coconut, head) to concentrate on something ◀Mex, Cuba, Col▶

quemarse (estrujarse) los sesos (to burn out [press] one's brain) to think about something over and over, rack one's brain ◀S. Cone, Sp▶

romperse la cabeza (los cascos) (to break the head [skulls]) to think a lot about something, beat one's brain out ◀Mex, DR, Sp▶
Me rompí la cabeza estudiando para el examen para nada. Al final, suspendí. I beat my brain out studying for the test for nothing. In the end, I flunked.

time

a la corta o a la larga (in the short or the long) sooner or later ◀L. Am., Sp▶

a estas alturas at this point or stage ◀L. Am., Sp▶

a la larga in the long run ◀L. Am., Sp▶

a la postre (at the dessert) last, at the end ◀Mex, DR, Sp▶
A la postre me vas a agradecer que te haya obligado a ir a la escuela. In the end you're going to thank (literally, be thankful to) me for making you go to school.

ahorita (diminutive of **ahora**) right now ◀L. Am. (not Cuba, S. Cone)▶

al primer envite at once, right off the bat, from the beginning ◀Sp▶

al tiro (at a shot) right now (Nic: one after another, in sequence) ◀CR, DR, Ch▶

colgarse (to hang, be suspended) to be hung up ◀Mex, ES▶
Se colgó una hora en el teléfono. He (She) was hung up on the telephone for an hour.

Me colgué una hora allí. I was hung up there for an hour.

de buenas a primeras (from good ones to first ones) from the beginning, at first sight, right away or on the spur of the moment ◀L. Am., Sp▶

de nuez again (sounds like **de nuevo**; **nuez** means nut) ◀Mex▶

de por vida, de toda la vida for life, lifelong ◀L. Am., Sp▶
Somos amigos de por vida. We're lifelong friends.

de pronto suddenly, soon ◀Mex, C. Am., Col, Arg, Ch, Sp▶

de sol a sol (from sun to sun) from sunup to sundown ◀L. Am., Sp▶

los días particulares (particular days) workdays, weekdays (Monday to Friday) ◀ES, Peru, Bol▶

estar atrás to be behind (in work, payments, etc.) ◀Mex, Cuba, DR, Col▶

el finde short for **fin de semana**, weekend ◀Arg, Sp▶
Hay una fiesta en casa de Julia el próximo finde. There's a party at Julia's house next weekend.

llegar a las raspas (to arrive at the scrapings) to get to a party or event when it's almost over (probably from **raspa**, as the scraping of the bottom of a pot) ◀CR▶

más días hay que longanizas (there are more days than pork sausages) there's no rush ◀Sp▶

no ver la hora de (+ inf.) (to not see the hour + inf.) to not be able to wait + inf. ◀L. Am., Sp▶
No veo la hora de ir. I can't wait to go.

el ostro sol (the other sun; **ostro** is used instead of **otro**) yesterday ◀Mex, Col▶

por de pronto, por lo pronto meanwhile, provisionally (Ch, Sp: **por lo pronto** only) ◀L. Am., Sp▶

la racha period of time, streak, run ◀L. Am., Sp▶
Hemos pasado una mala racha, pero creo que hoy vamos a ganar el partido. We've had a bad streak, but I think today we're going to win the game.

Say it with slang!

For the birds!

Parrots talk, and so in Spanish slang **una cotorra** (a parrot) means a talkative person, **un cotorreo** (a parroting) is a gabfest, and **cotorrear** or **hablar como papagayo** (to talk like a macaw) means to yak on and on. Some birds move in such a way as to suggest either grace and beauty or awkwardness and stupidity, which probably explains why in many parts of Latin America **creerse la divina garza** (to think oneself the divine heron) describes a conceited person and in Mexico **un guajalote** (a turkey) refers to a fool. In Chile, if you are told that you seem **pajarón(-a)** (big bird), it means that you appear absentminded and distracted. Perhaps you are **soñando con pájaros preñados** (literally, dreaming about pregnant birds—that is, thinking of something impossible), as they say in many parts of Latin America. The people who do that are often young innocents, who are still wet behind the ears, the ones usually referred to in Spanish as **caídos(-as) del nido** (just fallen from the nest).

ratón y queso (rat and cheese) used instead of **rato** ◀ Cuba ▶
¡Hola, socio! Hace ratón y queso que no nos vemos. Hi, pal! We haven't seen each other for ages.

las tantas an undetermined hour, late at night or in the day ◀ Mex, DR, Sp ▶

todo el santo día the whole live-long (holy) day ◀ L. Am., Sp ▶

el toque (touch) short time (Sp: also, **dar un toque**, to give notice) ◀ CR, Col, Sp ▶
Espérame un toquecito, porfa. Wait a sec, please.

a long time

añales many years ◀ ES, Nic ▶
Hace añales que no lo veo. I haven't seen him in years.

dilatar(se) to take a long time ◀ Mex, ES, CR, PR ▶
¡Cómo se dilata mi amiga! How long my friend is taking!

ir para rato (to go for a while) to be a while ◀ L. Am., Sp ▶
Ya va para rato que trabaja aquí. He (She) has been working here for a while.

el tiempal long time ◀ ES, Nic, CR ▶
Hace un tiempal que no estamos aquí. We haven't been here in ages.

in a little while

ahorita in a little while (different meaning than in rest of L. Am. See **ahorita**, page 235.) ◀ Cuba ▶

al chico rato, al ratón in a little while (that may never come) ◀ Mex, Col ▶

despuesito a little later than now ◀ Mex ▶

mero: Ya mero. Ya merito. Almost. It's (I'm, etc.) on the way, almost ready. ◀ Mex, G, ES, Nic ▶
¿Ya preparaste la comida? —Ya mero. Did you prepare the food (fix the meal) yet? —Almost.

Un momentico. Just a moment. ◀ CR, Col, Ven ▶

long ago

cuando las culebras andaban con chaleco (when snakes walked around in vests) a long time ago ◀ Ch ▶

cuando Franco era cabo (corneta) (when Franco was a corporal [a trumpet player]) a long time ago ◀ Sp ▶
Nos conocimos cuando Franco era cabo y aún me quedaba pelo en la cabeza. We met a long time ago when Franco was a corporal and I still had hair on my head.

cuando los perros se ataban con chorizos (when dogs were tied with sausages) long ago ◀ U ▶

en el año catapún (in the year **catapún**) a long time ago ◀ Sp ▶
Esa canción es del año catapún. That song is from ages ago.

en el año de la pera (in the year of the pear) a long time ago ◀ Ven, Peru, Ch, Sp ▶
¿Ves esta foto del colegio? Es del año de la pera. See this picture from school? It's from the Stone Age.

en tiempos del hilo azul (in the days of the blue thread) long, long ago ◀ Nic ▶

never

cuando la rana eche pelos (when the frog sprouts hair) the twelfth of never, when hell freezes over ◀ L. Am. ▶
¿Enrique te va a llamar? —Sí, cuando la rana eche pelos. Is Enrique going to call you? —Yes, when hell freezes over.

el día del pago de los bomberos (day when the firemen get paid) when hell freezes over, the twelfth of never ◀ Ch ▶

el día 30 de febrero (the 30th of February) never, the twelfth of never ◀ Mex, ES ▶
¿Cuándo te vas a casar conmigo? —El día 30 de febrero. When are you going to marry me? —The twelfth of never.

una y no más (santo Tomás) (once and no more [Saint Thomas]) never again ◀ Sp ▶

tobacco and smoking

Atácame un pulmón. (Attack my lung.) Give me a cigarette (or joint). ◀ Mex ▶

la bala, el prajo cigar ◀ Cuba ▶

la breva cigar ◀ Mex, Pan, Cuba, Peru ▶

fumar como un carretero (to smoke like a trucker) to smoke a lot ◀ Sp ▶

fumar como chacuaco (to smoke like a furnace or a cigarette butt) to smoke a lot ◀ Mex ▶

fumar como (una) chimenea to smoke like a chimney ◀ Mex, S. Cone, Sp ▶

fumar como murciélago (to smoke like a bat) to smoke a lot ◀ ES, DR, PR, S. Cone ▶
Su novio fuma como murciélago. Siempre tiene un cigarrillo en la mano. Her boyfriend smokes like a chimney. He always has a cigarette in his hand.

el pitillo cigarette ◀ Ch, Arg, Sp ▶

el pucho smoke, cigarette butt ◀ Arg, Ch ▶

travel and transportation

chinear to carry (usually a baby); also, to pamper ◀ C. Am. ▶
Su papá la llevaba chineada. Her dad was carrying her in his arms.

cruzar el charco (to cross the puddle) to cross a sea, usually to go to America or to the United States (Arg, U: to go over the Uruguay River or Río de la Plata) ◀ Mex, Cuba, DR, PR, Sp ▶

de la Ceca a la Meca (from Ceca to Mecca) from here to there, pillar to post ◀ Mex, ES, DR, PR, Ch, Sp ▶

estar con las botas puestas (to have one's boots on) to be ready for a trip ◀ Mex, Sp ▶

estar con un (el) pie en el estribo (to have one [the] foot in the stirrup) to be ready to take a trip ◀ Mex, ES, S. Cone, Sp ▶ **Te volveré a llamar, tía; ahorita estoy con un pie en el estribo.** I'll call you back (Aunt); right now I'm going out the door.

¿Hay alguien que canta aquí? Porque hay uno que está tocando. Is there someone who sings here? Because there is someone who touches (plays a musical instrument). (Said, for example, on a crowded subway or bus when someone is touching someone else unnecessarily.) ◀ ES ▶

turistear to go on an outing ◀ Mex, ES, CR, DR, Col ▶

cars

la cacharpa old car ◀ Nic, CR ▶

el cacharro old car ◀ Mex, DR, PR, Col, U, Arg, Sp ▶

los cafres del volante maniac drivers ◀ Mex, Col ▶

la carcacha old car, jalopy, old piece of junk ◀ Mex, G, ES, DR, Col ▶ **Ya es hora de que cambies esa carcacha por un carro nuevo.** It's time for you to trade in that piece of junk for a new car.

el carrazo nice big car ◀ Mex, ES, Col ▶

el carro car ◀ Mex, C. Am., Peru, Arg ▶

la carroza (carriage) car, new or old ◀ Col, Ec ▶

el chivo (kid goat) car ◀ Ec ▶

la garola old car ◀ ES ▶

la lámina (lata) car (use of part for the whole) ◀ Mex, Col ▶

la máquina machine; car ◀ Cuba ▶

la nave (ship) car, usually large ◀ Mex, G, Hond, CR, DR, PR, Col, Ven ▶

la ranfla car ◀ chicano, Mex ▶

el tuerca (metal nut in mechanics) grease monkey; car lover ◀ S. Cone ▶

hitchhiking, giving a lift

dar (pedir) un aventón to give (ask for) a lift ◀ Mex, ES, Nic ▶ **Nuestro carro estaba en el taller, pero un amigo nos dio un aventón.** Our car was in the shop, but a friend gave us a ride.

dar (pedir) una bola to give (ask for) a ride (ball) ◀ DR ▶ **¿Puedes darme una bola? Hoy ando a pie.** Can you give me a ride? I'm on foot today.

dar (pedir) una cola to give (ask for) a ride (tail) (Bol: **una colita**) ◀ Ven, Nic ▶

dar (pedir) un jalón to give (ask for) a lift (CR: **ir al jalón,** to hitchhike) ◀ ES, CR, Peru ▶

dar (pedir) pon to give (ask for) a ride ◀ PR, Col, Sp ▶ **Otra vez se me dañó el carro. Tengo que pedirle pon al vecino.** (PR) The car is out of commission (damaged) again. I have to ask the neighbor for a ride.

de paquete (as a package) referring to someone riding behind in a two-wheeled vehicle ◀ Sp ▶ **Yo no tengo moto; siempre voy de paquete.** I don't have a motorcycle; I always ride on the back.

hacer (viajar por) autostop to hitchhike ◀ Sp ▶

hacer dedo (to make thumb) to hitchhike, thumb a ride ◀ S. Cone, Sp ▶

on foot

a pata (by foot of an animal) walking ◀ Mex, C. Am., S. Cone, Sp ▶

a patín (from **a pata,** by foot of an animal) walking ◀ chicano, Mex, G ▶ **Fui al centro a patín.** I went downtown on foot.

a pincel (by paintbrush) by foot, walking (like **a pata**) ◀ Mex, Hond, Nic, CR ▶

andar en Dodge (to go in a Dodge) to walk ◀ Ec ▶

echar un patín (to throw a skate) to walk very fast ◀ Mex, Cuba ▶

ir en el coche de Armando: una vez a pie y la otra andando (to go in Armando's car: one way [once] on foot and the other walking) to walk ◀Ch▶

ir en el coche de San Fernando (to go in St. Ferdinand's car) to go on foot (U: ... Fernando: un poco a pie y otro poco caminando. ... Fernando: partway by foot and partway walking) ◀DR, U, Sp▶

patear to walk a lot, a long way ◀Sp▶

pistear to walk with no real destination, looking for a girl or guy, to be seen, or just for amusement ◀Cuba▶

volar pata (to fly foot) to walk a long way, a lot ◀CR, Col▶

other forms of transportation

la bici (short for bicicleta) bicycle ◀L. Am., Sp▶

el buga car ◀Sp▶

la burra (female donkey) bus ◀G▶

la burra (female donkey) bike (Sp: motorbike) ◀Col▶

el chivo (kid goat) bike ◀Cuba▶

el guajolotero (turkey carrier) tightly packed bus ◀Mex▶

la guagua bus ◀Caribbean▶
¿Cómo vas a la universidad? —En guagua. How do you go to the university? —By bus.

la lata (tin) bus ◀CR▶

la moto (short for motocicleta) motorcycle ◀L. Am., Sp▶

la rufa bus ◀Cuba▶

la troca truck (from English) ◀chicano, Mex, ES▶
Su troca es de último modelo. His (Her) truck is the newest model.

traffic jams

la galleta (cookie) traffic jam ◀Arg▶

la hora pico rush hour; peak hour of electricity use (Sp: hora punta) ◀Mex, Nic, DR▶

el taco (plug, wedge) traffic jam ◀Ch▶

truth

See also "certainty."

a calzón quitado (with underwear removed) openly, frankly ◀L. Am.▶

a flor de piel (at the flower of the skin) readily present in a person's expression and nature ◀L. Am., Sp▶
Ella tenía los nervios a flor de piel. Her nervousness was obvious.
Edgar mostró su amor a flor de piel. Edgar wore his heart on his sleeve.

a quema ropa (at burning of clothing) directly, straight out, point-blank ◀L. Am., Sp▶
Cuando lo vi, le di las noticias a quema ropa. When I saw him, I gave him the news straight out.

abrir su corazón a alguien to open one's heart to someone ◀Mex, DR, U, Arg, Sp▶

caer de cajón (to fall like a drawer) to go without saying, be obvious (also, ser de cajón) ◀Mex, Hond, Nic, Ven, Ec, Peru, S. Cone, Sp▶

con el corazón en la mano (with one's heart in one's hand) frankly and sincerely ◀L. Am., Sp▶

con razón (with reason) no wonder ◀L. Am., Sp▶

la hora de los quiubos (the time of the what-happeneds) the time for explanation, the moment of truth ◀Ch▶

ir a misa (to go to mass) to be correct, for real ◀Sp▶
Lo que dice mi padre va a misa. What my father says is for real.

la neta the truth ◀Mex▶

quitarse la careta (to take off one's mask) to stop acting or making a show, show one's true colors ◀Mex, ES, S. Cone▶
Quítate la careta, ya. Take off your mask. (Stop acting and be yourself.)

la verdad clara y desnuda (the clear and naked truth) the clear, unadulterated truth ◄ most of L. Am., Sp ►

la verdad de la milanesa (the truth of the Milanese chop) the real truth of the matter ◄ S. Cone ►

It's true. No joke.

Fuera de bromas. (Outside of jokes.) No joke. Seriously. ◄ Mex, ES, S. Cone, Sp ►
Ya fuera de bromas vamos a platicar de esto. Now let's talk about this seriously.

Ni que decir tiene. You don't have to say it (it's common knowledge). ◄ Mex, Peru, Sp ►

No hay que darle vueltas. (There's no need to turn it around.) It's just as it looks; it's obvious. ◄ Mex, ES, DR, S. Cone, Sp ►
Terminemos esta plática... no hay que darle vueltas al asunto. Let's finish this conversation . . . there's no need to dwell on the matter (look at it from other angles).

Pura verdad. (Pure truth.) True. Right you are. ◄ L. Am., Sp ►

Se (te) lo juro. I swear (it) to you. ◄ L. Am., Sp ►
Es la pura verdad, papá, te lo juro. It's the truth, dad, I swear to you.

Sin cachondeo(s). No joke. ◄ Sp ►

telling it like it is

See also "criticism."

cantar a alguien las cuarenta (to sing the forty to someone) to speak one's mind clearly, tell an unpleasant truth (U: **cantar las cuarentas**) ◄ Ec, Peru, Arg, Ch, Sp ►
Le canté las cuarenta cuando lo vi. I gave him a piece of my mind when I saw him.

cantar la justa (la pura) (to sing the just [the pure]) to speak frankly, tell it like it is ◄ U, Arg ►

cantarle a alguien la cartilla (el salmo) (to sing someone the primer [church card]) to set someone straight, read the riot act, lay down the law ◄ Mex, Ch, Sp ►

decir a alguien (las) cuatro verdades (to tell someone the four truths) to tell someone exactly what one thinks is the truth; to get it off one's chest ◄ ES, DR, PR, Ch, Sp ►

decir al pan pan y al vino vino (to call bread bread and wine wine) to tell something directly and without beating around the bush, tell it like it is ◄ L. Am., Sp ►

decir cuántos pares son tres moscas (to tell how many pairs three flies are) to read the riot act ◄ Ch ►
Le voy a decir cuántos pares son tres moscas. I'm going to give him (her) a piece of my mind.

decir cuatro cosas (to tell four things) to say what one really thinks, especially negative things, give (someone) a piece of one's mind (often used in anger) (ES: **decir tres o cuatro cosas**) ◄ ES, Nic, DR, PR, Ec, Peru, Ch ►
Estaba tan enojada que le dije cuatro cosas y la mandé al diablo. I was so mad that I gave her a piece of my mind and told her to go to the devil.

leerle a alguien la cartilla (to read the primer to someone) to set someone straight, read the riot act, lay down the law ◄ Mex, ES, DR, Ch, Sp ►
Le pedí permiso para andar con su hija y me leyó la cartilla. I asked him for permission to date his daughter and he laid down the law.

poner las cartas sobre la mesa (to put one's cards on the table) to be direct about a situation, explain it without concealing anything ◄ L. Am., Sp ►

poner los puntos sobre la mesa (to put one's points on the table) to lay things out clearly ◄ Mex, G ►
Pongamos los puntos sobre la mesa. Creo que hay muchas cosas que no saben. Let's put our cards on the table. I think there are a lot of things that you don't know.

ugliness

See also "bad."

chimbo(-a) ugly; low quality ◀ Ec ▶

el espantapájaro (scarecrow) ugly or skinny person ◀ L. Am., Sp ▶

feote (feota) very ugly or run-down (-ote, augmentative) ◀ L. Am., Sp ▶

el feto (fetus) ugly person ◀ Mex, U, Arg, Sp ▶

más feo(-a) que carracuca (uglier than carracuca) very ugly (vulgar) ◀ Sp ▶
Soy más feo que carracuca, ¿verdad? —**¡No digas eso, mi amor!** I'm ugly as hell, aren't I? —Don't say that, honey!

más feo(-a) que mandado a hacer (uglier than if designed for it) uglier than a toad ◀ CR ▶

ser un cardo borriquero (to be a cotton thistle) to be very ugly, used for people ◀ Sp ▶

ser un culo (to be an ass, asshole) to be ugly (vulgar) ◀ PR, U, Arg ▶

unusualness

echar una canita al aire (to throw a gray hair in the air) to let one's hair down ◀ ES, Ch, Sp ▶
Voy a salir a bailar. Voy a echar una canita al aire. I'm going to go out dancing (said by someone who doesn't usually go dancing). I'm going to let my hair down.

estrafalario(-a) strange, weird (usually referring mainly to dress) ◀ L. Am., Sp ▶
Esa chica siempre se ve muy estrafalaria. ¡Qué vestido más estrafalario! That girl always looks weird. What a weird dress!

medio raro (sort of unusual) kind of weird; possibly gay ◀ Mex, ES, DR, S. Cone, Sp ▶

re-que-te intensifiers used before adjectives, adverbs, and even verbs, meaning "very" ◀ L. Am., Sp ▶
rebien; retesimpático; requeteinteresante; very good; very nice; very, very interesting **¡Reteodio!** I really hate you!

vuelto loco(-a) y sin sentido (become crazy and without sense) said when someone has done something out of the ordinary ◀ DR ▶

extraordinary, tremendous

bárbaro(-a) (barbarous) abnormal, unusual, exceptional; badly done ◀ L. Am., Sp ▶

bestial great, tremendous, exaggerated (good or bad, but more likely bad in Mex) ◀ Mex, DR, PR, Col, Peru, U, Arg, Sp ▶
Fue una película bestial. It was an amazing film.

cagante (shitting) spectacular, fantastic, frightening (vulgar) ◀ Ven ▶

criminal (criminal) intelligent; well-done, extraordinary ◀ PR, G ▶

de primera (of first) first-class ◀ L. Am. ▶
Ese muchacho ha resultado de primera. That boy has turned out first-class.
Es un cabrón de primera. He's a first-class SOB.

de siete suelas (of seven soles/bases) true, for real (usually for something bad) ◀ Mex, U, Ch, Sp ▶
Es un pícaro de siete suelas. He's a real rascal.

del demonio (of the devil) extraordinary, tremendous ◀ Sp ▶

estar de quitar el hipo (to be such as to take away hiccups) to be amazing, breathtaking ◀ Mex, Sp ▶
Es tan bonita que quita el hipo. She's so pretty she takes your breath away.

jalado(-a) (pulled) exaggerated, ridiculous ◀ Mex ▶

matador(-a) ugly (often women), bad (Col, Mex: also, delightful, wonderful) ◀ Mex, G, Cuba, Col, S. Cone ▶
¡Qué trabajo matador! What a bad (exhausting) job!

mayúsculo(-a) (capital letter) major ◀ L. Am. ▶
Es un problema mayúsculo. It's a mega problem.

mortal (mortal, deadly) good, great, super ◀ Cuba, Col, S. Cone ▶

no estar en el mapa (to not be on the map) to be unusual, not ordinary ◀ ES, DR ▶
Esto no estaba en el mapa. This is off the wall. We couldn't have predicted this.

No tiene madre. (It has no mother.) Far-out! It's the best (worst)! No equal! ◀ Mex, ES ▶

por arte de birlibirloque as if by magic, through extraordinary or unnatural means (also, …**magia**) ◀ DR, PR, Ch, Sp ▶

pulento(-a) flashy, extraordinary (Peru, Arg: **pulenta**, invariable) ◀ Peru, Arg, Ch ▶

que te cagas (that you defecate) expression denoting something unusual or expensive (vulgar) ◀ Mex, Sp ▶
Hace un sol que te cagas. It's hot as hell.
Tiene una casa que te cagas. He (She) has a hell of a nice house.

ser un bicho raro (to be a strange bug, beast) to be an oddball ◀ Mex, S. Cone, Sp ▶
Esa persona es un bicho raro. That person is an oddball.

¡Tiene huevos (narices) la cosa! (The thing has eggs, meaning testicles [noses]!) How bizarre, abusive, unheard of! (vulgar with **huevos**) ◀ Sp ▶

tremendo(-a) tremendous, exaggerated, phenomenal ◀ L. Am., Sp ▶

getting carried away, going too far

botar la bola (pelota), botarla (to throw away the ball) to do or say something extraordinary or ridiculous ◀ Mex, Cuba, DR, PR ▶

Martín es un tonto, ¡pero Rafaelito botó la bola! Martín is a fool, but Rafaelito really went off the deep end!

darse un atracón (to give oneself a big assault) to do something in excess, go over the top ◀ Mex, ES, Ch, DR, Sp ▶

desmadrar (to dismother) to act immoderately, get a bit out of control ◀ ES, PR, Sp ▶
Esa chica era muy tímida, pero se está desmadrando últimamente. That girl was very shy, but she's getting out of control lately.

irse al chancho (to go to the pig) to go overboard, go too far, overdo it ◀ Ch ▶

pasarse (to pass oneself) to go beyond the limit, go too far ◀ Mex, ES, DR, S. Cone ▶
Yo soy feo, pero tú te pasaste. I'm ugly, but you've gone beyond the limit.
¡Ya te pasaste! You've gone too far!

pasarse de la raya to go beyond the limit (over the line) ◀ Mex, ES, DR, PR, S. Cone, Sp ▶

pasarse de rosca (to pass oneself as doughnut) to go above and beyond, go overboard ◀ Mex, Sp ▶
El maestro se pasó de rosca conmigo al darme un 6 de calificación en el examen. The teacher went too far giving me a 6 as a grade on the test.
Mi papá se pasó de rosca al no darme permiso para ir a la fiesta. My dad went too far by not giving me permission to go to the party.
No te pases de rosca con la repartición del pastel. Don't go overboard when you serve the cake (literally, with the giving out of the cake).

pasársele la mano (to have your hand slip on you) to go too far, overdo it ◀ L. Am., Sp ▶
Lo siento. Se me pasó la mano. I'm sorry. I went too far.

salir del tiesto (to go out of one's pot) to act beyond one's rights or obligations, do something not normal, go off one's rocker ◀ DR ▶

salirse de las casillas (to go out of the boxes) to go overboard, do something abnormal ◀ L. Am., Sp ▶

Agustín se enojó, se salió de las casillas y se puso a gritar a la gente. Agustín got angry, flipped out, and started yelling at people.

salirse de madre en algo (to go out of the mother in something) to go overboard, do something not normal ◀ Mex, Sp ▶
Cuando bebe, se sale de madre. When he drinks, he goes off his rocker.
Te estás saliendo de madre. You're overdoing it.

salirse del guacal (to go out of one's container) to act beyond one's rights or obligations, do something not normal ◀ Mex, ES ▶
Mi hijo se me salió del guacal... se portó muy mal. My son went beyond the limit... he behaved very badly.

tirarse para la calle del medio (to throw oneself toward the middle street) to behave without discretion, shamefully; also, **estar tirado(-a) para la calle del medio** ◀ Cuba, DR ▶
Desde que se enteró que su esposo tiene una amante, Rosa está tirada para la calle del medio. Todos los días se va a la discoteca y llega por la madrugada. Since she found out her husband has a lover, Rosa has gone off the deep end. Every day she goes to a disco and comes home in the early morning hours.

taking the cake

llevarse la palma (to carry away the palm, meaning the honors) to surpass, take the cake (Sp: also, to get ahead or go first in a line; **llevarse la bandera/joya/mapa** are also used there) ◀ Ch, Sp ▶
Dices que tu hijo saca malas notas, pero el mío se lleva la palma. Ha suspendido siete asignaturas esta evaluación. You say that your son gets bad grades, but mine takes the cake. He's failed seven subjects this term.

Me llevo el premio de... I win the prize for... (ironic, refers to bad habits such as always arriving late, etc.) ◀ Ch ▶

No se mide (te mides). (You don't measure yourself.) You're really something. You outdo yourself. ◀ Mex, Col ▶

pintarse solo(-a) (to paint oneself alone) to take the cake ◀ Mex, U ▶
Te pintas sola, m'hija. You're really something (my daughter).

ser la coña to be unusual, strange (people) (vulgar) ◀ Sp ▶

ser el despelote (to be the nakedness) to be unheard of, extraordinary (things) (vulgar) ◀ Sp ▶

ser la hostia (to be the Host) to be great, amazing, too much (people or things) (vulgar, with religious reference) (PR: to be annoying) ◀ Sp ▶
Ese tío es la hostia; le dije que me comprara cuatro entradas para el concierto y sólo me compró dos. That guy is too much; I told him to buy me four tickets to the concert and he only bought me two.
Universal Studios es la hostia. Universal Studios is the bomb (the greatest).

ser la leche (to be the milk) to be too much, be surprising (good or bad, people or things), unheard of ◀ Sp ▶
Fernando es la leche. Siempre consigue lo que quiere. Fernando's too much. He always gets what he wants.
Esa novela es la leche. That novel is really something.

ser la monda to be extraordinary (good or bad, said of things) ◀ Sp ▶

ser la pera to be the limit (the pear), too much ◀ Sp ▶
¡Eres la pera! You take the cake!

ser la polla to be unheard of, extraordinary (people or things) (vulgar) ◀ Sp ▶

ser la repanocha to be the height (of something) ◀ Sp ▶

uselessness

in vain

al cuete (to the fart) without a good result, in vain, for nothing ◀ Arg ▶
Fui allí al cuete. I went there for nothing.

arar en el mar (to plough in the sea) to do something useless ◀ Mex, DR, PR ▶
Es la tercera vez hoy que limpio la cocina. Es como arar en el mar. This is the third time I've cleaned the kitchen today. It's a lost cause.

echar agua en el mar (to throw water into the sea) to do something useless ◀ Sp ▶

echar perlas a los puercos to cast pearls before swine, give something to someone who doesn't appreciate or deserve it ◀ DR, PR, Sp ▶
Nena, no te vistas tan elegante. Vamos a casa de Juan Carlos y él ni siquiera lo va a notar. Es como echarle perlas a los puercos. Girl, don't dress so elegantly. We're going to Juan Carlos's house, and he won't even notice it. It's like casting pearls before swine.

echar sal al agua (to throw salt into water) to do something useless ◀ ES ▶
A ése no se le puede dar un consejo. Es como echar sal al agua. You can't give that guy any advice. It's like talking to a wall.

en balde (in bucket) in vain ◀ L. Am., Sp ▶

gastar pólvora en zopilotes (sanates) (to spend powder, as gunpowder, on vultures [blackbirds]) to waste time (e.g., trying to convince someone of something) ◀ ES, CR ▶

en balde

llevar leña al monte (to take wood [logs] to the woods or brush) to take coals to Newcastle (old saying) ◀ L. Am., Sp ▶

rizar el rizo (to curl the curl) to complicate something unnecessarily ◀ Sp ▶

not good for anything

See also "bad," "bad character."

al pedo (pe'o) (to the fart) worthless, bad ◀ U, Arg ▶

botella (bottle) someone who doesn't do anything ◀ DR, PR ▶
El presidente hizo diez nuevos nombramientos; ya estoy cansado de tantas botellas que no hacen nada. The president made ten new appointments; I'm sick of so many good-for-nothings who don't do anything.

estar como un cachivache to be useless (like a piece of junk) ◀ Mex, PR, Col, U ▶

ni para vestir santos (not even to dress saints) worthless ◀ Mex, PR, Col, U, Arg, Sp ▶

Ni pincha ni corta. (It doesn't pinch or cut.) It's useless, of no influence or importance. ◀ Arg, U, Sp ▶

No salva a nadie. (It doesn't save anyone.) It's not good for anything. ◀ Ch ▶

no ser carne ni pescado (to be neither meat nor fish) to be undefined, insipid, neither fish nor fowl ◀ Sp ▶

no ser ni chicha ni limonada (to be neither corn liquor nor lemonade) to be useless, superfluous, mediocre ◀ most of L. Am., Sp ▶
El nuevo director no me impresiona mucho. No es ni chicha ni limona'. The new director doesn't impress me much. He's mediocre.

no servir a Dios ni al diablo (to serve neither God nor the devil) to be useless or inept ◀ Mex, Ch ▶

no tener chiste (to not have any joke) to be blah, unappetizing; to be senseless or useless ◀ Mex, ES, Col, Ec, Peru ▶
No tiene chiste que hayamos salido a pasear; está lloviendo. It's a waste that we have come out to take a walk; it's raining.

¿Qué chiste tiene que mi esposo venga por mí si tú me vas a llevar a la casa? What sense does it make for my husband to come get me if you're going to take me home?

no valer un bledo (to not be worth a pigweed) to be worthless ◀ Mex, ES, U, Arg ▶

no valer un carajo to not be worth a damn (male organ) (vulgar) ◀ Mex, U, Arg ▶

no valer ni cacahuete (to not be worth a peanut) to be worthless ◀ Mex, ES ▶

papel mojado (wet paper) useless document or, in general, something useless or of little importance ◀ most of L. Am., Sp ▶
El famoso principio de que todos los hombres son iguales es papel mojado. Mira la situación de los indígenas. The famous principle that all men are equal is worthless. Look at the situation of the Native Americans.

ser un culo (to be an ass, asshole) to be useless (vulgar) ◀ PR, U, Arg ▶
Esa actriz es un culo. No sé por qué le dieron el papel principal. That actress is not worth a damn. I don't know why they gave her the main role.

ser un pedazo de carne con ojos (to be a piece of meat with eyes) to be useless ◀ DR, Sp ▶
Yo no sé para qué le pagan a ese asistente. No hace absolutamente nada en la oficina. Es un pedazo de carne con ojos. I don't know why they pay that assistant. He doesn't do anything in the office. He's deadwood.

ser la pura chapa (to be pure lock) to be useless ◀ ES, CR ▶
No seas pura chapa; hazme el paro, loco. (ES) Don't be useless; do me this favor, man.

la tusa (stripped cornstalk/cornsilk) something (or someone) worthless (Col: also, lie, deception) ◀ ES, CR, Col ▶

valer gorro (to be worth cap) to be worthless, unimportant ◀ Mex ▶
Me valen gorro tus problemas. I don't give a darn about your problems. (Your problems are of no importance to me.)

valer hongo, valer callampa (to be worth mushroom) to be worthless, not worth a dime ◀ Ch ▶

¿Qué te pareció la película? —Malísima, po'. ¡Vale hongo! What did you think of the movie? —Horrible. It's not worth beans.

valer papas (to be worth potatoes) to be worthless, worth beans ◀ Mex ▶

valer por tres tiritas (to be worth three little strips) to be worthless ◀ Col ▶

unnecessary, superfluous

ir de boyote to be superfluous, extra ◀ ES ▶

ir de pegoste (to go as an add-on) to be superfluous, extra ◀ Mex, ES, Nic ▶
Tu hermana vino de pegoste por culpa de tu mamá. It was your mother's fault that we got stuck with your sister (literally, that she came along stuck on to us).

ir de pegote (to go as an add-on) to be superfluous, extra ◀ Sp ▶
Iba al cine y mi hermanito fue de pegote. I was going to the movies and my little brother came along (stuck on to me).

meter de galleta a alguien (to put in someone as a cracker) to include someone not suitable in a group ◀ Ch ▶
A ese muchacho muy flaco lo metieron en el equipo de galleta porque es hijo del director. They put that skinny guy on the team as an extra because he's the coach's son.

warnings

El que con lobos anda a aullar aprende. (The person who walks with wolves will learn to howl.) Keeping bad company will teach you bad ways. ◀ Mex, Nic ▶

El que con niños se acuesta... (The person who sleeps with children . . .) If you sleep with children, you'll wake up wet (the second part is understood: ... amanece mojado). Be careful! If you take risks, you may suffer the consequences. ◀ Mex, ES, Nic, DR, S. Cone, Sp ▶

El que pestañea pierde. (The person who blinks loses.) He who hesitates is lost. If you snooze you lose. ◀ L. Am., Sp ▶

Hay moros en la costa. (There are Moors on the coast.) phrase warning that someone else may be listening ◀ L. Am., Sp ▶
¡Cállate! Hay moros en la costa. Be quiet! People are listening.

Hay ropa tendida. (There is clothing hung out to dry.) Be careful. The coast is not clear. ◀ Mex, U, Ch, Sp ▶

Juan Segura vivió muchos años. (John Security lived many years.) Better safe than sorry. ◀ Ch ▶

Mono sabe el palo que trepa. (The monkey knows the tree he climbs.) a threat ◀ PR ▶
Qué raro que Julio no te dijo nada. Parecía muy molesto contigo. —Mono sabe el palo que trepa; conmigo él no puede meterse. How strange that Julio didn't say anything to you. He seemed very upset with you. —He'd better watch it; he can't mix it up with me.

Mucho ojo, que la vista engaña. (Much eye; the sight deceives.) Be careful because appearances are deceptive. ◀ Mex, ES, U, Arg, Sp ▶

No la chifles que va cantada. (Don't whistle it; it's being sung.) euphemism for No la chingues. Don't mess it up. ◀ Mex ▶

No te rifes. (Don't join the raffle.) Don't take a risk (chance). Don't expose yourself to danger. ◀ U, Arg ▶

Mucho ojo, que la vista engaña.

Para luego es tarde. (For luego, then, it's late.) phrase to get someone else to act quickly and not wait ◀ Mex, ES, DR ▶
Vete ahora y háblale. Para luego es tarde. Go now and talk to him (her). Don't wait until it's too late.

Pica, lica y califica. (Poke, look, and judge.) Look before you leap (examine something before you buy it, or think carefully before deciding on something or someone). ◀ Mex, Col ▶

Picado que come miel, ¡ay de él! (Someone stung who eats honey, watch out!) Be careful not to lose control and like something too much. ◀ Nic ▶

Te conozco, bacalao, aunque vengas disfraza'o (disfrazado). (I know you, codfish, although you come in disguise.) I see you coming. I see what you're up to. ◀ Sp ▶

Te conozco, mosco. (I know you, fly.) You can't trick me. I see your intention. ◀ ES, Nic, Arg, Ch ▶

Te veo venir. (I see you coming.) I see your intention. ◀ Mex, U, Arg, Sp ▶

moderation

De lo bueno, poco. (Of the good, a little.) All things in moderation. ◀ L. Am., Sp ▶

Menos lobos (Caperucita). (Fewer wolves [Red Riding Hood].) Don't exaggerate so much. ◀ Sp ▶

Ni tan peludo ni tan pelado. (Not so hairy nor so bald.) All things in moderation. ◀ Arg ▶

Ni tanto ni tan poco. (Not so much nor so few.) Don't exaggerate. ◀ Mex, DR, PR, S. Cone, Sp ▶

Ni tanto que queme al santo, ni tanto que no lo alumbre. (Not so much as to burn the saint nor so much as not to illuminate it.) All things in moderation. ◀ Mex, DR ▶

warning or threatening

mostrar los dientes (to bare one's teeth) to threaten (L. Am.: also, **enseñar los dientes**) ◀ L. Am., Sp ▶

mostrar los dientes

Tuve que mostrar los dientes para que me hicieran caso. I had to make a bit of a threat so they would pay attention to me.

poner en mente (to put in mind) to warn, make (someone) aware ◀ Cuba, Col ▶
Me puso en mente que el jefe allí es muy antipático. He (She) warned me (made me aware) that the boss there is very unlikeable.

sacar las uñas to bare one's nails, show one's true colors (Ec, Peru: **mostrar las uñas**) ◀ Mex, DR, S. Cone, Sp ▶

Watch out!

¡Agua sucia! (Dirty water!) There's trouble! ◀ Mex, Col ▶

¡Aguas! (Waters!) Watch out! ◀ Mex, G, ES, Col ▶

¡Candela! (Candle! Fire!) Watch out! ◀ Ven ▶

Cuidado con la liebre. (Be careful of the hare.) Be careful of the enemy. ◀ Mex, ES, Col ▶

Ojo pelado. (Peeled eye.) Be watchful, keep your eyes peeled. ◀ Ven ▶

Ojo piojo. (Be careful flea.) Keep your eyes peeled. ◀ Ch ▶

¡Pilas! (Piles!) Watch out! ◀ Col ▶

¡Wacha! Watch out! (from English) ◀ chicano ▶

weakness

See also "fear."

enyemao(-a) (eñemao) weak (physically) ◀ PR ▶

estar todo(-a) derretido(-a) (to be all melted) to be completely under the spell ◀ most of L. Am. ▶
José está todo derretido con su nueva novia. José is completely under the spell of his new girlfriend.

pushover

el barco, el barcazo (ship) pushover, parent who never says no or professor who passes everyone or gives good grades ◀ Mex, Hond ▶
El profe de mi clase de literatura es un barco. The prof in my literature class is a pushover.
La mamá de Jaime es un barcazo; nunca le dice que no. Jaime's mom is a pushover; she never says no to him.

el/la blandengue (soft and squishy) person who can be easily influenced and who likes to help others; softie ◀ Mex, DR, Arg, Sp ▶

el calzonazos (oversized pants) man who is pushed around by his wife or girlfriend or overly attached to his mother; wimp; mama's boy ◀ Ch, Sp ▶

el calzonudo (oversized pants) man who is pushed around by his wife or girlfriend or overly attached to his mother; wimp; mama's boy ◀ Mex, ES, Peru, Arg, Ch ▶

el faldero henpecked man, from **falda**, skirt ◀ Mex, ES ▶

el mandilón (big commander, said in an ironic way) meek husband whose wife orders him around ◀ Mex, ES ▶
Mi hermano es un mandilón; su mujer lo manda. My brother is a wimp; his wife orders him around.

Say it with slang!

Tutti fruiti

Fruits are often used in descriptions in Spanish. In many countries, **una fresa** (a strawberry) is a naive girl from a sheltered background, and **un coco** (a coconut) or **una persona que tiene buen coco** (a person who has a good coconut, meaning head) is someone brainy. In parts of Latin America, a **guayaba** (guava) is a lie or scam (perhaps because of its seductive smell), and **un guayabero** is a liar or con artist. To describe someone with a bitter character, Mexicans and Salvadorans may say, **No es perita en dulce** (He [she] is not a little pear in sweet juice), and Colombians may say, **No es melocotón en almíbar** (He [she] is not a peach in syrup). In Mexico and El Salvador, such a person could be said to have **una cara de limón** (the face of a lemon). In many places a good-looking person of either sex is referred to as **un mango**, and in Mexico, Cuba, and Colombia, an attractive woman is **mamey** (a sweet and delicious fruit common in the Caribbean). When it comes to good health rather than looks, Spaniards say someone is **sano(-a) como una manzana** (healthy as an apple). Finally, when something wonderful comes our way we can say, **Me cae de perillas** (It falls to me like little pears).

---

el semáforo de medianoche (traffic light at midnight) person no one respects and whom everyone takes advantage of, pushover ◀ Ven ▶

---

wealth and poverty

See also "money."

broke, in debt

andar quebrado(-a) to be broke ◀ Mex ▶

arrancado(-a) (torn out) broke, penniless (CR: angry) ◀ Nic, Cuba, DR, Col ▶
Acho, 'mano, préstame cinco pesos, que ando arranca'o. Hey, bro', lend me five pesos; I'm broke.

en carne, en cuero (in meat, in hide) broke, penniless ◀ Cuba ▶

enculebra'o(-a) (snaked) in debt ◀ Col ▶

estar (quedarse) a dos velas (to be [remain] at two sails) to be broke ◀ Mex, Sp ▶

estar asfixiado(-a) to be without money (asphyxiated) ◀ Mex, Sp ▶

estar en las Malvinas (to be on the Falkland Islands) to be in a bad way economically, without money ◀ Nic ▶

estar endrogado(-a) (to be drugged) to be heavily in debt ◀ Mex ▶

estar ladrando (to be barking) to not have money and be trying to borrow, be hitting up ◀ Ven ▶

estar mamando (to be nursing at the breast) to not have money and be trying to borrow, be hitting up ◀ Ven ▶

estar pato (to be duck) to be broke ◀ Peru, S. Cone ▶

248

estar pelando (to be peeling) to not have money and be trying to borrow, be hitting up ◀Ven▶

estar seco(-a) (to be dry) to be broke, without money ◀U, Arg▶

estar sin cinco (to be without five) to be without money ◀Mex, ES, Sp▶

estar vendido(-a) (to be sold) to be deep in debt ◀Mex▶

la jarana debt; also, **enjaranarse**, to get into debt ◀ES, Nic, CR▶

más pelado(-a) que la rodilla de un cabro (more bald than a goat's knee) broke ◀PR▶

no tener blanca (to not have a white one, coin) to be broke ◀Sp▶

no tener un cuarto (to not have a fourth) to lack money, be broke ◀Sp▶

no tener donde caerse muerto (to not even have a place to fall dead in) to be very poor, destitute ◀L. Am., Sp▶

no tener ni cinco (to not have even five [cents]) to be broke ◀Mex, ES, DR, Sp▶
No tengo ni cinco para comprar comida. I don't have a plug nickel to buy food.

no tener ni papa (to not have even potato) to be broke ◀Mex, ES▶

no tener ni para pipas (to not have even for pipes [tobacco]) to be broke ◀Sp▶

no tener un quinto (to not have a fifth) to be broke ◀Mex, ES▶

pasmado(-a) broke, penniless; without a mate or significant other ◀Cuba, Col▶

pelado(-a) (peeled) broke, penniless ◀C. Am., PR, Cuba, DR, Col, Sp▶
¿Me prestas dinero? Estoy pelado. Will you loan me money? I'm broke.

quedar en la calle to be left in the street, left with nothing ◀Mex, C. Am., S. Cone▶

sin blanca (without a white one, meaning a coin) broke ◀Sp▶

tener sed (to be thirsty) to be broke, without money ◀Sp▶

poor

andar a patadas con los piojos (to go along kicking with fleas) to live from hand to mouth ◀Ch▶

andar al tres y al cuatro (to go to the three and the four) to get by on a shoestring ◀Ch▶

el/la atorrante tramp, bum ◀Peru, S. Cone▶

el bagayo (bag) bum, homeless man ◀Arg▶

la chilla poverty; **en la quinta chilla**, in the worst poverty ◀Mex▶

comerse un cable (to eat a cable) to be in a difficult situation economically ◀DR, PR, Pan, Cuba▶
Llevo tres meses sin trabajo, así que andamos comiéndonos un cable. I've been out of work for three months, so we're in a tight spot financially.

el hombre del saco (man of the jacket) bogeyman; homeless man ◀Ch, Sp▶

irse/pasar por el alambre (to go through the wire) to not eat for lack of money or time, tighten one's belt ◀Ch▶

misio(-a) poor, without money ◀Peru▶

el/la palomilla (little dove) street urchin, beggar child ◀Ch▶

el/la pela-bola (ball-peeler) penniless bum ◀Ven▶

la pelusa, el pelusón (la pelusona) (fluff) street urchin, beggar child ◀Ch▶

las poblaciones callampas (mushroom populations) slums ◀Ch▶

pobre como una rata poor as a (church)mouse (Sp: also, **más pobre que las ratas**; Pan: **más pobre que una rata**) ◀Mex, ES, Pan, S. Cone, Sp▶

el/la roto(-a) (broken) low-class person; jerk ◀Ch▶
Son unos rotos con plata. They're nouveaux riches (jerks with money).

ser gente de medio pelo (to be people by half a hair) to be barely middle-class ◀Mex, Nic, S. Cone, Sp▶

rich

el/la bienudo(-a) young man (woman) from a well-off family ◀Arg▶

el/la blanquito(-a) (white) person with money; high society ◀PR▶
Yo nunca voy al Caparra porque es un club de blanquitos. I never go to the Caparra because it's a club for rich people.

el burgués, la burguesa (bourgeois) ostentatious rich folks, moneybags ◀ ES, Nic, Ven, U, Arg ▶

el/la chico(-a) bien young man (woman) from a well-off family ◀ Mex, DR, U, Arg, Sp ▶

la crema y nata (cream and cream at the top of the milk) highest social class ◀ L. Am., Sp ▶
A esa boda va a ir gente de pura crema y nata. Only really upper-class people are going to go to that wedding.
A la inauguración del teatro acudió toda la crema y nata de la sociedad dominicana. The most distinguished of Dominican society attended the dedication of the theater.

El que tiene plata platica. (Whoever has money makes conversation.) Money gives you social importance. Money talks. ◀ Nic ▶

encontrar una mina (de oro) to find a (gold)mine (a way to live or get rich without working much) ◀ Mex, ES, Ch, Sp ▶

estar en la papa (to be in the potato) to be in the money, have some money ◀ Pan ▶
Mario siempre estaba en la papa porque tenía un padrino que estaba en el gobierno. Mario was always in the money because he had a godfather who was in the government.

estar podrido(-a) de dinero (to be rotten with money) to be filthy rich (CR: **estar podrido de plata**) ◀ Mex, ES, CR, DR, U, Arg, Sp ▶

forrado(-a) (lined) having money (as in pockets being lined) ◀ Mex, Cuba, DR, PR, U, Arg, Sp ▶
El novio de Lourdes está forrado. Creo que su mamá es la vice presidenta del banco. Lourdes's boyfriend is loaded. I think his mom is vice president of the bank.

forrarse (to make a lining for oneself, lined pockets) to become very rich ◀ Nic, DR, Sp ▶
Se forró de dinero en la bolsa de valores. He (She) made a lot of money in the stock market.

hacer su agosto (to make one's August) to make hay while the sun shines, take advantage of something, make a killing ◀ L. Am., Sp ▶
Doña María hizo su agosto en la bolsa el año pasado. Doña María made a killing in the stock market last year.

el/la hijo(-a) de papá (child of papa) kid who has everything solved for him or her by the parents' influence (U: **nene de papá**) ◀ Mex, Hond, ES, CR, Cuba, DR, Col, Peru, Sp ▶

el/la hijo(-a) de papi see **hijo de papá** ◀ Mex, G, ES, Col, Peru ▶

el junior spoiled brat, playboy, son of the wealthy ◀ Mex, Col ▶

el/la millonetis millionaire, rich person ◀ Sp ▶
Mi sueño es ir a Las Vegas para regresar a mi casa hecho un millonetis. My dream is to go to Las Vegas and come back home a millionaire.

la niña pija young, innocent upper-class or spoiled girl (not vulgar but pejorative) ◀ Sp ▶

el niño (la niña) bien well-brought-up (upper-class) boy (girl) ◀ L. Am., Sp ▶

los niños popis (stuck-up kids) rich brats ◀ Mex ▶
Es una escuela de puros niños popis. It's a school for rich brats.

pistudo(-a) having money (**pisto**) ◀ Hond, ES, CR ▶

platudo(-a) rich ◀ L. Am. ▶

Poderoso caballero es don Dinero. (A powerful gentleman is Sir Money.) Money is power. ◀ L. Am., Sp ▶

el ricachón, la ricachona very rich (person) ◀ L. Am., Sp ▶
Se casó con un ricachón que trabaja en una empresa. She married a moneybags who works in a big company.

el ricardo (richard) rich guy ◀ Mex ▶

ser de la jai lai (la jai jai) to be of the high life (from English), hoity-toity (U: **ser de la jai**) ◀ ES, Col ▶
Te crees como si fueras de la jai lai (jai jai) y en tu casa no tienes nada. You act like you were a fat cat and yet you don't have anything at your house.
Te la estás picando de la jai lai (jai jai). You're acting hoity-toity.

ser de sangre azul to be a blue blood, from an aristocratic family ◀ L. Am., Sp ▶

tener bolsillos alegres (to have cheerful pockets) to have lots of money ◀ Mex ▶

tener el billete largo (to have the long bill) to be loaded, rolling in dough ◀ Ch ▶

tener la guita loca (to have crazy money) to be loaded ◀ U, Arg ▶

weather

Aquí viene Elver... gazo de agua. (Here comes Elver . . . , **gazo** of water, a pun on the name Elver and the first syllables of **el ver-ga-zo**) Here comes a big rainfall. (slightly vulgar) ◀ ES, Nic ▶

caer un chinchín to sprinkle (rain) ◀ Cuba ▶

chiflar el mono (the monkey whistles) to be cold (weather) ◀ Mex, Cuba ▶
Anoche chifló el mono, ¿no? ¡Qué frío! Last night it was freezing, wasn't it? What cold weather!

como nalga de lavandera (like a washerwoman's buttock) very cold, (cold) as a witch's tit ◀ Nic ▶

estar achuchado(-a) to be cold, freezing (with chills) ◀ Para, U, Arg ▶
¡Qué frío! Estoy todo achuchado. What cold weather! I'm freezing.

estar erizo (to be hedgehog or sea urchin) to be cold, have goosebumps ◀ ES, CR, Col ▶

el gran cachimbazo (de agua) (big hit of water) big rainfall, cloudburst, big shower (vulgar in Nic, where **cachimba** refers to female organ) ◀ Nic, G, ES ▶

hecho(-a) una sopa (made a soup) very wet ◀ Mex, ES, CR, Col, S. Cone, Sp ▶
Ayer salí a pasear y quedé hecho una sopa. Yesterday I went out for a walk and ended up soaked.

llover a cántaros (to rain pitchers) to rain buckets ◀ L. Am., Sp ▶

el pacheco cold, low temperature ◀ Ven, Ec ▶
¡Qué pacheco hoy! No vamos a salir. What cold weather today! We're not going out.

sancocharse to be steaming hot (people) ◀ Mex, DR, PR, Col, Ch ▶
Me estoy sancochando del calor. ¡Abran las ventanas! I'm roasting hot. Open the windows!

Se caen los patos asados. (Ducks are falling already roasted.) It's a scorcher. ◀ Ch ▶

Test your slang power!

The working world

Relevant categories: agreement, authority, inactivity, money, success, technology and computers, work and effort

How much Spanish "slanguage" do you know related to this topic? Test yourself by completing the exercises. Answers and rating scale are on pages 263 and 264. (If you don't do very well, read through the categories listed above and try again. The items in each exercise occur in the same order as the categories.)

A. Something's missing. *Select the appropriate word to complete the sentence.*

1. To succeed there, you have to go along with what people want of you.
   Para tener éxito allí, tienes que bailar al (son / ritmo / piano)
   _____ **que te tocan.**

2. My neighbor is a big shot in the government. **Mi vecino es un pez
   (grande / gordo / largo)** _____ **en el gobierno.**

3. Mr. Hidalgo is the man in charge of this meeting. **El señor Hidalgo
   lleva la (nota / voz / mirada)** _____ **cantante en esta
   reunión.**

4. Those kids think that money grows on trees. **Esos muchachos creen
   que el dinero se encuentra debajo de las (nubes / flores / piedras)**
   _____ **.**

5. For my niece's fifteenth birthday, my sister blew the works.
   **En los quince años de mi sobrina, mi hermana tiró la casa por
   la (tierra / chimenea / ventana)** _____ **.**

6. Our project is going great guns. **Nuestro proyecto anda sobre
   (caminos / ruedas / maravillas)** _____ **.**

7. In Spain to tell someone you got the deal done really fast, you can say **Llegué y besé (la piedra / el billete / el santo)** _____.

8. My grandfather pulled himself up by his bootstraps. **Mi abuelo salió adelante a puro (tren / pulmón / zapato)** _____.

9. Those are occupational hazards. **Esos son los gajes del (producto / esfuerzo / oficio)** _____.

10. I'm going to finish the report tonight come hell or high water. **Voy a terminar el informe esta noche aunque (llueva / truene / queme)** _____ **o relampaguée.**

B. Pick a letter! *Choose the letter of the word or phrase that best completes each sentence. Write it in the blank.*

11. _____ The boss is a difficult person, and you have to humor him.
El jefe es una persona difícil y tienes que seguirle
a. **el sentimiento.**
b. **la sonrisa.**
c. **la intuición.**
d. **la corriente.**

12. _____ In Mexico, a guy who is in your company through connections and doesn't do any work is called
a. **un mecánico.**
b. **una girafa.**
c. **un aviador.**
d. **una calabaza.**

13. _____ Yesterday all the employees were twiddling their thumbs.
Ayer todos los empleados estaban allí con los brazos
a. **cruzados.**
b. **doblados.**
c. **en el aire.**
d. **en la mesa.**

14. _____ Prices are sky high. **Los precios están por**
a. **las calles.**
b. **las nubes.**
c. **los rieles.**
d. **los suelos.**

15. _____ A common way to refer to money in Latin America is **la plata**.
In Mexico, Central America, Cuba, and Peru, they also call it
   a. **el metal.**
   b. **la madera.**
   c. **el cristal.**
   d. **la lana.**

16. _____ In Mexico and El Salvador, to say that something is "in the bag"
or "a done deal," they say: **Ese _____ ya se coció.**
   a. **arroz**
   b. **plato**
   c. **cordero**
   d. **guiso**

17. _____ In Spain and Florida, **un emilio** is
   a. an illegal worker.
   b. an E-mail.
   c. a new job.
   d. an old client.

18. _____ In Spain if someone asks you, **¿En qué curras?**, you should
tell that person about your
   a. home.
   b. family.
   c. work.
   d. hobbies.

19. _____ One common slang verb for "to work" in many parts of Latin
America is **chambear**. Another one is
   a. **camellar.**
   b. **caballar.**
   c. **vaquear.**
   d. **perrear.**

20. _____ In many parts of Latin America people may describe someone
as **un vago** or **una vaga**. This means he or she is
   a. a traveler.
   b. a slacker.
   c. bossy.
   d. nosy.

work, effort

a medio palo (to the half stick) half done; inconclusive, up in the air ◀ Hond, Nic, CR, DR, Col ▶

el bisnes business (from English) ◀ ES, Nic, Sp ▶

calentar el asiento (to warm the seat) to be a short time in a job (usually in the negative) ◀ Mex, ES, U, Arg, Sp ▶
No calenté el asiento allí. (Sp) I didn't last long there.
Pablo no duró mucho en ese trabajo; sólo llegó a calentar el asiento. (ES) Pablo didn't last long in that job; he just barely warmed the seat.

la caña (cane) effort, intensity (with **darle** or **meterle**) ◀ Sp ▶
Luis le estuvo dando caña a su padre todo el día para que le comprara un coche. Al final su padre se enfadó. Luis was laying it on with his dad all day so his dad would buy him a car. Finally, his dad got angry.

colgarse (to hang, be suspended) to be behind in your work, with more work than time to do it ◀ Mex, Col ▶

el/la currante worker ◀ Sp ▶
Sólo soy un currante; díselo a mi jefe. I'm just a worker; tell (it to) my boss.

El que quiere celeste que le cueste. (Whoever wants baby blue, it will cost him.) If you want a good life, you have to work for it. There's no free lunch. No bees, no honey; no work, no money. ◀ ES, Nic, S. Cone ▶

¿En qué la giras? (In what do you spin [it]?) What do you do for a living? ◀ Mex, Col ▶

los gajes del oficio (matters of the trade) part and parcel of the job, occupational hazards ◀ Mex, ES, Nic, DR, S. Cone, Sp ▶

el laburante worker ◀ Arg ▶
Todos en esa fábrica son muy buenos laburantes. They're all good workers in that factory.

lo que ve la suegra (what the mother-in-law sees) superficial part of house to be cleaned (Ch: **mira** instead of **ve**) ◀ Mex, U, Arg, Ch, Sp ▶

los percances del oficio (chances of the trade) part and parcel of the job, occupational hazards ◀ ES, Nic, Sp ▶

por aquí pasó mi suegra (my mother-in-law passed by here) expression telling that one is working hard, from the idea of cleaning up; «**sólo por donde pasa la suegra**» (just where the mother-in-law will pass by or see things) ◀ Mex, Col ▶

los ratos perdidos (lost times) times when you do not have any obligatory thing to do and so do other chores or tasks, as opposed to **ratos libres**, free time ◀ Mex, Sp ▶

el ridículum vitae ironic for CV, curriculum vitae ◀ Mex, ES, DR, Col ▶

el sastre de campillo, que cosía de balde y ponía el hilo (the country tailor who sewed for free and paid for the thread) said of someone who works for free and suffers a cost ◀ Sp ▶

Se le da como curros. (It gives it to him or her like jobs.) He or she is very hardworking. ◀ Sp ▶

tomar sobre sí una cosa to take something upon oneself ◀ Sp ▶

el/la trabajólico(-a) workaholic, someone who works too hard or is addicted to work ◀ parts of L. Am. ▶

at any cost, come hell or high water

a rajatabla (to board breaking) at any cost, fanatical, strictly ◀ L. Am., Sp ▶
Es vegetariano a rajatabla. He's a strict vegetarian.
El plan saldrá bien si siguen las normas a rajatabla. The plan will turn out well if they follow the rules no matter what.

aunque truene y relampaguée (even if it thunders and lightnings) no matter what, come hell or high water ◀ Mex, ES, S. Cone ▶

contra viento y marea (against wind and tides) come what may, come hell or high water ◄ L. Am., Sp ►

Voy a luchar contra viento y marea para conseguir el papel en la película. I'm going to struggle to get the role in the film come hell or high water.

cueste lo que cueste (cost whatever it may cost) come what may, no matter what ◄ L. Am., Sp ►

mal que bien (badly as good, well) in any possible way, no matter what ◄ Mex, ES, DR, Peru, Sp ►

pese a quien pese at whatever cost, no matter what ◄ L. Am., Sp ►

doing the dirty work

cargar con el mochuelo (to carry the dirty work) to do the dirty work, get the job no one else wants (Sp, Ch: also, **cargar con el muerto,** carry the dead person) ◄ Mex, U, Arg, Sp ►

dar a alguien un hueso que roer (to give someone a bone to gnaw at) to give someone a task that is not very pleasant or useful ◄ Mex, Sp ►

pringar (to dip or soak in grease; to stab) to work more than others or do the most disagreeable tasks, be a pushover (vulgar) ◄ Sp ►

En esa empresa sólo hay uno que pringa. In that company there's only one person who works like a dog.

drudge

el/la chupatintas (ink sucker) paperpusher, drudge ◄ Mex, Ch, Sp ►

el/la goma (glue) lowest-paid person in an office who runs all the errands, gopher, step-and-fetch-it ◄ Ch ►

Soy el goma especialista en procesamiento digital de imágenes. I'm the drudge who specializes in digital image processing.

el/la pringado(-a) (soaked in grease) someone who is overworked or who always gets stuck with everything ◄ Sp ►

Es una pringada. Siempre trabaja los domingos y no se queja. She's a drudge. She always works on Sundays and doesn't complain.

putting out effort

bailar de coronilla (to dance on one's head) to do something very diligently, work hard ◄ L. Am., Sp ►

dar el callo (to give callus) to work hard ◄ Sp ►

darle (duro) (to give to it [hard]) to apply oneself, give it one's all ◄ Mex, C. Am., DR, S. Cone ►

¿Cómo te va? —Aquí, dándole (dándole duro). How's it going? —I'm here, at it.
¡Dale duro! Go for it! Give it all you've got!

doblar el lomo (to fold or bend the back) to do heavy work ◄ Mex, DR, PR, Col, U, Arg ►

echar huevos a un asunto, echarle huevos (to throw eggs or testicles to an issue) to throw oneself into something, applying energy or force, do something decisively or bravely (Ven: **echarle bolas;** Sp: **echarle pelotas;** Mex, Sp: **echarle cojones**) (vulgar) ◄ Mex, C. Am., Sp ►

Le vamos a echar huevos a este trabajo para salir temprano. We're going to really hustle and work hard so we can leave early.

echar la mula (to throw the mule) to work hard and fast to get ahead ◄ CR, Col ►

guapear to strive, try to get something ◄ Cuba ►

hacer la cacha (to make the effort) to do everything possible (to obtain something); to try or struggle for ◄ G, ES ►

hacer mil maromas para... (to do a thousand acrobatic tricks in order to . . .) to go to a lot of trouble to . . . ◄ most of L. Am., Sp ►

matarse por una cosa to kill oneself for something (figuratively) ◄ L. Am., Sp ►

meterle candela (to put a candle to it) to put some effort into it, get down to business ◄ Nic ►

Métele candela a ese trabajo y termina pronto. Get a move on with that work and finish it quickly.

Hay que meter candela para eso. ¡Es importante! You (We, They) have to get going on that. It's important!

montarse el rollo to use one's wits or find a way to get something ◀ Sp ▶

partir el brazo a alguien (to break someone's arm) to take advantage of the opportunity (to get something) ◀ Cuba ▶

partirse los cojones (to break one's testicles) to work very hard, work one's tail off (vulgar) ◀ Sp ▶

pegar (to glue or stick) to work ◀ Cuba ▶

pelar el ajo (to peel the garlic) to work like a dog ◀ Ch ▶

penquearse (to male organ oneself) to really put effort into something, hustle, push oneself (slightly vulgar) ◀ Nic ▶

poner el hombro (to put the shoulder) to get down to work, put one's shoulder to the wheel ◀ S. Cone ▶

ponerse las pilas (to put in one's batteries) to get with it, get going ◀ L. Am., Sp ▶
Pongámonos las pilas. Ya es tarde. Let's get moving. It's late.

rebuscarse (to relook for oneself) to hustle to get (e.g., work or money), get with it ◀ ES, Pan, U ▶
Mi marido se quedó sin trabajo y esta semana tiene que rebuscarse. My husband found himself without work and this week he has to hustle (to find work).

romperse los cuernos (to break the horns) to work very hard ◀ U, Sp ▶

soplar la tuba (to blow on the tuba) to put up with (something), work hard ◀ Nic ▶

sudar la gota gorda (to sweat the fat drop) to sweat bullets, sweat it out ◀ L. Am., Sp ▶
Yo aquí sudando la gota gorda y ella no hace nada. I'm here sweating it out and she isn't doing anything.

with effort, by force

a la brava by force, against one's will (like **a la fuerza**) ◀ chicano, Mex, ES, CR, DR, PR, Col, Sp ▶

Terminé el trabajo, pero lo hice a la brava. I finished the work, but I did it because I had to (not wanting to).
¡Qué tipo tan mal educado! Se metió en la fila a la brava. What a rude guy! He forced himself in line in front of everyone.

a brazo partido (to a broken arm) to the limit (describing how hard someone is working) ◀ L. Am., Sp ▶
Trabajamos todo el día a brazo partido. We worked all day to the max.

a la cañona by force ◀ Nic, DR, PR ▶
Tú no puedes conseguir que te hagan ese favor a la cañona. Mejor habla con ellos. You can't force them to do you that favor (get them to do you that favor by force). Talk to them instead.

a chaleco (at vest) by force, against one's will ◀ Mex ▶
Tenía que pasar el examen a chaleco. I had to pass the test no matter what.

a contrapelo (against the natural direction, the way the hair or fur grows) against one's will or against the norm ◀ DR, Ch, U, Sp ▶

a duras penas (at hard pains) with great difficulty ◀ Mex, DR, PR, S. Cone, Sp ▶
Luis pagó sus deudas a duras penas, pues no tiene trabajo desde hace tres meses. Luis paid his debts with great difficulty since he hasn't had any work for three months.

a empujones (at pushes) by (a) force (from outside) ◀ Mex, S. Cone ▶
La gente fue sacada a empujones. People were taken out forcibly.
Diego terminó su tesis a empujones. Diego finished his thesis because he had to (he was pushed to do it).

a (puro) huevo (at [pure] egg, testicle) with a lot of effort (vulgar); also, **a huevos** ◀ Mex, C. Am. ▶
Julia no quería ir, pero la hice ir a puro huevo. Julia didn't want to go, but I forced her to go (made her go by force).

a jalones y estirones (at pulls and stretches) with delays and difficulties, great effort ◀ Mex ▶
A jalones y estirones la llevé a misa. I took her to mass kicking and screaming.

a malas penas with great difficulty or effort ◀ Sp ▶

a (pura) penca (at pure male organ) by pure force of will (vulgar) ◀ Nic ▶
Marta era de una familia pobre y logró hacerse abogada a pura penca. Marta was from a poor family and managed to become a lawyer by pure force of will.

a puro pulmón (at pure lung) by working as hard as possible ◀ L. Am., Sp ▶
Lo hice a puro pulmón. I did it by sheer force of will.

a rastras forced, obligated ◀ Mex, Sp ▶

a trancas y barrancas (at beams and ravines/cliffs) passing over all obstacles ◀ Mex, Sp ▶

a tropezones (with trips, falling down) with delays and difficulties ◀ Mex, DR, Sp ▶
Miguelito lee a tropezones. Miguelito reads haltingly.

por pelotas (cojones) (by balls) by force; just because of a whim (vulgar) ◀ Sp ▶
Tuvo que hacerlo por pelotas. He (She) had to do it no matter what.

work, job

el ajetreo a lot of work; also, **ajetrear** ◀ Mex, ES, U, Arg ▶
Ay, ¡qué ajetreo! Ya vienen los invitados y no tengo la comida lista. Oh, what a lot of work! The guests are already arriving and I don't have the food ready.

el camello (camel) work, job ◀ Mex, ES, Col, Ec ▶
Ese camello me parece aburrido. That job sounds boring to me.

la chamba work ◀ Mex, C. Am., Col, Ven, Ec, Peru ▶

el chance work ◀ Mex, G ▶

las changas (female monkeys) odd jobs (different small jobs) ◀ U, Arg ▶
Juan no tiene trabajo fijo. Hace changas. Juan doesn't have steady work. He does odd jobs.

el curralo work ◀ Cuba ▶

el curro work ◀ Sp ▶

hacer algunas chapuzas to be working at odd jobs ◀ Sp ▶

¿Tienes trabajo? —Hago algunas chapuzas. Do you have a job? —I'm doing some odd jobs.

el hueso (bone) patronage job (for family or friends) ◀ Mex, ES ▶
Miriam tiene un puesto en el gobierno. Mordió un buen hueso allí. Miriam has a job in the government. She got a good deal (literally, bit a good bone) there.
No quiere soltar ese hueso. He (She) doesn't want to let go of that job.

el laburo work ◀ Bol, Para, U, Arg ▶
Este hijo mío me da un laburo tremendo. This son of mine gives me a lot of work.

el martilleo (hammering) work ◀ Mex, Col ▶

el miqueo very easy job (for a particular person), snap, breeze ◀ PR ▶
¡Este trabajo es un miqueo! This job is a breeze!

la pega (gluing) job, work ◀ Cuba, Ch ▶

el tajo short for **trabajo**, work ◀ Sp ▶

tener un guiso (to have a stew) to have a job on the side ◀ PR ▶

el trajín work, things to do ◀ L. Am., Sp ▶
¡Pobre Miriam! Vaya trajín se trae con la boda de su hija. (Sp) Poor Miriam! What a lot of work her daughter's wedding is giving her.
Con tanto trajín, no he tenido tiempo de llamar a mis amigos. With so much work, I haven't had time to call my friends.

working

camellar (to camel) to work (Col: also, to go out with friends) ◀ Mex, ES, Nic, CR, Col, Ec ▶

chambear (chambiar) to work ◀ Mex, C. Am., Col, Ven, Ec, Peru ▶
No puedo ir a la playa; tengo que chambear. I can't go to the beach; I have to work.

curralar to work ◀ Cuba ▶

currar to work ◀ Sp ▶
¿En qué curras? What kind of work do you do?

laburar to work ◀ Para, U, Arg ▶

martillar (to hammer) to work ◀ Mex, Col ▶
¿Qué tal, 'mano? —Por aquí, martillando. What's up, bro'? —I'm just here working.

Say it with slang!

Something's fishy.

¡Ponte trucha! (Become a trout!, meaning Look sharp!) Someone might give you this advice in Mexico or El Salvador if it seems that you need to be more alert to what's going on. Names of fish can mean different things in different places. A **bacalao** (codfish) is a pleasant, agreeable person in Colombia, but it means someone very skinny in Puerto Rico, Uruguay, and parts of Florida. A **piraña** in Mexico is a big eater, but in Costa Rica, El Salvador, or Colombia it means someone who has aggressive business practices. With that kind of business dealing, you would have to be careful not to **tragarte el anzuelo** (swallow the hook, meaning fall for a scam), especially if you want some day to become **un pez gordo** (a fat fish, meaning a bigshot); these two expressions are used almost everywhere in the Spanish-speaking world. On the other hand, you may prefer to say, as they do in some parts of Latin America, **¡Me río de los peces de colores!** (I laugh at colorful fish!—that is, I don't worry about anything!)

---

trabajar como burro (to work like a donkey) to work hard, work like a dog ◀ L. Am., Sp ▶

trabajar como enano (to work like a dwarf) to work very hard, work like the devil ◀ Ch, Sp ▶
Emilio trabaja como un enano. No para ni un segundo. Emilio works like the devil. He doesn't stop even for a second.

voltiar (from **voltear**, to turn) to work a lot ◀ Col ▶
Me tuvieron voltiando. They had me spinning (working hard).
Voltié todo el día. I worked hard all day.

worry

See also "difficulty," "problems."

coger lucha (to take fight) to worry excessively ◀ Cuba, DR ▶

Yo no voy a coger lucha. Si ella no quiere ir, que se quede. I'm not going to sweat it. If she doesn't want to go, she can stay.

¿(A)dónde vamos a parar? (Where are we going to end up?) phrase expressing worry about unforeseen developments ◀ Mex, ES, DR, S. Cone, Sp ▶
¿Qué vamos a hacer con esta crisis? ¿Adónde vamos a parar? What are we going to do with this crisis? Where are we going to end up?

estar más serio(-a) que un burro en lancha (to be more serious than a donkey in a rowboat) to look worried ◀ CR ▶

ir pisa'o(-a) (to go stepped on) to be under pressure ◀ DR ▶
Voy pisa'o en la escuela; tengo clases muy difíciles este año. I'm under a lot of pressure at school; I have very difficult classes this year.

no caber una cosa en el pecho (a thing won't fit in one's chest) said when something is weighing on one's mind ◀ Mex, ES, DR, Sp ▶

poner a alguien los nervios de punta (to make someone's nerves stand up) to put someone's nerves on edge ◄ L. Am., Sp ►
El mensaje me puso los nervios de punta. The message put my nerves on edge.

tener un careto (to have a white-faced mask) to look bad because of worry or lack of sleep ◄ Sp ►

tomarse las cosas a la tremenda (to take things to the tremendous) to give things too much importance ◄ U, Arg, Sp ►
Suspender un examen no es tan grave; no te lo tomes a la tremenda. Failing a test is not so serious; don't take it so hard.

volverse un ocho (to become an eight) to worry, get nervous ◄ PR, Col ►

anxiety

el calambre (cramp) anxiety attack ◄ Mex, Col ►

el corazón en un puño (the heart in a fist) situation of anxiety or depression ◄ most of L. Am., Sp ►

las ñáñaras heebie-jeebies, nervousness, willies ◄ Mex, ES ►

la preocupabilidad worry about guilt (**preocupar** and **culpabilidad**) ◄ Mex, ES, Col ►

sweating the small stuff

ahogarse en un vaso de agua (to drown in a glass of water) to worry about something unimportant ◄ L. Am., Sp ►

el corazón en un puño

buscarle tres (cinco) pies al gato (to look for three [five] feet on the cat) to get involved in something that can be harmful; to look for solutions or reasons that make no sense; to sweat the small stuff (U, Ch: **buscarle la quinta pata al gato**) ◄ L. Am., Sp ►
¿Para qué buscarle tres pies al gato si tiene cuatro? Why sweat the small stuff? (Literally, Why look for three feet on the cat if it has four?)

reparar en migajas (pelillos) (to notice crumbs [small hairs]) to pay attention to unimportant things instead of the bigger issue, split hairs ◄ Sp ►

(no) verle pelos a la sopa (to [not] see hairs in the soup) to (not) look for problems ◄ Mex ►
No le veas pelos a la sopa; no seas tan delicado. Don't look for problems; don't be so fussy.

worried, nervous

acelerado(-a) (sped up) high on alcohol or drugs; nervous from caffeine ◄ Mex, G, PR, Col, Ch, Sp ►
Tomé tres cafés y ahora estoy acelerado. I had three coffees and now I'm jittery.

como cocodrilo en fábrica de carteras (like a crocodile in a wallet factory) nervous ◄ PR ►
Tengo una entrevista de trabajo y me siento como cocodrilo en fábrica de carteras. I have a job interview and I feel really uptight.

como perro en canoa (like a dog in a canoe) nervous (U: **como perro en bote**) ◄ PR ►

estar como energúmeno (to be like one possessed) to be hysterical ◄ Mex, ES ►

estar con (tener) el alma en un hilo (to be with [have] the soul in a thread) to be very upset because of problems or danger; be nervous as a cat ◄ L. Am. ►
¿Qué pasa, Verónica? —Estoy con el alma en un hilo. Mi hijo está en el hospital. What's wrong, Verónica? —I'm a bundle of nerves. My son is in the hospital.

estar en ascuas (to be on embers) to be on edge, on pins and needles, anxiously awaiting something ◀ Mex, ES, Nic, S. Cone, Sp ▶
Estaba en ascuas hasta que me dieron la noticia. I was on pins and needles until they gave me the news.

friqueado(-a) (from English "freaked out") upset, freaked out ◀ Mex, DR, PR, Ven ▶

ponerse de los nervios (to become of the nerves) to get nervous ◀ ES, Sp ▶
Me puse de los nervios cuando vi que aún no había llegado a casa. I got nervous when I saw that he (she) had still not gotten home.

tener los nervios de punta (to have one's nerves standing) to have one's nerves on edge ◀ L. Am., Sp ▶

tener (andar con) cables pelados (to have or go around with frayed wires) to be nervous, on edge, strung out (ES: also, **tener los alambres pelados**) ◀ ES, Nic, S. Cone ▶

Se le pelan los alambres (cables). Tiene los cables (alambres) pelados. (ES) He (She) is a nervous wreck.

youth

See also "age."

la chaviza young folk (opposite of **momiza**, fogies) ◀ Mex, Col ▶
la edad del pavo (turkey age) change to adolescence, puberty ◀ S. Cone, Sp ▶
estar en pañales (to be in diapers) to be young ◀ L. Am., Sp ▶
la flor de la vida (flower of life) the prime of life ◀ L. Am., Sp ▶
A tus veinticinco años, estás en la flor de la vida. With your twenty-five years, you're in the prime of life.

Answer Key

Test your slang power! Celebrations, parties, and having fun

A. 1. sacudida 2. esqueleto 3. barril 4. blanco 5. buen diente 6. botana
7. movida 8. anchas 9. muerta 10. pachanga

B. 11. b 12. a 13. b 14. d 15. c 16. d 17. c 18. c 19. d 20. a

Test your slang power! Feelings and emotions

A. 1. chocolate 2. ladra 3. vacilando 4. pelo 5. emocionados (**Excitados** is
a false cognate that means "sexually aroused.") 6. punta 7. agua 8. pozo 9. vaso
10. ascuas

B. 11. b 12. d 13. d 14. a 15. c 16. a 17. b 18. c 19. b 20. b

Test your slang power! Learning and education

A. 1. botica 2. vecino 3. pelos 4. un acordeón 5. un ratón 6. calabaza
7. al sol 8. caigo 9. clavo 10. chispa

B. 11. d 12. c 13. c 14. c 15. a 16. b 17. d 18. c 19. a 20. d

Test your slang power! Sex, love, and romance

A. 1. alcahuetean 2. comérselo 3. freno 4. del alma 5. carne 6. el arpa
7. media naranja 8. perros 9. cuernos 10. polvo

B. 11. c 12. b 13. d 14. c 15. a 16. c 17. b 18. c 19. c 20. d

Test your slang power! The working world

A. 1. son 2. gordo 3. voz 4. piedras 5. ventana 6. ruedas 7. el santo
8. pulmón 9. oficio 10. truene

B. 11. d 12. c 13. a 14. b 15. d 16. a 17. b 18. c 19. a 20. b

Say it with slang!

page 19
chasgracias (**muchas gracias**), thank you; **chogusto (mucho gusto**),
pleased to meet you; **cole (colega)**, colleague or friend; **depre (depresión)**,
depression; **profe (profesor)**, professor

page 115
What's up, cousin (**primo**)? How are you?
Great! I'm going to see my woman (**mujer**).
I'll go with you up to the store on the corner (**esquina**).

Spanish-English Dictionary/Index

Numbers cross-refer to entries in the main the-saurus, where further details on register and us-age (polite, vulgar, pejorative, and so on), region of use, example sentences, and related terms may be found.

Note: The following words are not alphabetized within an entry:

definite and indefinite articles: **el, la, un(a), unos(-as);**
the prepositions **a (al), de (del),** and **en;**
the adverb **como;**
the object pronouns **la, lo, se,** and **te;**
the possessive adjectives **mi, tu,** and **su;**
the negatives **no** and **ni;**
the interrogative **qué;** and
ser/estar and their conjugated forms.

A

abatatarse to get upset and make mistakes 86
abatato(-a) goofball, silly fool 86
abordar to make a pass (at someone) 200
abrir su corazón a alguien to open one's heart to someone 239
abrir una raya to leave abruptly 66
en un abrir y cerrar de ojos in a blink of the eyes 221
abrirse to leave, go off 66; to break up a relationship, business or social 113
¡Tu abuela! expression of anger 140
aburrirse como una ostra to be or get very bored 39
abusado(-a) sharp, clever 141
el/la abusador(-a) opportunist, mooch 203
¡Qué abusadora! street compliment 24
el/la abusivo(-a) someone who takes advantage of others, mooch 203
el abusón, la abusona someone who takes advantage of others, sponge 203
acabar to do in; to frustrate or confuse 123, 210

acalorado(-a) hotheaded, temperamental 11
el/la acartonado(-a) stiff, unsociable person; pretentious person 181
acasito here 72
como el aceite y el vinagre like oil and water, said of two people who don't get along 129
acelerado(-a) high on alcohol or drugs 79; fast (not waiting an appropriate time before pressing for sex) 213; nervous from caffeine 260
ser de acero to be tough, inflexible, strong 222
achacoso(-a) hypochondriac 126
el/la achanchado(-a) slacker, loafer, underachiever 147
achancharse to be lazy, slack off, loaf around 147
el/la achantado(-a) person with no ambition, loser, slacker 147
achantar to frighten 91; to quiet 191
achantarse to comply, be quiet about something 191
el achantazón lack of spirit, apathy 147
¡Achará! What a shame! 230
achatado(-a) humbled or put down by some embarrassment 82; mediocre, blah, lackluster 167
achicarse to get scared and back down, chicken out 91
achicopalarse to be sad, depressed 202
acho word used to introduce a request, short form of **muchacho** 196
estar achuchado(-a) to be scared stiff 92; to be cold, freezing (with chills) 251
achumicarse to become shy, chicken out 82
estar achunchado(-a) to be embarrassed, shy, timid 83
achuncharse to become shy, embarrassed, timid 82
achurar to speak badly of, rip apart 56
ácido(-a) disagreeable (person), sourpuss 31
ser un acojonado to be a coward, timid 92
estar acojonado(-a) to be afraid 92
acolitar to help 126

el/la acomodado(-a) person with an "in" with the boss, government, etc. 102

el acomodo connection in government, business, etc. 102; bribe 160

Lo (La/Le) acompaño en su dolor (en sus sentimientos). Te acompaño en tu dolor. Please accept my condolences. 230

el acordeón crib sheet 81

actualizado(-a) "with it" 111

Adelante con la cruz. Hang in there. Let's not give up. 84

afanado(-a) zealously, with enthusiasm 85; in a hurry 219

el/la afanador(a) person involved in illegal business, shady deals 62

afanar to rob or mug without violence 56

el afano total rip-off 161

afilar con to be fooling around sexually with, making passes at 210

aflojar to give up (on), back down, give in 65

aflojar el billete to loosen the purse strings 161

aflojar la bolsa to loosen the purse strings 162

aflojar la cuerda to take a breather, loosen up discipline 197

aflojar las riendas to loosen the reins, loosen up 24

aflojar la torta to give in and have sex (a woman) 210

el/la agachado(-a) person good at avoiding (weaseling out of) things 87; submissive person 196

agandallar to take over, snatch 203

agarrado(-a) stingy, tight-fisted 205

agarrar a alguien en la maturranga to catch someone in the act of having illicit sex 211

agarrar el avión to go on a (drug) trip 76

agarrar el hilo to get the point 143

agarrar la onda to "get it," get with it 143

no agarrar la onda to not "get it" or get with it 133

agarrar su patín to find your path (opportunity) in life 166

agarrar viaje to accept an invitation or proposal 142

agarrar viento en la camiseta to get carried away 85

agarrarle el lado flaco to use someone's weak point, soft spot 123

agarrarse to get ready for a shock or surprise, hang on 227

agarrarse una chinche to get very angry, blow a gasket 12

agarrarse a un clavo ardiendo to clutch at straws 186

agarrarse a los faldones de alguien to cling to someone's skirts, accept protection or help 102

agarrarse una rabieta to have a fit, tantrum 13

agitarse to get upset, worked up 17

el/la agrandado(-a) conceited, self-important, person with a big ego 181

agringado(-a) having become like a gringo 173

estar como agua para (pa') chocolate to be at the boiling point, because of either anger or passion 10, 213

Al agua, pato(s). Let's go to it. 84

¡Agua sucia! There's trouble! 247

como el agua y el aceite like oil and water, said of two people who don't get along 129

aguacate foolish, stupid 224

aguacatero(-a) old-fashioned 29

aguacatón, aguacatona bore, party pooper 38; stupid 224

la aguacatona shy woman without much spirit 82

aguacatudo(-a) foolish, stupid 224

aguado(-a) simple, with no charm 38; tired or weak 88

el aguafiestas party pooper 38

aguaitar, estar al aguaite to be on one's toes, watching out for something 20

aguantar el chaparrón to get through or wait out something difficult, take your medicine 169

aguantar el nublado (el nubarrón) to wait patiently until someone (usually a superior) is no longer angry, wait it out 169

no aguantar pulgas to not tolerate problems 32

¡Aguas! Watch out! 247

agüitado(-a) down, tired, low 88

agüitarse to be down, tired, low 88

Ahí muere. No way. Absolutely not, period. 163

ahí nomasito very near 72

Ahí nos vidrios. See you. 113

estar ahogado(-a) to be drunk 78

ahogarse el ratón to take a drink during a hangover 76

ahogarse en un vaso de agua to be incompetent 131; to worry about something unimportant 260

Ahora caigo. Now I get it. 143

ahorcarse to get married, like **echarse la soga al cuello** 199

ahorita right now 235; in a little while 236

el/la ahuevado(-a) dope 223

ahuevarse to be sad or feel put down 202

el ahuevazón boredom 38

ahueviar to steal 56

ahuevonado(-a) boneheaded, dumb 224

ajá uh-huh 6

el ajetreo a lot of work 258

estar en el ajo to be in the know 143

ajumarse to get drunk 78

el/la alborotado(-a) troublemaker 14

alborotar las avispas (el panal, el gallinero) to upset the apple cart, get people riled up 158

alburear to talk with double meaning, confuse in a teasing way 47

el/la alcahuete(-a) person who spoils or pampers someone 5

alcahuetear to give in or go along (with something) 5

¡Ale, ale! Hurry up! 220

estar alegre como unas castañuelas to be happy as a lark 120

algodón a vague or evasive answer 48

¡Allí está el detalle! That's the point! 8

mi alma darling, dear 5

como alma que lleva el diablo with great agitation or speed 220

la almohada behind, rear end 36

Aló. phrase for answering the phone 117

alocado(-a) crazy for action, unpredictable 53

la alternadora girl who acts as hostess at bars to be invited for drinks 99

alucinante impressive, awesome 109

alucinar to be surprised or impressed; to dislike 227

el/la alzado(-a) pretentious, arrogant person 181

alzado(-a) in heat, horny 213

alzar vuelo to leave, take off 66

alzarse con el santo y la limosna to take everything, one's own and others' 203

amarrado(-a) married 199

amarrarse el cinturón to tighten one's belt (economically) 160

amarrarse los pantalones to make one's authority felt 25

el amarrete miser, stingy person 205

a la americana dutch treat 142

armarse una de todos los diablos to have a devil of a mess 159

¡Amigo! used to get a stranger's attention 20

los amigos (las amigas) del alma bosom buddies 101

No te amilanes. Don't be afraid. Don't back down. 91

amolado(-a) worn to a frazzle, ruined, exhausted 88

mi amor my love 5

mi amorciano my darling, my love 5

mi amorcito sweetheart 5

estar amormado(-a) to be sleepy 218

¡Qué amoroso(-a)! How sweet! How charmingly cute! 108

los amos del cotarro the people in charge, the ones with the power 25

amoscado(-a) irritated 13

amuermar to bore, put to sleep 38

añales many years 236

analfabestia lowlife, ignorant and proud of it 34

anárquico(-a) disorganized 158

¡Anda la hostia (leche, osa, puta)! expressions of surprise 228

las andadas old habits, tricks 28

¡Ándale! (¡Ándate!) Right! That's it! 8

Andando. Hurry up. 220

andar bien burro to be very drunk, smashed 77

andar de boca en boca to travel by word of mouth, be common knowledge 114

andar como bola sin manija to be going around in circles, any which way 39

andar de buenas pulgas to be in a good mood 108

andar cacheteando la banqueta to be drunk 78

andar con cables pelados to be nervous, on edge, strung out 261

andar con el diente largo to be dying of hunger 99

andar con el gorila to be drunk 78

andar con las hilachas colgando to be dressed in rags 74

andar con la mona to be drunk 79

andar con ojo to be always cautious and suspicious 20

andar en Dodge to walk 238

andar de farra to go out on the town 106

andar haciendo eses to be drunk 78

andar de maleta to be in a bad mood 28

andar mosca to be upset, annoyed 17

andar de novios to be engaged; to go steady 199

andar a palos to be at blows, always fighting 69

andar a patadas con los piojos to live from hand to mouth 249

andar como Pedro/Juan por su casa to feel or make oneself at home 188

andar como perro y gato to be enemies 129

andar por las ramas to beat around the bush 49

andar quebrado(-a) to be broke 248

andar sobre ruedas to be going smoothly, great 226

andar tras sus huesos to be on the prowl, out to get (a lover) 200

andar al tres y al cuatro to get by on a shoestring 249

arrojar la toalla to throw in the towel, give up 66
arrollado(-a) going without sex 212
arrollar los petates to leave, move 66
ser como arroz blanco to be everywhere 101
arrugarse to accept or put up with something 197
arruinar el estofado to ruin the plan, mess up the works 125
ser el as de la baraja to make oneself scarce 68
el asaltacunas cradle robber 198
ser un asco to be disgusting; to be worthless 154
estar en ascuas to be on pins and needles 261
estar asfixiado(-a) to be in love 200; to be broke 248
así como así just like that 219
Así me (te, nos) luce el pelo. phrase meaning that one is wasting time or not taking advantage of an opportunity 56
¡Así se hace! Way to go! That's the way to do it! 84
asomarse to show up 19
asombroso(-a) awesome 109
en las astas del toro in a dangerous position, in the lurch 185
Está el asunto feo. It's awful. 27
asustado(-a) half-cooked or -baked 96
asustón, asustona easily frightened, scaredy-cat 92
Atácame un pulmón. Give me a cigarette (or joint). 237
atacarse to begin to cry 203
el atado thorny problem or situation 186
el ataque de caspa fit, tantrum 13
atenido(-a) lazy, letting others do things 147
Atente a pan y no comas queso. Be content with one thing and don't wish for something else. 196
el atolladero mess, quagmire, bad situation 186
el/la atorrante tramp, bum 249
atracar to overcharge, take advantage of someone money-wise 63
estar atrás to be behind (in work, payments, etc.) 235
ser un atraso a la cultura to be old-fashioned, out of date 29
atravesado(-a) crazy 53
no atreverse a decir «esta boca es mía» to not dare open one's mouth 92
aunque truene y relampaguée no matter what, come hell or high water 255
¡Aupa! Go! (e.g., at a sports event) 84

¡Ave María! expression of surprise or other emotion 228
en una avemaría in an instant 221
aventado(-a) thrown into a course of action, risking oneself; (n.) risk taker 52
aventarse to take risks 52
la aventura love affair 198
el/la aviador(-a) said of someone who is paid for a job but doesn't really work 130
avispado(-a) alert, smart, clever 141
el ay de mí real worry, thorn in the flesh 186
¡Ay, bendito! Bless my soul!, expression of sympathy 230
estar en ayunas to be in the dark, unaware 145
el azote del barrio neighborhood troublemaker 54
No te azotes, que hay chayotes. Buck up! It's not that bad. 84
azurumbado(-a) confused 46

B

la babosada stupidity 225
baboso(-a) foolish, stupid 224
el bacalao lazy person 147; very skinny person, string bean 178
ser un bacalao to be an agreeable person 112
bacán super, great 109
el bacán shallow glamour boy, jerk (who has money) 32; successful player, achiever 226
bacano(-a) good, excellent, generous 109
la bachata party 168
bachatear to relax, joke around 106
el bache disappointment, obstacle (to success) 186
ser una bacteria en el horizonte to be of no consequence 138
el bagayo bum, homeless man 249
bailar a alguien to deceive someone 63
bailar al son que le tocan to go along with or do as others 7
bailar de coronilla to put out a lot of effort, work hard 256
bailar en la cuerda floja to try to do many things at once; to be in a difficult situation 39
el bailongo dance, dancing party 168
el bailorio party, dance 168
bajado(-a) del cielo perfect, excellent 109
Bájale. Don't exaggerate. Come off it. 58
Bájale de crema a tus tacos. Get off it! 58
Bájale de huevos a tu licuado. Get off it! 58
bajar la caña to charge an excessive price, rip off 63
bajar el moño to give in, concede 66

bajar un número to give (someone) bad news; to ask for something difficult to give 17

bajar las orejas to give in (during a dispute) 66

bajar a todos los santos to try everything in times of trouble 187

bajar el volumen to take it easy, cool down 146

bajarle el copete to take down a peg 58

bajarle los humos to take down a peg 58

bajarle el moño to take down a peg 58

bajarse del burro to back down 66

bajarse de la mula to give something in exchange for a favor, pay up 162

bajarse los humos to become disillusioned, lose hope or interest 202

bajo la cuerda under the table, through hidden means, on the sly 65

el bajón bad feeling, downer, bummer 202

el bajón de baterías arrival of bad news 165

bajoneado(-a) down and depressed 202

la bala cigar 237

balconear a alguien to embarrass someone in front of others 83

balconearse to strut one's stuff 35

de balde free of charge 161

en balde in vain 244

la ballena very corpulent person 178

balurde picky, fussy, uptight 32

balurdo(-a) weird, far-out, tacky 29

bambalán, bambalana foolish, stupid 224

a bañarse: mandar a alguien... to tell someone to get lost 139

no bancar to dislike 152

bancar(se) to cope or put up with; to bankroll, support financially 197

estar de bandera to be attractive 23

el/la baquiano(-a) neighborhood person, local yokel 173

barajar to explain, run (it) by again 48

barajárselas to keep trying (to solve a problem, for instance) 169

las baratijas baubles, trifles 232

ser un barbaján to be coarse, rude, a dope 34

el barbarazo Don Juan; someone who goes after someone else's woman 214

la barbaridad large amount 189

¡Qué barbaridad! Good grief! 16, 229

bárbaro(-a) abnormal, unusual, exceptional; badly done 241

¡Qué bárbaro! Good grief! 16, 229

barbero(-a) sucking up 96

el barco, el barcazo pushover 247

la barra group of friends 103

la barrabasada scandalous mistake 87

barrer con to take away from (someone) 198

barrigón, barrigona potbellied; pregnant 36

de barril draft (beer) 98

el barullo noisy fuss or mess, uproar 157

la basca, basquilla group of friends 103

basto(-a) raunchy, tacky, vulgar 29; selfish 203

el batacazo bad blow; bruise 121

la bataclana vulgar-looking woman wearing scanty or cheap-looking clothing, floozie 212

el/la batata loser, idiot 223

batear to fail, flunk 89; to eat a lot 99

el bato guy, dude 118

el bato loco crazy dude 53

el bayú party, get-together 168

la bayuncada remark out of context; antic 107

bayunco(-a) mischievous, with antics 226

el bazuquero drunkard 76

beber como una esponja to drink like a sponge 76

el bembé party 168

bendito(-a) "blessed," sometimes used ironically for the opposite 26

el berenjenal mess, disorder, fix 157

berreta cheap, low quality 29

el berro anger, bad temper 8

besar con la lengua to French-kiss 4

el beso de lengua French kiss 4

Lo (La) besó el diablo. He or she fell down, tripped. 121

besos y abrazos hugs and kisses (common ending for a letter to a friend) 4

los besotes smooches 4

ser bestia to be rude, a boor, ill-mannered 34

bestial great, tremendous, exaggerated (good or bad) 241

besuquearse to smooch 4

el besuqueo smooching, repeated kissing 4

la biblia en verso huge amount 189

el/la bicho(-a) kid 119

ser un bicho raro to be an oddball 242

¿Qué bicho te ha picado? What's bothering you? 14

la bici bicycle 239

el/la bienudo(-a) young person from a well-off family 249

el billullo lots of money 162

la birra beer 97

el/la birriondo(-a) dirty old man (woman) 210

el bisnes business 255

el bizcocho sexy, hot, good-looking person, usually woman 23; female organ 212

estar en blanco to have not eaten 96; to draw a blank, be unable to respond 133

el/la blandengue softie 247

el/la blanquito(-a) person with money, high society 249
bobo(-a) silly 226
el/la bobolóngolo(-a) fool 223
En boca cerrada no entran moscas. Talking can get you into trouble. Loose lips sink ships. 192
bocachón, bocachona with a big mouth, blabbermouth 114
ser un bocazas to be a blabbermouth 115
bochar to flunk 89
el bochinche (buchinche) noisy dispute; fuss 70
bochinchero(-a), bochinchoso(-a) argumentative, troublemaker; party animal 70
el bocón, la bocona big mouth, gossip 114
el bodrio stupid, boring thing or person 26
bofe unsociable, unlikeable, unpleasant 31
la bola gossip, rumor 115
¡De bola! Absolutely! Agreed! 8
¿Qué bolá? What's up? 117
en bolas naked 163
las bolas balls; testicles 214
boleado(-a) half crazy, flaky 53
de boleto on the fly, fast or while doing something else 220
el boli pen 232
el boliche nightclub for dancing; dive 105
el/la bolillo(-a) anglo 177; dumbbell, fool 223
el bollo female organ 212
estar bolo(-a) to be drunk 78
el/la bolsa dope, empty-headed person 223
bolsear to steal, pick pockets 56; to mooch, freeload 203
el/la boludo(-a) lazy dope, stupid jerk, deadhead 223
la bomba heart 35
estar (ser una) bomba to be very attractive 24
la bomba, el bombazo surprising piece of news, news flash 165
a bombo y platillo with a lot of fanfare 180
¡Qué bombón y yo con diabetes! street compliment 24
mi bomboncito my darling, love 6
el bonche party, celebration; mess or disorder 168; bunch, group 189
el bonitillo handsome boy; man who thinks he's good-looking 23
boquiabierto(-a) amazed, flabbergasted 227
el/la boquisabroso(-a) gourmand 96
las boquitas appetizers 100
borde stupid, ill-mannered 224
borrar to kill, wipe out 55
borrar a algo (alguien) del mapa to forget about something (someone) 100

borrarse, borrarse del mapa to leave or disappear, take off 66
el bostezo bore 38
la botana appetizers 100
botar la bola (pelota), botarla to do or say something extraordinary or ridiculous 242
botar la canica (la bola) to go crazy 54
botarse to outdo oneself; to have something special 45; to reveal one's true self 61
estar en el bote to be in jail 55
la botella what is memorized 80
botella someone who doesn't do anything 244
el botero large or robust person 178
¡Botones para los preguntones! Don't ask so many questions! 58
el boyo punch, hit 122
a la brava sloppily; using force 131; by force, against one's will 257
bravo(-a) angry 9
a brazo partido to the limit 257
el brete love affair 198
la breva cigar 237
el/la briago(-a) drunkard 76
brillar por su ausencia to be conspicuous by one's (its) absence 20
el brillar-hebilla close dancing with rhythmic movements (cheek to cheek) 59
brindar por las otras (cervezas que vienen) to toast the others (the other beers to come) 99
bróder (bródel) friend, pal 103
ser de bronce to be tough, inflexible, strong 222
el/la broncudo(-a) someone who gets in fights 70
bronquear to fight, fuss, argue 70
bronquearse to get angry or upset, argue, fight 70
el/la bronquinoso(-a) someone who gets in fights 70
brotar como callampas (hongos) to grow like mad 219
bruto(-a) stupid; rude 224
el buay guy 118
ser un buen partido to be a good match (for marriage) 199
¡Buen viaje! Good riddance! 113
a la buena de Dios at random, without a plan, without preparation 73
en buena forma in (good) shape 126
de buena gana gladly 152
buena gente nice, kind person or people 112
buena nota all right, good, great, cool 109
buena onda good deal, thing, idea 108
la buena portada honra la casa expression used to mean that large mouths are OK 35

el cachimbal bunch of things or people together 190

el cachimbazo blow, hit 122

ser cachimbón, cachimbona to be good at everything, competent 44

el cachito little bit 189

estar como un cachivache to be useless 244

los cachivaches junk, things of little value 232

cachondear to make out, indulge in foreplay 214

cachondearse (de alguien) to make fun of or tease (someone) 83

el cachondeo petting, foreplay 214

ser cachondo(-a) to be amusing, funny 105

estar cachondo(-a) to be horny, sexually excited, hot 213

ser un cachondo mental to be happy, agreeable, funny 120, 213; to be obsessed with sex 213

el/la cachorro(-a) kid 119

cachudo(-a) in poor taste 29

estar cachudo(-a) to be obsessed (with something) 234

el cachureo odds and ends, junk 232

cada hijo de vecino any person 46

Cada loco con su tema. There you go again! Same old thing! 234

cada muerte de un obispo once in a blue moon 101

cada nada constantly 101

Cada oveja con su pareja. Everyone with a partner. 198

Cada quien se rasque con sus propias uñas. Everyone for himself or herself, being without support. 133

a cada rato frequently 101

el/la ca'e pija (cara de pija) dickface, dope 139

el/la ca'e verga (cara de verga) dickface, dope 139

Se caen los patos asados. It's a scorcher. 251

caer to visit 19

estar al caer to be about to arrive 20

caer como bomba to fall like a bomb(shell); to arrive as a surprise, generally unpleasant 227

caer de cajón to go without saying, be obvious 239

caer un chinchín to sprinkle (rain) 251

caer en el chiste to figure out, wise up 143

caer con to pay up, fork up 162

caer en la cuenta to become aware of something, "get it" 143

caer como un gil (como un angelito) to be taken in, tricked, duped 137

caer de madre to be looked down upon 120

caer parado(-a) to land on one's feet, emerge unscathed 156

caer en la trampa (en la red) to fall into the trap 137

caer el veinte to "get it," understand 143

caerle (como una) bala to be a pain, disgusting to 152

caerle bien (mal) una persona to be likeable (not likeable) 152

caerle en el hígado (en los huevos) to be intolerable, distasteful to 152

caerle de la patada (pedrada) to be a pain, disgusting to, used like **gustar** 152

caerle como piedra (plomo) to be a pain, disgusting to 152

caerse to make a mistake 86

caerse en el amor propio euphemism for to fall on one's behind 36

caerse el casete to have a secret revealed 136

caerse con todo el equipo to fail totally 89

caerse de la mata to figure out, wise up 143

caerse del mecate to figure out, wise up 143

caerse muerto(-a) de miedo (susto) to be very afraid 92

caerse por acá (ahí) to drop in here (there) 19

caérsele a alguien el alma a los pies to lose heart 202

caérsele a alguien la baba to be very surprised, usually by something attractive 227

caérsele a alguien la casa encima to have something terrible happen 183

caérsele a alguien el mundo encima to have something terrible happen, have the world crumbling 183

caérsele un tornillo to have a screw loose 54

el cafiche pimp 214

cafre old-fashioned, outdated, bad 29; rude, lacking in respect 34; stupid, incompetent 132

la cafrería useless stuff, junk 232

los cafres del volante maniac drivers 238

la cagada dirty trick, piece of crap, betrayal 122

estar cagado(-a) to be ruined, messed up, screwed up 124

estar cagado(-a) (hasta los pelos) to be scared stiff, scared shitless 92

cagando leches hurriedly, in a hell of a rush 219

Ni cagando. Not on your life. No damn way. 164

cagante spectacular, fantastic, frightening 241

cagar to insult, ream out, rip apart 56; to give (someone) the shaft; to abuse, lie to, or cheat (on) 125

cagar(la) to make a mistake, blow it 86

cagar a pedos to insult, chew out 56

cagarse en la canción to ruin, destroy, mess up 125

cagarse en la olla to ruin, destroy, mess up 125

cagarse de la risa to die laughing, shit one's pants laughing 147

cagarse en el ventilador to mess up, ruin 125

que te cagas a hell of a, expression used for something unusual 242

¡Me cago en Dios! strong expression of anger 11

¡Me cago en tu madre (en la madre que te parió, en tus muertos)! strong insult 140

¡Me cago en la puta (diez, leche)! strong expression of anger 11

el cagón, la cagona scaredy-cat, chicken 92

cahuinear to insinuate, make an innuendo 50

caído(-a) de la cuna to be foolish, easily duped 224

como caído(-a) de las nubes unexpected 227

caído(-a) del catre not very bright, easily duped, soft in the head 224

caído(-a) del cielo describing a windfall, boon 227

caído(-a) del nido wet behind the ears, naive, clueless 137

caído(-a) del zarzo foolish, clueless, out of it 137, 224

Estoy que me caigo. I'm in bad shape (not well). 116

el caimán womanizer, Don Juan 215

la caja tonta television, boob tube 231

la cajetilla low-class braggart 34

ser de cajón to go without saying, be obvious 239

a cal y canto strong, tightly 222

¡Calabaza! The party's over! Time to go! 113

la calabaza failing grade 89

la calaca death 61

el calambre anxiety attack 260

la calentadita little workover (beating or sexual play) 123, 214

calentar(se) to heat up (become heated) with anger or sexual desire; to turn on 213

calentar el asiento to be a short time in a job (used mainly in the negative) 255

el calentón, la calentona hothead; person who is easily aroused sexually 11, 213

el/la caleta stingy person who hides things so as not to have to share them, tightwad 205

la caleta house, home 231

el caliche street slang 48

caliche, calichera (of the) street 48

cálida nice, kind 112

caliente fast (sexually), passionate, excited 213

el callejón sin salida dead end; problem or conflict that is difficult or impossible to resolve 186

la calva death 61

calzar a alguien to catch, bust, or arrest someone 55

a calzón quitado openly, frankly 239

el calzonazos wimp, henpecked man or mama's boy 247

el calzonudo wimp, henpecked man or mama's boy 247

calzonudo(-a) lazy 148

camao(-a) experienced 124

la cámara friend 103

¡Cámara! ¡Camaronchas! Wow! 4, 228

cambiar el agua a los peces (al pájaro) to make a pit stop, urinate 35

cambiar de canal to change pace or activity 43

cambiar de casaca to leave a group and go to a different one, be a turncoat 43

cambiar el cassette to change the subject 43

cambiar el chip to change one's way of thinking 233

camellar to work 258

el camello work, job 258

caminar con los codos to be stingy 205

con la camiseta puesta describing a real fan, enthusiast 85

el camorrero troublemaker, instigator of conflicts 70

el camote mess, trouble; fight, fit 157

estar camote con to be madly in love with, often referring to puppy love 200

las campanitas de la catedral lovely cash (from the sound of coins jingling) 162

camuflar la onda to keep a secret 191

estar en la cana to be in prison 55

la caña beer 98; effort, intensity 220, 255

el/la canalla vile person, creep 30

la canallada cheap shot, evil action 122

la cancha experience 79

En la cancha se ven los gallos. Actions speak louder than words. 3

el canchanchán, la canchanchana person with power in the community 25

la candela fiery woman 23

¡Candela! Watch out! 247

ser canela fina to be of great worth, be fine 108

el cangrejo hard case, tough nut to crack, problem; unsolved crime 186

la canilla leg, skinny leg 36

la cañona standing up of someone 194

a la cañona by force 257

Canta. Tell me. Do tell. 136

Canta, pajarito. No matter what you say I don't believe you. 71

¡Canta, pajarito! Tell the truth! 'Fess up! 136

el/la cantamañanas unreliable or irresponsible person, dreamer who doesn't get things done 32

cantar to denounce, inform 136

cantar a alguien las cuarenta to give someone a piece of one's mind, speak frankly 240

cantar como una almeja to call attention to oneself and look ridiculous 20

cantar la justa (la pura) to speak frankly, tell it like it is 240

cantar la pepa to inform on someone, squeal, rat on 136

cantar victoria to brag about or rejoice in a triumph 34

cantarle a alguien la cartilla (el salmo) to set someone straight, read the riot act, lay down the law 240

cantidad a lot 190

la cantinflada nonsense or hot air 107

cantinflear to speak a lot of nonsense 107

Cantó Gardel. Payday. Now we get paid. 160

el canuto marijuana cigarette 76

capar to punish, to kill (figuratively) 123

capar clase to cut class 81

ser capaz de dormir a un muerto to be very boring (people) 38

capear clases to cut class 81

la capirucha good old capital 179

ser capítulo aparte to be another kettle of fish, different topic 72

captar la onda to understand something insinuated 143

la cara nerve, pushiness 188

el/la cara de culo asshole 139

el/la cara dura person with a lot of nerve; someone who doesn't pay attention to criticism 188

el/la cara de limón unpleasant appearance; sourpuss 31

el/la cara de palo person with a lot of nerve 188

el/la cara de perro hostile appearance 31

el/la cara'e barro person with a lot of nerve; someone who doesn't pay attention to criticism 188

¡Caracoles! Darn it! 10

la carajada thingamajig, whatchamacallit 232

el carajal crowd, horde 170

carajear to fool around, dick around 222

el/la carajillo(-a) boy (girl), adolescent, young person 119

el/la carajito(-a) boy (girl), adolescent, young person 119

el/la carajo(-a) unknown person 174

del carajo super, fantastic, great(ly) 110

¡Carajo! common expletive, like Damn! 10

ser carajo(-a) to be difficult 69

al carajo: mandar a alguien... to tell someone to go to hell 139

el/la caralarga person with a sad appearance, sad sack 202

¡Caramba! Jeez! Darn it! 15

la carambada thing of little value; nonsense 232

el carambas young person; guy 118

de carambola by a lucky chance 156

ser un caramelo to be nice, kind, a sweetie 112

¡Caray! Jeez! Darn it! 15

la carcacha jalopy, old piece of junk 238

ser un cardo borriquero to be very ugly 241

el careto face that suggests fatigue or worry 35

carga good, great 109

la cargada joke, trick 107

cargar to steal 56; to make fun of 84; to make a pass at, hit on, come on to 200

cargar el arpa to go along with a couple on a date, be a fifth wheel 199

cargar con el mochuelo to do the dirty work, get the job no one else wants 256

cargar la lápida to be in danger of or singled out for death 61

No me cargues. Don't bother (bug) me. 15

caribear to take advantage of someone, con, scam 63

el/la carmelita mulatto 177

el carnaval fun time; street dance 168

no ser carne ni pescado to be undefined, insipid, neither fish nor fowl 244

en carne, en cuero broke, penniless 248

en carnes naked 163

el carrazo nice big car 238

como carreta en bajada fast, without much control, and no stopping it 220

el carro car 238

carros y carretas obstacles or problems that one puts up with 186

carroza old, mature; describing someone middle-aged who tries to be young 6

la carroza car, new or old 238

a carta cabal exactly, right; irreproachably or impeccably 175

la charanguiada party, dance 168
charanguiar to party, dance 168
charcha lame, worthless 29
charralero(-a) common, of little value 29
charro(-a) old-fashioned, out of it 29
Chasgracias. short for **Muchas gracias.** 231
chatear to chat on the Internet 231
chato(-a) affectionate nickname 5;
  pug-nosed 177
Chau, chau. Bye-bye. 113
la chaucha small change, just pennies 162
la chavala girl 117
el chavalo guy, boy 118
No chaves. Don't bother me. 15
la chaveta head 35
el/la chavito(-a) diminutive of **chavo(-a)** 119
la chaviza young folk 261
el chavo peso or dollar 162
el/la chavo(-a) boy (girl) 118
el/la chavo(-a) de onda gruesa young drug
  addict 76
chavón, chavona annoying, irritating 14
chayote bothersome 14
el chayote bribe 160
che friend, pal 104
los chécheres everyday objects of all sorts
  233
chele blue- or green-eyed, fair-complexioned
  177
la chela beer 98
el chele cent 162
los cheles things of little value 233
chelo(-a) fair, blue- or green-eyed 177
el chen chen money, dough 162
de chepa luckily, by pure luck or chance 156
Chepa la bola. Who knows? 73
chequear, chequar to check 20
el chesco soft drink 99
la cheve beer 98
chévere great, fantastic 109
el/la chibolo(-a) boy (girl), kid 119
chicato(-a) wearing glasses, blind (as a bat)
  178
la chicha anger 8
no ser ni chicha ni limonada to be useless,
  superfluous, mediocre 244
chichar to have sex 212
los chicharrones woman's breasts 36
los chiches breasts 36; knickknacks, trinkets,
  small toys 233
la chichi girl, girlfriend 201
el/la chichí baby 170
los chichis breasts 36
chicho(-a) good, nice, great 109
el chicle person who sticks like glue,
  annoying person 14
¡Chicles, muéganos y palomitas!
  exclamation of great surprise 228

Ni chicles. No. No way. 164
al chico rato, al ratón in a little while 236
chico(-a) friend, pal 104
el/la chico(-a) bien young person from
  a well-off family 250
el/la chicoco(-a) boy (girl), child 119
chido(-a) great, super 109
chido-uan super cool, super nice 109
chiflado(-a) crazy; foolish; like mad 53
estar chiflado(-a) del coco to be crazy in
  the head 53
chiflar to be crazy about, love 153
chiflar el mono to be cold (weather) 251
No la chifles, que va cantada. Don't mess
  things up. 246
¡Chihuahua! Darn! 15
el/la chilango(-a) person from Mexico City
  173
el chile male organ 214
la chilla poverty 249
chillar to squeal (inform on); to complain,
  cry, whine 45
chillar goma(s), chillarla to take off quickly
  67
chillón, chillona crybaby, complainer;
  person who yells a lot 45
el/la chilpayate(-a) kid, young person 119
chimba cool, super 109
en las chimbambas far away, on the
  outskirts 72
el chimbarón jerk, pest 33
el chimbero fraud, someone who doesn't
  give back money 62
chimbo(-a) stupid and out of style, lame 29;
  false 62; ugly; low quality 241
¡Chin! Darn! 15
¡Chin chin! Cheers! 98
el chin chin little bit 189
el/la chinchudo(-a) hothead, person with
  a short fuse 11
chinear to carry (usually a baby); to pamper
  237
estar de la chingada to be in deep trouble,
  screwed 125
a la chingada: mandar a alguien... to tell
  someone to go to hell 139
la chingadera thingamajig, worthless thing;
  trick; swear word 233
chingado(-a) (chinga'o[-a]) screwed 124
chingar to exploit; to screw 125; to break or
  screw up (a machine) 212
chingarse to suffer, exhaust oneself or wear
  out, get or be screwed 120
el chingo large amount 190
chingón, chingona annoying or bothersome
  14
ser un(a) chingón (chingona) to be
  competent, good 44

estar en chino to be incomprehensible, be Greek 132

chino(-a) curly haired 177

el chiquilín, la chiquilina kid, young person 119

chiquitico(-a) very, very tiny 178

el chiquitín, la chiquitina kid, small child 119

el chirimbolo doohickey, thingamabob 233

la chirimoya head 35

de chiripa by luck, by chance 156

el/la chiris child 119

chirolas something of little worth, small change 233

estar en chirona to be in jail 55

¡Chis! Jeez!, exclamation of annoyance, disgust 15; Shh! 192

los chismorreos gossip 116

la chispa smarts, intelligence, astuteness 140

¡Chispas! Darn! 15; Wow!, expression of surprise 228

el chiste colorado (rojo) off-color joke 50

el chiste pelado off-color joke 51

el chiste verde off-color joke 51

la chiva good luck 156; thing of little value 233

el chivato (chiva) traitor, fink, person who rats on others 136

chiveado(-a) inhibited, timid, overly proper person 32; false, fake 62

chivearse to act ashamed or inhibited, timid 83

el/la chivero(-a) lucky (person) 156; person who buys things in the United States and sells them in Mexico 160

chiviar to gamble, play dice 155

chivo(-a) pretty, elegant, attractive 108

el chivo crib sheet 81; die; dice game 155; womanizer, man who lives off women 215; car 238; bike 239

de chivo luckily 156

¡Chócala! Put it here! (said in greeting before a handshake) 117

chochear to dote on 4; to be a bit senile, forgetful because of age 6

el chocho (la chocha) female organ 212

chocho(-a) doting, proud, gaga; senile 4, 6

el chocolate hashish 75

Chogusto. short for **Mucho gusto.** 50

chollado(-a) not caring about anything 133

el chollo great chance or advantage; something very cheap 166

ser un chollo to be a bargain 161

choreado(-a) angry, mad 9

chorearse to lose patience, get angry 12

el chorizo male organ 214

choro(-a) brave, daring, admirable 52, 112

las chorradas stupidities, nonsense, pieces of junk 225

el chorro large amount, gobs 190

¡Chorro de mierda! Piece of shit! 140

chorrocientos(-as) many, an uncountable number 190

chotear to make someone look ridiculous 84

de choto for free 161

la choza house, home 231

¡La chucha! Crap! 10

a la chucha: mandar a alguien... to tell someone to go to hell 139

la chuchería fast food, junk food 100; something of little value, but cute 233

el chucho peso 162; pooch, dog 232

chueco(-a) crooked 54

chulear to make fun of 84

chulearle el dinero a alguien to rip someone's money off 63

chulis darling, my dear (between women) 104

el chulo man who lives off women 210

chulo(-a) cute, good 23

chulón, chulona naked 163

el chunche thing, thingamajig 233

chungo(-a) bad, inappropriate, crummy 26

estar chupado(-a) to be easy 80

el/la chupamedia(s) kiss ass, brownnoser 96

chupar to drink alcohol 99

el chuparosa, flor homosexual 172

no chuparse el dedo to not be naive or easily deceived 141

el/la chupatintas paper-pusher, drudge 256

el chupe small alcoholic drink 99; dish (of food) 100

el chupito small alcoholic drink 99

el churro attractive male 23

el chute shot (injection) of heroin or other drugs 75

chute nosy 114

mi cielo sweetheart, darling 6

¡Cielo verde! Holy smoke!, expression of surprise 228

a ciencia cierta for sure 43

ciento y la madre abundance (of people) 190

ciertas hierbas a certain someone 174

cilindro, cirilo, ciro, sirope used instead of **sí** 6

cincuentón, cincuentona fiftyish 6

de cine good, super 110

cinta(s) used instead of **sí** 6

cipeado(-a) dull 38

el/la cipote(-a) young person 118

el cirio upheaval; mess 157

Clarisa se llamaba... (la que me lavó el pañuelo). Right! Correct! 8

Claro, y los chanchos vuelan. Right, and that's likely. 71

clavado(-a) failing (in school); involved (in something) 89; stuck 182
clavar to swindle 63; to have sex 212
clavar el pico to fall asleep 217
clavar un examen to do well on an exam 80
clavarse to study hard 81; to fail; to get involved in a bad situation 89
ser un clavo to be bad, boring 38
el clavo problem, embarrassment 186
Un clavo saca otro clavo. One problem overshadows another, making it less important. 184
cliquear to click (e.g., on a key) 231
la coba lie; con, scam 62
cobar to lie; to cheat, to con 64
el/la cobero(-a) liar, scam artist, con man 62
cocerse en su propia salsa to stew in your own juice 120
el cochambre crowd, horde 170
cochambroso(-a) messy, like a slob, in ruins; dirty (e.g., mind) 158
la cochinada dirty trick 122
los cochos (cuchos) parents 170
el coco head 35
ser un coco to be difficult 69; to be smart, intelligent 141
como cocodrilo en fábrica de carteras nervous 260
el cocotazo blow to the head 122
codo(-a) stingy 205
coger to have sex 212
coger la baja a alguien to find someone's weak point and take advantage of it 123
coger un brei to take a break 197
coger un diez (un cinco) to take ten (five) 197
coger lucha to worry excessively 259
coger una trompa to tie one on, get blasted 78
cogerlo suave to take it easy, calmly 146
estar hasta el cogote to be fed up 16
la coima bribe 160
no ser cojo(-a) ni manco(-a) to be competent and experienced 44
el cojonal crowd, horde 170
estar hasta los cojones to be fed up 17
¡Cojones! Damn!, common expletive 10, 228
los cojones testicles 214
de los cojones awful, damn 27
Ni cojones. No damn way. Nothing. 164
¡Qué cojones! What nerve! 189
cojonudo(-a) brave 52; very good or admirable 110
el/la cojudo(-a) idiot 223
el cola gay, homosexual 172
en la cola de un venado once in a blue moon 101
el/la colado(-a) party or gate crasher 188

colarse to cut in line, squeeze in or through 188
el/la cole pal, short for **colega** 103
el/la colevaca someone who sneaks into a place, gate crasher 188
estar colgado(-a) to live without a notion of reality 47
colgado(-a) high on alcohol or drugs 79; failed (on an exam) 89; in love 200
estar colgado(-a) to be hanging or stood up 194
colgado(-a) del cuello in a bad situation, usually economic 185
colgar to die 60; to flunk 89
colgar los guantes to die; to retire 60
colgar el sable to die 60
colgar los tenis to die 60
colgar la toalla to throw in the towel 66
colgarse to fail, flunk 89; to fall in love 200; to be hung up 235; to be behind in your work, with more work than time to do it 255
la colita well-formed woman 24
colocarse (con) to get high, drunk 78
el colocón drunkenness 76
El comal le dijo a la olla: ¡Mira qué tiznada estás! The pot calls the kettle black. 216
No te comas un cable. Don't worry. Don't have a cow. 146
la comay (comadre) close female friend 101
el combo group of friends, band 103
el comelibros bookworm 82
el/la comemierda proud or stupid person, snob; fake 30
comer como chancho to eat fast and in a sloppy way, like a pig 99
comer el coco a alguien to influence or convince someone 175
comer a dos carrillos to serve two masters, work for two (often opposing) people or ends 64
comer delante de los pobres to show off in front of less fortunate people 35
comer en el mismo plato to be on very friendly terms 104
comer como niño Dios to wolf down food hungrily; to eat very carefully as though from an orphanage 99
no comer plátano por no tirar la cáscara to be miserly, especially with food 206
comer el sanduche antes del recreo to enjoy something before it should be enjoyed 210
A comer se ha dicho. Let's eat. 98
comer la torta antes de la fiesta to enjoy something before it should be enjoyed 210
no comer un huevo por no perder la cáscara to be miserly 206

comer vivo(-a) a alguien to treat badly, rip apart 121

Comer y callar. said when someone is benefiting from someone else and should not speak against them; Beggars can't be choosers. 196

comerse el buey to put up with something disagreeable 197

comerse un cable to be bored, with nothing to do, stood up 39; to be in a difficult situation economically 249

comerse el coco (el tarro, la olla) to worry or be preoccupied 234

no comerse una rosca to not find anyone to pick up, not have luck with the opposite sex 198

cometer una burrada to make a gaffe, mistake 86

la comida chatarra junk food, fast food 100

Comida hecha, amistad deshecha. said when someone eats and runs 98

comilón, comilona gluttonous 98

¿Cómo? Excuse me? What (did you say)? 133

¿Cómo le baila? What's up? 117

¿Cómo cree(s)? How can you think that? 71

¿Cómo (lo) diría? How should I put it (say this)? 128

¿Cómo diré? How shall I put it (say this)? 128

¿Cómo está la movida? How's the action? 117

¿Cómo te ha ido? How have you been? 117

¿Cómo lo llevas? How are things? 117

¿Cómo que...? What do you mean ...? 71

¿Cómo te va? How are you? 117

el comosellama thingamajig, whatchamacallit 233

comosellamear, chunchear to do something undefined 3

el compa close male friend 103

el compadrito young hustler, guy from mean streets 118

el compadrón arrogant macho man 173

el compi pal 103

el compiche, cómplice friend 103

el compinche friend, pal 103

completo(-a) high, stoned 79

la compu short for **la computadora** 231

comulgar con ruedas de molinos to believe the most unlikely things 137

estar con el alma en un hilo to be a bundle of nerves 260

estar con las antenas puestas to be listening (and ready for gossip) 114

estar con las botas puestas to be ready for a trip 238

con los brazos cruzados idle, doing nothing 130

con buen pie happily, with good fortune or luck 156

estar con cien (diez) ojos to be alert, suspicious 21

con el corazón en la mano frankly and sincerely 239

estar con la mente en blanco to have one's mind blank, daydream 131

estar con el mono to be in a state of abstinence from drugs 75

con el pie derecho in the right way, well 108

estar con un (el) pie en el estribo to be ready to leave 238; to be ready to die 61

con un pie en el hoyo near death 61

con un pie en el otro mundo with one foot in the grave, near death 61

con las manos en la masa caught in the act 55

Con mucho gusto. You're welcome. 231

El que con niños se acuesta (amanece mojado). Be careful! If you take risks, you may suffer the consequences. 245

estar con ojo to be alert, suspicious 21

con pelos y señales in great detail 45

estar con las pilas puestas to have one's act together, be on the ball 44

con puntos y comas meticulously 174

con razón no wonder 239

con la soga al cuello at risk, in a bad position or situation 185

Estoy con ustedes. expression of sympathy; I feel for you. 230

¡Coña! Damn! 10

estar de coña to fit well 74; to be joking 104

ser la coña to be unusual, strange (people) 243

Ni de coña. No damn way. 164

el coñazo drag, annoyance; hard time 15; blow or punch, impact, big fight 122

Concha. Who cares? (I don't give a damn.) 135

la concha shamelessness, insolence, nerve 188; female organ 212

la concha de tu madre insult, similar to son of a bitch 140

la conchuda pushy female 188

conchudo(-a) shameless or thick-skinned and insensitive person; con man 30

el conecte drug dealer 76; connection (social, political, etc.) 102

Conforme. OK. 8

confundir la gimnasia con la magnesia to confuse two very different things 71

coño devil, in the devil, in the hell 16

¡Coño! Damn!, interjection of anger, surprise, pain 10, 228

el coño de tu madre insult, similar to son of a bitch 140

conocer a alguien desde su (la) cuna to know someone from infancy 143

conocer como la palma de la mano to know like the back of one's hand 143

conocido(-a) en su casa unknown person 145

Te conozco, bacalao, aunque vengas disfraza'o (disfrazado). I see you coming. I see what you're up to. 246

Te conozco, mosco. You can't trick me. I see your intention. 246

consultar con la almohada to sleep on it, wait and think things over 233

contar batallitas to tell stories of one's life 49

Contigo ni a China me voy. I want nothing to do with you. 193

Contigo ni el saludo. used humorously, meaning that the other person is being unfriendly 193

Contigo ni a la vuelta de la esquina. I want nothing to do with you. 193

contra viento y marea come what may, come hell or high water 256

a contrapelo against one's will or against the norm 257

el contrapiropo comeback to a street compliment 24

ser un contreras to be contrary, always opposed 69

copado(-a) overwhelmed (usually with a positive emotion), happy 119

la coperacha pool of money used to buy something collectively 161

estar hasta el copete to be fed up 16

el copete cocktail, alcoholic drink 99

copetudo(-a) stuck-up 181

la copucha gossip 116

copuchar (copuchear) to gossip 114

el/la copuchento(-a) gossip 115

el coraje anger 8

corazón darling 5

el corazón en un puño situation of anxiety or depression 260

el corillo group, social gathering 168

la corneta nose 35

el/la cornudo(-a) cuckold 211

estar hasta la coronilla to be fed up 16

el corre-corre rat race, mess 39

Córrele. Go for it. 84

correr to run (someone) off or out; to fire 113

correrse to be said, rumored 114; to come (sexually) 210

ser una corriente to be coarse, rude, a dope (woman) 34

estar al corriente de to be up to date on 165

corriente y moliente everyday, normal 167

a la corta o a la larga sooner or later 235

¡Corta! ¡Corta! Be quiet!; Stop! Cut it out! 192

cortado(-a) por la misma tijera cut from the same cloth, very similar 216

cortado(-a) por (con) el mismo patrón cut from the same cloth, very similar 216

Córtala. Cut it out. 142

¡Córtala! Quiet! 192

cortante abrupt, giving short answers only 191

cortar to cut (class) 81; to cut off (a relationship) 101; to hang up (the phone) 113

cortar el hilo to interrupt a conversation, train of thought, etc. 141

cortar la nota to dampen one's spirits, knock someone out of kilter; to interrupt 141

cortar el queque to take control, cut to the chase 25

cortar el rollo to cut the jive 191

cortarse, sentirse cortado(-a) to be shy, embarrassed 83

las cortinas eyelids 35

ser de corto alcance to be narrow-minded, conventional 167

ser corto(-a) de genio to be timid, lacking in bravery 92

la cosa euphemism for male or female organ 210

Una cosa es con guitarra y otra con violín. That's a different story, another kettle of fish. 72

la cosa grandototota humongous thing 232

las cosas para picar appetizers 100

la coscolina loose woman 212

el coscolino dirty old man 215

ser coser y cantar to be child's play, a cinch 80

costar un huevo (y la mitad de otro) to cost a fortune or a lot of effort 161

costar más que un hijo tonto said when someone keeps showing up to eat or costs someone money excessively 161

costar un ojo de la cara to cost a fortune 161

costar un pastón to cost a fortune 161

el/la cotilla person who gossips 115

la cotorra chatterbox, someone who talks a lot 49

cotorrear to jabber away 49; to jive, feed a line 64

el cotorreo gab session 114

los coyoles testicles 214

el coyote someone who takes people across the U.S. border; intermediary to get things 54

cranear to think a lot 234

creer que el dinero se encuentra debajo de las piedras to think that money grows on trees 160

creerse to be proud or pretentious, stuck-up 182

creerse el choro de la playa to think one is hot stuff 182

creerse la divina garza to think one is God's gift 182

creerse la divina pomada to think one is God's gift 182

creerse la gran caca to think one is hot shit 182

creerse la gran cosa (cosota) to think one is hot stuff 182

creerse la gran mierda to think one is hot shit 182

creerse el hoyo del queque to think one is hot stuff 182

creerse el ombligo del mundo to think one is hot stuff 182

creerse la mamacita peluda (la maravilla peluda, la mamacita de Tarzán) to think one is hot stuff 182

creerse el (la) muy muy to think one is hot stuff 182

creerse la última chupada del mango (del mate) to think one is hot stuff 182

creerse la última Coca-Cola en el desierto to think one is hot stuff 182

¿Qué crees? Guess what. 50

creído(-a) stuck-up 181

la crema y nata highest social class, cream of the crop 250

estar en la cresta de la ola to be at one's high point 226

el/la cretino(-a) idiot 223

criado(-a) a puro machete badly brought up, brought up in a barn 30

criar margaritas to push up daisies, be dead 61

la criatura baby 170

criminal intelligent; well done, extraordinary 241

las croquetas de ave(rigua) mystery meat 100

la cruda hangover 79

estar crudo(-a) to be hung over 79

estar cruda to take an exam without studying; to not get it 80

¡Qué cruz! What a drag! 16

cruzado(-a) high, stoned (on drugs or alcohol) 79; very hungry 99

cruzar el charco to cross a sea, usually to go to America or the United States 237

cruzarse los cables to be or go crazy 53

el cuadernícolas very serious student who studies a lot 82

cuadrado corpulent, with a nice build (a man) 178

cuadrado(-a) complete, perfect 108; hooked up with, going steady with 199

cuadrar to suit; to agree with 153

cuadrar (la caja) con alguien to agree, make a deal, square things 7

la cuadratura del círculo the impossibility or overcomplication of something 130

el/la cuadre boyfriend (girlfriend) 201

cuando Franco era cabo (corneta) a long time ago 237

Cuando hay higos, hay amigos; cuando hay brevas... las huevas. Prosperity makes friends, adversity tries them. 102

¿Cuándo hemos comido en el mismo plato? Since when are we bosom buddies? 58

¿Cuándo hemos gastado el dinero juntos? Since when are we bosom buddies? 58

cuando la rana eche pelos the twelfth of never, when hell freezes over 237

cuando las culebras andaban con chaleco a long time ago 237

cuando los perros se ataban con chorizos long ago 237

el cuarto bate big eater 98

el cuarto de discusión chat room 231

el/la cuate(-a) good friend, pal 103

cuatrapear to get all messed or mixed up; to turn out badly 125

el/la cuatrojos person with glasses, four-eyes 178

el/la cuatro-pepas person with glasses, four-eyes 178

estar como una cuba to be drunk 78

cubrirse de mierda to dishonor oneself, screw up badly 83

la cuca female organ 212

cuchucientos(-as) (mil) a gazillion, uncountable number 190

Cuenta conmigo. You can count on me. 230

No me cuentes tu vida. Don't tell me your life story. 49

cuentiar to sweet-talk, butter up 175

¡Qué cuento! What nonsense!, expression of opposition 71

el cuento chino big lie, fishy story 62

el cuento del tío tall tale 71

el cuento de viejas old wives' tale 116

en cuernavaca naked 163

al cuerno: mandar a alguien... to tell someone to go to the devil 139

estar de cuerno uno con otro to be opposed or fighting with someone 69

el cuero attractive man or woman 24; bod 36; girl, woman; pretty woman 118; easy woman 212; male organ 214

en cueros naked 163

cuervear to take advantage of others financially, sponge 204

cueste lo que cueste come what may, no matter what 256

la cuestión thingamajig, whatchamacallit 233

al cuete in vain, for nothing 243

la cueva anus, ass 36; home 231

cuico(-a) ostentatious, snobbish 181

Cuidado con la liebre. Be careful (of the enemy). 247

Cuídame el changarro. Take my place for a few minutes. 126

cul calm in any situation (from cool) 145

culear to have sex 212

la culebra misunderstanding, tense disagreement 70

el culebrero charlatan 62

el culebrón soap opera 231

el/la culero(-a) lazy, uncooperative person, person who takes no initiative 33

el culito girl, woman; piece of ass; hot chick 210

el culo ass 36

ser un culo to be really ugly, butt-ugly 241; to be useless 245

como un (el) culo ugly, unpleasant 26

en el culo del mundo far away, in a godforsaken spot 72

¡Qué culos! Who gives a damn! 136

la cuña connection (social, political, etc.) 102

estar curado(-a) to be drunk 78

estar curado(-a) como huasca (tagua) to be dead drunk, drunk as a skunk 78

el/la curda drunk 78

la curda drunkenness 78

estar en curda to be drunk 79

curralar to work 258

el curralo work 258

el/la currante worker 255

currar to work 258

currar a alguien to con or cheat someone out of their money 64

el curro work 258

cursi corny, too sweet or sentimental 28

Qué curvas y yo sin freno. street compliment 24

cutre poor, low-quality 29; stingy 206

el cuzco pooch, cute little dog 232

el cuzquito pooch, cute little dog 232

D

Se le da como curros. He or she is very hardworking. 255

Le da la mano y se agarra hasta el codo. Give him (her) an inch and he'll (she'll) take a mile. 189

Le da el pie y le toma la mano. Give him (her) an inch and he'll (she'll) take a mile. 189

dabuten, dabuti very good, great 110

dale que dale phrase that expresses repetition 196

Dale saludo a la más vieja de tu casa. insult equivalent to ¡Tu madre! 140

Dame cinco dedos. Give me five. 117

el dame que te doy big fight, knock-down-drag-out 70

Dame. Give me five. 117

Te dan pon y ya quieres guiar. They give you a ride and you already want to steer (meaning take over). 189

no dar una to goof up constantly 87

dar una achurada to give (someone) a scolding or dirty deal 57

dar alas to stimulate, inspire 84

dar a alguien con la puerta en las narices to refuse someone something 129

dar a alguien un hueso que roer to give someone a task that is not very pleasant or useful 256

dar atole (atolillo) con el dedo a alguien to deceive someone, pull the wool over his or her eyes 64

dar un aventón to ask for a ride 238

dar ayotes to jilt; to stand (someone) up 194

dar bateo to oppose, fight against; to present a problem 69

dar una bola to give a ride 238

dar bola a alguien to pay attention to someone 21

dar la boleta to give someone their walking papers 113

dar el boleto to give someone their walking papers 113

dar bombo a alguien to praise someone with exaggeration 180

no dar el brazo a torcer to be stubborn, not give in 133

no dar ni los «Buenos días» to not even give (someone) the time of day 206

dar cabida to tease sexually 210

no dar calce to not give an opportunity or opening to 129

dar el callo to work hard 256

dar una cantaleta to give a sermon, repeat something ad nauseam 56

dar el cante to call attention to oneself and look ridiculous 20

dar carreta to flatter, deceive, feed a line 176

dar carrete a alguien to put someone off, make them wait or keep them dangling 17

dar chile to provoke, antagonize, excite 17

dar una clavada to charge more than what is proper or right, rip off 64

dar en el clavo to hit the nail on the head, figure out or be right 142

dar coba to flatter, usually to gain something, butter up, suck up 176

dar una cola to give a ride 238

no dar con ello to not get it 133

dar corte to be embarrassed or ashamed 83; to cut down (hit or kill) 123

dar un cortón (corte) a alguien to cut someone down to size in a sharp reply 58

dar cráneo (cabeza) to think a lot 234

dar cuartel to help (someone) 127

dar cuerda to string someone along, butter up, sweet-talk 176

dar curva to evade, throw a curve; to not know 47

dar diente con diente to be very cold or to be afraid, when teeth chatter 92

dar entrada to flirt 199

dar (un) esquinazo to go out of one's way to avoid (someone) 87

dar gato por liebre to deceive someone, giving them something inferior 64

dar el golpe to make a hit, steal or rob 56

no dar (un) golpe to be lazy, do nothing 130

dar hielo to treat coldly, give the cold shoulder 129

no dar ni la hora to not even give (someone) the time of day 206

dar igual, dar lo mismo to be indifferent, not care 134

dar un jalón to give a ride 238

dar jamón to exhibit part of one's body, sometimes to tease sexually 211

dar (la) lata to give someone a hard time; to annoy; to bore by talking a lot 17

dar leña to beat up, hit 123

dar a luz to give birth 37

dar en la madre to hit hard, hurt someone where he or she is vulnerable 123

dar manija to inspire enthusiasm (get enthusiastic about) 85

dar una mano to give (someone) a hand 128

dar marcha to give (someone) energy, a lift 84

dar la nota to stand out in a bad way 20

dar la nota alta to stand out in a bad way 20

dar un palo to strike; to make a hit, steal something 56; to get something really good, luck out 156

dar papaya to do or say something that exposes one to ridicule 222

dar pasaporte a alguien to kill 55; to break off with someone 113

dar la patada a la lata to kick the bucket, die 60; to be right 143

dar pelota a alguien to pay attention to someone 21

dar el pésame to express one's sympathy in times of misfortune 230

dar picones to provoke, antagonize, excite 17

no dar pie con bola to not be correct or do things right; to make a mess of things 132

dar piñazos to fight 70

dar (un) plantón to stand (someone) up 194

dar pon to give a ride 238

dar la puntilla to finish off, be the ruin of 123

dar saltos de alegría to jump for joy 120

dar tiempo al tiempo to be patient, wait for an opportunity 169

dar un toque to give notice 236

dar en la torre to knock (someone's) block off, fix (someone) 123

dar la última pincelada to put on the finishing touch 175

dar vuelta a la página to put the past behind you and go forward, turn over a new leaf 43

dar la vuelta a la tortilla to turn the tables 43

darle (duro) to apply oneself, give it one's all 256

darle a alguien el punto to feel like (doing something), get in a mood 153

darle a alguien la real gana to do exactly what one pleases 153

darle a alguien la regalada gana to do whatever one pleases 153

no darle a alguien vela en el entierro to not give someone authority or a reason to participate 129

darle una arrechera to upset, make "hot under the collar" 12

darle boleto to pay attention (to someone) 21

darle caña to beat up 123

darle al coco to think, study 234

darle con el palo al gato to beat a dead horse; to get the runaround 175

darle dos hostias a alguien to give someone a scolding or a piece of one's mind, chew someone out 57

darle mate to kill off, finish 123

darle palo to be disagreeable to, not want to 152

darse un atracón to do something in excess, go over the top 242

darse la buena (gran) vida (la vida padre) to live it up, enjoy oneself 106

darse de cabezazos to rack one's brain 234

darse una clavada to have a bad or boring (crummy) time 39

darse con la cabeza en la pared to be frustrated because of wasted effort 183

darse un cagazo to have a terrible fright 92

darse un cañangazo to drink a strong alcoholic beverage 99

darse un chucho to get scared or frightened 92

darse coba to brag, put on airs 180

darse una hostia to fall, have an accident 121

darse el lote (el filete) to hug and kiss 4

dar(se) manija to inspire enthusiasm (get enthusiastic about) 85

darse unas palizas to get all worn out and sore (e.g., from walking) 88

darse un palo, palito to have an alcoholic drink 99

darse paquete to put on airs 180

darse el piro to escape, go off 67

no darse por enterado(-a) (entendido[-a]) to pretend that one doesn't understand, play dumb 63

darse (por vencido) to give up 66

darse un quemón to show off something one has, e.g., something new 35; to study hard 81

darse en el queso to hit oneself in the face, fall on one's face 121

darse una rabieta to have a fit, tantrum 13

darse un susto de muerto to be very afraid 92

darse taco to put on airs 180

darse vuelta la chaqueta to be wishy-washy, change with the tide 43

dársela a alguien con queso to deceive, make fun of 84

dárselas de... to pretend to be or act like . . . 180

Date. Hurry up. 220

no decir «esta boca es mía» to not say a word 191

decir a alguien (las) cuatro verdades to tell it like it is, give someone a piece of one's mind 240

decir amén a todo to always agree, be a yes man 7

decir cuántos pares son tres moscas to read the riot act, tell it like it is 240

decir cuatro cosas to give (someone) a piece of one's mind 240

decir madres to say crude or stupid things, insult 138

no decir ni mu to not say a word 191

decir al pan pan y al vino vino to tell it like it is 240

no decir ni pío to not say a word 191

el decorado cuckold, man "decorated" by horns 211

defender a capa y espada to back up, take care of; to defend vehemently 128

defenderse to manage, get along 44

Deja de comer mierda. Stop with your foolishness. Stop letting people treat you badly. 222

Deja de decir fanfarrias (fanfarronadas). Stop bragging, tooting your horn. 34

Deja el friqueo. Stop freaking out. 91

dejado(-a) unworthy or irresponsible, loser 90

dejamestad laziness, boredom 147

dejar colgado(-a) to leave hanging or stood up 194

no dejar (ni) a sol ni a sombra a alguien to hound, pursue someone at all hours and in all places 18, 175

dejar a alguien en cueros to rob, leave someone without a shirt on his (her) back 56

dejar a alguien frío(-a) (helado[-a]) to shock, surprise, dumbfound 227

no dejar a alguien sentar el pie en el suelo to not let someone rest 18

dejar a alguien sin camisa to ruin someone, leave without a shirt on his (her) back 56

dejar de cama to wear (someone) out physically 88

dejar con los churquitos (colochos) hechos to stand (someone) up, leave waiting 194

dejar como Dios pintó al perico to make (someone) mad 8

dejar la escoba to screw (mess) something up 86; to disclose information that is shocking or embarrassing, let the cat out of the bag 136

dejar pegado(-a) (arrollado[-a]) to stand up, abandon 194

dejar pelando papas to leave (someone) waiting, stand up 194

dejar el pellejo to die 60

no dejar piedra sobre piedra to destroy completely 126

dejar planchado(-a) a alguien to leave someone dumbfounded, aghast 121

dejar plantado(-a) to stand (someone) up 194

no dejar títere con cabeza to destroy, blow away with insults 126

dejarle a alguien el tren to lose out; to be left a spinster 166

dejarse caer to drop by 19

Déjate de chiquilladas. Stop the foolishness. 222

dejarse de cuentos to stop telling stories, get to the point 70

¡Qué delicia! How delicious! 98

demasié short for **demasiado** 190

del demonio extraordinary, tremendous 241

al demonio: mandar a alguien... to tell someone to go to the devil 139

la depre depression 202

desbancar to push (someone) out of the way; to take a job away from (someone) 121

descachimbado(-a) slovenly, untidy; broken, screwed up 158

descachimbar to break, screw up 125

el/la descarado(-a) scoundrel, shameless person 30

la descarga scolding 8; good time; jam session 104

descargar to let loose with emotion, positive or negative, let it all out 9; to jam (play music) 104

¡Qué descaro! What nerve (brazenness)! 189

deschavado(-a) messy 158

deschavetado(-a) stupid 224

descojonado(-a) with problems; broke, screwed up, not working 124

descojonar to ruin, mess up, screw up 125

descojonarse de risa to laugh uncontrollably 147

descolgarse to appear suddenly 19

desconectar to avoid reality, relax, tune out 131

descoñetado(-a) trashed, messed up, badly hurt 124

descoñetar to trash, mess up, ruin, screw up 125

descontar to hit 123

descubrirse el pastel to have a secret revealed 143

el descueve super, fantastic 110

desembuchar to unload (problems, secrets) 136

Desgraciado en el juego, afortunado en amores. Unlucky in a game or gambling, lucky with love. 154

Las desgracias nunca vienen solas. Bad things never come alone (one at a time). 154

deshojando la margarita worrying "Does he/she love me or not?" 198

deslenguado(-a) using strong language, crude 51

desmadrar to beat up 123; to act immoderately, get a bit out of control 242

el desmadre mess, confusion 157

desmayar to keep quiet; to stop (talking or doing something) 191

desnudar a un santo para vestir a otro to take from Peter to pay Paul 187

la despedida de soltera send-off party for the bride before her wedding 169

despegar la boca to talk, open up 136

despelotado(-a) disorganized, messy 158

despelotarse to take off one's clothes 163

el despelote disorder, mess 157; nakedness, removal of clothes 163

ser el despelote to be unheard of, extraordinary (things) 243

despintarse to go away 67

estar despistado(-a) to be lost, off the track, clueless, forgetful 47

despuesito a little later than now 236

destaparse to open up, tell something 136

destripar a alguien el cuento to steal someone's thunder (telling a story he or she began) 48

el/la desubicado(-a) difficult person, pain in the neck 30

desubicado(-a) mistaken, wrong, all wet 86

estar detrás del palo to be uninformed, in the dark 145

devanarse los sesos to rack one's brain 234

devolver la pelota a alguien to counter someone with their own arguments or reasoning 48

el día del pago de los bomberos when hell freezes over, the twelfth of never 237

el día sándwich day off between a weekend and a holiday 108

el día 30 de febrero never, the twelfth of never 237

¡Diablo(s)! Holy smoke!, expression of surprise, anger, etc. 10, 228

El diablo anda suelto. The devil is loose. Evil is afoot. 26

el diablo vendiendo cruces hypocrite 33

¡Dianche!, ¡Diantre! Holy smoke!, expression of surprise, anger, etc. 10, 228

los días particulares weekdays (Monday to Friday) 235

¿Diay? But what can one do? 196

¡Qué dicha! What luck! 156

Del dicho al hecho hay mucho trecho. Easier said than done. 68

Dichosos los ojos (que te están viendo [que te ven]). Great to see you. 116

a diestra y siniestra helter-skelter 192

a dieta going without sex 212

Diga. Dígame. phrase for answering the phone 117

Como dijo Herodes, te jodes. phrase of resignation, something like: We're (I'm, you're) screwed. What can you do? 196

dilatar(se) to take a long time 236

como Dios manda in the proper way, perfectly, as it should be 109

¡Dios mío! My goodness! 228

¡Dios (nos) guarde! ¡Dios libre! God forbid! 73

¡Dios santo! My goodness! 228

la diosa verde marijuana 76

el/la dire director, principal 80
dirigir el cotarro to be in charge 25
disfrutar a lo loco to have a great time, have the time of one's life 106
no disparar un chícharo to not work, do nothing 130
el disparate nonsense 225
divertirse a sus anchas to enjoy oneself as much as possible 106
divis-divis divine, marvelous (very feminine expression) 110
doblar el lomo to do heavy work 256
doblar el pico to keep quiet, shut up 191
el doc drug dealer 76
dolerle hasta los huesos to ache all over (with tiredness) 88
los dolores used for dólares 162
la dolorosa check, bill 96
el don Juan Don Juan, womanizer 215
don Nadie unimportant person, with little influence or power 138
la dona doughnut 100
donde in the home of, where someone is 179
donde Cristo perdió el gorro far away 72
donde el diablo dio las tres voces/gritos far away 72
donde el diablo perdió el poncho y la diabla la chancleta in a far or out-of-the-way place 72
donde te dicen hijito sin conocerte bordello, house of prostitution 211
estar donde las papas queman to be where the action is, in the eye of the storm 185
¿Dónde va Vicente? Donde va (toda) la gente. phrase meaning that someone is just a follower 167
¿(A)dónde vamos a parar? Where are we going to end up? 259
el dormilón, la dormilona describing someone who sleeps a lot, sleepyhead 218
dormir a alguien to deceive someone 64
dormir a lo chancho chingo to sleep like a log 217
dormir con los ángeles to sleep well 218
dormir a cuerpo de rey to sleep like a king 217
dormir la juma to sleep it off 76
dormir como un lirón to sleep deeply 217
dormir la mona to sleep it off 76
dormir como un tronco (una leña) to sleep like a log 217
de dos caras two-faced 65
como dos gotas de agua like two peas in a pod 215
en dos monazos quickly 221
dos palabras short conversation 48
en dos patadas quickly 221

en un dos por tres quickly, in an instant 221
dos que tres so-so, not all that great 116
el dos que tres blow, punch 122
estar a dos velas to be broke 248
como dos y dos son cuatro as sure as shootin', as we're standing here 43
el dragón, la draga big eater, glutton 98
la drama, el dramón problem, difficult situation 186
el drogo drug addict 76
el/la drogota drug addict 76
ser un dulce (un bombón) to be a sweetie 112
dulzura sweetie, honey 5
dundo(-a) foolish 224
a duras penas with great difficulty 257
duro(-a) intelligent, very good at something 44; hard to convince, pig-headed 176; stingy 206
el duro five pesetas 162
ser un(a) duro(-a) to be the best, really good at something 44
duro(-a) de codo stingy 206
duro(-a) de pelar difficult to convince or get 176
al duro y sin guante pitilessly, without mercy 129
ser un durote to be sharp, have a lot of smarts 141

E

Ni ebrio(-a) ni dormido(-a). No way. 164
¡Échale ganas! Give it all you've got! 84
¡Échale lo que hay que echarle! Give it all you've got! 84
Echando a perder, se aprende. People learn by trial and error. 87
echar agua en el mar to do something useless 244
echar a alguien a escobazos to throw someone out 113
echar bala to make amorous conquests, put on the moves 200
echar una bronca to bawl out, reprimand 57
echar de cabeza to publicly reveal someone's secrets, let the cat out of the bag 136
echar una canita al aire to have an affair; to let one's hair down, do something unusual 198, 241
echar la capa to intervene, help out 128
echar un capote to intervene, help out 128
echar carreta to sweet-talk, butter up 176
echar la casa por la ventana to spend lavishly, blow the works 162
echar un casquete to have sex 212
echar chispas to show anger, to fume 11

echar la corta (la grande) to take a leak (a dump) 35
echar el cuento to sweet-talk, butter up 176
echar flores to compliment 180
echar un fonazo to make a phone call 48
echar fuego por los ojos to show fury or anger 11
echar huevos a un asunto, echarle huevos (bolas) to throw oneself into something, do something decisively or bravely 256
echar humo to be furious, steaming 11
echar leña al fuego to add fuel to the fire 121
echar un lukin to have a look 21
echar lumbre to show anger 11
echar madres (la madre) to curse, swear at 138
echar mal de ojo to try to cause (someone) bad luck, give the evil eye 121
echar una mano to give (someone) a hand 128
echar una manopla to lend a big helping hand 128
echar una meadita to take a leak 35
echar la mula to work hard and fast to get ahead 256
echar el ojo to eye, have one's eye on 21
echar pa'lante to move on, keep going after confronting a problem 175
echar un palo to have an alcoholic drink 99; to have sex 212
echar para atrás to put off 152
echar un patín to walk very fast 238
echar pedradas to criticize 57
echar perlas a los puercos to cast pearls before swine 244
echar los perros to call out the cavalry, go all out to win 200
echar una pestaña (pestañeada) to catch some winks (shut-eye) 218
echar un pie to dance, shake a leg 59
echar puteadas to insult with offensive names 138
echar rayos (y centellas) to show anger, be fuming 11
echar relajo to have a blast 106
echar un rollo to sling the bull, sweet-talk 176
echar el ruco to call out the cavalry, go all out to win 200
echar en saco roto to disregard completely 134
echar sal al agua to do something useless 244
echar un taco de ojo to look at (without obtaining) 21
echar los tejos to seduce, make passes, hit on 201

echar la vaca to chip in, pool money for a common cause 161
echar vaina to talk about nothing; to tease 48
echarle algo al buche (al pico) to eat, feed one's face 98
echarse to fail 90
echarse a alguien to kill someone 55; to fail someone (e.g., on an exam) 90; to have sex with someone 213
echarse un caldo to fart 35
echarse el día to cut class for the day 81
echarse ese trompo a la uña to perform an amazing feat 45
echarse flores to brag, praise oneself 34
echarse una mona encima to get drunk 79
echarse la pera to play hooky 81
echarse un pollo to scram, split 67
echar(se) un polvo to have sex 213
echarse la soga al cuello to get into trouble or debt; to get married 199
echón, echona pretentious, boastful, superior acting 34
la edad del pavo change to adolescence, puberty 261
¡Éjele! Listen! Hey! 20
el ostro sol yesterday 235
estar en ele olo (como chico zapote) to be completely out of it, in the dark, daydreaming 131
El que va pa' viejo va pa' pendejo. Old age brings woe. 6
elevado(-a) high (on drugs or alcohol) 79
el email (emilio) E-mail 231
emailear to E-mail 231
la embarrada embarrassment, problem 183
embarrado(-a) tainted, involved in shady business 183
embarrarla to goof up, make a mistake 86
embarretinarse to get complicated 184
embebido(-a) como una esponja drunk as a skunk 78
el/la embelequero(-a) busybody 115
embollado(-a) with too much to do 39
emborrachar la perdiz to beat around the bush 49
embotellarse to memorize, cram 81
el/la embustero(-a) fraud, cheat, liar 62
a la eme: mandar a alguien... to tell someone to go to the devil 139
¡Qué emoción! expression of amazement, like How wonderful! 108
emocionado(-a) excited 86
empaparse en algo to immerse oneself in something 143
emparrandarse to go out on the town, party 106
estar empatados to be a couple 199

empatar(se) to pair up, get together; to obtain or get 199

el/la empate girlfriend (boyfriend), partner, companion 201

emperrado(-a) wildly mad, angry 9

emperrarse to persist doggedly 175

empezar la casa por el tejado (techo) to put the cart before the horse 132

empilado(-a) dedicated to, enamored of 21

empilcharse to fix oneself up to go out to a party, primp 75

empinar el codo to have a drink, have a swig 99

empingado(-a) brave; with high values 52

empollar to memorize 81

el empollón, la empollona grind, student who studies a lot; someone who works all the time 82

a empujones by (a) force (from outside) 257

estar/quedarse en blanco to draw a blank, be unable to respond 133

en pleno vuelo high; stoned 79

estar en tránsito to be under way 3

enano(-a) short or small 178

encabronado(-a) angry 9

encabronar(se) to make angry, furious (to become furious) 12

encachimbarse to get enraged 12

encajarse to sponge, take advantage 204

encamarse con to go to bed and make love with 213

encanar to arrest, put behind bars 55

encantado(-a) de la vida very happy 120

encarnado(-a) singled out, being watched 20

encendérsele el bombillo/foco to have a brilliant idea 233

enchicharse to get mad 12

enchilado(-a) angry 9

encholarse to go wild (e.g., join a gang, etc.) 30

el/la enchufado(-a) teacher's pet 82

estar enchufado(-a) to have connections 102

enchufar to get laid, get lucky, have sex 213; to have connections 102

enchufarse to join in (conversation, etc.) 3, 48; to pay attention 21

enchuflar to have connections 102

enchulado(-a) in love 200

encimita and in addition, besides all that 50

encimoso(-a) insistent, pestering person 13

encohetado(-a) angry, furious 9

encojonado(-a) angry, furious 9

encojonarse to get angry, furious 12

encontrar la horma de su zapato to meet one's match 216

encontrar una mina (de oro) to find a way to live or get rich without working much 250

el/la encubridor(a) pal; someone who covers for you 103

enculado(-a) in love; enthusiastic 200

encularse to fall in love 200

enculebra'o(-a) in debt 248

estar endrogado(-a) to be heavily in debt 248

ene many, a great number, a lot 190

estar como energúmeno to be hysterical 10, 260

enfermo(-a) del mate (del chape) loose cannon, nutcase 53

enfiebrado(-a) passionately enthusiastic 86

enfogonarse to get angry 12

enganchar to attract (someone) from the start 22

engancharse to hook up with, hook someone up with; to be in love 199

engorilarse to get mad suddenly, snap, go ballistic 12

engranar to react angrily 12

engrifarse to smoke marijuana 76

engrupido(-a) pretentious, a bit snobbish 181

el/la engrupidor(a) person who deceives you with wit or charm, smooth talker, con man 62

engrupir to fool or trick with wit or charm, to con 64

estar enguayabado(-a) to be hung over 79

enguayabado(-a) madly in love 200

enhierrado(-a) armed, carrying a gun 55

enjaranarse to get into debt 249

enjaretar to force (on someone) 121

la enllave friend, connection 103

ennota'o(-a) high on drugs or alcohol 79

enojón, enojona hostile, easily angered 11

enpiernado(-a) sexually captivated by someone 200

enquilombar to make a mess or problem 159

estar enratonado(-a) to be hung over 79

enrollarse to sling the bull, talk at length, string along with talk or flattery, butter up 176

enrollarse con to get mixed up or involved with 3

enseñar los dientes to threaten 246

no entender ni jota (ni papa) to not understand anything 133

¡Que no te enteras, Contreras! phrase reproaching someone for not listening 130

entero(-a) pretty; good 108

enterrar a alguien to break off with someone for good 113

No se entienden ni se enteran. They don't get along. 129

como entierro de pobre quickly 220

entradito(-a) en años getting up there (euphemism) 6

entradito(-a) en carnes a little bit heavy, pleasingly plump (euphemism) 178

el/la entrador(-a) charmer, people person, one who fits in easily 102

entrar bizco y salir cojo to have things go from bad to worse 184

entrar como Pedro/Juan por su casa to feel or make oneself at home 188

entrarle a alguien a puños y patadas to beat someone up 123

entrarle una cosa por un oído y salirle por el otro to have something go in one ear and out the other 131

estar entre dos aguas to be undecided 65

entre la espada y la pared between a rock and a hard place 185

Entre nomás. C'mon in. 116

el/la entrometido(-a) busybody 115

entromparse to get angry 12; to get drunk 79

entuturutar (entotorotar) to confuse, brainwash 47

envolvente person who confuses others in a tricky way 47

envolver en razones to confuse (someone) 47

enyemao(-a) (eñemao) weak (physically) 247

enyoyarse to butter up 176

¡Epa! Hey! 20

¡Epa, Chepa! interjection of surprise and disbelief 228

¡Epa, epa! interjection expressing surprise or shock 228

estar erizo to be cold, have goosebumps 251

el error garrafal huge mistake 87

Esa se te zafó. You blew it. 87

escacharse to fail because of a wrong move or saying something wrong 86

escamado(-a) frightened, nervous, wary 92

escamarse to be frightened 92

escapar del trueno y dar con el relámpago to go from the frying pan to the fire 184

¡Escoba! Same to you, buddy! 58

escorchar to bother, annoy, bug 17

a escote dutch treat 142

el/la escuintle(-a) (escuincle[-a]) twerp, insignificant person or kid 119

escupir al asado to ruin a plan or situation, mess up 125

escurrir el bulto to avoid work or responsibility, pass the buck 88

Ese arroz ya se coció. It's in the bag. 226

Ese bicho, lo que está es frito (tosta'o). That guy's a nut. 53

Ése es otro rollo. That's another kettle of fish. 72

esfumarse to disappear into thin air 67

esnob snobbish 181

Eso es harina de otro costal. That's a horse of a different color. 72

Eso está hecho. That's for certain. It's a sure thing. (used for promises) 127

¡De eso nada, monada! mild expression of rejection 194

esos cinco the hand 35

el espantapájaro ugly or skinny person 241

espantar la mula to die; to go away, leave 60, 67

estar espeso(-a) to be slow, dull 219

las esposas handcuffs 55

No está en na'a (nada). He or she is out of it. 48

en la estacada in danger, in the lurch 185

en estado pregnant 37

el estantillo skinny person 178

a estas alturas at this point or stage 235

el estatequieto blow, punch, hit 122

Este... Uh . . . , Well . . . 128

Este disco tiene raya. (Este disco está rayado.) Same old story. It's like a broken record. 216

estirado(-a) uptight, snobbish 181

estirar la pata to kick the bucket, die 60

¡Esto es el colmo! This is the last straw! 10

Esto es la hostia. This is the damn limit. This is too much. 15

Esto resucita a un muerto. This livens, perks (a person, things) up. 111

estofa'o(-a), estofón (estofona) very studious 82

estofarse to study hard, cram 81

estrafalario(-a) strange, weird 241

estrellado(-a) with bad luck 154

la del estribo one for the road 100

estrujarse el coco to think, rack one's brain 234

estrujarse el melón to think, rack one's brain 235

evaporarse to disappear from the face of the earth 67

excitado(-a) aroused, excited 213

el excusado bathroom 36

explotarse to explode, blow up 12

ey yeah 6

F

la facha ridiculous dress, outfit 74

fachoso(-a) badly dressed; affected, trying to appear elegant 74

fácil easy (woman) 212

facilingo very easy 80

fajar to make out 4; to punish; to punch 121

el faldero henpecked man 247

fallarle la azotea to have bats in the belfry, be crazy 54

el/la falopero(-a) someone who takes drugs 76

falseta false 62

A falta de pan, buenas son tortas. One thing is as good as another. 216

¡Lo que faltaba para el duro! That's all we needed! 183

faltar a la palabra to not keep one's word 64

faltar el respeto a... to disrespect 24

faltarle a alguien un tornillo to have a screw loose 54

faltarle cinco para el peso to not be playing with a full deck 54

faltón, faltona irresponsible 32

el fandango party 168

la fanfarria party 168

fantasioso(-a) stuck-up 181

fantasma, fantasmón (fantasmona) hypocritical, artificial 33

fantasmear to promise something but not keep the promise 64

el/la fantoche(-a) presumptuous or ridiculous person; show-off 181

la farlopa heroine 75

el farol eye 35

el farolazo drink (alcoholic) 100

la farra party 168

farrear to go out on the town 106

fatal awful, the pits, not well done or said 27

Favor que usted me hace. How nice of you to say so. 180

el fax fax 231

faxear to fax 231

los féferes things of little value 233

feliciano(-a) tolerant, easy-going 112

feliz como una lombriz happy as a lark 120

fenomenal great, super 110

feote (feota) very ugly or run-down 241

la feria money 162

la festichola fantastic party 169

el feto ugly person 241

fichado(-a) (someone) known by all; (someone) being watched carefully 20

fiebre enthusiastic, fanatical 86

ser la fiel estampa/imagen de alguien to be the spitting image of someone 216

el/la fiestero(-a) party lover 169

fifí overly concerned with dressing in style 75; affected 181

¿Te fijas? See? Get it? 142

Fíjese (usted). Fíjate (tú). Just imagine. 21

filete very good, excellent 110

el/la filito(-a) lover, boyfriend (girlfriend) 202

el filo hunger, appetite 97

el finde short for **fin de semana** 235

fino(-a) great, cool, fantastic 110

fino(-a) como un coral astute, wise, bright as a dollar 141

finolis exaggeratedly refined, uppity 181

firme como el roble hard; strong 222

flaco(-a) affectionate nickname 5

flecharle to feel love at first sight 200

la flojera laziness, lack of spirit 147

flojo(-a) lazy, with no spirit; slacker, couch potato 148

ser flor de estufa to be overprotected 127

la flor de la vida the prime of life 261

a flor de labio on the tip of one's tongue 48

a flor de piel obvious 239

la flor y nata the cream of the crop 108

ser florero to be the center of attention 20

flotar to not be with it or in the world, not find out about things 47; to be lazy, goof off 130

flotar como el corcho en el agua to come out well despite adverse events or problems 226

la foca fat person 178

el foco eye 35

Qué foco. How boring. 38

follar to have sex, screw 213

el follón mess, confusion 157

fome dull, boring, lame 38

¡Fondo blanco! Bottoms up! 98

en forma in shape 126

formar un berrinche to have a fit, tantrum 13

forrado(-a) having money 250

forrarse to stuff oneself (with food) 99; to become rich 250

el forro good-looking person, male or female 23

fosforito quick-tempered, hotheaded 11

el fosforito easy woman, girl 212

el fósforo string bean, skinny person 178

fosforón, fosforona hot 213

el fracatán many, large amount 190

franelear to make out, pet, indulge in foreplay 214

la fregadera nagging, annoying 13; dirty trick 122; thingamajig 233

ser un(a) fregado(-a) to be an annoying, demanding, or bossy person 15

estar fregado(-a) to be useless, messed up, ruined 125

Qué fregado(-a) eres. How shameless (fresh, annoying) you are. 16

fregar to mess up, ruin, jerk around; to nag 125

fregón, fregona annoying 14

ser un(a) fregón (fregona) to be good at something 44

a freír buñuelos: mandar a alguien... to tell someone to get lost 139

a freír espárragos: mandar a alguien... to tell someone to get lost 139

a freír papas: mandar a alguien... to tell someone to get lost 139

la fresa innocent young woman, a bit disdainful or spoiled 137

fresco(-a) cynical 71; not worried, cool as a cucumber 145; shameless, unaffected by criticism 188

la fría beer 98

friqueado(-a) upset, freaked out 261

frito(-a) dead 61; toast, sunk, in trouble 185; asleep 218

ser un(a) fruncido(-a) to be very fussy, uptight and persnickety; to be a tightass 32

fruncir to be a coward, wimp 92

fu bad, bad news, yucky 27

ni fu ni fa neither good nor bad, expression of indifference 167

¡Fuchi! (¡Fúchila!) Yuck! 154

fuera de base (de órbita) out of it 47; in a state of hallucination 76

estar fuera de bola to be in the dark 145

Fuera de bromas. No joke, seriously. 240

estar fuera de liga to get excellent grades, be outstanding 80

fuera de onda out of it, totally unhip, old-fashioned 29

fuera de serie extraordinary, outstanding; (n.) outstanding person 110

fuerte surprising, shocking 227

Ni a la fuerza. Not on your life, no way. 164

fufurufo(-a) stuck-up 181

el/la fulano(-a), fulano(-a) de tal so-and-so, John or Jane Doe 174

Fulano, Mengano y Zutano Tom, Dick, and Harry (expression used to name unknown people) 174

la fumadita drag on a joint of marijuana 76

fumar como chacuaco/murciélago/un carretero to smoke a lot 237

fumar como (una) chimenea to smoke like a chimney 237

funar to see 21

No fuñas. Don't be a pain. 15

fundido(-a) exhausted 88

en el fundillo del diablo in a faraway and dreadful place, in a godforsaken spot 72

fundírsele a alguien los fusibles to go crazy 54

fúrico(-a) furious 10

furris bad, horrible 27

fututear to eat rapidly 99

G

la gaceta piece of news 165

gacho(-a) bad, unpleasant, of low quality or little worth 29

el gafe jinx 154

gafo(-a) silly, foolish 226

el/la gafudo(-a) person with glasses 178

los gajes del oficio part and parcel of the job, occupational hazards 255

el galanazo good-looking guy 23

la galleta traffic jam 239

el gallina coward 92

como gallina en corral ajeno in a poorly adjusted way, like a fish out of water 46

Gallina que come huevo, ni que le quemen el pico. Someone with a bad habit won't stop for anything. 28

el gallinazo womanizing 211

el gallo (galla) guy, dude 118

el gallo brave man; angry man 52

¡Qué gallo! What a (good-looking) guy! 24

como gallo en patio ajeno totally lost, like a fish out of water 46

¡Qué gambas! What (gorgeous) legs! 24

el/la gandalla loser, good-for-nothing 33

el ganso turkey, geek, introvert 171; freeloader 204

el gao house, home 232

el garabato swear word, bad word 51

al garete with no fixed direction or destination 192

el garito bar (usually small); place to gamble 105

la garola old car 238

el/la garra (garrapata) loser, unappealing or ugly person 33

gastar pólvora en zopilotes (en sanates) to waste time 244

Gato viejo, ratón tierno. phrase meaning that old geezers like sweet young things 198

el gavilán wolf, Don Juan 215

el gazpacho mess, mixup 157

geniudo(-a) bad tempered 31

ser gente de medio pelo to be barely middle-class 249

la gente del bronce happy, carefree people 120

estar geto(-a) to be drunk 78

el gil (la gila, el gilberto) chump, dupe, dope 223

la gilada stupid action; dirty trick 225

el/la gilipollas jerk, dope, asshole 223

las gilipolleces stupidities 225

el girador operator, guy involved in bad things 30

¿En qué la giras? What do you do for a living? 255

estar en la gloria to be in seventh heaven, on cloud nine 120

el glu-glú boozing, alcohol 99

la golfita easy woman 212

golfo(-a) living a disorganized life or being dishonest sexually; tramp 211

estar hasta el gollete to be fed up 16

el golpe bajo low blow 122

el golpe de teléfono phone call 48

el/la goma lowest-paid person in an office who runs all the errands, gopher 256

estar de goma to be hung over 79

a la goma: mandar a alguien... to tell someone to get lost 139

la gorda ten-cent coin 162

Ni gorda. Nothing. 164

gordito(-a) honey, dear 5

gordo(-a) fat plum; darling 5

el gorila barbaric person; very big person 34

de gorra free, at someone else's expense 204

gorrear to cheat, deceive 64; to sponge, not pay for things 205; to cheat on, be unfaithful to 211

estar hasta el gorro to be fed up 16

el gorrón, la gorrona sponge, mooch 205

Ni gota. Nothing. 164

gozar a millón to have a great time 106

el gozo en un pozo said when one's hopes for something have been dashed 202

Graciela. used instead of **Gracias.** 231

grajearse to make out 5

el gran cachimbazo (de agua) cloudburst, big shower 251

¡Qué gran cagada! What a piece of shit! What a dirty trick! What a big mistake! 11

gran cosota big deal 232

Gran puñado son tres moscas. expression pointing out the numerical scarcity of people or things 189

grasa low-class, common, rude 34

gratarola (gratirola) for free 161

greñudo(-a) longhaired, sloppy 30

la grifa marijuana 76

grifarse to smoke marijuana 76

grifo(-a) stoned on marijuana 76

Gringolandia the United States 179

a grito pelado yelling loudly 45

groncho(-a) low-class, common, rude 34

la grosería obscene word, swear word 51

el/la grupiento(-a) person who sells himself or herself well, smooth talker 176

¡Guaca! Yuck! 154

la guachafita silliness, goofing around 107

guacho(-a) orphan; fatherless child; single person 171

la guagua baby 170; bus 239

la guaguita little baby; babe 23

el/la guajiro(-a) country person, simple person from rural area 170

el/la guajolote(-a) fool, turkey 223

el guajolotero tightly packed bus 239

el guambra kid 119

el/la guanaco(-a) Salvadoran 173

el guanajo idiot, fool 223

guapear to strive, try to get something 256

el guapo arrogant braggart, macho man 173

guapo(-a) brave 52

el/la guaposo(-a) someone looking for a fight 70

la guarandinga thingamajig 233

guarango(-a) rude person with bad manners, boor 34

guardar to keep in jail 55

la guarra hussy, loose woman 212

la guarrada harmful action, dirty trick 122

las guarrerías junk, pieces of crap 233

el/la guarro(-a) person who is dirty or has loose morals 34

la guata paunch, beer belly, potbelly 36

la guata de callo (de foca) brownnose 96

guay (del Paraguay) great, super, cool 110

la guayaba lie 62

el guayabero fraud, liar 62

¡Qué güea! Oh, shit! 11

¿Qué güea? What's going on? 229

güero(-a) blond, fair 177

guevero(-a) opportunistic 205

el güey loser, dummy 223

gufeao(-a) funny, amusing 104

gufear to joke around, have a good time 106

el gufeo something fun or amusing 107

la guial, guialcita chick, babe, woman 118

el/la güila kid, baby 119

guillado(-a) not understanding or not wanting to admit understanding 63, 145

guillarse to cover something up, have a secret or secret relationship 61

el güiro child 119; party 169

ser un guiso to be corny 29; to be badly dressed 75; to be easy 80

la guita money 162

el guri young boy 118

la guriza young girl 118

H

ser una haba sin sal to be a boring person 38

haber una de todos los diablos to have a devil of a mess 159

no haber roto un plato to have the appearance of someone who's never made a mistake 86

habla que te habla talking or nattering on; blah, blah 49

¡No habla(s) en serio! You're not serious! 71

hacer el ridículo to appear foolish, act like a fool 222

hacer la rosca to flatter, butter up 176; to sleep anywhere, although it may not be comfortable 218

hacer una segunda to do a favor, help out 128

hacer serrucho to split a bill, go dutch 142

hacer de las suyas to do whatever one pleases 153

hacer tapa to say no to something 163

hacer teatro to act in a theatrical way 159

hacer tilín to be appealing; to like a little 153

hacer tortilla a una persona o cosa to crush or break someone or something, destroy 124

hacer de tripas corazón to pluck up one's courage 52

hacer tuto to go to sleep, go sleepy-bye 218

hacer un sinpa to leave without paying 205

hacer un tango to cause a scene, have a fit 159

hacer una vaca to chip in, pool money for a common cause 161

hacer el viacrucis to go from bar to bar 104

hacer la vista gorda to ignore, overlook 131

hacer zapping to change the channel 231

hacerla de pedo a alguien to give someone a hard time 17

hacerla de tos a alguien to give someone a hard time 17

hacerle agua la boca to have one's mouth watering 97

hacerle a alguien de chivo los tamales to cheat on someone, be unfaithful 211

hacerle la boca agua to have one's mouth watering 97

hacerle la cama a alguien to get ahead of someone, beat to the punch 123

hacerle la cruz a alguien to write someone off 113

hacerle la vida un yogurt a alguien to make someone's life bitter 18

hacerse añicos to be exhausted physically or mentally 88

hacerse bocho to obsess over something 234

hacerse bolas to get confused; to complicate one's life 46

hacerse caldo de cabeza to obsess or mull over (something), rack one's brain 234

hacerse camote to get confused 46

hacerse una chaqueta to masturbate (males) 214

hacerse (un) cráneo to get illusions about, obsess 234

hacerse el desentendido(-a) to pretend not to notice, play dumb 63

hacerse el chivo loco to pretend not to notice, play dumb 63

hacerse humo to disappear 67

hacerse el leso (la lesa) to pretend not to notice, play dumb 63

hacerse el loco (la loca) to pretend not to notice, play dumb 63

hacerse mala sangre to get upset, ticked off 17

hacerse el musiú to act in an unconcerned or condescending manner, be uppity 180

hacerse un ocho to complicate one's life, get balled up 46

hacerse un ovillo (una pelota) to shrink with fear, pain, etc.; to get confused or balled up 92

hacerse una paja to masturbate 214

hacerse pajas mentales to think a lot about something 234

hacerse pedazos to be exhausted physically or mentally 88

hacerse la pelada to play hooky, cut class 81

hacerse de(l) rogar to play hard to get, like to be begged 180

hacerse rosca to act sweet 63

hacerse un taco to get confused or balled up in difficulties 47

hacerse el tonto (la tonta) to pretend not to notice, play dumb 63

hacerse de la vista choncha to ignore, overlook 131

hacerse el vivo to get ahead, be clever at taking advantage of others 203

hacérsele to think, imagine 234

los hacheros police 26

la harina money 162

hartar to criticize 57

estar harto(-a) to be fed up 16

hartón, hartona gluttonous 98

¡Hasta ahí podríamos llegar! phrase of indignation facing a possible abuse 45

Hasta aquí llegó mi (el) amor. This was the last straw. 15

estar hasta atrás to be drunk 78

estar hasta las chanclas to be drunk 78

estar hasta el cepillo to be drunk 78

estar hasta el copete to be drunk 78

hasta el gorro drunk 78

estar hasta la madre to be fed up 16

estar hasta las manitas to be drunk 78

estar hasta el moño to be fed up 16

hasta las piedras all, without exception 46

hasta más no poder full-fledged; all possible 46

estar hasta el (mismísimo) coño to be fed up 16

hasta el quinto infierno far away 72

hasta en la sopa everywhere 101

hasta el tope entirely, completely, as far as it can go 46

Hasta que nos topemos. See you around. Catch you next time. 113

hasta los tuétanos down to the marrow 46

¿Hay alguien que canta aquí? Porque hay uno que está tocando. said in a crowd when someone is touching someone else unnecessarily 238

No hay bronca. No problem. 146

No hay casco. Forget it, let it go. 146

No hay más narices (cojones). There's no alternative. 197

Hay moros en la costa. The coast is not clear (someone else may be listening). 246

No hay que darle vueltas. It's just as it looks; it's obvious. 240

Hay que joderse. expression of opposition, something like "screw you" but not as strong 138; You have to put yourself out, put up with hard times. 197

Hay que jorobarse. expression of opposition, something like "screw you" but not as strong 138

Hay ropa tendida. Be careful. The coast is not clear. 246

Hay de todo como en botica. It takes all kinds. There's something here for everyone. 46

No hay tos. variant of **No hay problema.** 146

No hay vuelta de hoja. There's no turning back. 65

estar hecho(-a) un almíbar to act very friendly and affable 63

hecho(-a) añicos exhausted 89

estar hecho(-a) un asco to look dirty, decrepit 26

hecho(-a) atol worn out 88

estar hecho(-a) un cascajo to be decrepit 6

estar hecho(-a) una equis to be drunk 78

estar hecho(-a) un figurín to have a nice figure, look good physically 23

hecho(-a) (una) mierda worn down, exhausted 89

hecho(-a) la mocha very quickly 220

estar hecho(-a) un mulo to be very strong 222

hecho(-a) pedazos exhausted 89

estar hecho(-a) pelota to be all broken up and sad about something (a death or loss) 202

estar hecho(-a) un pimpollo to look good, youthful 126

hecho(-a) pinole ground down, exhausted 89

hecho(-a) polvo exhausted 89

hecho(-a) (un) puré exhausted, worn down 89

hecho(-a) la raya very quickly 220

hecho(-a) una sopa very wet 251

estar hecho(-a) unos zorros to be in bad shape or badly dressed 26, 74

Lo que se hereda no se roba (hurta). Like father, like son. Here's a chip off the old block. 217

el hermanazo close friendship 102

las hermanitas Bustos big boobs 36

el/la hermano(-a) carnal(a) close friend 103

la hierba marijuana 76

el hierro (yerro) pistol, revolver 232

ser un hígado to be a pain, jerk 33

de higos a brevas once in a blue moon 101

estar en la higuera to be distracted, daydreaming 131

¡Hijo de Dios! Good grief!, expression of surprise 228

¡Hijo de la gran chingada! Goddamn it to hell! 11

el/la hijo(-a) de la chingada son of a bitch (bitch) 140

el/la hijo(-a) de la gran puta son of a bitch (bitch) 140

el/la hijo(-a) de mil demonios (de mil desgracias) son of a bitch (bitch) 140

el/la hijo(-a) natural illegitimate child 171

el/la hijo(-a) de papá (de papi) kid who has everything solved for him or her by the parents' influence 250

el/la hijo(-a) de puta (hijueputa, hijoputa) son of a bitch (bitch) 140

el/la hijo(-a) de su SOB (bitch) 140

Hijo(-a) de tigre, sale rayado(-a). Like father, like son. 217

¡Híjole! Wow! Darn! 228

hijos de muchas madres describing the diversity of a group or community 71

el hijuemilpesos euphemism for **hijo de puta** 140

hijueputear to insult with offensive names 138

hincar los codos to study hard 81

el/la hincha fan (sports) 86

el/la hincha (hinchapelotas) irritating person, pest 14

estar hinchado(-a) (con) to be fed up (with) 16

hinchar (las pelotas) to bother, bug, pester 18

el hocicón, la hocicona loudmouth, gossip 115

hociconear to shoot off one's mouth 114

el hojaldra asshole 30

ser como las hojas del yagrumo to be two-faced 65

¡Hola! phrase for answering the phone 117

hombre term of address for either a man or a woman 104

el hombre del saco bogey man; homeless man 249

la home home 232

de hoquis for free 161

la hora de los quiubos the time for explanation, the moment of truth 239

la hora pico rush hour; peak hour of electricity use 239

la hora punta rush hour; peak hour of electricity use 239

ser la hostia to be great, amazing, too much 243

¡Hostia(s)! Hell! Damn!, expletive 15, 228

Ni hostia. No. Not a damn thing. 164

¡Hostia puta! Goddamn it! 10

hostigar to annoy, badger, bug 18

¡Huaca! (¡Huácala!) Yuck! 154

el hueco homosexual 172

hueco(-a) phony, superficial 33

ser un hueso to be very demanding 81

el hueso intelligent student 82; patronage job (for family or friends) 258

la huevada stupid action 225

¡Qué huevada! Oh, shit! 11

¿Qué huevada? What's going on? 229

las huevas testicles 214

huevear to goof off, mess around, dick around 147

el huevón, la huevona lazy, useless person 148; idiot 223

la huevonada stupidity, fooling or goofing around 225

¿Qué huevonada (verga) es ésta? What the hell is happening? What's going on? 11, 229

estar hasta los huevos to be fed up 17

los huevos testicles 214

a huevos with a lot of effort 257

Ni a huevos. No damn way. 164

¡Qué huevotes (huevos)! What nerve! 189

huir del fuego y caer en las brasas to go from the frying pan to the fire 184

¡Huy! Ouch! 13; Wow! Damn! 228

Huy, ¡qué flechazo! said when people fall in love at first sight 200

I

¡Ideay! interjection meaning What's happening?, How's it going? 116

Igual Pascual. Me too. The same. 8

Iguanas ranas. Me too. The same. 8

imbancable unbearable, intolerable 154

no importar un carajo to not give a damn 134

importarle madre to not give a damn 134

importarle un pito (un bledo)/un rábano to be unimportant, not care 134

importarle tres cojones/un comino/un pepino/un pimiento to be unimportant, not care 134

inaugurar el pastel to have sex with a virgin 213

¡Incúbalo! What a blunder! 87

la indirecta muy directa a very explicit hint meant not to be missed 50

las ínfulas airs 180

a la inglesa dutch treat 142

el insti high school 80

¡Qué invente! Baloney! 71

ir abajo to lose a position, be demoted 89

ir de boyote to be superfluous, extra 245

ir al chile to get to the point 50

ir en el coche de Armando: una vez a pie y la otra andando to walk 239

ir en el coche de San Fernando to go on foot 238

ir con viento en las velas to be doing fine, steaming along, progressing 226

ir contra la corriente to go against the current 52

ir de culo to be wrong; to fail 89

ir donde calienta el sol to go with the winner, change sides for benefit 96

ir al garete to fail 89

ir de gorra, de gorrón to go (somewhere) without having to pay, crash 205

ir al grano to get to the point 50

ir hecho(-a) (la/una) bala to go rapidly, like a speeding bullet 220

ir al jalón to hitchhike 238

ir de juerga to go out on the town, party 106

ir de miranda to guard, watch over 21

ir a misa to be correct, for real 239

ir (muy) lejos to go (very) far 226

ir (muy) lejos to be far from what is said or done 71

ir pa'la brea to go have a fight 70

ir para rato to be a while 236

ir de parche to go out on the town 106

ir de parranda to go out on the town, party 106

ir de pegoste to be superfluous, extra 245

ir de pegote to be superfluous, extra 245

ir a la pela to be stingy 206

ir en pira to leave, go away 67

ir pisa'o(-a) to go quickly 220; to be under pressure 259

ir por lana y volver (salir) trasquilado(-a) to have the tables turned on oneself 125

ir al rollo to get to the point 50

ir sobre ruedas to be going smoothly, great 226

ni ir ni venirle without it mattering (to someone) 134

lanzar un rollo to start a long story 49

la lapa person who is hard to shake off, pest 14

a la larga in the long run 235

largar to send to the devil, get rid of 67

largar los mangos to spend money 162

largarse to go away, move off 67

El que las hace las paga. You have to accept the consequences of an action. 197

como las huevas like crap, lousy 116

¡Qué lástima! What a shame! 230

lastimarse el amor propio euphemism for to hurt one's behind 36

la lata bus 239

ser una lata (ser pura lata) to be a pain, drag, bore, annoyance 15, 38

latero(-a) boring person or thing 38

latir to like 153

latirle to foresee, have a feeling about 234

estar en el latón to be in prison 55

latoso(-a) boring, bothersome, a pain 14

laxo(-a) not worried, laid back 146

ser la leche to be too much, be surprising (good or bad), unheard of 243

¡Qué leche! What luck! 156

lechero(-a) lucky 156

lechudo(-a) lucky, lucky stiff 156

la lechuga dollar; a thousand pesetas 162

leerle a alguien la cartilla to set someone straight, read the riot act, lay down the law 240

legal good, correct, right; good person 108

estar lejos to be far from what is said or done 71

lelo(-a) foolish, stupid 224

el/la lengua larga someone who reveals too much 115

el/la lentejo(-a) dope, idiot, fool 223

lento(-a) pero tardado(-a) very slow 219

el león wolf, womanizer 215

estar como un león (de bravo) to be very angry 10

la leperada low-class action or obscene expression 29

lépero(-a) low-class, rude 34

la lesera nonsense 225

ser levanta muertos to perk or liven things (or someone) up 111

levantar to rob, steal 56

levantar la antena to pay attention 21

levantar (el) vuelo to take flight; to raise spirits or imagination 84

levantarse a alguien to pick up (someone of the opposite sex) 200

levantarse con el pie izquierdo to get up on the wrong side of the bed, have a day of bad luck or be in a bad mood 154

el levante pickup, date 200

liar los bártulos to die 60; to move 67

liar el petate to die 60; to change residence 67

libar to drink 99

mi lic term of respect used jokingly, short for **mi licenciado** 104

ligar to make amorous conquests, pick up; to obtain, get 200

ligero(-a) de cascos frivolous, foolish 226

el ligón pickup, date; guy who flirts and is successful with women 201

limero(-a) hard, strict 80

los limones woman's breasts 36

limpiarse to pay (someone) back, be even 217

limpiarse el culo con algo to disdain something 180

linchar to kill, lynch; to punish, in a threat 55

Qué lindo que canta Polo cuando está bolo. Everything sounds simple when you're high and feeling good. 80

el lío mess 157

la lira guitar 232

liso y llano without difficulty 80

estar listo como el pisto to be ready 193

el listón, la listona a real smartie 141

la lisura obscene word, swear word 51

llamar a alguien a capítulo to call someone on the carpet, ask for an accounting, reprimand 57

la llave friend, connection 103

¡Llégale a la papa! Eat! 98

¡Llégale! Go for it! 84

llegar a las raspas to get to a party or event when it's almost over 235

llegar y besar (el santo) phrase describing how quickly something was obtained 226

llenar el buche to eat, feed one's face 98

Me lleva la chingada. I'm screwed. 125

estar que me (lo, la, etc.) lleva el diablo to be beside oneself, in a very bad mood 28

llevar a alguien al huerto (al baile) to deceive someone, lead them down the garden path 64

llevar la batuta to be in charge, be the main person, wear the pants 25

llevar bien puestos los pantalones to impose one's authority, especially in a home setting 25

llevar la contraria (contra) to contradict, oppose 69

llevar contra la pared (la tabla) to act cruelly (toward someone) or ask too much (of him or her) 124

llevar leña al monte to take coals to Newcastle 244

llevar en palmas (palmitas) to please, pamper 5

llevar la voz cantante to be in charge, call the shots 25

llevarla suave to take it easy, calmly 146

llevarle el apunte, llevar de apunte to pay attention 21

llevarle la carga to make a pass at, hit on 201

llevarse (a alguien) el demonio to be angry or very irritated 10

llevarse (a alguien) el diablo to be angry or very irritated 10

llevarse (a alguien) la trompada, la tostada, la trampa to be angry or very irritated 10

llevarse bien (con alguien) to get along well (with someone) 102

llevarse el demonio to fail, have a bad ending 89

llevarse el diablo to fail, have a bad ending 89

llevarse la palma to surpass, take the cake; to get ahead or in front 243

llevarse todo por delante to win at everything, take on all comers 44

Me llevo el premio de... I win the prize for . . . 243

Se lo llevó Pateta. He (She) went to the devil, said with reference to someone nasty who died 61

llorar a mares to cry a sea of tears, cry buckets 203

llorar a moco tendido to cry like a baby 203

llorar lágrimas de cocodrilo to cry crocodile tears 61

llorón, llorona crybaby, whiner 45

llover a cántaros to rain cats and dogs 251

llover sobre mojado to have one bad thing happen after another; to be repetitive or superfluous 155

No llueve pero gotea. Things are going OK, not as bad as it could be. 116

lo que ve (mira) la suegra superficial part of house to be cleaned 255

el lobo wolf, womanizer 215

lobo(-a) describing someone who doesn't dress well 75

loca effeminate; gay 211

la loca floozie, woman who likes sex 212

a lo loco (la loca) like crazy, without thinking 131

mi loco(-a) my friend 104

el loco(-a) guy (girl) 118

el/la loco(-a) perdido(-a) hopeless case, someone very stupid 223

estar loco(-a) de contento to be very happy, ecstatic 120

Ni loco(-a). No way. 164

el/la lolo(-a) teen, cool young person 119

el lomo bod, body 36

estar al loro to pay attention, be attentive 21

el loro radio cassette player 232

como los ángeles very good, excellent 108

la luca a thousand pesos or units of money 162

estar lucas (lurias) to be loony 54

lucir to suit, wear, or fit well 22

lucirse to stand out, do something unusual 45

lukear (luquear) to look 22

Le lukeo. (Le luqueo.) See you. 113

lukiar to look 22

estar en la luna (de Valencia) to be distracted, daydreaming 131

la luz money 162

La luz d'alante (de adelante) es la que alumbra. Take what's right in front of you when you have the chance. 166

ser la luz de los (sus) ojos to be the light of one's life 4

luz de mi vida light of my life, dear 5

M

la macana whopper, big lie 62; stupid act 222

macanear to talk nonsense; to tease 222

macanudo(-a) awesome, super 110

macarra vulgar, in bad taste 29

el/la macarra troublemaker, person with bad manners and/or violent tendencies 30

la maceta head 35

el/la maceta tightwad 206

maceta (maceteado[-a]) stacked, muscular, big (person) 222

la machachaca marijuana 76

machango describing a masculine woman 211

machetear to mooch off others 205

macho term of endearment among males 104

el machote macho man, male chauvinist pig 173

macizo(-a) muscular, well-built 222

madre nice, kind person 112

de madre difficult, bad, ugly 27

¡Tu madre! insult impugning the honor of one's mother 140

Ni madre. No. No way. 164

la madre del cordero the real reason for something 193

¡La madre que te parió! insult, similar to You SOB! 140

madrear to hit, beat up 124; to offend with bad language, swear at 138

madrugar to get ahead of someone, cut off at the pass, beat to the punch 123

el maestro middle-aged or older man, guy 118

el maestro Chasquila someone who can do a lot of things but none of them very well 132

El maestro Ciruela, que no sabe leer y pone escuela. said to censure someone who is talking about something he or she doesn't know much about 58

mafiar to steal 56

mafufo(-a) yucky, gross, weird 154

el maíz money 162

Ni maíz. Nothing. 164

majá (majado[-a]) lazy 148

majadero(-a) ill-mannered 34

el/la majadero(-a) fraud, liar 62

majasear to goof off 147

maje stupid 224

ser un mal bicho to have bad character 30

estar mal de la azotea/cholla to be crazy 53

estar de mal humor to be in a bad mood 28

mal nacido(-a) jerk, SOB 33

mal que bien in any possible way, no matter what 256

estar de mal talante to be in a bad mood 28

a la mala sloppily; using force 131

la mala ficha bad reputation 91

de mala gana gladly 152

la mala jugada dirty trick 122

estar de mala leche to be in a bad mood 28

de mala muerte crummy, poor quality 29

mala nota unpleasant thing or person; bad news; bad reputation 91

la mala pasada dirty trick 122

estar de mala uva to be in a bad mood 28

ser un malaje to have bad character 31

las malas juntas bad influence 26

las malas lenguas rumormongers, gossipers 115

a malas penas with great difficulty or effort 257

estar de malas pulgas to be in a bad mood 28

maldito(-a) damn(ed) 27; great, good 110

¡Maldito(-a) sea! Damn it! 10

el maletero dirty fighter, troublemaker 70

malhablado(-a) crude in speaking habits, using bad language 51

en la malle straight to the heart 121

el malón surprise party in which friends arrive with food 97

maluca (malena) kind of nasty, lame 27

estar en las Malvinas to be in a bad way economically 248

el/la mama'o(-a) fool 223

mamacita term of address derived from mamá 5

la mamada nonsense; lie, fib 225

estar mamado(-a) to be drunk 78

estar mamando to be trying to borrow money, be hitting up 248

mamar to have oral sex 214

mamar una cosa con la leche (en la leche) to learn something at a very young age 80

mamar gallo to tease 84

la mamasota good-looking woman; term to get a woman's attention 24

el mameluco oral sex 214

Qué mamera. How boring. 38

No mames. That's enough. Don't be so tiresome. 15

mamey good, high-quality 108

el mamey oral sex 214

ser un mamey to be easy 80

No mameyes en tiempos de melones. euphemism for ¡No mames! 15

mami, mamita term of affection for girl or woman 5; term used to get a woman's attention 20

el mamito handsome or elegant young fellow; mommy's boy 24

el mamitón guy who likes to be seen with girls 198

el mamo handsome guy, guy with a lot of women 24

el mamón, la mamona tiresome or annoying person 15; person who takes advantage of others 205

el/la man guy (girl) 118

ser un manazas to be a klutz 132

la mancha de plátano quality of being a real native of Puerto Rico 173

¡Manda huevo (cojones)! used to indicate impossibility, opposition, surprise, the height of something 228

mandar a alguien a... to tell someone to go to . . . 139

mandarse un discurso to deliver a sermon 56

¿Mande? Excuse me? What (did you say)? 133

el mandilón henpecked man, milktoast 247

mandón, mandona bossy 24

ser Mandraque el Mago to be a wonder worker 44

mandujano so-and-so 174

mangar to steal 56; to deceive 64

el mango money, dough 162

el mango, manguito good-looking person 23

la mani, manifa demonstration 232

ser un manitas to be good at doing things, handy 44

el manitas coward, sissy, wimp 92

la manito de gato touch-up, quick once-over to help someone look good 175

estar a mano to be even (with each other) 217

el/la mano(-a), manito(-a) close friend 104

la mano de santa effective remedy 126

ser mano de santo to work like a charm 108

el manotazo blow with the hand 122

Manuela masturbation 214

manyar to eat 98

el manzano young person who is innocent, not very active socially 137

la maña bad habit 28

no estar en el mapa to be unusual, not ordinary 242

la máquina machine; car 238

la maraca whore; bitch 31

ser una maraca sin palo to be incompetent, a ding-a-ling 132

la marca perra common low-quality brand in a product 232

la marca pistola common low-quality brand in a product 232

marcando ocupado out of it, not understanding anything 48

marchar requete bien to be going very well 226

marchar sobre ruedas to be going smoothly, great 226

el marica sissy 173

el maricón homosexual 173

la mariconada dirty trick 122; attitude or act of being effeminate or gay 173

la marimacho/la marimacha lesbian; tomboy 173

el mariposa homosexual 173

el mariposo, el mariposón homosexual 173

el mariquita sissy; euphemism for maricón 173

el marrano pig (dirty or fat); undesirable person 34

el marrón mess, bad situation, embarrassing situation 158

martes 13 Tuesday the 13th (unlucky) 155

martillar to work 258

el martilleo work 258

maruja homebody, home-loving 171

el marullo rip-off, setup, rigged election or game 62

ser más bueno que el pan to be as good as gold 112

más cerrado(-a) que un huevo de gallina (un tubo de radio) very stupid 224

ser más corto(-a) que las mangas de un chaleco to be stupid 225

¿Qué más da? Who cares? 136

ser más del campo que las amapolas to be a hick 170

ser más desgraciado(-a) que el Pupas to be very unlucky 155

estar más despistado(-a) que un pulpo en un garaje to be lost, off the track 47

más días hay que longanizas there's no rush 235

más duro(-a) que el cemento stingy 206

más feo(-a) que carracuca very ugly 241

más feo(-a) que mandado a hacer uglier than a toad 241

ser más (tan) fresco(-a) que una lechuga to be brazen, cool as a cucumber, fresh as a daisy 146

Era más grande (pequeño) el difunto. said to someone when they are wearing a large (small) article of clothing 74

más largo(-a) que la esperanza del pobre very tall 178

más lento(-a) que una caravana de cojos as slow as a snail 219

más lento(-a) que un suero de brea as slow as molasses 219

estar más liado(-a) que la pata de un romano (de una momia) to be a very messy or tangled situation, a can of worms 158

más listo(-a) que el hambre bright, quick-witted 141

más listo(-a) que un rayo (que el relámpago) smart, sharp as a tack 141

más loco(-a) que una cabra crazier than a she-goat 54

Más o menos. OK. 116

más pelado(-a) que la rodilla de un cabro broke 249

más pesado(-a) que cargar un elefante unpleasant (person) 31

más planchado(-a) que un sapo en la carretera with no wrinkles 177

ser más puta que las gallinas to be more of a slut than the hens are 212

más que la cresta very badly, a lot 152

más rápido(-a) que ligero(-a) hurriedly, in a rush 220

estar más serio(-a) que un burro en lancha to look worried 259

ser más sordo(-a) que una tapia to be deaf as a doornail 177

Más ven cuatro ojos que dos. Four eyes are better than two. 127

más viejo(-a) que Matusalén older than Methuselah 7

más viejo(-a) que el pargo de la meseta older than the snapper on the mesa 7

más viejo(-a) que el pinol as old as the hills 7

sus más y sus menos difficulties or complications that a matter gives 69

el mataburros dictionary 232
matado(-a) awful; graceless; boring 27; exhausting 88
matador(-a) exhausting 88; fabulous, wonderful 110; ugly, bad; delightful 242
el mátalas callando discreet womanizer who appears faithful 215
matar to finish off or up 97
matar al oso to masturbate 214
matar dos pájaros de un tiro to achieve two goals at once 45
matarse por una cosa to kill oneself for something 256
el/la matasanos doctor, quack 126
las mate math 80
el/la mateo(-a) bookworm 82
los mates attitude, customs 28
el matricidio matrimony, used in jest 199
ser lo máximo to be fantastic, the greatest, the best 111
mayúsculo(-a) major 242
mazo many, large amount 190
¿Qué me cuentas? What's happening? 165
mear fuera del tiesto (tarro) to make a mistake 86
mear(se) to urinate, pee 36
mearse de (la) risa to wet one's pants with laughter 147
mechado(-a) studious 82
mechar(se) to study very hard 81
mechudo(-a) with hair uncombed or very long 177
media cosita every little thing 232
la media naranja spouse, sweetheart, soul mate 198
medio mundo a lot of people 170
a medio palo half done; inconclusive, up in the air 255
medio raro kind of weird; possibly gay 241
medir calles to hang out in the street 130
el melón, la melona foolish, stupid 223
los melones woman's breasts 36
la memez stupid thing or idea, idiocy 225
memo(-a) foolish, stupid 224
mi (el/la) menda I, me 174
el/la menda so-and-so 174
menear el bote to dance 60
menear el esqueleto to dance 60
menearse to get moving, get a move on 4
el menjurje (menjunje) mess, confusion 158
Menos da una piedra. It's better than nothing. It could be worse. 197
Menos lobos (Caperucita). Don't exaggerate so much. 246
en menos que canta un gallo in very little time, in a jiffy 221
mensear to act like a fool; to confuse with silly talk 222

menso(-a) stupid, foolish 224
el/la mensolaco(-a) crazy retard 223
mentar la madre to insult someone by suggesting the moral impurity of his or her mother 138
la mente de alcantarilla dirty mind 234
el menudo número fine state of affairs, pretty picture 26
el/la mequetrefe just anyone, mediocre or pretentious person who won't amount to much 33
¡Mera mano! Hey, pal!, term of affection used to call a friend 116
el merequetengue disorder, confusion, mess 158
el merluzo dope, idiot 224
del mero bad, awful 27
el mero jodón big boss 25
el mero mero (la mera mera); el mero mero petatero main or most important person; head honcho 25
mero(-a) exact, this or that very (one) 43
mero: Ya mero. Ya merito. Almost. It's (I'm, etc.) on the way, almost ready. 236
la mescolanza confusion, mess 158
el metelón, la metelona busybody 115
metelón, metelona fearless 52
el/la métepatas busybody 115
meter to swallow, eat or drink 97
meter a alguien con cuchara una cosa to spoon-feed something to someone 127
meter baza to butt in 141
meter cabeza to pay attention; to persist in getting something 22
meter el cazo to be wrong 86
meter chala (fierro, pata) to step on it, accelerate 220
meter una chiva to make up a fib 64
meter el coco to concentrate on something 235
meter cuarta to step on it, step on the gas 220
meter la cuchara to butt in 142
meter fuego to activate or animate, fire up 84
meter de galleta a alguien to include someone not suitable in a group 245
meter el hocico en todo to stick one's nose into everything 114
meter mano to touch someone with sexual intentions 214
meter la mano hasta el codo en algo to do something with great dedication 3; to take something selfishly 203
meter las manos al fuego por alguien to vouch for someone 128
meter el pie to get into a house, business 188

meter en un puño a alguien to intimidate or oppress someone 121

meter la mula to betray, deceive, do a bad turn 64

meter un paquete to fine 55

meter la pata to put one's foot in one's mouth, make a mistake 86

meterle to step on it, step on the gas 220

meterle caña to study hard, put out some effort 81

meterle candela to put some effort into it, get down to business 256

meterle la chancla al pedal to step on it, step on the gas 220

meterle mano to take, undertake 4

meterle velocidad to hurry up 220

meterse algo en la cabeza to get an idea and cling to it 234

meterse algo entre ceja y ceja to get an idea and cling to it 234

meterse en la boca del lobo to expose oneself to unnecessary danger 185

meterse en camisa de once varas to bite off more than one can chew; to get mixed up in something unnecessarily 185

meterse en Honduras to get into deep trouble 185

meterse como la pobreza to appear all over and spread like wildfire 219

meterse en el sobre to go to bed 218

¡Métetelo donde te quepa (por el culo)! Up yours! 140

metiche nosy; busybody, buttinsky 115

la metida (metedura) de pata gaffe, mistake 87

el/la metido(-a) busybody 115

estar metido(-a) to be in love 200

estar metido(-a) en un rollo to be in a problem, bind 185

estar metido(-a) hasta los codos en algo to be up to one's elbows in something 39

México es un pañuelo. Mexico is a small world. 179

mezclar la velocidad con el tocino to mix things that are very different 71

No se mide (te mides). You're really something. You're too much. 243

de miedo awesome, super 110

miel sobre hojuelas expression meaning that one thing goes very well with another, adding to its attractiveness 22

¡Miércoles! Shoot!, euphemism for **¡Mierda!** 15

de mierda crappy, shitty 27

¡Mierda! Shit! 15

Ni mierda. No, nothing. 164

ser una mierda to be very bad, worthless, shitty 27

a la mierda: mandar a alguien... to tell someone to go to hell 139

¿Qué mierda es ésta? What the hell is happening? What's going on? 11, 229

la migra U.S. INS, immigration 232

Miguel(ito)/Tiburcio me/you 174

¡Mijito(-a) rico(-a)! Hey, babe! 24

m'ijo, m'ija short for **mi hijo, mi hija** 5

de mil (todos los) diablos very bad, a heck of a 27

de mil amores with pleasure 152

a las mil maravillas very good, excellent, perfectly 108

el mili short for **servicio militar** 25

el milico soldier 25

el/la millonetis millionaire, rich person 250

la mina girl, woman 118

la minga thank-you party for workers 169

el ministerio de guerra one's wife (ironic) 171

el minón gorgeous babe 24

miquear to take it easy, not work too hard 198; to flirt, draw attention 199

el miqueo easy job, snap, breeze 258

miquiar to cry 203

¡Mira quién habla! Look who's talking! 58

Mírame esta cara. phrase implying innocence or that the other person is unaware of one's merits 137

mírame y no me toques describing a very fussy person or things that break easily 32

mirar los toros desde la barrera to stay out of harm's way 87

mirar a alguien por encima del hombro to look down one's nose at someone 180

mirarse en alguien como en un espejo to love someone; to look like someone 4

Mírate en ese espejo. Let that be a lesson for you. 230

misio(-a) poor, without money 249

ser de la misma madera to be of the same nature (wood) or in the same condition 216

ser el mismísimo demonio to be the devil himself, very perverse or cunning 30

el mismo (la misma) que viste y calza yours truly 174

Lo mismo es Chana que Juana. There's no choice. Two of the same. 217

miti-miti (miti-mota) halves on a bill, dutch treat 142

el mitote gossip, rumor 116; party; mess 158

la mocha fight 70

el/la mocho(-a) overly religious in appearances, always in church 171

Ni mocho. No, no way, used instead of **Ni modo.** 165

el/la mocoso(-a) kid 119

a la moda "with it" 111
Ni módulo (como dijo el astronauta). No way. 165
el mogollón disorder, exaggeration, abundance 190
mojado(-a) wetback, illegal(ly) 173
no mojarse to not take any risk 91
mojarse el culo en algo to get involved in something 4
el mojón turd 36
el/la mojonero(-a) liar, deceitful person 62
molar to please, be pleasing to 154
molar cantidad to be very pleasing to; to "rock" 154
de molde fitting, perfectly 109
molido(-a) exhausted 89
molón, molona bothersome, annoying 15
el molote tumult; crowd 170
Un momentico. Just a moment. 236
la momia geezer, old fogy 7
la momiza geriatric set, fogies 7
estar como la mona to be feeling bad (physically or mentally), be under the weather 116
ser una monada to be cute, pretty, darling 23
ser la monda to be extraordinary (good or bad, things) 243
el mono sketch, drawing 232
Mono mayor. Monkey see, monkey do. 217
Mono sabe el palo que trepa. a threat, like Watch it! 246
mono(-a) cute 23; blond or with light brown hair 178
montar un cirio to raise a fuss, do something that gets attention 159
montar un cotorreo to start a gab session 114
montar un numerito to cause a scene, do something that gets attention 159
montar un número to behave badly, have a fit, cause a scene 159
montar el rapeo (montar rancho) to sweet-talk 176
montarse el rollo to use one's wits or find a way to get something 257
el monte marijuana 76
ser del montón to be common, mediocre 167
el montón (los montones) a lot (of), heaps 190
a montones abundantly, in big quantities 189
moqueado(-a) sad 202
moquiar to cry, snivel 203
morder to understand 143
morder el cordobán (la soga) to bite the bullet, do something one has to do 197

morderse la lengua to bite one's tongue, avoid saying something 191
la mordida bribe 161
estar mordido(-a) to be angry 10
moreno(-a) black (person) 178
morir con las botas puestas to keep on working up to the end of one's life 60
morir pollo to keep quiet, keep one's lips sealed 191
morir vestido(-a) to die violently 60
morirse de risa to die of laughter 147
morocho(-a) brunette 178
el moropo head 35
el morro brazenness, nerve 188
el/la morro(-a), morrito(-a) young person, kid 119
morrocotudo(-a) great, fantastic 110
mortadela great, good; (n.) pretty girl 110
ser mortal to be difficult 69
mortal good, great, super 242
estar mosca to be suspicious and alert to avoid something 21
mosquear to bother, pester 18
la mosquita (mosca) muerta snake in the grass, hypocrite 63
mostrar los dientes to smile 147; to threaten 246
mostrar las uñas to bare one's nails, show one's true colors 247
la mota marijuana 76
motearse to smoke marijuana 76
el motivito party among friends 169
la moto motorcycle, short for **motocicleta** 239
el mouse mouse (computer) 231
no mover un dedo to not lift a finger 130
mover el esqueleto to get going, get a move on 4; to dance 60
la movida unlawful business 55; influential friend 102; the action, the scene, fun 104; romance, prospect 202
en la movida "with it" 111
la muchachada group of young people 170
Mucho ojo, que la vista engaña. Be careful because appearances are deceptive. 246
mucho ruido y pocas nueces said when something yields very little despite appearances or expectations 26
la muela talk, chat, sweet-talk 176
ser un muermo to be a drag, a snooze 39
estar de muerte to be very attractive (a woman) 24
la muerte excellent, incredible, super 110
ser la muerte en bicicleta to be as slow as a snail 219
El muerto al hoyo y el vivo al bollo. The dead person in the hole and the opportunist at the widow. 204

muerto(-a) empty, boring 38; slow, with no initiative 219

andar (estar) muerto(-a) de hambre to be starving to death 99

estar muerto(-a) de risa to be dying of laughter 147

la mujer de mal vivir prostitute 212

la mujer fatal femme fatale 24

la mujer rabo verde dirty old woman 212

el mujeriego (mujerero) womanizer 214

muletear to deceive, fool 64

multiplicarse por cero to keep quiet 191

El mundo es un ranchón (una hacienda). It's a small world. 179

la muñeca pretty girl 23; connections, pull 102

el muñeco good-looking man 23

muñeco(-a) term of affection 6

muñeco viejo old hat 48

muñequear to use connections, pull 102

la música sacudida lively music 59

ser muy cabrón (cabrona) para algo to be very good at something 44

el/la muy condenado(-a) that darn guy (girl, man, woman, etc.) 14

muy especial expression sometimes used ironically to mean difficult 26

estar muy lejos to be far from what is said or done 71

ni muy muy ni tan tan mediocre, blah, happy medium 167

estar muy potable to look good physically 23

estar muy verde to be innocent, immature, not socially active 137

ser muy vivo(-a) to be a go-getter, good at getting ahead 203

N

Nacaradas conchas. Nothing. No way. 163

nacer con el pie derecho to be born lucky 156

nacer de pie to be born lucky 156

naco(-a) jerk, uneducated or rude person 33

Nada de eso. Not at all. 164

Nada, pescadito mojado. Zero, nothing. 164

no ser nada (cosa) del otro jueves to not be extraordinary 167

no ser nada del otro mundo to be nothing to write home about, not rare 167

nadar contra la corriente to go against the current 52

¡Nadie lo (la) salva! Nothing can be done. It's a hopeless case. 183

como nalga de lavandera very cold, cold as a witch's tit 251

¡Naranjas de la China! No! Nothing doing! 164

Naranjas. No. No way. 164

el/la narco drug dealer 76

estar hasta las narices to be fed up 17

narices dickens, often a euphemism for **cojones** 11, 140

la nave car, usually large 238

navegar con bandera de inocente (de tonto) to pretend to be innocent or foolish but have a motive for it 63

los negocios chuecos monkey business 225

negro(-a) term of affection, used for people of any skin color 6

estar negro(-a) to be fed up, sick of 16

Nel. Nel, pastel. No. No way. 164

el/la nene(-a) used instead of **niño(-a)** 119

el/la nene(-a) de papá kid who has everything solved for him or her by the parents' influence 250

el nerdo nerd 171

la neta the truth 239

el/la nica Nicaraguan, short for **nicaragüense** 173

Nicaragua es un ranchón (una hacienda). Nicaragua is a small world. 179

De ninguna manguera (como dijo el bombero). Absolutely not. 163

ningunear to treat (someone) badly, as a nobody 129

la niña fresa naive, conservative girl 137

ser la niña de los (sus) ojos to be the apple of one's eyes 4

la niña pija young, innocent upper-class or spoiled girl 250

el niño (la niña) bien well-brought-up (upper-class) boy (girl) 250

como niño con juguete nuevo happy, like a kid in a candy store 119

como niño con zapatos nuevos happy, like a kid in a candy store 119

los niños popis rich brats 250

nítido(-a) great, perfect, correct, very acceptable 110

nitidón, nitidona really great 110

En la noche todos los gatos son pardos. It is hard to see any difference between some things. 216

la noche toledana sleepless night, night of insomnia 218

¡Nones! No! 165

¡Nones para los preguntones! Don't ask too many questions! 58

Al nopal lo van a ver sólo cuando tiene tunas. saying that means people call on others only when they're doing well 203

norteado(-a) disoriented, confused 47

la nota drunkenness 77

en nota high, inebriated 79
¡Qué nota! How nice! 108
la(s) nota(s) news 165
¿Qué notas me cuentas? What news can you tell me? 165
estar en las nubes to be daydreaming 131
de nuez again 235
estar como nunca to look better than ever 23
Nunca falta un pelo en la sopa. There's always a hitch, problem. 183

Ñ

las ñáñaras heebie-jeebies, nervousness, willies 260
el/la ñato(-a) guy, gal 118
mi ñeco my friend 104
el/la ñero(-a) buddy, pal 103
el ñero Mataratas dirty Dan or any name of disrespect 138
ñien cool, good 110
el/la ñis buddy, pal 103
ñor, ñora short for **señor, señora** 118

O

O sea... That is . . . 128
¿Somos o no somos? Are we on or not? Are you with me or not? 50
O somos o no somos. phrase meaning that because we are who we are we can or should act in a certain way or do a certain thing 50
ser una obra maestra to be great, wonderful 108
el ocho rear end 36
ser la octava maravilla to be the eighth wonder (of the world), said of things 108
¡Qué ocurrencia! The very idea! 71
¡Oiga! Excuse me, may I speak to you? 20
Oigo. phrase for answering the phone 117
el ojete asshole 30
estar ojo al charqui to take special care with something 21
Ojo pelado. Keep your eyes peeled. 247
Ojo piojo. Keep your eyes peeled. 247
Okei. OK. 8
no oler bien una cosa, oler mal to seem suspicious 26
estar en la olla to be in hot water, in trouble 185
en la onda "with it" 111
estar de/en onda to be "in," cool, "with it" 111
la onda gruesa heavy (difficult, scary, dangerous) thing, situation 186
¿Qué onda(s)? What's happening? 117
Oquey, maguey. Okey-dokey. 8

Órale. used to get someone to do something or accept an invitation; all right; that's it; OK 84
Estoy a sus órdenes. I am at your service. 127
ordinario(-a) common, low-class, tacky 167
el/la oreja spy, informer 136
¡La osa! Jeez!, exclamation of surprise 228
¡Qué oso! How embarrassing! 82
¡Ostras! Darn! 11; Holy cow! 229
estar en otra to feel spaced out, detached 47
ser de la otra acera to be homosexual 173
de la otra banqueta homosexual 172
ser otra canción (otro cantar) to be another kettle of fish 72
Otra cosa es con guitarra. That's a different thing. 72
A otra cosa, mariposa. That's that, forget it. On to a new topic. 43, 193
Otra cosa, mariposa. Not the same thing. 72
La otra patita. Let's move on now. 84
del otro barrio homosexual 172
del otro lado (bando) homosexual 172
del otro Laredo homosexual 172
Óyeme manito. Hey, pal!, term of affection used to call a friend 116

P

p'allacito; de la mierda p'allacito in some godforsaken place 73
pa' (para) que sepas just so you know 144
la pachanga, el pachangón party 169
el pacheco cold, low temperature 251
la pachocha dough, money 162
el pachuco someone who dresses in a bizarre or unacceptable way; slang 75
los pacos police 26
de pacotilla of bad quality or little importance 29
la pacotilla gang, crowd 170
padre, padrísimo(-a) fantastic, super 110
¡Tu padre! expression of anger 140
padrote good, great 111
el padrote pimp 214
pagar con la misma moneda to give tit for tat 217
pagar el pato (los patos) to pay for something unfairly, be left holding the bag 137
pagar los platos/vidrios rotos to pay for something unfairly, be left holding the bag 138
pagar el piso to pick up the tab or get the worst of the lot because of lack of seniority 162
pagar por sustos to buy something on credit 162

el/la **paisa** person from the same place or country 103

la **paja** lie, nonsense 62

pajarear to observe, look at 22

el **pájaro** effeminate man; homosexual 173; male organ 214

pajarón, pajarona absentminded, forgetful 101

el/la **pajero(-a)** liar; someone who talks a lot with no point 62

¡Pa'joderte! Screw you! 140

el/la **pajoso(-a)** liar; someone who talks a lot with no point 62

Ni pa'l carajo. No damn way. 165

Son palabras mayores. There's something very serious or difficult that has to be talked about. 184

palabrear to try to persuade, talk a lot 176

la **palabrota** swearword, vulgar word 51

la **palanca** someone who helps someone, uses his or her influence to their benefit 102

palancón, palancona very tall, from **palanca** 178

palanquear to help, e.g., get a job 102

la **paleta** one who does favors, helps out 128

ser paleta to be slow, a bit inept 132

en paleta abundantly, a lot 190

la **paleteada** favor 128

la **paliza** boring time 38

palmarse (palmarla) to die 60

ser un palo to be boring, a drag (people or things) 39

el **palo** male organ 214

el **palo de escoba** person who is too skinny 178

el **palo grueso** big cheese 25

la **paloma** male organ 214

el/la **palomilla** street urchin, beggar child 249

Ni a palos. No way. 164

el **paltón, la paltona** well-dressed person 75

las **pamplinas** stupidities, trivia 225

ser un pan to be kind, unselfish 112

ser pan comido to be very easy, a piece of cake 80

ser (un) pan de Dios to be good, an angel 112

ser como el pan sin sal to be bland, unattractive 38

el/la **pana** friend, buddy, pal 103

mi **pana-burda** my dear pal, my special buddy 103

el **panal** long-term group of friends 103

estar en pañales to have little or no knowledge (of something) 145; to be young 261

la **panda** band, gang 170

pando(-a) unlucky 155

la **pandura** bad luck 155

panetela good, kind, nice 112

la **panocha** female organ 212

ser una papa to be easy, a piece of cake 80

la **papa** food, especially used for children 100

estar en la papa to be in the money, have some money 250

ser una papa sin sal to be bland, unattractive 39

ser una papa suave (una papita) to be easy 80

Ni papa(s). No, nothing. 165

papacito term of affection for a man 6

estar papando (cachando) moscas to be acting foolish, goofing off 222

¡Papas! Great! You're on! Agreed! 8

la **papaya** female organ 212

papazote big daddy 6

papear to eat 98

papel mojado something useless or of little importance 245

papi term of affection often used by women to men 6

el **papisongo, papichulín, papisón, papisuqui, papito, papazote** handsome guy 23

papucho daddy-o, big daddy (for boyfriends, not dads) 6

el **paquete** lie, fraud 63

de paquete riding behind in a two-wheeled vehicle 238

paquete(-a) elegant, nicely turned out (people or things) 23, 75

ser un paquete to be very attractive, chic 23

paquetear to deceive 64

el/la **paquetero(-a)** fraud; liar 62

para acabarla de joder to make matters worse 184

no estar para bromas to not be in a joking mood 28

ser para chuparse los dedos to be delicious 97

para colmo; para colmo de desgracias (de males) to top it all off, on top of everything else 184

estar para comérselo to be very attractive 23

para dar y regalar in abundance 190

para dar y tomar in abundance 190

Para luego es tarde. He who hesitates is lost. 246

para parar un tren very strong 222

para puro paladar curtivo for gourmets 152

¿Para qué? You're welcome. 231

¡Para los (las) que amamos! For those whom we love! (a toast) 98

estar para sopitas y buen vino to be up in years, very elderly 6

No es para tanto. It's not as bad as all that. 146

para tirar pa' (para) arriba in abundance 190

ni para vestir santos worthless 244

el/la paracaidista freeloader, party crasher 205

parar (la) oreja (parar las orejas) to prick up one's ears, listen carefully 22

parar bolas to pay attention 22

parar de decir paridas to stop saying ridiculous things 222

parar los pelos de punta to make someone's hair stand on end (from fear) 91

parar(se) en seco to stop cold (stop in one's tracks) 142

pararle el carro a to firmly prevent (someone from doing something), put one's foot down 142

parcelero(-a) ridiculous, uneducated 170

el/la parcero(-a) friend, member of a certain group 103

parchar to have sex 213

el parche group of friends, band 103

¿Qué te parece (si...)? How does it seem to you (if...)? How about (if...)? How do you like...? 152

parece Volkswagen con las puertas abiertas having very large ears 177

parecer araña fumigada to be suffering from the effects of too much partying or drinking 79

parecer un arroz con bicicleta to seem absurd 3

parecer chiva loca to be running around like crazy 53

parecer un pato mareado to seem confused or dim-witted 47

parecer que alguien está empollando huevos to seem like a homebody 171

parecer que se ha tragado un palo de escoba to be hard to deal with, uppity or arrogant 182

parecer siete pisos to seem or look very tall 178

parecerse una cosa a otra como un huevo a una castaña to be very different 72

parar la antena to listen 22

Parió la mula. It was a surprise. It hit the fan. 155, 227

parir chayotes to do something very difficult 69

parla conversation, way of speaking 48

parlar to talk 48

en un parpadeo fast 221

estar parquiado(-a) (parqueado) to be bored stiff 39

la parrafada long, uninterrupted conversation 49

el/la parrandista party lover 169

partes euphemism for private parts 211

partido effeminate (adj.) 211

partido(-a) very hungry 99

partir el brazo a alguien to take advantage of the opportunity (to get something) 257

partirle a alguien el alma to break someone's heart 230

partirle a alguien la cara to beat someone up 124

partirse de risa to break up with laughter 147

partirse los cojones to work very hard, work one's tail off 257

el parto de los montes something very difficult 68

el/la pasa rato boyfriend or girlfriend who's just OK for now; in the feminine, slut 202

¿Qué pasa, panita? How ya doin', my friend? 117

pasable tolerable, so-so 167

ser una pasada to be expensive, overpriced 161

de pasada on the fly, fast and while doing something else 220

pasado(-a) stoned 76

pasadón, pasadona out of date, old-fashioned 29

Pasáme el mate. Let me get a word in. 142

pasar to pass (on something), decline 88; to be indifferent 134

no pasar a alguien to not be able to stand someone 152

pasar a mejor vida to pass away 60

pasar de castaño oscuro to be or get too serious or troublesome (things) 186

pasar la bola to pass the buck in conversation 88

pasar las de Caín to have a rough time, often financially 184

pasar la cuenta (a alguien) to reprimand; to settle accounts 124

pasar gato por liebre to deceive (someone), giving him or her something inferior 64

pasar muchas navidades y sin nochebuena describing a bitter person 202

pasar la noche contando estrellas (cabritos) to spend the night counting sheep, be sleepless 218

pasar la noche en blanco/en claro/en vela to spend a sleepless night 218

pasar plancha to suffer an awkward moment 83

pasar por alto to go over one's head; to forget or not realize, miss 101

pasar por el alambre to not eat for lack of money or time 249

pasarla de peluche to have a great time 106

pasarlas negras (canutas) to have a rough time 184

pasarlas putas to have a hell of a time 184

pasarlo(-a) bien to have a good time 106

pasarlo bomba to have a great time 106

pasarlo caballo/regio/chancho to have a great time, a blast 106

pasarlo en (a lo) grande to have a great time 106

pasarlo piola to take it easy, keep cool 146

pasarlo pipa to have a great time 106

pasarse to go beyond the limit, go too far 242

pasarse con ficha to pass, avoid a response 88

pasarse de listo(-a) to try to show oneself (erroneously) to be smarter than others 203

pasarse de la raya to go beyond the limit, over the line 242

pasarse de rosca to go above and beyond, go overboard 242

pasarse de vivo(-a), de víbora to try to show oneself (erroneously) to be smarter than others 203

pasársele la mano to go too far, overdo it 242

Te pasaste. You did something wrong, goofed. 87

estar como unas pascuas to be very happy 120

de Pascuas a Ramos once in a blue moon 101

pasearse en algo to ruin something 126

Pasemos a otro patín. Let's change the subject. 43

a paseo: mandar a alguien... to tell someone to get lost 139

¿Qué pasión? variant of ¿Qué pasó? 117

la pasma police 26

pasmado(-a) foolish, stupid 225; broke, penniless; without a significant other 249

pasmar to dumbfound or surprise; to scold 227

el pasme problem, embarrassment, stupefaction 186

a paso de tortuga slow as a snail, at a snail's pace 218

Pasó la vieja. said to mean that someone missed out on something, missed the boat 166

Pasó un ángel. said when there is silence in a conversation 191

el/la pasota someone who doesn't care about anything, slacker 134, 148

la pasta money 163

la pasta gansa a lot of money, a fortune 163

pastelear to make out 5

a pata walking 238

la pata de perro (pata'eperro) gadabout, person on the go 106

a pata pelada barefoot 74

estar de la patada to be in a bad way 125

patalear to die; to end 60

la pataleta fit, tantrum 13

el patán lowlife 34

las patas feet 37

patas pa'arriba (patas arriba) topsy-turvy, disorganized 159

la patata caliente very delicate matter 186

el patatús tantrum, (fainting) fit 13

patear to walk a lot, a long way 239

patear la perra to do something as an outlet for repressed anger, blow off some steam 13

el/la patialegre party lover 169

a patín walking 238

¿En qué patín andas? How are things? 117

patinarle a alguien el coco to be crazy, have a slipped gear mentally 54

patinarle a alguien el embrague to be crazy, have a slipped gear mentally 54

Patitas, ¿pa' qué te [las] quiero? said when one is about to flee from danger 68

el pato sissy; homosexual 173

estar pato to be broke 248

el patojo homosexual, gay 173

el/la patojo(-a) guy (girl) 118

patón, patona person who can't dance 59

como patos cagados easy to capture or kill, like sitting ducks 137

los patos malos bad guys 30

la patota bunch of people 170

las patriarcas feet 37

las patrullas feet 37

el/la patudo(-a) pushy or nervy person 188

la pava girl, woman 118; easy woman 212

la pavera silly giggling, childish nonsense 146

el pavo boring or socially inept person 38

la payasada silly thing or action 107

ser como payaso de circo to be silly 105

el/la payuco(-a) country bumpkin 170

de pe a pa entirely; from beginning to end 46

el pe'o drunkenness 77

la pechocha well-endowed woman, with a large bust 24

el/la pechoño(-a) very religious person 171

la pechuga almendrada appetizing bust 37

la pechugona big-breasted woman 24

pedazo de... used to intensify an insult 58
el pedazo de alcornoque blockhead, fool 224
ser un pedazo de carne con ojos to be useless 245
ser un pedazo de pan to be affable, good-natured 112
pedir un aventón/jalón to ask for a lift 238
a pedir de boca exactly as one wishes, just right or perfect 175
pedir una bola/cola to ask for a ride 238
pedir cacao to give up in a fight, say "uncle" 66
En pedir no hay engaño. No harm in asking. 196
pedir la luna to ask for something in vain 130
pedir peras al olmo to ask for something in vain 130
pedir pon to ask for a ride 238
pedirle cobija al frío to ask for the impossible 130
pedirle comida al hambre to ask for the impossible 130
el pedo problem 186
al pedo (pe'o) worthless, bad 244
estar (en) pedo(-a) to be drunk 78
¿Qué pedo? youth slang for **¿Qué pasa?** 117
la pega job, work 258
pegado(-a) a las faldas clinging to the skirt, dependent 102
pegado(-a) a la pared confused, not able to react 47
pegajoso(-a) pesky, always at one's side (person); catchy or sticking in one's mind (things) 15
pega-pega pesky; catchy or sticking in one's mind 15; attractive 22
pegar to work 257
pegar la gorra to eat at someone else's house, sponge 205
pegar el grito to protest, cry out 45
no pegar una to goof up constantly 87
pegar una cosa como guitarra en un entierro to be out of time or place 3
no pegar los ojos en toda la noche, no pegar ojo to not sleep a wink the whole night 218
pegarle en la nuca to have an affair with someone's partner 211
pegarle en la pera to freeload a meal from someone 205
pegarse unos cuantos pititos to have a few joints (of marijuana) 76
pegarse la gran picada to have sex 213
pegarse la vida padre to live it up 106
pegársele a alguien las sábanas to oversleep 218

pegársele a alguien la silla (el asiento) to stay somewhere for a long time, settle in 130
el pegue appeal; sex appeal 22
el/la pela-bola penniless bum 249
la pelada haircut 35
pelado(-a) shameless, rude 33; broke, penniless 249
el/la pelagatos jerk 33
estar pelando to be trying to borrow money, be hitting up 249
pelao(-a) como un guineo dying of laughter 147
pelar el ajo to work like a dog 257
pelar cable to talk nonsense 223
pelar los dientes to smile or make smile 147
pelársela to do nothing 130; to not give a damn 134
pelárselas to do something quickly or intensely 221
peleados(-as) angry, treating each other as enemies 129
la peli movie 105
de película great, fantastic 110
la película verde erotic movie 105
el pellejo old geezer 7; body, bod 36
estar en el pellejo de otro to be in someone else's shoes 216
el pellizco pinch, small adjustment, tweaking 189
el pelma (pelmazo) idiot, boring person 14
al pelo exactly, just right 175
el pelo, pelito little bit, tad 189
el pelón mistake, goof up, snafu 87
el pelón, la pelona someone who can't make a joke or laughs at things that are not funny 146
la pelona death 61
de pelos great, fantastic, good 110
los pelos de la cola loose ends 232
en pelota(s) naked 163
Ni pelotas. No way, not at all. 165
pelotear to bounce around (e.g., from office to office) 121
la pelotera mess 158
pelotudo(-a) jerk (bitch), schmuck 140
la pelu beauty shop, barber shop 232
de peluche fantastic 110
estar peludo(-a) to be difficult or complicated 68
la pelusa the masses, hordes 170
la pelusa, el pelusón (la pelusona) street urchin, beggar child 249
penca lame, boring; low-quality 30
la penca euphemism for male organ 214
a (pura) penca by pure force of will 257
el/la penco(-a) coward 92

pencón(-a) dynamic, full of chutzpah, hustler in a good sense 52

la pendejada silly or stupid thing to do; trick 225

pendejear to behave in a foolish or stupid way 223

a lo pendejo like crazy, without thinking 131

el/la pendejo(-a) kid, child 119

pendejo(-a) foolish, stupid 224

pender de un hilo to hang from a thread 185

el/la pendex boy (girl); childish person 118

penquearse to really put effort into something, hustle 257

el/la pensante dope, idiot 224

Ni pensarlo. Don't even think about it. 165

la peña group of friends 103

Peor es chile y agua lejos. Things could be worse. 197

Peor es nada. It's better than nothing. 197

el/la peoresnada phrase used in jest to describe a boyfriend or girlfriend chosen because there was no one better 202

pepepato(-a) pretentious, arrogant 181

peque short for **pequeño(-a)** 178

ser la pera to be the limit, too much 243

los percances del oficio part and parcel of the job, occupational hazards 255

perder la chaveta to go crazy, be off one's rocker 54

perder el culo to do the impossible (for someone) 127; to move fast 220

perder los estribos to lose patience, lose your cool 12

perder el hilo to lose the thread (e.g., of a conversation) 48

perder el norte to be disoriented in what one says or does 47

perder el (último) tren to miss the boat, lose out 166

perder de vista to escape from or stop seeing (someone or something) 67

perderse de vista to be very superior; to be astute or clever 108

¡A la perica! expression of surprise 228

de perilla easy 80

de perillas timely or opportune 156

no ser perita en dulce to be difficult, disagreeable 31

ser una perla to be perfect, good 111

de perlas perfectly, great 110

Pero bendito... But please . . . 196

la perra bitchy woman 31; ten-cent coin 162

el perrillo de todas bodas person who likes to be at all social events and parties 106

perro(-a) rotten, mean, a bitch, difficult 27

como perro en canoa (en bote) nervous 260

ser como perro y gato to be enemies 129

los perros police 26

de perros very disagreeable, a bitch of a + noun 27

como perros y gatos like enemies 129

la persona tiliche perfect person, person who has everything 174

ser pesado(-a) to be a pain, a drag, boring or unpleasant 15, 38

a pesar de los pesares in spite of everything 183

pescar (un marido, etc.) to trap (a husband, etc.) 198

pescar un resfriado (un resfrío) to catch a cold 126

pescar en río revuelto to take advantage of confusion or disorder and profit from it 166

pese a quien pese at whatever cost, no matter what 256

El que pestañea pierde. He who hesitates is lost. If you snooze you lose. 246

ser un pestiño to be a bore 39

ser un petardo to be bad quality, boring or ugly 28

el petardo fart 35; idiot 224

petizo(-a) short, small 178

estar como pez en el agua to be in one's element 120

el pez gordo big shot, big cheese 25

el/la pibe(-a) kid, young person 119

Pica, lica y califica. Look before you leap. 246

las picadas appetizers 100

picado(-a) annoyed, resentful 14; enthusiastic or curious 86

picado(-a) de la araña fickle and flirtatious 30

Picado que come miel, ¡ay de él! Be careful not to lose control and like something too much. 246

el picaflor fickle and flirtatious person 30; playboy 198

picante tacky, low-class, in bad taste 30

el picao thing 233

estar pica'o(-a) to be drunk 78

picar a alguien to upset someone 18

picarla to go away 67

picarle to hurry up, get a move on 221

picarle a alguien una mosca to be bothered, have something be the matter 17

picarse to get angry, mad 13; to get annoyed, upset 17; to get drunk 79; to get caught up with, be interested, enthusiastic, or curious 86

picarse de... to pretend to be or act like . . . 180

la pichicata illegal drug 75

pichicato(-a) stingy 206
el/la pichiruche unimportant person who fusses about small details, lower civil servant 32
mi pichón my turtledove, love 6
el pico kiss 5; mouth 35; male organ 214
ser un pico to be a good talker 49
estar en la picota to be embarrassed 84
picudo(-a) well connected and clever 141
al pie de la letra exactly, to the letter 174
estar al pie del cañón to be ready and waiting 192
no ser de piedra to be vulnerable to sexual provocation 211
la piel girl 118
ser de la piel del diablo to be very mischievous, a little dickens 30
la pierde tiempo floozie 212
¡Piérdete! Go away! Get lost! Scram! 113
ser la pierna de alguien to be someone's main squeeze, be going out with that person 199
las piernas de canario skinny legs 36
¡Qué piernón! What shapely legs! 24
de (los) pies a (la) cabeza from head to toe, entirely 46
Pies, ¿para qué os quiero? said when one is about to flee from danger 68
la pija male organ 214
¡Pilas! Watch out! 247
pillar to catch, get 55
Te pillo mañana. Catch you tomorrow. 113
pillo(-a) sharp, alert, clever 141
piloso(-a) someone who studies a lot and does well in school 82
la piña clique, select group, two or more people who act as one 170
a pincel on foot, walking 238
los pinceles feet 37
Ni pincha ni corta. It's useless, of no influence or importance. 244
pinchar to get, take 56
pinche blasted, damn 27
pinche buey jerk, loser 33
pinche cabrón rotten bastard 140
la pinga male organ 214
de pinga, de pinguísima great, exciting, fantastic 110
a la pinta super, awesome 109
pintando varillas unemployed, out of work 130
pintar monos to show off, call attention to oneself; to be out of place 35
no pintar nada to not care, not get involved 133
pintar su calaverita to disappear 67
pintarlo (de) color de rosa to make it sound and look great, gild the lily 61

pintarse to go away, leave 67
pintarse solo(-a) to take the cake 243
pintarse solo(-a) para una cosa to be very skillful at something 44
pintárselo bonito to gild the lily, present a pretty picture 61
Píntate (de colores). Go away. 113
el/la piojo(-a) chico(-a) kid 119
el/la piola sponge, someone who wants a free ride 205
pipa (pepa) intelligent 141
de pipa y guante all dressed up 75
pipiris nais highfalutin, chic 108
el piquete shot of alcohol put in coffee 100
estar pirado(-a) to be crazy 53
la piraña person who eats a lot 98
el/la piraña shark; someone astute in business, taking advantage of others 205
pirar to disappear 67
pirarse to leave, go away, beat it 67
estar piripi to be drunk 78
piropear to compliment 180
la pirula male organ (children) 214
pisado(-a) son of a bitch (bitch) 140
pisado(-a), pisa'o(-a) dominated 121
pisar to have sex 213
pisarle los callos a alguien to bother, be all over someone 18
Pisémonos. Let's go. 68
pistear to drink (alcohol) 99; to bribe 161; to walk with no real destination, just for amusement or to be seen 239
el pisto money 163
la pistola male organ 214
pistudo(-a) having money 250
pitar to go, go away, run away 67
el pitillo marijuana joint 76; cigarette 237
el pito marijuana joint 76; male organ 214
la pitopausia male menopause 211
pituco(-a) affected, snobbish 181
pitudo(-a) with a very high voice, like a **pito** 177
el pitusa bluejeans 74
ni pizca de not even a shred of 165
planchar to fail (e.g., an exam) 90
planchar la oreja to go to bed, sleep 218
las planchas big feet 37
de plano for sure 43
plantar cara a alguien to oppose, defy, resist someone 69
el plantón standing up; someone who stands someone else up 194
estar de plantón to be stuck somewhere for a while, stood up 194
la plasta piece of excrement 36
plástico(-a) hypocritical, artificial or superficial 33
la plata money 162

el platal a lot of money 163
ser un plato to be funny, amusing, a real character 105
ser plato de segunda mesa to be or feel put off or not treated with consideration, play second fiddle 83
(no) ser plato del gusto de alguien to (not) be one's cup of tea 152
platudo(-a) rich 250
pleno(-a) good, great, good-looking; high 111
el plomazo lead balloon, a drag 38
ser un plomo to be boring 39
de un plumazo at the stroke of a pen 220
el pó fanny, bottom 36
po' short for **pues** 50
las poblaciones callampas slums 249
pobre como una rata poor as a churchmouse 249
pobre pero caballero/honrado poor but dignified 112
¡Pobrecito(-a)! Poor (little) thing! 230
ser de pocas pulgas to be fussy, delicate 32
el/la pocho(-a) someone of Mexican descent, usually those living in the United States 174
Un poco de respeto. A little respect. polite way of criticizing someone 59
poco espléndido(-a) tightfisted, stingy 206
a pocos pasos close by; without much effort 72
no poder alguien con sus huesos to be very tired 88
no poder más to not be able to take any more, be fed up 16
no poder ver a alguien ni en pintura (ni pintado) to not be able to stand the sight of someone 152
Poderoso caballero es don Dinero. Money is power. 250
estar podrido(-a) de dinero (de plata) to be filthy rich 250
la polilla de biblioteca bookworm 82
los polis policemen, coppers 26
la polla male organ 214
ser la polla to be unheard of, extraordinary 243
el/la pollo(-a) young person 118
pololear to go steady with someone 199
el/la pololo(-a) sweetheart, steady boyfriend (girlfriend) 202
el polvo blanco (polvo de ángel) cocaine 75
el pompis (pompas) rear end, derriere 36
Pon los pies sobre la tierra. Put your feet on the ground. 58
ponchar to fail (an exam); to puncture, as a tire 90

El que pone el baile que pague la marimba. The one who thinks up an idea should take care of implementing it. 197
poner a alguien a cien to excite or exasperate someone 18
poner a alguien como lazo de cochino/palo de gallinero/percha de perico to ream out, rip apart with insults 57
poner a alguien los nervios de punta to put someone's nerves on edge 260
poner a alguien los pelos de punta to make someone's hair stand on end 91
poner a alguien en su sitio (en su lugar) to put someone in his or her place 58
poner a alguien como un trapo (viejo) to bawl someone out with offensive and angry words 57
poner a alguien de vuelta y media to treat someone badly, heap insults on 57
poner la antena to listen 22
poner a caldo to criticize, say bad things about 57
poner como camote a alguien to give someone his or her due (dressing down, beating) 124
poner un candado a la boca to keep a secret or keep quiet 191
poner las cartas sobre la mesa to lay things out clearly 240
poner el cascabel al gato to bell the cat (do something difficult or dangerous) 69
poner en el cielo to praise highly 180
poner cuadrado(-a) to flatten, beat to a pulp 124
poner un cuatro to do the test for drunkenness 77
poner en los cuernos de la luna to praise (someone or something) a great deal 180
poner como dado to scold, chew out, hurt 124
poner el dedo a alguien to point the finger at someone 137
poner freno a algo to put a stop to something 142
poner el gorro to cheat on, be unfaithful to 211
poner gorro a alguien said of lovers who make out in someone else's presence, make someone feel like a fifth wheel 199
poner el grito en el cielo to complain or cry out loudly 45
poner el hombro to get down to work, put one's shoulder to the wheel 257
poner un huevo to make a mistake 87
poner en mente to warn, make (someone) aware 247
poner parejo to flatten, beat to a pulp 124
poner en la picota to embarrass 84

315

poner pies con cabezas las cosas to confuse things or mix them up 159

poner pies en polvorosa to run away 67

poner los puntos sobre las íes to dot the "i"s (and cross the "t"s), explain in detail 174

poner los puntos sobre la mesa to lay things out clearly 240

poner a raya to draw the line (when someone is trying to take advantage) 58

poner toda la carne en el asador to put all one's eggs in one basket 156

poner en tres y dos to give an ultimatum, put on the spot 65

poner una vela a San Miguel (a Dios) y otra al diablo to try to keep one's options open to profit from either of two people or groups 166

poner verde to heap insults on 57

poner un zíper en la boca to zip up one's mouth, keep quiet 191

ponerle algo en (una) charola de plata (bandeja de plata) to give someone a great opportunity 166

ponerle los cachos a alguien to cheat on someone, be unfaithful 211

ponerle los cuernos a alguien to cheat on someone, be unfaithful 211

ponerles la mosca detrás de las orejas to put a bug in someone's ear 176

ponerse águila to be on the lookout, keep one's eyes peeled 22

ponerse en algo to get with it 4

ponerse borde to go too far 224

ponerse las botas to indulge in something (food, sex, etc.); to make a killing (financially) 203

ponerse un bozal to be quiet 191

ponerse en buena to make up, reconcile 8

ponerse buzo to be alert; to be suspicious 22

ponerse la cara como un chile to turn red, blush 82

ponerse carcamán to be getting old-looking 7

ponerse como una fiera to get very angry 13

ponerse en curda to get drunk 79

ponerse hasta el gorro to eat and drink one's fill 99

ponerse al hilo/en onda to get with it, become aware, wise up 143

ponerse mosca to be suspicious and alert to avoid something 21

ponerse de los nervios to get nervous 261

ponerse las pilas to get with it, get going 257

ponerse los pantalones to take charge of a situation 25

ponerse para to show a lot of interest in, concentrate on 22

ponerse al rojo vivo to get red hot (a situation), heat up 184

ponerse como un tomate to blush, turn red 82

ponerse al tiro to face the music, prepare for a fight 69

ponerse trucha to be aware, alert 22

ponerse un zíper to be quiet 191

ponérsele to suppose, think 234

No te pongas cerril. Don't get uptight. 146

¿Qué le pongo? What shall I serve you? 97

popis high-class (adj.) 108; high-class, snooty 181

popoff posh, upper-class, snooty 181

a poquitos bit by bit 219

Por aquí (trabajando, estudiando). Nothing is new. 117

Por aquí pasándola. Just getting along, so-so. 116

por aquí pasó mi suegra expression telling that one is working hard 255

Por aquí, vagando. I'm just goofing around. 117

por arte de birlibirloque (de magia) as if by magic, through extraordinary or unnatural means 242

Ni por asomo. No way, not by a longshot. 165

por lo bajini (bajo) in secret 191

por las buenas o por las malas one way or another, by force or voluntarily 152

por su cara bonita for no good reason 193

por chiripa by luck, by chance 156

por debajo del agua/tapete under the table, sneakily 65

por debajo de cuerda under the table, through hidden means, on the sly 65

por debajo de la mesa in a corrupt way, under the table 65

por encima very good 111

por favorciano pretty please (por favorciano, mi amorciano) 196

¡Por la flauta! By heaven! 229

Ni por el forro. Nothing, not at all. 165

por la goma correct 175

por gusto, de puro gusto for the fun of it, as a whim 193

por hache o por be one way or another 192

por el librito right, well done 174

por el libro (la libreta) right, good, well done, perfect 175

por su linda cara for no good reason 193

estar por las nubes to be sky-high, very expensive 161

por un pelo by a little bit 189

por pelotas (cojones) by force; just because of a whim 258

por la (su) pinta because of his (her, their, etc.) appearance 177

por pitos o por flautas for one reason or another 193

por poco by a miracle, by a hair 154

por de pronto, por lo pronto meanwhile, provisionally 235

por las puras alverjas just for the heck of it, for no reason at all 193

por un «quítame allá esas pajas» for nothing, for no reason at all 193

por real decreto because that's how it is, it's not to be appealed 193

de por sí anyhow 50

por si las moscas just in case 73

Está por el suelo. It's in the pits, in a bad way. 27

estar por los suelos to be dirt cheap 161

por la tremenda violently, with no respect 129

por un tubo abundantly 190

por un tubo: mandar a alguien... to get rid of someone; to dump 139

de por vida, de toda la vida for life, lifelong 235

porfa please 196

porfia'o(-a) not believing, obstinate 71

la porno short for **pornografía** 211

porque la abuela fuma for no good reason, meaning that someone is inventing an excuse for something 193

porque voló la mosca just for the heck of it, for no reason at all 193

la(s) porquería(s) junk, trash; junk food 100, 233

a la porra: mandar a alguien... to tell someone to go to the devil 139

¡Porras! Darn! 15

el porro marijuana joint 76

postalita boastful 34

ser un poste to be deaf; to be slow, dim-witted 177

a la postre last, at the end 235

el potaje complicated or difficult situation 158

el poto base, bottom, rear end 36

la potranca pretty girl 118

el potro guy who's always following girls around 215

el prajo cigar 237

a precio cómodo cheap(ly) 161

a precio de huevo dirt cheap 161

prender to turn on (sexually) 213

Le prendió la vacuna. She got pregnant. 37

la preocupabilidad worry about guilt 260

el/la presentado(-a) busybody 115

presentar armas to have a hard-on 214

Préstame la guitarra. Let me get a word in. 142

prestar pa' la orquesta to chip in for some cooperative event 161

prieto(-a) black or dark (person) 178

al primer envite at once, right off the bat, from the beginning 235

de primera first-class 241

el/la primerísimo(-a) sweetheart 202

no ser el primero phrase used to excuse an action because there are other examples 87

Primero Dios. God willing. 73

el/la primo(-a) naive person, hick 170

primordial terrific 111

el príncipe azul prince charming, ideal man 202

el/la pringado(-a) someone who is overworked, always gets stuck with everything 256

pringar to work more than others or do the most disagreeable tasks, be a drudge 256

pringarla to make a mistake, blow it 87

el privado the john, bathroom 36

privarse to fall into a deep sleep 218

ser un problema mayúsculo to be a major problem 186

La procesión va por dentro. said when one feels pain or sadness but covers it up 202

el/la profe prof 80; smart person, said in jest, short for **profesor(a)** 141

de pronto suddenly, soon 235

en su propia salsa in your (his, her, their) element 120

lo propio (y lo chimbo) what's "in" (and what's "out") 112

provocarle algo a alguien to feel like having something 154

¡Pucha! ¡La pucha! Darn it! 16; Holy cow!, euphemism for **¡La puta!** 229

¡Púchica! Holy cow! 229

¡Puchis! Holy cow! 229

el pucho smoke, cigarette butt 237

No se puede contigo. Things are impossible with you. 69

Ni puel putas. No freaking way. 165

pueque maybe 73

a las puertas de la muerte at death's door 61

Pues... Uh..., Well... 128

estar puesto(-a) to have a lot of knowledge (about something) or a talent for it 144; to be ready 193

el pujo bad joke, groaner 51

como pujo (en vendaval) bothered, uncomfortable, frustrated 121

el pul fame 90

pulento(-a) flashy, extraordinary 242
el pulir-hebilla close dancing with rhythmic movements (cheek to cheek) 59
el pulpo very aggressive or selfish person 205; wolf, guy who likes to touch women inappropriately 215
la puñeta hand job, masturbation 214
¡Puñeta! Damn! 16
puñeta(s) devil, dickens 16
puñetero(-a) lousy, terrible 27
estar de punta uno con otro to be at odds or on bad terms with 69
la puntada clever remark or something unusual and amusing that someone does 105
Punto acabado. (Punto final.) Absolutely not, period. 165
ser punto y aparte to be against (something) 69
puntudo(-a) overly sensitive, finicky 32
pupuluco(-a) indecisive, wishy-washy 65
de pura cepa genuine (people) 112
ser la pura chapa to be useless 245
¡Pura chepa! Nonsense! 71
ser pura lata to be a pain, drag, bore 15
¡Pura leche! Nonsense! 71
ser pura mierda to be very bad, worthless, shitty 27
¡Pura paja! Nonsense! 71
la pura papa cash 162
Pura verdad. True. Right you are. 240
pura vida great, nice, fantastic 111
a (pura) penca by pure force of will 257
puras madres things of little value 233
¡Puras vainas! Nonsense! 71
puritito(-a) pure, sheer 46
¡Puro cuento! What a whopper! What a fib! 63
a puro pulmón by working as hard as possible 258
ser puro Satanás to be Satan himself 30
a (puro) huevo with a lot of effort 257
la puta bitch 31
en puta in abundance, a shitload of 190
¡Puta! Damn! 11, 229
¡Puta la huevada (güea)! Goddamn it to hell! 11
puta madre very good, great 111
¡Puta madre! expression of surprise or anger 11, 229
¡La puta que te parió! insult something like You son of a bitch! 140
de una puta vez at once, definitively 220
la putada dirty trick; piece of crap 122
ser el putas to be really good at something 44
del putas excellent, the best 110
Ni a putas. No damn way. 164

putear to annoy, harass 18; to insult with offensive names 138
el puto homosexual 173; pimp 214
puto(-a) blasted, damn 27
ser un putón verbenero to be a real slut 212
puyar to bother, annoy, pressure 18

Q

Está que arde. It's at fever pitch and getting worse and worse. 26
estar que cortar las huinchas to be in desperate straits, ready to lose control 17
El que con lobos anda a aullar aprende. Keeping bad company will teach you bad ways. 245
Ni que decir tiene. You don't have to say it (it's common knowledge). 240
estar que ladra to be angry 10
Que lo haga Rita. Let George (someone else) do it. 147
Que lo pase(s) bien. Have a good day (time). Have a good one. 113
el que más y el que menos everyone 46
¡A mí que me registren! Search me! Check me out! (I'm innocent.) 137
que si patatín que si patatán blah, blah, blah; excuses for someone who beats around the bush 49
a la que te criaste as well as possible, with a hope and a prayer 192
quebrado(-a) stuck-up 181
el quebrador womanizer 214
quebrarse to turn one's nose up at others, act like a snob 182
la quedada get-together 169
el/la quedado(-a) loser, fool 90
quedar to leave it, agree, decide 65
quedar bien (mal) parado(-a) to have good (bad) luck, come out well (badly) 154
quedar como semáforo to be stood up, left hanging 194
quedar de cama to get worn out 88
quedar en la calle to be left with nothing 248
quedar en la página dos to break, get ruined or eliminated 125
quedar en un quedar to be stood up, left hanging 195
quedar flechado(-a) to end up hit by an arrow (that is, Cupid's), be in love 200
quedar limpio(-a) to be cleaned out, without money 56
quedar pasmado(-a) to be dumbfounded, surprised 227
quedar pintado(-a) to fit very well 74
no quedar títere con cara (cabeza) to be totally destroyed, often because of verbal abuse 126

quedarse a dos velas to be broke 248

quedarse a medio camino to not finish 3

quedarse a oscuras to not understand 145

quedarse en blanco to draw a blank, be unable to respond 133

quedarse chiquito(-a) to be afraid 92

quedarse como en misa to be quiet 191

quedarse con el moño hecho to be stood up, left hanging 195

quedarse con la cara cuadrada to be very surprised 227

quedarse con la copla to realize what someone was trying to do secretively, find out 143

quedarse con la mente en blanco to have one's mind blank, daydream 131

quedarse con los crespos hechos to be stood up, left hanging 195

quedarse en el aparato to be left behind in life, miss the boat, be a loser 166

quedarse en la estacada to come out of a business badly; to have been gotten the better of in a dispute 184

quedarse frío(-a) (helado[-a]) to be stunned, flabbergasted 228

quedarse pa'adentro to be left speechless 192

quedarse para vestir santos (imágenes) to be left behind; to be a spinster 166

quedarse patidifuso(-a) (y perplejo[-a]) to be (end up) confused 47

quedarse ruqueando en la caleta to hang out at home 130

quedarse tirado(-a) to be left (somewhere); to be stood up; to lose everything 195

estar (quedarse) a dos velas to not understand something, not get it 132

estar (quedarse) detrás del palo to not understand anything, not get it 132

Quedó la escoba (la crema). It was a total disaster. 183

a quema ropa directly, straight out, point-blank 239

la quemada put-down, disparaging remark 58

quemado(-a) exhausted; burned out 89; damaged (usually in reputation) 125

el/la quemado(-a) has-been, someone who's lost his or her abilities 90

quemar el tenis to leave quickly, hotfoot it 67

quemar el último cartucho to go to the last resort, play one's last trick 187

quemar las naves to burn one's bridges 65

quemarse to burn out physically 88; to fail or flunk 90; to get involved in a problem; to blow it; to discredit oneself 183

quemarse (estrujarse) los sesos to rack one's brain 235

quemarse las pestañas (cejas) to study hard, burn the midnight oil, cram 81

ser un queque to be easy, a piece of cake 80

¿Qué querétanos? variant of **¿Qué quieres?** 196

estar querido phrase indicating that there is no problem, something will be resolved 84

¿Quién es? phrase for answering the phone 117

¡Quién lo diría! Oh, come on! 71

¿Quién quita que...? expression used to indicate the probability or chance of something happening 73

¿Quién te mete, Juan Bonete? This isn't your affair. None of your business! 59

Como quiera(s). As you like. If you want. 152

El que quiere celeste que le cueste. There's no free lunch. No bees, no honey; no work, no money. 255

¡Estás como quieres! You look great! 116

no estar quieto(-a) ni a la de tres to not be quiet for even one minute 3

el quilombo mess 158

en las quimbambas far away, on the outskirts 72

en la quinta puñeta far away 72

en el quinto coño (carajo)/infierno far away 72

el quinto pino far away 73

estar en el quinto sueño to be fast asleep 218

estar de quitar el hipo to be amazing, breath-taking 241

quitar hierro to take away the importance of something that one thinks was exaggerated 59

quitar lo bailado to take away what has been enjoyed (danced) 105

quitarse la careta to stop acting or making a show, show one's true colors 239

quitarse un peso de encima to take a load off; to sit down 145

quitarle a alguien hasta la camisa to ruin someone, leave without a shirt on his (her) back 56

en la quinta chilla in the worst poverty 249

R

¡Un rábano! expression of rejecting or declining something 194

de rabo a cabo from top to bottom, from beginning to end, completely 46

con el rabo entre las piernas in a humiliated, embarrassed manner 83

el rabo verde dirty old man 215

la raca marijuana 76

reparar en migajas (pelillos) to pay attention to unimportant things instead of the bigger issue, split hairs 260

repatear to repel, bother; to dislike 153

repelón, repelona describing someone who refuses to do things, is always negative 69

repetirlo hasta el cansancio (hasta el agotamiento) to keep saying something again and again, go on and on 196

requeñequero(-a) stingy 206

re-que-te intensifiers used before adjectives, adverbs, and even verbs, meaning "very" 241

la resaca hangover 79

resbalarle algo a alguien to be indifferent, to roll off one's back 134

resondrar a alguien to scold or yell at someone 57

respondón, respondona uppity, describing someone who talks back unjustifiably when reprimanded 69

Retaca la buchaca. Eat your fill. Stuff your face. 98

retar (a un niño, a un subordinado) to scold 57

retorcer el hígado to get angry 13

reventado(-a) exhausted, wiped out 89

reventar de risa to crack up with laughter 147

el reventón (de primera) a (first-class) bash 169

el revoltijo disorder, mess 158

el revolú disorder, mess, brawl 158

el revoluto disorder 158

revolver a alguien las tripas (el estómago) to cause disgust, repugnance 153

revolver el gallinero to cause a big fuss, stir things up 159

revolverla to stir things up, rock the boat 159

mi rey (reina) my dear, sweetheart 6

el ricachón, la ricachona very rich (person) 250

el ricardo rich guy 250

¡Qué rico! used for agreement 108

rico(-a) delicious (food); hot, sexy 108

el ridículum vitae curriculum vitae (ironic) 255

a rienda suelta with free rein, freely or quickly 219

Riendo se va aprendiendo. Humor helps learning. 81

rifarse to fight 70

No te rifes. Don't take a risk (chance). Don't expose yourself to danger. 246

el rin rin gossip 116

el ripio male organ 214

rizar el rizo to complicate something unnecessarily 244

robar el show (la película) to steal the show; to steal someone's thunder 121

rocharse, rochearse to be upset or depressed 202

No te rochées (e.g., con los padres). Don't let things (e.g., your parents) get you down. 84

el rocheo problem, mental conflict, something bad or boring 186

ser un rodeo to be a cutup, amusing person 105

al rojo vivo red hot (passions) 213

a rolete in great quantities, in droves, tons 189

el rollo long story; bull; complicated situation; way of being 49

el rollo macabeo lie, deception 63

el rollo patatero lie, deception 63

romancear to get romantic 5

No te rompas la cabeza. Don't worry about it. 146

¡Qué rompe grupo! said of someone who is not sociable 32

de rompe y rasga determined and angry 9

romper con alguien to break up with someone 113

romper el hielo to break the ice 48

romper una lanza to defend absolutely, to the hilt 128

romper (partir) la madre to hit hard, hurt someone where he or she is vulnerable 123

romperle los huevos a alguien to bug, pester, get someone very upset 18

romperse la cabeza (los cascos) to think a lot about something, beat one's brain out 235

romperse los codos to study diligently 82

romperse los cuernos to work very hard 257

rondar los cincuenta (cuarenta, etc.) to be pushing fifty (forty, etc.) years old 7

la ropa de semanear (de dominguear) clothes for weekdays (Sundays) 74

La ropa sucia se lava en casa. Let's not air the dirty laundry in public. 114

como una rosa perfectly, very good 108

la rosca circle, closed group 170

el rostro brazenness, nerve 188

el/la roto(-a) low-class person; jerk 249

la ruca girl; woman; broad 118; house, home 232

el ruco, rucailo geezer, old guy 7

los rucos old folks, fogies 7

la rufa bus 239

estar con la ruler to have one's menstrual period 37

A rumbear (tomar, tirar, etc.)... que el mundo se va a acabar. Hey, let's have a good time (drink, make love, etc.) because life is short. 104

rumbiarse to French-kiss 5

el rumbón spontaneous party 169

S

el/la sabe de letras intelligent person, egghead 141

Sabe Dios. God knows. 73

A saber. Who knows? 73

saber de buena fuente to know from a good source 144

saber de buena tinta una cosa to know something from a reliable source, have it on good authority 144

no saber a qué carta quedarse to be in doubt 73

saber a cuerno quemado to make a bad impression or give a bad feeling 26

saber al dedillo to know to a "T," have knowledge at one's fingertips 144

saber dónde le aprieta el zapato to know what is suitable or appropriate for one 144

no saber dónde se tiene la mano derecha (la nariz) to be inept, of little talent 132

saber a gloria to be very pleasant 108

no saber de la misa la mitad to not know (something) 145

no saber ni papa to know nothing, not know beans 145

saber de qué pie cojea to know how the cookie crumbles, what someone's weak point is 142

saberse la cartilla to know the score, know how to behave 144

sabiondo(-a) (sabihondo[-a]) know-it-all 144

el sablazo loan; bad loan scam 160

sacar agua de las piedras to get blood from a turnip 130

sacar a alguien de sus casillas (de quicio) to drive someone crazy, rattle someone's cage 14

sacar (apagar) un fuego con otro fuego to forget one bad thing because of another bad thing 184

sacar canas verdes to do in, give someone gray hair, make him or her despair 124

sacar la cara por alguien to go to bat for someone, defend openly 128

sacar las castañas del fuego to help (someone) out at one's own expense 128

sacar con los pies adelante (por delante) a alguien to take someone to be buried 60

sacar el jugo to take maximum advantage, get the best or most (from) 121, 166

sacar la lotería to have a windfall, luck out 157

sacar de onda to knock out of kilter, throw off 18

sacar partido to take maximum advantage, get or make the most of 166

sacar la piedra to bother, try someone's patience 19

sacar punta a una cosa to attribute something bad to something wrongly, twist; to use it for a purpose that wasn't intended 26

sacar los trapos al sol to give someone the lowdown, air the dirty laundry 114

sacar las uñas to bare one's nails, show one's true colors 247

No se lo sacarán ni con pinzas. They won't get it out of him (her, them) even with tweezers. 191

sacarle a alguien de un apuro to get someone out of a jam 187

sacarse el clavo to get even 217

sacarle el cuero a alguien to rip someone to shreds with gossip, bad comments 57

sacarle la piel a tiras to speak badly (of someone) 57

sacarle las tiras del cuero a alguien to rip someone to shreds with gossip, bad comments 57

sacarse un peso de encima to take a load off; to sit down 145

sacarse la polilla to dance 60

el saco (mata) de huevas dickhead, fool 224

sacudir el polvo a alguien to hit or verbally assault someone 124

sacudirse to dance 60

sae (sa, tusa, tusabe) you know 144

el sal pa'fuera commotion, mess 158

Sal quiere el huevo. said when someone wants to be praised for something or to mean that a business is close to coming to perfection 174

salado(-a) unlucky; kind, nice 155; pricey 161

salarse to be unlucky 155

Sale (y vale). It's a deal. 8

a lo que salga without knowing or caring about the result 192

salga pato o gallareta whatever may happen, come what may 192

Se me salió un zapato. said by someone who has had a fright or shock 91

salir adelante to get ahead 226

salir bien (mal) parado(-a) to come out well (badly), have good (bad) luck 154

salir como un bólido to leave or take off quickly 67

salir como un cohete to take off like a rocket 68

salir con su domingo siete to have bad luck (often, to be pregnant); to say stupid things 155

salir de Guatemala para entrar en Guatepeor to go from the frying pan into the fire 184

salir de marcha to go out and have a good time 106

salir pitando to take off quickly; to show anger in a conversation 68

salir por la ventana to get out of a place or business in a disgraceful way 183

salir del tiesto to do something abnormal, go off one's rocker 242

salir como tío Coyote to make a fast getaway 67

salir el tiro por la culata to backfire (e.g., a plan) 155

(no) salirle a alguien algo de los cojones (los huevos, las narices) to (not) be in the mood, (not) feel like 153

no salirle a alguien la(s) cuenta(s) to not turn out right for someone, not work 86

salirle la baba (por litros) to have one's tongue hanging out, drooling with admiration 23

salirse con la suya to get one's way 153

salirse de las casillas to go overboard, do something abnormal 242

salirse del guacal to do something abnormal, go off one's rocker 243

salirse de madre en algo to go overboard, do something abnormal 243

salirse por el cuello de la camisa to be very skinny 179

salirse por la tangente to sidestep or avoid 88

el salmón idiot, fool 224

¡Salud! (¡Salucitas!) To your health!, said as a toast 98; Gesundheit!, said after a sneeze 126

No salva a nadie. It's not good for anything. 244

salvaje affected talk for fabulous, super 111

salvar el pellejo to save one's skin 185

salvarse en el anca de una pulga to be saved at the last minute, have a close call 186

salvarse por un pelo to be saved by the bell, escape by a hair 186

salvarse en tablitas to be saved by a miracle, get out of danger or a difficult task 186

San Lunes Monday taken off after partying on the weekend 108

sanano(-a) stupid, foolish 225

sancocharse to be steaming hot (people) 251

las sandeces nonsense 226

ser de sangre azul to be a blue blood, from an aristocratic family 251

a sangre y fuego violently 129

sangrón, sangrona bad tempered, unpleasant, annoying 32

sano(-a) como una manzana healthy, fit as a fiddle 126

Sanseacabó. That's that, phrase used to end a discussion 43

ser como Santa Elena, cada día más buena to be like Saint Elena, better every day 108

la Santa Inquisición one's (inquiring) wife 171

Santas pascuas. That's that, phrase used to end a discussion 43

en un santiamén in an instant 221

¡Santísima Trinidad! expression of surprise or fright 230

el santito good boy (sometimes sarcastic) 112

como a un santo cristo un par de pistolas inappropriate, out of place 3

ser santo de su devoción to be someone looked up to, an idol 4

Santo que no me quiere, basta con no rezarle. There's no need to bother with someone who doesn't care about me. 197

santo(-a) y bueno(-a) great, good 112

el santurrón, la santurrona (santulón, santulona) goody-two-shoes, goody-goody 171

sapear to meddle, get in the way 121; to tell on someone, squeal; to spy on 137

el sapo informer, stool pigeon, fink 136

sapotocientos(-as) (mil) a gazillion, uncountable number 190

como sardina en lata, como una lata de sardinas like sardines in a can, crowded or packed 190

el sastre de campillo, que cosía de balde y ponía el hilo said of someone who works for free and ends up putting out money 255

sato(-a) stupid, foolish; mixed breed animal 225

Se me caen las medias (los calzones). I'm excited by that good-looking guy. 22

Se te están cayendo las pestañas. Your eyes are going to pop out. 22

a secas only; alone, and that's all 133

estar seco(-a) to be broke, without money 249

seguir en sus trece to persist in an opinion or in doing something 175

seguir las huellas de alguien to follow in someone's footsteps 216

seguirle a alguien la corriente to follow someone and agree with him or her, go along 8

el segundo frente mistress, lover of a married man 211

el semáforo de medianoche person no one respects, pushover 248

señalar a alguien con el dedo to point the finger at someone 137

la senda de elefantes areas in a city where there are a lot of bars 105

sendo(-a) big, great 190

seño short for **señorita** 118

estar sentado to be dominated by a wife or girlfriend 121

sentar cabeza to settle down 43

sentirse en plena forma to feel great 126

Sepa Chepa/Judás/Moya. Who knows? 73

sepetecientos(-as) many, an uncountable number 190

serrucharle el piso a alguien to undermine, say bad things about someone to others 57

el serrucho pool of money to buy something collectively 161

los servicios públicos public washrooms 36

no servir a Dios ni al diablo to be useless or inept 244

servir lo mismo para un fregado que para un barrido to be all-purpose; to serve for different uses 109

sholón, sholona foolish, stupid 225

Si Dios quiere. God willing. 73

como si nada just like that, without giving the matter any importance 133

Si no lo veo, ¡no lo creo! I can't believe my eyes! Incredible! 230

que si pito que si flauta yada, yada, yada; one thing and then another 49

¡Que si quieres arroz, Catalina! sarcastic remark said when someone hasn't gotten something expected (for example, a promise has been broken) 69

Si se quema la casa, no pierde nada. If the house burns down, he or she won't lose anything. 74

Siempre pa'lante. I'm plugging along. 117

Lo siento muchísimo. I am very, very sorry. 230

el siete rear end 36

ser un siete to be the best, a ten 111

de siete suelas true, for real (usually negative characteristic) 241

sifón variant of **sí** 6

sifrinito(-a) snobbish, pretentious 181

Que siga rodando la bola. Let things happen as they may. 136

Sigue con la cruz a cuestas. Keep going in spite of problems. 85

simón used instead of **sí** 6

simonetes used instead of **sí** 6

sin blanca broke 249

Sin cachondeo(s). No joke, seriously. 240

sin chiste blah, unappetizing 167

estar sin cinco to not have a dime 249

sin co short for **sin comentarios** 192

sin faltar una coma (jota) with accuracy 175

la sin hueso tongue 35

sin padre ni madre, ni perro que me ladre alone, independent or without support 133

sin paracaídas without prior notice, casually 20

sin ton ni son without rhyme or reason 159

sincho of course 6

sirol used instead of **sí** 6

el sistema jodicial screwed-up system, corruption of **judicial** 55

siútico(-a) affected, pretentious 181

el sobaco de la confianza absolute trust or confidentiality 112

sobado(-a) touched in the head 54

sobar to sleep 218

¡Sóbate! Oopsy-daisy! 127

sobrado(-a) stuck-up 181

sobrar (haber) tela que cortar to have plenty of material to deal with an issue 190

la sobremesa after-dinner conversation at the table 48

Sobres. Right. 8

socado(-a) tight (clothing) 74

el/la socio(-a) friend, pal, often used in direct address 103

la soda café that sells reasonably priced food 97

ser una soda to be terrific 111

sofocarse to get upset, worked up 13

de sol a sol from sunup to sundown 235

Ni el sol te va a dar. Don't get big ideas. 58

sollado(-a) good, first-class 111

solano(-a) alone 133

solapiao(-a) alone 133

soltar la cuerda to confess, implicate someone in something 136

soltar la culebra to talk on and on 50

soltar la lengua to open up, spill the beans 136

soltar la pepa to inform on, squeal, rat on 136

soltar el rollo to tell a long story or tell all that one knows 50

estar a la sombra to be in jail 55

no ser ni la sombra de lo que era to be a shadow of one's former self 43

el sombrero (el gorro) condom 211

¿A(l) son de qué? For what reason? 193

Son habas contadas. They're a sure thing. They're scarce and with a fixed number. 43

sonado(-a) in big trouble 185
sonar to hit 123
sonar (como tarro) to try and fail (at something), fall (flat) on your face 90
sonsacar to distract someone or get them to go out 105
estar sopa to be asleep; to be stunned 218
soñar con pájaros preñados to be crazy, thinking of the impossible 53
Ni soñarlo. Don't even dream about it. 165
la sopa boba life lived at others' expense, without working 147
la sopa de letras confusion 158
el sopapo blow 122
¡Sopla! You don't say! 50
soplado(-a) good, excellent 111; quickly, fast as the wind 220
soplar to squeal, inform on, tattle; to whisper a test answer 137
No es soplar e inflar (y hacer) botellas. It's not that easy. 68
soplar la tuba to put up with (something), work hard 257
soplarse to make love to a virgin 213
el soplón, la soplona informer, tattle-tale, rat; someone who whispers a test answer 136
suave good, nice, easy, pleasant 109
Suave. Chill out. Easy does it. 146
¡Suave! used to get someone to stop or wait 20
suave y sin sudar calmly 145
Súbete a la micro. Join in the conversation. 136
subir el diapasón to raise one's voice 69
estar subido(-a) en la poltrona to be in charge, give orders 25
subido(-a) de tono strong language, implying vulgar expressions 48
subirse por las paredes to be crawling up the walls 17
subírsele a alguien el apellido/la mostaza to get angry 13
subírsele a alguien los huevos to lose one's courage 91
subírsele a alguien el humo a las narices (a la cabeza) to be very annoyed, steamed 11
Me la suda. I don't give a damn. 135
sudar frío to break out in a cold sweat, be fearful 92
sudar la gota gorda to sweat bullets, sweat it out, work hard 257
el sueño dorado heart's desire, dream 152
Ni en sueños. No way. Not even in his (her) dreams. 164
a la suerte de la olla potluck 96

sufrir un ataque de cuernos to be very jealous and react violently 198
sulfurarse to get steamed up 13
el supermuertario cemetery 60
surfear la Red (la Internet) to surf the Internet 231
suspender to flunk 90

T

¿'Tá la vaina? How's everything? What's up? 116
el tablazo straight-up-and-down guy (with no hips) 178
el tacho hair 35
el taco bad word, swear word 51; traffic jam 239
el tajo short for **trabajo** 258
¿Qué tal andas? How are things? 117
tal para cual made for each other, birds of a feather 217
tal por cual out-and-out, dyed-in-the-wool 46
¿Qué tal? How are things? 117
el talego a thousand pesetas 163
tallar to sweet-talk, talk with wit and charm 177
el tambembe rear end, backside 36
estar en el tambo to be in jail 55
Ni tan peludo ni tan pelado. All things in moderation. 246
la tandeada big lead, victory 226
tandear to win with a big advantage or lead 226
estar como un tanque to be attractive, strong, a hunk 222
las tantas an undetermined hour, late at night or in the day 236
Ni tanto ni tan poco. Don't exaggerate. 246
Ni tanto que queme al santo, ni tanto que no lo alumbre. All things in moderation. 246
ser la tapa to be tops 111
tapando el sol con un dedo covering things up, trying to keep up appearances 184
el tapis alcoholic drink 100
la taquilla "in" person or thing, fad 111
taquillero(-a) cool, "in" 111
la tarabilla nonstop talker 50
tarado(-a) foolish, stupid 225
el tarambana undisciplined (person, kid) 26
el tarro head 35
la tartamuda machine gun, automatic weapon 232
tarugo(-a) stupid 225
el tata (taita) father; grandfather 171
los tatas parents; grandparents 171
el techo hair 35
¿Qué se teje? How's it going? What's up? 117

el tejemeneje problem, scheme, bad business 186

la tele television 231

la teleculebra TV program that tells a silly story in installments, cheesy soap opera 231

el telele foolishness 226

ser un telele to be foolish 226

temático(-a) obsessive, monomaniacal, crazy 54

tener a alguien en el alma to feel for someone 230

tener a alguien frito(-a) to tire someone out, bothering him or her 19

tener (sus) abriles to have a certain age 7

tener agallas to have guts, nerve 52

tener los alambres pelados to be nervous, on edge, strung out 261

tener alma de acero to be without feelings, cold 230

tener el alma en un hilo to be a bundle of nerves 260

tener ángel to have that special something, be a good person 112

tener las antenas puestas to be listening (and ready for gossip) 114

tener aprendida la cartilla to know the score, know how to behave 144

no tener arte ni parte to have no part in, nothing to do with 133

tener un ataque de hígado to get angry 13

tener banca to have influence, power, worth 25

tener bien puestas las pilas to have one's act together, be on the ball 44

tener bien puestos los calzones (pantalones) to be worthy, have character or valor 52

tener el billete largo to be loaded, rolling in dough 251

no tener blanca to be broke 249

tener bolas to be bold, brave 52

tener las bolas bien puestas to be brave, bold 52

tener las bolas llenas to be fed up 16

tener en el bolsillo a alguien to have someone at one's beck and call, be able to count on that person 25

tener bolsillos alegres to have lots of money 251

tener bonita letra to not be too smart (ironic) 222

tener en el bote to sweet-talk or pick up, to convince 177

tener una bronca to have a fight, dispute 70

tener buen coco to be smart 141

tener buen diente to be a big eater 98

tener buen lejos to be or look good from a distance, not too much fun to have around 32

tener buena barra a alguien to like someone 152

tener buena cuchara to be a good cook 97

tener buena mano para to have the skill for something, have the knack, the right touch 44

tener buena prensa to have good press or reputation 90

tener buena sombra to be pleasant, a good influence; to be lucky 109

tener buena vibración to give good vibes, inspire confidence 112

tener la cabeza hueca to be brainless, an airhead 225

tener la cabeza llena de humos to be full of oneself, have one's head swollen 181

tener cabeza de mosquito to be brainless 225

tener la cabeza a las tres o a las once to be absentminded, a little bit out of it 48

tener cables pelados to be nervous, on edge, strung out 261

tener una calentura to be really excited sexually, be turned on, hot 213

tener cancha to be on one's home court 79

no tener cara to have no shame, be shameless 188

tener cara de cemento armado to have a lot of nerve, brazenness 188

tener cara de chiste to look ridiculous 222

tener cara de mala leche to look like one is in a bad mood 28

tener cara de poco amigos to look hostile, unfriendly 128

tener una cara de teléfono ocupado to look angry, annoyed 10

tener cara de «yo no fui» to have a humble or innocent-looking face, contrary to truth 63

tener un cacao mental to have a confusion of ideas 47

tener un careto to look really bad because of worry or lack of sleep 89, 260

no tener chiste to be blah, unappetizing 167; to be senseless or useless 244

tener chuchaqui to be hung over 79

no tener ni cinco to be broke 249

tener clara la película to have a clear picture of some situation, understand it in full 144

tener los cojones (tenerlos) por corbata to be fearful, timid, scared 91

tener los cojones bien puestos to be bold, brave 53

tener colmillo to be astute in business 45

tener un corazón de oro to have a heart of gold 112

tener un corazón de piedra to have a heart of stone 230

tener crudo algo to have something be difficult to do or get 69

no tener un cuarto to be broke 249

tener cuernos to be a cuckold (with horns) 212

tener una curda to be drunk 79

no tener donde caerse muerto to be very poor, destitute 249

no tener dos dedos de frente to be stupid, brainless 225

tener duende to have charm, be enchanting 109

tener una empanada mental to not have clear ideas or thinking 47

tener un enchufe to have a connection 103

tener estrella to be lucky and easily accepted by people 156

tener la farmacia abierta (y el doctor dormido) to have an open fly in one's pants 74

tener flojos los tornillos to have a screw loose 54

tener gancho to fascinate, seduce, captivate 23

tener guayabo to be hung over 79

tener un guiso to have a party 106; to have a job on the side 258

tener la guita loca to be loaded 251

tener hambre de león to be really hungry 99

tener hormigas en el culo to be impatient, have ants in your pants 17

tener huevos to be bold, brave 52

no tener huevos to be a coward 91

tener los huevos bien puestos to be bold, brave 53

tener los huevos de corbata to be fearful, timid, scared 92

tener los huevos cuadrados to be very bold 53

tener los nervios de punta to have one's nerves on edge 261

tener un jabón to be afraid 92

tener leche to be lucky 156

tener la leche cortada to be in a bad mood 28

tener un ligue to have a date, relationship 199

tener madera to have strength, aptitude, have what it takes (to do something) 45; to have good or a strong character 112

tener mal rollo (con alguien) to lead a bad life (with someone) 183

tener mala barra a alguien to dislike someone 152

tener mala leche to have bad intentions 31; to be bad tempered, disagreeable; to be unlucky 155

tener mala pata to have bad luck 155

tener mala prensa to have bad press or reputation 90

tener mala sangre to be bad tempered, disagreeable 32

tener mala sombra to be unpleasant, a bad influence; to be unlucky 27

tener mala uva to have a gruff or severe demeanor 32

tener mambo en la cabeza to be confused, disoriented 47

tener mano to be competent 45

tener mano de guagua to be very tight with money, tight-fisted 206

tener mano de monja to be a good cook, have the gourmet touch 97

tener manos de hacha to be clumsy, a klutz 132

tener más cojones que nadie to be very brave, bold 53

tener más vidas que un gato to have more lives than a cat 156

tener a menos to disdain 180

tener la mente en blanco to be daydreaming, have one's mind blank 131

tener la mona to be drunk 78

tener mucha cara (mucha jeta) to have a lot of nerve, be an opportunist 188

tener mucha chorra to have good luck 157

tener mucha cuerda to look very healthy 126

tener mucha mollera to be bright 225

tener mucho coco to be smart 141

tener mucho culo to be very lucky 157

tener mucho rollo to talk a lot without saying much 50

tener mucho rostro (mucho morro) to have a lot of nerve, be an opportunist 188

tener muchos humos to be full of oneself 181

tener un muermo to be sleepy 218

tener narices to be brave, bold 53

tener la nota to be drunk 78

tener una nota to be stoned 76

no tener ni papa to be broke 249

no tener ni para pipas to be broke 249

tener patas to be brash or bold 53

no tener pelos en la lengua to talk clearly, without mincing words 136

tener pelotas to be brave, bold 53

tener una pelotera to have a fight, blowup, brawl 70

tener pena to be shy, embarrassed 83

tener un pico de oro to be a good talker, gifted speaker 50

no tener pies ni cabeza to have no order or logic 159

tener pinta (de) to look (like) 177

tener poca mollera to be stupid 225

tener en poco a una persona o cosa to have little regard for someone or something 180

tener una polilla to be sleepy 218

no tener por donde agarrarlo (cogerlo) to be difficult to comprehend or grasp 132

no tener un quinto to be broke 249

no tener remedio to be hopeless, beyond help 183

tener resaca to be hung over 79

tener un rollo con alguien to have an affair with someone; to have a disagreement 211

no tener sal en la mollera to not be very bright 225

tener el santo de cabeza to ask for something until you get it 196

tener el santo de cara to have good luck 156

tener el santo de espaldas to have bad luck 155

tener santos en la corte to have connections 103

tener la sartén por el mango to be in charge, have the upper hand 26

tener sed to be broke, without money 249

tener siete vidas como los gatos (como el gato) to have seven lives like a cat 157

tener tablas to be experienced or poised; to lose one's timidity in public 45

no tener tiempo ni para rascarse to be very busy 39

tener un tío en las Indias to have a wealthy or influential connection 103

no tener vela en el entierro to not have authority or a reason to participate 129

tener la vida en un hilo to be in great danger 185

tener ya dura la mollera to no longer be able to learn 225

tenerle una bronca a alguien to be upset with someone 9

tenerlos de corbata to be fearful, timid, scared 92

tenérsela pelada to tire someone out repeating or insisting on something 19

Tengamos la fiesta en paz. Don't cause trouble. 8

¿Tengo monos en la cara? Why are you staring at me? 14

Tenías que ser de alquilar, como tu madre, ¡huevón! You are useless, you son of a bitch! 140

el tenorio womanizer, Don Juan 215

el tentempié (tente en pie) mid-morning snack 100

el tequemeneje problem, scheme, bad business 186

mi tesoro my dear 6

las tetas tits 37

tetona big-breasted (woman) 37

tetuda big-breasted (woman) 37

el tiburón wolf, womanizer 215

el/la tico(-a) Costa Rican 174

el tiempal long time 236

en tiempos del hilo azul long, long ago 237

No tiene agua para beber y quiere bañarse. said of someone who wants to be more than he or she can be 182

¡Tiene huevos (narices) la cosa! How bizarre, abusive, unheard of! 242

No tiene madre. It's the best (worst)! No equal! 242

El que tiene plata platica. Money talks. 250

No tiene(s) que jurarlo. said when something is agreed, obvious 8

los tiesos the dead 61

tifitear, tifitifi to thieve 56

el tigre aggressive person 188

el tigre (bárbaro) wolf, womanizer 215

la tíguera clever bitch, heartbreaker, sleazy gal 212

tijerear a alguien to criticize, cut down with words 57

los tiliches things, stuff 233

el tilín tilín noise, talk 50

el/la timador(a) rip-off artist, con man 62

la timba big stomach, belly 36

la tincada hunch 234

tincarle to think, have a hunch 234

tío(-a) term of affection 104

el tío, la tía guy, fellow (girl, woman) 118

el tipazo handsome guy 23

el tipo guy, fellow 118

el/la tiquis miquis fussy or high-class person, not easily pleased by just anything 181

el tiquismo Costa Rican word or expression 48

la tira police 26

tira y afloja back and forth negotiations between two people or groups having trouble agreeing 69

estar tirado(-a) to be easy 80

tirado(-a) cheap, a steal (at such a good price) 161

tirado(-a) de las mechas absurd, crazy 3

Tirando. Hanging in, getting along. 117

tirar arroz to criticize 57

tirar la baba (por litros) to have one's tongue hanging out, drooling with admiration 23

tirar bomba to stand (someone) up 195
tirar la casa por la ventana to spend lavishly, blow the works 162
tirar (de) la cuerda a alguien to pull someone back, control 26
tirar la esponja to throw in the towel 66
tirar a los leones to leave in a bad position, do in 124
tirar de manoletina to masturbate (males) 214
tirar un palo to give a hint 50
tirar para colina (la cola) to back out of some plan or commitment at the last minute 88
tirar la piedra y esconder la mano to hurt someone but cover up one's action, be a hypocrite 121
tirar piedras to criticize 57
a tirar piedras al río: mandar a alguien... to tell someone to get lost 139
tirar pinta to dress to impress 75
tirar rostro to make a good impression 109
A tirar (rumbear, tomar, etc.)... que el mundo se va a acabar. Hey, let's make love (have a good time, drink, etc.) because life is short. 104
tirar los tejos to seduce, make passes, hit on 201
tirar la toalla to throw in the towel, give up 66
tirarse to fail 90
tirarse a alguien to have sex with someone 213
tirarse un caldo to fart 35
tirarse el lance to take a stab or chance at 52
tirarse para la calle del medio to behave badly, without discretion 243
tirarse el pegote to brag or boast 34; to lie or deceive 64
tirarse el rollo to lie, brag 34
la tirijala (tira y jala) mess, confusion 158
al tiro right now; in sequence 235
el tiro al aire unreliable or unpredictable person, loose cannon; slacker 32
el tiro de gracia fatal blow, coup de grace 60
de un tirón at once, all at one time 220
Ni a tiros. Not a chance. 164
tocado(-a) elegant; bad smelling; high 79
tocado(-a) (de la cabeza) touched in the head, a bit crazy 54
tocar fondo to touch bottom, hit rock bottom; to get to the bottom of something 184
tocar la flauta to be right, guess correctly 143
tocar los cojones (huevos) a alguien to bother someone continually 19

tocar madera to touch (knock on) wood 73
tocar muchas teclas to push a lot of buttons (to solve a problem) 187
tocar el violín to go out with a couple and have the feeling they really want to be alone, be a fifth wheel 199
tocarle a alguien la lotería to have a windfall, luck out 157
tocarse las narices (los cojones) to goof off, not do anything 130
a tocateja in cash 162
de tocho morocho at any rate 50
a toda hostia/leche fast, quickly 219
a toda madre far out, fantastic 109; at full blast, fast 219
a toda máquina quickly, fast 219
a toda marcha/mecha very quickly 219
a toda pastilla quickly 219
a todas margaritas fantastic, great 109
todititito(-a) everything 46
a todo chancho intensely 219
todo lo contrario just the opposite 165
a todo dar great, fantastic 109; fast 219
a todo esto by the way; meanwhile 50
todo fresas calm, not worried 146
a todo ful fast; at full volume 219
a todo gas fast 219
a todo mamón fast, like mad, like a house afire 219
Todo marchando. Everything's fine, OK. 117
a todo meter fast, with vehemence, at full blast 219
Todo pasando. Everything's going OK. 117
a todo lo que da going great guns, like a house afire 219
todo quisque everyone 46
Todo me sale torcido (al revés). Everything turns out badly for me. 155
todo el santo día the whole live-long day 236
a todo trapo with style or class 75
a todo vapor fast, with vehemence, at full blast 219
estar todo(-a) derretido(-a) to be completely under the spell 247
estar como todos los diablos to be beside oneself, in a very bad mood 28
To'el tiempo pa'lante. Onward and upward. 175
el tolete male organ 214
¡Toma! Take that! (in a discussion); So what? 194
¡Toma castaña! (¡Toma del frasco, Carrasco!) Take that! (in a discussion); So what? 194
¡Tomá tu muñeca, muchacha ñoñeca! Have it your way (but I think it's a mistake)! 59
Toma tu tomate. Take what's coming to you. What goes around comes around. 59

estar tomado(-a) to be drunk 78
tomar a coña algo to not take something seriously 145
tomar algo con soda to take something calmly 145
tomar algo con un grano de sal to take something with a grain of salt 71
tomar una copa to have a drink 99
tomar once to have tea, a snack in the afternoon 97
tomar el pelo a alguien to pull someone's leg, tease 84
tomar el portante to disappear quickly 68
tomar el rábano por las hojas to jump in any which way 192
A tomar (rumbear, tirar, etc.)... que el mundo se va a acabar. Hey, let's drink (have a good time, make love, etc.) because life is short. 104
tomar sobre sí una cosa to take something upon oneself 255
tomar las de Villadiego to take to one's heels, beat it 68
tomar vuelo to take flight, make progress 226
tomarse el quirse to leave, get a move on 68
tomarse las cosas a la tremenda to take something too hard 260
los tombos police 26
a tontas y a locas recklessly, like crazy, without thought 131
tontear to behave in a foolish or stupid way 223
¡Qué tontería(s)! What nonsense! 71
a lo tonto like crazy, without thinking 131
tonto(-a) de capirote extremely stupid, dope 225
el/la tonto(-a) perdido(-a) hopeless case, someone very stupid 223
el top the best 111
topado(-a) stupid 225
estar hasta el tope to be fed up 16
a tope totally; with all one's energy; fast 45
estar hasta los topes to be fed up 17
el toque hit of cocaine 75; hit of marijuana 76; little bit 189; short time 236
el toquesín hit of marijuana 76
el toqui leader of the pack, head honcho 25
torear to manage, manipulate people or a situation 3; to provoke, upset 19
torpe dim-witted, slow 225
torreja low-class 34
la torta face, fat face (round) 35; female organ 212
Ni torta. Nothing. 165
la tortillera lesbian 173
la tortuga slow person 219
a lo torugo like crazy, without thinking 131

to'tirao (todo tirado) messy, disorderly 158
trabajar como burro to work hard, work like a dog 259
trabajar como enano to work very hard, work like the devil 259
el/la trabajólico(-a) workaholic 255
la tracalada large quantity; crowd 191
el/la tracalero(-a) swindler, cheat 62
traer de una ala to have (someone) helplessly in love 200
traer a alguien de acá para allá (aquí para allí) to keep someone very busy, on the run 39
traer a alguien frito(-a) to tire someone out, bothering them 19
traer azorrillado(-a) to have (someone) helplessly in love 200
traer cola (coleta) to bring serious consequences 183
traer de culo a alguien to upset someone 19
traerlo (tenerlo) entre ojos to have a grudge against someone, dislike 153
traer una nota to be high on drugs or alcohol 79
traer la tripa amarrada to be faint with hunger 99
tráfalo(-a) low-class, like a bum 34
el/la tragaldabas glutton, guzzler 98
el tragalibros bookworm 82
tragar to study 82; to accept, put up with 197
no tragar to not (be able to) stand 153
tragar(se) algo to believe (swallow) something 137
tragarse de alguien to have a crush on someone 200
tragar el anzuelo to be deceived 137
tragar camote to have to put up with something quietly; to be unable to express oneself 197
tragarle la tierra a alguien used to express embarrassment, a wish to disappear from view 83
tragarse la píldora (la bola) to believe a lie, fall for something 137
tragárselo a alguien la tierra to disappear from places one usually frequents 68
el trago drink (often alcoholic drink) 100
el tragón serious student 82
el tragón, la tragona big eater 98
el trajín butt of a joke or of mockery 83; work, things to do 258
el/la tramposo(-a) dirty player, cheater 62
la tranca hangup, block, inhibition 234
trancarse to be dumbfounded, unable to respond 234
a trancas y barrancas passing over all obstacles 258

Tranquilo(-a). (Tranqui.) No problem, relax. 146

los tranquilos the dead 61

la transa ruse, trick, con 63

transar to swindle, cheat 64

el/la transista con man, con woman 62

los trapos clothing 74

traqueteado(-a) old, used or worn out 7

el traqueteo intense activity, mess, transaction; drug deal 158

el trasero rear end 36

trasnochar to stay out or up late at night 105

la trastada dirty trick 122

el traste rear end, backside 36

tratar con la punta del pie to treat badly, treat like dirt 124

Trato hecho. It's a deal. 8

el trauco unknown father 171

tremendo(-a) tremendous, exaggerated, phenomenal 242

estar como un tren to be attractive, strong, a hunk 222

treprársele a la cabeza to take advantage of 121

de tres al cuarto so-so, no great shakes 167

estar en tres y dos to be in a decisive moment, on the spot 65

Ni a la de tres. No way. 164

ser trililís to be of bad quality, junky 30

tripón, tripona potbellied, heavy 36

la troca truck 239

a troche y moche (trochemoche) willy-nilly, pell-mell 192

la trompa mouth (often in reference to an angry person) 35

estar trompa (trompeta, tururú) to be drunk 78

el trompabulario bad language 51

el trompazo hard blow 122

trompudo(-a) loudmouthed or bigmouthed; someone sounding off threats 10

el/la trompudo(-a) with a big mouth 115

tronado(-a) stoned 76

tronar to reprimand 57; to fail (e.g., an exam, a project, in love) 90

tronar como (un) ejote to end badly, fail 90

troncharse de risa to break up laughing, crack up 147

el trono (de los césares) toilet seat 36

a tropezones with delays and difficulties 258

trucho(-a) fake, phony 62

tuanis (tuani) great, nice; greeting among young people 111

el tuerca grease monkey; car lover 238

el tugurio dive, bar; slum 105

tumbado(-a) victim of a robbery 56

tumbar to kill; to convince or persuade; to deceive 55; to mug, rob 56

tumbarse to make love 213

al tuntún haphazardly, without thinking, without a plan 192

tupirle to hurry up, get a move on 221

tupirse to get spaced out, confused 47

el/la turista someone who rarely goes to class 82

turistear to go on an outing 238

la tusa worthless thing or person 245

tutifruti describing someone who changes often 43

U

la u university 81

Ubícate. Straighten up. Behave yourself. 59

¡Qui úbole!, ¡Qui úbo! a greeting, like Hi! 116

¡Úchala! Yuck! 154

¡Uff! Oh dear! Oops! 16, 230

¡Újule! expression indicating a put-down, often followed by a disparaging remark 59

ser la última gota to be the last straw 15

estar en las últimas to be on one's last legs 61

ser el último mono to be insignificant, not count (people) 138

el último toque finishing (last) touch 175

ser uña y carne to be bosom buddies 104

ser uña y mugre to be bosom buddies 104

la uni university 81

del uno super, great 110

uva good 111

de uvas a peras once in a blue moon 101

¡Qué uvas! Hi! 116

V

¡Qué va! Oh, come on! 71

No va pa'l baile. He (She) is a loser, not wanted. 33

estar de vacaciones en el bote to be in jail 55

el/la vacacionista someone who rarely goes to class 82

la vacilada deceit, con, trick 63; joke, trick 107

el/la vacilador(-a) someone who enjoys life, jokes around or makes fun of others; deceitful person 105

vacilar to tease, trick, con, make a fool of 84; to joke around, have a good time; to put someone on, tease 106

vacilar a alguien to eye, hit on, put the moves on 201

vacilar con (alguien) to fool around with, have fun with (someone) 107

el vacilón funny comment used to tease repeatedly 105

ser un vacilón to be a comic, entertaining person 105

el vacilón party, fun, diversion 169

vacunar to deceive or cheat 64

el/la vago(-a) slacker, drifter; drug addict or alcoholic 148

la vaina problem, mess; situation 186; thing 233

¡Qué vaina! expression of surprise, anger, annoyance, disagreement 16, 230

Ni de vaina. No. No way. 164

¿Qué vaina es ésta? What the hell is happening? What's going on? 11, 229

el vale male friend, guy 103

Vale. All right. OK. 8

Me vale. I don't give a damn. 135

el valedor casual drinking buddy 103

el valemadrismo attitude of indifference 134

valer gorro to be worthless, unimportant 245

no valer un bledo to be worthless 245

no valer ni cacahuete to be worthless 244

no valer un carajo to not be worth a damn 245

valer hongo, valer callampa to be worthless, not worth a dime 245

valer un imperio (un mundo, un Potosí) to be worth a fortune 161

valer papas to be worthless, worth beans 245

valer su peso en oro to be worth its weight in gold 161

valer por tres tiritas to be worthless 245

valerle huevo to not care, not give a damn 135

valerle madre to not give a damn 134

valerle pinga (verga) to not care, not give a damn 135

¡Válgame Dios! Good grief! 16

la valona favor 128

No van por ahí los tiros. You're off the track, cold. 87

la vara thing 233

estar en varas dulces to be pregnant 37

el vato guy, dude 118

el vato loco crazy dude 53

Vaya. Good. Agreed. Understood. 8

Vaya a contárselo a su tía (abuela). Oh, come on! 71

Vaya a decírselo a su abuela. Oh, come on! 71

Que te (le, les) vaya bien. Have a nice day (time). (May all go well.) 113

Vaya uno a saber. Who knows? 74

Vaya usted (Vete) a saber. Who knows? 74

Váyalo. All right. Agreed. 8

los vegetales parents 171

vejestorio(-a) geezer, fogy 7

el vejete old man 6

la venada fit 13

vender la pomada to do a hard sell, sell snake oil 160

no vender una escoba to fail, not accomplish what was intended 90

venderle a alguien to sell someone out 61

venderse como pan caliente to sell very well, sell like hot cakes 160

vendido(-a) sellout, person who sells out 61

estar vendido(-a) to be deep in debt 249

Venga. way of ending conversation on the phone; word used instead of **vale** 113

venir a alguien en bandeja to come without effort 166

venir con cuentos to tell tall tales 64

venir a menos to deteriorate 121

venir(se) to come sexually 211

venirle grande to be too much (for someone) 132

ventajoso(-a) opportunistic 205

el ventaneo cheating on an exam by looking at another's paper 81

Te veo venir. I see what you're up to. 246

¿A ver? phrase for answering the phone 117

no ver ni gorda to not see anything 131

no ver la hora de (+ inf.) to not be able to wait (+ inf.) 235

ver los toros desde la barrera to stay out of harm's way 87

no ver ni tres en un burro to not see anything 131

la verdad clara y desnuda the clear, unadulterated truth 240

la verdad de la milanesa the real truth of the matter 240

verde natural, referring to sex 211

el verde very studious person, nerd 171

de la verde marijuana 76

los verdes soldiers 25

la verga male organ 214; thing, piece of crap 233

¡A la verga! interjection of anger or surprise 10

a la verga: mandar a alguien... to tell someone to go to hell 139

el vergazo hard blow 122

la vergueada blow, beating 122

estar vergueado(-a) to be really down and out 184

verguear to hit, strike 124

la de la vergüenza the last portion of food on a plate that no one dares to take 96

verla peluda to find oneself in a jam, pinch 184

verle la cara a alguien to deceive or take advantage of someone 64

(no) verle pelos a la sopa to (not) look for problems, be too fussy 260

verse a palitos to find oneself in a jam 185

vérselas negras to have a problem, have trouble 185

no vérsele a alguien el pelo to not see hide nor hair of someone 67

el/la versero(-a) liar, big talker 62

vestido(-a) y calzado(-a) dressed and shod, ready for interaction with others 74

los veteranos parents 171

vetusto(-a) old and worn out, old goat 7

viajar por autostop to hitchhike 238

víbora bad, insidious 30

mi vida sweetheart, darling 6

¡La vida me sonríe! What a stroke of luck! 157

estar la vida muy achuchá (achuchada) to be very difficult, expensive 68

el/la viejo(-a) father (mother); husband (wife), partner; term of endearment 171

el viejo verde (viejo caliente) old man who is still involved in romantic relationships 215

viene como el tiburón here comes the opportunist, fraud 62

vientos, vientísimos great, super 111

¡Virgen santísima! Good heavens! 230

el virote euphemism for male organ 214

visitar al señor Roca to go to the rest room 36

¿Viste? See? 142

la viuda verde dirty old woman 212

ser la viva imagen de alguien to be the spitting image of someone 216

vivaracho(-a) sharp, astute; fresh 203

vivazo(-a) astute, liable to take advantage 203

vivir como escopeta de hacienda to be always pregnant 37

vivir de panza to enjoy life without working 203

vivito(-a) y coleando living and breathing 126

ser el vivo retrato de alguien to be the spitting image of someone 216

vocea'o(-a) much voiced or commented on 91

la volada favor 128

de volada quickly, on the fly or run 220

volado(-a) stoned; spaced out; high 76; daydreaming 131; in a hurry 220

el/la volador(a) someone who is disorganized, forgetful, scatterbrained 48

volar to rob; to be robbed 56; to flunk, fail 90

volar lengua (lata) to talk, converse 50

volar pata to walk a long way, a lot 239

volarle to hurry it up, take off 221

volarse la barda to do something very impressive, usually good 45

Voló la paloma. said when something escapes unexpectedly from one's grasp 155

de volón pinpón on the fly, fast or while doing something else 220

el volteado homosexual; pervert 173

voltiar to work hard 259

volver a alguien tarumba (turumba) to confuse, bewilder 47

volverse un etcétera to be confused 47

volverse un ocho to be confused 47; to worry, get nervous 260

No voy a tragar carros y carretas. I'm not swallowing that nonsense. 71

No voy a tragarme esa guayaba. I'm not going to swallow that nonsense. 71

¡Vóytelas! interjection of surprise 230

a vuelta de ruedas slow(ly) 219

No me vuelve loco(-a). It doesn't do a thing for me. 134

vuelto loco(-a) y sin sentido said when someone has done something out of the ordinary 241

W

¡Waca! Yuck! 154

wach(e)ar to watch, look 22

¡Wacha! Watch out! 247

Nos wachamos. See you. 113

el water toilet, toilet bowl 36

Y

Y dale la burra al trigo. said when someone keeps repeating the same thing 196

¿Y eso? What does that mean? What's that all about? 133, 228

Y en paz. That's that, phrase said to end a discussion 44

Y de la vida, ¿qué más? What else is happening in your life? 165

una y no más (santo Tomás) never again 237

y pico and a bit, small amount 189

Ya. OK. 8

Ya apareció (el) peine. greeting for a person who has been missing 116

Ya lo creo. I should say so. I believe you. 8

Ya está bien de cuentos. Enough stories (nonsense). 71

Ya me gana. said when one has to urinate 36

Ya le han caído cincuenta castañas (tacos). He or she is fifty. 7

Ya maté a lo que me estaba matando. I'm full. 98

Ya sábanas (sabadabas). You know (already). 144

ya tener una pata allí to have earned a place somewhere, have your foot in the door 166

ya tú sabe' you know (already) 144

Ya vas, Barrabás. All right. Agreed. There you go again. 8

Ya se ve. expression of agreement, I see. 8

de yapa for free 161

la yapa freebie; free gift 232

Yo soy como (Juan) Orozco; cuando como no conozco. said of someone who is too absorbed in eating 98

yo que tú if I were you 174

ser yoyo to be a suck-up 176

yuma foreign(er) 174

yumático(-a) United States 179

mi yunta my best friend (used by youth) 103

Z

¡Zafa! Get out of here! 114

zafado(-a) crazy 54; sassy, fresh, disrespectful 189

zafarse (de) to excuse oneself, avoid or get out of; get rid of 88

¡Záfate! Go away! 114

ser un zafio to be a blunderer 132

el zambrote mess 158

el/la zanahorio(-a) young person who is innocent, immature, not socially active; health nut 137

zángano(-a) foolish, silly 225

el/la zángano(-a) lazybones, slacker 148

Zapatero a tus zapatos. Mind your own business. Let's stick to what we know best. 3

¡Zape! Shoo! Go away! 114

el zaperoco mess, mixup 158

zarrapastroso(-a) badly dressed, dirty, sloppy 75

en un zas quickly, in an instant 221

zoncear to behave stupidly 223

zonzo(-a) silly, stupid 225

zoquete (zoqueta) stupid, foolish 225

la zorra foxy lady, party girl; female organ 24; bitch, nasty woman 31

zorro(-a) sly, clever like a fox 141

en zumba habitually drunk 78

a la zumba marumba spontaneously, without advanced plans 192

el/la zurdo(-a) someone who is slow or inept at a certain activity 132

zurumbado(-a) confused 46

English Topic Index